The Au...
Wine
Annual
2007

The Essential Guide to Australian Wine

Your complete guide to drinking pleasure
with nearly 10,000 wines rated

- Many more wines and wineries than ever before
- Tasting notes for every new release
- Australia's best under-$20 wines
- Labels for all wines in full colour

Published and designed in Australia.

Jeremy Oliver Pty Ltd
565 Burwood Rd Hawthorn, Victoria, 3122 Australia
Tel: 61 3 9819 4400   Fax: 61 3 9819 5322

Printed by   KHL Printing Co Pte Ltd, Singapore

Design and Layout by   Artifishal Studios, Melbourne, Victoria, Australia

Distributed to book   Macmillan Publishing Services
retailers in Australia by   Free call 1800 684 459
                                  Free fax 1800 241 310

Distributed to wine   Fine Wine Partners
retailers in Australia by   Tel: 1300 668 712
                                  Fax: 1300 668 512

Copyright © Jeremy Oliver 2006

ISBN 0-9581032-7-5

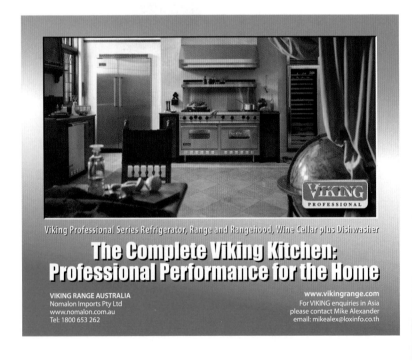

Contents

There is a silver lining...

Welcome to the tenth edition of The Australian Wine Annual. Like me, the Australian wine industry is now a decade older, and it is certainly a decade wiser.

The past decade has finally put to bed the notion that growing and making wine is a 'lifestyle choice'. The reality check now being felt by many growers and makers is as widespread as it is painful, and we have not yet seen the end of the damage caused by the Australian wine industry's swinging boom-bust pendulum.

While writing the introduction to the first edition in 1996, I mentioned the Winemakers Federation of Australia's then recently released Strategy 2025 document. Back then, most commentators considered it a wildly ambitious and unrealistic proposal by the Australian wine industry to become a world player. Optimistically, I thought the industry would succeed, but I could never have guessed to what extent. Or at what cost, to many.

Read virtually any publication commenting on wine these days and the news sounds bad for Australia. Scandinavians could be forgiven for thinking there are riots in Adelaide; New Yorkers for thinking the place is for sale and Londoners for thinking that Australians are forsaking their fixation on wine for football.

But if everything is taken into account, Australia's wine industry is still doing very well, especially when measured against other wine-producing nations. Australia's wine sales are increasing. It's true that the value per litre has fallen over the past four years, but Australia's share of most important wine markets is going upwards, not downwards. Exports rose 12% in 2005/06. Certain large European countries would gladly be in that position.

What makes this performance even more laudable is that Australia is certainly not being granted any favours by the world's wine media, which, like a large predatory cat, has largely taken to sharpening its claws on Australian wine. Every gain the industry makes is won the hard way.

Back home, the domestic wine market is struggling to hold ground. Grape-growers across the country are doing it tough, and the next two years are likely to see a large number of vineyard and winery closures. The industry will be treading water financially for several years before being able to strike out for profit again.

But if wineries can survive the next two to three years, Australian wine will be in a strongly competitive shape. Most estimates suggest the oversupply will have eased significantly, the remaining vines will have matured and the resulting wines will be better, making the industry even more competitive across a range of prices.

By then, of course, it is possible that winemakers will be running short of some grape varieties and that another wave of plantings will begin. One hopes that this would take place in a rather more considered fashion than last time around.

More wines of world class

In the meantime, there is much happening in Australian wine to get excited about. Firstly, there is the emergence of a new breed of elite Australian wine producer. Thirty years ago it was possible for new wineries to succeed simply because they were there. It was a bonus if their wine was any good. That's no longer the case because the market is now overcrowded with small wineries. Newcomers need to over-provide significantly against established opposition, regardless of price bracket.

A list of recent entrants to the top end of Australian winemaking includes names like Andrew Thomas, Balnaves, Bindi, Capercaillie, Castagna, Clayfield, Epis, Glaetzer, Hurley Vineyard, Kilikanoon, Kooyong, mesh, Tappanappa, Woodlands and Woodside Valley Estate. These makers are dramatically expanding Australia's offering of world-class wine. Even a label like Torbreck, which seems to have been with us forever, crushed its first vintage as recently as 1996. There is indeed action aplenty at the top end.

Additionally, many long-established brands, large and small, have made changes that have elevated their wines to another quality level. This list includes such names as Bowen Estate, d'Arenberg, Henschke, Seppelt, Wantirna Estate, Woodstock, Wynns and Zema Estate. Again, it's a fairly formidable collection, leaving little doubt that there is more top-end wine being made in Australia today than ever before.

Great wines from 2004 and 2005

The 2004 vintage made the task of compiling this book even happier than usual. As predicted in the 2005 edition, this vintage has delivered a number of genuine highlights. South Australia, which produces roughly half of Australia's wine, enjoyed a fine red wine vintage, especially for cabernet sauvignon, and especially in areas like McLaren Vale and Coonawarra. There is some truly outstanding Barossa cabernet sauvignon from 2004, plus some very handy Barossa shiraz.

2004 was also possibly the best year yet for McLaren Vale shiraz, certainly the best since 1995 and 1998. I have never tasted so many McLaren Vale shirazes of gold medal standard from a single vintage. Coonawarra experienced a late but even vintage, producing truly regional reds of exceptional intensity and elegance. The finest will live on and on, just like the great releases from the 1950s and 1960s.

Similarly, the better low-cropped vineyards in Margaret River enjoyed an exceptional 2004 vintage. While several of its better makes found chardonnay a challenge, the region has delivered more top-class cabernet than ever.

Furthermore, the early signs from Coonawarra, southern Victoria and Margaret River are that another great cabernet vintage is on the way. If Australia's best from 2004 and 2005 don't get people talking about cabernet again, I don't know what will.

As more 2005 releases come on to the market, it will be possible to see what a marvellous vintage that was for Tasmania. It has taken Tasmania a long time to fulfil the undoubted potential of its better sites, but today its wine industry is significantly better equipped, better resourced, more experienced and more technically capable than it was just a decade ago. It's also one of those parts of the world whose viticulture will doubtless benefit from global warming.

From the Government and here to help?

While climate change is undoubtedly assisting genuine cool-climate viticulture, an even more unexpected source of assistance to Australian wine is the Federal Treasury. The Federal Government increased the rebate per winery from the Wine Equalisation Tax from $290,000 to $500,000. Intended to restore some measure of profitability to small players, most or all wineries will simply use this money to reduce prices and retain distribution, benefiting nobody. One day, perhaps, the Government will apply a tax policy to Australian wine that shows more than a kindergarten-level understanding of the industry. But at least it is thinking well of wine, for a change!

The natural wine supplier to Asian markets

My recent experiences in Asia have given me further cause for optimism about Australian wine. Having spent time with many of the region's leading wine professionals, I am not only impressed by the thoroughness and depth of their knowledge and enthusiasm for wine, but by their willingness to experience wine sourced from countries outside wine's Old World.

Australia needs to showcase its best wine around the world, in Asia especially. The profile of top-level Australian wine lags well below its European competition in Asian markets. It is encouraging that the top buyers and sommeliers are prepared to give Australian wine a chance, but our wine producers need to give them compelling reasons to buy Australian.

Why is this so important? A few years ago I was hosting an Australian wine event at the Ritz-Carlton Millenia in Singapore. Two of the guests were American businessmen fascinated by the wines I was presenting. Having introduced myself, I asked them what would bring two Americans to an Australian wine dinner in Singapore. 'When you're in the region, you drink the regional wines,' I was told. Nothing else could quite put it so clearly. Australia is the logical local supplier of wine to Asia, and its winemakers should not rest until this ambition becomes reality.

Vale, Dr John

Looking over this introduction, I can't help being reminded of another annual publication, in which a very deep-thinking and not entirely unopinionated individual would forthrightly comment on just about anything he could relate to wine. It was the only winery newsletter I actually read in full, and it's a sad thought that I have read the last Mount Mary newsletter written by John Middleton.

Dr John would address his subject with the subtlety of a marksman taking target practice from six feet, with a Gatling gun. He made an enormous contribution to Australian wine, not just through the legacy of great wine he leaves behind. While Robert Parker recently took apart several vintages of Mount Mary wines, I firmly believe that Parker was wrong. Mount Mary is and will hopefully remain one of the New World's greatest and most important wineries. John Middleton is already missed by his thousands of devotees.

I have written this guide with the same energy and enthusiasm for Australian wine with which I began my first. It is still written for wine drinkers, and not winemakers.

The sheer number of Australian wines made today has made it harder than ever to research, and to decide which wines are in, and which are out. I realise I can never please everybody. And while it is no longer possible for a single individual to cover every Australian wine, I can assure you that there is no Jeremy Oliver tasting panel, and no scores, thoughts or comments in this guide that are anything other than 100% my own.

Thank you for picking up this book. I hope it helps you understand Australian wine better and enjoy it more.

Acknowledgements

This book would not have been created without the dedicated assistance provided by a number of people. Thanks to Toby Hines, Stephen O'Connor, Robyn Heald and Frank Ameneiro of Artifishal Studios. Special thanks also to Michael Wollan, Robyn Lee and Roslyn Grundy as well as my father, Rodney Oliver. It's a finicky and demanding process, but a worthwhile one! Thanks again to my wife, Jennifer, and son, Benjamin, who will now have to adjust to my reappearance in their lives!

How to use this book

Finding the wine or winery

It's dead easy to find the wine you're after in *The Australian Wine Annual*. Each winery or brand of wine is presented in alphabetic order. Under the winery heading, each of its wines or labels is then listed alphabetically. To find the tasting note and ratings for Rosemount Estate Roxburgh Chardonnay, for example, simply search for the start of Rosemount Estate's entries, which begin on page 238 then turn alphabetically through the pages to the Roxburgh Chardonnay, which appears on page 240.

Winery information

Wherever possible, the actual address of each winery is listed in this book — not its head office or marketing office — plus its region, telephone number, fax number and web site and e-mail address if appropriate. On those occasions where the entries refer to a vineyard whose wines are made elsewhere, the address usually supplied is for the vineyard itself. So, if you're thinking of visiting a vineyard and wish to be sure whether or not it is open for public inspection, I suggest you telephone the company using the number provided.

Each winery included is accompanied by a listing of its winemaker, viticulturist and chief executive, plus brief details concerning any recent changes of ownership or direction, key wines and recent developments of interest.

The Wine Ranking

The Australian Wine Annual provides the only Australian classification of nearly all major Australian wine brands determined on the most important aspect of all: quality. Unlike the very worthwhile Langtons' Classification of Distinguished Australian Wine, which presents a more limited overview of the super-premium market and which is largely based on resale price and performance at auction, the Wine Rankings in this book are not influenced in any way by price or other secondary factors. Being a secondary market, the auction market is usually slow to respond to the emergence of new quality wines, while in some cases, for example the plethora of so-called 'cult' shirazes from the Barossa and McLaren Vale, it can produce excessive prices grossly disproportionate to genuine wine quality.

The Wine Ranking is your easiest and most convenient guide to wine quality. This book allocates to the best wines in Australia a Wine Ranking from 1 to 5, based on the scores they constantly receive in my tastings, which are printed adjacent to each entry. Unless I have good reason to do otherwise, such as opening a bottle spoiled for some reason, the scores printed in this edition relate to the most recent occasion on which I have tasted each wine. Any wine to be allocated a Wine Ranking at all must have scored consistently well in my tastings. So, even if its Ranking is a lowly 5, the wine might still represent excellent value for money.

To provide a rough basis for comparison, a Wine Ranking of 1 is broadly equivalent to a Grand Cru classification in France. A large number of wines included in this book are not given Wine Rankings, since the minimum requirement for a ranking of 5 is still pretty steep.

At the head of the next page is a rough guide to the way Wine Rankings relate to scores out of 100, and how they compare to different medal standards used in the Australian wine show system.

Wine Ranking	Regular Score in Jeremy Oliver's Tastings	Approximate Medal Equivalent
RATING **1**	96+	**Top gold medal**
RATING **2**	94–95	**Regular gold medal**
RATING **3**	92–93	**Top silver medal**
RATING **4**	90–91	**Regular silver medal**
RATING **5**	87–89	**Top bronze medal**

See the flap on the inside front cover for further information.

As far as this book is concerned, if a brand of wine improves over time, so will its Wine Ranking. Similarly, if its standard declines, so will its ranking. Since Wine Rankings are largely a reflection of each label's performance over the last four years, they are unlikely to change immediately as a result of a single especially poor or exceptionally good year.

Reassessing back vintages

While I taste thousands of current and forthcoming releases each year, I also taste hundreds of back vintages. I have the classic wine writer's cellar, comprising single bottles of many wines, which I open regularly. If a wine is drinking significantly differently to the details I have previously published, I update them.Throughout the year I also attend a large number of tastings which give me the chance to refresh my views on entire verticals of wines. These are invaluable, since they tend to even out the changes in wine fashion, viticulture and winemaking techniques that inevitably occur over time.

I believe it is important for critics to re-evaluate wine, and to be prepared to alter scores if necessary. There are so many variables that can affect the way even the most professional taster can perceive a wine from one tasting to the next that it is ludicrous for anyone to expect a wine to attract precisely the same score, time and again.

Current Price Range

All the wines listed are allocated a price range within which you can usually expect to find their latest releases.

When to drink each wine

To the right hand side of the wine listings is a column that features the suggested drinking range for every vintage of each wine included, within which I would expect each wine to reach its peak. If a '+' sign appears after a range of years, it is quite possible that well-cellared bottles may happily endure after the later year of the specified range.

These drinking windows are my estimations alone, since it's apparent that different people enjoy their wines at different stages of development. Some of us prefer the primary flavours of young wine, while others would rather the virtually decayed qualities of extremely old bottles. However, it's a day-to-day tragedy how few top Australian cellaring wines of all types and persuasions are actually opened at or even close to their prime.

For quick and easy reference, a broad indication of each vintage's maturity is provided with a simple colour background. The chart inside the front cover explains how the colours indicate whether a wine is drinking at its best now, will improve further if left alone, or if it is likely to be past its best.

Best Australian Wines Under $20

There has never been a better time to buy Australian wine under $20. Each of these wines has achieved a score of 90-plus, and in my estimation qualifies for at least Silver Medal status. These wines are listed here because their normal retail price is under $20, so this list does not take into account the walk-in specials, or 'loss-leaders' deployed by the large chains to attract you to shop in their stores. On any given day, some amazing wine or other is being sold somewhere for well below its genuine value.

Yet again, riesling is the strongest variety by some margin. While the prices of the better rieslings are steadily rising, there is still plenty of spectacular value with this variety for around $15, and even below.

Cabernets and Blends

Devil's Lair Fifth Leg Red 2005	90
Huntington Estate Cabernet Sauvignon 2002	90
Mildara Coonawarra Cabernet Sauvignon 2002	92
St Huberts Cabernet Merlot 2004	90
Taltarni Three Monks Cabernet Merlot 2004	90
Water Wheel Cabernet Sauvignon 2004	90
Woodlands Cabernet Merlot 2004	93

Chardonnay

Barwang Chardonnay 2005	91
Coldstream Hills Chardonnay 2005	90
Blue Pyrenees Chardonnay 2005	90
Westend Three Bridges Chardonnay 2004	90
Wynns Coonawarra Estate Chardonnay 2005	90

Riesling

3drops Riesling 2005	91
Brown Brothers Victoria Riesling 2005	90
Delatite Riesling 2005	91
Feathertop Riesling 2005	91
Ferngrove Riesling 2004	90
Geoff Weaver Riesling 2005	93
Heggies Riesling 2005	95
Hewitson Eden Valley Riesling 2005	92
Jacobs Creek Reserve Riesling 2004	93
Jim Barry Watervale Riesling 2005	91
Knappstein Riesling 2005	93
Leasingham Bin 7 Riesling 2005	94
Leo Buring Eden Valley Riesling 2005	95
McWilliams Clare Valley Riesling 2005	92
Mitchell Watervale Riesling 2005	95
Orlando St Helga Riesling 2005	95
Pauletts Riesling 2005	93
Peter Lehmann Eden Valley Riesling 2005	93
Pewsey Vale Riesling 2005	93
Pikes Riesling 2005	92
Plantagenet Riesling 2005	95
Reillys Watervale Riesling 2005	93
Sevenhill St Aloysius Riesling 2005	92
Taylors Jaraman Riesling 2005	94
Wirra Wirra Hand Picked Riesling 2005	90

Sauvignon Blanc

Amberley Sauvignon Blanc 2005	93
d'Arenberg The Broken Fishplate Sauvignon Blanc 2005	91
Grant Burge Kraft Sauvignon Blanc 2005	92
Omrah Sauvignon Blanc 2005	90
Redgate Reserve Sauvignon Blanc 2005	91
Starvedog Lane Sauvignon Blanc 2005	94
Voyager Estate Sauvignon Blanc Semillon 2005	91

Semillon and Blends

Allandale Semillon 2005	90
Bethany Semillon 2004	90
Brokenwood Semillon 2005	90
Crofters Semillon Sauvignon Blanc 2005	90
Lindemans Hunter Valley Bin 0455 Semillon 2004	92
St Hallett Semillon 2003	92
Wandin Valley Reserve Semillon 2005	91

Shiraz and Blends

d'Arenberg d'Arrys Original Shiraz Grenache 2004	92
Huntington Estate Shiraz 2002	90
Jacobs Creek Reserve Shiraz 2003	90
Jacobs Creek Shiraz Cabernet 2004	90
Lindemans Hunter Valley Bin 0403 Shiraz 2004	90
Metala Shiraz Cabernet 2004	90
Morris Shiraz 2002	90
Peter Lehmann Barossa Shiraz 2004	90
Richmond Grove Limited Release Barossa Shiraz 2001	90
Seppelt Victoria Shiraz 2004	90
Tahbilk Shiraz 2003	91
Water Wheel Shiraz 2004	90

Other Reds

Discovery Road Pinot Noir 2004	90
Heatland Dolcetto Langrein 2004	91
Richard Hamilton Lot 148 Merlot 2004	90

Other Whites

Domain Day Garganega 2005	90
Gramp's Botrytis Semillon 2004	90
Lillydale Estate Gewürztraminer 2005	93
Madew Pinot Gris 2005	92
Margan Botrytis Semillon 2005	91
Skillogalee Gewürztraminer 2005	90

Current Trends in Australian Wine

One of Australia's largest wine companies recently exhibited a number of its wines at a public food and wine show in Melbourne. Its most popular wine, by far, was a slightly sweet and very effervescent rosé. They ran out of it.

While there's little doubt that the serious wine-drinking segment of the Australian population is becoming more sophisticated, the appeal of wine is significantly broader than just to those who sniff and swirl. Just as some people buy cars simply to get around, others buy them for prestige, price, perceived quality and style. It's no different with wine.

Two of the hottest segments within Australian wine retail are sauvignon blanc and rosé. While New Zealand sauvignon blanc dominates its category, by and large it is now a simpler, more confectionary and sweeter wine than that on which its reputation was forged. Most today lack the cut, the shape and the raciness of which the best are capable.

While neither denying their popularity nor attempting to understand it, rosés are back in force. I'm old enough to remember the phenomenon of Mateus and its raft of imitators in the late 1970s, and contrary to the opinion expressed a few years later by Split Enz, history does repeat. I receive hundreds of bottles of Australian rosé each year and while I find most to be excessively cloying, candied and alcoholic, there are clearly countless other drinkers who do not.

The other fad of the moment is pinot gris, or grigio, or whatever. Far too much Australian pinot gris is thick, oily, hard and flabby, while most pinot grigio is so dull, flat and uninteresting that bottled water looks complex by comparison. The fact that there are fine Australian examples of these styles makes it harder to understand why so many ordinary ones sell so well.

Because it remains tarnished by its fat, oaky past, many Australian wine drinkers still ignore chardonnay. Indeed, it has become as fashionable to publicly decry chardonnay as it is to choose an inferior pinot gris (or grigio). That's frustrating for many wineries, whose chardonnays are today less oaky, more restrained and with more refreshing acid balances than those of yesteryear. However, it's possible that the days are numbered for that wine born of economic necessity, unwooded chardonnay. Today, winemakers are using oak so deftly that this extreme (and largely deficient) wine has lost its raison d'être.

As I noted last year, the red wine fad of the moment is the shiraz-viognier blend. While there is still too much viognier in most of these wines, the species has certainly improved over the past twelve months. There is, however, a danger that winemakers might throw out the baby with the bathwater, adding viognier to their shiraz in circumstances that actually diminish the wine. Fashion can sometimes come at a cost.

I have never been one to talk up the virtues of wines made from newly introduced varieties before their time. As we saw with the introduction of pinot noir to Australia, it takes time for the right clones to be matched to the right sites, for grape growers to learn how best to capitalise on the new variety and for winemakers to understand how to deal with it in the cellar.

With a few exceptions, it took the better part of two decades before Australia could consistently make good pinot, so while it's exciting to see people serious about their sangiovese, nebbiolo, barbera, tempranillo, graciano, garganega, petit manseng et al, it's not realistic to expect miracles overnight. That said, some makers have done the research, are getting the right clones, and beginning to make some startling wine. This is good news because not only does it expand the diversity of Australian wine — which was frankly looking rather narrow a decade ago — but many of these varieties come from European regions where they produce dry and savoury wines that are better-equipped to handle various expressions of Australia's widely diverse cuisine. No wines go better with traditional Italian cuisine, for instance, than Italian wines — or fine Australian examples made from the same grape varieties.

It's no coincidence that sales of imported wines — many of which are significantly leaner, tighter and more savoury than the average Australian offering — continue to grow apace. I'm thoroughly in favour of this. Not only do imported wines provide more diversity for Australian wine drinkers, but they act as a reality check — and an inspiration — for our own winemakers.

One trend that is troubling more Australian winemakers is the high level of alcohol evident in wine, reds especially. More are aware that alcoholic strengths over 14% have the potential to unbalance most wines.

Reds have become more alcoholic for several reasons. Modern viticultural techniques that expose fruit to the elements appear to accelerate the accumulation of sugar, so genuinely ripe fruit flavours do not appear in grapes until higher sugar concentrations are present. Furthermore, modern winemaking yeasts are converting sugar into more alcohol more efficiently. And compounding the issue, many opinion leaders are still talking up the virtues of wines that are frankly out of balance, frequently dehydrated and lacking length and brightness of fruit. These 'dead grape' wines, as they could more accurately be described, also have far shorter cellaring lives than wines made from fruit harvested at its peak of ripeness.

As more over-ripe Australian wines made since 1997 are opened after a few years in the bottle, their flaws are becoming apparent. Frankly, some of us were preaching this back then. In response, more winemakers are talking about balance in the vineyards and adjusting viticultural practices in an effort to achieve the flavours they are seeking with less sugar in the fruit. Furthermore, the companies that own the machines that selectively remove alcohol from wine are having a day out.

Wine is such a precise reflection of a country's culture. Australian culture is energetic, industrious, creative and innovative. Once we're convinced of the merits of something, we adopt it as our own. We like our good life, but at the same time, we find excessive displays of opulence or ego distasteful. We enjoy our culture, but fine art, opera and theatre struggle more than they should in an economy and society like ours. Our restaurants, whether traditional or fashionable, are frequently excellent. But most are stylish cafés and bistros, not fine dining restaurants.

Our wine mirrors that precisely. We are doing well, better than we have been, but it could be so much better. Many vineyards are performing well below their potential because their makers and growers are nervous about moving too upmarket. The challenge for Australian wine is to create the environment for more people to do so, and profitably. Then we will really see what this country can do. But, until this happens, there's no cause for complacency or self-congratulation.

The Top Tens...

People are always asking wine writers for their 'best of' lists. These questions typically draw a blank from me, for I'm always nervous about missing something out. So here are some predetermined lists of Top Tens, with a special emphasis on the most important wine varieties made in Australia today. Where I recommend a wine, it's one I have tasted within the last twelve months and, to the best of my knowledge, is still currently available at the time of publication of this issue.

The Top Ten Bargain Ranges

- Angoves Long Row
- Deakin Estate
- De Bortoli Windy Peak
- Jacob's Creek
- Hardy's Oomoo
- Lindemans Bin Series
- McWilliams Hanwood
- Preece
- Rosemount Diamond Series
- Yalumba Y

The Top Ten Chardonnays

1.	Leeuwin Estate 2003 (Margaret River)	97
2.	Wantirna Estate 2005 (Yarra Valley)	97
3.	Lake's Folly 2004 (Lower Hunter Valley)	96
4.	Yeringberg 2005 (Yarra Valley)	96
5.	Stonier KBS 2004 (Mornington Peninsula)	96
6.	Tyrrell's Vat 47 2004 (Lower Hunter Valley)	96
7.	Seville Estate Reserve 2004 (Yarra Valley)	96
8.	TarraWarra Estate 2004 (Yarra Valley)	96
9.	Voyager Estate 2004 (Margaret River)	96
10.	Bindi Quartz (Macedon Ranges)	95

The Top Ten Rieslings

1.	Grosset Polish Hill 2005 (Clare Valley)	98
2.	Jacob's Creek Steingarten 2003 (Eden Valley)	98
3.	mesh 2005 (Eden Valley)	97
4.	Seppelt Drumborg 2005 (Henty)	97
5.	Grosset Watervale 2005 (Clare Valley)	96
6.	Knappstein Ackland Vineyard 2005 (Clare Valley)	96
7.	Forest Hill 2005 (Mount Barker)	95
8.	Plantagenet 2005 (Mount Barker)	95
9.	Leasingham Classic Clare 2005 (Clare Valley)	95
10.	Pipers Brook 2005 (Pipers River)	95

The Top Ten Cabernets and Blends

1.	Balnaves The Tally Reserve Cabernet Sauvignon 2004 (Coonawarra)	97
2.	Cullen Diana Madeline Cabernet Sauvignon Merlot 2004 (Margaret River)	97
3.	Woodlands Cabernet Sauvignon 2004 (Margaret River)	97
4.	Yarra Yarra The Yarra Yarra 2003 (Yarra Valley)	97
5.	Saltram Winemaker Selection Cabernet Sauvignon 2002 (Barossa)	97
6.	Wantirna Estate Amelia Cabernet Sauvignon Merlot 2004 (Yarra Valley)	97
7.	Mount Mary Quintet (Yarra Valley)	97
8.	Woodlands Margaret Reserve Cabernet Merlot (Margaret River)	97
9.	Dalwhinnie Cabernet Sauvignon 2004 (Pyrenees)	97
10.	Henschke Cyril Henschke Cabernet Sauvignon 2002 (Eden Valley)	96

The Top Ten Pinot Noirs

1.	Bass Phillip Reserve 2004 (Gippsland)	97
2.	Main Ridge Estate Half Acre Pinot Noir 2004	97
3.	Epis Pinot Noir 2004 (Macedon Ranges)	97
4.	Mount Mary Pinot Noir 2004 (Yarra Valley)	96
5.	Bindi Block 5 2004 (Macedon Ranges)	96
6.	Wantirna Estate Lily Pinot Noir 2005 (Yarra Valley)	96
7.	Stonier Windmill Pinot Noir 2004 (Mornington Peninsula)	96
8.	Stefano Lubiana 2004 (Derwent Valley)	95
9.	Yarra Yering 2004 (Yarra Valley)	95
10.	By Farr 2004 (Geelong)	95

The Top Ten Dry Semillons

1. Tyrrell's Vat 1 1999 (Lower Hunter Valley) — 97
2. Thomas Braemore 2005 (Lower Hunter Valley) — 95
3. Brokenwood ILR 1999 (Lower Hunter Valley) — 95
4. Mount Horrocks 2005 (Clare Valley) — 95
5. Tyrrell's Reserve HVD 1999 (Lower Hunter Valley) — 94
6. Mount Pleasant Lovedale 2002 (Lower Hunter Valley) — 94
7. Capercaillie 1999 (Lower Hunter Valley) — 93
8. Tower Estate Hunter Valley 2006 (Lower Hunter Valley) — 93
9. Tyrrell's Reserve Belford 1999 (Lower Hunter Valley) — 93
10. Sandstone 2004 (Margaret River) — 93

The Top Ten Shiraz

1. Seppelt St Peters Shiraz 2004 (Great Western) — 97
2. Wendouree Shiraz 2004 (Clare Valley) — 97
3. Dalwhinnie Shiraz 2004 (Pyrenees) — 97
4. Saltram The Eighth Maker Shiraz 2002 (Barossa Valley) — 97
5. Yarra Yering Dry Red No. 2 (Shiraz Viognier) 2004 (Yarra Valley) — 97
6. Penfolds St Henri Shiraz 2002 (South Australia) — 97

7. d'Arenberg The Dead Arm 2004 (McLaren Vale) — 96
8. Thomas Kiss Shiraz 2004 (Lower Hunter Valley) — 96
9. Coriole Lloyd Reserve 2004 (McLaren Vale) — 96
10. Giaconda Warner Vineyard 2004 (Beechworth) — 96

The Top Ten Wines from New Varieties

1. Castagna La Chiave Sangiovese 2004 (Beechworth) — 95
2. Jasper Hill Georgia's Paddock Nebbiolo 2004 (Heathcote) — 94
3. Primo Estate Joseph Nebbiolo 2002 (McLaren Vale) — 94
4. Pizzini Sangiovese 2004 (King Valley) — 93
5. Coriole Sangiovese 2004 (McLaren Vale) — 92
6. Montrose Barbera 2002 (Mudgee) — 92
7. Yalumba Tempranillo Grenache Viognier 2005 (Barossa) — 92
8. d'Arenberg The Sticks & Stones Tempranillo Grenache Souzao (McLaren Vale) — 92
9. Mt Surmon Wines Reserve Nebbiolo 2003 (Clare Valley) — 91
10. Heartland Dolcetto Lagrein 2004 (Langhorne Creek) — 91

The Top Ten Tips for Wine Investment

- Stick with established brands, large and small.
- Avoid poor or ordinary vintages like they're carrying a communicable disease.
- If you buy in dozens, unopened boxes are best.
- The market, especially the overseas component, is spending big on older vintages of top labels and good years.
- Just because a currently available wine may be expensive, it doesn't mean that
  (a) it is any good, and
  (b) that it will appreciate in value.
- Shiraz is still king, locally and overseas.
- Magnums cost more than they should in Australia, but they do appreciate more quickly.
- Check the track record of the agent or auction house, plus the selling and buying commissions applicable.
- Buy at or before release if you can, for the lowest possible price.
- Check on provenance whenever and wherever you can.

Australia's Perfect 1s

Of the thousands of table wines made in Australia today, I have allocated the highest possible wine ranking of 1 to a mere 18. These are the benchmarks, the Grand Cru standards, the wines against which all others can be measured. As a group, they are continually improving, but together they define the limits of contemporary Australian wine.

Each has its particular stamp. Each certainly reflects vintage variation from year to year, usually without compromising the special qualities associated with the label.

Bass Phillip Reserve Pinot Noir

Australia's best and longest-living pinot noir, made in Gippsland, by Phillip Jones. is a frustratingly rare, full orchestra wine capable of stunning evolution and expression of briary, meaty complexity and layered structure.

Clarendon Hills Astralis Syrah

Sourced from ancient vines near Clarendon, Roman Bratasiuk's ultimate red has performed exceptionally well in recent years, rising to extraordinary levels of strength and finesse. A powerful statement at the more sumptuous end of the shiraz spectrum.

Clonakilla Shiraz Viognier

Tim Kirk is succeeding in his ambition of creating an exotically perfumed, deeply scented and powerfully flavoured shiraz-viognier blend in a style faithful to the best from the northern Rhône Valley. Poles apart from mainstream Australian shiraz, this savoury, firm and fine-grained red has spawned a generation of imitators.

Cullen Diana Madeline Cabernet Sauvignon Merlot

An essay in concentration, elegance and refinement from Margaret River, this wine is not without power and presence. The piercing intensity, refined structure and enormous potential of Vanya Cullen's premier wine leaves little to the imagination.

Giaconda Chardonnay

My pick as Australia's finest chardonnay, this is extraordinarily well structured, meaty, savoury and complete. Expressing a heritage more Burgundian than Australian, it is made by Rick Kinzbrunner at Beechworth in Victoria.

Grosset Polish Hill

A modern icon in Australian wine, Jeffrey Grosset's standout Clare Valley Riesling stretches the limits of what this most traditional of Australian varieties is able to achieve.

Henschke Hill of Grace

In a country full of spectacular single-vineyard shiraz wines, Steven Henschke's signature wine from this individual Eden Valley vineyard marries firmness with velvet-like fineness; vitality with longevity.

Jacob's Creek Steingarten Riesling

This apogee of the great riesling vineyard resources and experience within Orlando Wyndham (now Pernod Ricard Pacific) marries exceptional fruit intensity and fragrance with mouth-watering minerality and tight acidity.

Leeuwin Estate Chardonnay

At the forefront of Australian chardonnay since its first vintage in 1980, this luscious and long-living Margaret River wine has been for many palates the real 'white Grange'.

Leo Buring Leonay Eden Valley Riesling

A classic and traditional Australian label, whose most recent releases — erratic as their appearances may have been — have invariably proved spectacular. The cellaring potential of these wines is simply legendary.

Mount Mary Cabernet 'Quintet'

An inspiration by John Middleton in Victoria's Yarra Valley, this is the nearest Australian wine to a premier Bordeaux red and a global standard in its own right. Recent vintages have been downright brilliant.

Penfolds Bin 707 Cabernet Sauvignon

Penfolds' most eloquent expression of cabernet sauvignon. This multi-regional blend, matured in new American oak, represents the pick of Penfolds' entire South Australian cabernet crop.

Penfolds Grange

Australia's definitive red wine has been a model of style and consistency since 1951. Based on Barossa shiraz, it incorporates contributions from other regions and small amounts of cabernet sauvignon.

Petaluma Tiers Chardonnay

A single-vineyard chardonnay, sourced from the mature block immediately above Petaluma's winery. Very fine and restrained, exceptionally long and mineral, it reveals a surprisingly concentrated core of explosive fruit.

Pierro Chardonnay

The role model for so many of Australia's more opulent and hedonistically proportioned chardonnays, this stunning expression of Margaret River chardonnay by Mike Peterkin is now becoming more elegant and mineral.

Seppelt St Peters Shiraz

A definitive Great Western shiraz from the Grampians region of western Victoria. Arthur O'Connor and his team are unashamedly seeking Grand Cru status for this wine, sourced from the low-yielding St Peters, Imperial and Police vineyards.

Wendouree Shiraz

A fastidiously maintained ancient dryland vineyard in Clare is at the heart of this great wine. The past ten years have seen the development of more fruit sweetness in new releases without compromising the legendary structure and longevity of this wine.

Wolf Blass Platinum Label Shiraz

Proof positive that Australia's largest winemakers are working as hard as ever to make the country's leading wine. Sourced from a collection of small vineyards in the Eden Valley, Barossa floor and Adelaide Hills, this is consistently complex and musky, delivering intensely pure and vibrant shiraz flavour.

Jeremy Oliver's Wine of the Year

This edition marks the eighth naming of Jeremy Oliver's Wine of the Year, drawn from the ten best current-release Australian wines I have tasted throughout the previous year.

In sequence, the previous winners have been Rosemount Estate's 1996 Mountain Blue Shiraz Cabernet Sauvignon, Cullen's 1998 Cabernet Sauvignon Merlot 1998, Hardy's Eileen Hardy Shiraz 1998, Mount Mary Quintet 2000, Lake's Folly's Cabernet Blend 2001, Wolf Blass Platinum Label Shiraz 2001 and Leeuwin Estate's Art Series Chardonnay 2002.

While quality clearly remains paramount in making this award, the winning wine must be commercially available around or shortly after the time of publication and represent some special characteristic of individuality, innovation, maturity or longevity. Wines selected must make a positive statement about style, terroir and winemaking direction.

Here are the finalists for Jeremy Oliver's 2006 Wine of the Year, including the winner itself.

Wine of the Year

Balnaves The Tally Reserve Cabernet Sauvignon 2004 (97)

Australian wine is busily promoting its shiraz all around the world, and I go and name another cabernet as Wine of the Year. Is there a subplot? Not on your life! This is a marvellous wine and there are plenty of winemakers in this country for whom it should be mandatory tasting.

A straight cabernet sauvignon, it has been skilfully grown and superbly crafted, marrying the purest varietal fruit with some pretty snazzy oak and some of the best tannin going around in Australian wine. It's one of those rare cabernets that honestly doesn't need anything else thrown into the mix. And it will live and develop for decades.

Made by artisan winemaker Pete Bissell, The Tally is the top-grade cabernet from Balnaves. Bissell was understudy to Peter Douglas at Wynn's Coonawarra when Doug Balnaves poached him in 1995. Bissell began separating out reserve parcels in 1996 and 1997, but wasn't allowed to bottle them separately. Then, in 1998, he showed Doug Balnaves a wine, saying 'That's the super-premium I'm not allowed to make. We have 200 cases of it. Do you want me to blend it away?' The Tally was born.

The 2004 vintage is typically deep, withdrawn and layered, and takes its time to unfold. It's already perfumed, but you sense there is so much more to come. It's concentrated without being cloying, firm without being aggressive, sumptuous and savoury without being heavy. It's utterly complete, balanced and perfectly structured, with the sort of fine, drying and tightly integrated tannins that are only evident from top vineyards.

Sourced from Balnaves' Walker block (77%), Dead Morris Vineyard (21%) and Rise Vineyard (2%), it spent 20 months in new fine-grained barrels from Seguin Moreau, Saury and Taransaud cooperages before a light egg fining and bottling in March 2006.

Finalists

Bass Phillip Reserve Pinot Noir 2004 (97)

Phillip Jones remains at the cutting edge of Australian pinot noir. From the original plantings near his winery at Leongatha comes this tiny two-barrel selection whose significance and impact far outweighs the volume of its make. This is a typically powerful and opulent young Bass Phillip pinot that is anything but ready to drink. When it is, it will blow you away.

Clarendon Hills Astralis Syrah 2004 (97)

This is the second consecutive year in which Astralis has made this list. It's a wine of extremities, but everything it does, it does exceptionally well. Despite its overt opulence, oak and ripeness, it's controlled, balanced and very together. In fact, its sour-edged flavours of cassis, dark plums, blackberries and cherries offer about as much as McLaren Vale shiraz is ever going to give, without even a hint of over-ripeness or dead fruit.

Cullen Diana Madeline Cabernet Sauvignon Merlot 2004 (97)

An almost perpetual inclusion in this list, and another triumph from Vanya Cullen, this cabernet blend effortlessly marries structure and power with elegance, tightness and fineness. It's deeply scented and alluring, and is another of the top echelon of Australian cabernets to experience the means by which intensely flavoured and succulent fruit can be supported by assertive and even astringent tannins.

Grosset Polish Hill Riesling 2005 (98)

This exceptional wine thoroughly deserves its extraordinary score. It's one of the most approachable and early-drinking Polish Hills, but one that will cellar for as long as the rest of them. It combines the richness and roundness of 2002 with the structure of the 2003 vintage. Few rieslings are genuinely great, but I believe this, the highest-ever scoring Polish Hill, to be just that. If you get some, try to keep it.

Jacob's Creek Steingarten Riesling 2003 (98)

A better wine even than the excellent 2002 vintage, which previously made the finals for this award. This edition is even more smoky, complex and mineral. Exceptionally tight, beautifully sculpted, chalky and deeply scented, it's the best of its kind yet made in Australia, and went very close to collecting this award. Rieslings of this kind change perceptions of what is possible from Australia's best mature vineyards.

Leeuwin Estate Art Series Chardonnay 2003 (97)

Last year's release picked up the award. Now Leeuwin Estate has followed it up with another outstanding wine. Here is a chardonnay that marries the opulence and generosity of the 2002 edition with the texture and underlying mineral spine of the 1995. Its perfectly focused and tightly integrated fruit, oak and acidity are nothing short of exemplary. Leeuwin Estate's track record with this wine is perhaps without peer anywhere in the world.

Seppelt St Peters Shiraz 2004 (97)

Arthur O'Connor's attention to detail continues to pay off with this wine, now recognised as being in the top echelons of Australian shiraz. This is a more substantial and profoundly structured wine than the 2002 vintage, also a finalist for this award. It's packed with pepper and spice, deeply stained with sour-edged fruit and framed by firm but silky tannins.

Woodlands Cabernet Sauvignon 2004 (97)

Unashamedly made in a fine, elegant and lightly herbal fashion by Stuart Watson, this wine eloquently states the case for more restrained, complex and finessed cabernets. Australia needs more champions of the red Bordeaux varieties right now, and Woodlands has certainly stepped up to the mark.

Yarra Yarra
The Yarra Yarra Cabernet Blend 2003 (97)

If, like many, you grew up thinking that cabernet was thin, lean and greenish, you need to try this wine. It's an aristocrat among Australian cool-climate reds, based on deep, dark and brooding fruit depth that knits seamlessly with new oak and firm, powdery tannins. It's a classic cabernet blend whose qualities are the very things you look for in fine Paulliac.

Cellaring Wine

If you're going to cellar wine...

Keep your wine upside down. While some scientists suggest that the partial pressure of water between the wine's surface and the cork in an upright bottle is enough to keep the cork sufficiently moist, I'm not prepared to take the risk. If corks dry out, air gets it. This is ruinous. An added advantage of the growing number of white wines packaged with screwcap seals for longevity and to guard against cork taint is that you can actually cellar them upright without concern. I have been amazed at the ability of both whites and reds to mature with these seals.

Keep your wine in the dark. Ultra-violet light can penetrate most glass bottles to some degree (especially the clear ones) and oxidise the wine inside. This is why so many cellars are dimly lit. If you haven't the space for a dark cellar, keep your bottles in their boxes or else behind a heavy curtain.

Keep your wine still and undisturbed. Regular vibrations accelerate the ageing process with wine. Furthermore, there's no need to turn your bottles every morning, as some people regularly do. This habit began when English gentlemen needed an unobtrusive means of checking that their household staff hadn't secreted any away from their premises, so they actually did this to count their stock.

Temperature should be both constant and low. There is debate about the ideal cellaring temperature. In my experience, if wine is cellared above 18 degrees Celsius it ages too quickly. If it is cellared at around 10–12 degrees, it ages very slowly, perhaps too slowly for some of us. Around 14 degrees is probably ideal, which means that in most parts of Australia, you will need some temperature control. Most importantly, changes in temperature from day to night and from season to season must be avoided if wine is to be kept for even a few months. So keep wine well away from windows and external walls, unless they're very thick.

Think about humidity. If a cellar is too humid then labels and racks may go mouldy. It's unlikely that the wines themselves will be adversely affected, but it's not worth the risk with rare and expensive wines. If there's not enough humidity in the cellar, the outward ends of wine corks may shrink and reduce their ability to impart a seal. This can considerably shorten a bottle's longevity. If there's too much humidity, a small fan can help to keep air moving.

If there's not enough, a bowl of water, or even water tipped onto a gravel floor, can help.

To make the most of your cellar...

Start by keeping good records. Book-keeping is essential unless you can readily remember the name and age of every wine you own. There's nothing worse than finding a good wine left beyond its peak, so a record-keeping system is crucial. Do it on the computer. There are several cellar management systems available to choose from. Use one that enables you to customise its logic to suit your own cellar. There's another big advantage if your cellar is computerised: you don't have to worry about the bin size or having to construct single bottle slots. All you do is search for a wine by name in your database and its location will automatically appear. Furthermore, in the unfortunate event of fire or flood, your records will at least give you a sporting chance when you make an insurance claim for your cellar contents.

Think about your buying and drinking habits. If you regularly buy wine by the dozen, you'll need bins for twelve bottles, bins for half-dozens and perhaps single bottle slots. That way you can put a new dozen straight into the system, move it along when you're half way through, and then insert the remaining bottles into their own slots. If you're designing a cellar this way, keep between 40–50% for single bottles.

Try to buy by the dozen. Most of us miss wine at its peak by purchasing a small amount and drinking it too soon. With a dozen bottles it has more of a chance and besides, some of us can only summon sufficient resistance with the sight of an unopened box. But if you've bought a dozen, don't rest on your laurels for a decade or more without taking a peep at the wine. Sometimes it's possible to wait too long. Sample a bottle about four years before the wine is expected to peak and then, all being well, about two years before. Your expectations will then be confirmed, or you should alter your approach towards the wine in question. Then, once you expect the time is near, try a bottle every six months or so. That way you should not only have enjoyed watching the wine develop, but have about six or seven bottles left to experience at their best.

So if your dream home wasn't built with a cellar...

Think about a temperature and humidity-controlled wine cabinet. Then you won't have a worry in the world about the health of your wine or your ability to access it. Some of these units are particularly impressive. Factors you might take into account if considering this option include your ability to change temperature settings, the ease of access to the wines inside, possible temperature zoning within the unit to provide different compartments for 'drink now' wines, whether or not fresh air circulates throughout the unit, that the inside of the unit is dark, that it is lockable, that any glass doors are UV-treated, and that the degree of vibration caused by motor units is minimal.

Find yourself a commercial cellaring facility. When choosing which cellaring facility to go with, ask about the temperature and humidity issues, find out about their data keeping facilities, how much and on what basis you will be charged, the security against theft, flood and fire and what sort of pick-up and delivery service you're offered. Will you be told when a wine is nearing its peak? Will you have the ability to buy from and trade with other customers? Some of these operations are equipped with professional standard tasting rooms and commercial kitchens and even offer club-style memberships to their customers, including newsletters, tastings and dinners. Other leading operations of this kind are networked over the entire country, so you can keep wine in different cities, depending on where you bought it.

Seasonal Variation and Quality

It's clear just by glancing through this book that the same grapes from the same vineyard invariably produce very different wines from year to year. Traditionally, vintage variation in Australia has been considered merely a fraction of that encountered in most European wine regions of any quality, but the last five years have proven it to be a very significant variable that demands consideration when buying wine.

Even if all other variables were consistent from year to year, which they certainly are not, weather provides the greatest single influence in wine quality and style from season to season. Weather can influence wine in an infinite number of ways, from determining whether conditions at flowering are favourable or not, all the way through to whether final ripening and harvest occur in the warmth of sunshine or through the midst of damaging rains. If viticulturists were to turn pagan, it would be to a god of weather that they would build their first shrine.

Weather-influenced variation is nearly always more pronounced and more frequent in the cooler, more marginal viticultural regions. While Australia is principally a warm to hot wine producing nation, a significant proportion of the country's premium wine now comes from cooler regions in the southwestern and southeastern corners of the continent. The spectrum of diverse weather encountered in these regions far exceeds that of the traditional Australian wine growing areas like the Barossa Valley, McLaren Vale, central Victoria and the Clare Valley. Paradoxically, the best years in cool climates are typically the warmer seasons that accelerate the ripening period, creating a finer acid balance, superior sugar levels, flavours and better-defined colours.

Variety by variety, this is how Australia's premium wine grapes are affected by seasonal conditions:

White wines

Chardonnay

Cool years cause chardonnay and most white varieties to accumulate higher levels of mineral acids, resulting in lean, tight wines with potential longevity, provided they have sufficient intensity of fruit. Cool year chardonnays can display greenish, herbal and green cashew flavours, and can resemble grapefruit and other citrus fruit, especially lemon. Warmer year wines become richer and rounder, with fruit flavours more suggestive of apple, pear, quince and cumquat. In hot seasons, chardonnays become flabbier, faster-maturing wines with flavours of peach, green olive, melon and tobacco.

Riesling

Although riesling does not need to ripen to the sugar levels necessary for a premium chardonnay, cool-season riesling tends to be lean and tight with hard steely acids, possibly lacking in length and persistence of flavour. Better rieslings from superior years have succulent youthful primary fruit flavours of lime juice, ripe pears and apples, with musky, citrus rind undertones. Significantly broader and less complex than wines from better seasons, warmer year rieslings tend to mature faster, occasionally becoming broad and fat on the palate after a short time.

Sauvignon Blanc

Cool season sauvignon blancs tend to be hard-edged wines with steely acids, with over-exaggerated and undesirable herbaceous flavours suggestive of asparagus and 'cat pee', a description for which I have yet to find a polite alternative even half as succinct. The warmer the season the riper the fruit becomes and the less grassy and vegetal the aroma. The downside is often a reduction in the intensity of the wine's primary fruit flavours. Expect sweet blackcurrants, gooseberries and passionfruit from sauvignon blancs in good seasons, with at least a light capsicum note. Warmer seasons create broader, occasionally oily and less grassy wines, with more emphasis on passionfruit, lychee and tropical fruit flavours.

Semillon

Semillon tends to react to cooler seasons by creating very tight, lean wines with more obvious grassy influences, but perhaps lacking in primary fruit character. On occasions, these rather one-dimensional young wines can develop stunning flavours in the bottle over many years, as classically unwooded Hunter semillon proves time and again. The best cellaring examples need length on the palate and an absence of green characters while young.

Red wines

Cabernet Sauvignon

A late-ripening grape variety which reacts very poorly to cool, late seasons, cabernet sauvignon has traditionally and wisely been blended with varieties like merlot (in Bordeaux) and shiraz (commonly, until recently in Australia). Cool season cabernet sauvignon makes the classic doughnut wine: intense cassis/raspberry fruit at the front of the palate with greenish, extractive tannin at the back and a hole in the middle. Under-ripe cabernet sauvignon reveals less colour and a thin, bitter finish. Its tannins are often greenish and under-ripe, tasting sappy or metallic, while its flavour can be dominated by greenish snow pea influences more suggestive of cool-climate sauvignon blanc.

Warmer seasons create much better cabernet, with genuinely ripe cassis/plum flavours, a superior middle palate and fine-grained, fully-ripened tannins, although a slight capsicum note can still be evident. In really hot years, the wines tend to become jammy and porty, suggestive of stewed, dehydrated prune and currant-like fruit flavours and lacking in any real definition and fineness of tannin.

Pinot Noir

Pinot noir does not react well to very cool seasons, becoming herbal and leafy, with a brackish, greenish palate and simple sweet raspberry confection fruit. Warmer seasons produce the more sought-after primary characters of sweet cherries and plums, fine-grained tannins and spicy, fleshy middle palate. Too warm a season and the wine turns out to be undefined, simple and fast maturing, often with unbalanced and hard-edged tannins.

Shiraz

Thin and often quite greenish — but rarely to the same extent as cabernet sauvignon — cool-season shiraz often acquires leafy white pepper characters, with spicy, herby influences plus metallic, sappy and green-edged tannins. Provided there's sufficient fruit, which may not be the case in cool seasons, it can still be a worthwhile wine, although not one likely to mature for long in the bottle. Warmer years create shiraz with characteristic richness and sweetness, with riper plum, cassis and chocolate flavours and fully-ripened tannins. Hot year shiraz is often typified by earthy flavours suggestive of bitumen and leather, with dehydrated prune juice and meaty characters.

2006 Australian Vintage Report

A vintage that caught most producers by surprise, 2006 was the earliest ever recorded — and by some margin — all over Australia with the very distinct exception of Western Australia. The early onset of warm, mild conditions caused rapid ripening through South Australia and the east coast. Once the sequence of events from flowering and fruit set onwards that leads to grape ripening is actually in train, very little can happen to slow it down.

White grapes ripened extremely quickly, and reds followed exceptionally shortly thereafter. In many cases reds accumulated sugar well in advance of genuine flavour development, so it is extremely likely that there will be a large number of 2006 reds with very high levels of alcohol, and with the presence of cooked and raisined flavours. Vineyards affected by drought conditions, or those which for whatever reason missed the very brief window of optimal flavour ripeness, will have more difficulties than others.

On a positive note, the vintage was largely free of significant vine diseases, and some very good wines were indeed made when grapes were harvested at their peak ripeness of flavour.

From a numerical perspective, the total national harvest was 1.846 million tones, 79,000 tonnes less than 2005. These figures do not yet take into account the amount of fruit either left on the vine or dropped onto the ground, which accounted for 50,000 tonnes in 2005. Estimates for 2006 at time of writing range between 100,000 and 200,000 tonnes. The Murray Valley Winegrowers, whose members produce just under a quarter of Australia's crop, estimate their own members left a minimum of 50,000 tonnes unsold, and believe the overall national figure could be well in excess of 200,000 tonnes, more than 10% of the national crop.

New South Wales

Other than some of the cooler inland regions, New South Wales' vintage was largely dominated by the ongoing period of extreme heat that began in late December. The vintage was early, compact and while it was without many genuine highlights, the average standard of wine made was surprisingly good. The better, older vineyards in the Hunter Valley handled the season best. Orange managed to avoid much of the heat, and enjoyed a solid vintage for white wines and cabernet sauvignon.

Queensland

Queensland's vintage was above average in quality, better than 2003 and 2004, but not as good as 2005. Highlights from the Granite Belt include sauvignon blanc and verdelho, while some growers there found it too hot for white wines, producing reds of good expectation. South Burnett growers enjoyed drier conditions than normal.

South Australia

South Australia's vintage was very early, warm and compact. Unusually, shiraz ripened later than cabernet sauvignon in several districts.

Cabernet sauvignon appreciated the Barossa Valley's early season better than did shiraz, whose wines lack the flesh and density of top vintages. Cabernet, however, appears to have good fruit expression and intensity. Eden Valley white wines are good, but not exceptional, while its reds are below average in standard. Clare Valley white wines tended to suffer from the early harvest. Its rieslings are deeply coloured and while many are quite concentrated, they will age for as long as usual. Clare Valley reds are solid but unexceptional.

While the overall standard of McLaren Vale reds is rather disappointing, the best old vine vineyards on top sites actually made some stunning wine. It's a vineyard-dependent thing in this region.

The south-east of the state performed well and quite evenly. Despite the earliness of the season, Coonawarra performed as well as it has done in recent years, while Padthaway and Wrattonbully produced solid wines of acceptable standard.

Tasmania

Tasmania experienced an exceptional season across all regions, styles and varieties. Despite one of the earliest seasons on record, northern Tasmania tended to harvest its crop with no alteration to its usual levels of flavours and acids. Red wines show excellent concentration and colour, while sparkling wines reveal excellent levels of acidity and flavour richness. Sauvignon blancs are ripe and fruit-driven, while the pinots could be first-rate.

While the southern Tasmanian vintage finished a month earlier than ever before, it has not come at any cost to flavour or quality. Crops were down by 15-20%, so flavours were intense, pinots deeply coloured and aromas fresh and vibrant in riesling, pinot gris and sauvignon blanc. The vintage could be even better than 2005.

Victoria

Exceptionally early, the Victorian vintage was a very mixed bag. The cooler regions were around a month earlier than usual, but that hasn't prevented some exceptional parcels of chardonnay and pinot noir from the Yarra Valley, the Macedon Ranges and the Mornington Peninsula.

North of the Great Dividing Range, the vintage was very hot, dry and quick. Wine quality will depend to a greater extent than usual on the management of the vineyards. Those which were allowed to avoid water stress and were harvested at the peak of flavour ripeness should produce good wine. The practical difficulty facing many wineries was that most varieties ripened together, which meant that the later of them were left on the vine past optimal ripeness because of inadequate processing and storage capacity.

The cooler alpine regions in the north-east were better able to retain brightness and freshness than those in central Victoria, and provided the fruit was harvested at slightly lower sugar levels than usual, should produce fresh and vibrant reds and whites. It was a very difficult season for the fortified makers of the north-east.

Overall, the vintage should rate above 2002 and 2003, but well below 2004.

Western Australia

An extremely cool, late and frustrating vintage for Western Australia has broken several climatic records of the wrong kind. It began later than any vintage in living memory and became progressively cooler as the 'summer' went on. It was a challenge to get sugar ripeness in white fruit and flavour ripeness in reds. A lot of red fruit was made into white wine.

It was a struggle for Margaret River cabernet to ripen, while merlot managed to produce some spectacular wines. The vineyards around the northern parts of Yallingup and Willyabrup fared better. Some of the crisp, aromatic whites look tight and vibrant, especially those from the warmer northerly parts of the region, while shiraz had a disaster season. The better vineyards should produce very good chardonnay.

The Great Southern struggled in the cool conditions, but the better-managed sites might have got over the line. Many stressed vineyards defoliated early in the cool weather. Shiraz was an enormous challenge. Pemberton should produce some good chardonnay.

Alkoomi

A

RMB 234, Wingebellup Road, Frankland WA 6396. Tel: (08) 9855 2229. Fax: (08) 9855 2284.
Website: www.alkoomiwines.com.au Email: info@alkoomiwines.com.au

Region: **Frankland River** Winemaker: **Michael Staniford** Viticulturist: **Wayne Lange** Chief Executive: **Merv Lange**

Alkoomi recently celebrated its 30th anniversary with the release of a special edition of one it its most distinctive wines, a perfumed, smooth and silky Malbec from 2004. One of its region's founding vineyards and wineries, Alkoomi makes very aromatic white wines, especially its Riesling, while its signature reds are intensely focused, offering a slightly jammy expression of mulberry and small berry flavours supported by firm, drying tannins. Its 'reserve' level Blackbutt blend of red Bordeaux varieties and its Jarrah Shiraz offer most complexity and definition of fruit, while its spicy Shiraz Viognier is evolving into a pleasing marriage of these varieties.

BLACKBUTT RED BLEND
RATING 3

Frankland River $30–$49
Current vintage: 2004   92

A polished, smooth and elegant cabernet blend of Alkoomi's typically unctuous and dark-fruited style. Its confiture-like fragrance of blackberries, dark plums and cassis reveals herbal undertones of crushed vine leaves and cedary oak. Silky and refined, the palate's deep fruit flavours and dusty, lightly smoky vanilla oak are coated by fine tannins. Tightly focused, it finishes with a tangy note of dark olives.

2004	93	2012	2026
2002	92	2010	2014+
2001	93	2013	2021
1999	88	2004	2007
1998	92	2006	2010+

CABERNET SAUVIGNON
RATING 5

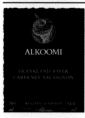

Frankland River $20–$29
Current vintage: 2004   89

An elegant, slightly herbal cabernet with floral aromas of small black and red berries over leafy, greenish and capsicum-like influences. The palate is initially bright and vibrant, with intense berry and plum fruit and emerging cedar/cigarbox undertones, but thins out a little towards a green-edged finish. It offers some genuine structure and vitality of fruit.

2004	89	2012	2016
2003	84	2005	2008+
2002	86	2007	2010
2001	89	2009	2013
1999	92	2011	2019
1998	92	2010	2018
1996	81	2001	2004
1995	82	2003	2007
1994	89	2002	2006
1993	88	1998	2001
1992	88	1997	2000
1991	89	2003	2011
1990	90	2002	2010
1989	88	2001	2009
1988	87	2000	2005

CHARDONNAY
RATING 5

Frankland River $20–$29
Current vintage: 2004   89

Fine and complex, this smooth, juicy and fruit-driven wine just lacks the impact for a higher score. There's some funky mineral and wheatmeal complexity beneath its smoky aromas of grapefruit, melon and matchstick oak. Long and smooth, with a light babyfat texture, its bright citrus, melon and lightly tropical fruit finishes with delicacy and freshness.

2004	89	2006	2009
2003	86	2005	2008
2002	93	2007	2010
2001	89	2003	2006+
2000	88	2002	2005
1998	87	2000	2003
1997	92	2002	2005
1996	88	1998	2001

JARRAH SHIRAZ
RATING 3

Frankland River $30–$49
Current vintage: 2003   89

Dark, spicy, deeply flavoured and brooding, this leathery and rustic shiraz presents meaty flavours of blackberries, mulberries and plums with cedary oak over musky and rather reductive undertones. It's long, linear, fine and quite restrained, marrying sweet berry fruit with pencil shavings-like oak, but appears to have been slightly over-protected from oxygen, of which it could perhaps have used more.

2003	89	2011	2015+
2002	92	2010	2014+
2001	89	2006	2009
2000	86	2005	2008
1999	93	2007	2011+

B C D E F G H I J K L M N O P Q R S T U V W X Y Z

RIESLING

Frankland River	$12–$19
Current vintage: 2005	**86**

Lightly herbal and dusty, with musky, floral aromas of lime juice preceding a smooth, elegant and fluffy palate. Tight-knit and elegant, its lively expression of lime, apple and pear flavours just finishes a little too herbal for a higher rating.

2005	86	2007	2010
2004	90	2009	2012+
2003	93	2011	2015+
2002	89	2004	2007
2001	93	2009	2013
1999	88	2001	2004+
1998	90	2006	2010
1997	91	2005	2009
1996	91	2004	2008
1995	91	2000	2003+
1994	94	2002	2006
1993	87	1998	2001

SAUVIGNON BLANC

RATING 5

Frankland River	$20–$29
Current vintage: 2005	**82**

Simple and confectionary, with lightly grassy aromas of passionfruit before a rather cloying palate that finishes without length or intensity.

2005	82	2005	2006+
2004	89	2005	2006
2003	87	2003	2004
2002	82	2003	2004
2001	89	2002	2003
2000	93	2001	2002
1999	87	2001	2004
1998	88	2000	2003
1997	90	1998	1999

SHIRAZ VIOGNIER (Shiraz pre 2002)

RATING 4

Frankland River	$20–$29
Current vintage: 2004	**91**

Smooth, deeply fruited and savoury, this spicy young shiraz has a floral, slightly meaty and viognier-aided bouquet of intense berry aromas and vanilla oak. It's deeply fruited and elegant, with blackberry, plum, cassis and licorice-like fruit seamlessly integrated with fine-grained oak and framed by silky tannins. It finishes with length and persistence of fruit.

2004	91	2009	2012
2003	91	2008	2011+
2002	91	2007	2010+
2001	87	2003	2006+
2000	81	2002	2005
1999	89	2007	2011
1998	86	2003	2006
1997	87	1999	2002

All Saints Estate

All Saints Road, Wahgunyah Vic 3687. Tel: (02) 6035 2222. Fax: (02) 6035 2200.
Website: www.allsaintswine.com.au Email: wine@allsaintswine.com.au
Region: **Rutherglen** Winemaker: **Dan Crane** Viticulturist: **Tim Trimble** Chief Executive: **Eliza Brown**
All Saints Estate is one of the grand original properties of the Rutherglen region, today owned by the family of Peter Brown, one of the Brown Brothers of Milawa fame. Peter died tragically and prematurely in November, 2005. All Saints is one of the classic historic cellars in Australia and boasts a rich stock of mature fortified wines. It also creates a wide range of generously flavoured and early maturing table wines, including the local regional specialities of shiraz and marsanne.

CARLYLE SHIRAZ (formerly St Leonards)

RATING 5

Rutherglen	$30–$49
Current vintage: 1999	**83**

Very ripe, very oaky red whose jammy plum and blackcurrant aromas reveal suggestions of mocha, treacle and currants. Rather porty, its over-ripened palate marries stressed fruit characters with ashtray-like oak.

1999	83	2001	2004
1998	77	2000	2003
1997	91	2005	2009
1996	89	1998	2001
1995	86	2000	2003
1994	91	2004	2008

SHIRAZ

RATING **5**

Rutherglen	$20–$29
Current vintage: 2004	**87**

Meaty, rather cooked and very oaky, this rustic shiraz has a very ripe and porty aroma backed by cinnamon, cloves, white pepper and spirity nuances of alcohol. Firm, slightly raw and blocky, its palate of sweet, jammy blackberry fruit culminates in a dusty, earthy finish. It needs time to settle.

2004	87	2009	2012
2003	80	2005	2008
2002	85	2007	2010
2000	87	2005	2008
1999	88	2004	2007
1998	87	2003	2006
1997	88	2002	2005
1996	87	1998	2001
1994	92	2002	2006+
1993	90	2001	2005
1992	88	2000	2004
1989	88	1997	2003

Allandale

132 Lovedale Road, Lovedale NSW 2320. Tel: (02) 4990 4526. Fax: (02) 4990 1714.
Website: www.allandalewinery.com.au Email: wines@allandalewinery.com.au
Region: **Lower Hunter Valley** Winemakers: **Bill Sneddon, Rod Russell** Viticulturist: **Bill Sneddon**
Chief Executive: **Wally Atallah**

Allandale makes reliable and affordable traditional Hunter Valley white wines, but sources its Cabernet Sauvignon from Mudgee and the Hilltops regions of New South Wales. The delightfully powdery and refreshing 2005 Semillon is one of a very strong set produced across the Hunter in 2005.

CHARDONNAY

RATING **5**

Lower Hunter Valley	$12–$19
Current vintage: 2004	**85**

A creamy and peachy chardonnay whose rather simple and confectionary aromas of melon, toasty oak and marmalade precede a forward but then rather lean and hollow palate that reveals some under-and over-ripe characters. Its buttery, citrusy expression of cumquat-like flavour reveals herbal and tobaccoey undertones.

2004	85	2006	2009
2003	87	2004	2005+
2002	86	2003	2004
2001	87	2002	2003+
2000	90	2002	2005
1999	89	2004	2007
1998	80	1999	2000

SEMILLON

RATING **4**

Lower Hunter Valley	$12–$19
Current vintage: 2005	**90**

Delicate, lightly herbal and powdery aromas of fresh honeydew melon precede a moderately long and refreshing palate whose pleasing length of slightly candied fruit culminates in a lemon sherbet finish. Likely to develop well.

2005	90	2010	2013+
2003	87	2005	2008
2002	88	2007	2010
2001	90	2006	2009
2000	93	2005	2008+
1998	86	2000	2003+
1997	89	2002	2005
1996	92	2004	2008
1995	90	2000	2003
1993	94	2001	2005

A B C D E F G H I J K L M N O P Q R S T U V W X Y Z

Amberley

Thornton Road, Yallingup WA 6282. Tel: (08) 9366 3900. Fax: (08) 9321 6281.
Website: www.amberleyestate.com.au Email: pauld@amberley-estate.com.au
Region: **Margaret River** Winemaker: **Paul Dunnewyk** Viticulturist: **Phil Smith** Chief Executive: **Eddie Price**
Amberley today finds itself in the same stable as Houghton, Western Australia's largest wine producer, because
its previous owner, the Canadian wine producer and distributor Vincor (which also owned another significant
Western Australian producer in Goundrey), was recently taken over by Houghton's ultimate parent,
Constellation Brands. From a wine perspective, Amberley continues its steady improvement, as exemplified
by its best-ever red in the First Selection Cabernet Sauvignon 2001 and the delicious 2005 Sauvignon Blanc.

FIRST SELECTION CABERNET SAUVIGNON
(formerly Reserve)

RATING **3**

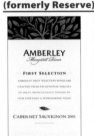

Margaret River	$30–$49
Current vintage: 2001	94

Possibly the finest red wine yet from Amberley,
this searingly intense and finely balanced young
cabernet offers plenty of vibrant and tightly
focused flavour. Its floral, lightly earthy and
gamey aromas of violets, dark cherries, boysen-
berries and blackberries are supported by cedary
oak, while its long, juicy palate shows delightful
integration between fruit, oak, tannin and acidity.
Give it time.

2001	94	2013	2021
2000	92	2008	2012+
1997	87	2005	2009
1996	88	2008	2016
1995	91	2007	2015
1993	85	2001	2005
1992	87	2000	2004+

FIRST SELECTION CHARDONNAY

RATING **5**

Margaret River	$20–$29
Current vintage: 2004	90

Polished, round and generous, this sumptuously
flavoured, smooth and creamy chardonnay easily
handles a healthy measure of winemaker-induced
complexity. Its reserved peach/grapefruit aromas
are backed by creamy, nutty leesy influences and
fresh vanilla oak, while its substantial palate of juicy,
tangy fruit culminates in a warm, slightly spirity
and savoury finish.

2004	90	2006	2009
2003	87	2005	2008
2002	81	2003	2004
2001	87	2003	2006

FIRST SELECTION SHIRAZ

RATING **5**

Margaret River	$20–$29
Current vintage: 2003	88

Meaty, lightly herbal aromas of plums, cassis
and cedary oak reveal nuances of white pepper
and tomato stalk. Full-flavoured, smooth and
juicy, the palate begins with intense flavours of
raspberries, cassis and redcurrants before becoming
more tomato-like and meaty towards the finish.
Backed by toasty, cedary oak and framed by rather
blocky tannins and slightly metallic acids, it
should evolve in a more complex way. A wine I
half expect to score more highly in future.

2003	88	2008	2011+
2002	88	2004	2007+
2001	82	2003	2006
2000	86	2002	2005+
1999	88	2004	2007
1998	81	2000	2003
1997	89	2002	2005

SAUVIGNON BLANC

RATING **5**

Margaret River	$12–$19
Current vintage: 2005	93

A delightfully tangy and regional wine whose
delicate, slightly musky, herbal and grassy aromas
of cassis and gooseberries are lifted by a floral scent.
Elegant and unctuous, smooth and even, its
long and vibrant palate of juicy flavour finishes
fresh and tight, with very soft acids and gentle
phenolics.

2005	93	2006	2007+
2004	83	2004	2005
2002	89	2003	2004
2001	85	2002	2003+
2000	82	2001	2002

Annie's Lane

Quelltaler Estate, Quelltaler Road, Watervale SA 5452. Tel: (08) 8843 0003. Fax: (08) 8843 0096.
Website: www.annieslane.com.au Email: cellardoor@annieslane.com.au

Region: **Clare Valley** Winemaker: **Mark Robertson** Viticulturist: **Peter Pawelski** Chief Executive: **Jamie Odell**

A consistent and often under-rated Clare Valley brand within the Beringer Blass stable whose wines are overseen by Kiwi winemaker Mark Robertson. The 'reserve' level Copper Trail wines are the label's finest, presenting a typically slatey and minerally Riesling and a fine-grained, spicy shiraz with a firm tannic backbone. The 2005 white collection, the Riesling especially, doesn't do justice to the brand's tradition and potential.

CABERNET MERLOT
RATING 5

Clare Valley			**$20–$29**
Current vintage: 2002			**91**

Elegant and harmonious, medium to full in weight, with a sweet earthy perfume of red berries and cassis, backed by hints of herbaceousness and restrained vanilla oak. Smooth, fine and stylish, presenting a lively palate of pristine small berry fruit supported by oak and fine-grained tannins. Great value for the cellar.

2002	91	2010	2014
2001	85	2003	2006
2000	87	2002	2005
1999	86	2001	2004
1998	90	2003	2006
1997	87	2002	2005
1996	82	1998	2001
1995	94	2003	2007

COPPER TRAIL RIESLING
RATING 3

Clare Valley			**$20–$29**
Current vintage: 2005			**91**

Delicate aromas of lime juice, lemon rind and chalky, powdery mineral influences overlie a floral, rose garden-like perfume. Fine and juicy, its effortlessly smooth expression of delicate citrus and mineral character culminates in a lingering and silky finish whose lively core of fruit and refreshing acidity help to conceal a hint of sweetness.

2005	91	2010	2013+
2004	92	2009	2012+
2003	94	2008	2011
2002	95	2010	2014+

COPPER TRAIL SHIRAZ (formerly The Contour)
RATING 3

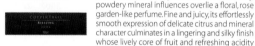

Clare Valley			**$50–$99**
Current vintage: 2000			**88**

A typical 2000 vintage wine whose meaty mulberry, cassis and plum-like fruit presents some under- and over-ripe influences. Laced with herbal and spicy notes of cinnamon and cloves, it's given sweetness and length through some fine-grained cedar/vanilla oak, before finishing slightly green-edged and sappy.

2000	88	2002	2005+
1999	92	2007	2011
1998	93	2006	2010
1997	93	2005	2009
1996	95	2004	2008+
1995	90	2003	2007

RIESLING
RATING 5

Clare Valley			**$12–$19**
Current vintage: 2005			**87**

Simple bath powder and lemon sherbet-like aromas with some floral qualities precede a forward, chalky palate with slightly sweet and confectionary qualities. Lacks genuine varietal definition and frankly rather disappointing from such a fine vintage.

2005	87	2007	2010+
2004	86	2004	2005+
2003	89	2005	2008
2002	93	2007	2010+
2001	89	2006	2009
2000	89	2002	2005
1999	81	2000	2001
1998	94	2003	2006+
1997	90	2005	2009

SEMILLON
RATING 5

Clare Valley			**$12–$19**
Current vintage: 2005			**87**

Clean and refreshing, this simple and austere semillon has a dusty, creamy nose of green melon and butter with grassy undertones, which gradually reveals floral suggestions and hints of sweet oak. There's a chalkiness beneath its melon/lemon fruit and restrained vanilla oak, while it finishes with tangy, citrusy acids.

2005	87	2006	2007+
2004	90	2006	2009
2003	89	2005	2008
2002	88	2004	2007+
2001	88	2003	2006
2000	82	2001	2002
1999	87	2004	2007
1998	91	2000	2003
1997	87	1999	2002
1996	93	2004	2008

2007 THE AUSTRALIAN WINE ANNUAL
www.jeremyoliver.com.au _____ **29**

SHIRAZ

Clare Valley	$12–$19
Current vintage: 2003	89

A firm, robust and typically minty, menthol-like Clare Valley shiraz whose sweet, slightly jammy aromas of cassis and red berries, sweet cedar/vanilla oak are backed by spicy notes of cloves and cinnamon. Opening up with depth and length, its intense, juicy expression of ripe berry fruit knits tightly with choco-latey oak influences and a firm, fine-grained astringency. Good length and strength.

2003	89	2011	2015+
2002	82	2004	2007
2001	90	2006	2009
2000	88	2002	2005+
1999	86	2001	2004
1998	90	2003	2006
1997	89	2002	2005
1996	90	2001	2004
1995	88	2000	2003

Armstrong

Military Road, Armstrong Vic 3377. Tel: (08) 8277 6073. Fax: (08) 8277 6035. Email: armstrong@picknowl.com.au

Region: **Grampians, Great Western** Winemaker: **Tony Royal** Viticulturist: **Stan Royal** Chief Executive: **Tony Royal**

Armstrong is the pet project of experienced winemaker Tony Royal, a long-time senior winemaker for Seppelt. The Shiraz and Shiraz Viognier often reveal a herbal thread, but as the vineyard gains maturity, they are becoming longer, finer, more elegant and complete, acquiring the typical longevity of Great Western shiraz.

SHIRAZ

Great Western	$30–$49
Current vintage: 2002	89

A minty perfume of violets, cassis and dark plums is tightly integrated with lightly smoky scents of fine-grained vanilla oak, with meaty undertones of cloves, cinnamon and menthol. Long, smooth and structured, the palate delivers intense cassis and dark plum flavours framed by a slightly drying extract of firm, but fine-grained tannins. It finishes long and savoury, with nuances of menthol, but doesn't quite appear to be able to shake an underlying herbal thread.

2002	89	2010	2014
2001	93	2009	2013
2000	93	2008	2012
1999	89	2007	2011
1998	83	2000	2003
1996	88	2001	2004+

Arundel

Arundel Road, Keilor Vic 3036. Tel: (03) 9335 3422. Fax: (03) 9335 4912.
Website: www.arundel.com.au Email: bianca@arundel.com.au

Region: **Sunbury** Winemaker: **Bianca Hayes** Viticulturist: **Mark Hayes** Chief Executive: **Bianca Hayes**

A tiny vineyard near Keilor, Victoria, Arundel is proving that its early promise was no fluke. While its Viognier still requires some fine-tuning, its Shiraz is usually a spicy, peppery, fine-grained and savoury Rhône-inspired wine delivering dark, briary and penetrative fruit. It offers a higher level of tightness and acidity than most other Australian shirazes.

SHIRAZ

Sunbury	$30–$49
Current vintage: 2004	91

A spicy, regional Sunbury shiraz whose lifted floral perfume of fresh small red berries is scented with lightly smoky vanilla oak plus minty, spicy com-plexity. Long and even, its creamy and oaky palate of spicy red and black berries knit tightly with creamy vanilla oak, finishing with lingering suggestions of fennel and anise. Framed by charming and supple tannins, it takes time to fully open in the glass.

2004	91	2009	2012
2003	90	2008	2011+
2002	90	2007	2010+
2001	92	2009	2013
2000	93	2005	2008+
1999	89	2001	2004+
1997	77	1998	1999

Baileys of Glenrowan

RMB 4160 Taminick Gap Road, Glenrowan Vic 3675. Tel: (03) 5766 2392. Fax: (03) 5766 2596.
Website: www.baileysofglenrowan.com.au Email: paul.dahlenburg@beringerblass.com.au

Region: **NE Victoria** Winemaker: **Paul Dahlenburg** Viticulturist: **Paul Dahlenburg** Chief Executive: **Jamie Odell**

Baileys is a fine example of how a small and relatively idiosyncratic brand of rustic red wines and luscious fortifieds can thrive and prosper in a multinational environment. Located in the picturesque northeast corner of Victoria, it produces a trio of shirazes, the elder two of which are named according to the age of their vineyards. The common thread is their richness, ripeness and meaty, spicy expression of varietal flavour. Typically firm, often closed in their youth, they open up to reveal generous depth and flavour. In sporting parlance, they're fighting above their weight.

1904 BLOCK SHIRAZ

RATING **3**

NE Victoria $30–$49
Current vintage: 2004   94

A sumptuous, long and varietal shiraz whose deeply spicy, meaty and plummy aromas of small dark berries, cloves and cinnamon are backed by earthy, rustic nuances and hints of white pepper. Its deeply fruited palate of sweet, dark plums and berries overlies a tight, firm spine of powdery tannins, finishing long and persistent, with lingering sweet fruit and leathery undertones.

2004	94	2016	2024
2003	90	2015	2023
2000	90	2005	2008
1999	93	2011	2019+
1998	91	2010	2018

1920s BLOCK SHIRAZ

RATING **4**

NE Victoria $20–$29
Current vintage: 2005   93

A natural, stable and well-made wine with a future. Its smoky fragrance of sweet blackberries, cassis and violets is backed by spicy nuances of cloves, cinnamon and nutmeg, with a whiff of rosemary. Sumptuous and deeply concentrated, its thick, full-bodied palate backs its evenly ripened fruit with a firm spine of chalky tannin and meaty, mineral undertones. Rustic but well crafted, with a touch of attitude.

2005	93	2017	2025+
2003	91	2015	2023
2001	87	2003	2006
2000	92	2005	2008+
1999	91	2011	2019
1998	89	2006	2010+
1997	87	2002	2005
1996	88	2001	2004
1995	86	2000	2003
1994	93	2006	2014
1993	87	1998	2001
1992	90	2000	2004
1991	94	2003	2011

SHIRAZ

RATING **5**

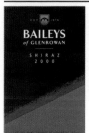

NE Victoria $12–$19
Current vintage: 2004   89

A firm, rustic shiraz that makes up in depth and strength what it might lack in complexity. Sweet aromas of blackberries and slightly raisined fruit are assertively backed by smoky, coffee-like dark chocolate oak. Ripe and sumptuous, its lingering palate of dark berries, plums and spice is coated with drying, powdery tannins and reveals a meaty aspect.

2005	89	2010	2013+
2004	89	2012	2016+
2003	90	2008	2011
2002	91	2010	2014+
2000	89	2005	2008
1999	87	2004	2007

A
B
C
D
E
F
G
H
I
J
K
L
M
N
O
P
Q
R
S
T
U
V
W
X
Y
Z

Balgownie Estate

Hermitage Road, Maiden Gully Vic 3551. Tel: (03) 5449 6222. Fax: (03) 5449 6506.
Website: www.balgownieestate.com.au Email: info@balgownieestate.com.au

Region: **Bendigo** Winemaker: **Tobias Ansted** Viticulturist: **John Monteath** Chief Executive: **Des Forrester**

Balgownie began in the 1970s as a small domaine-like vineyard producing small amounts of handcrafted wine by former Bendigo chemist, oboe player and Bugatti enthusiast, Stuart Anderson. The brand fell into the doldrums after its purchase by Mildara Blass, but under its present ownership has been reincarnated to an astonishing degree. Its Bendigo-based reds are among the finest of their kind, and its new Yarra Valley operation is enhancing its reputation for quality.

CABERNET SAUVIGNON

RATING **3**

Bendigo	$30–$49
Current vintage: 2004	93

A traditional Bendigo cabernet of tremendous depth, ripeness and regional intensity. Scented with spicy, menthol-like aromas of cassis, dark plums and sweet oak, it reveals floral, violet-like undertones. Firm and fine-grained, its profound expression of ripe, slightly jammy red and black berry/plum fruit is framed by firm, fine tannins and finishes with minty suggestions of eucalypt. Modestly alcoholic, given its richness and ripeness.

2004	93	2016	2024
2003	93	2015	2023
2002	93	2014	2022+
2001	89	2013	2021
2000	90	2012	2020
1999	89	2004	2007
1998	87	2006	2010+
1997	86	2005	2009
1996	90	2008	2016
1995	88	2007	2015
1994	87	2002	2006
1993	88	2005	2013
1992	93	2004	2012
1991	88	2011	2021
1990	95	2010	2020

SHIRAZ

RATING **3**

Bendigo	$30–$49
Current vintage: 2004	91

A minty central Victorian shiraz whose intense aromas of cassis, dark plums, dark chocolate and cedar oak are backed by suggestions of menthol, white pepper, cloves and cinnamon. Its firm, somewhat bony palate is slightly closed, but still delivers ripe dark fruit flavours and polished cedar/vanilla oak over nuances of dried herbs. Finishing tight and savoury, it lacks the depth and complexity of previous recent vintages, but delivers pleasing weight and structure.

2004	91	2012	2016+
2003	95	2011	2015+
2002	94	2010	2014+
2001	92	2009	2013
2000	89	2005	2008
1999	89	2004	2007
1998	89	2003	2006+
1997	93	2009	2017
1996	93	2004	2008+
1995	94	2007	2015
1994	90	2002	2006
1993	93	2005	2013
1990	94	2002	2010

Balnaves

Main Road, Coonawarra SA 5263. Tel: (08) 8737 2946. Fax: (08) 8737 2945.
Website: www.balnaves.com.au Email: kirsty.balnaves@balnaves.com.au

Region: **Coonawarra** Winemaker: **Peter Bissell** Viticulturist: **Peter Balnaves** Chief Executive: **Doug Balnaves**

Peter Bissell and his team at Balnaves have made a solid impression, along with some truly outstanding wine, from recent difficult Coonawarra vintages, but in 2004 they had the chance to really strut their stuff. The results are spectacular, and again it's impossible to taste them without wondering if Coonawarra has really fulfilled its potential. Buy as much of the Shiraz, the Cabernet Sauvignon Merlot and The Tally as your budget permits. Coonawarra cabernet is in the process of being reinvented.

CABERNET SAUVIGNON MERLOT

RATING **4**

Coonawarra	$30–$49
Current vintage: 2004	95

Deeply flavoured, firm and fine-grained, this is precisely the sort of wine that Coonawarra should be making more of. Its heady perfume of violets, small berries, plums and blackcurrants reveals smoky undertones of cedar/vanilla oak and a minty whiff of dried herbs. Full in weight, its palate-staining and sour-edged flavours of intense dark cherry/berry fruit, tobacco and cedary oak are harmoniously supported by an assertive but pliant backbone of drying tannins.

2004	95	2016	2024
2002	87	2007	2010+
2001	90	2009	2013
2000	88	2002	2005+
1998	93	2006	2010

CABERNET SAUVIGNON

RATING 4

Coonawarra $30–$49
Current vintage: 2002 91

Tightly knit and focused cabernet with a violet-like fragrance of lightly minty cassis and redcurrant aromas supported by sweet creamy and cedary oak. Austere and fine-grained, its long, briary and brightly lit palate of pristine plum, mulberry and blackcurrant flavours is framed by firm, bony tannins. Although there's a suggestion of wildness, the palate is stylish and elegant.

2002	91	2010	2014+
2001	88	2006	2009
2000	86	2002	2005
1999	89	2007	2011
1998	92	2006	2010+
1997	87	2002	2005
1996	90	2004	2008+

CHARDONNAY

RATING **5**

Coonawarra $20–$29
Current vintage: 2004 87

A well-made, smooth and savoury chardonnay that just lacks in genuine fruit brightness. Its slightly cooked, citrusy aromas of cumquat and quince overlie vanilla and clove-like oak, with undertones of butterscotch. Medium in weight, it's dusty and herbal, with lemon/grapefruit flavours finishing dry and nutty.

2004	87	2006	2009
2003	91	2005	2008
2002	88	2004	2007
2001	83	2006	2009+
1999	86	2000	2001+

SHIRAZ

RATING **4**

Coonawarra $20–$29
Current vintage: 2004 95

A first-rate, supple and elegant shiraz whose deep, brooding aromas of blackberries, dark plums, cassis and chocolate/cedary oak are lifted by fragrances of spice and pepper. Full to medium in weight, it's long and smooth, bursting with briary flavours of dark berries and plums, and framed by powdery, fine-grained tannins. It finishes long and vibrant, with an appealing fruit sourness.

2004	95	2012	2016+
2002	87	2007	2010
2001	90	2003	2006
1999	89	2001	2004+

THE BLEND

Coonawarra $20–$29
Current vintage: 2004 93

Fine, firm and elegant, this generously flavoured Coonawarra red marries its lively flavours of cassis, dark plums and cherries with restrained cedar/vanilla oak, herbal undertones and a fine-grained spine of firm but loosely knit tannins. Its slightly stewy aromas reveal a hint of mineral, while its palate delivers plumpness and roundness without compromising its freshness or restraint.

2004	93	2012	2016+
2002	86	2004	2007+
2001	86	2006	2009
2000	86	2002	2005+

THE TALLY RESERVE CABERNET SAUVIGNON

RATING **3**

Coonawarra $50–$99
Current vintage: 2004 97

Powerfully structured, richly fruited and handsomely crafted, this is a cabernet of First Growth attitude and presence. Alluring and lightly smoky, its perfume of dark plums, black and red berries, violets, spicy and cedary/vanilla/chocolate new oak reveals a hint of dried herbs. Profound in its impact, its still closed but densely concentrated palate of deep blackberry, blueberry and dark olive flavour is tightly integrated with new oak and a drying, powdery spine of firm tannin. Perfectly honed, with great strength and longevity.

2004	97	2024	2034
2001	96	2013	2021
2000	91	2008	2012+
1998	93	2010	2018

A B C D E F G H I J K L M N O P Q R S T U V W X Y Z

Bannockburn

1750 Midland Highway, Bannockburn Vic 3331. Tel: (03) 5281 1363. Fax: (03) 5281 1349.
Website: www.bannockburnvineyards.com Email: info@bannockburnvineyards.com
Region: **Geelong** Winemaker: **Michael Glover** Viticulturist: **Lucas Grigsby** Chief Executive: **Phillip Harrison**

Mike Glover, the former winemaker for Moorilla Estate, has taken over the reins as full-time winemaker at Bannockburn.
While his first role has been to rationalise the various unfinished wines remaining in the cellar from the previous
regime, he has already taken a hand in the development of some very surprising red and white wines from
2005. It's entirely possible that in a decade's time, Bannockburn might actually be famous for an entirely different
range of wines to those that crafted its initial reputation. Watch this space.

CHARDONNAY

RATING

Geelong $30–$49
Current vintage: 2004   88

A deeply flavoured and richly textured chardonnay that lacks genuine freshness and brightness.
Its dusty, nutty aromas of peach, citrus and
melon-like fruit are underpinned by clove and
vanilla-like oak, while its rather brassy palate has
almost a syrupy lusciousness. Slightly cooked and
cloying, its finishes a little short.

2004	88	2006	2009
2003	93	2008	2011+
2002	94	2007	2010+
2001	88	2006	2009+
2000	90	2002	2005+
1999	94	2004	2007
1998	93	2006	2010
1997	94	2002	2005+
1996	95	2001	2004
1995	96	1997	2000
1994	95	2002	2006
1993	96	2001	2005
1992	94	2000	2004

PINOT NOIR

RATING

Geelong $50–$99
Current vintage: 2004   88

Spicy and rather herbal aromas of maraschino
cherries, plums and berries are lifted by lightly smoky
cedar/vanilla oak with musky, meaty undertones. Forward and juicy, its slightly candied
palate of redcurrants, plums and cherries finishes
slightly short and sappy, with lingering nuances
of dried herbs and meatiness. Lacks a genuine core
of fruit and likely to age quickly.

2004	88	2006	2009+
2003	86	2005	2008
2002	91	2007	2010+
2001	90	2006	2009
2000	91	2005	2008
1999	94	2007	2011
1998	94	2003	2006
1997	94	2005	2009
1996	93	2004	2008+
1995	93	2003	2007+
1994	94	2002	2006+
1993	88	1998	2001+
1992	96	2004	2012

SERRÉ PINOT NOIR

RATING

Geelong $50–$99
Current vintage: 2003   92

Wild, meaty and floral, this heady, earthy and early-
maturing pinot presents a rustic fragrance suggestive of violets, smoked meats and briar.
Smooth and juicy, it's deeply and lavishly flavoured,
presenting a long and luscious palate of cherries,
plums and cassis backed by savoury, meaty and
earthy complexity. Framed by tight, fine-grained
tannins, it's polished and supple. Its underlying
brett-derived influences might be contributing
to some tightening of palate length.

2003	92	2005	2008
2000	88	2005	2008
1999	96	2007	2011+
1998	96	2006	2010+
1997	95	2005	2009
1996	92	2004	2008+
1995	95	2003	2007
1994	96	2006	2014
1993	93	2001	2005
1991	72	1993	1996
1990	88	1998	2002+

SHIRAZ

Geelong		$30–$49	2004	89	2009	2012

Geelong	$30–$49
Current vintage: 2004	**89**

Wild, spicy and deeply flavoured, this smooth and fine-grained shiraz lacks genuine length of fruit and conviction. Its musky, charcuterie-like aromas of blackberry confiture, dark plums, cinnamon and pepper reveal cedary undertones. Finished with excellent oak, its juicy and forward palate of sumptuous berry flavour is coated by hard and slightly gritty tannin, with lingering herbal suggestions.

2004	89	2009	2012
2003	89	2008	2011+
2002	88	2004	2007+
2001	95	2009	2013+
2000	96	2012	2020
1999	89	2001	2004+
1998	95	2006	2010
1997	95	2009	2017
1996	93	2004	2008
1995	87	2000	2003
1994	95	2002	2006
1993	90	1998	2001
1992	95	2000	2004
1991	94	1999	2003+
1990	90	1998	2002

SRH CHARDONNAY

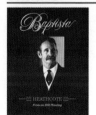

Geelong	$50–$99
Current vintage: 2000	**95**

Revelling in its customary palate fatness, toasty oak and savoury qualities, this steadily maturing and genuinely complex chardonnay backs its slightly edgy and oxidative expression of floral, nutty, melon-like and citrusy fruit with appealingly smoky, nougat-like undertones. Supported by smart, spicy new cooperage, it's chewy and viscous, but finishes long and waxy, with lingering fruit and matchstick-like oak.

2000	95	2005	2008+
1999	95	2004	2007
1995	94	1997	2000
1994	93	1996	1999
1993	97	1998	2001

Baptista

139 High Street, Nagambie Vic 3608. Tel: (03) 5794 2514. Fax: (03) 5794 1776.
Website: www.dromanaestate.com.au Email: DTW1@bigpond.com

Region: **Heathcote** Winemaker: **David Traeger** Viticulturist: **David Traeger** Chief Executive: **David Traeger**

Winemaker David Traeger has redeveloped one of Victoria's oldest shiraz vineyards, from which he crafts this rare wine. Located near the central Victorian village of Graytown, which was recently admitted into the Heathcote wine region in the face of most viticultural intelligence, it creates intense, minty and tightly focused wines made in a very protective manner. Personally, I'd like to see more oxygen involved in their upbringing.

SHIRAZ

Graytown	$50–$99
Current vintage: 2000	**91**

Meaty, savoury and peppery, this slightly retentive shiraz might seem to need a good aeration but backs its minty, menthol-like berry and plum-like fruit with cedary, dark chocolate oak, herbal undertones and dusty, leathery complexity. Highlights of cassis and violets punctuate its substantial and slightly gamey palate, coated with smooth oak and firm layers of drying tannins. It finishes with spicy nuances of cloves and licorice.

2000	91	2008	2012+
1999	92	2011	2019
1998	90	2006	2010+
1997	88	2005	2009+

Barossa Valley Estate

Seppeltsfield Road, Marananga SA 5355. Tel: (08) 8562 3599. Fax: (08) 8562 4255.
Website: www.bve.com.au Email: sales@bve.com.au
Region: **Barossa Valley** Winemaker: **Stuart Bourne** Viticulturist: **Kirsty Waller** General Manager: **Christine Hahn**
The Barossa Valley Estate releases three tiers of wine, atop of which are rightly perched the E&E shirazes, one still, the other sparkling. These are modern Barossa classics, full of vibrant, often jammy, meaty fruit and supported by American oak. The Ebenezer wines are more approachable, yet can still present good underlying structure and cellaring opportunity.

E&E BLACK PEPPER SHIRAZ
RATING **3**

Barossa Valley　　$50–$99
Current vintage: 2002　　94

A very fine, restrained and velvet-smooth expression of Barossa shiraz whose relatively delicate fragrance of small berry fruit, sweet smoky vanilla oak, cloves, cinnamon and white pepper exudes charming gaminess and complexity. It gradually opens to reveal a long and elegant palate whose concentrated dark fruit flavours are delivered with surprising deftness of touch, assertively but carefully offset by well-seasoned American oak. It finishes almost savoury, with a lingering core of dark fruit.

2002	94	2010	2014+
2001	94	2013	2021
2000	87	2002	2005+
1999	91	2004	2007+
1998	96	2010	2018
1997	90	2005	2009
1996	96	2004	2008+
1995	93	2007	2015
1994	93	2002	2006
1993	93	2001	2005
1992	91	2000	2004
1991	95	2003	2011

E&E SPARKLING SHIRAZ
RATING **3**

Barossa Valley　　$50–$99
Current vintage: 2001　　90

Spicy aromas of dark plums, currants, prunes and blackberries with gamey, chocolatey undertones. Sumptuous, rich and savoury, it's smooth and round, with lingering meaty, earthy flavours of plums and prunes framed by firm, powdery tannins. Very good, but showing signs of maturity, so drink soon.

2001	90	2006	2009
1999	88	2007	2011+
1998	95	2006	2010
1996	93	2001	2004+
1995	91	2000	2003
1994	94	1999	2002+

EBENEZER CABERNET SAUVIGNON MERLOT
RATING **5**

Barossa Valley　　$20–$29
Current vintage: 2002　　89

An elegant, fine cooler year cabernet with just a hint of greenness. Its slightly herbal aromas of brightly lit small red and black berry fruits are enhanced with restrained vanilla oak, while its evenly measured palate of vibrant fruit and cedary oak is tightly wound around fine-grained tannins.

2002	89	2010	2014
2001	86	2003	2006+
2000	85	2002	2005
1999	90	2004	2007
1998	87	2003	2006
1997	80	1999	2002
1996	91	2001	2004

EBENEZER CHARDONNAY
RATING **5**

Barossa Valley　　$12–$19
Current vintage: 2002　　89

A round, soft and generously flavoured, modern style of easy-drinking chardonnay. Its fresh peachy aromas are backed by nuances of buttery vanilla oak and wheatmeal, while its palate offers pleasing freshness and roundness. Its buttery expression of peaches and cream finishes soft and toasty, with a lingering hint of honey.

2002	89	2004	2007
2001	87	2003	2006
2000	86	2001	2002

EBENEZER SHIRAZ
RATING **5**

Barossa Valley　　$20–$29
Current vintage: 2002　　87

Dark, meaty aromas of raisined, currant-like fruit with undertones of plums and berries are lifted by assertive nuances of smoky oak. It's juicy and richly textured, lacking in balance and harmony, and its frankly dull and dehydrated fruit reflects an unusual measure of stress for this vintage. Drink soon.

2002	87	2004	2007+
2001	87	2006	2009
2000	83	2002	2005+
1999	88	2004	2007
1998	90	2003	2006
1997	88	2002	2005
1996	88	2001	2004
1995	92	2000	2003
1994	91	1999	2002
1993	86	1998	2001

Barwang

Barwang Road, Young NSW 2190. Tel: (02) 6382 3594. Fax: (02) 6382 3594.
Website: www.mcwilliams.com.au   Email: mcwines@mcwilliams.com.au

Region: **Hilltops** Winemaker: **Jim Brayne** Viticulturist: **Murray Pulleine** Chief Executive: **George Wahby**

Barwang is an individual vineyard site that has become the flag-bearer for the emerging Hilltops region of New South Wales. While recent releases have been affected by the ongoing drought which has caused a distinctly evident level of fruit stress, the Barwang label has established a reliable reputation for its mineral, grainy Chardonnay and long-living, deeply flavoured and robust red wines.

CABERNET SAUVIGNON   RATING 4

Hilltops	$20–$29
Current vintage: 2003	**91**

A sumptuously ripened, concentrated and robust cabernet whose rich and minty expression of briary cassis, dark plum and blackberry-like fruit and sweet mocha/vanilla oak are framed by firm, chalky tannins. While it reveals some pleasing herbal undertones, it's almost but not quite overcooked, retaining plenty of fruit brightness and intensity.

2003	91	2011	2015
2002	88	2010	2014
2001	92	2009	2013
2000	91	2012	2020
1999	90	2004	2007
1998	90	2006	2010+
1997	94	2005	2009+
1996	87	2001	2004
1995	89	2003	2007
1994	90	2002	2006
1993	91	2001	2005
1992	90	2000	2004
1991	95	1999	2003

CHARDONNAY   RATING 5

Hilltops	$12–$19
Current vintage: 2005	**91**

Delicate, grainy, wheatmeal aromas are accompanied by nuances pf peach, quince and apple and a hint of lanolin. Fine, taut and savoury, its long and elegant palate delivers a restrained expression of nutty fruit flavours before a tightly focused, lingering and mineral finish. Attractively reserved and lean.

2005	91	2007	2010+
2004	84	2005	2006
2002	87	2004	2007
2001	87	2003	2006
2000	90	2002	2005
1999	87	2001	2004
1998	94	2003	2006
1997	90	2002	2005
1996	92	2001	2004
1995	88	1997	2000
1994	91	1996	1999
1993	89	1995	1998

MERLOT   RATING 5

Hilltops	$20–$29
Current vintage: 2002	**91**

Powerful, grippy merlot whose sweet aromas of cherries, plums and blackberries, violets, mint and menthol are backed by fragrant, smoky suggestions of vanilla oak. It's rather firm and oaky, with smoky mocha qualities beneath deep, brightly flavoured dark fruits.

2002	91	2010	2014
2001	84	2006	2009+
2000	87	2002	2005+

SHIRAZ   RATING 4

Hilltops	$20–$29
Current vintage: 2003	**86**

A deeply flavoured and firmly structured shiraz whose powerfully spiced, meaty fruit profile of under-and over-ripe flavour does suggest some stress in the vineyard prior to harvest. Spicy clove and cinnamon-like aromas of raisined fruit are lifted by cedary oak, while the palate is rather raw and sappy, with a metallic extract of drying tannin.

2003	86	2008	2011
2002	88	2007	2010+
2001	93	2009	2013
2000	89	2005	2008+
1999	88	2004	2007
1998	94	2006	2010
1997	94	2005	2009
1996	87	1998	2001
1995	93	2003	2005
1994	92	1999	2002
1993	94	1998	2001
1992	89	2000	2004

Bass Phillip

Tosch's Road, Leongatha South Vic 3953. Tel: (03) 5664 3341. Fax: (03) 5664 3209. Email: bpwines@tpg.com.au
Region: **South Gippsland** Winemaker: **Phillip Jones** Viticulturist: **Phillip Jones** Chief Executive: **Phillip Jones**
Aside from being one of the most instinctive pinot winemakers to walk this earth, Phillip Jones is possessed with such disarming honesty that he recently staged a comprehensive tasting of most of the wine he made from 1989 onwards. This event confirmed beyond doubt the special nature of his home site at Leongatha, the source of the Estate, Premium and Reserve pinots. Bass Phillip has its critics and doubters, but no other winery in Australia could have staged such a show of excellence with pinot noir.

CROWN PRINCE PINOT NOIR — RATING 3

South Gippsland $50–$99
Current vintage: 2003   82

Slightly cooked, stewy and varnishy, with over-ripened fruit partnered by raw oak. Very forward, lacking length and structure, delivering a thick, cloying and syrupy expression of fruit.

2003	82	2005	2008
2001	93	2003	2006+
2000	91	2005	2008
1999	93	2001	2004

ESTATE PINOT NOIR — RATING 3

South Gippsland $50–$99
Current vintage: 2004   91

Spicy, slightly varnishy aromas of plums and cherries reveal slightly stressed, dried out and currant-like undertones, although it steadily opens in the glass to reveal layers of red cherries and blood plums backed by dusty, nutty oak. Presently rather closed and tight, it has the underlying depth and length of fruit, plus a fullish drying and fine-grained structure, and should gradually unfold in the bottle.

2004	91	2009	2012
2003	83	2005	2008+
2002	93	2010	2014+
2001	95	2006	2009
2000	89	2005	2008
1999	94	2004	2007
1998	92	2003	2006
1997	93	2002	2005

PREMIUM PINOT NOIR — RATING 2

South Gippsland $100–$199
Current vintage: 2004   95

A little unpolished, but a very impressively fruited and structured pinot with a floral and slightly meaty bouquet that slowly unfolds aromas of red cherries, plums and berries. Sumptuous and very approachable, the palate is heavily laden with ripe cherry and plum flavours supported by a firm but fine-grained chalky backbone. A powerful and concentrated wine in the traditional spicy and complex Bass Phillip style.

2004	95	2009	2012+
2003	95	2011	2015+
2002	93	2014	2022+
2001	93	2009	2013
2000	87	2005	2008
1999	96	2007	2011
1998	88	2003	2006
1997	96	2009	2017
1996	90	2004	2008
1995	88	2003	2007
1994	96	2002	2006+
1993	95	1998	2001+

RESERVE PINOT NOIR — RATING 1

South Gippsland $200+
Current vintage: 2004   97

An opulently flavoured, sumptuously concentrated and lusciously proportioned pinot of exceptional power. Its deep fragrance of red plums and cherries reveals undertones of marzipan and fig, with an assertive background of walnut-like oak. Very smooth and velvet-like, its powerful and substantially oaked palate of pristine fruit is framed by robust, chalky tannins, but remains evenly balanced and focused. It finishes long and savoury, with an appealing suggestion of meatiness.

2004	97	2012	2016+
2003	96	2015	2023
2001	96	2013	2021
2000	87	2002	2005
1999	83	2001	2004+
1998	93	2003	2006+
1997	97	2009	2017+
1996	95	2004	2008+
1995	93	2003	2007+
1994	93	2002	2006
1991	95	2003	2011
1989	95	2001	2009

VILLAGE PINOT NOIR

RATING 4

South Gippsland	$30–$49
Current vintage: 2004	90

2004	90	2006	2009+
2003	95	2008	2011
2001	92	2003	2006
1999	89	2001	2004

Slightly unpolished, this delicious young pinot has a heady, perfumed bouquet of rose garden fragrances, raspberries and sweet red cherries over subtle suggestions of caramel and spearmint. Round and sumptuous, its juicy and slightly confectionary expression of pristine pinot flavour is long and luscious, supported by fine and supple tannins. It finishes with characteristically soft acids.

Batista Estate

Franklin Road, Middlesex WA 6258. Tel: (08) 9772 3530. Fax: (08) 9772 3530.

Region: **Pemberton** Winemaker: **Bob Peruch** Chief Executive: **Bob Peruch**

Batista is one of the leading small vineyards in the Pemberton/Manjimup/Warren Valley region, whose Pinot Noir and Shiraz are deeply flavoured, herbal and spicy. No Pinot Noir was made in 2003.

PINOT NOIR

RATING 5

Warren Valley	$30–$49
Current vintage: 2002	86

2002	86	2004	2007
2000	89	2002	2005
1999	86	2001	2004
1998	89	2003	2006
1997	87	2002	2005

Herbal, meaty pinot with a white pepper-like fragrance of slightly tomatoey berry fruit, undergrowth and herbaceous undertones. Fine and supple, its juicy palate of raspberry, plum and tomato-like fruit finishes soft and sappy but slightly hot, with herbal, greenish edges.

Battle of Bosworth

Edgehill Vineyards, Gaffney Road, Willunga SA 5171. Tel: (08) 8556 2441. Fax: (08) 8556 4881.
Website: www.battleofbosworth.com.au Email: bosworth@edgehill-vineyards.com.au

Region: **McLaren Vale** Winemaker: **Joch Bosworth** Viticulturist: **Joch Bosworth**
Chief Executives: **Peter & Anthea Bosworth**

The Bosworth family has been growing grapes in McLaren Vale since the 1840s, while this generation has been involved since the early 1970s. They earn their place in this book because of their evident determination to make top-level wine, as shown by the dramatic improvement seen in their 2004 reds.

CABERNET SAUVIGNON

RATING 5

McLaren Vale	$20–$29
Current vintage: 2004	90

2004	90	2009	2012+
2003	80	2005	2008
2002	79	2004	2007

A fine, elegant cabernet whose sweet aromas of plums, cassis and cedary oak reveal faint herbal undertones. Smooth and fine-grained, its rather polished palate finishes with attractive length and a pleasing core of vibrant berry/plum flavour.

SHIRAZ

RATING 5

McLaren Vale	$20–$29
Current vintage: 2004	90

2004	90	2012	2016
2003	82	2008	2011
2002	80	2004	2007

Rich and sumptuous, this polished and handsomely fruited shiraz has depth and character to burn. A smoky fragrance of dark berries, plums, plain chocolate and vanilla is lifted by spicy nuances of cloves and cinnamon, with nuances of treacle. Its smooth and generous palate of deep, dark fruits and sweet vanilla oak is coated by firm, but pliant tannins. True to region and variety.

2007 THE AUSTRALIAN WINE ANNUAL
www.jeremyoliver.com.au
39

Best's

Best's Road, Great Western Vic 3377. Tel: (03) 5356 2250. Fax: (03) 5356 2430.
Website: www.bestswines.com Email: info@bestswines.com
Region: **Grampians, Great Western** Winemakers: **Viv Thomson, Adam Wadewitz**
Viticulturist: **Ben Thomson** Chief Executive: **Viv Thomson**

An icon in Australian wine, Best's is an historic winery in western Victoria whose shirazes rate among Australia's finest. Recent seasons have also seen significant developments with the winery's perfumed and elegant Cabernet Sauvignon and its Riesling which, like the 2004 and 2005 wines, have become chalkier and more mineral. As happened in other sites with similar climates, the very hot 2001 and 2003 vintages produced robust and rather more dehydrated shirazes than typical for Best's. There was no Pinot Meunier made in 2003.

BIN No. 'O' SHIRAZ

RATING **3**

Grampians, Great Western	$30–$49
Current vintage: 2003	87

Lacking its customary brightness and freshness, this rather meaty shiraz of medium to full weight presents a rather cooked expression of varietal flavour entwined around a firm and youthful spine of fine tannins. Its slightly dehydrated aromas of prunes and currants reveal undertones of dried herbs, leather and treacle, while there is a little more fruit sweetness on the palate than the bouquet might suggest. Its lingering flavours of cooked plums and cassis finish with herbal, licorice-like undertones.

2003	87	2011	2015
2002	87	2010	2012
2001	92	2009	2013+
2000	93	2008	2012
1998	95	2010	2018+
1997	90	2005	2009
1996	95	2004	2008
1995	95	2007	2015
1994	88	2006	2014+
1993	86	1998	2001
1992	95	2004	2012
1991	91	1999	2003

CABERNET SAUVIGNON

RATING **4**

Grampians, Great Western	$20–$29
Current vintage: 2001	91

A piercing violet-like perfume of cassis and red berries, restrained vanilla oak and delicate herbal notes precedes a supple and silky palate of vibrant small berry flavours. Delightfully ripened, it's long and smooth, bursting with fruit and harmoniously entwined with tight, fine-grained tannins. Restrained but hardly lacking presence or structure, it should develop more elegance and complexity.

2001	91	2009	2013+
2000	87	2005	2008
1999	91	2011	2019
1998	91	2010	2018
1997	90	2005	2009+
1996	88	1998	2001
1995	90	2007	2015
1993	87	2001	2005
1992	90	2004	2012
1991	90	1999	2003+
1990	92	1998	2002
1989	82	1991	1994

CHARDONNAY

RATING **5**

Grampians, Great Western	$20–$29
Current vintage: 2003	87

Ripe, slightly confected and forward, with a sweet fragrance of peaches and melon, lemon sherbet, green olives, oatmeal and vanilla oak. Tropical, forward and juicy, it should settle back into a finer and more reserved style.

2003	87	2005	2008
2001	92	2006	2009
2000	84	2002	2005
1998	86	2003	2006
1997	88	2002	2005
1996	89	1998	2001
1995	93	2003	2007
1994	94	2006	2014

PINOT MEUNIER

RATING **5**

Grampians, Great Western	$20–$29
Current vintage: 2002	87

Peppery, spicy aromas of fresh basil, minty dark cherries and plums with slightly reductive, leathery and musky undertones. Its lively, flavoursome palate of dark cherries and plums, mint and eucalypt is juicy and vibrant. Supported by sweet vanilla/chocolate oak and modest tannins, it finishes with lingering boiled lolly-like berry fruits.

2002	87	2007	2010+
2001	87	2003	2006
1999	90	2004	2007
1998	89	2003	2006
1997	87	2005	2009
1996	90	2004	2008
1995	88	2003	2007
1994	89	2002	2006

PINOT NOIR

RATING 5

Grampians, Great Western	**$20–$29**	2001	88	2003	2006+
Current vintage: 2001	**88**	2000	87	2005	2008

2001	88	2003	2006+
2000	87	2005	2008
1999	87	2001	2004
1998	89	2000	2003+
1997	77	1998	1999
1996	89	2001	2004

Modestly structured, slightly candied pinot whose sweet red cherry and plum flavours are scented with musky spices and supported by fine, slightly bony tannins. It finishes with bright acidity and undergrowth-like complexity, and should build in the bottle.

RIESLING

RATING 4

Great Western	**$20–$29**
Current vintage: 2005	**91**

2005	91	2013	2017
2004	90	2009	2012+
2003	92	2011	2015
2002	93	2010	2014
2001	88	2003	2006+
2000	88	2005	2008
1999	93	2007	2011
1998	88	2003	2006
1997	82	1999	2002
1996	89	1998	2001
1995	94	2003	2007
1994	94	2006	2014
1993	83	1995	1998
1992	89	2000	2004

A fresh and shapely riesling whose floral perfume of pear, apple and lime juice reveals a musky aspect. Smooth and supple, it's long and tangy, delivering a juicy cut of spotlessly clean pear, apple and lemony flavour over a fine chassis of chalky phenolics. It finishes long and bright, with limey acids.

THOMSON FAMILY SHIRAZ

RATING 2

Grampians, Great Western	**$50–$99**
Current vintage: 2001	**93**

2001	93	2013	2021
1998	93	2006	2010
1997	94	2005	2009+
1996	97	2008	2016
1995	96	2007	2015+
1994	93	2004	2012
1992	96	2004	2012

Fragrant aromas of dark cherries, cassis, mulberries and plums are supported by sweet cedar/chocolate oak. There's also plenty of varietal pepper and spice, with an underlying violet-like perfume. Long, very smooth and velvet-like, with a ripe, succulent mouthfeel of berry/plum flavours bordering ever so marginally on the over-cooked. Its length and tight-knit spine of powdery tannins will ensure a strong future.

Bethany

Bethany Road, Bethany via Tanunda SA 5352. Tel: (08) 8563 2086. Fax: (08) 8563 0046.
Website: www.bethany.com.au Email: bethany@bethany.com.au

Region: **Barossa Valley** Winemakers: **Geoff & Robert Schrapel, Colin Slater**
Viticulturists: **Geoff & Robert Schrapel** Chief Executives: **Geoff & Robert Schrapel**

Bethany is a Barossa-based vineyard and winery with a long family tradition that is beginning to return to the quality levels on which it created such a strong following during the 1980s. There is still a way to travel, but wines like the Semillon 2004 and Riesling 2005 represent a move in the right direction. Its reds have recently shown an excess of over-and under-ripe influences.

CABERNET MERLOT

Barossa Valley	**$12–$19**
Current vintage: 2004	**80**

2004	80	2006	2009
2002	82	2004	2007
2001	82	2003	2006
2000	88	2002	2005+
1999	82	2001	2004
1998	87	2003	2006
1997	81	1999	2002
1996	84	1998	2001
1995	87	1997	2000
1994	90	2002	2006
1993	82	1995	1998

Simple, stewy aromas of plums, cranberries and currants with greenish, stressed undertones precede a forward and rather lifeless palate of prunes and currants that is loosely framed by green and metallic edges.

A B C D E F G H I J K L M N O P Q R S T U V W X Y Z

EDEN VALLEY RIESLING

Barossa Valley $12–$19
Current vintage: 2003 90

Citrusy, pineapple-like aromas with a suggestion of wet steel. Its restrained but willowy palate of slightly confectionary-like lime, apple and pear flavours is supported by a lightly powdery, chalky spine.

2003	90	2008	2011
2002	82	2004	2007
2001	89	2006	2009
2000	82	2001	2002
1999	88	2001	2004
1998	84	2000	2003
1997	83	1998	1999
1996	90	2001	2004+
1995	87	2000	2003+

GR RESERVE RED

Barossa Valley $50–$99
Current vintage: 1999 82

Earthy, leafy and dusty aromas of sweet red berries and cedary oak precede a sappy, rather hollow and skinny palate lacking brightness, depth and structure.

1999	82	2001	2004
1998	81	2000	2003+
1997	77	1999	2002
1996	90	2001	2004
1995	86	2000	2003
1994	92	1999	2002+
1992	90	1997	2000

RIESLING

Barossa Valley $12–$19
Current vintage: 2005 88

A generous, round and soft Barossa riesling whose floral and slightly spicy and estery aromas of lime juice and lemon rind overlie nuances of tropical fruit. Its approachable, clean and mouth-filling palate of apple, pear and lemony fruit has a light, chalky coating of phenolic extract, finishing with a refreshing cut of citrusy acidity.

2005	88	2007	2010+
2004	91	2006	2009
2003	87	2004	2005+
2002	89	2004	2007+
2001	87	2003	2006
2000	87	2001	2002+
1999	89	2001	2004
1998	88	2000	2003
1997	81	1999	2002
1996	90	2001	2004
1995	87	2000	2003

SELECT LATE HARVEST RIESLING

Barossa Valley $20–$29
Current vintage: 2005 86

Spicy, marmalade-like aromas of citrusy fruit precede a forward, rather cloying, candied and luscious palate. It's very sweet and juicy, but lacks a little freshness and brightness, finishing without much acid definition and tightness.

2005	86	2007	2010
2004	86	2005	2006+
2003	89	2004	2005+
2002	87	2003	2004+
1999	90	2001	2004
1998	89	2000	2003+
1997	90	1999	2002
1996	91	2001	2004
1995	87	1997	2000

SEMILLON

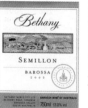

Barossa Valley $12–$19
Current vintage: 2004 90

A tangy and varietal semillon whose fresh, fruit-driven aroma of melon, lemon, hints of quince and cumquat overlies a light background of toasty vanilla oak. Round, soft and generous, its lightly oaked palate of smooth, juicy fruit is as approachable as it is fresh and lively. It finishes with a faint hint of ashtray-like oak.

2004	90	2006	2009+
2003	88	2005	2008
2002	89	2004	2007
2001	86	2003	2006
2000	88	2002	2005
1999	89	2001	2004
1998	89	2000	2003

THE AUSTRALIAN WINE ANNUAL
www.jeremyoliver.com.au **2007**

Bindi

343 Melton Road, Gisborne Vic 3437. Tel: (03) 5428 2564. Fax: (03) 5428 2564.
Region: **Macedon Ranges** Winemakers: **Stuart Anderson, Michael Dhillon** Viticulturist: **Bill Dhillon**
Chief Executive: **Bill Dhillon**

Bindi is one of the best and most important vineyards in Victoria. Found just south of the town of Gisborne, it is planted to pinot noir and chardonnay on a variety of sites, soils and aspects. With increasing vine age now providing more underlying richness and complexity, its low-cropped wines are entering a new phase of excellence. Frankly, they are probably being helped by global warming, but there is no denying that for such a cool site, it is regularly achieving in its fruit a rare combination of richness, intensity and focus.

BLOCK 5 PINOT NOIR
RATING 2

Macedon Ranges	$50–$99
Current vintage: 2004	96

Brooding and tight-fisted, this sumptuously flavoured and elegantly composed pinot is simply waiting to explode with fruit and complexity. It reveals an accentuated sweet and heady rose petal perfume of red cherries and raspberries before a long, finely crafted and ethereal palate. Framed by silky tannins, it builds in volume before a lingering, savoury finish of pure pinot fruit and charcuterie-like undertones.

2004	96	2012	2016
2003	97	2011	2015
2002	89	2004	2007
2001	94	2006	2009+
2000	87	2002	2005+
1998	92	2003	2006
1997	96	2005	2009

COMPOSITION CHARDONNAY (formerly Chardonnay)
RATING 3

Macedon Ranges	$30–$49
Current vintage: 2004	91

A floral and lightly herbal fragrance of citrus, white peach and buttery aromas overlies creamy, leesy nuances and a whiff of minerality. Its juicy and generous, with a rather slippery and almost viscous palate of lively fruit and cashew oak that culminates with bracingly clean acids and an austere, Macon-like mineral finish.

2004	91	2006	2009
2003	95	2008	2011+
2002	95	2007	2010+
2001	89	2003	2006+
2000	87	2002	2005+
1999	86	2001	2004
1998	88	2003	2006
1997	93	2002	2005
1996	87	1998	2001
1995	93	2000	2003
1994	95	2002	2006

ORIGINAL VINEYARD PINOT NOIR
RATING 3

Macedon Ranges	$50–$99
Current vintage: 2004	95

Finely crafted and deliciously spicy, this silky young pinot has a slightly meaty aroma of fresh red cherries, dark plums, rose petals, cloves and cinnamon over sweet nuances of cedary oak and faint suggestions of mint and undergrowth. Long and smooth, with a lingering core of bright, sappy fruit, it's generously flavoured, long and savoury. Despite its elegance, it reveals genuine structure and texture.

2004	95	2009	2012
2003	95	2008	2011
2002	90	2007	2010
2001	90	2006	2009
2000	87	2005	2008
1999	86	2001	2004
1998	91	2003	2006
1997	95	2002	2005
1996	95	2004	2008
1995	94	2000	2003
1994	94	2002	2006
1993	93	1998	2001

QUARTZ CHARDONNAY
RATING 2

Macedon Ranges	$50–$99
Current vintage: 2004	95

A richly textured and handsomely structured chardonnay that simply needs time. Its floral perfume of citrus and melon fruit overlies tightly knit, spicy new vanilla oak influences, while its long, juicy palate has a babyfat-like texture that culminates in a typical mineral finish of tightness and austerity. Delightfully complex, finely balanced and tightly focused.

2004	95	2009	2012
2003	97	2011	2015
2002	97	2007	2010+
2001	93	2006	2009
2000	93	2005	2008+
1999	90	2001	2004+
1998	95	2003	2006+
1995	95	2000	2003

Blackjack

Calder Highway, Harcourt Vic 3453. Tel: (03) 5474 2355. Fax: (03) 5474 2355.
Website: www.blackjackwines.com.au Email: sales@blackjackwines.com.au
Region: **Bendigo** Winemakers: **Ian McKenzie, Ken Pollock** Viticulturist: **Ian McKenzie**
Chief Executive: **Ian McKenzie**

The 2004 vintage has seen Blackjack produce a series of surprisingly elegant and fine-grained red wines, of which the Cabernet Merlot is especially restrained and focused. Blackjack is now an established Bendigo producer with a solid track record that dates back to the early 1990s. However, I'm still not convinced that the Block 6 Shiraz justifies being separated from the 'standard' edition, which could use more depth and stuffing.

BLOCK 6 SHIRAZ

RATING 5

| Bendigo | $30–$49 |
| Current vintage: 2004 | 89 |

Just a little simple and sweet for a higher score, this smooth and polished shiraz has a spicy and slightly minty aroma of cassis, blackberries, red-currants and sweet vanilla oak, backed by nuances of cloves, cinnamon and leather. It's smooth, generously fruited and has a background of sweet vanilla and a pliant structure of tight tannins. It finishes with nuances of mint and menthol, with pleasing intensity and balance.

2004	89	2009	2012
2003	88	2008	2011
2002	91	2007	2010

CABERNET MERLOT

RATING 5

| Bendigo | $20–$29 |
| Current vintage: 2004 | 90 |

Effortlessly natural and stable, this fine, elegant and very varietal cabernet has a dusty, lightly herbal fragrance of cassis, blackberries and dark plums backed by fresh cedary oak and undertones of violets, mint and menthol. Smooth and elegant, its tightly focused fruit, oak and silky tannins culminate in a charming and vibrant finish.

2004	90	2012	2016
2003	85	2005	2008+
2002	89	2007	2010
2001	90	2009	2013+
2000	89	2005	2008+
1999	83	2001	2004
1998	89	2003	2006
1997	90	2005	2009
1996	87	2001	2004
1995	85	1997	2000

SHIRAZ

RATING 5

| Bendigo | $30–$49 |
| Current vintage: 2004 | 88 |

A pretty and smooth shiraz of full to medium weight whose lightly spiced aromas of fresh red berries, raspberries and plums are supported by vanilla oak and nuances of white pepper. Fine and silky, it's vibrant and approachable, but perhaps deserved a little better than its simple nutty/vanilla oak.

2004	88	2006	2009+
2003	87	2005	2008
2002	87	2004	2007+
2001	92	2006	2009+
2000	90	2002	2005+
1999	88	2004	2007
1998	89	2003	2006+
1997	90	2002	2005
1996	90	2001	2004
1995	82	1997	2000

Bleasdale

Wellington Road, Langhorne Creek SA 5255. Tel: (08) 8537 3001. Fax: (08) 8537 3224.
Website: www.bleasdale.com.au Email: bleasdale@bleasdale.com.au

Region: **Langhorne Creek** Winemakers: **Michael Potts, Renae Hirsch** Viticulturist: **Robert Potts**
Chief Executive: **David Foreman**

Bleasdale is a stalwart of Langhorne Creek, whose wines are typically ripe, generous, approachable and relatively long-living. They're also among the most affordable of their kind. The 2003 Malbec is a perfect example of this — a delicious wine that will improve in the bottle for many a year. The 2004 Frank Potts blend is another finely crafted, silky and balanced wine, while the Mulberry Tree Cabernet Sauvignon from the same vintage is a little jammy and simple. Some wines still reflect some ongoing vine stress in the Langhorne Creek region.

BREMERVIEW SHIRAZ

RATING **5**

Langhorne Creek	$12–$19
Current vintage: 2003	85

Firm, meaty and unyielding, this robust and leathery shiraz has a pungent aroma of musk, dark plums and blackberries over nuances of briar and undergrowth. Slightly cooked and tough, its raisined palate of plums and currants is framed by drying tannin and slightly raw oak. It finishes with a hint of saltiness.

2003	85	2008	2011
2002	87	2007	2010+
2001	89	2003	2006+
2000	90	2008	2012
1999	89	2004	2007
1998	87	2003	2006
1997	92	2005	2009
1996	89	2001	2004
1995	90	2000	2003
1993	82	1995	1998
1992	88	2000	2004

FRANK POTTS CABERNET BLEND

RATING **4**

Langhorne Creek	$20–$29
Current vintage: 2004	90

Lightly floral aromas of violets, blackberries, cranberries and sweet red plums are backed by cedar/vanilla oak, with underlying herbal complexity. Long, fine and supple, the smooth and polished palate of vibrant, surprisingly generous and brightly lit small berry fruit is backed by silky tannin and sweet cedar/vanilla oak. Its natural balance and stability will assist its likely longevity.

2004	90	2012	2016+
2003	90	2011	2015
2002	89	2010	2014+
2001	89	2009	2013
2000	89	2005	2008+
1999	93	2007	2011
1998	90	2003	2006+
1997	90	2005	2009
1996	92	2004	2008+
1995	92	2003	2007
1994	87	1999	2002

MALBEC

RATING **5**

Langhorne Creek	$12–$19
Current vintage: 2003	90

A sound, firm and well-balanced malbec with a sweet, earthy and slightly confectionary aroma of cassis and raspberries that reveals floral undertones of mint and violets. Smooth and generous, it's pleasingly bright and spicy, with lingering flavours of ripe berry fruit framed by a drying and fine-grained astringency plus light oak influences.

2003	90	2011	2015
2002	82	2004	2007
2001	90	2006	2009
2000	89	2005	2008
1999	87	2004	2007
1998	88	2000	2003
1997	85	1998	2001
1996	84	1998	2001
1994	88	1999	2003
1992	82	1997	2000

MULBERRY TREE CABERNET SAUVIGNON

RATING **5**

Langhorne Creek	$12–$19
Current vintage: 2004	87

Jammy, sweet and simple, this long, firm and fine-grained young cabernet has a slightly cooked aroma of dark plums, red berries, blackberries and cedary oak with light minty undertones. Sumptuously backed by chocolate/cedary oak, its juicy and slightly sweet palate of dark berry and plum-like flavours is firm and fine-grained, but just a little simple and straightforward.

2004	87	2009	2012
2003	87	2005	2008+
2002	87	2010	2014
2001	87	2006	2009
2000	87	2005	2008
1999	90	2004	2007
1998	88	2003	2006
1997	88	2002	2005+
1996	89	2004	2008
1995	82	1997	2000
1993	87	2001	2005
1992	89	2000	2004

Blue Pyrenees

Vinoca Road, Avoca Vic 3467. Tel: (03) 5465 3202. Fax: (03) 5465 3529.
Website: www.bluepyrenees.com.au Email: info@bluepyrenees.com.au
Region: **Pyrenees** Winemaker: **Andrew Koerner** Chief Executive: **John B. Ellis**

While its table wines have been affected by recent hot and dry vintages, there is still plenty of evidence that Andrew Koerner is turning around one of the largest quality wine operations in central Victoria. The very fine Chardonnays from 2004 are ample proof of that. A handsome facility that was significantly expanded by its previous owner, Remy Martin, Blue Pyrenees is blessed with exceptional infrastructure and vineyard resource.

CABERNET SAUVIGNON
RATING **5**

Pyrenees	$12–$19
Current vintage: 2004	**89**

An honest, vibrant, minty and violet-like cabernet with pleasing length, tightness and elegance. Its fragrance of blackberries, dark plums, plain chocolate and dark olives precedes a long and dusty palate whose bright, minty berry/plum flavours knit tightly with polished oak and tannin.

Vintage	Score	Drink	
2004	89	2009	2012+
2003	82	2005	2008
2002	81	2007	2010
2001	88	2003	2006+
2000	83	2002	2005
1999	89	2001	2004

CHARDONNAY
RATING **4**

Pyrenees	$12–$19
Current vintage: 2005	**81**

A simple, short and ordinary chardonnay whose sweet, over malo-ed aromas of butterscotch, wheatmeal and sweet corn precede a candied palate that lacks length and freshness.

Vintage	Score	Drink	
2005	81	2006	2007
2004	90	2005	2006+
2003	90	2005	2008
2002	84	2003	2004
2001	82	2002	2003
2000	87	2002	2005

ESTATE RESERVE CHARDONNAY
RATING **3**

Pyrenees	$30–$49
Current vintage: 2004	**95**

Pleasing indeed to see this important Victorian winery back in top form. This spotless and tightly crafted chardonnay reveals a complex floral perfume whose white peach and honeydew melon aromas are supported by fine-grained, spicy oak. Long and silky, its tightly focused palate boasts a pristine core of vibrant nutty fruit punctuated by refreshing but unusually soft acids.

Vintage	Score	Drink	
2004	95	2006	2009+
2001	95	2006	2009
2000	86	2001	2002+
1999	93	2004	2007
1998	88	2000	2003
1997	93	2002	2005
1996	91	2001	2004+
1995	88	1997	2000
1994	89	1999	2002

ESTATE RESERVE (Cabernet Blend)
RATING **5**

Pyrenees	$30–$49
Current vintage: 2002	**86**

Rustic, old-fashioned central Victorian red whose minty expression of plums and small berries is backed by eucalypt and menthol-like undertones. A little dull and meaty on the nose, it reveals more fruit sweetness on the palate, where structure and firm, drying tannins are also evident. With lingering nuances of leather and chocolate, it's a little too lean and hard-edged.

Vintage	Score	Drink	
2002	86	2007	2010+
2001	87	2009	2013+
2000	84	2005	2008
1999	93	2007	2011+
1998	93	2010	2018
1997	89	2005	2009
1996	93	2008	2016
1995	93	2003	2007
1994	95	2002	2006+
1993	94	2001	2005
1992	92	2000	2004

SHIRAZ
RATING **5**

Pyrenees	$12–$19
Current vintage: 2003	**86**

Meaty, spicy and slightly tarry aromas of currants and raisins are lifted by the perfume of blueberries and plums, cedary oak and regional minty nuances. Smooth, rather polished and elegant, it presents a palate featuring some brightly lit berry/plum flavour, some overcooked aspects and some under-ripe and greenish, metallic acids. Lacks harmony and balance.

Vintage	Score	Drink	
2003	86	2005	2008+
2002	85	2004	2007
2001	90	2006	2009
2000	90	2002	2005+
1999	82	2001	2004

Bowen Estate

Riddoch Highway, Coonawarra SA 5263. Tel: (08) 8737 2229. Fax: (08) 8737 2173.
Website: www.coonawarra.org/wineries/bowen/ Email: bowen@bowenestate.com.au
Region: **Coonawarra** Winemakers: **Doug Bowen, Emma Bowen** Viticulturist: **Doug Bowen**
Chief Executive: **Joy Bowen**

The rebirth of Bowen Estate continues apace with the release of two more exceptional Coonawarra red wines and a fine and surprisingly integrated Chardonnay. The in-house combination of Doug Bowen's experience and daughter Emma Bowen's enthusiasm is resulting in deeply flavoured and finely balanced wines of classical elegance and the promise of exceptional longevity. The benchmark Bowen Cabernet Sauvignon was always the very refined and Bordeaux-like 1984 vintage, but it might have met its equal from 2004.

CABERNET SAUVIGNON
RATING **3**

Coonawarra $30–$49
Current vintage: 2004 95

A very fine, tightly focused and classical Coonawarra cabernet likely to age exceptionally well. Its dusty perfume of violets, cassis, cedar and vanilla overlies some complex and gamey oak-derived aromas. Smooth and silky, its long and fine-grained palate delivers a lingering core of intense cassis, blueberry and dark plum flavour tightly knit with cedar/vanilla oak and framed by firm, powdery tannin. It finishes long and dusty, with undertones of dried herbs and dark olives.

2004	95	2016	2024+
2003	90	2011	2015
2002	92	2010	2014
2001	94	2006	2009+
2000	90	2005	2008
1999	82	2001	2004
1998	95	2010	2018
1997	87	2005	2009
1996	88	2008	2016+
1995	77	1997	2000
1994	90	2002	2006
1993	84	1998	2001
1992	93	2000	2004+
1991	93	1999	2003
1990	94	1995	1998

CHARDONNAY
RATING **5**

Coonawarra $20–$29
Current vintage: 2005 90

Frankly, a surprise. This refreshingly clean, elegant and crisply defined chardonnay has tightness and focus. Its lightly floral aromas of lime juice, peach, melon and dusty cinnamon/cloves undertones precedes a smooth and vibrant but tangy palate in which fresh butter/vanilla oak is content to play second fiddle.

2005	90	2007	2010+
2004	89	2006	2009
2003	89	2005	2008
2001	86	2002	2003
2000	77	2002	2005
1999	89	2001	2004

SHIRAZ
RATING **2**

Coonawarra $30–$49
Current vintage: 2004 94

Elegant, fine-grained and deeply fruited, this is a marvellously long, firm and sumptuous modern shiraz. Laced with the scent of violets, its deep aromas of blackberries, blueberries, dark chocolate and meaty complexity reveal spicy undertones of cloves, cinnamon and dark olives. Its long and sour-edged palate is framed by fine, drying tannins, finishing with a tangy note of mineral salt.

2004	94	2012	2016+
2003	93	2011	2015
2002	95	2014	2020
2001	95	2009	2013+
2000	94	2008	2012+
1999	81	2001	2004
1998	93	2010	2018
1997	88	2005	2009
1996	88	2001	2004
1995	90	2003	2007
1994	93	2002	2006
1993	94	2001	2005
1992	95	2000	2004
1991	94	1996	1999
1990	87	1998	2002

Boynton's

6619 Great Alpine Road, Porepunkah Vic 3740. Tel: (03) 5756 2356. Fax: (03) 5756 2610.
Website: www.boynton.com.au Email: boynton@boynton.com.au
Region: **Alpine Valleys** Winemaker: **Kel Boynton** Viticulturist: **Kel Boynton** Chief Executive: **Kel Boynton**

2003 was a very difficult year for vineyards in alpine Victoria. Long, hot and dry, it also affected many wines with the ashtray-like characters associated with smoke taint. In my experience, regardless of how subtle they might be in a wine's early life, they tend to dominate it after a few years. The cooler and more moderate 2005 season has enabled Kel Boynton to produce wine of more fragrance and freshness.

FEATHERTOP CABERNET SAUVIGNON

RATING 5

FEATHERTOP

Alpine Valleys   **$20–$29**
Current vintage: 2003   **83**

Rather cooked and raw, this smooth but slightly dehydrated cabernet has a closed bouquet of small black and red berries over cedar/vanilla oak and herbal undertones. It's rather jammy, with a moderately long palate whose initially sweet flavours of black and red berries dries out towards a currant-like and raisined finish backed by suggestions of dried herbs. Lacks freshness and brightness.

2003	83	2005	2008
2002	87	2007	2010
2000	82	2002	2005+
1998	89	2003	2006
1997	91	2005	2009
1996	86	2005	2009
1995	75	1997	2000
1994	94	2002	2006
1993	93	2001	2005+
1992	92	2000	2004
1991	87	1996	1999
1990	95	1998	2002

FEATHERTOP MERLOT

RATING 5

FEATHERTOP

Alpine Valleys   **$20–$29**
Current vintage: 2003   **77**

Juicy, confiture-like aromas of blackberries, plums and cherries are backed by cedar/vanilla oak and smoky undertones. Rather closed, the palate does reveal some dark and brooding fruit, but is totally dominated by ashtray-like bushfire taint.

2003	77	2005	2008
2002	89	2007	2010+
2000	90	2005	2008
1998	89	2000	2003
1997	88	1999	2002+
1996	90	2001	2004

FEATHERTOP RIESLING

RATING 4

FEATHERTOP

Alpine Valleys   **$12–$19**
Current vintage: 2005   **91**

Fresh aromas of apple, pear and tropical fruits precede a juicy palate that becomes long, tight and slightly chalky. Its lingering expression of tangy fruit finishes clean and refreshing, with a light sweetness similar to the German halbtrocken style. Should flesh out and develop well.

2005	91	2010	2013
2002	87	2004	2007
2001	90	2006	2009
2000	86	2002	2005
1998	85	2000	2003

Brand's

Main Road, Coonawarra SA 5263. Tel: (08) 8736 3260. Fax: (08) 8736 3208.
Website: www.mcwilliams.com.au Email: brands_office@mcwilliams.com.au
Region: **Coonawarra** Winemaker: **Peter Weinberg** Viticulturist: **Trent Brand** Chief Executive: **George Wahby**

Brand's is the Coonawarra base for the McWilliam family. Its wines are typically fine, full to medium in weight, smooth and elegant. While they have more intensity, oak and volume, much the same can be said for the Patron's Reserve and Stentiford's Reserve wines. The first red releases from 2004 look very encouraging.

CABERNET SAUVIGNON

RATING 4

BRAND'S
OF COONAWARRA

COONAWARRA
CABERNET SAUVIGNON
2000

Coonawarra   **$20–$29**
Current vintage: 2004   **90**

A floral, lightly minty and violet-like perfume of sweet black berries, raspberries and vanilla/cedar oak precedes a smooth, supple and elegant palate whose pristine berry flavours are framed by fine, tightly knit tannins. It's medium in weight, polished and very finely balanced, with vanilla and cedary oak playing a reserved second fiddle.

2004	90	2009	2012+
2003	82	2005	2008+
2002	84	2004	2007
2001	91	2006	2009+
2000	91	2002	2005+
1999	91	2004	2007+
1998	92	2006	2010
1997	90	2002	2005
1996	82	1998	2001
1995	87	2000	2003
1994	91	1999	2002
1993	93	1998	2001

CHARDONNAY

Coonawarra	$12–$19
Current vintage: 2005	**87**

Generously flavoured, but sweet, oaky and rather confectionary. Lively peachy fruit, vanilla oak and cashew nut aromas reveal dusty, herbal undertones before a forward, slightly cloying and simple palate.

2005	87	2006	2007+
2004	88	2005	2006+
2003	88	2004	2005+
2002	83	2003	2004
2001	87	2002	2003+
1998	87	1999	2000
1997	88	1999	2002
1996	86	1998	2001
1995	88	2000	2003
1994	87	1996	1999

MERLOT

Coonawarra	$20–$29
Current vintage: 2004	**90**

Smooth, effortless, pretty and easy-drinking, this supple young merlot marries pleasingly sour-edged dark cherry and plum-like fruit with sweet, creamy and chocolaty oak. Its spicy, floral perfume of sweet varietal fruit and cedary oak precedes a restrained palate whose juicy flavours and fine tannins finish with bright, clean acids.

2004	90	2009	2012
2003	90	2008	2011
2002	84	2004	2007+
2001	93	2006	2009
2000	90	2002	2005+
1999	90	2001	2004
1997	90	1999	2002

PATRON'S RESERVE RED

Coonawarra	$50–$99
Current vintage: 2002	**86**

Full to medium in weight, with some pleasing fruit brightness and intensity, this moderately firm but slightly sappy red lacks genuine ripeness and balance. There's a herbal thread beneath its slightly dull aromas of plums, berries and cedar/vanilla oak, while it finishes rather greenish, with some modest fruit intensity and length.

2002	86	2007	2010+
2001	90	2009	2013
2000	92	2008	2012
1999	95	2007	2011+
1998	94	2006	2010+
1997	88	2002	2005+
1996	95	2004	2008+
1991	92	1999	2003+
1990	85	1995	1998

SHIRAZ

Coonawarra	$20–$29
Current vintage: 2003	**88**

Leathery and lightly meaty aromas of red cherries, raspberries, fresh plums and sweet vanilla oak are backed by spicy nuances of cloves and cinnamon. Medium to full in weight, it's moderately fleshy, with a lively flavours of red berries and plums framed by slightly sappy and metallic tannins. Pleasing for the shorter term.

2003	88	2005	2008
2002	86	2004	2007
2001	92	2006	2009+
2000	87	2002	2005+
1999	89	2001	2004
1998	90	2000	2003+
1997	91	2002	2005
1996	89	1998	2001
1995	86	1997	2000
1994	82	1996	1999

STENTIFORD'S RESERVE OLD VINES SHIRAZ

Coonawarra	$50–$99
Current vintage: 2002	**87**

Dusty, herbal and minty aromas of jammy plums and berries are backed by meaty, leathery undertones. Initially forward and juicy, it presents some fruit attractive sweetness and depth, but lacks conviction. It finishes with slightly raw and metallic tannins and green-edged fruit.

2002	87	2007	2010
2000	89	2005	2008+
1999	95	2007	2011+
1998	96	2010	2018
1997	94	2005	2009
1996	95	2004	2008
1995	91	2003	2007
1991	87	1996	1999
1990	86	1992	1995+
1988	87	1996	2000
1987	79	1992	1995
1986	91	1994	1998+
1985	92	1997	2005

A B C D E F G H I J K L M N O P Q R S T U V W X Y Z

Bremerton

Strathalbyn Road, Langhorne Creek SA 5255. Tel: (08) 8537 3093. Fax: (08) 8537 3109.
Website: www.bremerton.com.au Email: info@bremerton.com.au

Region: **Langhorne Creek** Winemaker: **Rebecca Willson** Viticulturist: **Tom Keelan** Chief Executive: **Craig Willson**

A family affair at Langhorne Creek, Bremerton has struggled a little to maintain the freshness and brightness of its red wines due to some very challenging seasons. These are typically quite assertive wines, with layers of rich, minty fruit supported by assertive and grainy oak. It will be interesting to see how the Willsons have handled the 2004 and 2005 seasons, which should have made red winemaking rather more satisfying.

OLD ADAM SHIRAZ

RATING **5**

Langhorne Creek $30–$49
Current vintage: 2002   87

Sweet, slightly medicinal and menthol-like aromas of cassis, plums and restrained vanilla oak present a rather chemical note. The palate, however, has depth and richness of dark berry/plum fruit framed by a firm grip of drying tannins and supported by toasty vanilla oak. There's a hint of rawness and saltiness, but it's solid and firm, with lingering mint/menthol characters.

2002	87	2007	2010
2001	89	2006	2009
1999	86	2001	2004+
1998	88	2000	2003
1997	83	2002	2005
1996	90	2001	2004

RESERVE CABERNET SAUVIGNON (formerly Walter's)

RATING **5**

Langhorne Creek $20–$29
Current vintage: 2002   87

A firm but tiring cabernet whose earthy, leathery and slightly tarry aromas of dark plums, blackberries and cassis are handsomely backed by cedary, dark chocolate and cigarboxy oak. It delivers length, intensity and regionality, with an initially smooth expression of dark plums and berries framed by smooth, dusty tannin. It finishes savoury but restrained, with its fruit just beginning to dry out.

2002	87	2007	2010
2001	89	2009	2013+
2000	86	2002	2005
1999	88	2004	2007
1998	90	2006	2010
1997	86	1999	2002
1996	89	2004	2008

SELKIRK SHIRAZ

RATING **5**

Langhorne Creek $20–$29
Current vintage: 2003   87

A competent, modern and oaky wine from a tough vintage. Its slightly cooked and jammy aromas of black and red berries, plums and mocha/chocolate oak overlie meaty, pruney influences. Smooth and persistent, it's moderately long and juicy, with some pleasing fruit sweetness, but reveals more raisined and currant-like flavours towards its slightly dehydrated and salty finish.

2003	87	2005	2008
2002	87	2004	2007+
2000	92	2005	2008+
1999	86	2001	2004
1998	85	2000	2003
1997	80	1999	2002
1996	89	2004	2008

VERDELHO

RATING **5**

Langhorne Creek $20–$29
Current vintage: 2005   88

A tangy, herbal and citrusy verdelho whose dusty and lightly mineral aromas of lemony and tropical fruit precede a clean and refreshing palate whose lively varietal flavours finish with zesty, bright acidity and a hint of minerality.

2005	88	2006	2007
2004	87	2004	2005+
2003	87	2003	2004+
2002	88	2003	2004+

Brian Barry

Juds Hill Vineyard, Clare SA 5453. Tel: (08) 8363 6211. Fax: (08) 8362 0498.
Website: www.brianbarrywines.com Email: brianbarrywines@optusnet.com.au

Region: **Clare Valley** Winemakers: **Brian Barry, Judson Barry** Viticulturist: **Brian Barry** Chief Executive: **Brian Barry**

Brian Barry is a long-established and traditional maker of regional Clare Valley wines, with a particular focus on its Juds Hill Riesling. Rather more spicy and estery than is typical for the region, it's often quite spiky, forward and candied. The 2004 Juds Hill Cabernet does reveal lightly under-and over-ripe fruit qualities.

JUDS HILL VINEYARD CABERNET BLEND

RATING **4**

Clare Valley	$20–$29		
Current vintage: 2004	86		

Rich, flavoursome but rather cooked cabernet whose meaty and slightly tarry aromas of blackcurrants, currants, plums and raisins are backed by herbal, minty undertones. Its forward and treacle-like palate is thick and chewy, but doesn't offer any great length.

2004	86	2009	2012+
2002	89	2010	2014+
2000	93	2008	2012
1999	91	2007	2011
1997	81	1999	2002
1996	89	2008	2016
1995	88	2007	2015
1994	87	2006	2014
1993	83	1995	1998

JUDS HILL VINEYARD RIESLING

RATING **4**

Clare Valley	$20–$29		
Current vintage: 2005	86		

Spicy, spiky and slightly oxidative and varnishy aromas of lemon blossom and apricots have a rather syrupy aspect. Its juicy, but rather candied flavours of apple and pear overlie a minerally backbone. It improves significantly with breathing, but remains a little too sweet and spiky.

2005	86	2010	2013
2004	89	2006	2009+
2003	88	2005	2008+
2002	90	2007	2010+
2001	94	2009	2013+
2000	86	2002	2005
1999	80	1999	2000
1998	94	2003	2006+
1997	80	1998	1999
1996	93	2001	2004+
1995	93	2003	2007
1994	95	2002	2006

Briar Ridge

593 Mount View Road, Mount View NSW 2325. Tel: (02) 4990 3670. Fax: (02) 4990 7802.
Website: www.briarridge.com.au Email: indulge@briarridge.com.au

Region: **Lower Hunter Valley** Winemakers: **Mark Woods, Karl Stockhausen** Viticulturist: **Derek Smith** Chief Executive: **John Davis**

Briar Ridge is one of my favourite small Hunter makers. Its wines are very true to the region's long-held traditions of elegance and complexity. They are typically generously fruited and stylishly made. Most can be enjoyed in their youth — the Chairman's Selection Chardonnay from 2004 especially, but like the 2005 Karl Stockhausen Semillon, they can also cellar for many years.

KARL STOCKHAUSEN SEMILLON

RATING **4**

Lower Hunter Valley	$20–$29		
Current vintage: 2005	90		

A tangy, fine and lively semillon whose fresh aromas of lime, honeydew melon and lemon are backed by herbal suggestions of tobacco. Supple, dry and zesty, it's lightly chalky, delivering a long, fresh and vibrant palate, finishing with racy, citrusy acids.

2005	90	2010	2013+
2003	82	2005	2008
2002	93	2010	2014

KARL STOCKHAUSEN SHIRAZ

RATING **3**

Lower Hunter Valley	$20–$29		
Current vintage: 2002	90		

Old-fashioned, restrained and very elegant Hunter burgundy style whose earthy, spicy and leathery bouquet of slightly stewed plum-like fruit, red berries and cherries is lifted by hints of tar and white pepper. Its palate is restrained and almost shy, but offers an excellent length of reserved berry flavours, creamy oak and fine tannins.

2002	90	2007	2010+
2001	89	2003	2006
2000	85	2005	2008
1999	95	2007	2011
1998	95	2006	2010+
1997	94	2005	2009
1996	84	2001	2004
1995	92	2007	2015
1994	88	1999	2002
1993	93	2001	2005

ROCK PILE CHARDONNAY

RATING 5

Lower Hunter Valley		**$20–$29**	
Current vintage: 2005		**87**	

Slightly over and under-ripe, this rich, round and generously flavoured chardonnay reveals some slightly cooked fruit as well as greenish elements. Its toasty aromas of melon, quince, cumquat and butter/vanilla oak reveal creamy, leesy and lightly funky undertones. Smooth and forward, its long and creamy palate finishes soft and refreshing.

2005	87	2007	2010
2004	88	2006	2009
2003	76	2003	2004
2002	87	2004	2007
2001	90	2003	2006+
2000	87	2002	2005
1999	82	2001	2004
1998	90	2000	2003+
1997	88	1999	2002
1996	93	2001	2004

Bridgewater Mill

Mount Barker Road, Bridgewater SA 5155. Tel: (08) 8339 9200. Fax: (08) 8339 5311.
Website: www.petalumalimited.com.au Email: bridgewatermill@petaluma.com.au
Region: **Adelaide Hills** Winemaker: **Andrew Hardy** Viticulturist: **Mike Harms** Chief Executive: **Peter Cowan**

Its owners have finally returned Bridgewater Mill, whose home is a delightful sparkling wine cellar and restaurant high in the Adelaide Hills, to again being a label for freshly flavoured and varietal wines from its region. As the current white releases illustrate, this should help to refresh the brand, which began its existence as a rather credible second label for Petaluma.

CHARDONNAY

RATING

Adelaide Hills		**$20–$29**	
Current vintage: 2004		**92**	

An elegant, fine and supple chardonnay exuding freshness, restraint and harmony. With a nutty, floral aroma of citrus fruit and sweet vanilla and buttery oak, it reveals a generous, smooth and delightfully vibrant palate whose peach, melon, apple and grapefruit flavours are neatly integrated with fresh oak influences and finished with fresh acids.

2004	92	2006	2009+
2002	83	2003	2004+
2001	81	2002	2003
2000	88	2002	2005
1999	87	2001	2004
1998	81	1999	2000
1997	90	1999	2002
1996	86	1998	2001
1995	90	1997	2000

MILLSTONE SHIRAZ

RATING 5

Various, SA		**$20–$29**	
Current vintage: 2001		**91**	

A very good shiraz from this challengingly hot vintage, whose deeply spiced and earthy bouquet of dark chocolate, plums and blackberries reveals some pleasingly meaty undertones. Medium to full in weight, it's smooth and savoury, presenting a delightfully sour-edged expression of plum and cherry flavour beneath leathery and chocolate-like qualities. Pleasingly evolved in a Rhône-like fashion.

2001	91	2006	2009
2000	89	2002	2005+
1997	86	2002	2005
1996	90	2001	2004
1995	88	2000	2003
1994	91	1999	2002
1993	92	2001	2005
1992	93	1997	2000
1991	88	1996	1999

SAUVIGNON BLANC

RATING

Adelaide Hills		**$12–$19**	
Current vintage: 2005		**88**	

A little candied but nevertheless clean and refreshing, this vibrant and tangy sauvignon blanc has a fresh aroma of tropical fruit, gooseberries and passionfruit backed by a light grassiness and a hint of mineral. Its palate is fresh and moderately racy, but slightly too confectionary.

2005	88	2005	2006
2004	87	2004	2005+
2003	87	2003	2004
2002	89	2002	2003
2001	87	2001	2002
2000	90	2001	2002
1999	90	2000	2003
1998	87	1998	1999

Brokenwood

McDonalds Road, Pokolbin NSW 2320. Tel: (02) 4998 7559. Fax: (02) 4998 7893.
Website: www.brokenwood.com.au Email: sales@brokenwood.com.au
Regions: **Various** Winemaker: **Peter-James Charteris** Viticulturist: **Keith Barry** Chief Executive: **Iain Riggs**

Recent vertical tastings of Brokenwood's key prestige labels, the Graveyard (shiraz) and ILR Reserve Semillon, confirmed not only their lofty status as benchmark Hunter wines, but also revealed an observant ongoing process of fine-tuning. Brokenwood's Hunter reds suffered a little with the bushfires in 2003, but the winery still turned out a delightfully sumptuous, smooth and sour-edged Rayner Vineyard Shiraz from McLaren Vale.

CABERNET BLEND   RATING 4

Beechworth, King Valley,
McLaren Vale $20–$29
Current vintage: 2003   83

Lightly smoky and earthy aromas of sweet red plums, berries and undertones of menthol precede a firm and sinewy palate whose slightly stewed expression of plums, red cherries, redcurrants and cranberries finishes flat and stale, framed by a drying astringency. Given that two of the three wine regions (Beechworth and King Valley) that contributed to this blend were to some extent affected by bushfires, the presence of ashtray-like smoke taint does not come as a surprise.

2003	83	2005	2008
2002	91	2007	2010+
2000	89	2005	2008
1999	90	2004	2007+
1997	90	2000	2005
1996	87	2004	2008
1994	90	2002	2006
1992	93	2000	2004
1991	93	1996	1999
1990	92	1995	1998

CHARDONNAY   RATING 4

Various $20–$29
Current vintage: 2004   90

Fine, elegant and refreshing chardonnay with a delicate fragrance of peach, melon and citrusy fruit supported by lightly buttery and creamy nuances of fine-grained vanilla oak. Smooth and supple, it's moderately long and chalky, with vibrant fruit and tightly knit oak finishing clean and dusty with lively acids. Good shape and tightness.

2004	90	2006	2009
2003	85	2004	2005
2001	89	2003	2006
2000	89	2002	2005
1998	93	2000	2003+
1997	94	2002	2005
1995	91	2000	2003

GRAVEYARD VINEYARD (Shiraz)   RATING 2

Lower Hunter Valley $50–$99
Current vintage: 2004   95

Fine and silky, this heady and perfumed Hunter shiraz has an intense and floral aroma of violets and raspberries, cherries and cedar/vanilla oak backed by cinnamon-like spices. Smooth and restrained, with a pleasing youthful sappiness, its pristine palate of fresh blackcurrant, raspberry and cherry flavours is framed by velvet tannins. Delightfully long and elegant, it is likely to build in flavour and structure, while remaining a finer and less overt style.

2004	95	2016	2024
2003	92	2015	2023
2002	93	2014	2022
2001	86	2006	2009
2000	97	2012	2020
1999	94	2011	2019
1998	95	2010	2018
1997	86	2002	2005+
1996	89	2004	2008+
1995	91	2003	2007
1994	88	2006	2014
1993	84	1998	2001+
1991	94	2003	2011+
1990	89	2002	2010
1989	87	1997	2001
1988	91	2000	2008

ILR RESERVE SEMILLON   RATING 3

Lower Hunter Valley $30–$49
Current vintage: 1999   95

Smooth, supple and silky, this maturing semillon has a smoky and perfumed bouquet developing some nutty, honeyed, toasty and beeswax-like complexity beneath its punchy melon aromas. Its finely textured palate is exceptionally long, medium to full in weight, and its toasty, buttery expression of honeydew melon and nutty flavour culminates in a lingering dry and savoury finish of punctuation and freshness.

2001	91	2009	2013
2000	88	2005	2008+
1999	95	2007	2011+
1998	87	2003	2006+
1997	92	2005	2009
1996	90	2004	2008
1995	87	2000	2003
1994	93	2006	2014
1993	91	2001	2005

RAYNER VINEYARD SHIRAZ

RATING 3

McLaren Vale	$50–$99
Current vintage: 2003	**93**

Deeply flavoured and faultless, this stylish modern McLaren Vale shiraz marries dark and slightly treacle-like fruit with smoked oyster-like oak and velvet tannins. Its spicy fragrance of sour cherries, dark plums, cassis and smoky vanilla oak reveals undertones of bitumen and cloves, while its moderately full palate is smooth and velvet-fine. Sumptuous, sour-edged and concentrated, it finishes with a lingering core of fruit and dark olives.

2003	93	2011	2015+
2002	94	2010	2014+
2001	93	2009	2013
2000	91	2005	2008
1999	89	2001	2004+
1996	93	2004	2008

SEMILLON

RATING 4

Lower Hunter Valley	$12–$19
Current vintage: 2005	**90**

Lightly herbal and grassy aromas of fresh melon, gooseberry and hints of rosewater precede a juicy and very intense, mouthfilling and tangy palate whose herbaceous expression of intense melon fruit culminates in a vibrant acid finish. There's a lightly chalky spine beneath the fruit and the promise of some development.

2005	90	2007	2010
2004	91	2005	2006+
2003	86	2004	2005+
2002	90	2004	2007
2001	91	2002	2003
2000	91	2001	2004+
1998	95	2003	2006+
1997	91	2002	2005
1995	94	2003	2007
1994	93	2002	2006
1993	88	2001	2005
1992	87	2000	2004

SHIRAZ

RATING 4

Various	$20–$29
Current vintage: 2003	**82**

A smoke-tainted shiraz whose dark, meaty and menthol-like aromas of plums and dark berries overlie smoky nuances of salami and ashtray. Its rather cooked and cedary palate packs plenty of impact and power, but retains a blockiness and smoky bitterness. It finishes rather acrid, lacking regional character.

2003	82	2005	2008
2001	92	2006	2009
2000	87	2002	2005
1998	90	2003	2006
1996	88	2001	2004

Brown Brothers

239 Milawa-Bobinawarrah Road, Milawa Vic 3678. Tel: (03) 5720 5500. Fax: (03) 5720 5511
Website: www.brown-brothers.com.au Email: bbmv@brown-brothers.com.au

Region: **NE Victoria** Winemakers: **Wendy Cameron, Hamish Seabrook, Marc Scalzo, Joel Tilbrook, Cate Looney** Viticulturist: **Mark Walpole** Chief Executive: **Ross Brown**

Brown Brothers occupies a unique place in Australian wine, largely because it has continually shown a determination to make table wines out of virtually every variety grown commercially in this country. While there have been some steady improvements with its Italian varieties, I think Brown Brothers deserves most credit for the consistency and quality of the Patricia Pinot Chardonnay Brut. Its more basic range of Victorian and King Valley varietals just lacks a little brightness and vitality.

CABERNET SHIRAZ MONDEUSE BLEND

RATING 4

NE Victoria	$20–$29
Current vintage: 1998	**90**

Deep, dark and chocolatey, with intense aromas of cassis, plums, black olives and fruitcake, plus slightly ashtray-like smoky oak. Powerful and extracted, massively concentrated, with rich, meaty raisin and spicecake qualities supported by smoky oak and a firm, bony spine of robust and presently unyielding tannins.

1998	90	2010	2018+
1997	90	2009	2017+
1996	91	2008	2016
1995	87	2007	2015
1992	92	2004	2012
1990	91	2002	2010
1989	90	2001	2009
1988	90	2000	2005
1987	90	1999	2004
1986	91	2006	2016
1985	91	2015	2025
1984	85	1992	1996
1983	91	2003	2013
1982	90	1994	1999
1981	90	1993	1998
1980	94	2010	2020

KING VALLEY BARBERA

RATING 5

| King Valley | $12–$19 |
| Current vintage: 2002 | 87 |

Honest, varietal but slightly greenish barbera with a spicy, confectionary aroma of sweet red cherries and berries, with meaty undertones of diesel oil and nicotine. Smooth and supple, its lively and pristine fruit is supported by fine, tight tannins, before finishing slightly herbal and green-edged.

2002	87	2004	2007
2001	91	2003	2006
1999	87	2001	2004+
1998	81	1999	2000
1997	85	1998	1999
1996	88	1998	2001

PATRICIA NOBLE RIESLING

RATING 3

| King Valley | $30–$49 |
| Current vintage: 2002 | 93 |

A luscious, intensely flavoured and pristine dessert wine that avoids the cloying nature of so many of its kind. Its honeyed aromas of tinned tropical fruits, pear and apricot reveal complex undertones of pastry. Slightly buttery, very ripe and concentrated, the palate delivers an elegant, smooth and juicy expression of stonefruits, honeycomb and tropical flavours before finishing fresh and clean with zesty lemony acidity.

2002	93	2007	2010+
2000	93	2005	2008+
1999	89	2004	2007
1998	89	2003	2006
1997	85	1998	1999
1996	81	1998	2001
1994	82	1999	2002
1993	92	1998	2001

PATRICIA PINOT CHARDONNAY BRUT

RATING 2

| King Valley | $30–$49 |
| Current vintage: 2000 | 95 |

A classy, complex and slightly meaty sparkling wine that ably marries fresh citrus and melon-like fruit with complex, leesy and slightly aldehydic nuances. It's floral and highly aromatic, with a fresh, crackly and creamy palate whose vibrant fruit eases into a luxuriantly long and savoury finish. Very accomplished, with a pleasing undercurrent of dusty chalkiness.

2000	95	2005	2008+
1999	90	2004	2007+
1998	94	2003	2006+
1997	88	2002	2005
1996	90	2001	2004
1995	95	2000	2003+
1994	89	1999	2002
1993	79	1995	1998

VICTORIA CABERNET SAUVIGNON

RATING 5

| Victoria | $12–$19 |
| Current vintage: 2003 | 86 |

An honest, relatively simple but flavoursome cabernet whose rather closed, lightly oaked and meaty aromas of dark plums and blackberries precedes a supple, smooth and fine-grained palate. Its bright flavours of plums and small berries with undertones of dried herbs are rather let down by raw and cardboard-like oak extract.

2003	86	2008	2011
2002	87	2007	2010
2001	89	2006	2009+
2000	82	2002	2005
1999	82	2001	2004
1998	85	2000	2003
1997	88	2002	2005
1996	90	2001	2004
1994	89	2002	2006
1993	90	2005	2013

VICTORIA CHARDONNAY

RATING 5

| Victoria | $12–$19 |
| Current vintage: 2004 | 87 |

Floral aromas of grapefruit, peach and melon with smoky, meaty and leesy undertones are barked by sweet vanilla oak and creamy, butterscotch-like malolactic influences. Rather fast-developing, with toffee-like influences affecting the brightness and freshness of melon and peachy fruit, it's smooth and creamy, but lacks genuine length and tightness.

2004	87	2006	2009
2003	85	2004	2005
2001	83	2002	2003+
2000	89	2002	2005
1999	80	2000	2001
1998	82	2000	2003
1997	88	1999	2002

A B C D E F G H I J K L M N O P Q R S T U V W X Y Z

RATING 5

Victoria	$12–$19
Current vintage: 2005	**90**

A crisp, clearly and cleanly defined riesling whose fresh floral aromas of apple, lime and lemon sherbet have a slightly confectionary note. Its palate has a lightly chalky structure beneath vibrant lemony flavours, and finishes with clean, lively acidity.

2005	90	2010	2013+
2004	87	2006	2009
2003	87	2004	2005+
2002	90	2004	2007
2001	80	2001	2002
2000	84	2002	2005
1999	87	2001	2004
1997	87	1999	2002
1996	86	1998	2001
1995	85	2000	2003

Burge Family

Barossa Valley Way, Lyndoch SA 5351. Tel: (08) 8524 4644. Fax: (08) 8524 4444.
Website: www.burgefamily.com.au Email: draycott@burgefamily.com.au
Region: **Barossa Valley** Winemaker: **Rick Burge** Viticulturist: **Rick Burge** Chief Executive: **Rick Burge**

Rick Burge has strengthened his reputation with some first-rate 2004 reds, the pick of which is not entirely unexpected — the Draycott Shiraz. Sumptuous and velvet-like, it's the best wine I have ever tasted from this maker, a classic expression of what used to be known as the Australian 'burgundy'. The Garnacha is just a little confectionary and spirity for a higher rating, but will please enthusiasts of this style. I actually prefer the palate-staining and rather grenache-dominant Olive Hill red blend from this vintage.

DRAYCOTT SHIRAZ

RATING 3

Barossa Valley	$30–$49
Current vintage: 2004	**95**

A classic Australian burgundy style whose exotically spicy and leathery aromas of deep red and black berries, plums and cranberries are laced with musk and pepper. Its powerful core of deep, sumptuous black and red berry flavour effortlessly handles its restrained oak, while it finishes with rare intensity and mouthwatering acids. Tightly framed by velvet tannins that reveal a fine, bony edge, it's exceptionally elegant and already quite complex. Beneath its lingering fruit lie rustic nuances of mint, menthol and sweet leather.

2004	95	2016	2024+
2003	80	2005	2008
2001	93	2009	2013
2000	88	2005	2008
1999	95	2007	2011

OLD VINES GARNACHA

RATING 4

Barossa Valley	$20–$29
Current vintage: 2004	**88**

Meaty, spicy and rather alcoholic, this ripe and confectionary grenache delivers a punchy palate full of vibrant and slightly jammy cherry, blueberry and raspberry flavour that dries out towards a velvet-smooth and savoury finish. Exactly what you expect from Barossa grenache.

2004	88	2006	2009+
2003	90	2008	2011+
2001	92	2006	2009+
2000	92	2005	2008
1999	90	2003	2006+

OLIVE HILL SEMILLON

RATING 4

Barossa Valley	$20–$29
Current vintage: 2005	**90**

Ripe melon and citrusy aromas are backed by oaky suggestions of vanilla and grilled nuts, with slightly pungent and reductive undertones of dried flowers and oatmeal. Smooth and generous, it's seamless and quite viscous, delivering pristine ripe varietal fruit carefully backed with oak and finished with clean but soft acidity.

2005	90	2007	2010
2004	81	2004	2005
2002	90	2004	2007
2001	87	2002	2003
2000	86	2001	2002
1999	90	2004	2007

OLIVE HILL SHIRAZ MOURVÈDRE GRENACHE

RATING **3**

	Barossa Valley	$30–$49
	Current vintage: 2004	**92**

Delightfully rustic and complex, dominated by grenache, this finely crafted wine has a funky bouquet of red plums, cherries and berries over nuances of forest floor and animal hide. Long and concentrated, its dark, pristine and slightly jammy palate becomes smooth and elegant, finishing with a bright core of fruit framed by velvet tannins.

2004	92	2009	2012+
2003	91	2011	2015+
2002	93	2007	2010+
2001	94	2006	2009+
2000	87	2002	2005
1999	94	2007	2011
1998	89	2000	2003

By Farr

101 Kelly Lane, Bannockburn, Vic, 3331 Tel: (03) 5281 1933. Fax: (03) 5281 1433.
Website: www.byfarr.com.au Email: kalvos@datafast.net.au
Region: **Geelong** Winemakers: **Gary Farr, Nick Farr** Viticulturist: **Gary Farr** Chief Executive: **Gary Farr**

By Farr is the label owned by Gary Farr, whose fruit is sourced from his own vineyards adjacent to those of Bannockburn, where for many years he was the winemaker, and where the By Farr wines were made. A recent tasting of By Farr wines showed what a stellar vintage 2004 was for the brand, and also illustrated that the 1999 releases of Chardonnay, Pinot Noir and Shiraz are not to be sneezed at either!

CHARDONNAY

RATING **3**

	Geelong	$50–$99
	Current vintage: 2004	**95**

Sumptuous, generous and fine-grained, this complex and meaty chardonnay unfolds a floral perfume of grapefruit, lime and lemon backed by nutty, melon-like undertones. Long, taut and mineral, its vivacious expression of citrus fruit has a juicy, creamy core that culminates in a lingering, flavoursome and tightly focused finish.

2004	95	2009	2012
2003	87	2005	2008
2002	93	2007	2010
2001	87	2003	2006
2000	91	2005	2008
1999	91	2004	2007

SANGREAL (formerly Pinot Noir)

RATING **4**

	Geelong	$50–$99
	Current vintage: 2004	**95**

A finely crafted, supple and satiny pinot whose heady, floral perfume of sweet cherries, plums and berries is backed by meaty, musky undertones. Smooth and silky, its pristine palate of intense cherry/plum fruit finishes long and spicy. Supported by very fine-grained tannin, it's long and savoury.

2004	95	2009	2012
2003	88	2005	2008
2002	82	2004	2007
2001	89	2006	2009
2000	87	2002	2005
1999	94	2004	2007+

SHIRAZ

RATING **4**

	Geelong	$30–$49
	Current vintage: 2004	**93**

Wild, peppery aromas of briary black and red berries overlie heady, spicy scents of cloves, cinnamon and sweet oak. Full to medium weight, it's tightly crafted and supple, with a restrained and savoury expression of spicy fruit that reveals some greenish, herbal undertones as well as just a hint of cooked fruit.

2004	93	2009	2012+
2003	86	2005	2008
2002	86	2004	2007+
2001	91	2006	2009+
2000	89	2005	2008
1999	94	2004	2007+

VIOGNIER

RATING **4**

	Geelong	$30–$49
	Current vintage: 2004	**92**

A powerful, assertive and impactful viognier of the fuller style whose very perfumed and musky aromas reveal deeply floral and spicy scents of apricot and blossom. Very juicy, almost unctuous and slightly fat, it's smooth, creamy and savoury.

2004	92	2006	2009
2003	88	2005	2008
2002	87	2004	2007
2001	93	2003	2006
2000	89	2002	2005
1999	87	2001	2004

Campbells

Murray Valley Highway, Rutherglen Vic 3685. Tel: (02) 6032 9458. Fax: (02) 6032 9870.
Website: www.campbellswines.com.au Email: wine@campbellswines.com.au
Region: **Rutherglen** Winemaker: **Colin Campbell** Viticulturist: **Malcolm Campbell**
Chief Executives: **Colin & Malcolm Campbell**

Campbells is a long-established family winery in Rutherglen, best known for its richly flavoured, but soft and smooth duo of Bobbie Burns Shiraz and The Barkly Durif. Campbells' whites are generous, fruity and early to mature, and the 2005 releases are delightfully fresh expressions of their varieties. Like many others of the region, Campbells has a well-deserved reputation for fortified wine, muscat and tokay especially. Its style is rich, soft, sweet and generous, with a distinctive lightness and elegance.

BOBBIE BURNS SHIRAZ   RATING 4

Rutherglen	**$20–$29**		
Current vintage: 2003	**91**		

Sweet and juicy, this warmer season's impression of Bobbie Burns is full-bodied, round and generous, with juicy, mouthfilling fruit, and firmish but pliant tannins. Its jammy aromas of raspberries, redcurrants, violets and sweet vanilla oak have a spicy background of cloves and nutmeg. Smooth and approachable, its spicy, juicy palate of blackberry and cassis, blueberry and raspberry, licorice and vanilla oak is coated with fine and pliant tannin.

2003	91	2011	2015
2002	87	2007	2010
2001	90	2006	2009
2000	90	2008	2012
1999	89	2004	2007
1998	90	2006	2010
1997	89	2002	2005+
1996	90	2008	2016
1995	93	2003	2007+
1994	91	2002	2006+
1993	88	2001	2005+
1992	92	2000	2004+

CHARDONNAY   RATING 5

Rutherglen	**$12–$19**		
Current vintage: 2005	**77**		

Spicy, lightly spiky aromas of peach, citrus and tropical fruit with a nutty background of cashew-like oak. Its initially juicy, tangy palate of rather spicy fruit lacks freshness and length, finishing sour-edged, flat and stale.

2005	77	2005	2006
2004	87	2005	2006
2002	87	2003	2004+
2001	86	2002	2003
2000	86	2002	2005
1999	83	2001	2004
1998	87	1999	2000

RIESLING   RATING 5

Rutherglen	**$12–$19**		
Current vintage: 2005	**88**		

Lightly toasty and confectionary, with lemon sherbet aromas of apple and lime over delicate teabag-like nuances. Round, generous and juicy, its long, shapely and rather succulent palate of tangy lime, apple and lemony flavour finishes with tight, citrusy acids. Simple, clean and refreshing.

2005	88	2010	2013+
2004	87	2006	2009
2003	79	2004	2005
2002	86	2003	2004+
2001	87	2006	2009
2000	87	2005	2008
1999	87	2004	2007
1998	86	2003	2006
1997	83	2002	2005
1996	88	2001	2004

THE BARKLY DURIF   RATING 4

Rutherglen	**$30–$49**		
Current vintage: 2002	**89**		

A rustic, meaty durif with an evolving, leathery bouquet of currants, plums and raisins backed by a hint of cedar. Forward and intense, with a suggestion of overcooked character, its smooth, generous expression of lingering flavour is framed by gentle tannins and soft acids. Attractive and regional, but not hugely complex.

2002	89	2010	2014+
2001	90	2006	2009
1998	89	2003	2006
1997	89	2002	2005
1996	91	2001	2004+
1995	89	2000	2003
1994	93	2002	2006
1993	88	2001	2005
1992	94	2000	2004+
1991	90	1999	2003
1990	91	2002	2010

Cannibal Creek

260 Tynong North Road, Tynong North Vic 3813. Tel: (03) 5942 8380. Fax: (08) 5942 8202.
Website: www.cannibalcreek.com.au Email: wine@cannibalcreek.com.au
Region: **Gippsland** Winemaker: **Patrick Hardiker** Viticulturist: **Patrick Hardiker**
Chief Executives: **Patrick, Kirsten & Kath Hardiker**

There isn't a lot of Australian varietal sauvignon blanc of international standard, but Cannibal Creek makes a wine of intense passionfruit and gooseberry flavour and nervy acidity that is usually supported by a fine, powdery and mineral backbone of tightly knit phenolics. It's one of the few Australian makers whose sauvignon blancs can rival the best from Marlborough in New Zealand.

SAUVIGNON BLANC

RATING 4

Gippsland	$20–$29				
Current vintage: 2005	**93**	2005	93	2005	2006+
		2004	92	2004	2005+
		2003	91	2003	2004+

A long, tangy and powdery sauvignon blanc whose limey aromas of passionfruit, gooseberry and honeysuckle reveal mineral undertones. Smooth and juicy, but with some mineral texture beneath, the palate is punchy, clean and refreshing, finishing with plenty of bright melon/passionfruit flavour and a tangy, schisty quality.

Cape Mentelle

Wallcliffe Road, Margaret River WA 6285. Tel: (08) 9757 0888. Fax: (08) 9757 3233.
Website: www.capementelle.com.au Email: info@capementelle.com.au
Region: **Margaret River** Winemaker: **Robert Mann** Viticulturist: **Steve Meckiff** Chief Executive: **Tony Jordan**

While its 2002 Cabernet Sauvignon is too herbaceous to warrant a higher score and its 2004 Chardonnay is very disappointing, Cape Mentelle has made great strides with its 2004 Shiraz — a stellar wine saturated with fruit that will improve for at least a decade. The company is also finding much more consistency with a wine that has been a regional benchmark for several years, the Sauvignon Blanc Semillon blend.

CABERNET MERLOT 'TRINDERS'

RATING 5

Margaret River	$20–$29				
Current vintage: 2004	**91**	2004	91	2012	2016
		2003	89	2005	2008+
		2002	86	2004	2007
		2001	91	2006	2009
		2000	86	2005	2008
		1999	82	2001	2004
		1998	86	2000	2003
		1997	83	1999	2002+
		1996	90	2004	2008
		1995	90	2003	2007
		1994	90	1999	2002

Finely balanced, firm and focused, this harmonious young wine has cellaring potential aplenty. Its dark-fruited fragrance of blackberries, cassis, plums and cherries overlies suggestions of violets and currants against a fresh background of cedar/vanilla oak. Smooth, elegant and intensely fruited, its vibrant palate of dark fruits, dried herbs and menthol knits tightly with cedary oak and a tight, firm cut of chalky tannin.

CABERNET SAUVIGNON

RATING 3

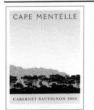

Margaret River	$50–$99				
Current vintage: 2002	**87**	2002	87	2010	2014
		2001	95	2013	2021+
		2000	93	2008	2012+
		1999	93	2007	2011+
		1998	93	2010	2018
		1996	92	2004	2008+
		1995	88	2003	2007
		1994	93	2014	2024
		1993	94	2005	2013
		1992	94	2004	2012
		1991	96	2003	2011
		1990	94	1998	2002
		1989	94	1997	2001
		1988	92	2000	2008
		1987	94	2007	2017
		1986	91	1998	2006
		1985	90	1993	1997
		1984	93	1996	2001

A finely crafted but herbaceous cabernet of sufficient asparagus and capsicum-like greenness not to be marked higher. Its cedary aromas of light blackcurrants, mulberries and plums reveal dusty, leafy undertones of dried herbs and white cheese mould. Like many Australian cabernets of the early 1980s, its pretty berry/plum fruit does offer richness and intensity, but remains overshadowed by greenish influences. Handsomely oaked and framed by tight, fine tannins.

CHARDONNAY

RATING 4

Margaret River $30–$49
Current vintage: 2004 87

Spicy aromas of melon and grapefruit are quite restrained, with buttery undertones of sweet vanilla oak. Smooth and slightly oily, its somewhat candied palate of juicy chardonnay fruit is forward and simple, lacking its customary structure, length and polish.

2004	87	2006	2009
2003	91	2005	2008+
2002	90	2004	2007+
2001	93	2003	2006
2000	93	2005	2008
1999	95	2004	2007+
1998	95	2003	2006+
1997	90	2002	2005
1996	95	2001	2004
1995	96	2003	2007
1994	94	2002	2006

SAUVIGNON BLANC SEMILLON

RATING 3

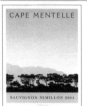

Margaret River $20–$29
Current vintage: 2005 94

A wine that captures the racy acidity and intensity missing since the late 1990s, it's exactly what this fruit-driven Margaret River style should be. Its surprisingly complex, dusty and herbaceous aromas of passionfruit and gooseberries reveal suggestions of asparagus and nettles, although the pure and penetrative palate is enticingly vibrant and dominated by its intense and persistent core of tropical and gooseberry-like fruit.

2005	94	2006	2007+
2004	93	2004	2005+
2003	94	2004	2005+
2002	90	2002	2003+
2001	87	2001	2002
2000	88	2001	2002
1999	88	1999	2000
1998	95	2000	2003

SHIRAZ

RATING 3

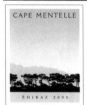

Margaret River $30–$49
Current vintage: 2004 96

A very vibrant, savoury, intensely flavoured and stylish modern shiraz whose spicy, dark-fruited fragrance of cassis, blackberries and plums is handsomely backed by vanilla/cedar/dark chocolate oak and peppery nuances of cloves and cinnamon. It's powerful, sumptuous and opulent, but manages to retain elegance, smoothness and tightness. Framed by firm, powdery tannins, it finishes long and savoury, gradually revealing layers of fruit and complexity.

2004	96	2012	2016+
2003	91	2011	2015
2002	92	2010	2014+
2001	94	2009	2013+
2000	90	2005	2008+
1999	93	2007	2011
1998	93	2010	2018
1997	94	2009	2017
1996	93	2004	2008+
1995	92	2007	2015
1994	95	2006	2014
1993	89	2001	2005
1992	95	2004	2012+

WALLCLIFFE SAUVIGNON BLANC SEMILLON

RATING 3

Margaret River $30–$49
Current vintage: 2003 93

A smooth, smoky white blend whose toasty aromas of vanilla oak and pristine gooseberry, passionfruit and cassis-like fruit overlie funky, reductive influences and hints of dusty herbaceousness. Juicy melon and tropical flavours and lightly charry, buttery oak deliver a sumptuous palate punctuated by mineral acids. It finishes just a touch hot and spirity for a higher score.

2003	93	2005	2008+
2002	93	2004	2007+
2001	95	2003	2006
2000	87	2001	2002
1999	88	2001	2004

ZINFANDEL

RATING 3

Margaret River $30–$49
Current vintage: 2004 92

A very elegant, fine and modern zinfandel whose meaty expression of jujube-like blackberry, blueberry and tomato-like fruit is framed by a smooth and fine-grained cut of moderately astringent tannin. It's spicy, floral and confiture-like, with a vibrant palate tightly knit with assertive cedar/vanilla oak, finishing with flavours of dark berries and ripe tomato. I'd prefer a drier and more savoury finish.

2004	92	2012	2016+
2003	94	2011	2015+
2002	94	2010	2014+
2001	87	2009	2013
2000	92	2008	2012
1999	93	2007	2011
1998	95	2006	2010+
1997	94	2005	2009+
1996	87	2001	2004
1995	94	2003	2007
1994	89	2002	2006
1993	88	1998	2001

Capel Vale

Lot 5 Stirling Estate, Mallokup Road, Capel WA 6271. Tel: (08) 9727 1986. Fax: (08) 9727 1904.
Website: www.capelvale.com Email: winery@capelvale.com

Regions: **Geographe, Mount Barker, Pemberton, Margaret River** Winemaker: **Rebecca Catlin**
Viticulturists: **Neil Delroy, Steve Partridge** Chief Executive: **Peter Pratten**

Its stunningly aromatic and very Germanic Whispering Hill Riesling from 2005 underlines the potential inherent at Capel Vale. Its more expensive Reserve level wines are still fighting that battle between the development of a pleasing level of funky winemaking complexity and the encouragement of winemaking-related faultiness. I've no doubt that once the pendulum swings a little further towards slightly cleaner wines, Capel Vale has the vineyard resources to produce outstanding wine.

CABERNET SAUVIGNON

RATING **5**

Various, WA	$20–$29
Current vintage: 2002	88

Firm, rustic and generous, this developing cabernet has a meaty bouquet of blackberries, dark plums, mint and violets with leathery under-tones. Firm and drying, with a little rawness at the finish, the palate marries an intense but earthy expression of plum and cassis flavour with cedary oak. Unpolished, but flavoursome and assertive.

2002	88	2010	2014
2001	88	2003	2006
2000	86	2005	2008
1999	84	2000	2001+
1998	81	2000	2003
1997	81	1999	2002
1996	87	1998	2001
1995	93	2003	2007
1994	92	2002	2006

KINNAIRD RESERVE SHIRAZ

RATING **5**

Mount Barker	$50–$99
Current vintage: 2002	89

Smoky, charcuterie-like aromas of cassis and cooked plums over herbal and Bovril-like nuances. Long, smooth and succulent, it's very briary and gamey, with distinctive smoky, gunpowder-like oak. Very rustic, with a slightly green undercurrent beneath its succulent small berry flavours. A rather wild and meaty effort at a Rhône Valley style.

2002	89	2007	2010
2001	75	2003	2006
2000	72	2002	2005
1998	87	2003	2006
1997	88	2002	2005
1996	90	2001	2004

MERLOT

RATING **4**

Geographe	$20–$29
Current vintage: 2002	88

Richly fruited and minty, this robust and blocky merlot has a cooked aroma of stewed berries over earthy undertones of cedar, menthol and eucalypt. Its sumptuous palate offers some softness and approachability, but is framed by a firm astringency, finishing long and minty.

2002	88	2007	2010
2001	90	2003	2006+
2000	91	2005	2008
1999	89	2001	2004
1998	76	2000	2003+
1997	81	1999	2002
1996	80	1997	1998

RIESLING

RATING **5**

Mount Barker	$12–$19
Current vintage: 2004	86

A perfume of pear, apple, white peach and tangerine precedes a smooth, juicy and gener-ously flavoured palate whose pear/apple flavours finish with green-edged metallic acids and a notion of tinned tropical fruit. Good length and intensity.

2004	86	2006	2009+
2003	90	2008	2011
2002	91	2007	2010
2001	84	2002	2003+
2000	87	2005	2008
1999	77	2000	2001
1998	87	2000	2003
1997	80	1997	1998
1996	87	2001	2004
1995	89	2003	2007
1994	90	1999	2002
1993	94	2001	2005
1992	87	1997	2000

SBS SAUVIGNON BLANC SEMILLON

RATING 5

Pemberton $20–$29
Current vintage: 2005   **82**

Leafy, capsicum-like aromas of tinned pineapple, passionfruit and paw paw are backed by hints of asparagus. Very intense and forward, but ultimately lacking length and freshness, the palate begins with bright flavours of pineapple and passion-fruit but finishes flat and herbaceous, with slightly tinny acids.

2005	82	2005	2006
2004	82	2005	2006
2003	85	2004	2005
2002	87	2003	2004
2001	83	2002	2003
2000	90	2001	2002+
1999	77	2000	2000

WHISPERING HILL RIESLING

RATING 4

Mount Barker $20–$29
Current vintage: 2004   **94**

This austere, shapely and Germanic riesling offers excellent depth of flavour, austerity and balance. Its penetrative, floral and lightly smoky aromas of lime juice and lemon zest are backed by talcum-like undertones of mineral and wet steel. Long, taut and elegant, its racy palate of lime and apple flavour overlies a fine chalkiness, finishing dry and savoury.

2004	94	2012	2016
2003	87	2005	2008
2002	86	2004	2007
2001	86	2003	2006
2000	92	2008	2012
1998	87	2000	2003+
1997	93	2002	2005
1996	94	2004	2008

Capercaillie

Londons Road, Lovedale, NSW 2325. Tel: (02) 4990 2904. Fax: (02) 4991 1886.
Website: www.capercailliewine.com.au   Email: capercaillie@hunterlink.net.au

Region: **Hunter Valley** Winemakers: **Alasdair Sutherland, Daniel Binet** Viticulturist: **Alasdair Sutherland** Chief Executives: **Alasdair & Patricia Sutherland**

Alasdair Sutherland is an experienced winemaker who has been able to craft classic regional Hunter wines from some very good mature vineyards and it is to be hoped that he can continue to source fruit of the standard seen so far for his red flagship, The Ghillie Shiraz. His semillons age finely, and his red blends with fruit from other regions are typically briary and complex.

CEILIDH SHIRAZ

RATING 5

McLaren Vale, Hunter Valley $30–$49
Current vintage: 2003   **88**

A cheerful marriage between the sour-edged cassis and plum-like flavours of McLaren Vale shiraz with the more leathery qualities of the same variety from the Hunter Valley. Its wild, briary aromas of dark berries, plums, dark chocolate and restrained oak precede a long, vibrant and persistent palate that will settle down and find more balance in the short to medium term.

2003	88	2008	2011+
2001	94	2009	2013
2000	82	2002	2005

SEMILLON

RATING 5

Lower Hunter Valley $20–$29
Current vintage: 2002   **90**

Austere, tight and spotlessly clean, this herbal Hunter semillon presents a tangy cut of slightly con-fectionary melon, apple and lemon flavours before a clean and refreshing finish. It has pleasing shape and fine cellaring potential.

2002	90	2010	2014
2001	91	2011	2015
1999	93	2011	2019

THE CLAN (Cabernet Blend)

RATING 5

McLaren Vale, Orange	$20–$29
Current vintage: 2004	90

2004	90	2012	2016+
2002	81	2004	2007
2001	90	2009	2013

Deep, dark and intense, this interesting but rather closed and brooding wine has the structure and balance to develop in the bottle. Its penetrative aromas of dark berries, plums and currants are dusted with pepper and backed by mocha/vanilla oak. Firmish but pliant tannins frame slightly jammy, palate-staining flavours of cassis, dark plums, dark cherries and blackberries, finishing with brightness of flavour and acid balance.

THE GHILLIE SHIRAZ

RATING 3

Lower Hunter Valley	$30–$49
Current vintage: 2003	95

2003	95	2015	2023
2002	95	2014	2022+
2000	90	2008	2012+

Something of a revelation, this exceptional Hunter shiraz has a violet-like perfume of sweet, spicy raspberries, plums, cherries and cassis, backed by sweet vanilla/mocha oak and appealing varietal nuances of black pepper. Smooth, sumptuous and concentrated, but full to medium in weight, its inky palate is saturated with penetrative flavours of dark plums and berries, with undertones of spice, leather and smart new oak. It has structure and focus aplenty.

Carramar Estate

Wakley Road, Yenda NSW 2681. Tel: (02) 6968 1346. Fax: (02) 6968 1196.
Website: www.casellawine.com.au
Region: **Riverina** Winemakers: **Alan Kennet, Phillip Casella** Viticulturist: **Marcello Casella**
Chief Executive: **John Casella**

Carramar Estate is a label owned by the Casella family, owners of the [yellow tail] wine phenomenon. Its leading wine is this typical Griffith-grown late harvest semillon, which John Casella prefers to craft in a finer, more elegant and less syrupy style than many local expressions of this style. The bottle retasted for this edition was certainly in much better condition than that opened a year ago.

BOTRYTIS SEMILLON

RATING 5

Riverina	$20–$29 (375 ml)
Current vintage: 2002	90

2002	90	2004	2007
2000	89	2002	2005
1999	92	2004	2007
1998	86	2000	2003
1997	83	1998	1999

Lightly honeyed, toasty aromas of slightly candied apricots, orange rind and custard tart reveal undertones of vanilla and brioche. Smooth and lusciously, it's intensely flavoured and slightly candied but neither excessively concentrated nor sugary. It's long, generous and clean to finish, with a lingering slightly savoury finish of lingering fruit and pastry.

Cascabel

Rogers Road, Willunga SA 5172. Tel: (08) 8557 4434. Fax: (08) 8557 4435. Email: cascabel@intertech.net.au

Region: **McLaren Vale** Winemakers: **Susana Fernandez, Duncan Ferguson** Viticulturist: **Robert Ferguson**
Chief Executive: **Duncan Ferguson**

Susana Fernandez' Spanish background imparts a real point of difference at Cascabel, a recent arrival on the McLaren Vale scene. Tempranillo, graciano and mataro (or monastrell) were among the varieties first planted in 1997. While I am very enthusiastic about what Cascabel is doing to fashion its unique styles, recent reds have perhaps been given too free a rein to develop complexity by the time of their release.

RIESLING

RATING 5

Eden Valley	$20–$29	2005	88	2007	2010+
Current vintage: 2005	**88**	2004	92	2009	2012
		2003	89	2008	2011
		2001	83	2003	2006+
		2000	89	2008	2012

Slightly sweet-sour, this austere and savoury riesling has a minerally bouquet of stony, limey fruit and a long, steely palate of some viscosity. It's smoky and funky, with tangy citrus fruit culminating in a briney and phenolic finish.

SHIRAZ

Fleurieu	$20–$29	2003	84	2005	2008+
Current vintage: 2003	**84**	2002	80	2004	2007
		2001	89	2003	2006+
		2000	83	2005	2008
		1999	83	2001	2004

Rustic, earthy and meaty shiraz whose rather cooked and currant-like aromas of plums and raisins are given sweetness through mocha and chocolate oak. Moderately rich, it's a combination of dead, meaty and under-ripe green-edged fruit that tends to lack freshness and vitality.

TIPICO GRENACHE MONASTRELL SHIRAZ

RATING 5

McLaren Vale	$20–$29	2003	89	2006	2009
Current vintage: 2003	**89**	2002	75	2004	2007
		2001	89	2003	2006
		2000	80	2001	2002

A charming and old-fashioned red blend with plenty of rustic complexity. Perfumed grenache aromas lift an earthy, meaty bouquet whose underlying raisin-like fruit also reveals greenish aspects. The palate presents a long and lingering core of fruit over a bony chassis of finely astringent tannins, delivering spicy plum, raisin and currant-like flavours, with undertones of cranberries.

Cassegrain

764 Fernbank Creek Road, Port Macquarie NSW 2444. Tel: (02) 6582 8377. Fax: (02) 6582 8378.
Website: www.cassegrainwines.com.au Email: info@cassegrainwines.com.au

Region: **Hastings River** Winemaker: **John Cassegrain** Viticulturist: **John Cassegrain**
Chief Executive: **John Cassegrain**

Cassegrain has embraced the hybrid French variety chambourcin as a cornerstone of its identity, a decision
I admire more for its bravery than its wisdom. Its best wine, the Fromenteau Vineyard Chardonnay, is a complex
and heavily worked expression of this variety with genuine character, and the meaty, savoury 2004 vintage
is again reminiscent of the excellent wines under this label of a decade ago. The Reserve Shiraz from 2003 is
another highly complex, rustic and firmly structured wine of great drinkability.

FROMENTEAU RESERVE CHARDONNAY   RATING 4

Hastings Valley $20–$29
Current vintage: 2004   91

Typically evolved, wild and complex, this is
certainly not a chardonnay for the technocrats.
Its toasty aromas of melon and citrus fruit reveal
funky lanolin-like undertones. Heavily worked, with
sumptuous flavours of cumquat, figs and butterscotch, its smooth and creamy palate finishes
with pronounced savoury and meaty attributes.

2004	91	2006	2009
2003	89	2005	2008
2002	93	2004	2007+
2001	89	2003	2006
2000	91	2002	2005+
1998	80	1999	2000
1996	88	1998	2001
1995	91	2000	2003
1993	88	1998	2001
1991	94	1996	1999

RESERVE CHAMBOURCIN

Hastings River $20–$29
Current vintage: 2002   81

Meaty, earthy, herbal aromas of plums, raspberries
and cherries, before a lean, green-edged palate
whose light small berry fruit is underpinned by
sweet vanilla oak but wrapped in searing,
steely decay.

2002	81	2004	2007
2001	79	2003	2006
2000	82	2002	2005
1998	87	2003	2008
1997	79	1999	2002
1996	87	1998	2001
1995	83	1997	2000

RESERVE SHIRAZ   RATING 5

Northern Slopes, Cowra $20–$29
Current vintage: 2003   91

Deeply spicy, musky and peppery aromas of dark
plums and blackberries are backed by meaty, earthy
undertones. Very firm and bony, it's deeply
fruited, evolved and gamey, with brambly, leathery
and spicy fruit tightly knit with robust, sinewy tannins.
It finishes long and savoury, and has the fruit and
structure to develop further.

2003	91	2011	2015+
2001	84	2006	2009
2000	88	2005	2008

SEMILLON   RATING 5

Hunter Valley,
Hastings River $12–$19
Current vintage: 2005   83

Rather angular and herbaceous, this early-drinking
semillon reveals citrusy aromas of passionfruit, apricot
and tropical fruits. Its juicy, tropical and candied
palate quickly broadens out towards a syrupy and
ill-defined finish that lacks shape and tightness.

2005	83	2006	2007
2004	89	2006	2009+
2003	87	2005	2008
2002	87	2004	2007
2001	89	2003	2006+
2000	85	2001	2002
1998	88	2000	2003
1997	87	2002	2005
1996	88	2001	2004
1993	90	2001	2005
1992	87	1997	2000

Castagna

Ressom Lane, Beechworth Vic 3747. Tel: (03) 5728 2888. Fax: (03) 5728 2898.
Website: www.castagna.com.au Email: castagna@enigma.com.au

Region: **Beechworth** Winemaker: **Julian Castagna** Viticulturist: **Julian Castagna**
Chief Executive: **Julian Castagna**

Castagna is one of Beechworth's emergent clan of high-quality and high-elevation small vineyards, whose principal wine is a very spicy, Rhône-like shiraz of fineness, elegance and complexity. The superlative 2002 and 2004 vintages of La Chiave Sangiovese, wines packed with sour plum and cherry fruit and framed by a powdery cut of astringent tannin, are in my opinion the finest and most varietally correct sangioveses yet released in Australia.

GENESIS SYRAH

RATING **2**

Beechworth	$50–$99
Current vintage: 2004	95

A Cornas-like shiraz whose ethereal, exotically spicy and meaty bouquet of dark cherries, cassis and sweet oak reveals nuances of fennel and cloves, cinnamon and black pepper. Moderately rich, its silky palate of fully ripened dark fruits, spices, smoky oak and powdery tannins finishes with hints of charcuterie.

2004	95	2009	2012+
2002	95	2010	2014+
2001	91	2003	2006+
2000	90	2002	2005
1999	95	2006	2007

LA CHIAVE SANGIOVESE

RATING **3**

Beechworth	$50–$99
Current vintage: 2004	95

Closed and brooding, this tight-fisted sangiovese reveals a dusty and slightly minty fragrance of sour cherries, plums, chocolate and meaty, forest floor-like undertones. Its typically sour-edged dark fruit knits with a firmish spine of astringent tannins, finishing long, with nuances of nicotine.

2004	95	2009	2012+
2002	95	2007	2010
2001	87	2002	2003+

Castle Rock Estate

Porongorup Road, Porongorup WA 6324. Tel: (08) 9853 1035. Fax: (08) 9853 1010.
Website: www.castlerockestate.com.au Email: diletti@castlerockestate.com.au

Region: **Porongorup** Winemaker: **Robert Diletti** Viticulturist: **Angelo Diletti** Chief Executive: **Angelo Diletti**

This small cool-climate estate in the Porongorups is forging a solid reputation for its very stylish and sculpted Riesling, but also for its steady progress as the leading producer of pinot noir in Western Australia. While its 2005 Riesling doesn't meet the standards of recent releases, it has certainly become one of the Great Southern's better makers of its specialist white variety. Not unsurprisingly, the Cabernet Sauvignon Merlot is less consistent.

CABERNET SAUVIGNON MERLOT

Porongorup	$20–$29
Current vintage: 2001	89

Elegant, fine-grained and supple, this restrained and lightly herbal blend reveals cedary aromas of sweet red berries, violets and dark plums. Framed by fine, powdery tannins, its reserved palate of vibrant small berry fruits and cedar/dark chocolate oak finishes with length and style, but a faintly greenish acidity.

2001	89	2006	2009+
2000	72	2002	2005
1999	81	2001	2004
1998	88	2003	2006+
1997	87	2002	2005
1996	84	2001	2004

PINOT NOIR

RATING **5**

Porongorup	$20–$29
Current vintage: 2004	88

A vibrant and charming young pinot with a spicy, floral fragrance of sweet dark and red cherries and earthiness backed by nuances of forest floor. Its smooth, pristine palate of slightly candied cherry/raspberry/plum flavours is long and supple, but finishes with a hint of dried herbs. It might develop into something more substantial.

2004	88	2006	2009
2003	90	2005	2008
2002	86	2004	2007
2001	90	2003	2006
2000	84	2001	2002
1999	84	2000	2001
1998	88	2000	2003

RIESLING

Porongorup	$12–$19
Current vintage: 2005	**84**

Delicate tropical and floral aromas of mango and pawpaw precede a smooth and rather herbal palate whose flavours of tinned tropical fruits and asparagus reveal herbaceous undertones, finishing under-ripened and slightly metallic.

2005	84	2007	2010
2004	93	2009	2012
2003	94	2008	2011+
2002	90	2007	2010+
2001	86	2006	2009
2000	89	2008	2012
1999	80	2000	2001
1998	93	2006	2010
1997	88	2002	2005

Chandon

Green Point Maroondah Highway, Coldstream Vic 3770. Tel: (03) 9738 9200. Fax: (03) 9738 9201.
Website: www.chandon.com.au Email: info@domainechandon.com.au

Region: **Southern Australia** Winemakers: **Tony Jordan, James Gosper, John Harris, Matt Steel**
Viticulturist: **Bernie Wood** Managing Director: **Tony Jordan**

With its opening in the mid 1980s, Domaine Chandon not only reinvented Australia's approach and attitude towards sparkling wine, but it single-handedly created a market for cool climate-grown wines from classic Champagne varieties. This edition welcomes the ZD Chardonnay, a complex, rather wild and edgy chardonnay bottled without any sugar at expedition. Chandon also continues its great form with its other chardonnay, the Vintage Blanc de Blancs.

GREEN POINT CUVÉE (formerly Prestige Cuvée)

RATING 2

Southern Australia	$30–$49
Current vintage: 1995	**91**

A developed mushroomy, toasty, buttery and honeyed fragrance of floral fruit and hay-like aromas. Rich, chewy and toasty, it's smooth and mature, with an assertive and creamy palate still revealing small berry fruit flavours.

1995	91	2000	2003
1994	95	1999	2002
1993	95	1998	2001+
1992	95	1997	2000
1989	95	1997	2001+

TASMANIAN CUVÉE

RATING 3

Tasmania	$30–$49
Current vintage: 2003	**93**

A fine, creamy and very elegant aperitif style, with a lightly tropical, herbal and floral fragrance of tangerine, creamy leesy undertones, honeysuckle and butter. Long, smooth and refreshing, with a tight, silky texture and a fine effervescence, it retains its intense core of fruit flavour long after its clean and bracing finish.

2003	93	2005	2008+
2002	89	2004	2007+
1998	91	2003	2006
1995	94	2000	2003

VINTAGE BLANC DE BLANCS

RATING 3

Southern Australia	$30–$49
Current vintage: 2003	**94**

A class act. Clean, crackly and creamy, with a fragrant floral perfume of lemongrass and white peach over bakery-like yeasty undertones, it's long, round and generous but ever so tightly focused. Long, smooth and stylish, with a lingering core of stonefruit and citrus, it becomes nutty and savoury towards a finish of refreshing acidity.

2003	94	2005	2008+
2002	94	2004	2007+
2000	85	2002	2005
1999	89	2004	2007
1998	95	2003	2006
1997	94	2002	2005
1996	91	1998	2001
1995	93	2000	2003
1993	95	1998	2001+
1992	93	1997	2000

VINTAGE BLANC DE NOIRS

Southern Australia $30–$49
Current vintage: 1999   93

A maturing and complex wine whose lightly meaty and creamy, earthy bouquet still reveals nuances of raspberry confection. Its generous and deeply textured palate delivers gamey, toasty flavour that finishes long and savoury, with a lingering pastry-like aspect. An authentic blanc de noirs style.

1999	93	2004	2007
1997	95	2002	2005+
1996	89	2001	2004
1994	95	1999	2002
1993	94	1998	2001
1992	95	1997	2000

VINTAGE BRUT

RATING 4

Southern Australia $30–$49
Current vintage: 2003   91

Long, dry and savoury, this moderately rich sparkling wine has a floral and nutty fragrance of vibrant peach, apple and pear-like fruit backed by fresh creamy and yeasty complexity. Smooth and crackly, its lightly toasty expression of white peach and melon finishes with lingering fruit and yeast-derived qualities but just lacks a little mid-palate freshness and substance.

2003	91	2005	2008
2002	90	2004	2007
2001	95	2003	2006+
1999	94	2004	2007
1998	89	2003	2006+
1997	89	1999	2002+
1996	87	1998	2001+
1995	89	1997	2000
1994	94	1999	2002
1993	93	1998	2001

VINTAGE BRUT ROSÉ

RATING 3

Southern Australia $30–$49
Current vintage: 2001   88

Perhaps lacking its customary freshness and brightness, this deeply pigmented rosé is long and creamy, offering its typical richness and presence on the palate. It presents a meaty expression of slightly cooked currant, red cherry and raspberry flavour backed by earthy, bakery yeasty undertones.

2001	88	2003	2006+
1999	87	2001	2004+
1998	94	2003	2006
1997	94	2002	2005
1996	93	2001	2004
1995	91	2000	2003
1994	94	1996	1999

ZD CHARDONNAY

RATING 3

Southern Australia $30–$49
Current vintage: 2003   91

Very dry and refreshing, with a floral, peachy and grapefruit-like bouquet backed by complex undertones of butter, honey and oatmeal. Fine, silky and restrained, it delivers a vibrant, nutty palate of stonefruit and citrus flavour, finishing with zesty acids and a lingering core of melon fruit.

2003	91	2005	2008+
2002	95	2004	2007+
2001	92	2006	2009
2000	88	2005	2008

Chapel Hill

Chapel Hill Road, McLaren Vale SA 5171. Tel: (08) 8323 8429. Fax: (08) 8323 9245.
Website: www.chapelhillwine.com.au Email: winery@chapelhillwine.com.au

Region: **McLaren Vale** Winemakers: **Michael Fragos, Bryn Richards** Viticulturist: **Danny Higgins**
Chief Executive: **Jim Humphrys**

Chapel Hill is a consistent maker of ripe, juicy and slightly old-fashioned, oaky reds from McLaren Vale and Coonawarra fruit. The enterprise today features a gourmet retreat, featuring a cooking school and conference venue. While its currently released wines are not of the same standard as those responsible for the winery's strong reputation, recent developments suggest that future releases should be more exciting.

CABERNET SAUVIGNON

RATING 5

McLaren Vale, Coonawarra $30–$49
Current vintage: 2002   86

Firm but slightly green-edged, this briary and cedary cabernet has a light bouquet of berry and plum aromas with herbal, capsicum-like undertones. Some livery and forward flavours of small berries and plums get some benefit from cedary oak, but finish rather green and sappy, with a grippy extract.

2002	86	2004	2007+
2001	88	2006	2009+
2000	87	2005	2008
1999	88	2001	2004
1998	83	2003	2006
1997	93	2005	2009
1996	93	2004	2008+
1995	89	2000	2003
1994	92	2002	2006
1993	93	2001	2005
1992	92	1997	2000

McLAREN VALE SHIRAZ

RATING 4

McLaren Vale		$30–$49	
Current vintage: 2002		**87**	

Tiring, slightly cooked aromas of plums, currants and raisins depend a little excessively on sweet vanilla oak for impact and brightness, while the moderately firm and reasonably long palate delivers a little more freshness with black and red berry flavours and cedary oak framed by tightly knit tannins. It's just too advanced and even slightly varnishy for a higher score.

2002	87	2007	2010
2001	89	2009	2013
2000	86	2003	2005+
1999	90	2004	2007
1998	92	2006	2010+
1997	94	2005	2009
1996	94	2001	2004+
1995	92	2000	2003
1994	93	1999	2002
1993	94	2001	2005
1992	93	2000	2004
1991	94	1999	2003
1990	91	2002	2010

RESERVE CHARDONNAY

RATING 5

McLaren Vale		$20–$29	
Current vintage: 2003		**89**	

A generously flavoured, round and approachable drink-me-soon chardonnay. Fresh aromas of sweet peachy, buttery fruit with nuances of lemon and tobacco precede a soft, unctuous palate whose voluptuous expression of varietal fruit is cleverly balanced with oak and acidity.

2003	89	2005	2008
2002	90	2004	2007
2001	89	2003	2006
2000	86	2001	2002+
1999	87	2000	2001
1998	89	2000	2003+
1997	89	1999	2002
1996	93	2001	2004
1995	92	2000	2003
1994	95	2002	2006

THE VICAR

RATING 4

McLaren Vale		$30–$49	
Current vintage: 2001		**89**	

Firm, old-fashioned, rather jammy and oaky red blend with a fractionally green-edged and salty finish. Its earthy, cedary bouquet of cassis, dark olives and violets reveals a whiff of white pepper and cinnamon. Tarry, rather jammy and licorice-like berry, currant and plum-like fruit is handsomely wrapped in smoky chocolate oak, before a slightly sappy, but savoury finish. It should settle down with time.

2001	89	2009	2013+
1998	90	2003	2006
1996	94	2004	2008+
1994	92	2002	2006
1993	89	1998	2001

UNWOODED CHARDONNAY

RATING 5

Padthaway		$12–$19	
Current vintage: 2005		**88**	

A finely crafted unwooded chardonnay with surprising length and style. Its nutty, cashew-like aromas of peaches, butter and cream reveal light herbal undertones, while its palate culminates in a tangy, citrusy finish of pleasing acidity and tightness.

2005	88	2006	2007
2003	89	2004	2005
2002	90	2003	2004
2001	82	2002	2003
2000	86	2001	2002

VERDELHO

RATING 5

McLaren Vale		$12–$19	
Current vintage: 2005		**83**	

Spicy, estery and slightly varnishy aromas of tropical and melon-like fruit precede a slightly herbal and lemony palate that finishes slightly awkwardly, with fractionally sweet and spiky nuances.

2005	83	2005	2006+
2004	87	2005	2006
2003	86	2003	2004+
2002	87	2003	2004
2001	89	2002	2003+
2000	84	2001	2002
1999	86	2000	2001
1998	91	2000	2003

Charles Melton

Krondorf Road, Tanunda SA 5352. Tel: (08) 8563 3606. Fax: (08) 8563 3422.
Website: www.charlesmeltonwines.com.au Email:cmw@charlesmeltonwines.com.au

Region: **Barossa Valley** Winemaker: **Graeme Melton** Viticulturist: **Peter Wills** Chief Executive: **Graeme Melton**

Charles Melton is a champion of traditional Barossa styles, although in its mischievously named Nine Popes it was one of the first to 'rediscover' the virtues of the blend of shiraz, grenache and mourvèdre. The generous, slightly meaty and spicy 2003 vintage release is a fine effort from yet another challenging season for Barossa growers. Travellers can always be assured of a warm and friendly welcome at Charles Melton.

CABERNET SAUVIGNON (Cabernet Shiraz in 2000)

RATING **5**

Barossa Valley $30–$49
Current vintage: 2003   87

Rather cooked and porty, this rich and chewy cabernet is very typical of this Barossa vintage. Its meaty, rather stewy aromas of plums, currants, prunes and treacle overlie slightly caramel-like mocha and vanilla oak. Slightly spirity, its sumptuously ripened palate just avoids being overcooked, delivering meaty but not excessively dehydrated flavours.

2003	87	2008	2011
2002	86	2007	2010
2001	87	2006	2009
2000	87	2002	2005
1999	82	2001	2004
1998	93	2003	2006+
1996	87	2001	2004
1993	87	2001	2005

GRENACHE

RATING **5**

Barossa Valley $20–$29
Current vintage: 2000   88

A meaty, herbal and savoury wine whose boiled lolly-like aromas of raspberries and red cherries are backed by cedary nuances of vanilla oak. Smooth and elegant, it's earthy but lively, with familiar grenache flavours. An honest, shorter-term wine with some green edges, and a slightly thin finish.

2000	88	2002	2005
1999	88	2001	2004+
1998	88	2000	2003
1996	93	2004	2008
1994	87	1996	1999

NINE POPES

RATING **4**

Barossa Valley $30–$49
Current vintage: 2003   90

A very good wine from a challenging vintage, with a spicy, lightly herbal and floral bouquet whose sweet aromas of plums, cherries and berries are backed by fine, cedary oak. Generous, smooth and even, its long, spicy and meaty palate of slightly raisined and plummy fruit reveals vibrant notes of blackberry, blueberry and plum. Finishing with lingering notes of licorice and currant-like fruit, it's framed by sandpapery tannins.

2003	90	2008	2011
2002	92	2010	2014
2001	88	2003	2006+
2000	86	2002	2005
1999	89	2004	2007
1998	92	2006	2010
1997	88	1999	2002
1996	95	2004	2008
1995	94	2003	2007+
1994	89	1999	2002
1993	87	2001	2005
1990	92	1998	2002

BAROSSA SHIRAZ

RATING **4**

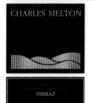

Barossa Valley $30–$49
Current vintage: 2003   89

Firm, robust and sinewy, this intense and forward shiraz offers a floral, confiture-like bouquet of blackberries, plums, prunes and currants backed by sweet vanilla oak, meaty and spicy undertones. Moderately long, rich and concentrated, it reveals a slightly cooked and currant-like expression of plum, blackberry and cranberry flavour. While its does dry out a little towards its astringent and slightly raw finish, it offers a surprisingly bright and intense core of fruit.

2003	89	2008	2011
2002	88	2004	2007+
2001	85	2003	2006
2000	88	2005	2008
1999	90	2004	2007+
1998	92	2003	2006
1997	89	2005	2009
1995	94	2003	2007
1990	92	1998	2002+

Chateau Reynella

Reynell Road, Reynella SA 5161. Tel: (08) 8392 2222. Fax: (08) 8392 2202.

Region: **McLaren Vale** Winemakers: **Paul Lapsley, Robert Mann** Viticulturist: **Brenton Baker**
Chief Executive: **David Woods**

Chateau Reynella has traditionally made the expression of Australian 'Vintage Port' against which others are compared. As the exceptional 1998 vintage illustrates, it has nothing to do with the Portuguese style, but is a typically ripe, jammy and astringent wine, usually fortified with fabulous spirit, that can develop in the bottle for decades. The Cabernet Sauvignon and Shiraz are found under the 'Reynell' entry.

VINTAGE PORT

RATING 2

McLaren Vale	$30–$49
Current vintage: 1998	**97**

About as good as it gets for traditional Australian vintage port. A heady, spicy and deeply concentrated aroma of briary cassis, plums and violets overlies a tarry, treacle-like background and chocolate/vanilla oak. Warm, ripe and spirity, its velvet-smooth and sumptuous palate reveals layers of dark plum and berry fruit before finishing long and savoury with a firm spine of powdery tannins. Excellent balance and integration.

1998	97	2018	2028
1997	90	2009	2017
1996	93	2008	2016
1994	96	2014	2024
1993	94	2013	2023
1990	95	2010	2020
1987	96	2007	2017
1983	93	2003	2013
1982	90	2002	2012
1981	93	2001	2009
1980	90	2000	2005

Chestnut Grove

Chestnut Grove Road, Manjimup WA 6258. Tel: (08) 9758 5999. Fax: (08) 9758 5988.
Website: www.chestnutgrove.com.au Email: winery@chestnutgrove.com.au

Region: **Manjimup** Winemaker: **Jarrad Olsen** Viticulturist: **Southern Viticultural Services**
Chief Executive: **Mike Calneggia**

Initially established by the Kordic family, Chestnut Grove is today a part of Australian Wine Holdings Ltd, an operation that includes other Western Australian brands such as Alexandra Bridge, Bunker Bay and Hay Shed Hill. While it produces a full range of table wines, Chestnut Grove has been most successful on the show circuit with its rather oaky, tomatoey and very herbaceous Merlot.

MERLOT

RATING 5

Pemberton	$30–$49
Current vintage: 2003	**86**

Quite firm and flavoursome, but rather simple and lacking genuine depth of fruit, this slightly herbaceous merlot marries sweet, tobaccoey flavours of red berries, tomato over cedar/vanilla oak with both meaty and lightly herbal undertones.

2003	86	2005	2008+
2002	87	2004	2007
2001	88	2003	2006+
2000	87	2002	2005
1999	89	2001	2004
1998	75	1999	2000
1997	81	1998	1999

Clairault

Caves Road, Willyabrup WA 6280. Tel: (08) 9755 6225. Fax: (08) 9755 6229.
Website: www.clairaultwines.com.au Email: clairault@clairaultwines.com.au
Region: **Margaret River** Winemaker: **Will Shields** Viticulturist: **Nick Macpherson** Chief Executive: **Bill Martin**

With its 2002 Estate Cabernet Sauvignon, made in anything but a great year for Margaret River cabernet, Clairault has created its best red since since the 1998 edition of the same wine. I view this as a strong sign that Clairault is heading back to the quality standards of the 1980s and mid 1990s, when it was one of the region's finer makers. Alas, the 2005 whites are a little disappointing.

ESTATE CABERNET SAUVIGNON
(formerly 'Reserve', also 'The Clairault')

RATING 5

Margaret River		$50–$99	2002	91	2010	2014

Margaret River		$50–$99
Current vintage: 2002		91

A fine and quite stylish Margaret River cabernet whose typically dark-fruited qualities and smart new oak combine smoothly with a fine-grained tannic backbone. Its briary and slightly meaty aromas of cassis, dark plums are backed by suggestions of dried herbs and slightly gamey undertones of chocolate/mocha oak. Long and lively, its palate sumptuously delivers dark berry, dark cherry and plum-like fruit ably supported by dark chocolate/vanilla oak. The slight green edges about the wine's acidity should soften with time.

Year	Score		
2002	91	2010	2014
2001	89	2006	2009+
2000	86	2005	2008+
1999	81	2001	2004+
1998	92	2006	2010+
1997	81	2002	2005
1996	87	2001	2004+
1995	94	2003	2007
1994	94	2006	2014
1993	88	2001	2005
1991	95	2003	2011
1990	93	2002	2010
1989	91	1997	2001
1988	91	1996	2000
1987	87	1995	1999
1986	93	1998	2006

SAUVIGNON BLANC

RATING 5

Margaret River	$12–$19
Current vintage: 2005	86

An honest, clean and fruity sauvignon blanc, whose grassy and lightly sweaty aromas of gooseberry and passionfruit are backed by suggestions of dried herbs. Initially generous and juicy, it finishes taut and austere, with lingering flavours of gooseberry and passionfruit punctuated by assertive acidity.

Year	Score		
2005	86	2006	2007+
2004	87	2005	2006
2003	87	2004	2005
2002	85	2003	2004
2001	87	2002	2003
2000	87	2002	2005
1999	84	2000	2001
1998	89	1999	2000
1997	92	1999	2002
1996	95	1998	2001
1995	94	2000	2003
1994	94	1996	1999

SEMILLON SAUVIGNON BLANC

RATING 5

Margaret River	$12–$19
Current vintage: 2005	83

A rather raw and hard-edged blend of these two varieties whose grassy green melon and gooseberry fruit is backed by undertones of green beans and capsicum. There's some generous flavour, but the phenolic extract is just too dominant and likely to tend to fatness and hardness with time.

Year	Score		
2005	83	2006	2007+
2003	86	2004	2005
2002	86	2002	2003
2001	92	2006	2009
2000	88	2002	2005
1998	90	2000	2003
1997	94	1999	2002+
1996	93	1998	2001
1995	89	1997	2000
1994	94	1999	2002

Clarendon Hills

Lot 11 Brookman Road, Blewitt Springs SA 5171. Tel: (08) 8383 0544. Fax: (08) 8383 0544.
Website: www.clarendonhills.com.au Email: clarendonhills@bigpond.com

Region: **McLaren Vale** Winemaker: **Roman Bratasiuk** Viticulturists: **Various** Chief Executive: **Roman Bratasiuk**

Clarendon Hills enjoyed a stellar 2004, producing some of the best and most interesting wines of my year's tasting. Among the most memorable are the seamless Astralis Syrah (a fraction better even than the superb 2003 edition), the silky, meaty and essence-like Romas Grenache, the sinewy but concentrated Blewitt Springs Grenache and the sumptuously ripened Brookman Syrah. This is a small maker that keeps separate a number of different fruit parcels sourced from different sites in the Clarendon area. At their best, they are exceptional.

ASTRALIS SYRAH

RATING **1**

McLaren Vale	$200+
Current vintage: 2004	97

About as perfect as the more pronounced expression of Australian shiraz can be, this is a remarkable wine of seamless length, strength and harmony. Steeped in briary aromas of cassis, dark plums, berries and cherries, its meaty bouquet also reveals oak-derived suggestions of dark chocolate, mocha and smoked oyster. Incredibly concentrated, its sumptuous palate of dark plum and berry flavours soaks up some fairly assertive new oak with ease, leaving a substantial and seamless expression of sour-edged fruit framed by mouth-coating tannins and finishing with spicy nuances of licorice, cloves and cinnamon. Manages to retain aspects of elegance despite its power and structure.

2004	97	2016	2024
2003	97	2015	2023+
2002	93	2010	2014+
1999	96	2011	2019
1998	93	2010	2018
1997	93	2009	2017
1996	95	2008	2016
1995	96	2007	2015
1994	94	2006	2014

BLEWITT SPRINGS GRENACHE

RATING **3**

McLaren Vale	$50–$99
Current vintage: 2004	95

A robust, palate-staining grenache whose wild and quite funky complexity adds to its impressive power and concentration. Pungent and meaty, its deep, spicy aromas of dark plums, blackberries and blueberries are backed by cedar/vanilla oak. Underpinned by ultra-ripe flavours of currants and prunes, its rich and robust palate of concentrated berry/plum flavour is framed by chalky, sinewy tannins, finishing with exceptional length and persistence.

2004	95	2009	2012+
2003	92	2008	2011
2002	88	2004	2007+
1999	87	2001	2004+
1998	92	2003	2006
1997	90	2002	2005
1995	95	2003	2007+
1994	91	2002	2006

BROOKMAN MERLOT

RATING **5**

McLaren Vale	$50–$99
Current vintage: 2004	82

Herbal, autumnal and leafy, with greenish but concentrated cassis and mulberry-like fruit over raisined, shrivelled currant-like influences suggestive of an extended hang time. Generally lacking fruit brightness and framed by raw, greenish tannins.

2004	82	2006	2009
2003	85	2005	2008+
2002	87	2010	2014+
2001	88	2013	2021
1998	87	2003	2006

BROOKMAN SYRAH

RATING **4**

McLaren Vale	$50–$99
Current vintage: 2004	96

A deeply flavoured and impactful shiraz of excellent balance and rustic charm. Its smoky, fruitcake-like aromas of currants, prunes and cassis reveal some ultra-ripeness of fruit, but appealingly complex undertones of game meats, black pepper and vanilla/walnut oak. Sumptuously concentrated and steeped in black berry flavour, it flirts with over-ripeness, but retains a juicy, vibrant core of genuinely ripe fruit, finishing savoury and spicy.

2004	96	2012	2016
2003	87	2005	2008+
2002	90	2007	2010+
1999	89	2004	2007
1998	87	2003	2006
1997	87	2005	2009

CLARENDON GRENACHE

RATING 4

McLaren Vale	$50–$99
Current vintage: 2004	**93**

Smoky, raisiny and spicy aromas of meaty blackberries, plums and fresh chocolate/vanilla oak precede a moderately rich and jammy palate whose intense, slightly raisined fruit overlies a subtle spine of powdery tannins whose profound astringency steadily catches up with you, finishing long and firm with a slightly salty minerality.

2004	93	2009	2012+
2003	94	2008	2011+
2002	89	2004	2007+
2001	89	2006	2009
1999	89	2001	2004+
1998	92	2003	2006
1997	80	1999	2002
1996	85	2004	2008

HICKINBOTHAM SYRAH

RATING 3

McLaren Vale	$100–$199
Current vintage: 2004	**92**

Profoundly assertive and searingly concentrated, this sumptuous shiraz builds a massive presence on the palate but never loses its silkiness and charm. Rather closed, its dark and meaty aromas of berries and plums are cloaked by oaky influences of mocha and vanilla. Its rich, dark-fruited palate is coated by firm but velvet-like tannins and creamy oak. Backed by suggestions of mint, menthol and black olives, its impact lasts and lasts.

2004	92	2009	2012
2003	95	2011	2015
2002	95	2010	2014+
2001	83	2006	2009
1999	88	2004	2007
1998	91	2003	2006

LIANDRA SYRAH

RATING 5

McLaren Vale	$50–$99
Current vintage: 2004	**87**

Heady aromas of plums, cassis and mulberries reveal leafy, herbal undertones of candied fruits and menthol. Medium to full in weight, it's supple and smooth, delivering a lively but green-edged spectrum of shiraz fruit that lacks genuine ripeness and finishes rather thin. A most un-Clarendon Hills-like wine.

2004	87	2006	2009+
2003	88	2005	2008+
2002	88	2010	2014
2001	89	2006	2009
1999	95	2007	2011
1998	91	2003	2006
1997	93	2005	2009+

MORITZ SYRAH

RATING 5

McLaren Vale	$50–$99
Current vintage: 2004	**90**

Wild and meaty, rustic and complex, this heavily worked shiraz marries its slightly over-ripened currant and raisin-like expression of stewed plum and dark cherry flavour with assertive mocha/vanilla oak. There's a kirsch-like aspect to its heady bouquet, while its sumptuously ripened palate finishes slightly flat and overcooked, rather reliant on its spicy new oak for sweetness. Charming to drink, but would have been better if harvested earlier.

2004	90	2009	2012
2003	91	2008	2011
2002	88	2007	2010
2001	84	2003	2006+
1999	89	2004	2007+

PIGGOTT RANGE SYRAH

RATING 3

McLaren Vale	$200+
Current vintage: 2004	**92**

A powerful modern shiraz whose ultra-ripe fruitcake-like flavours of spicy, meaty fruit retains enough freshness to ensure it drinks well now and into the medium term. It's smoky, dark and pruney, with powerful currant and chocolate aromas over herbal nuances of spearmint and sage. Thick, firm and sumptuous, its slightly warm and spirity palate is densely packed with fruit and flaunts its impressive oak. Just a fraction hard-edged and metallic at the finish.

2004	92	2012	2016
2003	97	2015	2023
2002	89	2010	2014+
1999	94	2007	2011
1998	90	2003	2006+
1997	88	2002	2005+

Clayfield

25 Wilde Lane, Moyston Vic 3377. Tel: (03) 5354 2689. Fax: (03) 5354 2679.
Website: www.clayfieldwines.com Email:clayfieldwines@netconnect.com.au

Region: **Grampians** Winemaker: **Simon Clayfield** Viticulturist: **Simon Clayfield** Chief Executive: **Simon Clayfield**

Simon Clayfield is an experienced and talented maker of Victorian red wines, and under his own label he crafts classically elegant and exotically spiced Shiraz of considerable finesse and longevity. The 2004 wine is a return to its tightly focused, spicy and deeply flavoured best. Like the other top vintages of 2001 and 2002, it will mature with grace and complexity.

SHIRAZ

RATING **2**

Grampians	$30–$49
Current vintage: 2004	**95**

A rather hermitage-like shiraz whose spicy, peppery and floral fragrance of dark-fruited plums, blackberries remains closed and rather brooding. Full to medium in weight, it's sumptuously flavoured but hides its strength behind a tightly knit but firm and fine-grained backbone that will become more velvet-like with time. It's well-ripened and generously flavoured, finishing long and savoury, with lingering fruit brightness and peppery undertones.

2004	95	2016	2024
2003	89	2008	2011
2002	95	2014	2022
2001	95	2009	2013+
2000	87	2005	2008

Clonakilla

Crisps Lane off Murrumbateman Road, Murrumbateman NSW 2582. Tel: (02) 6227 5877.
Fax: (02) 6227 5871. Website: www.clonakilla.com.au Email: wine@clonakilla.com.au

Region: **Canberra** Winemaker: **Tim Kirk** Viticulturist: **Michael Lahiff** Chief Executive: **John Kirk**

Clonakilla is a small producer in the Canberra wine region that has pioneered the Côte-Rôtie-styled expression of shiraz and viognier blend in Australia. The intensely flavoured and pliant 2005 edition will build on the reputation of this wine. Its Viognier is one of this country's finest, with the 2005 release the vineyard's best yet. This release also includes a typically long and tightly sculpted Riesling, plus the best Hilltops Shiraz yet made.

BALINDERRY CABERNET BLEND

RATING **3**

Canberra	$30–$49
Current vintage: 2005	**91**

Likely to smooth out into a fine and cultivated wine, this fragrant, firmish young cabernet blend has a spicy, lightly herbal and confiture-like aroma of blackberries, cassis and dark cherries backed by cedar/vanilla oak. Fine-grained and gravelly tannins frame its deeply ripened palate of sweet red and black berries and measured cedary oak.

2005	91	2013	2017
2004	90	2009	2012+
2003	86	2008	2011+
2002	90	2007	2010
2001	93	2009	2013+
2000	93	2008	2012+
1999	91	2007	2011
1998	93	2003	2006+
1997	88	2005	2009+
1996	84	1998	2001
1995	88	2003	2007
1994	92	2002	2006

HILLTOPS SHIRAZ

RATING **4**

Hilltops	$20–$29
Current vintage: 2005	**92**

The best release yet from this emergent red label is a vibrant and enticingly varietal shiraz that marries brightly presented fruit with a fine and powdery structure. Its slightly meaty aromas of sweet red and black berries, plums, cherries and cedar/vanilla oak reveal musky, earthy undertones. It's assertive and quite sumptuous, but despite its weight of dark berry and plum flavours and its handsome dark chocolate oak, it retains a savoury elegance.

2005	92	2010	2013+
2004	89	2006	2009
2003	87	2005	2008
2002	87	2004	2007
2001	92	2003	2006+
2000	91	2002	2005+

RIESLING

RATING **3**

Clonakilla

CANBERRA DISTRICT
RIESLING
750 mL

Canberra	$20–$29
Current vintage: 2005	**93**

A tightly sculpted, long and brittle riesling whose floral, rocky and mineral aromas of fresh lime juice and green apples precede a crunchy, slightly reductive and chewy palate of length and austerity. Finely crafted, with pristine flavours of lime juice over a chalky spine, it finishes with length, drive and lingering mineral qualities.

2005	93	2013	2017+
2004	91	2006	2009+
2003	88	2005	2008+
2002	93	2004	2007+
2001	88	2003	2006+
2000	92	2008	2012
1999	95	2004	2007+
1998	94	2003	2006+
1997	93	2005	2009
1996	94	2001	2004
1995	92	2003	2007

SHIRAZ VIOGNIER

RATING **1**

Clonakilla

SHIRAZ
VIOGNIER
2001
750 mL

Canberra	$50–$99
Current vintage: 2005	**96**

Dusty, musky aromas of dried herbs, raspberries, cassis and blackberries are backed by polished cedar/vanilla oak and lifted by floral undertones suggestive of cherries and cranberries, plus and exotic, spicy lift from viognier. Supple, fine and silky, it's surprisingly sumptuous and generous, with a vibrant presence of intense fruit over a tightly knit chassis of firm, but particularly pliant tannins. Likely to build more richness and structure with bottle-age, showing exemplary integration of fruit, oak and tannin.

2005	96	2013	2017
2004	97	2012	2016+
2003	96	2011	2015+
2002	96	2010	2014
2001	97	2009	2013+
2000	90	2005	2008+
1999	89	2003	2007
1998	96	2010	2018
1997	95	2009	2017
1996	90	2001	2004+
1995	89	2003	2007+
1994	93	2002	2006
1993	89	1998	2001+
1992	89	1997	2000
1991	88	1996	1999
1990	82	1992	1995

VIOGNIER

RATING **3**

Clonakilla

CANBERRA DISTRICT
VIOGNIER
750 mL

Canberra	$50–$99
Current vintage: 2005	**95**

An outstanding wine receiving the highest score I am yet to post for an Australian viognier. Its spicy aromas of apricots, cinnamon and cloves are backed by a pleasingly restrained background of reductive and meaty undertones. The generous palate delivers exceptional viscosity and vinosity, but has the tightness and focus to avoid any semblance of overblown characters. Fine and silky, it's seamlessly long and persistent, with a refreshing and savoury finish.

2005	95	2007	2010
2004	84	2005	2006
2003	94	2004	2005+
2002	95	2004	2007
2001	92	2003	2006
2000	93	2002	2005
1999	92	2000	2003

Clover Hill

60 Clover Hill Road, Lebrina Tas 7254. Tel: (03) 6395 6114. Fax: (03) 6395 6257.
Website: www.taltarni.com.au Email: enquiries@taltarni.com.au
Region: **Pipers River** Winemakers: **Leigh Clarnette, Loic le Calvez, Louella McPhan**
Viticulturist: **Kym Ludvigsen** Chief Executive: **Adam Torpy**

Clover Hill is a Taltarni-owned operation in northern Tasmania that specialises in sparkling wine. Its wines are typically fragrant, creamy and crisply defined, with a fruit profile often slightly herbaceous and tropical. The 2001 vintage is one of the label's finest, and one of the best available in Australia today.

VINTAGE

RATING **3**

Pipers River	$30–$49
Current vintage: 2001	**94**

A very complex, smooth and stylish aperitif style with a nutty, floral and creamy bouquet of peach and tropical fruit over bakery-like autolytic complexity. Long, fresh and racy, its fine and crackly palate presents a very fine mousse and persistent effervescence. Punctuated by refreshing acidity, it finishes very long and clean.

2001	94	2006	2009
2000	87	2005	2008
1999	94	2004	2007+
1998	87	2000	2003+
1997	82	1999	2002
1996	92	2001	2004
1995	91	1997	2000
1994	94	1999	2002

Coldstream Hills

31 Maddens Lane, Coldstream Vic 3770. Tel: (03) 5964 9388. Fax: (03) 5964 9389.
Website: www.coldstreamhills.com.au

Region: **Yarra Valley** Winemaker: **Andrew Fleming** Viticulturist: **Richard Shenfield** Chief Executive: **Jamie Odell**

Founded by wine scribe James Halliday, who remains a consultant to this label, Coldstream Hills became part of the Southcorp empire that is today owned by Foster's. With the possible exception of some rather herbaceous Reserve Cabernet Sauvignons, Coldstream Hills has maintained an honesty and integrity with its reserve wines, which are simply not released from inadequate seasons. As shown by some delightful 2005 releases, the 'standard' labels, the Chardonnay and Pinot Noir especially, can reveal delightful varietal qualities and winemaking polish.

CHARDONNAY   RATING 4

Yarra Valley	$20–$29
Current vintage: 2005	**90**

Elegant, restrained and refreshing, this vibrant young chardonnay is made with sensitivity and style. Its floral aromas of peach/melon fruit reveal undertones of citrus blossom and wheatmeal, while its tightly focused palate of stonefruit, apple and pear flavour culminates in a zesty finish of lemony acids.

2005	90	2007	2010
2004	90	2005	2006+
2003	90	2004	2005+
2001	92	2003	2006
2000	88	2002	2005
1999	87	2001	2004
1998	90	2000	2003
1997	92	1999	2002
1996	91	1998	2001

MERLOT   RATING 5

Yarra Valley	$20–$29
Current vintage: 2004	**86**

Briary, earthy and meaty aromas of plums, dark cherries and restrained cedary oak precede a forward, simple and fruity palate that thins out towards the finish. It lacks depth, richness of fruit and structure.

2004	86	2006	2009
2003	91	2005	2008
2001	89	2003	2006+
2000	83	2002	2005
1997	89	1999	2002

PINOT NOIR   RATING 4

Yarra Valley	$20–$29
Current vintage: 2005	**93**

Absolutely charming early-drinking pinot noir, with genuine underlying structure and texture. Its floral perfume of rose petals, red cherries and cedar/chocolate/vanilla oak reveals spicy, clove-like undertones, while its smooth, silky and pristine palate explodes with the brightness of youthful pinot fruit. Supple and succulent, it's long and juicy, but finishes clean and savoury.

2005	93	2007	2010+
2003	90	2005	2008+
2002	86	2003	2004
2001	90	2003	2006
2000	91	2002	2005+
1999	93	2001	2004
1998	86	1999	2000
1997	91	2002	2005
1996	92	1998	2001

RESERVE CABERNET SAUVIGNON   RATING 4

Yarra Valley	$30–$49
Current vintage: 2003	**89**

A fine, supple, smooth and elegant cabernet whose vibrant violet-like tones of cassis, mulberries and dark plums reveal just a little too much herbaceous character for a higher rating. It's fragrant, heady and handsomely oaked, with an assertive but integrated background of cedar, dark chocolate and vanilla influences before finishing just a fraction green and sappy.

2003	89	2011	2015
2001	93	2009	2013+
2000	95	2008	2012+
1998	82	2000	2003
1997	84	2002	2005
1995	90	2000	2003
1994	91	2002	2006
1993	93	1998	2002
1992	96	2004	2012+
1991	93	1999	2003

RESERVE CHARDONNAY

Yarra Valley $30–$49
Current vintage: 2003   90

A big, round and spirity chardonnay with a lightly smoky fragrance of heavily worked melon and peach fruit backed by suggestions of grilled cashews, spices and butterscotch. There's also a whiff of lime juice and a hint of mineral. Powerfully concentrated and structured, the palate delivers ample melon and citrus-like flavour with genuine complexity and character, but tends towards broadness and hotness.

2003	90	2005	2008
2000	90	2002	2005
1999	90	2001	2004+
1998	94	2003	2006
1997	90	2002	2005
1996	93	2001	2004+
1995	94	2000	2003
1994	95	1999	2002
1993	90	1995	1998
1992	96	2000	2004

RESERVE MERLOT

Yarra Valley $30–$49
Current vintage: 2000   93

Very smart merlot with strength, ripeness and structure. There's some tobaccoey and herbal complexity behind its varietally correct expression of dark cherries, mulberries and plums, while its assertive vanilla and mocha oak is tightly integrated. It has perfume, length and finish, with pleasing balance and texture.

2000	93	2005	2008
1998	92	2003	2006
1997	87	2002	2005+

RESERVE PINOT NOIR

Yarra Valley $50–$99
Current vintage: 2002   90

Medium to full red with very faint browning edges. A fragrance of raspberries, cherries and confection reveals herbal, greenish undertones and a hint of meatiness. Dusty, long and elegant, but beneath its rich pristine and sumptuous expression of cherry/berry flavours lies a layer of sappy herbal influence.

2002	90	2007	2010
2000	93	2008	2012
1998	95	2006	2010+
1997	95	2005	2009
1996	93	2001	2004+
1995	90	1997	2000
1994	93	2002	2014
1993	88	1995	1998
1992	95	2004	2012

Coriole

Chaffeys Road, McLaren Vale SA 5171. Tel: (08) 8323 8305. Fax: (08) 8323 9136.
Website: www.coriole.com Email: info@coriole.com

Region: **McLaren Vale** Winemaker: **Grant Harrison** Viticulturist: **Rachel Steer** Chief Executive: **Mark Lloyd**

Coriole is a McLaren Vale vineyard whose winemakers have resisted the temptation to pursue the ultra-ripe flavours and porty alcoholic strengths so common today among its neighbours. Instead, Coriole's wines are tightly focused and elegant, although they can be quite rustic, earthy and complex. 2004 was indeed a stellar vintage for Coriole, producing a superlative Lloyd Reserve Shiraz, the company's best Sangiovese by far, and a delightfully fragrant and tightly focused Shiraz.

CHENIN BLANC

McLaren Vale $12–$19
Current vintage: 2005   88

A clean and refreshing wine whose herbaceous aromas of tinned tropical fruits are backed by shaded nuances of capsicum. Forward, juicy and slightly sweet, it's both very ripe and herbal, with some pleasingly intense tropical and lemon flavours backed by grassy influences. Finishes clean and refreshing, with lingering pear-like fruit.

2005	88	2006	2007
2003	89	2004	2005+
2002	87	2003	2004+
2001	87	2002	2003
2000	88	2000	2001
1999	89	2001	2004

LLOYD RESERVE SHIRAZ

RATING **2**

McLaren Vale	$50–$99
Current vintage: 2004	96

An exemplary shiraz whose perfumed and spicy aromas of violets, cassis, dark plums, cloves and cinnamon are backed by sweet chocolate/vanilla oak and undertones of dried herbs. Supremely fine-grained and elegant, the palate delivers an intense, fully ripened and sour-edged expression of dark cherries, cassis and dark plums evenly matched by coconut ice/chocolate oak and framed by tightly woven powdery tannins. Superbly long and balanced, it finishes with a hint of mineral salt.

2004	96	2016	2024
2002	89	2007	2010+
2001	94	2013	2021
2000	87	2005	2008+
1999	94	2007	2011+
1998	96	2010	2018+
1997	90	2005	2009
1996	95	2008	2016
1995	95	2007	2015
1994	94	2006	2012
1993	89	2001	2005
1992	95	2004	2012
1991	94	2003	2011+
1990	91	2002	2010
1989	93	2001	2009

MARY KATHLEEN RESERVE CABERNET MERLOT

RATING **3**

McLaren Vale	$30–$49
Current vintage: 2003	93

Fine and elegant, smooth and supple, this is a fine regional expression of the Bordeaux blend whose violet-like fragrance of blackcurrants, raspberries, dark cherries and plums are backed by a measured expression of tightly knit cedar/vanilla oak. Pristine and sharply focused, its penetrative red and black cherry/berry flavours are tightly knit with fine, drying and powdery tannins, finishing with lingering nuances of dried herbs.

2003	93	2011	2015+
2002	90	2010	2014
2001	91	2013	2021
2000	88	2005	2008
1999	92	2011	2019
1998	93	2010	2018
1997	89	2005	2009
1996	93	2004	2008+
1995	90	2003	2007
1994	89	2002	2006

REDSTONE SHIRAZ CABERNET

RATING **4**

McLaren Vale	$20–$29
Current vintage: 2003	89

An honest, generous and flavoursome red that should improve in the bottle. Its spicy aromas of blackberries, plums, cinnamon and cloves overlie meaty and slightly earthy nuances of treacle, spice and blueberry. Full to medium in weight, it's moderately rich palate of dark plums, berries and dark olives is backed by cedar/vanilla oak, before a spicy finish of black fruit, minerals and star anise.

2003	89	2011	2015
2002	89	2007	2010
2001	91	2006	2009
2000	91	2005	2008+
1999	87	2004	2007
1998	89	2003	2006+
1997	87	2002	2005
1996	87	2004	2008
1995	89	2001	2004
1994	91	2002	2006
1993	86	1998	2001
1992	89	2000	2004

SANGIOVESE

RATING **4**

McLaren Vale	$20–$29
Current vintage: 2004	92

A finely honed sangiovese whose appealing and varietally correct qualities are presented in a precisely focused, tightly astringent and savoury wine. Its perfume of plums, red and dark cherries is floral, dusty and earthy, with meaty undertones. Supple, smooth and sour-edged, its pure core of vibrant fruit is backed by meaty, earthy undertones, framed by fine-grained and drying tannin, and finished with delightfully refreshing acidity.

2004	92	2009	2012+
2003	91	2008	2011
2002	89	2004	2007+
2001	87	2003	2006+
1999	88	2004	2007
1998	86	2000	2003
1997	90	2002	2005
1996	90	2001	2004
1995	90	2003	2007
1994	89	1999	2002
1993	88	2001	2005
1992	84	1997	2000

A B C D E F G H I J K L M N O P Q R S T U V W X Y Z

SEMILLON (formerly Lalla Rookh Semillon)   RATING 5

McLaren Vale	$20–$29
Current vintage: 2005	**89**

A lively, fresh and tangy semillon whose lightly herbal aromas of honeydew melon precede a long and almost creamy palate whose pristine sherbet-like fruit has a powdery, chalky undercarriage of fine phenolics. It finishes pleasingly clean, crisp and taut.

2005	89	2007	2010+
2002	88	2004	2007+
2001	90	2006	2009
2000	89	2002	2005
1999	88	2001	2004+
1998	94	2003	2006
1997	91	2002	2005
1996	89	2001	2004
1995	90	1997	2000

SHIRAZ   RATING 3

McLaren Vale	$20–$29
Current vintage: 2004	**92**

A fragrant, almost heady perfume of spicy, peppery small red and black berries reveals attractive floral and lightly meaty undertones. Long, supple and silky-smooth, the vibrant, juicy palate presents a pristine spectrum of small berry flavour backed by nuances of spice and carefully handled oak. Framed by particularly tight tannins, this wine offers exceptional value.

2004	92	2009	2012+
2002	93	2007	2010+
2001	92	2006	2009+
2000	86	2002	2005+
1999	89	2004	2007
1998	89	2006	2010
1997	89	2002	2005
1996	92	2001	2004
1995	93	2002	2007
1994	89	2002	2006
1993	91	2001	2005
1992	93	1997	2000

Craiglee

Sunbury Road, Sunbury Vic 3429. Tel: (03) 9744 4489. Fax: (03) 9744 4489.
Website: www.craiglee.com.au Email: patatcraiglee@hotmail.com

Region: **Sunbury** Winemaker: **Patrick Carmody** Viticulturist: **Patrick Carmody** Chief Executive: **Patrick Carmody**
Craiglee is responsible for one of Australia's most sought-after individual vineyard shirazes. The wine is very derivative of its season, which it tends to reflect with unfailing honesty. Recent vintages, most of which have been very dry and warm, have produced atypically rich and robust wines that are stylistically quite distinct from the finer and sappier wines of the early 1990s. 2004 was another drier season, from which Pat Carmody has deftly crafted an impressively concentrated and mineral Shiraz.

CHARDONNAY   RATING 5

Sunbury	$20–$29
Current vintage: 2005	**89**

Juicy aromas of melon, nectarine and sweet, buttery and vanilla oak are just slightly candied, with pleasingly pungent and slightly funky undertones of wheatmeal and reduction. Ripe and juicy, the palate is rich, round and buttery. Its long and persistent core of fruit finishes with savoury, nutty complexity, but with a slightly overt spirity warmth.

2005	89	2007	2010
2004	89	2006	2009
2003	88	2005	2008+
2002	93	2007	2010
2001	89	2003	2006+
2000	88	2002	2005+
1999	90	2001	2004
1998	80	1999	2000
1997	90	2002	2005
1996	91	2001	2004
1995	91	2000	2003
1994	94	2002	2006

SHIRAZ   RATING 2

Sunbury	$30–$49
Current vintage: 2004	**91**

Powerfully ripened, this robust and tannic shiraz has a slightly stewed and meaty bouquet of blackberries, blueberries, cassis and dark plums with spicy undertones of cinnamon, star anise, white pepper and cedar/vanilla oak. Concentrated and quite astringent for this vineyard, its dark and mineral palate of deep plum and blackberry fruit finishes long and drying, with a sour-edged aspect and a hint of iodide.

2004	91	2012	2016
2003	90	2011	2015
2002	94	2010	2014
2001	93	2009	2013
2000	95	2012	2020
1999	91	2004	2007+
1998	89	2003	2006+
1997	95	2005	2009
1996	93	2004	2008
1995	88	2000	2003+
1994	95	2002	2006+
1993	95	2001	2005
1992	89	1997	2000
1991	91	1999	2003
1990	93	2002	2010
1989	91	1991	1994

Crawford River

Upper Hotspur Road, Crawford via Condah Vic 3303. Tel: (03) 5578 2267. Fax: (03) 5578 2240.
Email: crawfordriver@h140.aone.net.au

Region: **Western Victoria** Winemaker: **John Thomson** Viticulturist: **John Thomson** Chief Executive: **John Thomson**

Located in the pastoral country of western Victoria, Crawford River's most popular wine is perhaps its rather accentuated, estery and spicy Riesling. However, its elegant, succulent and shapely Cabernet Sauvignon (and occasional reserve releases of this wine) are often its finest. Occasional releases of Nektar, a late-harvest dessert wine from riesling grapes, can also be spectacular.

CABERNET MERLOT

RATING **5**

Western Victoria	$30–$49
Current vintage: 2003	**81**

A vegetal, herbal blend whose initial impression of sweet raspberry and blackberry fruit and smooth, creamy oak gives way to more sappy and under-ripe characters. Atypical for this maker.

2003	81	2005	2008+
2002	87	2007	2010
2001	89	2006	2009
1999	89	2004	2007

CABERNET SAUVIGNON

RATING **3**

Western Victoria	$30–$49
Current vintage: 2001	**93**

A perfume of violets, cassis and cedary/vanilla oak precedes a smooth, elegant palate of pristine berry flavours harmoniously integrated with fine, silky tannins. Its sweet oak and earthy, meaty undertones of forest floor provide complexity and a creamy texture, but the wine is a shade too herbal for an even higher rating.

2001	93	2009	2013+
2000	89	2005	2008
1999	95	2007	2011+
1997	90	2005	2009
1996	95	2004	2008+
1995	93	2003	2007+
1992	89	2000	2004
1991	95	1999	2003+
1990	89	1995	1998
1989	88	1994	1997

RIESLING

RATING **3**

Western Victoria	$20–$29
Current vintage: 2005	**89**

Delicate musky floral scents of apple and pear precede a restrained and elegant palate whose intense and vibrant core of citrus and deciduous fruits culminates in a long, tangy and juicy finish.

2005	89	2010	2013+
2004	90	2009	2012+
2003	90	2005	2008+
2001	94	2006	2009
2000	87	2002	2005
1999	92	2004	2007
1995	91	2003	2007+
1994	94	2002	2006
1993	95	2001	2005
1992	94	1997	2000
1991	90	1996	1999
1990	93	1999	2002

SAUVIGNON BLANC SEMILLON BLEND

RATING **4**

Western Victoria	$20–$29
Current vintage: 2005	**87**

Lightly grassy, herbaceous aromas of gooseberries and lychees with lightly sweaty undertones precede a warm, juicy palate of passionfruit, lychees and gooseberry flavours. It's moderately long, clean and tangy, and backed by a measured expression of slightly toasty vanilla oak. It's pleasingly fresh and austere to finish, but just lacks a little finesse.

2005	87	2006	2007
2004	89	2006	2009+
2003	90	2004	2005+
2002	82	2002	2003
2001	93	2003	2006
2000	89	2002	2005+

Cullen

Caves Road, Willyabrup via Cowaramup WA 6284. Tel: (08) 9755 5277. Fax: (08) 9755 5550.
Website: www.cullenwines.com.au Email: enquiries@cullenwines.com.au
Region: **Margaret River** Winemakers: **Vanya Cullen, Trevor Kent** Viticulturist: **Michael Sleegers**
Chief Executive: **Vanya Cullen**

Cullen's signature wine, the Diana Madeline cabernet blend, produced another cracker in 2004 — a wine of exceptional substance and stuffing, along with the deeply layered expression of fruit and oak. The present releases also include a first-rate Sauvignon Blanc Semillon from 2005, a spicy and astringent 2004 Mangan blend, and a 2004 Chardonnay that doesn't quite meet expectations. Cullen is today respected as one of Australia's finest wineries.

CHARDONNAY

RATING **2**

Margaret River	$50–$99
Current vintage: 2004	**88**

Dusty, nutty and lightly juicy aromas of apricot and grapefruit overlie spicy nuances of cloves and cinnamon. Forward and candied, its crystalline expression of sugar-cured citrusy fruit thins out, lacks its customary shape, richness and structure, finishing sweet and rather cloying despite the presence of some rather tight acids.

2004	88	2006	2009
2003	83	2005	2008
2002	96	2007	2010+
2001	95	2006	2009+
2000	94	2005	2008
1999	95	2004	2007
1998	94	2000	2003
1997	96	2002	2005+
1996	95	2001	2004+
1995	94	2000	2003
1994	95	2002	2006

DIANA MADELINE CABERNET SAUVIGNON MERLOT

RATING **1**

Margaret River	$50–$99
Current vintage: 2004	**97**

An extremely elegant but powerfully constructed cabernet blend whose alluring fragrance reveals layer after layer of dark berries, black cherries, cranberries, plums and dark chocolate/vanilla oak. Its profoundly intense expression of bright cherry/berry fruit reveals classical notes of dried herbs and superlative oak, all framed by chalky, drying and faintly bony tannins. First-rate length and structure, with a persistent core of pristine flavour.

2004	97	2024	2034
2003	95	2015	2023
2002	95	2014	2022
2001	97	2013	2021+
2000	97	2012	2020+
1999	97	2019	2029
1998	96	2010	2018+
1997	93	2009	2017
1996	95	2008	2016
1995	96	2015	2025
1994	95	2006	2014
1993	94	2005	2013+
1992	94	2004	2012+
1991	89	2003	2011
1990	90	2002	2010
1989	95	2001	2009

MANGAN (Malbec, Petit Verdot blend)

RATING **4**

Margaret River	$30–$49
Current vintage: 2004	**92**

An exuberant young wine with a heady perfume of blackberries, black cherries and blueberries laced with aromas of violets, spices and sweet vanilla/bubblegum oak. Medium in weight, it's smooth and silky, delivering a delightful length of spicy jujube-like flavours of small dark berries over an undercarriage of moderately firm and astringent tannins. Appealing balance and structure.

2004	92	2009	2012
2003	88	2005	2008
2002	93	2007	2010
2001	89	2004	2007

SAUVIGNON BLANC SEMILLON

RATING **2**

Margaret River	$30–$49
Current vintage: 2005	**95**

A supple, elegant and persistent white blend with a lightly smoky, herbal and subtle bouquet of melon and passionfruit, cloves and cinnamon. It's textural wine, with a smooth, vibrant and evenly measured palate whose tangy flavours of melon, citrus, passionfruit and gooseberries are backed by toasty vanilla oak. Long and creamy, with dusty edges and a light herbal presence, it finishes nutty and savoury. Very stylish and delicious.

2005	95	2010	2013
2004	90	2006	2009
2003	89	2005	2008
2002	96	2004	2007+
2001	96	2006	2009
2000	95	2002	2005+
1999	96	2007	2011
1998	91	2000	2003
1997	94	2005	2009
1995	91	2000	2003
1994	93	1996	1999
1993	95	1998	2001

Curlewis

55 Navarre Road, Curlewis Vic 3222. Tel: (03) 5250 4567. Fax: (03) 5250 4567.
Website: www.curlewiswinery.com.au Email: curlewis@datafast.net.au

Region: **Bellarine Peninsula** Winemaker: **Rainer Breit**
Viticulturists: **Rainer Breit, Wendy Oliver** Chief Executives: **Rainer Breit, Wendy Oliver**

Curlewis is presently riding high on a crest of popularity. Its owners fell in love with the more funky and wild expressions of Burgundy, then wanted to make similar wines in Australia. They also felt that the only way to make an initial impact in the market was to pursue an extremely rustic style. This they have done, but their wines are now showing more class as they become more vibrant and less risky, without compromising their intentions of making pinots of structure, richness and complexity.

CHARDONNAY
RATING 4

Bellarine Peninsula		$30–$49
Current vintage: 2004		**89**

Nutty, lightly floral aromas of melon and nectarine reveal an underlying meatiness and wild mealy, cheesy, leesy complexity. Round, juicy and slightly viscous, its slightly candied and juicy fruit, buttery oak and butterscotch malolactic influences finish with a faint spirity hotness and minerally acids.

2004	89	2006	2009
2003	95	2005	2008+
2002	83	2003	2004+
2001	90	2003	2006+

PINOT NOIR

Bellarine Peninsula		$30–$49
Current vintage: 2003		**86**

A spicy, meaty pinot whose aromas of animal hide and undergrowth present underlying nuances of slightly cooked red cherries and plums. Ripe and meaty, its slightly cooked and stressed palate of currant-like fruit dries off slightly towards a flat, green-edged finish. The wine has pleasing depth, but lacks an evenness of ripeness.

2003	86	2005	2008
2002	87	2004	2007
2001	89	2006	2009
2000	86	2002	2005

RESERVE PINOT NOIR

Bellarine Peninsula		$50–$99
Current vintage: 2003		**89**

Elegant, supple and more vibrant than previous releases, it opens with a floral perfume of cherries and raspberries over smoky suggestions of walnuts and slightly raw oak. Quite intense, with currant-like flavours beneath more vibrant cherry/berry fruit, it's framed by firm, drying and powdery tannins. There's a hint of greenness beneath the fruit, but there's also freshness and brightness.

2003	89	2006	2009
2002	82	2004	2007
2001	82	2003	2006
2000	80	2002	2005+
1998	77	2000	2003

d'Arenberg

Osborn Road, McLaren Vale SA 5171. Tel: (08) 8329 4888. Fax: (08) 8323 8423.
Website: www.darenberg.com.au   Email: winery@darenberg.com.au

Regions: **McLaren Vale, Fleurieu Peninsula, Adelaide Hills**   Winemakers: **Chester Osborn, Phillip Dean**
Viticulturists: **Chester Osborn, Giulio Dimasi**   Managing Director: **d'Arry Osborn**

d'Arenberg enjoyed its best vintage ever in 2004, creating a stellar range of wines with tremendous depth of fruit, terrific balance and varietal integrity. They are less wild and funky, and considerably better finished than recent years of d'Arenberg wine. The Dead Arm Shiraz, for instance, is handsomely the best red released under this label, and probably the best d'Arenberg wine ever made. Congratulations to Chester and the team for raising the bar so significantly. Now all they have to do is keep it there!

D'ARRY'S ORIGINAL SHIRAZ GRENACHE   RATING 4

McLaren Vale $12–$19
Current vintage: 2004   92

Vibrant and youthful, this ripe and old-fashioned Australian burgundy style has a spicy fragrance of red and black cherry/plum fruit with undertones of cloves, cinnamon and restrained older oak. Long and smooth, it's soft and charming, with deep, bright blackberry/blueberry fruit framed by velvet tannin and finished with soft acids.

2004	92	2016	2024+
2003	87	2008	2011+
2002	90	2010	2014+
2001	87	2006	2009
2000	90	2005	2008+
1999	89	2004	2007+
1998	90	2006	2010+
1997	89	2002	2005+
1996	89	2004	2008
1995	92	2003	2007
1994	92	2002	2006
1993	89	2001	2005
1992	91	2000	2004
1991	88	1999	2003
1990	91	1998	2002
1989	87	1997	2001
1988	93	2000	2008

THE BROKEN FISHPLATE SAUVIGNON BLANC   RATING 5

Adelaide Hills $12–$19
Current vintage: 2005   91

An honest, vibrant and grassy sauvignon blanc whose intense gooseberry/passionfruit flavours burst their way down a long, juicy palate that finishes with mineral cut and definition. There's a pungent, sweaty aspect to the aroma, while the finish is long and tangy.

2005	91	2006	2007+
2004	85	2004	2005
2003	86	2003	2004+
2002	90	2003	2004
2001	87	2001	2002
2000	90	2001	2002
1999	90	2001	2004
1998	82	1999	2000

THE COPPERMINE ROAD CABERNET SAUVIGNON   RATING 3

McLaren Vale $50–$99
Current vintage: 2004   93

Long, firm and tightly focused, this lean, sinewy but powerfully fruited cabernet simply needs time. Its brooding, rather closed bouquet of dark plum and berries, bitumen and dark olives reveals some floral perfume while its tightly muscled and astringent palate suggests deeply ripened fruit and baked earth.

2004	93	2016	2024+
2003	93	2015	2023
2002	93	2014	2022
2001	93	2009	2013+
2000	93	2012	2020
1999	89	2007	2011+
1998	94	2010	2018+
1997	90	2005	2009+
1996	89	2008	2016

THE CUSTODIAN GRENACHE   RATING 4

McLaren Vale $20–$29
Current vintage: 2004   90

A spicy, floral perfume of blueberry confiture, rose petals, cherries and blackcurrants offers just a hint of confection. Smooth and tightly focused, its vibrant and juicy palate of intense black berry fruit is neatly framed by a supple grade of fine tannin, harmoniously finishing with length of fruit, refreshing acidity and brightness.

2004	90	2006	2009+
2002	92	2010	2014+
2001	89	2009	2013
2000	92	2005	2008+
1999	91	2004	2007+
1998	87	2003	2006
1997	92	2002	2005
1996	91	2004	2008
1995	93	2003	2007

THE DEAD ARM SHIRAZ

McLaren Vale   **$50–$99**
Current vintage: 2004   **96**

The finest Dead Arm ever made has a smoky, ethereal and spicy bouquet of slightly meaty dark plums and berries scented with violets, licorice and black pepper, cloves and cinnamon. Smooth and sumptuous, its powerful and searingly intense palate of black berry fruit has a salty/mineral edge and a sophisticated marriage with new oak. Despite its intense fruit sweetness, the wine finishes long and savoury, with lingering sour edges, terrific acids and overall balance. A traditional wine, with cut and polish.

2004	96	2016	2024+
2003	92	2015	2023
2002	94	2010	2014
2001	93	2013	2021+
2000	93	2012	2020
1999	89	2007	2011
1998	93	2010	2018
1997	92	2005	2009
1996	95	2008	2016
1995	95	2007	2015
1994	93	2006	2014

THE DRY DAM RIESLING

McLaren Vale   **$12–$19**
Current vintage: 2005   **87**

A trim, lean riesling whose fresh, floral and citrusy aromas have a slightly confectionary aspect. Long and restrained, it's a tart and high acid style whose lively expression of citrus and apple fruit finishes clean and austere. Well made, and needing time in the bottle.

2005	87	2010	2013
2004	87	2006	2009
2003	90	2008	2011+
2002	90	2007	2010
2001	87	2003	2006
2000	87	2005	2008
1999	92	2004	2007
1997	87	2002	2005

THE FOOTBOLT SHIRAZ

McLaren Vale   **$20–$29**
Current vintage: 2004   **90**

A juicy, assertive and brightly presented young shiraz without a hint of over-ripeness. Its sweet fragrance of small black and red berries, black pepper, cloves and cinnamon is neatly balanced with vanilla oak, while its palate represents a step forwards in brightness and focus for this label. Searingly intense, with a background of coconut and vanilla oak, it's vibrant and juicy, finishing with refreshing acidity.

2004	90	2012	2016+
2003	85	2005	2008+
2001	87	2003	2006+
2000	87	2002	2005+
1999	89	2004	2007+
1998	90	2006	2010
1997	87	2002	2005+
1996	90	2004	2008
1995	90	2003	2007
1994	91	2006	2014
1993	90	2001	2005
1992	90	2004	2012
1991	93	2003	2011

THE GALVO GARAGE CABERNET BLEND

McLaren Vale, Adel. Hills   **$30–$49**
Current vintage: 2004   **91**

Tightly balanced, finely polished and presented, this smooth and pliant red marries piercing and penetrative blackberry and plum-like flavour with newish mocha/dark chocolate oak and firm, powdery tannin. Its minty small berry/cherry aromas reveal undertones of eucalypt, menthol and a faint meatiness, while its sumptuous palate is long, even and finely balanced.

2004	91	2016	2024
2003	90	2008	2011+
2002	90	2010	2014
2001	90	2009	2013

THE HIGH TRELLIS CABERNET SAUVIGNON

McLaren Vale   **$20–$29**
Current vintage: 2004   **89**

Sweet aromas of small black and red berries, restrained vanilla oak and minty, lightly herbal and menthol-like aromas precede a vibrant, juicy and intensely fruited palate neatly entwined around firmish tannins. Tightly crafted, it's long and bright, well focused and balanced.

2004	89	2009	2012+
2003	89	2011	2015
2002	89	2007	2010+
2001	85	2006	2009
2000	87	2005	2008
1999	87	2004	2007
1998	93	2006	2010
1997	88	2002	2005+
1995	92	2003	2007
1994	88	1999	2002
1993	87	2001	2005

THE IRONSTONE PRESSINGS (Grenache Shiraz Mourvèdre) RATING 3

McLaren Vale $50–$99
Current vintage: 2004 95

A step up in brightness and elegance for this label. There's a confectionary note to its vibrant, floral aromas of blueberries, blackberries and redcurrants, plus undertones of licorice and spice. Smooth and silky, the palate delivers a penetrative and spicy cut of intense, confiture-like fruit backed by nuances of black pepper. Framed by fine, bony tannins, it's long, evenly balanced and deeply concentrated.

2004	95	2016	2024+
2003	91	2011	2015+
2002	94	2014	2022+
2001	92	2013	2021
2000	89	2005	2008
1999	89	2007	2011
1998	89	2010	2018
1997	91	2005	2009
1996	94	2008	2016
1995	93	2007	2015
1994	89	2006	2014
1993	91	2005	2013
1992	95	2000	2004
1991	91	2003	2011
1990	90	2002	2010

THE LAST DITCH VIOGNIER RATING 5

McLaren Vale $12–$19
Current vintage: 2005 88

A funky, wild and meaty viognier whose smoky, spicy perfume of toasty, caramel-like and musky fruit precedes a broad, round and oily palate of considerable evolution. Its chewy mouthful of stone-fruit and lemony flavour has length and dryness, and culminates in a rather angular and savoury finish that lacks a little conviction.

2005	88	2006	2007+
2004	87	2005	2006
2003	82	2004	2005
2002	87	2003	2004+
2001	89	2003	2006

THE LAUGHING MAGPIE (Shiraz Viognier) RATING 4

McLaren Vale $20–$29
Current vintage: 2004 92

Spicy, earthy and charcuterie-like aromas of dark plums, blackberries and musky spices precede a long, vibrant and dark-fruited palate framed by firmish, fine and drying tannins. It's ever so slightly cooked, but steeped in flavours of blackberries and plums backed by chocolate oak, finishing with faint meaty, savoury notes, lingering dark fruit and spiciness.

2004	92	2009	2012+
2003	90	2005	2008+
2002	92	2007	2010+
2001	90	2006	2009
2000	87	2005	2008

THE NOBLE RIESLING RATING 5

McLaren Vale $20–$29 (375 ml)
Current vintage: 2003 84

Made from a vintage all but impossible for this style of wine, with rather a dried out and varnishy bouquet of citrus fruit, apricot and marzipan. Very sweet but stale and flat, the palate is forward and oily, with a syrupy expression of dehydrated fruit than finishes rather coarse and syrupy.

2003	84	2004	2005
2002	88	2004	2007+
2001	86	2003	2006
2000	88	2002	2005+
1999	88	2001	2004+
1998	84	2000	2003
1997	90	2002	2005
1996	87	1998	2001
1995	90	2000	2003
1994	93	2002	2006
1993	89	1995	1998

THE OLIVE GROVE CHARDONNAY

RATING 5

McLaren Vale, Adel. Hills $12–$19
Current vintage: 2005 88

Juicy, warm and spirity, this ripe and slightly confectionary chardonnay has a bright, floral aroma of peaches, citrus and tropical fruit backed by buttery oak and nutty, mealy undertones. Long and smooth, its creamy and handsomely ripened palate of green melon and peachy flavours culminates in a lingering nutty, savoury finish.

2005	88	2007	2010
2004	88	2005	2006+
2003	87	2005	2008
2002	90	2004	2007
2001	81	2002	2003
2000	88	2002	2005
1999	92	2001	2004+
1998	92	2003	2006
1997	88	1999	2002

THE STUMP JUMP RED BLEND

RATING 5

McLaren Vale $12–$19
Current vintage: 2004 88

A spicy, grenache-driven southern Rhône style with a sweet fragrance of earthy cherry, plum and blueberry aromas with a restrained hint of oak. Juicy and forward, its flavoursome and powdery palate finishes with lingering dark fruit flavours refreshingly framed by lively acids and fine tannins. Pleasing elegance and brightness.

2004	88	2005	2006+
2002	89	2004	2007+
2001	86	2003	2006
2000	86	2002	2005
1999	77	1999	2000

THE TWENTYEIGHT ROAD MOURVÈDRE

RATING 4

McLaren Vale $30–$49
Current vintage: 2004 91

Deeply flavoured, this savoury and harmoniously balanced red wine has a lightly herbal, violet-like aroma of dark red and black berry fruits that reveals earthy, stony undertones of cloves and cinnamon. Framed by fine, bony tannins, its firm and slightly meaty expression of prunes and plums reveals a measure of support from older oak. It just needs time.

2004	91	2012	2016+
2002	90	2010	2024+
2001	93	2009	2013+
2000	87	2005	2008
1999	88	2007	2011
1998	89	2003	2006+
1997	87	2002	2005
1996	92	2004	2008+
1995	89	2003	2007

VINTAGE DECLARED FORTIFIED SHIRAZ
(formerly Vintage Port)

RATING 3

McLaren Vale $30–$49
Current vintage: 2004 94

Deep, dark and spicy aromas of dark plums, currants and cassis overlie nuances of licorice, cloves and cinnamon, with a very clean and aromatic lift of spirit. Very clean, restrained and fine-grained, its savoury and spicy palate is partially reminiscent of the Portuguese expression of vintage port. Its tannins are tight and powdery, its lingering finish slightly meaty and spicy.

2004	94	2016	2024
2003	93	2015	2023+
2002	93	2014	2022+
2001	94	2013	2021+
2000	95	2020	2030+
1999	90	2011	2019+
1998	93	2010	2018
1997	93	2005	2009+
1995	94	2007	2015
1993	93	2005	2013
1987	94	2007	2017
1978	90	1998	2008
1976	93	1996	2006
1975	93	1995	2005
2004	89	2009	2012
2003	87	2005	2008+
2001	89	2009	2013
2000	83	2005	2008
1999	84	2004	2007+
1998	87	2003	2006
1997	87	2002	2005
1996	91	2004	2008+
1995	92	2003	2007+
1994	89	2006	2014
1993	84	2001	2005
1992	88	2000	2004

Dalwhinnie

448 Taltarni Road, Moonambel Vic 3478. Tel: (03) 5467 2388. Fax: (03) 5467 2237.
Website: www.dalwhinnie.com.au Email: dalwines@iinet.net.au

Region: **Pyrenees** Winemaker: **David Jones** Viticulturist: **David Jones** Chief Executive: **David Jones**

Simply brilliant is the brief description of Dalwhinnie's 2004 vintage, which produced what are likely to be recognised as its finest ever wines from Shiraz and Cabernet Sauvignon. Dalwhinnie's exposed dryland site is more suited to shiraz than cabernet, but in later seasons with even temperatures, it has proven capable of making growing flavoured and tightly structured cabernets of exceptional balance and longevity.

CHARDONNAY

RATING 3

Pyrenees $30–$49
Current vintage: 2004   93

A long, smooth, austere and minerally chardonnay whose delicate aromas of citrus fruit, honeydew melon, guava and wheatmeal overlie dusty nuances of vanilla oak and lifted floral scents. Seamless, savoury and nutty, it's a generous but restrained marriage of lime and melon fruit with fresh vanilla oak and lees-derived complexity punctuated by slightly sour-edged and steely acids.

2004	93	2009	2012
2003	92	2005	2008
2002	89	2004	2007+
2001	93	2006	2009
2000	92	2002	2005+
1999	87	2001	2004
1998	94	2003	2006
1997	94	2002	2005
1996	92	2001	2004
1995	94	2000	2003
1994	94	2002	2006
1993	95	1998	2001
1992	93	2000	2004
1991	93	1999	2003
1990	94	1998	2002

EAGLE SERIES SHIRAZ

RATING 2

Pyrenees $100–$199
Current vintage: 2001   86

A hot year wine whose peppery aromas of boiled lollies, cherries and raspberries reveal undertones of musk, spice, cinnamon and fresh vanilla oak. The palate delivers some up-front and uncomplicated confectionary fruit, before drying out rather dramatically to a lean finish of underripe tannins, with lingering flavours of baked fruit and marzipan. Not a stellar moment for this label.

2001	86	2003	2006
2000	95	2012	2020
1998	93	2003	2006
1997	97	2005	2009
1992	94	2000	2004
1986	93	1998	2006

MOONAMBEL CABERNET

RATING 3

Pyrenees $30–$49
Current vintage: 2004   97

A superb cabernet whose deep and pure expression of spotless varietal fruit is handsomely partnered by finely handled oak and supported by a classically firm and powdery spine of drying astringency. Its heady bouquet of cassis, small red berries, plums and mulberries is backed by dusty cedar/vanilla oak against a faint background of black olives, mint and menthol. Long and grainy, it's sumptuous and deeply layered, revealing intense and complex dark fruits with dusty suggestions of dried herbs and cedar. Beautifully complete, balanced and very stable; set for the long term.

2004	97	2016	2024+
2003	90	2011	2015
2002	92	2014	2022
2000	91	2012	2020
1999	93	2011	2019
1998	94	2010	2018
1997	92	2009	2017
1996	86	2004	2008
1995	93	2003	2007+
1994	90	2002	2006
1993	85	2001	2005+
1992	94	2004	2012+
1991	92	2003	2011
1990	88	2002	2010
1989	91	1997	2001
1988	89	1996	2000+
1987	82	1992	1995
1986	93	1998	2006
1985	86	1990	1993
1984	80	1989	1992
1983	87	1995	2003

MOONAMBEL SHIRAZ

RATING 2

Pyrenees	**$50–$99**	2004	97	2012	2016+

Pyrenees $50–$99
Current vintage: 2004   97

Heady, wild, floral and musky aromas of cassis, plums, redcurrants and cranberries are handsomely supported by dusty new vanilla oak and backed by minty nuances of menthol, licorice and treacle. Sumptuous and smooth, its seamless palate unfolds layers of sour-edged dark berries and plums with mocha and vanilla oak framed by tightly knit, fine-grained tannins. Tremendous depth, tightness and balance.

2004	97	2012	2016+
2003	89	2008	2011+
2002	90	2007	2010+
2001	94	2009	2013+
2000	95	2008	2012+
1999	94	2007	2011+
1998	95	2006	2010
1997	94	2005	2009
1996	95	2004	2008
1995	92	2003	2007
1994	93	2002	2006
1993	87	2001	2005
1992	97	2004	2012
1991	95	1999	2003+
1990	95	2002	2010
1989	82	1994	1997
1988	89	2000	2008
1987	83	1995	1999

David Traeger

139 High Street, Nagambie Vic 3608. Tel: (03) 5794 2514. Fax: (03) 5794 1776. Email: DTW1@bigpond.com
Region: **Nagambie Lakes** Winemaker: **David Traeger** Viticulturist: **David Traeger**
Chief Executive: **Richard Green**

Now owned by Dromana Estate Ltd, the David Traeger label has made a name for some juicy, if slightly sweet central Victorian Verdelho, as well as some finely crafted, leaner expressions of Cabernet Sauvignon and Shiraz. Its reds, which are in danger of being released to the market after they have lost their brightness and intensity, are typically tight, lean and protected, and slowly acquire roundness and softness with age.

CABERNET MERLOT

RATING 5

Goulburn Valley $20–$29
Current vintage: 2003   83

Rather varnishy, raisined and meaty aromas of currants and plums precede a robust, thick and chewy palate whose prune-like fruit lacks length of sweetness, drying out towards a hard, tough-edged finish.

2003	83	2008	2011
1999	87	2004	2007+
1998	90	2010	2018
1997	86	2005	2009
1996	89	2004	2008
1995	88	2003	2007
1993	91	2001	2005
1992	94	2004	2012
1990	93	2002	2010
1989	92	1997	2001
1988	88	1996	2000

SHIRAZ

RATING 3

Nagambie Lakes $20–$29
Current vintage: 2002   83

An ageing shiraz apparently made from stressed fruit. Its dusty autumnal aromas of currants, blackberries and plums are backed by sweet cedary oak and meaty, herbal and leafy undertones. Its initial impression of richness and fruit sweetness dries out towards a green-edged finish lifted by sweet cedary oak. Lacks length and brightness.

2002	83	2004	2007+
2001	85	2005	2009
2000	92	2005	2008+
1999	88	2004	2007+
1998	92	2006	2010+
1997	93	2005	2009+
1996	92	2004	2008
1995	90	2003	2007
1993	85	1998	2001
1992	88	2000	2004
1990	89	1998	2002
1988	93	1996	2000

VERDELHO

RATING 4

Various, Victoria $12–$19
Current vintage: 2004   82

Slightly candied aromas of gooseberries, citrus fruits and honeydew melon with a spicy background of green cashew precede a juicy but underripe and syrupy palate whose citrusy tropical fruit finishes with green edges. Lacks its customary brightness and freshness.

2004	82	2004	2005+
2002	87	2003	2004
2001	90	2003	2006+
2000	82	2001	2002
1999	93	2004	2007
1998	91	2003	2006
1997	88	1999	2002

De Bortoli

De Bortoli Road, Bilbul NSW 2680. Tel: (02) 6966 0100. Fax: (02) 6966 0199.
Website: www.debortoli.com.au Email: reception_bilbul@debortoli.com.au

Region: **Riverina** Winemaker: **Julie Mortlock** Viticulturist: **Kevin De Bortoli** Chief Executive: **Darren De Bortoli**

De Bortoli actually created the genre of late-harvest semillon in Australia with the release of the first vintage of what was then labelled 'Semillon Sauterne' in 1982. Since then the wine has been renamed 'Noble One', and has become virtually mandatory on Australian wine lists. The 2004 release lacks the wine's usual cut and polish.

NOBLE ONE RATING 2

Riverina	$20–$29 (375 ml)
Current vintage: 2004	**89**

Very oaky and quite varnishy, this very sweet dessert wine offers concentrated and mouthfilling flavours of citrus and melon backed by nuances of wheatmeal, honey and pastry. It's luscious and creamy, but also quite cloying, finishing with oaky rawness. A little awkward, and lacking its usual finesse.

2004	89	2006	2009+
2003	92	2005	2008+
2002	96	2010	2014
2001	90	2003	2006
2000	93	2005	2008
1999	93	2004	2007
1998	95	2010	2018
1997	89	2002	2005
1996	95	2004	2008
1995	95	2003	2007
1994	96	2002	2006

De Bortoli Yarra Valley

Pinnacle Lane, Dixon's Creek Vic 3775. Tel: (03) 5965 2271. Fax: (03) 5965 2442.
Website: www.debortoli.com.au Email: Yarra_Cellar_Door@debortoli.com.au

Region: **Yarra Valley** Winemakers: **Stephen Webber, David Slingsby-Smith** Viticulturist: **Philip Lobley**
Chief Executive: **Darren De Bortoli**

De Bortoli is one of the Yarra Valley's largest winemakers, and while recent vintage are not quite up to the brand's established standard, given the scale of its operations it does an excellent job in delivering consistently flavoursome wines of quality and distinction. De Bortoli's team has never been afraid to administer a decent measure of newish oak to its riper and richer reds. Its restaurant has long been a benchmark in the region.

CABERNET SAUVIGNON RATING 4

Yarra Valley	$30–$49
Current vintage: 2001	**85**

Floral aromas of small red berries, blackberries and restrained cedary oak precede a forward, moderately full palate that dries out quickly towards a meaty, herbal finish of sappy tannins. Lacks structure and fruit substance.

2001	85	2003	2006+
2000	92	2008	2012
1999	89	2004	2007
1998	90	2003	2006
1997	92	2005	2009
1996	91	2001	2004
1995	95	2007	2015
1994	89	1999	2002

CHARDONNAY RATING 4

Yarra Valley	$20–$29
Current vintage: 2005	**88**

Complex, smooth and very slightly sweet, this juicy young chardonnay has a floral fragrance of grapefruit, melon and lemon rind backed by dusty clove and vanilla-like oak. Its intense expression of melon, peach and banana is long, fine and fluffy, with restrained vanilla oak plus undertones of sweet corn and herbaceous, reductive influences.

2005	88	2007	2010
2004	86	2006	2009
2003	89	2005	2008
2002	94	2007	2010
2001	89	2003	2006
2000	93	2002	2005+
1999	93	2004	2007
1998	93	2003	2006
1997	90	1999	2002+
1996	94	2001	2004+

PINOT NOIR RATING 5

Yarra Valley	$30–$49
Current vintage: 2003	**83**

Earthy, herbaceous aromas of raspberries, cherries and plums reveal meaty nuances, with undertones of cloves and cinnamon. Juicy and forward, but drying out down the palate, it finishes thin, green and hard-edged, lacking ripeness and freshness.

2003	83	2005	2008
2002	89	2004	2007+
2001	85	2002	2003+
2000	87	2002	2005
1999	89	2001	2004
1998	89	2000	2003
1997	94	2002	2005
1996	95	2001	2004

SHIRAZ

RATING 4

Yarra Valley		**$30–$49**	2003	88	2008	2011
Current vintage: 2003		**88**	2002	90	2007	2010

2003	88	2008	2011
2002	90	2007	2010
2001	89	2006	2009
2000	88	2002	2005+
1999	90	2004	2007
1998	89	2003	2006+
1997	93	2005	2009
1996	93	2001	2004
1995	93	2003	2007
1994	93	1999	2002
1993	90	1998	2001

A smooth and savoury shiraz whose confiture-like aromas of cassis, mulberries and raspberries are backed by nuances of cedar/vanilla oak, white pepper, dusty and earthy complexity and some gamey development. Medium to full in weight, it's finely structured and elegant, delivering a supple and restrained palate of spicy fruit and chocolate/vanilla oak supported by fine tannins. It finishes savoury, with some herbal edges.

Deakin Estate

Kulkyne Way, Iraak via Red Cliffs Vic 3496. Tel: (03) 5029 1666. Fax: (03) 5024 3316.
Website: www.deakinestate.com.au Email: deakin@wingara.com.au
Region: **Murray Darling** Winemaker: **Phil Spillman** Viticulturist: **Craig Thornton**
Chief Executive: **David Yunghanns**

Every year, or so it seems, I am happily surprised by the flavours, the freshness, the balance and the finesse of Deakin Estate's wine. Even the fresh and peachy 2005 Chardonnay offers great value for money, while the Reserve Chardonnay from 2004 is frankly quite sophisticated and classy. I am convinced by the value and consistency of this brand, which is part of the group that owns Katnook Estate.

CABERNET SAUVIGNON

RATING 5

Murray Darling	**$5–$11**
Current vintage: 2004	**87**

2004	87	2006	2009
2003	87	2005	2008+
2002	87	2004	2007
2001	84	2002	2003
2000	86	2001	2002
1999	81	2000	2001

Attractively balanced and composed, its slightly stewy expression of dark plums, cranberries and dark berries is backed by dusty vanilla oak and framed by fine tannins. Pleasing length and freshness.

MERLOT

RATING 5

Murray Darling	**$5–$11**
Current vintage: 2003	**82**

2003	82	2004	2005
2002	87	2003	2004
2001	88	2002	2003+
2000	84	2001	2002
1999	87	2000	2001+
1998	82	1999	2000
1997	85	1998	1999

Earthy, meaty and spicy, with simple and slightly confectionary dark plum and cherry fruit backed by earthy, cedary and chocolate-like undertones. Lacks genuine length and varietal character, finishing a little flat and green-edged.

SAUVIGNON BLANC

RATING 5

Murray Darling	**$5–$11**
Current vintage: 2005	**88**

2005	88	2005	2006
2004	87	2004	2005
2003	83	2003	2004
2002	84	2002	2003
2001	87	2001	2002

Vibrant and herbaceous, this generously flavoured, round and juicy sauvignon blanc delivers punchy flavours of gooseberries and passionfruit along a slightly chalky palate, finishing with tangy lemony acids and a hint of sweetness.

RESERVE CHARDONNAY (formerly Select)

RATING 5

Murray Darling	**$12–$19**
Current vintage: 2004	**89**

2004	89	2006	2009
2003	86	2004	2005+
2002	89	2003	2004
2000	83	2001	2002
1998	80	1998	1999
1997	87	1998	1999

An exceptional wine for its price, revealing a slightly funky bouquet of pineapple, melon and peach over pronounced smoky and leesy bound sulphide-like undertones. Its penetrative palate of pear, apple and lemon zest is creamy and generous, delivering a lingering core of tangy citrus and stonefruit flavour before a nutty and slightly savoury finish.

SELECT SHIRAZ

Murray Darling	$12–$19
Current vintage: 2002	87

It takes a little breathing for its full depth of lively spicy black and red berry fruit to emerge, but this slightly meaty, lightly herbaceous and cedary shiraz does present a generous and well-structured mouthful of fruit. It's framed by firmish tannins and supported by tight-knit chocolate/vanilla oak with more than a hint of toastiness.

2002	87	2004	2007+
2001	86	2003	2006
1999	88	2001	2004
1998	89	2000	2003+

SHIRAZ

Murray Darling	$5–$11
Current vintage: 2004	88

A supple, elegant and easy-drinking shiraz of genuine structure and style. Its spicy, floral aromas of fresh small red and black berries, vanilla and cedary oak are lifted by nuances of white pepper. Surprisingly long and tightly focused, its smooth, spicy and brightly lit palate of delicate berry flavours and lightly toasty oak has a fine-grained coating of pliant and powdery tannin.

2004	88	2006	2009
2003	87	2005	2008
2002	86	2004	2007
2001	86	2002	2003+
2000	87	2001	2002
1999	82	2000	2001
1998	83	1999	2000

Delatite

Corner Stoney's & Pollard Roads, Mansfield Vic 3722. Tel: (03) 5775 2922. Fax: (03) 5775 2911.
Website: www.delatitewinery.com.au Email: info@delatitewinery.com.au
Region: **Mansfield** Winemakers: **Jane Donat, David Ritchie** Viticulturist: **Andrew Storrie**
Chief Executive: **David Ritchie**

While it produces a wide range of different wines from an impressively broad range of varieties, Delatite's best wines are its perfumed and mineral Rieslings, occasionally deeply floral Dead Man's Hill Gewürztraminer and refreshing Demelza sparkling wine. The estate's red wines often reveal powerful mint and menthol-like characters, while the Sauvignon Blanc can be vibrant and tightly sculpted. Delatite is one of the coolest vineyards in Victoria, and occupies a superb site overlooking the Victorian high country.

DEAD MAN'S HILL GEWÜRZTRAMINER

Mansfield	$20–$29
Current vintage: 2005	88

A rather sweet and phenolic traminer whose floral perfume of rose oil, lychees and dusty, musky spices precedes a long, smooth and juicy palate of brightly lit varietal flavour. Rather chalky and richly textured, it's likely to become quite broad in future.

2005	88	2007	2010+
2004	85	2006	2009
2003	89	2005	2008+
2002	87	2003	2004+
2001	94	2006	2009
2000	91	2005	2008
1999	87	2001	2004
1998	88	2000	2003
1997	89	1999	2002
1996	91	2004	2008
1995	87	2000	2003
1994	93	1999	2002
1992	91	2000	2004+

DEMELZA

Mansfield	$30–$49
Current vintage: 2002	88

Toasty, floral, buttery and creamy aromas are backed by nuances of honey, citrus and wheatmeal. Rather broad, thick and cloying, with crackly, creamy yeast-derived influences, its simple, buttery and rather herbal palate lacks its customary freshness and charm.

2002	88	2004	2007+
2001	92	2006	2009
2000	87	2002	2005
1996	93	2001	2004+
94–95	93	1999	2002+
1991	84	1996	1999
87–88	87	1995	1997

RIESLING

Mansfield		$12–$19	2005	91	2010	2013+
Current vintage: 2005		**91**	2004	93	2012	2016
			2003	89	2005	2008+
			2002	92	2007	2010+
			2001	90	2006	2009
			2000	91	2005	2008+
			1999	92	2007	2011
			1998	94	2006	2010
			1997	88	2005	2009
			1996	93	2004	2008
			1995	93	2000	2003
			1994	94	2002	2005
			1993	95	2001	2005
			1992	95	2000	2004

An elegant, mineral riesling in a Germanic style that presents a spicy, estery, honeysuckle-like perfume and a juicy, tangy palate whose apple and lemon rind flavours finish crisp and crunchy. It's long, chalky and finely phenolic, with lingering lime juice flavours.

SAUVIGNON BLANC

2005	75	2005	2006
2004	86	2005	2006
2003	91	2003	2004+
2002	87	2002	2003
2001	89	2002	2003+
2000	90	2001	2002
1999	89	2000	2001+
1998	88	1999	2002+
1997	92	1999	2002

Mansfield $20–$29
Current vintage: 2005 **75**

Flat, stale, herbal and sweet; possibly the result of a stuck ferment.

VS LIMITED EDITION RIESLING

Mansfield	$12–$19	2004	92	2012	2016
Current vintage: 2004	**92**	2001	95	2009	2013
		1999	95	2007	2011+

A delicate floral perfume with lime and mineral undertones heralds a tight, long and moderately phenolic and chalky palate whose pristine fresh lemon rind and lime juice flavours culminate in a taut and racy finish of just slightly exaggerated minerality.

Devil's Lair

Rocky Road, via Margaret River WA 6285. Tel: (08) 9757 7573. Fax: (08) 9757 7533. Website: www.devils-lair.com
Region: **Margaret River** Winemaker: **Stuart Pym** Viticulturist: **Simon Robertson** Chief Executive: **Jamie Odell**

Its southerly location in Margaret River hampers cabernet vintages from time to time, but followers of Devil's Lair's cabernet blend could be excused for thinking that some opportunities have slipped through the net. With two disappointing wines under the premium label, the only bright light in this range today is the juicy, fruit-driven Fifth Leg red blend.

CHARDONNAY

Margaret River	$30–$49	2004	87	2006	2009
Current vintage: 2004	**87**	2003	94	2005	2008
		2002	90	2004	2007+
		2001	91	2003	2005+
		2000	95	2005	2008
		1999	95	2004	2007
		1998	89	2000	2003+
		1997	95	2002	2005
		1996	88	1998	2001
		1995	93	2000	2003
		1994	94	1996	1999

A mineral fragrance of lemon sherbet, lime and grapefruit overlies spicy, oak-derived nuances of clove and nutmeg. Smooth and creamy, its tangy palate of forward, citrusy fruit finishes rather drying and oaky, with a lingering powdery aspect. Rather hollow, lacking generosity and mouthfeel.

FIFTH LEG RED

RATING **5**

Margaret River $12–$19
Current vintage: 2005   90

A delicious young and early-drinking red packed with genuinely ripe but not overcooked flavours of dark berries, cherries and plums. Its bouquet has a floral aspect, with undertones of dark chocolate/cedar oak and nuances of dried herbs. Medium to full in weight, its fruit-driven palate is framed by very fine, dusty tannins. It finishes long and lingering with fresh dark fruit and lively acidity.

2005	90	2007	2010
2004	89	2006	2009
2003	83	2004	2005+
2002	89	2004	2007
2001	89	2003	2006+
2000	92	2002	2005+
1999	92	2001	2004
1997	80	1998	1999
1996	90	1998	2001

FIFTH LEG WHITE

RATING **5**

Margaret River $12–$19
Current vintage: 2005   88

Dusty, herbal and slightly asparagus and nettle-like aromas of gooseberries and passionfruit are backed by undertones of green cashew. Smooth, long and elegant, its fresh and vibrant palate offers a juicy, lingering core of fruit supported by hints of creamy lees and restrained oaky complexity. It finishes clean, with refreshing acidity.

2005	88	2006	2007
2004	88	2005	2006
2003	82	2003	2004+
2002	89	2003	2004
2000	86	2001	2002
1998	89	1999	2000

MARGARET RIVER CABERNET (Cabernet Merlot)

RATING **5**

Margaret River $50–$99
Current vintage: 2003   87

Lacking genuine conviction, ripeness and structure, with rather dusty, leafy aromas of cassis, mulberries and dark cherries, backed by cedar/dark chocolate oak and a hint of blue mould cheese. Medium to full in weight, it's supple, fine and elegant, delivering rather a herbaceous expression of cherry/plum fruit framed by a slightly insipid spine of green-edged tannin.

2003	87	2008	2011+
2002	84	2007	2010
2001	84	2006	2009
2000	89	2008	2012+
1999	93	2007	2011
1998	95	2010	2018
1997	89	2002	2005+
1996	95	2004	2008
1995	94	2003	2007
1994	93	2002	2006
1993	94	2001	2005
1992	93	2004	2012
1991	91	1999	2003

Diamond Valley

PO Box 4255, Croydon Hills Vic 3136. Tel: (03) 9722 0840. Fax: (03) 9722 2373.
Website: www.diamondvalley.com.au   Email: enq@diamondvalley.com.au

Region: **Yarra Valley** Winemaker: **James Lance** Viticulturist: **David Lance** Chief Executive: **Graeme Rathbone**

Diamond Valley was originally developed by David and Cathy Lance. Now owned by Graeme Rathbone, its home vineyard occupies a site capable of fine chardonnay, pinot and red Bordeaux varieties. The Close Planted vineyard (for pinot) is a separate planting on the same site, but will apparently be sold under a different brand in future. The blue labelled Yarra Valley wines are sourced from various sites in the Yarra Valley region. Without question, its best wines are made from pinot noir.

CLOSE-PLANTED PINOT NOIR

RATING **2**

Yarra Valley $50–$99
Current vintage: 2002   95

Silky, velvet-like pinot whose deep aromas of dark cherries and berries reveal earthy, charcuterie-like undertones. Its complete and succulent palate reveals layers of dark fruits harmoniously interwoven with restrained oak. With meaty complexity and undertones of forest floor, it finishes long and savoury.

2002	95	2007	2010+
2001	95	2006	2009
2000	88	2002	2005+
1999	91	2002	2005
1997	94	1999	2002
1996	94	2001	2004
1995	93	1997	2000

ESTATE CABERNET MERLOT

RATING **3**

Yarra Valley $30–$49
Current vintage: 2000 93

A lightly herbal, but stylish blend of elegance and balance. Its violet-like perfume of raspberries, red-currants and slightly meaty, cedary oak reveals nuances of dried herbs. Medium to full weight, it's smooth and supple, with a sweet and lively expression of small red berries, cherries and plums framed by fine tannins and restrained oak.

2000	93	2012	2020
1999	92	2007	2011+
1998	92	2003	2006+
1997	93	2005	2009+
1996	88	2001	2004+
1994	90	2002	2006+
1992	85	2000	2004
1991	85	1999	2003
1990	93	1998	2002

ESTATE CHARDONNAY

RATING **3**

Yarra Valley $30–$49
Current vintage: 2004 88

A pretty, buttery, lightly herbal and shorter-term chardonnay whose floral, peach and melon-like aromas are backed by nuances of grapefruit, quince, restrained oak and light, creamy and leesy under-tones. Soft and smooth, it is already revealing some toasty development, finishing with pleasing length, brightness of fruit and clean acidity.

2004	88	2006	2009
2003	93	2005	2008+
2002	94	2007	2010
2001	87	2003	2006
2000	92	2005	2008
1999	88	2001	2004
1998	89	2000	2003
1997	88	1999	2002
1996	87	1998	2001
1995	92	2000	2003
1994	93	2002	2006

ESTATE PINOT NOIR

RATING **3**

Yarra Valley $50–$99
Current vintage: 2004 88

A flavoursome but slightly unconvincing pinot whose floral, spicy and slightly confectionary perfume of raspberries, cherries and sweet vanilla oak precedes a juicy, smooth and generous palate with slightly under and over-ripe charac-ters. Vibrant flavours of red cherries and berries are backed by currant-like influences and framed by slightly metallic tannins with greenish edges.

2004	88	2006	2009+
2003	90	2005	2008
2002	93	2007	2010
2001	90	2003	2006+
1999	93	2007	2011
1998	94	2003	2006
1997	96	2002	2005+
1996	89	2001	2004
1995	90	2000	2003
1994	88	1996	1999

YARRA VALLEY CABERNET MERLOT

RATING **5**

Yarra Valley $20–$29
Current vintage: 2002 90

A smooth, fine and very attractive early-drinking blend with a light herbal aroma of sweet red berries, forest floor nuances and cedar/vanilla oak. Long and creamy, it's supple and restrained, delivering pristine, if slightly minty berry/plum fruit and lightly smoky oak with fine, tight tannins and refresh-ing acids.

2002	90	2004	2007+
2001	82	2003	2006
2000	87	2002	2005
1999	87	2001	2004+

YARRA VALLEY CHARDONNAY

RATING **4**

Yarra Valley $20–$29
Current vintage: 2004 89

Complex, smoky and lightly funky aromas of lime and melon, with nutty, creamy and oatmeal-like undertones of leesy complexity and minerals. Moderately generous and juicy, it's smooth and even, delivering vibrant chardonnay flavour, pleasing oak influences and finishing dry and savoury, with attractive tightness and balance.

2004	89	2006	2009
2003	90	2005	2008
2002	90	2003	2004+
2000	90	2002	2005
1999	90	2001	2004
1998	88	2000	2003
1997	91	1999	2000
1996	89	1998	2001

YARRA VALLEY PINOT NOIR

RATING **5**

Yarra Valley $20–$29
Current vintage: 2004 86

An unusually peppery and spicy perfume of tomato-like red cherries and plums is backed by wild, almost funky undertones, plus nuances of cloves and cinnamon. An initial burst of spicy raspberry and maraschino cherry flavour then becomes rather thin and hollow, finishing quite simple and deficient in fruit.

2004	86	2006	2009
2003	90	2005	2008
2002	89	2004	2007
2001	89	2003	2006
2000	89	2002	2005
1999	90	2001	2004
1998	90	2000	2003
1997	94	1998	2001
1996	91	1998	2001
1994	85	1996	1999

Domaine A

105 Tea Tree Road, Campania Tas 7026. Tel: (03) 6260 4174. Fax: (03) 6260 4390.
Website: www.domaine-a.com.au Email: althaus@domaine-a.com.au

Region: **Coal River Valley** Winemaker: **Peter Althaus** Viticulturist: **Peter Althaus** Chief Executive: **Peter Althaus**

Domaine A is the label for the small volumes of handcrafted wines Peter Althaus bottles from his Stoney Vineyard in the Coal River Valley. Perhaps extraordinarily for a Tasmanian vineyard, its most consistent performer is its Cabernet Sauvignon, which in years like 1991, 1994, 1995, 1998, 2000 and 2001 has acquired the depth of flavour and structure one might expect from a good Bordeaux growth. The Pinot Noir can also be excellent, while the Lady A Fumé Blanc (a varietal but wood-aged sauvignon blanc) is an exciting addition to this book.

CABERNET SAUVIGNON

RATING **3**

Coal River Valley $50–$99
Current vintage: 2001 94

A long, firm and cedary cabernet likely to become deeper, more profound and impactful before it becomes finer and more elegant with longer cellaring. It opens with a dusty fragrance of cedar, mulberries and ripe black and red berries before revealing nuances of mint, dried herbs and chocolate/vanilla oak. Firm, tight and powdery, its slightly sour-edged palate of dark berry/plum flavours, fine-grained oak and meaty, lightly reductive complexity finishes with mineral undertones.

2001	94	2013	2021
2000	96	2012	2020+
1999	90	2007	2011+
1998	93	2010	2018
1997	87	2005	2009
1995	94	2007	2015
1994	93	2006	2014
1993	89	2005	2013
1992	90	2004	2012
1991	95	2003	2011
1990	87	1995	1998

LADY A FUMÉ BLANC

RATING **4**

Coal River Valley $30–$49
Current vintage: 2003 91

Smoky, complex and savoury, this heavily worked sauvignon blanc has a wild, floral and slightly meaty fragrance of lime marmalade, passionfruit and tropical aromas backed by lightly grassy, bacony undertones and sweet vanilla oak. Smooth and richly textured, its fruit is presently slightly subdued beneath a weight of meaty, spicy and smoky oak complexity, but finishes with a salty suggestion of soy sauce and a refreshing lemon rind acidity.

2003	91	2008	2011+
2002	94	2007	2010
2001	82	2003	2006

PINOT NOIR

RATING **3**

Coal River Valley $50–$99
Current vintage: 2003 90

An assertive, powerful and slightly hard-edged pinot whose spicy clove and cinnamon-like fragrance of cherries, red plums and sweet cedar/vanilla oak is backed by nuances of mint and menthol. Its firm, polished palate of sour-edged cherry, currant and plum flavours is framed by fine, drying tannins. Backed by smoky oak and minty undertones of forest floor, it should become brighter and more elegant with time.

2003	90	2008	2001+
2001	92	2009	2013
2000	92	2005	2008+
1999	89	2004	2007
1998	95	2003	2006+
1997	94	2005	2009
1995	89	1997	2000
1994	95	1999	2002+
1992	94	1997	2000+

Dominique Portet

870 Maroondah Highway, Coldstream Vic 3770. Tel: (03) 5962 5760. Fax: (03) 5962 4938.
Website: www.dominiqueportet.com.au Email: dominique@dominiqueportet.com.au

Regions: **Yarra Valley, Heathcote** Winemakers: **Dominique Portet, Scott Baker** Chief Executive: **Dominique Portet**

Dominique Portet is the highly experienced and affable French winemaker whose long association with Taltarni introduced him to thousands of Australian wine drinkers. Now, having gone out on his own, he is based on the Maroondah Highway, where he makes a number of regional wines from the Yarra Valley and Heathcote. While Portet's natural inclination is to make reds of finesse and polish, recent Heathcote vintages have been too hot to avoid cooked and soupy characters. The Yarra Valley Sauvignon Blanc offers a real point of difference.

CABERNET SAUVIGNON
RATING **5**

Heathcote (or Yarra Valley)	$30–$49	2004	89	2009	2012
Current vintage: 2004	89	2002	86	2004	2007+
		2001	90	2006	2009+
		2000	88	2005	2008

Sweet-fruited, smooth and elegant, this honest and flavoursome cabernet has a juicy aroma of blackberries, red berries and fragrant cedar/dark chocolate and vanilla oak influences. Long and even, its fine-grained palate of vibrant berry fruit is framed by dusty, silky tannins, finishing with a pleasing lengthy of flavour.

HEATHCOTE SHIRAZ
RATING **5**

Heathcote	$30–$49	2004	77	2006	2009+
Current vintage: 2004	77	2003	83	2005	2008
		2002	89	2004	2007+
		2001	82	2003	2006
		2000	89	2005	2008

Meaty, cooked and dull, with a spicy and rather flat aroma of dehydrated fruit. It offers some fruit towards the front of the palate but dries out, lacking length, freshness and intensity.

SAUVIGNON BLANC
RATING **4**

Yarra Valley	$20–$29	2005	93	2005	2006
Current vintage: 2005	93	2004	91	2004	2005+
		2003	90	2003	2004+
		2002	81	2002	2003
		2000	87	2000	2000

This finely structured and very drinkable sauvignon blanc has a lightly dusty, herbal and restrained aroma of pristine gooseberry, melon, passionfruit and cassis-like flavour backed by light suggestions of vanilla oak. Supple and elegant, its vibrant palate offers lively fruit flavour and clarity offset by herbal undertones and light oak qualities, finishing long, clean and citrusy.

Dromana Estate

555 Old Moorooduc Road, Tuerong Vic 3933. Tel: (03) 5974 4400. Fax: (03) 5974 1155.
Website: www.dromanaestate.com.au Email: info@dromanaestate.com.au

Region: **Mornington Peninsula** Winemaker: **Rollo Crittenden** Viticulturist: **Rollo Crittenden**
Chief Executive: **Richard Green**

Now part of a publicly listed company and based in a new winery, Dromana Estate was one of the first producers on Victoria's Mornington Peninsula. Its wines are sound and competent, but lack the pace-setting flair that helped to launch the brand. Given that the region experienced such good vintages in 2004 and 2005, it's fair to expect some exciting new releases under this label.

CABERNET MERLOT
RATING **3**

Mornington Peninsula	$20–$29	2003	89	2008	2011
Current vintage: 2003	89	2002	81	2004	2007
		2001	93	2009	2013
		2000	93	2008	2012+
		1999	92	2007	2011
		1998	90	2006	2010
		1997	92	2005	2009
		1996	83	1998	2001+
		1995	86	2000	2003
		1994	86	1999	2002+
		1993	86	1998	2001+

A supple and silky-smooth cabernet blend with floral aromas of small red and black berries, dried herbs and dusty cedar/vanilla oak. Its vibrant and medium-weight expression of mulberries and black berry flavours reveals lightly herbaceous undertones.

RATING **4**

Mornington Peninsula $20–$29
Current vintage: 2003 92

Smoky, meaty and savoury, this generous and maturing chardonnay reveals wild, funky, charcuterie-like aromas of matchstick, dried flowers, minerals and a hint of wet wool. Sumptuous and richly textured, its exotically complex expression of melon and citrusy fruit builds in fruit sweetness as it opens up, finishing with refreshing acids.

2003	92	2005	2008
2002	89	2004	2007
2001	89	2003	2006
2000	82	2001	2002
1999	93	2001	2004
1998	90	2000	2003
1997	87	1999	2002
1996	88	1998	2001
1995	90	1997	2000

PINOT NOIR

RATING **5**

Mornington Peninsula $20–$29
Current vintage: 2003 82

Dull and meaty, with rather cooked aromas of plums and cherries, this rather sappy pinot noir is simple and green-edged. Medium in weight, it lacks length and genuine ripeness.

2003	82	2005	2008
2002	89	2004	2007
2001	85	2002	2003+
2000	90	2005	2008
1999	87	2001	2004
1998	88	1999	2000
1997	91	2002	2005
1996	93	2001	2004

RESERVE CHARDONNAY

RATING **4**

Mornington Peninsula $30–$49
Current vintage: 2002 92

A more powerful expression than the 'standard' chardonnay, with a closed, but creamy leesy bouquet of oatmeal, melon and green olives, lifted by vanilla oak. Sumptuous but very restrained and stylish, with concentrated peach/pineapple and green olive flavours elegantly presented before a tangy finish of soft, vibrant acids. Tightly integrated, with good refinement.

2002	92	2004	2007+
2001	91	2003	2006+
2000	90	2002	2005
1998	91	2003	2006
1997	95	2002	2005
1996	91	2001	2004
1995	92	1997	2000
1994	94	1996	1999

RESERVE PINOT NOIR

RATING **4**

Mornington Peninsula $30–$49
Current vintage: 2002 88

Dusty, leafy aromas of cherries and slightly stewed plums are tightly integrated with restrained scents of cedary chocolate/vanilla oak. Forward and intense, its slightly meaty, pruney palate does present some sweet currant, plum and berry flavours, offering a good length of velvet-like texture.

2002	88	2004	2007
2001	89	2003	2006
2000	85	2002	2005
1998	91	2000	2003+
1997	95	2002	2005+
1996	94	2001	2005+
1995	93	2000	2003+

Elderton

3–5 Tanunda Road, Nuriootpa SA 5355. Tel: (08) 8568 7878. Fax: (08) 8568 7879.
Website: www.eldertonwines.com.au Email: elderton@eldertonwines.com.au
Region: **Barossa Valley** Winemaker: **Richard Langford** Viticulturist: **David Young** Chief Executive: **Lorraine Ashmead**
Elderton is a very successful Barossa wine producer with significant export markets. Best known for its smooth, spicy and ultra-ripe reds, it can produce the occasionally elegant and polished surprise like the beautifully balanced and brambly Ashmead Cabernet Sauvignon from 2002 and the sumptuous but ultra-ripe Command Shiraz from 2004. I also have a soft spot for the meaty and smoky Shiraz 2004.

ASHMEAD CABERNET SAUVIGNON

RATING **5**

Barossa Valley $50–$99
Current vintage: 2002 93

A deeply accentuated, heady and minty aroma of dark olives and plums, cassis and menthol, backed by nuances of graphite and iodide. Medium to full in weight, it's concentrated but surprisingly elegant and polished, even finely crafted and restrained. It easily carries its chocolate/vanilla oak, while there's just a hint of currant about its brambly fruit. Framed by firmish, but velvet-smooth tannins.

2002	93	2010	2014+
2000	88	2002	2005+
1999	89	2007	2011+
1998	89	2006	2010

CABERNET SAUVIGNON

RATING **5**

Barossa Valley $20–$29
Current vintage: 2002 91

A smooth, minty and regional Barossa red whose lively and generous small berry flavours are offset by measured oak treatment and refreshing acids. Its violet-like aromas of briary berry and plum fruit, sweet oak and a whiff of capsicum overlie a hint of meatiness, while its smooth and harmonious palate has length and vitality.

2002	91	2007	2010+
2001	86	2003	2006
2000	89	2005	2008
1999	87	2004	2007
1998	91	2003	2006
1997	87	1999	2002+
1996	89	2001	2004
1995	88	2000	2003
1994	93	1999	2002
1993	91	1998	2001
1992	88	1997	2000
1991	91	1996	1999

COMMAND SHIRAZ

RATING **4**

Barossa Valley $50–$99
Current vintage: 2002 93

Quite a sophisticated but extremely ripe shiraz that has retained plenty of vibrant, bright fruit character. Its juicy notes of cassis, dark plums, blackberries and sweet cedar/mocha oak are backed by spicy nuances, with suggestions of mint and menthol. Smooth and sumptuous, its oaky and velvet-like palate underpins its blackberry and dark plum flavours with riper, meaty currant-like influences and assertive, smoky and dark chocolate oak. It finishes with lingering spicy, raisined and savoury characters.

2002	93	2014	2022
2001	89	2009	2013
2000	93	2008	2012+
1999	90	2004	2007
1998	89	2006	2010
1997	83	2002	2005
1996	89	2004	2008
1995	91	2003	2007
1994	94	2002	2006
1993	89	2001	2005
1992	95	2000	2004+
1990	92	1995	1998
1988	87	1996	2000
1987	94	1999	2004

CSM CABERNET SAUVIGNON SHIRAZ MERLOT

RATING **5**

Barossa Valley $30–$49
Current vintage: 2001 83

Rather clumsy and both over-and under-ripe, with jammy, cooked aromas of stressed fruit backed by greenish suggestions of mint and menthol. Simultaneously herbal and meaty, with a slightly metallic grip of sappy tannin, the palate relies on its oak for sweetness. It's built with a firm spine of gritty tannin, but lacks sufficient fruit for it to be genuinely balanced.

2001	83	2006	2009
2000	86	2002	2005
1999	90	2004	2007+
1998	86	2003	2006
1997	88	1999	2002
1996	87	2001	2004
1995	88	1998	2001
1994	90	1999	2002

SHIRAZ

RATING **5**

Barossa Valley $20–$29
Current vintage: 2004 90

Meaty, ripe and mouthfilling, this smooth and pliant shiraz has a floral aroma of raspberries, blackberries and cassis backed by assertive and lightly toasty vanilla oak, with undertones of cloves, cinnamon and white pepper. Round and generous, its juicy, vibrant palate of slightly jammy and sour-edged fruit is tightly knit with smoky savoury oak and framed by firm but gentle tannins.

2004	90	2009	2012
2003	88	2005	2008+
2002	89	2004	2007+
2001	89	2003	2006+
2000	90	2005	2008
1999	83	2001	2004
1998	90	2003	2006
1997	87	1999	2002
1996	87	1998	2003+
1995	90	2000	2003
1994	89	1999	2002
1993	90	1995	1998
1992	88	2000	2004
1991	90	1999	2003

A
B
C
D
E
F
G
H
I
J
K
L
M
N
O
P
Q
R
S
T
U
V
W
X
Y
Z

Epis

812 Black Forest Drive, Woodend Vic 3442. Tel: (03) 5427 1204. Fax: (03) 5427 1204
Email: domaineepis@iprimus.com.au
Region: **Macedon Ranges** Winemaker: **Stuart Anderson** Viticulturist: **Alec Epis** Chief Executive: **Alec Epis**

Epis is a small Macedon Ranges wine producer that is starting to create an impact on Victorian wine many times the size and scale of its production. The 'home' chardonnay and pinot noir vineyard near Woodend is the site of the winery, and produces tiny yields of deeply fruited and tightly structured wine. Its owner, Alec Epis, also owns the original Flynn & Williams cabernet sauvignon plantings at Kyneton, to which he has added the merlot that has successfully fleshed out this individual vineyard Bordeaux blend.

CHARDONNAY

RATING 2

Macedon Ranges	$30–$49
Current vintage: 2004	95

A fine, austere and sculpted chardonnay with minerality and brightness to burn. Its youthful aromas of peach and grapefruit are slightly over-awed by fresh, fine-grained vanilla oak, with undertones of dried flowers, cloves and cinnamon. Long, taut and savoury, its palate marries restrained flavours of peach, pear and apple with crunchy acids and a lingering minerality. It should flesh out in the bottle, allowing the fruit to become richer and more expressive.

2004	95	2009	2012+
2003	95	2008	2011
2001	96	2006	2009+
2000	95	2005	2008+
1998	95	2003	2006+

EPIS & WILLIAMS CABERNET MERLOT

RATING 3

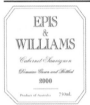

Macedon Ranges	$30–$49
Current vintage: 2004	95

Fine-grained and seamless, this exemplary cool climate cabernet blend has a vibrant perfume of blackberries, violets, dark plums and cherries backed by cedar/vanilla oak and minty, smoky, dark chocolate-like undertones. Merlot contributes to the wine's plumpness and sweet dark cherry-like fruit, ably supporting the cabernet's tightly focused and palate-staining blackberry and plum flavours. Excellent length, with lingering undertones of dried herbs and a hint of mint.

2004	95	2012	2016+
2003	93	2011	2015+
2002	89	2007	2010+
2001	94	2013	2021
2000	95	2008	2012+
1999	93	2007	2011+

PINOT NOIR

RATING 2

Macedon Ranges	$30–$49
Current vintage: 2004	97

A pinot whose striking depth of fruit and silky texture are very suggestive of Vosne-Romanée. Its heady perfume of rose petals, sweet red cherries and plums reveals undertones of cinnamon and nutmeg, caramel and butter. Its pristine, juicy palate of powerful cherry-like fruit delivers exceptional depth and richness, with a luscious viscosity neatly framed by fine tannins and refreshing acids. Long and savoury, with lingering fruit sweetness and meaty nuances.

2004	97	2006	2009+
2003	96	2008	2011
2001	96	2006	2009+
2000	93	2005	2008+
1998	94	2003	2006+

Evans & Tate

Corner Caves & Metricup Roads, Willyabrup WA 6280. Tel: (08) 9755 6244. Fax: (08) 9755 4362.
Website: www.evansandtate.com.au Email: et@evansandtate.com.au

Region: **Margaret River** Winemaker: **Richard Rowe** Viticulturist: **Murray Edmonds** Chief Executive: **Franklin Tate**

Evans & Tate's financial issues are well known to readers of business columns. This Margaret River-based wine producer now appears very reliant on its four vineyards located in the warmer eastern segment of the Margaret River region. Well handled in the cellar, its wines are relatively simple, lacking intensity and definition. One hopes the company can steer its way to safer waters.

GNANGARA SHIRAZ RATING **5**

Swan Valley $12–$19
Current vintage: 2003   88

Slightly confectionary aromas of sweet raspberries, plums and cassis over peppery suggestions of cloves and cinnamon supported by a light background of chocolate and vanilla oak. A soft and supple expression of a traditional 'Australian Burgundy' style, with a lively core of slightly sour-edged cassis, plums and raspberries framed by fine tannins and soft acids. Finishes with lingering notes of licorice and leather.

2003	88	2008	2011
2002	82	2003	2004
2000	87	2002	2005
1999	80	2000	2000
1998	88	2000	2003+
1997	80	1999	2002
1996	89	1998	2001

MARGARET RIVER CLASSIC RATING **5**

Margaret River $12–$19
Current vintage: 2005   88

A flavoursome, fresh and fruity dry white blend with a lightly grassy and faintly dusty aroma of honeydew melon and passionfruit. Its punchy, forward palate becomes quite fine and shapely towards its lingering, limey finish of refreshing acidity and lemon sherbet flavour. It lacks the opulence of some years, but is tight and shapely.

2005	88	2005	2006+
2004	88	2004	2005
2003	86	2003	2003
2002	88	2002	2003
2001	82	2001	2002
2000	89	2000	2000

MARGARET RIVER SAUVIGNON BLANC SEMILLON RATING **4**

Margaret River $20–$29
Current vintage: 2005   88

Lightly sweaty, herbaceous aromas of melon, citrus and tropical fruits precede a clean, juicy palate whose pleasingly restrained but penetrative fruit finish slightly sappy and metallic. Flavoursome and early-drinking.

2005	88	2006	2007
2004	90	2005	2006
2003	88	2003	2006+
2002	89	2003	2004+
2000	90	2000	2000
1999	90	2000	2000
1998	90	1999	2000

MARGARET RIVER SHIRAZ RATING **4**

Margaret River $20–$29
Current vintage: 2003   84

Light, rather flat aromas of spicy red berries, cloves and cinnamon reveal earthy, meaty undertones. Medium to full in weight, it's smooth but slightly hollow palate of plum and tomato-like fruit lacks real depth and focus. Framed by rather raw and metallic tannins, it finishes slightly dilute.

2003	84	2005	2008+
2002	87	2004	2007+
2001	90	2006	2009
2000	90	2005	2008
1999	90	2004	2007
1998	91	2003	2006+
1997	89	2005	2009
1996	90	2004	2008
1995	92	2007	2015
1994	94	2002	2006
1993	86	2001	2005
1992	93	2000	2004
1991	93	1999	2003

A B C D E F G H I J K L M N O P Q R S T U V W X Y Z

Farr Rising

101 Kelly Lane, Bannockburn, Vic 3331. Tel: (03) 5281 1733. Fax: (03) 5281 1433.
Website: www.byfarr.com.au Email: kalvos@datafast.net.au

Region: **Geelong** Winemaker: **Nick Farr** Viticulturist: **Nick Farr Chief Execuive: Gary Farr**

Nick Farr is the son of Gary Farr, the winemaker who made his reputation at Bannockburn in Victoria. He makes wine at his parents' By Farr winery alongside his father, but has the necessary strength of character to do things his own way. It's early days, but so far the results are particularly encouraging.

CHARDONNAY

RATING **4**

Geelong	$30–$49	2004	90	2006	2009+
Current vintage: 2004	**90**	2003	87	2004	2005+
		2002	91	2004	2007
		2001	89	2003	2006+

A warm, smooth, generous and creamy chardonnay whose fresh aromas of quince, melon and cumquat are backed by suggestions of fig, wheatmeal and lightly charry, buttery vanilla oak. There's perhaps some excessive bacony and toffee-like malolactic influence on the palate, but its broad and juicy expression of peach/melon fruit culminates in a nutty, savoury finish. It finishes a little warm and spirity, but with a lingering core of fruit.

PINOT NOIR

RATING **4**

Geelong	$30–$49	2004	93	2006	2009+
Current vintage: 2004	**93**	2003	90	2008	2011
		2002	85	2004	2007
		2001	85	2003	2006

Supple, sappy and fine-grained, this spicy, meaty and rather funky young pinot reveals an aroma of slightly stewed red cherries backed by earthy and slightly vegetal undertones. Smooth and silky, the palate presents a pleasingly deep core of bright red cherry and plum flavours tightly knit with pliant tannins and restrained oak. Give it time.

Ferngrove

Ferngrove Road, Frankland WA 6396. Tel: (08) 955 2378. Fax: (08) 9855 2368.
Website: www.ferngrove.com.au Email: info@ferngrove.com.au

Region: **Frankland River** Winemaker: **Kim Horton** Viticulturist: **Chris Zur** Chief Executive: **Anthony Wilkes**

Ferngrove's philosophy has obviously been to build its market share by over-delivering on quality at every price-point. It's early days for this emergent winery, and while there's still plenty of refinement to be achieved, I've little doubt that given its present approach, it will become a benchmark operation. From the very affordable 'Symbols' range of varietal wines to the flagship 'The Stirlings' blend of red Bordeaux varieties, Ferngrove's hallmark is its presentation of bright, focused varietal qualities, which it typically delivers with a combination of elegance and structure.

COSSACK RIESLING

RATING **4**

Frankland River	$20–$29	2005	93	2013	2017
Current vintage: 2005	**93**	2004	90	2009	2012+
		2003	90	2005	2008
		2002	94	2007	2010+
		2001	86	2003	2006

A taut, high acid expression of austere and mineral riesling whose lime juice and lemon sherbet aromas reveal lightly musky and smoky undertones of wet stones. Its long and sculpted palate of juicy citrus flavour is tightly harnessed by its acidity, culminating in a lingering and refreshing schisty finish of lingering smoky, reductive complexity.

Fox Creek

Malpas Road, McLaren Vale SA 5171. Tel: (08) 8556 2403. Fax: (08) 8556 2104.
Website: www.foxcreekwines.com Email: brenda@@foxcreekwines.com
Region: **McLaren Vale** Winemakers: **Chris Dix, Scott Zrna** Viticulturist: **Paul Watts**
Chief Executives: **Jim & Helen Watts**

Like several other wineries in McLaren Vale, Fox Creek produced some spectacular red wine in 2004. Its Reserve Shiraz continues to grow in stature, while the earlier-drinking Short Row Shiraz is acquiring consistent quality. These wine share the deep, very meaty and sour-edged fruit characters so typical of the region. Wisely choosing not to release a Reserve Cabernet Sauvignon from 2003, Fox Creek has maintained the standard of this very reliable label.

DUET CABERNET MERLOT

RATING 5

| McLaren Vale | $20–$29 |
| Current vintage: 2004 | 88 |

Brambly, confiture-like aromas of plums, cranberries and blackberries are backed by sweet vanilla and cedary oak with slightly meaty undertones of prunes and dark olives. It's forward, jammy and slightly cooked, with an initially rich expression of plum and berry flavour that loses some freshness down the palate, finishing rather tannic and chewy, with mint and menthol undertones.

2004	88	2009	2012
2003	87	2003	2006+
2002	88	2004	2007
2001	87	2005	2008

JSM SHIRAZ CABERNET FRANC

RATING 4

| McLaren Vale | $20–$29 |
| Current vintage: 2004 | 89 |

An attractive, generous and spicy wine with a grenache-like complement of spicy, blueberry character. Fresh aromas of blackberries, plums and sweet vanilla/cedar oak are lifted by floral and spicy clove and cinnamon influences. Smooth, supple and moderately rich, it's intense, tight and focused, offering a pleasing length of fruit framed by dusty, chalky tannins.

2004	89	2006	2009+
2003	87	2008	2011
2002	88	2004	2007+
2001	91	2003	2006+
2000	90	2002	2005+
1999	89	2001	2004
1998	89	2003	2006
1997	87	1999	2002
1996	84	1998	2001+

RESERVE CABERNET SAUVIGNON

RATING 4

| McLaren Vale | $30–$49 |
| Current vintage: 2004 | 90 |

A sumptuous, deeply flavoured, rather jammy and slightly meaty cabernet whose slightly raw grip of firm tannin should settle down with time. Intense aromas of plums and cassis are backed by mint, menthol and dark chocolate/vanilla oak. Framed by powdery tannin, its briary palate of mulberries, blackberries and dark plums knits tightly with cedary oak, finishing with meaty, dark olive influences.

2004	90	2012	2016+
2002	92	2010	2014+
2001	92	2009	2013+
2000	89	2005	2008
1999	90	2004	2007+
1998	89	2006	2010
1997	90	2005	2009+
1996	92	2004	2008+
1995	88	2000	2003

RESERVE MERLOT

RATING 4

| McLaren Vale | $30–$49 |
| Current vintage: 2001 | 92 |

A firm, generous and honest merlot with a fresh and lightly perfumed bouquet of black and red cherries and sweet, smoky vanilla and mocha oak. Its vibrant, up-front flavours of dark cherries, plums and cassis then reveal more interesting nuances of licorice, tar and game meats. Framed by fine-grained but drying tannins, it finishes with lingering clove and nutmeg-like flavours with balanced chocolate/vanilla oak.

2001	92	2006	2009
2000	90	2005	2008+
1999	88	2001	2004
1998	87	2003	2006+
1997	87	2002	2005+

RESERVE SHIRAZ

RATING **2**

McLaren Vale	$50–$99
Current vintage: 2004	95

A luscious, long and stylish modern shiraz steeped in musky, spicy aromas of blackberries and plums, black pepper, cloves and cinnamon with an assertive but finely integrated background of smoky fine-grained vanilla oak. Its smooth and chocolatey palate of concentrated, briary fruit and spicy oak finishes with savoury, dark olive notes and minerals, plus a lingering core of black fruits.

Year	Score	Drink	Drink
2004	95	2016	2024
2002	93	2010	2014+
2001	96	2013	2021
2000	88	2005	2008
1999	95	2007	2011+
1998	90	2003	2006+
1997	88	2002	2005+
1996	95	2008	2016
1995	89	1997	2002
1994	94	2006	2014

SHORT ROW SHIRAZ

RATING **3**

McLaren Vale	$20–$29
Current vintage: 2004	93

A deliciously intense, vibrant and smooth shiraz packed with penetrative varietal flavour. Deep aromas of plums, cassis and blueberries are laced with spices and backed by smoky, gamey mocha/vanilla oak, with slightly cooked, currant-like undertones. Framed by fine, pliant tannins, its pristine and moderately rich palate of deep, dark and spicy fruit and dark chocolate oak culminates in a lingering dark-fruited finish with minerally undertones of smoked oyster.

Year	Score	Drink	Drink
2004	93	2009	2012
2003	93	2008	2011
2002	88	2004	2007
2001	91	2003	2006+
2000	87	2002	2005
1999	90	2001	2004

VERDELHO

RATING **5**

South Australia	$12–$19
Current vintage: 2005	89

A tangy, fresh and mineral verdelho whose lemon sherbet-like aromas are backed by stony, flinty nuances. Juicy, round and generous, its ripe citrusy and tropical flavours are tightly backed by mineral undertones, finishing clean and refreshing, with a lingering core of intense fruit.

Year	Score	Drink	Drink
2005	89	2007	2010
2004	88	2005	2006+
2003	90	2004	2005+
2002	86	2003	2004
2001	86	2002	2003+
2000	82	2001	2002

Frankland Estate

Frankland Road, Frankland WA 6396. Tel: (08) 9855 1544. Fax: (08) 9855 1549.
Website: www.franklandestate.com.au Email: info@franklandestate.com.au
Region: **Frankland River** Winemakers: **Barrie Smith, Judi Cullam** Viticulturist: **Elizabeth Smith**
Chief Executives: **Barrie Smith, Judi Cullam**

Frankland Estate is a little like two wine companies in one. On one hand, it is a fastidious maker of several individual vineyard rieslings that are made with passion, flair and some inherent measure of risk. On the other, it makes several red wines and a Chardonnay that appear to lack the same levels of attention and dedication. Frankland Estate also deserves huge credit for staging major riesling events around Australia every two years that have done much to increase the awareness of the variety amongst makers, trade and public.

COOLADERRA VINEYARD RIESLING

RATING **3**

Frankland River	$20–$29
Current vintage: 2005	93

Juicy and generous, this tight and mineral riesling has a zesty perfume of lemon, apple and pear and a penetrative, citrusy palate finishing with powdery, slate-like undertones and a lively cut of refreshing acids. It easily has the brightness of fruit to carry its reductive complexity.

Year	Score	Drink	Drink
2005	93	2010	2013
2004	93	2006	2009
2002	94	2007	2010+
2001	94	2006	2009+

ISOLATION RIDGE CABERNET SAUVIGNON

RATING **5**

Frankland River $20–$29
Current vintage: 2003 86

Rustic, earthy and astringent, this meaty and reductive cabernet reveals plenty of dark plum and blackberry flavours, but could perhaps have received some better oak and been bottled in fresher condition.

2003	86	2008	2011+
2002	87	2007	2010
2001	83	2006	2009
1998	84	2003	2006
1997	89	2002	2005
1996	91	2008	2016
1995	87	2007	2015
1994	87	1999	2002
1993	91	2005	2013
1992	88	1997	2000
1991	88	1996	1999

ISOLATION RIDGE RIESLING

RATING **3**

Frankland River $20–$29
Current vintage: 2005 86

Lustrous, spicy and crystalline aromas of lime juice and floral perfume precede a lean and candied palate whose rather varnishy expression of citrusy flavours finishes thin, green and spiky.

2005	86	2007	2010
2004	93	2009	2012
2003	93	2008	2011+
2002	89	2004	2007
2001	95	2006	2009+
2000	93	2005	2008
1999	85	2001	2004
1998	93	2006	2010
1997	88	2002	2005
1996	91	2001	2004
1995	91	2000	2003
1994	88	1999	2002
1993	87	1995	1998
1992	89	1997	2000
1991	90	1993	1996

POISON HILL VINEYARD RIESLING

RATING **3**

Frankland River $20–$29
Current vintage: 2005 88

An unusually complex, meaty and heavily worked riesling whose zesty apple, lime and lemon fruit has a mineral, bath powder-like aspect and whose finish is not merely savoury and reductive, but borders on bitter. That said, the wine's rose petal perfume, slatey texture and overt wild complexity are by no means without interest and individual charm.

2005	88	2007	2010
2004	86	2005	2006
2002	93	2007	2010
2001	95	2006	2009+

Freycinet Vineyard

15919 Tasman Highway, Bicheno Tas 7215. Tel: (03) 6257 8574. Fax: (03) 6257 8454.
Website: www.freycinetvineyard.com.au Email: freycinetwines@tassie.net.au

Region: **East Coast Tasmania** Winemaker: **Claudio Radenti** Viticulturists: **Claudio Radenti & Lindy Bull**
Chief Executive: **Geoff Bull**

Its heat-trap vineyard on Tasmania's temperate east coast provides Freycinet with a fine climate for the ripening of wine grapes, with special preference to chardonnay, pinot noir and riesling. The red Bordeaux varieties do well occasionally, but generally require a very warm and late vintage. Freycinet's Pinot Noir is one of Australia's best and most long-living expressions of the variety, developing genuine gamey character with age.

CABERNET MERLOT

RATING **5**

East Coast Tasmania $30–$49
Current vintage: 2003 86

Earthy, meaty and herbaceous aromas of red cherries, plums and small berries have a sweet oaky background, while its smooth and supple palate of rather shaded fruit offers some elegance and brightness, but finishes slightly under-ripe, green-edged and sappy.

2003	86	2008	2011
2002	81	2004	2007
2001	88	2006	2009
2000	95	2012	2020
1999	89	2005	2007+
1998	93	2006	2010+
1997	87	2002	2005
1995	87	2000	2003
1994	94	2002	2006

CHARDONNAY

RATING **3**

East Coast Tasmania	$30–$49
Current vintage: 2005	**93**

Tightly crafted, this pristine and piercingly flavoured chardonnay has an intense bouquet of pineapple, grapefruit, lemon blossom and melon aromas over creamy, leesy undertones of spicy clove and vanilla oak. Its long and crystalline expression of concentrated citrus and melon fruit overlies a fine chalkiness before finishing with clean, austere and lemony acids.

2005	93	2010	2013+
2004	88	2006	2009
2003	96	2005	2008+
2002	87	2004	2007
2001	88	2003	2006
2000	87	2002	2005
1999	93	2004	2007
1998	90	2000	2003+
1997	87	1999	2002
1996	89	1998	2001
1995	95	2003	2007

PINOT NOIR

RATING **2**

East Coast Tasmania	$50–$99
Current vintage: 2004	**90**

Backed by a firm, drying chassis of powdery tannins, this fragrant and floral pinot reveals vibrant, delicate and confiture-like aromas of cherries, raspberries and underlying spicy elements. Long, lean and supple, it's a linear and high acid style whose deep cherry/berry flavours knit tightly with cedary oak. It should develop well.

2004	90	2009	2012
2003	94	2008	2011+
2002	90	2004	2007+
2001	95	2006	2009+
2000	92	2005	2008
1999	93	2004	2007+
1998	95	2006	2010
1997	93	2005	2009
1996	89	2001	2004
1995	93	2000	2003+
1994	95	1999	2002+

RIESLING

RATING **3**

East Coast Tasmania	$20–$29
Current vintage: 2005	**93**

An elegant, modern riesling whose floral aromas of lime juice, mineral and bath powder reveal candy-like undertones. Long, lean and elegant, its tightly focused lime juice and lemon flavours are tartly wrapped with fresh acids, culminating in a drying, austere and sculpted finish.

2005	93	2010	2013+
2004	94	2009	2012+
2003	95	2011	2015+
2002	93	2007	2010
2001	88	2003	2006+
2000	95	2005	2008
1999	92	2004	2007
1998	94	2006	2010

Gapsted Wines

Great Alpine Road, Gapsted Vic 3737. Tel: (03) 5751 1383. Fax: (03) 5751 1368.
website: www.gapstedwines.com.au Email: admin@gapstedwines.com.au

Regions: **King Valley, Alpine Valleys** Winemakers: **Shayne Cunningham & Michael Cope-Williams**
Viticulturist: **John Cavedon** Chief Executive: **Shayne Cunningham**

Gapsted is the brand owned by a contract wine producer in northern Victoria, the Victorian Alps Wine Company, whose wines feature the canopy system chosen to maximise sunlight penetration and fruit exposure in this chilly segment of the viticultural world. The company has made a feature of relatively new varieties for the Australian scene, such as barbera, petit manseng, saperavi and tempranillo. In my view its best wines still come from the more traditional varieties, cabernet sauvignon especially. The 2002 release is another polished example.

BALLERINA CANOPY CABERNET SAUVIGNON

RATING **4**

King Valley	$20–$29
Current vintage: 2002	**91**

Framed by fine, loose-knit firm tannins and backed by cedar/vanilla oak, this elegant and handsomely crafted cabernet has a fresh perfume of violets, cassis and dark plums backed by undertones of dried herbs, chocolate and vanilla. Medium to full in weight, it's brightly lit, delivering an intense and pristine expression of lightly herbal cool climate flavours of cassis, mulberry and dark plums.

2002	91	2010	2014+
2001	88	2006	2009+
2000	92	2008	2012+
1999	87	2007	2011
1998	90	2006	2010+

BALLERINA CANOPY MERLOT

King Valley, Alpine Valleys	$20–$29	2002	88	2007	2010
Current vintage: 2002	88	2001	89	2006	2009
		2000	87	2005	2008
		1999	90	2007	2011

A pretty varietal merlot whose herbal, tobaccoey aromas of red cherries, plums and restrained cedar/vanilla oak precede a soft, plump and juicy palate of cherry/plum flavours backed by restrained vanilla oak and framed by fine-grained, powdery tannins. There's a faint herbaceousness that is likely to become more cigarboxy in time.

Gembrook Hill

2850 Launching Place Road, Gembrook Vic 3783. Tel: (03) 5968 1622. Fax: (03) 5968 1699.
Website: www.gembrookhill.com.au Email: enquiries@gembrookhill.com.au
Region: **Yarra Valley** Winemaker: **Timo Mayer** Viticulturist: **Ian Marks** Chief Executive: **Ian Marks**

Gembrook Hill is a genuinely cool-climate and high altitude Yarra Valley vineyard that is steadily coming of age. Its Sauvignon Blanc can be spectacular; its Chardonnay long and mineral. The company has recently added a second but generally richer and meatier pinot noir to its range. It's sourced from the vineyard owned by its winemaker, Timo Mayer, and is named after him.

CHARDONNAY

Yarra Valley	$30–$49	2004	87	2006	2009+
Current vintage: 2004	87	2003	87	2005	2008
		2002	84	2004	2007
		2001	95	2006	2009
		2000	92	2005	2008
		1997	86	1999	2002
		1995	91	2000	2003
		1994	89	1999	2002
		1993	92	1998	2001

A simple, rather herbal chardonnay whose cashew-like aromas of tropical fruits, melon and citrus reveal candied, sweet corn-like and butterscotch elements. Lacking great length and ripeness, its confectionary palate finishes greenish and steely, but should flesh out for the short to medium term.

MAYER VINEYARD PINOT NOIR

Yarra Valley	$30–$49	2004	90	2009	2012
Current vintage: 2004	90	2003	93	2005	2008
		2002	92	2007	2010+

A very well made and stylish pinot. While it could use a little more ripeness and stuffing, it's likely to build in colour, structure and intensity with time in the bottle. There's a hint of dried herbs beneath its aromas of rose petals, raspberries and red cherries, while its palate is fine and silky, with a pleasing sappiness. Sweet red berry/cherry fruit with undertones of mint and menthol are supported by a genuine structure of firmish and slightly drying tannins.

PINOT NOIR

Yarra Valley	$30–$49	2004	88	2006	2009
Current vintage: 2004	88	2003	91	2008	2011
		2002	87	2007	2010
		2001	93	2003	2006+
		2000	94	2005	2008
		1998	91	2003	2006
		1997	89	1999	2002

Funky and perfumed, with some reductive charcuterie-like complexity, this sappy, charming and smoky pinot has an earthy bouquet of sweet red berries and cherries. Smooth and silky, its slightly forward and sappy palate of pleasingly sweet red fruit falls a little short, before a slightly green-edged and herbaceous finish.

SAUVIGNON BLANC

RATING 3

Yarra Valley	$30–$49		
Current vintage: 2004	**87**		

Just lacking the sought-after brightness and vivaciousness expected of this variety, this otherwise honest and flavoursome wine presents rather a pungent and slightly sweaty aroma of passionfruit and gooseberries with grassy and floral undertones. Generous and oily, it culminates in a slightly metallic finish of steely acids.

2004	87	2005	2006+
2003	93	2005	2008
2002	93	2004	2007
2001	90	2003	2006
2000	90	2002	2005
1999	86	2000	2001
1998	94	2000	2003

Geoff Weaver

2 Gilpin Lane, Mitcham SA 5062. Tel: (08) 8272 2105. Fax: (08) 8271 0177.
Website: www.geoffweaver.com.au Email: weaver@adelaide.on.net
Region: **Lenswood** Winemaker: **Geoff Weaver** Viticulturist: **Geoff Weaver** Chief Executive: **Geoff Weaver**
Sadly, Geoff Weaver no longer makes his Cabernet Merlot blend. I agree that recent wines have been rather herbaceous, but had hoped that with increasing vine age (not to mention the effects of global warming), the fruit might ripen more fully. That said, Weaver is a very convincing maker of white wines whose Chardonnay, finely sculpted Riesling and savoury Sauvignon Blanc are each very consistent and vibrant.

CHARDONNAY

RATING 4

Lenswood	$30–$49		
Current vintage: 2005	**91**		

Complex and oxidative, with a polished, oaky fragrance of delicate lemony fruit backed by nuances of wheatmeal, lime juice and minerals, this dry and elegant chardonnay should develop even more complexity. Long and smooth, its newish creamy, nutty oak influences support its attractive flavours of apple, pear and peach, before a lingering dry, austere and shapely finish of vibrant acidity.

2005	91	2007	2010+
2001	93	2003	2006+
2000	86	2002	2005
1999	84	2001	2004
1998	88	2003	2006
1997	94	2002	2005+
1996	92	1998	2001
1995	94	2000	2003+
1994	90	1999	2002

RIESLING

RATING 3

Adelaide Hills	$20–$29		
Current vintage: 2005	**93**		

Delicate floral aromas of lime juice and minerals precede a fine, supple, clear and stylish palate that delivers a lingering core of juicy citrus fruit culminating in a chalky, dry and slaty finish of some austerity. There's plenty of concentrated flavour and some admirable elegance and refinement.

2005	93	2013	2017
2004	91	2009	2012+
2003	93	2008	2011+
2001	91	2006	2009+
2000	93	2008	2012+
1999	92	2007	2011
1998	93	2003	2006
1997	94	2005	2009
1996	87	1998	2001
1995	92	2003	2007
1994	77	1995	1996

SAUVIGNON BLANC

RATING 4

Lenswood	$20–$29		
Current vintage: 2005	**93**		

A spicy, complex and shapely sauvignon blanc with a delicate and lightly grassy perfume of gooseberries and citrusy fruit plus a supple, taut and chalky palate that finishes with definition and austerity. Long and dry, with persistent flavours of melon, gooseberries and lemon, it reveals undertones of minerals and licorice, before a lingering briney finish.

2005	93	2007	2010
2004	91	2005	2006+
2003	89	2004	2005+
2002	94	2003	2004+
2001	87	2001	2002
2000	87	2001	2002
1999	84	2000	2001
1998	94	2000	2003

Giaconda

Corner Wangaratta & McClay Roads, Beechworth Vic 3747. Tel: (03) 5727 0246. Fax: (03) 5727 0246.
Website: www.giaconda.com.au Email: sales@giaconda.com.au

Region: **Beechworth** Winemaker: **Rick Kinzbrunner** Viticulturist: **Rick Kinzbrunner**
Chief Executive: **Rick Kinzbrunner**

After a year virtually out of the trade due to the bushfire-affected 2003 vintage, Giaconda enjoyed a fine but rather different season in 2004. Pick of the wines for mine is the Shiraz, another smoky, seamless and exotically spiced wine in its short but strong lineage. The Cabernet Sauvignon also fared especially well, delivering intense, classically varietal qualities framed by an excellent spine of fine, drying tannin. A little more sumptuous and perhaps a shade more advanced — although I would like to taste it again in future to confirm these impressions — the Chardonnay is again richly complex and smooth. The Pinot Noir is another very promising wine, and a worthy successor to the excellent 2002 vintage.

AEOLIA ROUSSANNE

RATING 2

Beechworth $50–$99
Current vintage: 2005   93

Musky and floral, with aromas of pears and a heady perfume of almost traminer-like spiciness, this generous and savoury roussanne has its share of wild, meaty development. Its lingering, juicy core of citrus and pawpaw flavour is underpinned by a fine, powdery texture, while it culminates in a fractionally sweet finish of tangy, mineral acids. Not as punchy as some of its predecessors; but perhaps a little tighter.

2005	93	2007	2010
2004	94	2006	2009+
2003	94	2005	2008
2002	92	2004	2007
2001	94	2003	2006
2000	95	2002	2005+

CABERNET SAUVIGNON

RATING 3

Beechworth $50–$99
Current vintage: 2004   95

Smooth and seamless, this finely crafted cabernet has a lightly herbal aroma that opens with nuances of dried herbs and snap pea, but gradually reveals a greater volume of cassis, blackberries and sweet cedar/vanilla oak. Tightly knit around a firm spine of dusty, drying tannin, it's lightly jammy, with intense small berry fruit backed by undertones of mint and dried herbs. Beautifully focused, it's reminiscent of the delightful 1991 vintage, although the oak and tannin are better this time.

2004	95	2016	2024+
2003	80	2005	2008
2002	95	2014	2022
2001	90	2006	2009+
1999	96	2011	2019
1998	93	2006	2010
1997	92	2005	2009
1996	90	2004	2008+
1995	94	2003	2007
1994	87	1999	2002+
1993	83	1995	1998
1992	87	1997	2000+
1991	93	2003	2011
1990	93	2002	2010

CHARDONNAY

RATING 1

Beechworth $100–$199
Current vintage: 2004   93

Stylistically, perhaps, this wine has more to do with Puligny than the more Meursault-like vintages of the past. Its lightly smoky and floral aromas of grapefruit and lemon rind, honeysuckle and nougat reveal mineral undertones of wet stones and meaty suggestions of leesy complexity. Typically concentrated, long, creamy and effortlessly smooth, the elegant and almost fluffy palate delivers deep flavours of peach, nectarine, melon and grapefruit with a slightly brassy and candied aspect. It finishes long, savoury and harmonious, with perhaps a shade more development than expected.

2004	93	2009	2012
2002	97	2007	2010+
2001	91	2003	2006
2000	94	2005	2008
1999	94	2001	2004+
1998	97	2006	2010
1997	92	2002	2005
1996	98	2001	2004+
1995	96	2000	2004+
1994	95	2002	2006
1993	94	1998	2001+
1992	96	2000	2004+
1991	95	1999	2003
1990	95	1998	2002
1989	91	1994	1997+

NANTUA LES DEUX (Chardonnay Roussanne)

RATING 4

Beechworth	$50–$99
Current vintage: 2005	**89**

Very generous and quite advanced, with a spicy, mealy fragrance of flowers and fresh bark, melon and grapefruit, plus smoky, creamy, leesy undertones of nutty and clove-like complexity. Forward and buttery, its juicy and honeyed palate of vibrant citrus/melon fruit is framed by a slightly hard-edged acidity, finishing with a note of buttered corn.

2005	89	2007	2010
2004	91	2006	2009
2002	88	2003	2004+
2000	91	2002	2005

PINOT NOIR

RATING 5

Beechworth	$50–$99
Current vintage: 2004	**94**

Fine and silky, this elegant and tightly knit wine needs time to evolve into a Volnay-like expression of pinot. Already quite evolved, it reveals rustic, reductive and briary scents of dark plums, red cherries, smoked meats and dried herbs. Dark and penetrative, supported by dusty, grainy tannins, it's supple and restrained, delivering pristine cherry/plum fruit that should steadily build with time in the bottle.

2004	94	2012	2016
2002	95	2010	2014
2001	88	2003	2006
2000	86	2002	2005
1999	84	2001	2004
1998	89	2003	2006
1997	86	1999	2002
1996	83	1998	2001
1995	77	1996	1997
1994	82	1996	1999
1993	86	1995	1998
1992	93	2000	2004+
1991	94	1996	1999
1990	87	1995	1998
1989	97	2001	2009

WARNER VINEYARD SHIRAZ

RATING 2

Beechworth	$100–$199
Current vintage: 2004	**96**

Heady, musky and exotically spiced, its ethereal and peppery perfume of blackberries, dark plums, cassis and mocha/dark chocolate oak has a meaty ripeness and an undercurrent of dried herbs. Full to medium in weight, its bright, briary flavours of sour-edged blackberries and dark plums reveal smoky, rustic and charcuterie-like nuances and spicy suggestions of licorice. The tannins are fine, drying and bony. Very seamless and balanced, it's complete, complex and savoury, with more than a suggestion of Hermitage.

2004	96	2012	2016+
2002	98	2014	2022
2001	95	2009	2013
2000	93	2008	2012
1999	96	2007	2011
1998	88	2000	2003+

Giant Steps

10–12 Briarty Road, Coldstream Vic 3770. Tel: (03) 5962 6111. Fax: (03) 5962 6199.
Website: www.giant-steps.com.au Email: mail@giant-steps.com.au

Region: **Yarra Valley** Winemaker: **Steve Flamsteed** Viticulturist: **Sharon Hebbard** Chief Executive: **Phil Sexton**

Phil Sexton, founder of the Devil's Lair vineyard and winery in Margaret River and an experienced operator in the small brewery and hospitality industry, has crossed the Nullarbor with his wife, Allison, to establish this 47 hectare vineyard on ancient rocky gravel-clay soils overlooking the Yarra Valley. The first few vintages have shown that the site can produce some spectacular Chardonnay and some fine, structured Pinot Noir.

CHARDONNAY

RATING 5

Yarra Valley	$20–$29
Current vintage: 2004	**92**

A pristine and stylish chardonnay whose generous flavours of cumquat, peach, nectarine and melon are supported by toasty vanilla oak and a complex background of creamy, leesy influences. There's a light smokiness about the bouquet, with some earthy, reductive undertones, but the fruit is vibrant and penetrative. Smooth and elegant, the palate is long, tightly focused and creamy, finishing with lingering citrusy acids.

2004	92	2006	2009
2003	87	2005	2008
2002	86	2003	2004+

PINOT NOIR

RATING 5

	Yarra Valley	$20–$29
	Current vintage: 2004	90

2004	90	2006	2009+
2003	86	2005	2008
2002	87	2003	2004+

A varietally correct and tightly structured pinot whose delicate musky perfume of rose petals, red and black cherries and restrained, cedar/vanilla oak precedes a long, round and generous palate with an assertive mouthfeel of ripe flavours and fine-grained, powdery tannins. It presents a deep core of ripe cherries and plums and should flesh out even further over the short term.

Glaetzer

34 Barossa Valley Way, Tanunda SA 5352. Tel: (08) 8563 0288. Fax: (08) 8563 0218.
Website: www.glaetzer.com Email: admin@glaetzer.com
Region: **Barossa Valley** Winemakers: **Colin & Ben Glaetzer** Chief Executive: **Colin Glaetzer**

Among the dozens of wines made by Ben Glaetzer at the Barossa Vintners winery are several that find their way under the Glaetzer label. At the top of the tree sits the sumptuous and finely crafted Amon-Ra Shiraz, which makes its debut in this guide at a very high level, and deservedly so. The second red, the Godolphin Shiraz Cabernet Sauvignon, rates 95 points (drink 2012–2016+) for its inaugural 2004 release. As for the other shirazes from 2004? Simply delicious.

AMON-RA SHIRAZ

RATING 2

	Barossa Valley	$100–$200
	Current vintage: 2004	94

2004	94	2012	2016
2003	95	2011	2015+
2002	96	2014	2022+

A supremely ripe and confiture-like modern Barossa shiraz whose ethereal, musky and briary aromas of blackcurrant, dark Swiss chocolate, dark olives, stewed plums, nutmeg and cinnamon are backed by smoky nuances of mocha/vanilla oak. Deeply ripened and slightly meaty, its substantial and luxuriant palate of sumptuous fruit is framed by firm but silky-smooth tannins, finishing long, savoury and slightly mineral.

BISHOP SHIRAZ

RATING 4

	Barossa Valley	$30–$49
	Current vintage: 2004	91

2004	91	2006	2009
2002	89	2004	2007+
2001	90	2006	2009
1999	88	2004	2007

A seductive, smooth and sumptuous easy and early-drinking red with a violet-like perfume of cassis, spearmint and cedar/chocolate oak. Its vibrant berry flavours are unobtrusively supported by oak and framed by supple, gentle tannins. Very sexy.

SHIRAZ

RATING 5

	Barossa Valley	$50–$99
	Current vintage: 2004	93

2004	93	2012	2016+
2002	89	2010	2014
2001	89	2009	2013
1999	86	2001	2004+
1998	91	2010	2018
1997	88	1999	2002

Smooth, polished and artfully balanced, with a spicy and floral fragrance of violets, white pepper and cloves beneath pristine aromas of cassis, plums and blackberries. Restrained cedar/vanilla oak also underpins its silky palate of deep blackberry, dark plum and blueberry flavours, along with nuances of dark olives and minerals.

Goundrey

Langton, Muir Highway, Mount Barker WA 6324. Tel: (08) 9892 1777. Fax: (08) 9851 1997.
Website: www.goundreywines.com.au Email: info@goundreywines.com.au

Region: **Great Southern, Mount Barker** Winemakers: **David Martin, Stephen Craig, Mick Perkins**
Viticulturists: **Cate Finlay, Rob Hayes** Chief Executive: **Rich Hanen**

Changing ownership yet again, this time into the Hardy Wine Company stable through mutual new owner Constellation Brands, Goundrey is a reliable maker of elegant and flavoursome regional styles from the Great Southern. Its current Reserve releases are typically strong and true to form. I believe this brand has the potential to take the next step upwards, provided, of course, the motivation exists within.

RESERVE CABERNET SAUVIGNON   RATING 5

Mount Barker	**$20–$29**
Current vintage: 2003	**91**

A finely balanced, elegant and lightly herbal cabernet whose dusty, slightly cedary aromas of sweet red plums and small dark berries reveal scents of violets and forest floor with slightly meaty undertones. Smooth, polished and fine-grained, its brightly lit palate of sweet red and black berry and plum flavour is assertively backed by cedar/vanilla oak and framed by fine, chalky tannins.

2003	91	2011	2015
2002	87	2004	2007+
1998	78	2000	2003
1997	80	1999	2002
1996	90	2002	2008
1995	90	2003	2007
1993	87	2001	2005
1992	85	1997	2000
1991	93	2003	2011
1990	85	1998	2002

RESERVE CHARDONNAY   RATING 5

Mount Barker	**$20–$29**
Current vintage: 2004	**90**

Tightly crafted in a juicy, fruity style, this pleasingly bright and fluffy chardonnay has a lightly tropical and herbal bouquet backed by nuances of butter and sweet corn. Its fresh, restrained and creamy palate of peach and nectarine flavour marries with toffee-like malolactic notes before a clean and lingering finish of soft acids. Should flesh out nicely.

2004	90	2006	2009+
2003	85	2005	2008
2002	91	2004	2007
2001	86	2003	2006
1999	81	2000	2001
1998	85	2000	2003
1997	88	1999	2002
1995	87	1997	2000

RESERVE RIESLING   RATING 5

Mount Barker	**$20–$29**
Current vintage: 2005	**91**

Smoky, slightly reductive aromas of lime juice and minerals are lifted by a complex floral perfume. Long, taut and lean, its crystalline expression of vibrant citrusy fruit and reductive complexity overlies a chalky mineral texture and a crackly, almost brittle acidity at the finish. It's fresh, clean and racy.

2005	91	2010	2013+
2004	87	2006	2009
2003	93	2008	2011
2002	84	2002	2004
2000	84	2005	2008
1999	82	2001	2004
1998	88	2000	2003
1997	90	2002	2005
1996	93	2004	2008
1995	87	2003	2007
1994	94	2002	2006
1993	95	1998	2001

RESERVE SHIRAZ   RATING 5

Mount Barker	**$20–$29**
Current vintage: 2002	**90**

Smooth, approachable and savoury, this very supple short to medium-term shiraz has a smoky, char-cuterie-like bouquet of red currants, red plums and cranberries over spicy nuances of white pepper. Slightly herbal to finish, its cedary palate of fresh berry/plum fruit and vanilla oak is finely structured and balanced. A faint green note prevents it from being rated higher.

2002	90	2007	2010
2001	82	2003	2006
2000	85	2002	2005+
1999	90	2004	2007
1998	80	2000	2003
1997	83	1999	2002
1996	81	1997	1998
1994	93	2002	2006
1993	91	2001	2005
1992	94	2000	2004

Gramp's

Barossa Valley Way, Rowland Flat SA 5352. Tel: (08) 8521 3111. Fax: (08) 8521 3100.
Website: www.gramps.com.au
Region: **Barossa Valley** Winemakers: **Don Young, Hylton McLean, Nick Bruer** Viticulturist: **Joy Dick**
Chief Executive: **Laurent Lacassgne**

The logic behind the labelling of Pernod Ricard's best dessert wine, a semillon from Griffith, under its Barossa-based Gramp's label still eludes me, but the 2004 release continues its consistent run of restrained and elegant vintages made without excessive sweetness or fatness. These are dessert wines you can enjoy. The remaining wines are well-made and sound, but frankly rather uninteresting. Perhaps the Gramps deserve better.

BOTRYTIS SEMILLON   RATING 4

Griffith $12–$19 (375 ml)
Current vintage: 2004   **90**

Floral, lightly candied, citrusy and crème brulée-like aromas of peachy fruit are quite restrained and closed. Tangy and vibrant, its long, smooth and moderately lusciouspalate of restrained peach, citrus and nectarine flavours and pastry-like undertones is neither excessively sweet nor cloying, finishing clean and fresh with citrusy acids.

Year	Score		
2004	90	2005	2008+
2003	90	2005	2008+
2002	91	2004	2007+
2001	88	2003	2006
1999	90	2001	2004+
1998	83	1999	2000
1997	89	1999	2002
1996	89	1998	2001
1994	82	1995	1996

CABERNET MERLOT   RATING 5

Barossa Valley $12–$19
Current vintage: 2003   **88**

An honest, approachable and vibrant wine whose floral and juicy aromas of fresh plums and dark berries are supported by fresh vanilla and chocolate oak. Smooth, elegant and slightly jammy, its generously fruited and carefully oaked palate is framed by fine and lightly powdery tannins.

Year	Score		
2003	88	2008	2011
2002	82	2004	2007
2001	82	2002	2005
1999	86	2001	2004
1998	88	2003	2006
1997	89	2002	2005
1996	86	1998	2001
1995	85	1997	2000
1994	82	1999	2002
1993	75	1995	1998

CHARDONNAY   RATING 5

Barossa Valley $12–$19
Current vintage: 2005   **87**

A ripe, syrupy chardonnay whose sweet, juicy aromas of candied peach, tropical fruit and creamy, buttery oak reveal faint undertones of sweet corn. Generous, round and buttery, its juicy and slightly oily palate of sumptuous peach/nectarine fruit offers plenty of flavour.

Year	Score		
2005	87	2006	2007
2003	85	2004	2005
2002	89	2004	2007
2001	80	2002	2003
2000	87	2001	2002
1999	87	2001	2004
1998	82	1999	2000

GRENACHE   RATING 5

Barossa Valley $12–$19
Current vintage: 2004   **88**

A flavoursome but relatively uncomplicated grenache whose herbal, slightly jammy and confectionary aromas of cooked plums, blueberries and raspberries reveal spicy undertones of cloves and cinnamon. Smooth, supple and elegant, its juicy palate of sweet berry and currant-like fruit is elegant and approachable, with almost exaggerated varietal flavours.

Year	Score		
2004	88	2006	2009+
2002	86	2004	2007
1999	89	2004	2007
1998	87	2000	2003+
1997	88	1999	2002

Granite Hills

1481 Burke & Wills Track, Baynton Vic 3444. Tel: (03) 5423 7264. Fax: (03) 5423 7288.
Website: www.granitehills.com.au Email: knights@granitehills.com.au
Region: **Macedon Ranges** Winemakers: **Llew Knight, Ian Gunter**
Chief Executives: **Gordon, Heather & Llew Knight**

Located at one of the coolest and latest-ripening vineyard sites on mainland Australia, Knight has a history of deeply perfumed, intensely flavoured and minerally Riesling, an elegant, fine-grained Cabernet Sauvignon plus a sneezy black pepper Shiraz from riper years. The 2005 Riesling appears to reflect difficulties encountered during fermentation, and lacks the raciness and floral lift typical of the label.

CABERNET SAUVIGNON

RATING **5**

Macedon Ranges	$20–$29
Current vintage: 2001	**82**

Earthy, herbal and meaty, cedary aromas precede an up-front palate of green-edged small red berries, finishing lean and sappy.

2001	82	2003	2006
2000	77	2002	2005
1999	94	2007	2011+
1998	90	2006	2010
1997	86	2002	2005
1996	84	2001	2004
1995	89	2003	2007
1992	86	1997	2000
1991	87	2003	2011
1989	86	1991	1994
1988	82	1996	2000

CHARDONNAY

RATING **5**

Macedon Ranges	$20–$29
Current vintage: 2004	**87**

A charming, brightly flavoured and early-drinking chardonnay with a fresh, tropical aroma of melon and peaches backed by light vanilla and cashew-like oak. Smooth and supple, it's bright and forward, with attractive if uncomplicated primary fruit finishing a little greenish with slightly tinny acids.

2004	87	2006	2009
2003	88	2005	2008
2002	88	2003	2006
2001	82	2002	2003
2000	87	2002	2005
1999	85	2000	2001
1998	86	2000	2003
1997	83	1999	2002
1996	90	2001	2004
1995	93	2003	2007
1994	83	1996	1999
1993	92	1998	2001

RIESLING

RATING **3**

Macedon Ranges	$20–$29
Current vintage: 2005	**88**

Lacking its customary perfume and freshness, with delicate, estery and spicy aromas of pear, apple and honeysuckle backed by nuances of lemon sherbet and tropical fruit. Supported by powdery phenolics, its juicy, generous and faintly sweet palate presents slightly candied flavours of apple, pear that culminate in a taut and spicy finish.

2005	88	2010	2013
2004	94	2009	2012+
2003	96	2011	2015
2002	92	2007	2010
2001	89	2003	2006
2000	87	2002	2005
1999	92	2007	2011
1998	91	2003	2006+
1997	94	2009	2017
1995	93	2003	2007
1994	89	2002	2006
1993	85	1998	2001
1992	94	2000	2004

SHIRAZ

RATING **5**

Macedon Ranges	$20–$29
Current vintage: 2002	**80**

Already browning in colour, this fast-ageing and herbaceous shiraz has a jammy, rather cooked and capsicum aspect. Spicy and peppery, it's forward and rather thin in flavour.

2002	80	2004	2007
2001	89	2009	2013+
2000	88	2005	2008
1999	86	2001	2004+
1998	87	2003	2006
1997	82	1999	2002
1996	80	1998	2003

Grant Burge

Barossa Valley Way, Jacob's Creek, Tanunda SA 5352. Tel: (08) 8563 3700. Fax: (08) 8563 2807.
Website: www.grantburgewines.com.au Email: admin@grantburgewines.com.au

Region: **Barossa Valley** Winemaker: **Grant Burge** Viticulturist: **Michael Schrapel** Chief Executive: **Grant Burge**

This significant family-owned wine company has developed several tiers of wine, plus a number of special run labels along the lines of big company limited releases. Its wines are typically consistent and flavoursome, with a slightly old-fashioned Australian approach evident in its steadily expanding folio of red wines. The company's highlight is again its flagship red, the Meshach Shiraz, a deeply flavoured, firm, savoury but exceptionally fine and elegant wine, with similar finesse to the spectacular 1998 vintage.

BAROSSA VINES SHIRAZ

Barossa Valley	**$12–$19**	
Current vintage: 2004	**86**	

An honest, flavoursome shiraz of moderate weight and fresh, but simple varietal character. Its spicy, earthy, rather jammy and slightly floral aromas of plums and berries overlie creamy nuances of vanilla oak. Juicy and fresh, supported by a grainy backbone, its lively palate lacks great length, but finishes with fresh acids.

Year	Score		
2004	86	2006	2009
2003	86	2005	2008
2002	87	2003	2004+
2001	86	2003	2006
2000	82	2001	2002
1999	88	2001	2004
1998	85	1999	2000

CAMERON VALE CABERNET SAUVIGNON

RATING **5**

Barossa Valley	**$12–$19**
Current vintage: 2003	**82**

A dull and old-fashioned cabernet whose minty, meaty dark plum, prune and raisin-like fruit offers some jammy brightness but finishes rather stewed and stale. Both fruit and oak could use more freshness.

Year	Score		
2003	82	2008	2011
2002	87	2007	2010
2001	89	2006	2009
2000	82	2002	2005
1999	82	2001	2004
1998	88	2006	2010
1997	87	2002	2005
1996	91	2004	2008
1995	91	2003	2007
1994	89	2002	2006
1993	88	2001	2005

FILSELL SHIRAZ

RATING **3**

Barossa Valley	**$20–$29**
Current vintage: 2003	**94**

A firm, deeply flavoured and seductive Barossa shiraz built around profoundly ripened and slightly meaty fruit of brightness and intensity. Its vibrant aromas of plums, cassis and blackberries overlie sweet vanilla/chocolate oak and undertones of currants. Concentrated and voluptuous, it's sumptuous but silky-smooth, framed by firm fine-grained tannins. Delivering a punchy mouthful of plums, cassis and dark olives, it finishes long and savoury with meaty, mineral and clove-like undertones.

Year	Score		
2003	94	2011	2015+
2002	90	2010	2014+
2001	86	2003	2006+
2000	93	2008	2012
1999	88	2001	2004+
1998	94	2006	2010
1997	88	2002	2005
1996	95	2004	2008+
1995	91	2000	2003
1994	95	2002	2006+
1993	82	1998	2001
1992	90	2000	2004
1991	93	2003	2011

KRAFT SAUVIGNON BLANC

RATING **5**

Barossa Valley,	
Adelaide Hills	**$12–$19**
Current vintage: 2005	**92**

Punchy, grassy aromas of gooseberries, passionfruit and lychees show a lightly estery and sweaty aspect, while its long and tangy palate of juicy varietal flavour finishes clean and zesty. It's neatly sculpted, with a lingering powdery and mineral quality.

Year	Score		
2005	92	2005	2006+
2004	92	2005	2006+
2003	81	2003	2004
2002	89	2002	2003+
2001	83	2001	2002
2000	87	2001	2002
1999	84	2000	2000
1998	90	1999	2000

MESHACH

RATING 2

Barossa Valley	$50–$99
Current vintage: 2002	95

An elegant Meshach, but no shrinking violet, either. Very intense and assertively oaked, with dark plums, blackcurrants and dark chocolate backed by toasty aromas of vanilla, coconut ice, cedar and cigarboxes, it's also perfumed and floral. Surprisingly fine, elegant and seamless, its palate is saturated with jammy black and red berry flavours and supported by fine, firm tannins of genuine strength. It finishes long and savoury, with lingering suggestions of licorice, cloves and minerals.

2002	95	2014	2022
2001	88	2009	2013
2000	93	2008	2012+
1999	96	2007	2011+
1998	97	2010	2018+
1996	93	2008	2016
1995	96	2007	2015
1994	95	2006	2014
1993	93	2001	2005
1992	93	2000	2004
1991	95	2003	2011
1990	93	1998	2002+

MIAMBA SHIRAZ

RATING 5

Barossa Valley	$12–$19
Current vintage: 2004	89

A typically spicy and measured red-fruited Lyndoch shiraz whose pleasingly rich but not exaggerated expression of raspberry, red cherry and plum-like qualities reveals undertones of menthol and mint. It's lightly dusted with cloves and cinnamon, with rather a polished measure of creamy vanilla oak to boot. With a pleasing underlying structure, it will develop for a few years yet.

2004	89	2009	2012
2003	91	2005	2008+
2002	84	2004	2007
2001	87	2003	2006
2000	88	2002	2005+
1999	89	2001	2004+

MSJ RESERVE CABERNET SHIRAZ BLEND

RATING 3

Barossa Valley	$50–$99
Current vintage: 1998	91

Slightly old-fashioned Barossa blend, with an earthy, meaty aroma of sweet cassis, plums and mulberries, suggestions of pepper and spice, and a healthy dollop of new chocolate and vanilla oak. Smooth and cedary, with a pleasingly long palate of intense berry fruit and earthy complexity supported by rather a firm, rod-like spine of drying tannins.

1998	91	2006	2010
1996	93	2004	2008+
1994	95	2006	2014

SHADRACH CABERNET SAUVIGNON

RATING 4

Barossa Valley	$50–$99
Current vintage: 2001	88

Generous and concentrated, but rather old-fashioned and lacking finesse, this rather blocky and sinewy cabernet reveals a ripe, jammy and slightly meaty bouquet. Earthy aromas of dark plums, cassis and sweet chocolate/mocha/vanilla oak reveal undertones of currant and raisins. Initially intense, but lacking genuine mid-palate depth and presence, it dries out towards an astringent, slightly sappy and mineral finish.

2001	88	2009	2013
2000	82	2005	2008
1999	87	2004	2007
1998	93	2006	2010+
1996	92	2008	2016
1994	93	2006	2014
1993	90	2013	2023

SUMMERS CHARDONNAY

RATING 5

Eden Valley, Adelaide Hills	$12–$19
Current vintage: 2004	87

Soft, juicy chardonnay with a closed and slightly oaky aroma of peach and citrus fruits backed by undertones of green olives. Long and smooth, with a lightly herbal thread beneath its lively fruit, it finishes with refreshing acids.

2004	87	2005	2006
2003	87	2004	2005
2002	88	2002	2004+
2001	80	2002	2003
2000	88	2002	2005
1999	87	2001	2004

THE HOLY TRINITY (Grenache Shiraz Mourvèdre) — RATING 5

Barossa Valley $30–$49
Current vintage: 2002   88

A rather old-fashioned and sweet-fruited red blend whose floral and slight confectionary aromas of cranberries and plums reveal earthy, spicy undertones and suggestions of mint and menthol. Smooth and supple, its vibrant expression of spicy blueberry and plum-like fruit is framed by tight, fine and powdery tannin. Restrained and savoury, it's just beginning to age and dry out.

2002	88	2007	2010
2001	85	2003	2006+
2000	87	2002	2005
1999	92	2004	2007
1998	90	2000	2003+
1997	89	1999	2002
1996	89	1998	2001
1995	86	1997	2000

THORN RIESLING — RATING 4

Eden Valley $12–$19
Current vintage: 2005   88

A slightly advanced, toasty and oily riesling whose floral and honeyed aromas of lemon rind and lime juice are backed by suggestions of baby powder and butter. Rich and juicy, broad and generous, it's an assertive wine whose vibrant citrus flavours are coated by powdery phenolics before a clean finish of citrusy acids. Just lacks a little delicacy and freshness.

2005	88	2007	2010+
2004	93	2009	2012+
2002	90	2007	2010
2001	91	2006	2009+
2000	87	2002	2005+
1999	88	2001	2004+
1998	93	2003	2006
1997	87	1999	2002

ZERK SEMILLON — RATING 5

Barossa Valley $12–$19
Current vintage: 2005   89

A delicate fragrance of apple, pear and melon with lightly grassy undertones precedes a round, generous and slightly viscous palate of attractive length and crunchy, refreshing acidity that ably cleans up a slight fattiness. It finishes slightly phenolic and quite dry.

2005	89	2006	2007+
2004	86	2005	2006
2002	92	2003	2004+
2001	84	2002	2003
2000	87	2001	2002
1999	92	2001	2004+
1998	88	2000	2003
1997	87	2002	2005

Green Point

Green Point Maroondah Highway, Coldstream Vic 3770. Tel: (03) 9738 9200. Fax: (03) 9738 9201.
Website: www.greenpointwines.com.au
Regions: **Yarra Valley, Various** Winemakers: **Tony Jordan, James Gosper, John Harris, Matt Steel**
Viticulturist: **Bernie Wood** Managing Director: **Tony Jordan**

Green Point is the label by which Domaine Chandon's Australian sparkling wines are sold in overseas markets, as well as the company's brand of still table wines sold in Australia. Its range is now sourced exclusively from Victoria. As a group, they are very carefully constructed and technically sound, but just lack a little presence and richness of genuinely ripe flavour.

RESERVE CHARDONNAY — RATING 5

Yarra Valley $20–$29
Current vintage: 2004   89

A very oaky and slightly oxidative chardonnay whose delicate aromas of wheatmeal, dried flowers and vanilla precede a rather viscous and slippery palate whose juicy melon and peach-like fruit is presently rather overshadowed by its rather showy, dusty and vanilla oak. It does build in fruit weight and concentration towards the finish and should settle down with more balance.

2004	89	2006	2009
2003	88	2005	2008+
2002	89	2007	2010
2001	88	2003	2006
2000	87	2002	2005

RESERVE PINOT NOIR

RATING **5**

Yarra Valley	$20–$29
Current vintage: 2003	82

Rather soupy, meaty and smoky, with light floral aromas of plums and cherries overwhelmed by charry oak. Soft and juicy, sweet and syrupy, its confectionary palate of simple berry/cherry fruit lacks length and structure, finishing green and under-ripe.

2003	82	2005	2008
2002	90	2004	2007
2001	87	2003	2006
2000	89	2005	2008

VICTORIA SHIRAZ

RATING **5**

Victoria	$20–$29
Current vintage: 2004	87

Dusty and lightly herbal aromas of blood plums and slightly confectionary-like red berries with a background of white pepper and restrained oak precede a fine, spicy and savoury palate framed by measured oak, fine tannins and green-edged acids. Its small berry and plum-like flavours finish with a lingering impression of cloves and licorice.

2004	87	2006	2009
2003	86	2005	2008
2002	90	2004	2007

YARRA VALLEY CHARDONNAY

RATING **5**

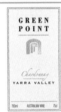

Yarra Valley	$20–$29
Current vintage: 2004	89

An uncomplicated but well constructed chardonnay with floral, spicy aromas of peach, apple and nuances of tropical fruits before a supple and refreshing palate whose lively peaches-and-cream flavours and dusty vanilla oak finish with pleasing length and clean, refreshing acidity.

2004	89	2006	2009
2003	90	2005	2008
2002	87	2004	2007
2001	84	2003	2006
2000	86	2000	2003
1999	81	2000	2001
1998	83	2000	2003
1996	82	1996	1997
1995	93	2000	2003
1994	92	1999	2002
1993	89	1998	2001
1992	92	1997	2000

Grey Sands

6 Kerrisons Road, Glengarry Tas 7275. Tel: (03) 6396 1167. Fax: (03) 6396 1153.
Website: www.greysands.com.au Email: info@greysands.com.au
Region: **Tamar Valley** Winemakers: **Fran Austin, Andrew Pirie** Viticulturist: **Bob Richter**
Chief Executive: **Bob Richter**

Grey Sands is a 2.5 hectare close-spaced vineyard planted exclusively to pinot gris and merlot. Its Pinot Gris is a ripe and sumptuous style given full malolactic fermentation and four months of lees contact to develop texture and complexity. The 2005 vintage is typically smoky and complex, long and savoury. The vineyard is open to visitors by appointment.

PINOT GRIS

RATING **3**

Tamar Valley	$30–$49
Current vintage: 2005	94

A smooth, generous and intensely fruited pinot gris whose musky perfume of rose oil, pear and apple-like fruit is backed by nutty undertones. It's chalky and powdery, with some smoky, charcuterie-like reductive complexity beneath its pristine, juicy flavours. It finishes long and savoury, with lingering citrus notes and soft acids. Lovely balance and varietal purity.

2005	94	2007	2010
2004	93	2005	2006+
2003	80	2003	2004
2001	81	2002	2003
2000	94	2002	2005

Grosset

King Street, Auburn SA 5451. Tel: (08) 8849 2175. Fax: (08) 8849 2292.
Website: www.grosset.com.au Email: info@grosset.com.au

Region: **Clare Valley** Winemaker: **Jeffrey Grosset** Viticulturist: **Jeffrey Grosset** Chief Executive: **Jeffrey Grosset**

2005 was a brilliant vintage for Jeff Grosset's exceptional pair of rieslings, and possibly the finest ever for the benchmark Polish Hill. While this winery is best known for these wines, I am also very impressed with the top-level performance of the silky and sensuous Piccadilly Chardonnay, which now deserves ranking among Australia's top ten wines from this variety. Recently, in Tokyo, I also mistook the tight, powdery and astringent 1995 Gaia for an Italian red. I think Jeff Grosset would see the humour in that.

GAIA (Cabernet blend)

RATING **3**

| Clare Valley | $30–$49 |
| Current vintage: 2003 | 93 |

A ripe and profoundly structured cabernet blend whose depth of fruit and measured balance should set it up for at least a decade's cellaring. Dark, ripe and juicy, its deep, earthy aromas of dark plums, cassis and red berries are backed by cedar/chocolate oak with smoky undertones. Tightly wound about a firm, powdery spine of astringent tannin, its assertive and drying palate of rich plum and berry flavour reveals undertones of mint and dried herbs. A well-measured warm-year wine.

2003	93	2011	2015+
2002	90	2014	2022+
2001	94	2013	2021
2000	91	2008	2012+
1999	90	2007	2011
1998	95	2010	2018
1996	91	2004	2008
1995	93	2007	2015
1994	94	2006	2014
1993	94	2005	2013
1992	95	2004	2012
1991	88	1996	1999
1990	89	2002	2010

PICCADILLY (Chardonnay)

RATING **2**

| Adelaide Hills | $30–$49 |
| Current vintage: 2004 | 95 |

A particularly stylish, smooth and seamless chardonnay of elegance, brightness and intensity. Its delicate floral perfume of pear, apple and white peach is enhanced by tightly integrated vanilla and spicy oak, with creamy, leesy nuances of cashew and wheatmeal. Long and silky, it effortlessly delivers pristine, vibrant chardonnay fruit, culminating in a lingering finish of soft acids and faint undertones of sweet corn.

2004	95	2009	2012
2003	96	2008	2011
2002	95	2007	2010
2001	94	2006	2009
2000	95	2005	2008
1999	95	2004	2007+
1998	90	2003	2006
1997	94	2002	2005
1996	95	2001	2004
1995	94	2000	2003
1994	94	2002	2006

PINOT NOIR

RATING **3**

| Adelaide Hills | $30–$49 |
| Current vintage: 2004 | 91 |

A pristine, perfumed and precisely flavoured pinot noir whose delicate perfume of rose petals, raspberries, strawberries and lightly toasty vanilla oak reveals nuances of confectionary and bacon. Despite its fineness and silkiness, it's deeply fruited and surprisingly astringent; likely to build more depth of flavour and firmness of structure with time in the bottle. It finishes long, with earthy undertones.

2004	91	2009	2012
2003	93	2005	2008+
2002	92	2007	2010+
2001	88	2003	2006
2000	82	2002	2005
1998	93	2003	2006
1997	95	2002	2005+
1996	94	2004	2008
1995	91	1997	2000
1994	93	1999	2002
1993	90	1998	2001

POLISH HILL

RATING **1**

| Clare Valley | $30–$49 |
| Current vintage: 2005 | 98 |

A beautifully presented and tightly structured riesling with the openness and seamless quality of the famous 2002 vintage. A heady rose petal-like perfume with layers of spotlessly clean lime, apple and mineral qualities precedes a long and luscious palate whose juicy expression of near-perfect riesling flavour overlies a super-fine undercarriage of powdery phenolics. Tremendous depth of fruit and structure, with a lingering finish reminiscent of wet slate.

2005	98	2017	2025
2004	95	2012	2016+
2003	96	2015	2023
2002	97	2014	2022
2001	96	2009	2013+
2000	95	2008	2012
1999	95	2007	2011+
1998	92	2006	2010
1997	97	2009	2017+
1996	94	2004	2008
1995	93	2003	2007+
1994	95	2006	2014
1993	90	2001	2005
1992	93	2004	2012

SEMILLON SAUVIGNON BLANC

RATING 4

Clare Valley, Adelaide Hills $20–$29
Current vintage: 2005   **90**

Delicate lemony, buttery and lightly grassy aromas of melon and gooseberry, citrus and tropical fruit precede a smooth and fleshy palate that finishes nutty and savoury, dry and refreshing. It might lack a little punch and impact, but offers a pleasing length of fruit punctuated by smooth acids.

2005	90	2007	2010+
2004	89	2004	2005+
2003	92	2004	2005+
2002	90	2004	2007
2001	92	2006	2009
2000	91	2002	2005
1999	90	2004	2007
1998	93	2003	2006
1997	90	1998	1999
1996	93	1998	2001
1995	94	1997	2000
1994	94	1999	2003
1993	94	2001	2005
1992	91	1997	2000

WATERVALE RIESLING

RATING 2

Clare Valley $30–$49
Current vintage: 2005   **96**

A stylish and tightly presented riesling with balance, brightness and focus. Its pristine perfume of lime juice and lemon rind reveals undertones of tropical fruit and stonefruit. Laced with suggestions of melon and peach, its fine, taut and minerally palate is underpinned by fine, powdery phenolics, delivering almost an opulent expression of primary citrus-like flavour. Terrific persistence and chalkiness; a top effort.

2005	96	2013	2017+
2004	93	2009	2012+
2003	95	2008	2011+
2002	96	2010	2014+
2001	95	2009	2013
2000	95	2008	2012+
1999	95	2004	2007+
1998	90	2003	2006+
1997	95	2002	2005+
1996	94	2001	2004+
1995	92	2000	2003
1994	94	2002	2006
1993	90	1998	2001
1992	90	1997	2000
1991	96	2003	2011
1990	94	2002	2010

Gulf Station

Pinnacle Lane, Dixon's Creek Vic 3775. Tel: (03) 5965 2271. Fax: (03) 5965 2442.
Website: www.debortoli.com.au   Email: dbw@debortoli.com.au
Region: **Yarra Valley** Winemakers: **Stephen Webber, David Slingsby-Smith** Viticulturist: **Philip Lobley**
Chief Executive: **Darren De Bortoli**

Gulf Station is a De Bortoli label that offers affordable and sometimes upmarket drinking from Yarra Valley vineyards. Its easy-drinking Shiraz and floral Riesling often deliver qualities more associated with European styles, while the usually refreshing Chardonnay appears to have skipped a beat in 2005.

CHARDONNAY

RATING 5

Yarra Valley $12–$19
Current vintage: 2005   **80**

A little greenish, oily and lacking freshness, with smoky, reductive and confectionary aromas of melon, grapefruit and pineapple plus a slightly cooked and forward palate with greenish undertones and a sweet corn-like finish. Lacks length and brightness.

2005	80	2006	2007
2004	87	2005	2006
2003	89	2004	2005+
2002	89	2003	2004+
2001	81	2002	2003
2000	80	2001	2002
1999	90	2000	2001

RIESLING

Yarra Valley $12–$19
Current vintage: 2006   **89**

A surprisingly genuine and varietal riesling whose floral perfume of pear, apple and lime juice precedes a clean, juicy and slightly chalky palate. Its vibrant fruit overlies a tight-knit spine of fine phenolics, while it finishes with length, freshness and crisp acidity.

2006	89	2008	2011
2005	77	2006	2007
2004	87	2006	2009
2003	81	2003	2004
2002	87	2002	2003
2001	77	2001	2002
2000	82	2001	2002
1999	80	2000	2001
1998	91	2003	2006
1997	87	2002	2005

SHIRAZ RATING 5

Yarra Valley $12–$19
Current vintage: 2003   88

Moderately firm, this savoury and slightly meaty shiraz has a spicy, briary aroma of small, earthy black and red berries over lightly cedary oak and nuances of undergrowth. Medium to full in weight, its juicy and slightly sour-edged cherry/plum fruit is well supported by chocolate/mocha oak and its bony extract.

2003	88	2005	2008+
2002	89	2004	2007
2001	87	2006	2009
2000	88	2001	2002+
1999	83	2001	2004
1998	83	2000	2003
1996	92	2008	2016

Hanging Rock

88 Jim Road, Newham Vic 3442. Tel: (03) 5427 0542. Fax: (03) 5427 0310.
Website: www.hangingrock.com.au Email: hrw@hangingrock.com.au
Region: **Macedon Ranges** Winemaker: **John Ellis** Viticulturist: **John Ellis** Chief Executive: **John Ellis**

Hanging Rock creates a wide range of inexpensive wines under its Victoria label, but I am more interested in its steadily expanding top tier of slightly idiosyncratic wines sourced from a number of regions, with a developing focus on Heathcote. While recent vintages of Heathcote Shiraz have handled the warmth of recent seasons with some aplomb, I am concerned that the Macedon Brut, an extremely evolved and meaty wine, has become almost totally dominated by its aldehydic influences.

HEATHCOTE SHIRAZ   RATING 3

Heathcote $50–$99
Current vintage: 2003   91

While it carries its 15% alcohol quite well, it could show more finesse. Ripe, concentrated and briary aromas of blackberries and dark plums reveal some dehydrated nuances of currants and tar, with a spicy background of cloves and nutmeg. Firmly coated by aggressive and astringent tannins, it has the length, strength and grip to underpin its vigorous expression of black fruit.

2003	91	2015	2023
2002	93	2010	2014+
2001	89	2006	2009
2000	91	2008	2012+
1999	93	2011	2019
1998	93	2010	2018
1997	90	2005	2009
1992	95	2012	2022
1991	95	2003	2011+
1990	95	2002	2010+
1989	89	1997	2001+
1988	91	2000	2008

MACEDON   RATING 4

Macedon Ranges $30–$49
Current vintage: Cuvée XI   86

A deliberately extreme expression of sparkling style fashioned in an overtly oxidative and aldehydic style. Its very evolved, toasty, honeyed and buttery bouquet is very fragrant and meaty, while its palate is richly textured, chewy and rather stale, finishing with a lingering suggestion of apple cider. I admire the style and the ambitions behind it, but believe this wine has gone too far.

Cuvée XI	86	2005	2008
Cuvée X	86	2004	2007
Cuvée IX	87	2003	2005
Cuvée VIII	91	2002	2006+
Cuvée VII	94	2000	2003
Cuvée VI	88	1999	2002
Cuvée V	87	1997	2000
Cuvée IV	94	1996	1999
Cuvée III	91	1995	1999

THE JIM JIM SAUVIGNON BLANC   RATING 5

Macedon Ranges $20–$29
Current vintage: 2005   88

Delicate, lightly grassy aromas of lychees and gooseberries are backed by lightly sweaty and nutty undertones. It's clean and juicy, but its melon and gooseberry-like palate lacks great impact, finishing a little thin, with green cashew-like notes and a hint of minerality. A little green and simple.

2005	88	2006	2007
2004	94	2005	2006+
2003	88	2004	2005
2002	87	2003	2003
2001	90	2003	2006
2000	87	2001	2002
1999	86	2000	2001
1998	90	2000	2003

Hardys

Reynell Road, Reynella SA 5161. Tel: (08) 8392 2222. Fax: (08) 8392 2202.
Website: www.hardywines.com.au Email: corporate@hardywines.com.au

Regions: **South Australia, Tasmania, Victoria** Winemakers: **Peter Dawson (chief), Paul Lapsley (red), Tom Newton (white), Ed Carr (sparkling)** Viticulturist: **Brenton Baker** Chief Executive: **David Woods**

Part of one of the world's largest wine companies in Constellation Wines, The Hardy Wine Company still produces a number of apparently disparate wines under its original name. The flagship Eileen Hardy wines have again delivered handsomely, especially the ultra-stylish 2002 Shiraz. Oddly, though, the 2002 Tintara Shiraz, which is usually one of my favourite wines from this stable, is extremely disappointing. Other highlights are the largely Margaret River-sourced 2001 Thomas Hardy Cabernet Sauvignon and another excellent Arras release.

ARRAS SPARKLING CHARDONNAY PINOT NOIR   RATING 2

Tasmania		$50–$99	2000	94	2005	2008
Current vintage: 2000		**94**	1999	95	2007	2011
			1998	94	2003	2006+
			1997	90	1999	2002
			1995	95	2003	2007

A very good, richly favoured, complex and slightly meaty sparkling wine of intensity and structure. Scented with a floral perfume and creamy bakery yeast, its nutty and citrusy aromas show some toasty, honeyed development. Chewy and toasty, its crackly, crunchy palate is full of impact and complexity. It might lack the polish of the 1999 release, but retains plenty of lingering lemon sherbet and apple-like flavour, finishing with a pleasing balance of sweetness and acidity.

EILEEN HARDY CHARDONNAY   RATING 2

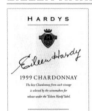

H A R D Y S

Eileen Hardy

1999 CHARDONNAY

The best Chardonnay from each vintage is selected by the winemakers for release under the 'Eileen Hardy' label.

750ml

Tasmania, Yarra Valley, Tumbarumba,			2004	93	2009	2012
Adelaide Hills		$50–$99	2003	95	2008	2011+
Current vintage: 2004		**93**	2002	94	2007	2010
			2001	95	2006	2009+
			2000	95	2005	2008
			1999	96	2004	2007+
			1998	94	2003	2006
			1997	92	1999	2002
			1996	95	2001	2004+
			1995	93	2000	2003
			1994	91	1996	1999
			1993	90	1998	2001
			1992	85	1997	2000
			1991	93	1996	1999+

Complex and toasty, with smoky, mineral and creamy leesy notes beneath honeysuckle-like scents of grapefruit, lemon and melon, this finely crafted chardonnay is just a fraction herbal for a higher rating. Its long, elegant and tightly knit palate marries fresh nectarine, peach, honeydew melon and grapefruit notes with creamy, matchstick oak, a light minerality and acids that just lack a little cut and definition.

EILEEN HARDY SHIRAZ   RATING 2

H A R D Y S

Eileen Hardy

2000 SHIRAZ

The best Shiraz from each vintage is selected by the winemakers for release under the 'Eileen Hardy' label.

750ml

McLaren Vale	$50–$99	2002	95	2014	2022
Current vintage: 2002	**95**	2001	95	2013	2021
		2000	93	2008	2012+
		1999	96	2011	2019
		1998	97	2010	2018
		1997	93	2005	2009
		1996	96	2016	2026
		1995	95	2003	2007
		1994	95	2006	2014
		1993	89	2001	2005
		1992	90	2000	2004
		1991	92	1999	2003
		1990	93	2002	2010+
		1989	90	1997	2001
		1988	93	2000	2008+
		1987	91	1995	1999

A sumptuous and stylish modern shiraz and a classic reflection of its vintage. Its floral perfume of accentuated cassis, redcurrants, raspberries, plums and dark cherries has a faintly meaty aspect and overlies tightly knit cedar/dark chocolate/vanilla oak with musky undertones of violets, cinnamon and cloves. Silky-smooth and fine-grained, its slightly sour-edged fruit, savoury oak and velvet tannins combine effortlessly, culminating in a long and persistent finish.

NOTTAGE HILL CABERNET SHIRAZ

South Australia $12–$19
Current vintage: 2004 86

Sweet spicy, confection-like aromas of fresh berries and plums are backed by cedar/vanilla oak and floral, earthy undertones. The palate begins with sweet, juicy and jammy berry/plum flavours, supported by fine tannins and thinning out a little towards the finish.

2004	86	2006	2009
2003	87	2005	2008
2002	81	2003	2004+
2001	78	2002	2003
2000	80	2001	2002
1999	80	2000	2001
1998	88	2000	2003+
1996	82	2001	2004
1995	83	1997	2000
1994	85	1996	1999

SIEGERSDORF RIESLING

RATING **5**

Clare Valley $12–$19
Current vintage: 2005 88

Fresh confectionary, floral and lemon sherbet-like aromas of lime and apple, with bath powder-like undertones precede a clean, zesty and mouth-filling palate of vibrant riesling flavour. It's long and vibrant, finishing with refreshing acids.

2005	88	2007	2010+
2004	89	2009	2012
2003	84	2004	2005+
2002	89	2007	2010
2001	89	2003	2006+
2000	89	2005	2008
1999	80	2004	2007+
1998	89	2003	2006+
1997	89	2002	2005
1996	88	2001	2004
1995	86	1996	1997

THOMAS HARDY CABERNET SAUVIGNON

RATING **3**

Margaret River, Coonawarra $50–$99
Current vintage: 2001 92

Floral aromas of sweet red cherries, raspberries and violets overlie cedar/vanilla oak and undertones of dried herbs and dark olives. Full to medium in weight, it's firm and fine-grained, with a vibrant length of restrained small black and red berry flavours, over chalky tannins and dusty, fine-grained chocolate-like oak. Elegant and harmonious, it finishes with a slightly greenish aspect.

2001	92	2009	2013+
2000	89	2008	2012+
1999	93	2011	2019
1996	94	2008	2016
1995	92	2003	2007+
1994	94	2006	2012
1993	90	2001	2005
1992	93	2000	2004
1991	94	2003	2011
1990	95	2002	2010
1989	94	2001	2009

TINTARA GRENACHE

RATING **4**

McLaren Vale $30–$49
Current vintage: 2003 92

A fine, deeply flavoured, focused and savoury grenache with a briary, spicy bouquet of cranberries, redcurrants and red plums with slightly meaty undertones of blueberries and fennel. Smooth and supple, its moderately deep palate of meaty fruit is wrapped in fine, slightly bony tannins. It finishes with pleasing length of vibrant licorice-like fruit.

2003	92	2008	2011
2002	90	2007	2010+
1999	89	2004	2007
1998	95	2003	2006+
1997	89	2002	2005
1996	92	2001	2004+
1995	93	2003	2007

TINTARA SHIRAZ

RATING **5**

McLaren Vale $30–$49
Current vintage: 2002 86

A rather old-fashioned bouquet of smoky, meaty and leathery aromas of plums and blackberries is backed by smoked oyster and mocha-like oak. Its palate is of the ethereal kind, excessively so, since it lacks a presence of fruit along its entirety, finishing short, rather insipid and carried by oak. Finely crafted, but already ageing and drying out.

2002	86	2004	2007
2001	90	2006	2009+
2000	89	2005	2008
1999	88	2004	2007
1998	95	2006	2010+
1997	89	2002	2005
1996	94	2004	2008
1995	95	2000	2003+

Heartland Wines

34 Barossa Valley Way, Tanunda SA 5352. Tel: (08) 8357 9344. Fax: (08) 8357 9388.
Website: www.heartlandwines.com.au Email: admin@heartlandwines.com.au

Region: **Langhorne Creek** Winemaker: **Ben Glaetzer** Viticulturist: **Geoff Hardy** Chief Executive: **Grant Tilbrook**

Heartland Wines sources its fruit from mature vineyards at Langhorne Creek and the Limestone Coast. Made under the guidance of one of its partners, Ben Glaetzer, it releases an interesting and eclectic series of wines deliberately made to be ready for early enjoyment, such as the innovative blends of Dolcetto Lagrein (delicious and savoury) and Viognier Pinot Gris (up-front and refreshing). Its premier wine is the Director's Cut Shiraz, which makes its debut in this edition.

DIRECTOR'S CUT SHIRAZ

RATING **3**

Langhorne Creek,		2004	90	2012	2016
Limestone Coast	$30–$49	2003	85	2008	2011+
Current vintage: 2004	90	2002	87	2010	2014

Sweet aromas of violets, cassis and dark plums are backed by dark chocolate and vanilla oak with leathery undertones of cinnamon, cloves, nutmeg and mint. Sumptuous, smooth and polished, with bright jujube-like flavours of blackberries, dark plums, it reveals spicy, minty and meaty undertones. Its pleasingly long core of fruit is framed by firm but pliant tannins with tightly integrated nuances of dark chocolate and cedary oak. Very elegant, despite its profound richness and weight.

Heathcote Estate

Drummonds Lane, Heathcote Vic 3523. Tel: (03) 5433 2107. Fax: (03) 5433 2152.
Website: www.heathcoteestate.com Email: info@heathcoteestate.com

Region: **Heathcote** Winemakers: **Tod Dexter, Larry McKenna** Chief Executive: **Louis Bialkower**

Louis Bialkower, the founder of Yarra Ridge, and Robert Kirby have combined to create this ambitious new brand whose home is nearly 40 hectares of vineyard adjacent to Jasper Hill. It's largely planted to shiraz, with a small area of grenache. The wines are made by a very experienced duo in Tod Dexter (formerly Stonier) and Larry McKenna (formerly Martinborough Vineyard). The 2004 release is easily the best yet.

SHIRAZ

RATING **3**

Heathcote	$30–$49	2004	93	2012	2016+
Current vintage: 2004	93	2003	92	2011	2015
		2002	89	2007	2010

A deeply and richly flavoured shiraz from Heathcote with none of the overcooked and porty characters so common today among the species. Its floral aromas of raspberries, cassis, dark plums and polished vanilla oak are backed by spicy nuances of cloves, cinnamon and black pepper, with an underlying charcuterie-like note. Full to medium weight, it's sumptuously and deeply flavoured, with vibrant black and red berries and plums handsomely backed by excellent cedary and savoury oak. Long and pliant, it's framed by tightly constructed and powder-fine tannins.

Heathcote Winery

183 High Street, Heathcote Vic 3523. Tel: (03) 5433 2595. Fax: (03) 5433 3081.
Website: www.heathcotewinery.com.au Email: winemaker@heathcotewinery.com.au

Region: **Heathcote** Winemaker: **Jonathan Mepham** Viticulturist: **Brett Winslow** Chief Executive: **Steve Wilkins**

Heathcote Winery is a shiraz and viognier specialist with more experience than most Australian wineries in the art of using viognier to add complexity and lift to shiraz without making it patently obvious that you have done so. The Curagee Shiraz from 2004 is a classic examples of this — a firm and floral wine with classic mineral undertones. While the 2004 Mail Coach is a slightly riper and meatier wine, neither approach the excessive ripeness and portiness that so many local growers and makers are repeatedly mistaking for Heathcote regional character.

CURAGEE SHIRAZ

RATING **3**

Heathcote	$30–$49
Current vintage: 2004	**95**

Closed and brooding, this mineral and savoury shiraz slowly reveals a delicate, floral and spicy perfume of vibrant and brambly blackberry, dark plum and blackcurrant fruit backed by fresh cedar/dark chocolate oak. Full to medium weight, its sumptuous, meaty layers of deep dark plum and slightly sour-edged berry fruits are tightly wound around a firm, powdery spine of fine-grained tannins. It finishes with minty nuances of dried herbs.

2004	95	2016	2024
2003	91	2011	2015
2002	91	2010	2014
2001	95	2009	2013
1999	87	2004	2007+
1998	95	2006	2010+
1997	94	2005	2009

MAIL COACH SHIRAZ VIOGNIER

RATING **4**

Heathcote	$20–$29
Current vintage: 2004	**90**

Musky, peppery scents of blackberry confiture, cassis and dark cherries reveal undertones of cloves, cinnamon and sweet cedar/vanilla oak. Smooth and spicy, its peppery expression of jujube-like fruit reveals some ultra-ripe suggestions of currants, treacle and tar, backed by nuances of mint, menthol and licorice. Robustly framed by fine-grained tannin, it's long, spicy, juicy and slightly meaty.

2004	90	2009	2012+
2003	88	2008	2011
2002	89	2010	2014
2001	91	2006	2009+
2000	93	2008	2012
1999	92	2007	2011
1998	93	2006	2010+
1997	93	2002	2005+
1995	85	1997	2000
1994	91	1999	2002

MAIL COACH VIOGNIER (formerly Curagee Viognier)

RATING **5**

Heathcote	$20–$29
Current vintage: 2005	**87**

Forward and early maturing, this rather spirity young viognier has a slightly wild and spicy bouquet of apricot and honeysuckle with floral undertones. Juicy, long and rather viscous, the slightly phenolic palate of peach and apricot flavours becomes quite dusty, nutty and savoury towards the finish.

2005	87	2006	2007+
2004	87	2005	2006+
2003	86	2004	2005
2002	86	2003	2004+
2001	88	2003	2006
2000	91	2002	2005
1998	89	2000	2003

Heggies Vineyard

Heggies Range Road, Eden Valley SA 5235. Tel: (08) 8561 3200. Fax: (08) 8561 3393.
Website: www.heggiesvineyard.com Email: info@heggiesvineyard.com
Region: **Eden Valley** Winemaker: **Peter Gambetta** Viticulturist: **Robin Nettelbeck** Chief Executive: **Robert Hill Smith**
If, for whatever reason, the cause of the excitement presently surrounding Australian riesling still eludes you, open a bottle of the Heggies 2005. It was love at first sniff, for me at least! As this remarkable wine shows, this mature Eden Valley vineyard can mix it with the best. It's also proving time and again to be a consistent producer of a soft, fluffy Chardonnay and an exotically spicy Viognier.

CHARDONNAY

RATING 4

Eden Valley $20–$29
Current vintage: 2004 92

An elegant, fine-grained and refreshing chardonnay of brightness and intensity. Its pungent aromas of ripe melon, honeysuckle and lemon butter are supported by sweet, but fine-grained oak and undertones of minerals. Soft and fluffy, its palate bursts with a lingering core of juicy melon and stonefruit flavour before a clean and tangy finish.

2004	92	2006	2009
2003	90	2005	2008
2002	93	2004	2007
2001	90	2003	2006
2000	85	2002	2005
1998	89	2000	2003+
1997	87	1999	2002
1996	87	1998	2001
1995	91	2000	2003

MERLOT (formerly Cabernet Blend)

RATING 4

Eden Valley $20–$29
Current vintage: 2002 89

A finely balanced, lightly herbal merlot whose floral aromas of sweet black and red cherries and cedar/vanilla oak are pristine and perfumed. Silky-smooth, its moderately rich palate of confiture-like fruit and well-handed chocolate/cedary oak is framed by a competent structure of slightly greenish tannins and acids, finishing with nuances of mint and menthol.

2002	89	2007	2010+
2001	93	2008	2013
2000	87	2002	2005+
1999	88	2001	2004+
1998	89	2003	2006
1996	90	2001	2004
1995	90	2000	2003+
1994	93	2002	2006
1993	94	2001	2005
1992	87	2000	2004
1991	88	1996	1999
1990	91	1998	2002

RIESLING

RATING 3

Eden Valley $12–$19
Current vintage: 2005 95

Exceptionally long and shapely, this tightly sculpted and focused riesling marries pristine varietal fruit and perfume with wet stone-like minerality and texture. Its floral, lime juice aromas of musk and wet slate precede a silky smooth palate of vibrant, mouthfilling lemon, apple and pear-like flavour over a precisely honed and powdery chassis of mineral influences. Exceptional length and a long future.

2005	95	2013	2017
2004	93	2009	2012+
2003	92	2008	2011+
2002	92	2010	2024+
2001	90	2006	2009
2000	90	2005	2008+
1999	95	2007	2011
1998	96	2006	2010+
1997	89	2002	2005
1996	88	2003	2007
1995	94	2003	2007
1994	77	1996	1999

VIOGNIER

RATING 4

Eden Valley $20–$29
Current vintage: 2004 92

A soft, smooth and gentle viognier with an alluringly spicy perfume of honeysuckle and apricot, cloves and cinnamon. Long and voluptuous, its creamy, buttery palate presents delightfully vibrant fruit before a clean and savoury finish. Genuinely varietal, with attractive nutty and spicy complexity.

2004	92	2005	2006+
2003	89	2004	2005+
2002	94	2004	2007
2001	90	2002	2003+
2000	89	2002	2005
1999	82	2001	2004
1998	93	2000	2003
1997	92	1999	2002
1996	86	1997	1998
1995	80	1996	1997
1994	90	1999	2002

Henschke

Henschke Road, Keyneton SA 5353. Tel: (08) 8564 8223. Fax: (08) 8564 8294.
Website: www.henschke.com.au Email: info@henschke.com.au
Region: **Eden Valley** Winemaker: **Stephen Henschke** Viticulturist: **Prue Henschke**
Chief Executive: **Stephen Henschke**

Henschke is a small and iconic Australian winery in Eden Valley with access to several landmark old vine vineyards in the Eden Valley itself, plus some steep but relatively modern plantings at Lenswood in the Adelaide Hills. The ongoing release of the company's premier red wines from the watershed 2002 vintage has continued with the deeply flavoured and beautifully structured Cyril Henschke Cabernet Sauvignon, the best wine ever released under this label. And, as if to show that 2002 was no fluke, the 2003 Mount Edelstone is certainly one of the finest South Australian reds from a vintage that was very challenging except in the state's southeast.

ABBOTTS PRAYER

RATING **4**

Lenswood		$50–$99
Current vintage: 2001		**90**

Sweet aromas of mulberries, blackberry confiture and earthy, herbal undertones of dark plums and cherries are supported by creamy vanilla oak. Fine and elegant, its smooth and silky palate of dark, slightly jammy fruit and tight-knit oak finishes savoury and slightly meaty, with lingering suggestions of licorice and dried herbs. A fraction greenish.

2001	90	2009	2013
2000	85	2002	2005
1999	92	2011	2019
1998	82	2000	2003
1997	87	2005	2009
1996	94	2004	2008+
1995	94	2003	2007
1994	95	2006	2014
1993	94	2005	2013
1992	92	2000	2004
1991	93	2003	2011
1990	96	2002	2010

CRANES EDEN VALLEY CHARDONNAY

RATING **4**

Eden Valley		$20–$29
Current vintage: 2002		**87**

A generous, older-style chardonnay whose slightly brassy and toasty aromas of pungent melon-like fruit are very buttery and honeyed. Smooth, soft and oaky, its juicy palate of peach/melon fruit is ably supported by sweet vanilla/buttery oak, finishing with some phenolic firmness.

2002	87	2004	2007
2000	82	2002	2005
1999	82	2000	2001
1998	92	2003	2006
1997	90	2002	2005
1996	93	2001	2004
1995	90	1997	2000
1994	93	1999	2002
1993	91	1995	1998
1992	92	1997	2000
1991	94	1996	1999
1990	95	1998	2002

CROFT CHARDONNAY

RATING **5**

Lenswood		$30–$49
Current vintage: 2004		**92**

Generously flavoured with a slightly minerally expression of grapefruit, honeydew melon and stonefruit, this round and juicy chardonnay shows an improved measure of oak integration and balance over previous Henschke Chardonnays. There's some creamy, dusty and smoky complexity and some buttery oak beneath its ripe aromas, while the rich, barrel-fermented palate culminates in a lingering, nutty and savoury finish with a persistent core of limey fruit. Wrapped in soft acids, it's a fraction spirity and lacks the complexity for a higher rating.

2004	92	2006	2009
2002	87	2004	2007
2000	87	2002	2005
1999	84	2001	2004
1998	94	2003	2006+
1997	87	2002	2005
1996	94	2001	2004
1995	90	1997	2000
1994	94	1999	2003
1993	89	1995	1998
1990	94	1995	1998

CYRIL HENSCHKE CABERNET SAUVIGNON

RATING 4

Eden Valley	**$100–$200**		
Current vintage: 2002	**96**		

A stunning return to form for one of Australia's most significant cabernet labels. Its dusty and complex fragrance of sweet cassis, black olives, dark plums and fine-grained vanilla and walnut-like oak reveals a distinctive heady and floral quality, with undertones of rosemary and cedar. Firm and mouthfilling, it's long and smooth, beautifully structured and deeply fruited with well-ripened varietal flavours of blackberries and dark plums framed by firm but pliant tannins. Newish oak adds texture and structure, while nuances of cedar and undergrowth contribute to its appealing complexity. It has balance, elegance and cellaring potential aplenty.

2002	96	2014	2022
2001	88	2009	2013
2000	88	2005	2008
1999	81	2004	2007
1997	88	2005	2009
1996	95	2008	2016+
1995	91	2003	2007
1994	89	2002	2006+
1993	87	2001	2005
1992	94	2004	2012
1991	95	2003	2011
1990	95	2002	2010
1989	91	2001	2009
1988	96	1996	2000
1987	87	1992	1995
1986	92	1998	2003
1985	93	1997	2002
1984	95	1992	1996
1983	90	1995	2000
1982	87	1987	1990
1981	94	1993	1998
1980	90	1992	1997
1979	87	1987	1991
1978	91	1990	2000

EUPHONIUM KEYNETON ESTATE

RATING 3

Eden Valley	**$50–$99**		
Current vintage: 2002	**95**		

Briary aromas of blackberry and mulberry confiture are supported by sweet vanilla oak and lightly herbal undertones of white pepper and spices. Smooth, fine and silky, its tightly focused and pristine palate is stained with juicy dark berry, cherry and plum-like flavours tightly knit with lightly smoky vanilla/chocolate oak and fine-grained tannins. Finishes long and savoury, with structure and balance.

2002	95	2014	2022+
2001	86	2006	2009
1999	86	2004	2007
1998	92	2006	2010
1997	87	2002	2005
1996	93	2004	2008+
1994	93	2002	2006
1993	94	2005	2013
1992	93	1997	2000
1991	95	2003	2011
1990	88	1995	1998
1989	87	1994	1997
1988	93	1996	2000
1987	85	1992	1995
1986	94	1998	2003

GILES PINOT NOIR

RATING 5

Lenswood	**$30–$49**		
Current vintage: 2004	**88**		

Slightly jammy and confectionary aromas of wild berries, plums and sweet vanilla oak reveal reductive and meaty undertones. Supple and sappy, its juicy Beaune-like palate reveals some pure berry/cherry fruit, but lacks genuine length and follow-through, finishing quite oaky and porty, with creamy, mouth-coating tannins.

2004	88	2006	2009+
2003	87	2005	2008
2002	82	2004	2007
2001	87	2003	2006+
1999	89	2004	2007
1998	84	2003	2006+
1997	90	2002	2005
1996	90	2001	2004
1994	89	1999	2002

GREEN'S HILL RIESLING

RATING 4

Lenswood	**$20–$29**		
Current vintage: 2004	**90**		

A refreshing, juicy and mineral cool climate riesling with a lightly pungent and perfumed aroma of lime juice, lemon rind and apple backed by spicy hints of musk and cloves. Its tangy and supple palate finishes with lingering fruit, a faint sweetness and a suggestion of wet stone.

2004	90	2006	2009
2002	87	2004	2007
2001	82	2003	2006
2000	87	2002	2005+
1999	90	2001	2004
1998	93	2003	2006+
1997	94	2005	2009
1996	95	2004	2008
1995	93	2003	2007
1994	93	2002	2006
1993	94	1998	2001

HENRY'S SEVEN (Shiraz, Grenache, Viognier)

RATING 4

Barossa, Eden Valley $20–$29
Current vintage: 2004   93

2004	93	2009	2012
2003	91	2005	2008
2002	89	2004	2007+
2001	90	2003	2006

Ripe and savoury; another fine release under this emergent label. Its deeply scented and spicy aromas of plums, cherries, blueberries and cranberries are backed by sweet vanilla oak, white pepper and meaty influences. Richly flavoured, warm and smooth, its long and meaty palate of dark plum and berry flavours reveals underlying suggestions of currants and raisins before a slightly tarry and spirity finish. Framed by firmish, powdery tannins, it has grip and structure.

HILL OF GRACE

RATING 1

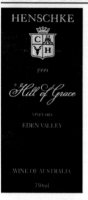

Eden Valley $200+
Current vintage: 2001   91

2001	91	2009	2013+
1999	90	2011	2019
1998	96	2018	2028
1997	95	2017	2027
1996	97	2008	2016+
1995	93	2015	2025
1994	93	2002	2006+
1993	91	2013	2023
1992	95	2012	2022
1991	95	2011	2021
1990	94	2002	2010+
1989	87	1994	1997
1988	96	2008	2018
1987	88	1999	2007+
1986	97	2006	2016
1985	91	2005	2015
1984	88	1996	2004
1983	84	1991	1995
1982	89	1994	2002
1981	84	1986	1989
1980	89	1992	2000
1979	90	1991	1999
1978	95	1998	2008
1977	90	1989	1997+
1976	94	1996	2006
1975	87	1983	1987
1973	95	1993	2003
1972	94	1992	2002

A plush, smooth and densely flavoured shiraz whose slightly jammy expression of redcurrants, liqueur cherries, mulberries and cassis-like fruit reflects the exceptionally hot 2001 vintage. Its aromas reveal undertones of cedar and sweet leather, with coconut ice-like oak, while its palate presents a rich array of spicy fruit backed by dark chocolate oak influences. There's a herbal edge beneath the fruit, while the savoury finish is just slightly attenuated and lacking definition.

JOHANN'S GARDEN (Grenache, Shiraz & Mourvèdre)

RATING 3

Barossa Valley $30–$49
Current vintage: 2004   91

2004	91	2006	2009+
2003	95	2008	2011+
2002	90	2004	2007+
2001	93	2006	2009

A spicy, finely structured and early-drinking red blend whose juicy flavours are framed by silky tannins. There's a floral aspect about its perfume of star anise, blueberries, cranberries and ripe plums, with a subtle background of lightly dusty vanilla oak. Tightly integrated, long and lively, its summer pudding-like delivery of dark berry and plum flavours and vanilla/coconut oak culminates in a lingering finish of licorice-like fruit and dried herbs.

A B C D E F G H I J K L M N O P Q R S T U V W X Y Z

JULIUS RIESLING

RATING **3**

Eden Valley		$20–$29
Current vintage: 2005		**93**

A typically charming Eden Valley riesling fragrance of lime juice and musky rose petals with undertones of wet slate and suggestions of mineral precede a lean and tight-knit palate of focus and freshness. Its charmingly soft and supple expression of lime, lemon rind and minerally flavour is underpinned by a fine, powdery chalkiness, while it finishes long and tangy.

2005	93	2013	2017+
2004	93	2009	2012+
2003	90	2008	2011
2002	94	2010	2014
2001	88	2009	2013
2000	84	2002	2005
1999	93	2004	2007
1998	91	2006	2010
1997	94	2005	2009
1996	94	2004	2008
1995	91	1997	2000
1994	95	2006	2014
1993	95	2000	2005
1992	94	2000	2004
1991	95	1999	2003
1990	95	1995	1998
1989	87	1994	1997
1988	88	1993	1996
1987	94	1999	2007
1986	90	1991	1994

LOUIS EDEN VALLEY SEMILLON

RATING **4**

Eden Valley		$20–$29
Current vintage: 2005		**90**

Lightly herbal, dusty and chalky aromas of green melon and chalk reveal floral undertones, while its restrained palate of lemony, honeydew melon flavour has a pleasing length and a dusty, chalky finish. It's a pretty wine, bright and lively, with balance and focus, but should become considerably richer and rounder with time in the bottle.

2005	90	2010	2013
2002	90	2007	2010
2000	87	2002	2005
1999	83	2001	2004
1998	88	2003	2006
1997	90	2002	2005
1996	86	1998	2003
1995	94	2000	2003
1994	93	2002	2006
1993	95	1998	2001

MOUNT EDELSTONE

RATING **3**

Eden Valley		$50–$99
Current vintage: 2003		**95**

An excellent wine from a challenging vintage. Its deep aromas of slightly jammy redcurrants, cranberries, cassis and candied red cherries are fully but not over-ripe, with spicy undertones of cloves and cinnamon, plus a smoky background of creamy coconut ice-like oak. There's a hint of spirit that is also found on the deeply concentrated and sumptuous palate, whose jujube-like berry and plum-like fruit and newish, assertive and slippery oak are neatly framed by loose-knit tannins. Its lingering core of intense flavour finishes licorice-like, with savoury and mineral notes. A richer and more profound Mount Edelstone than ever seen before, and lacking the cooked or dehydrated flavours common from this vintage, it just lacks the exceptional length for a higher rating.

2003	95	2015	2023+
2002	97	2014	2022+
2001	92	2009	2013
2000	82	2002	2005+
1999	92	2007	2011
1998	88	2000	2003+
1997	87	2005	2009
1996	90	2004	2008
1995	93	2007	2015
1994	92	2002	2006
1993	95	2005	2013
1992	94	2004	2012
1991	95	2003	2011
1990	95	2002	2010
1989	89	1997	2003
1988	94	2000	2005
1987	87	1995	2001
1986	93	1998	2003
1985	87	2005	2015
1984	88	1996	2001
1983	90	1995	2000
1982	90	1994	1999

Hewitson

66 London Road, Mile End SA 5031. Tel: (08) 8443 6466. Fax: (08) 8443 6866.
Website: www.hewitson.com.au Email: dean@hewitson.com.au

Regions: **Barossa Valley, Fleurieu Peninsula** Winemaker: **Dean Hewitson** Chief Executive: **Dean Hewitson**

Dean Hewitson appears to be enjoying himself thoroughly at his self-appointed task of making small parcels of distinctive wine from ancient vineyards. His wines reflect not only a technical stability and correctness, but a level of artisanship rare in Australian wine. Typically full-flavoured, firm and tightly structured, his savoury and earthy reds combine deep, complex and concentrated fruit quality with rusticity and flair.

EDEN VALLEY RIESLING   RATING 4

Eden Valley $20–$29
Current vintage: 2005 92

Zesty aromas of lime and lemon rind reveal floral and mineral undertones. Surprisingly viscous, this generous, round and sumptuous expression of concentrated apple, pear and lime juice flavour ends with a tangy note of lemon meringue. Finishes long, with underlying chalky phenolics.

2005	92	2010	2013+
2004	90	2009	2012
2003	91	2008	2011
2002	88	2004	2007
1998	90	2003	2006

THE MAD HATTER SHIRAZ (formerly l'Oizeau)   RATING 4

McLaren Vale $30–$49
Current vintage: 2004 90

Powerfully reductive, this rustic and leathery shiraz marries sour-edged dark plum, cherry and blackberry fruit with musky, peppery and licorice-like spices and tightly knit oak. There's a heady cinnamon and clove-like quality to its meaty bouquet, while the sumptuous palate is deeply but not overly ripened, with just a hint of meatiness. It's full in weight but fine and silky, with a lingering savoury finish.

2004	90	2012	2016+
2002	93	2010	2014+
2001	88	2003	2006+
2000	93	2008	2012+
1999	86	2004	2007
1997	87	1999	2002
1996	86	2001	2004

MISS HARRY (Grenache Shiraz Mourvèdre)   RATING 4

Barossa Valley $20–$29
Current vintage: 2005 91

Smooth, spicy and savoury, this typically regional blend of southern Rhône varieties is deliciously and deeply fruited, with a restrained expression of grenache that doesn't dominate the other varieties. Deep aromas of plums, cherries and dark berries have a slightly confectionary aspect, with dusty undertones of cinnamon, cloves and nutmeg. Smooth and polished, its palate is spicy, long and finishes with a note of licorice.

2005	91	2007	2010
2004	90	2005	2006+
2003	93	2004	2005+
2002	91	2003	2004+
2001	90	2003	2006

NED & HENRY'S SHIRAZ   RATING 4

Barossa Valley $30–$49
Current vintage: 2005 89

A sumptuous, smooth and spicy shiraz with a spicy, peppery and cinnamon-like fragrance of red cherries, raspberries and sweet plums. Full to medium in weight, its rich and juicy flavours of blackberries, plums and currants are backed by tarry, treacle-like nuances, while the palate shows pleasing persistence and length. Very generous, but drink relatively soon.

2005	89	2007	2010
2004	90	2007	2009
2002	90	2004	2007+

OLD GARDEN MOURVÈDRE

RATING 3

Barossa Valley	$30–$49	2004	87	2006	2009
Current vintage: 2004	87	2003	91	2005	2008+

2004	87	2006	2009
2003	91	2005	2008+
2002	92	2010	2014+
2001	91	2009	2013
2000	95	2012	2020

Barossa Valley $30–$49
Current vintage: 2004 87

A meaty, slightly cooked and jammy old-style red whose slightly funky, spicy and peppery aromas of red and black plums, dark pepper and olives precede a forward, juicy and currant-like palate just lacking in focus and freshness. Earthy and leathery, quite evolved, it's a touch awkward and lacking in tightness.

Hill Smith Estate

Flagman Valley Road, Eden Valley SA 5235. Tel: (08) 8561 3200. Fax: (08) 8561 3393.
Website: www.hillsmithestate.com Email: info@hillsmithestate.com

Region: **Eden Valley** Winemaker: **Louisa Rose** Viticulturist: **Robin Nettelbeck** Chief Executive: **Robert Hill Smith**

Hill Smith Estate is a mature Eden Valley vineyard linked through ownership to the Yalumba winery. Its typically grassy Sauvignon Blanc — its sole remaining wine — is typically refreshing and tightly defined.

SAUVIGNON BLANC

RATING 5

Eden Valley $20–$29
Current vintage: 2005 90

Punchy and slightly confectionary aromas of gooseberries, lychees and passionfruit are backed by varietal herbaceous undertones. Its juicy and slightly phenolic palate delivers a fine length of grassy, lychee-like flavour, finishing herbal and clean. Quite shapely, with pleasing texture and definition.

2005	90	2006	2007
2004	89	2005	2006+
2003	90	2004	2005+
2002	88	2003	2004
2001	81	2001	2002
2000	81	2001	2002
1999	92	2000	2001

Hollick

Corner Ravenswood Lane & Riddoch Highway, Coonawarra SA 5263. Tel: (08) 8737 2318.
Fax: (08) 8737 2952. Website: www.hollick.com Email: admin@hollick.com

Region: **Coonawarra** Winemakers: **Ian Hollick, David Norman** Viticulturist: **Ian Hollick** Chief Executive: **Ian Hollick**

The disappointing scores given to most of Hollick's current wines reflect my view that the company is not making the most of its mature vineyard resource in the heart of Coonawarra. Too many of the wines are lacking fruit density and sweetness, and reveal green, metallic, under-ripe characters that are impossible to conceal in finished wines. I would also question the oak selection for a number of the red wines.

RAVENSWOOD (Cabernet Sauvignon)

RATING 5

Coonawarra $50–$99
Current vintage: 2001 84

Moderately long, but raw-edged and herbaceous, this leafy expression of small red and blackberry-like cabernet is supported by fine-grained cedary oak, but finishes with green-edged tannins and acids.

2001	84	2006	2009
2000	89	2005	2008
1999	84	2004	2007
1998	94	2006	2010+
1996	87	2001	2004
1994	89	2002	2006+
1993	92	2001	2005
1992	93	2000	2004
1991	95	2003	2011
1990	94	2002	2010
1989	92	2001	2009
1988	93	2000	2005

RESERVE CHARDONNAY

RATING 5

Coonawarra $20–$29
Current vintage: 2004 80

Rather brassy, nutty and meaty aromas of peaches and sweet corn precede a herbal, forward palate of cashews and butterscotch. Very deficient in fruit.

2004	80	2004	2005
2003	87	2005	2008
2002	89	2003	2004+
2001	84	2002	2003
2000	82	2001	2002
1999	89	2001	2004
1998	83	2000	2003
1997	82	1998	1999
1996	87	1998	2001
1995	83	2000	2003

RIESLING

Coonawarra $12–$19
Current vintage: 2004 87

An early-drinking riesling whose honeyed aromas of pear, peaches and lemon detergent precede a juicy, forward palate of generous lime/lemon and apricot-like flavours. It finishes with some tightness, but with a metallic hint of green acidity.

Year	Score		
2004	87	2005	2006+
2003	87	2005	2008
2002	85	2003	2004
2001	86	2003	2006
2000	87	2002	2005
1999	86	2001	2004
1998	85	2000	2003
1997	83	1999	2002
1995	88	2000	2003
1994	88	1999	2002
1992	94	1997	2000
1991	91	1993	1996

SHIRAZ CABERNET SAUVIGNON

RATING 5

Coonawarra $20–$29
Current vintage: 2004 86

Pleasingly sweet and juicy, with a slightly peppery bouquet of small black and red berries, plums and ashtray/cardboard-like oak. Fine and elegant, medium to full in weight and framed by fine, tightly knit tannins, its vibrant palate of small berry flavours and underlying savoury and herbal qualities are rather flattened by its unusual oak treatment.

Year	Score		
2004	86	2006	2009
2002	84	2004	2007
2001	83	2003	2006
2000	90	2001	2002
1998	90	2000	2003+
1997	82	1999	2002

WILGHA SHIRAZ

RATING 5

Coonawarra $30–$49
Current vintage: 2003 89

Spicy and slightly jammy aromas of blackberries, raspberries, cloves and nutmeg overlie lightly varnishy, cardboard-like oak influences. Long and elegant, its briary palate of black and red berries is lively and fine-grained, with undertones of dried herbs and lingering nuances of sweet fruit and star anise. The oak is just a little underwhelming and cardboardy.

Year	Score		
2003	89	2008	2011
2002	83	2004	2007
2000	87	2002	2005
1999	88	2001	2004+
1998	81	2000	2003
1997	86	1999	2002
1996	82	1998	2001
1994	91	1996	1999
1993	90	1998	2001
1992	89	1997	2000
1991	92	1996	1999
1990	91	1995	1998

Houghton

Dale Road, Middle Swan WA 6056. Tel: (08) 9274 5100. Fax: (08) 9250 3872.
Website: www.houghton-wines.com.au

Regions: **Various WA** Winemakers: **Robert Bowen, Ross Pamment, Simon Osicka** Viticulturist: **Ron Page**
Chief Executive: **David Woods**

Having given Houghton a loud and deserved rap last edition, I'm finding it a little hard to sound as enthusiastic this time around about Western Australia's largest producer. It hasn't escaped my attention that the only current release to rate more highly than that of the previous year was for the wine formerly known as White Burgundy, whose name has thankfully — and finally — been changed to White Classic. Then again, perhaps that is simply a reflection of the ground made by Houghton in recent years and the reality with viticulture that you can't always do it year in, year out.

CROFTERS CABERNET MERLOT

RATING 5

Western Australia $12–$19
Current vintage: 2003 86

Slightly hollow and weedy, this young cabernet blend of moderate weight has a simple but slightly stewy aroma of plums, berries and sweet vanilla oak over attractive nuances of flowers and forest floor. Rather forward, its initially vibrant plum confiture-like flavour palate thins out towards a herbal and minty finish.

Year	Score		
2003	86	2008	2011
2002	86	2007	2010
2001	87	2006	2009
2000	90	2008	2012+
1999	87	2007	2011
1998	88	2003	2006

CROFTERS SEMILLON SAUVIGNON BLANC

RATING 5

Margaret River, Pemberton Mount Barker $12–$19
Current vintage: 2005 **90**

A lively, tangy and brightly flavoured blend whose delicate aromas of passionfruit, lemon and tropical fruits reveal nettle-like herbal undertones, with a suggestion of vanilla oak. Tightly focused and refreshing, its long and restrained palate of mouthfilling and lightly herbal fruit fits neatly with a hint of oak and a crisp acidity.

2005	90	2006	2007+
2004	90	2005	2006+
2003	84	2004	2005
2002	88	2004	2007
2001	85	2002	2003

FRANKLAND RIVER SHIRAZ

RATING 5

Frankland River $20–$29
Current vintage: 2003 **86**

This rather firm, unfinished and old-fashioned shiraz has very ripe, jammy and lightly spicy aromas of plums and blackcurrants backed by chocolate/mocha oak. Its porty, leathery and chocolate-like flavour is overwhelmed by an excessively raw and astringent coating of tannin. Lacks length and brightness.

2003	86	2008	2011
2002	88	2007	2010
2001	87	2006	2009+
2000	89	2008	2012
1999	90	2004	2007

GLADSTONES SHIRAZ

RATING 3

Frankland River $50–$99
Current vintage: 2003 **89**

A robust and meaty shiraz whose deep flavours of red and black berries are perhaps overwhelmed by an even more assertive extract and oakiness. Its smoky, charcuterie-like aromas of raspberries, dark cherries and cassis reveal undertones of dried herbs, while its deep, robust palate is framed by slightly blocky and raw-edged tannins. It finishes with gamey and tomato-like undertones.

2003	89	2008	2011
2002	90	2010	2014+
2001	88	2009	2013+
2000	95	2012	2020
1999	96	2007	2011+

JACK MANN RED

RATING 2

Various WA, mainly Great Southern $50–$99
Current vintage: 2001 **94**

A deep, closed, brooding and rather old-fashioned wine with dark, minty aromas of cassis, plums and violets tightly knit with sweet vanilla and cedary oak. It's long, very firm and tight-fisted, with a dark, powerful core of concentrated fruit firmly wrapped around an astringent spine of drying, powdery tannin. Give it plenty of time to breath if you're thinking of opening it before it's really ready.

2003	91	2015	2023
2002	95	2014	2022+
2001	94	2011	2021+
2000	86	2008	2012+
1999	93	2011	2019
1998	96	2018	2028
1996	91	2008	2016
1995	93	2007	2015+
1994	95	2006	2014+

MARGARET RIVER CABERNET SAUVIGNON

RATING 4

Margaret River $20–$29
Current vintage: 2002 **88**

Rather overpowering, mouth-coating tannins grip this slightly heavy-handed and juicy expression of blackberry, cherry and plum-like fruit. Its cedary bouquet reveals dusty, herbal and slightly cheesy undertones, while the firm and tightly-knit palate opens with richness and depth, but lacks great length and penetration.

2002	88	2007	2010+
2001	92	2009	2013
2000	90	2005	2008+
1999	85	2001	2004+

PEMBERTON CHARDONNAY

RATING 4

Pemberton	**$20–$29**		
Current vintage: 2005	**88**		

A competent chardonnay that is almost very much better. Its smoky aromas of grapefruit, pineapple and melon is backed by vanilla and matchstick-like oak, with undertones of butterscotch and lemon zest. Generous and juicy, it marries brightly lit fruit with malolactic undertones, assertive but measured oak and refreshing acidity. The only drawback is a slightly acrid and smoky presence that emerges after the finish.

2005	88	2007	2010
2004	90	2006	2009
2003	93	2005	2008+
2002	91	2004	2007+
2001	92	2003	2006

PEMBERTON SAUVIGNON BLANC

RATING 3

Pemberton	**$20–$29**		
Current vintage: 2005	**90**		

A highly acidic sauvignon blanc whose lightly herba-ceous aromas of passionfruit, gooseberries and tropical fruits reveal a faint sweatiness. Its essence-like palate of concentrated, almost exaggerated varietal fruit is tightly punctuated by a rather brisk and overt acidity. Would rate even higher if its acids were better integrated.

2005	90	2006	2007+
2004	93	2005	2006+
2003	91	2003	2004+
2002	93	2003	2004+
2001	85	2002	2003

WHITE CLASSIC (formerly White Burgundy)

RATING 5

Western Australia	**$12–$19**		
Current vintage: 2006	**87**		

Tropical, passionfruit-like and lightly grassy aromas precede a juicy, vibrant and early-drinking palate whose attractive bright fruit finishes with clean acids and a faint lingering sweetness.

2006	87	2006	2007
2005	86	2005	2006
2004	86	2005	2006
2003	87	2003	2004+
2002	82	2002	2003
2001	87	2002	2003+
2000	77	2001	2002
1999	87	2001	2004
1998	87	2000	2003

Howard Park

Lot 377, Scotsdale Road, Denmark WA 6333. Tel: (08) 9848 2345. Fax: (08) 9848 2064.
Miamup Road, Cowaramup, WA, 6284 Tel: (08) 9756 5200. Fax: (08) 9756 5222.
Website: www.howardparkwines.com.au Email:hpw@hpw.com.au.

Regions: **Great Southern, Margaret River** Winemakers: **Michael Kerrigan, Andy Browning** Chief Executive: **Jeff Burch**

To me, at least, Howard Park is an enigmatic wine company. I find its Margaret River reds from the Leston vineyard to be more complete and balanced than its Cabernet Sauvignon flagship wine, an issue that puts me at odds with most wine critics, not to mention the folks at Howard Park itself. The drying, hard edges and rawness of the 2003 Cabernet Sauvignon contrast unfavourably with the richness and brightness of the 2004 Leston reds. Special mention, however, must be made of the 2004 Chardonnay, easily the best ever released by Howard Park, and a seamless chardonnay of suppleness and smoothness.

CABERNET SAUVIGNON

RATING 4

Great Southern,			
Margaret River	**$50–$99**		
Current vintage: 2003	**88**		

A slightly meaty bouquet of blackberries, currants and prunes, dusty cedar/dark chocolate oak and earthy undertones reveals evolving undertones of sweet leather. Lacking generosity and fruit sweetness, the palate presents stewy suggestions of currants, plums and raisins framed by firm, drying and kernel-like tannins with a metallic hardness. Firm and linear, lean and tight, it reflects rather green-edged fruit.

2003	88	2008	2011+
2002	88	2007	2010+
2001	89	2009	2013+
2000	90	2005	2008+
1999	92	2004	2007+
1998	83	2003	2006
1997	86	2002	2005+
1996	96	2008	2016
1995	83	2000	2003
1994	96	2014	2024
1993	92	2001	2005+
1992	97	2004	2012+
1991	93	2003	2011
1990	90	1998	2002
1989	95	2001	2009
1988	96	2008	2018
1987	90	1995	1999+
1986	95	2006	2016

CHARDONNAY

Great Southern $30–$49
Current vintage: 2004 95

A polished and beautifully integrated chardonnay whose crystal-bright flavours of grapefruit, pineapple and quince knit harmoniously with dusty, nutty vanilla oak and refreshingly citrusy acids. Its aroma reveals undertones of cloves and cinnamon, while its smooth, supple and creamy palate culminates in a tightly focused and mineral finish.

2004	95	2009	2012
2003	89	2005	2008
2002	87	2004	2007
2001	86	2006	2009
2000	89	2002	2005
1999	90	2001	2004
1998	90	2000	2003
1997	87	1999	2002
1996	91	1998	2001
1995	94	2000	2003
1994	94	1999	2002
1993	93	1998	2001

LESTON CABERNET SAUVIGNON

RATING **4**

Margaret River $30–$49
Current vintage: 2004 93

Elegant, stylish and tightly crafted, this balanced and firmish cabernet has an intense bouquet of slightly meaty and gamey dark plum, blackberry and cassis-like aromas overlying sweet cedary oak and nuances of mint, mineral and dried herbs. Long, supple and deeply flavoured, its handsomely oaked and sumptuous palate is intermeshed with a firm spine of drying, bony tannins.

2004	93	2012	2016+
2003	93	2011	2015+
2002	89	2007	2010+
2001	90	2006	2009
2000	89	2005	2008+

LESTON SHIRAZ

RATING **5**

Margaret River $30–$49
Current vintage: 2004 92

A violet-like perfume of cassis, raspberries, red-currant and sweet cedar/vanilla oak is backed by spicy, licorice-like undertones. Fine, polished and elegant, its smooth, willowy and spotless palate of medium to full weight bursts with intense flavours of red and black berries with nuances of dark plums and tomato stalk. It finishes savoury, with a fine coating of tight-knit tannins.

2004	92	2009	2012
2003	89	2008	2011
2002	88	2004	2007+
2001	88	2003	2006+
2000	91	2005	2008
1999	87	2001	2004

RIESLING

RATING **4**

Great Southern $20–$29
Current vintage: 2005 93

A fine, shapely and tightly focused riesling of elegance and intensity. Its piercing, floral perfume of lime juice and lemon rind reveals a hint of mineral, while its long and marginally candied palate of lemon/lime flavour and bath powder-like undertones delivers plenty of juicy fruit sweetness. The finish is long and persistent, punctuated by slightly sour-edged acids.

2005	93	2010	2013+
2004	87	2006	2009
2003	95	2011	2015
2002	84	2004	2007+
2001	88	2006	2009
2000	87	2008	2012
1999	86	2001	2004+
1998	92	2003	2006
1997	94	2005	2009+
1996	93	2004	2008
1995	94	2000	2003+
1994	92	2002	2006
1993	95	2001	2005
1992	95	2004	2012
1991	94	2003	2011

SCOTSDALE CABERNET SAUVIGNON

RATING **5**

Great Southern $30–$49
Current vintage: 2004 81

Hollow, thin and green, with a polished cut of sweet vanilla and cedary oak that fails to compensate for the greenish and under-ripe small red berry flavours that are framed by a sappy extract of metallic tannin.

2004	81	2006	2009
2003	86	2008	2011
2001	93	2006	2009+
2000	82	2002	2005
1999	87	2001	2004

SCOTSDALE SHIRAZ

RATING **5**

Great Southern	$30–$49
Current vintage: 2004	86

Rather simple, cooked and oaky, with herbal undertones. Ground coffee and mocha oak tends to dominate meaty aromas of prune and currant-like fruit, while the palate is excessively reliant on its sweet oak for brightness and length. Meaty and dehydrated, it falls away towards a flat and sappy finish of lingering herbal influences.

2004	86	2006	2009
2003	89	2005	2008
2002	93	2007	2010
2001	88	2003	2006+
2000	91	2002	2005+

Huntington Estate

Cassilis Road, Mudgee NSW 2850. Tel: (02) 6373 3825. Fax: (02) 6373 3730. Email: huntwine@hwy.com.au

Region: **Mudgee** Winemaker: **Tim Stevens** Viticulturist: **Colin Millott** Chief Executive: **Tim Stevens**

Now owned by Tim and Connie Stevens of nearby Abercorn, Huntington Estate makes ripe, firm and rustic red wines that offer both value and character. Its Special Reserve releases offer an extra degree of intensity, evolution and structure, and receive additional time in newer oak. 2002 is the best red vintage for several years, delivering plenty of dark, leathery and chocolatey flavour as well as Huntington's customary longevity.

CABERNET SAUVIGNON

RATING **5**

Mudgee	$12–$19
Current vintage: 2002	90

Earthy, meaty aromas of redcurrants and blackberry jam, with undertones of dark chocolates and polished leather. Soft, round and generous, its long palate of intense cassis, plum and blackberry flavour culminates in a savoury, earthy finish and a firm grip of supple tannins and restrained oak. Delightfully rustic, with plenty of character.

2002	90	2010	2014+
2001	87	2009	2013
1999	89	2007	2011+
1998	88	2006	2010
1997	85	2002	2005+
1995	88	2003	2007
1994	88	2002	2006
1993	89	2001	2005
1992	93	2004	2012
1991	90	1996	1999

RESERVE CABERNET SAUVIGNON

RATING **4**

Mudgee	$20–$29
Current vintage: 2002	91

An old-fashioned, concentrated red whose heady aromas of plums, cassis and blackberries are backed by assertive smoky vanilla oak and undertones of licorice, tar and treacle. Ripe and sumptuous, it's thickly laden with dark fruit and gripped by firm, furry tannin. The oak is fairly intrusive right now, but should ease back with time.

2002	91	2014	2022
2001	93	2013	2021
1999	92	2011	2019
1997	87	2005	2009
1994	80	2002	2006

RESERVE SHIRAZ

RATING **5**

Mudgee	$20–$29
Current vintage: 2002	89

An oaky and spirity Mudgee red that needs time. Its assertively wooded and slightly meaty aromas of blackberry and redcurrant confiture reveal nuances of polished leather and clove-like spiciness. Firm and sinewy, its deeply fruited palate of black and red berries is presently overawed by its rather raw and angular oak, but should have what it takes to come together.

2002	89	2010	2014+
2001	87	2006	2009
1999	86	2004	2007

SEMILLON

Mudgee	$12–$19	2005	89	2007	2010+
Current vintage: 2005	**89**	2004	82	2005	2006

Zesty aromas of lemon sherbet, lime marmalade and bath powder precede a fresh, forward and slightly candied palate whose vibrant melon-like fruit finishes with a lingering minerality and lemony acids. Fresh and lively, but just a fraction sweet.

2003	83	2005	2008
2002	87	2004	2007
2000	90	2002	2005
1999	84	2001	2004
1998	86	2000	2003
1997	90	2002	2005
1996	93	2001	2004
1995	92	2000	2003

SHIRAZ

Mudgee	$12–$19	2002	90	2010	2014+
Current vintage: 2002	**90**	2001	84	2003	2006+

An honest regional cellaring shiraz from Mudgee, with slightly porty and meaty aromas of brambly berry/plum fruit, backed by sweet oak and lifted by a floral perfume. Firm and drying, its rustic and evolving palate is already showing some earthy maturity, but steadily reveals more depth of fruit with time in the glass.

1999	87	2004	2007+
1998	81	2003	2006
1997	90	2005	2009
1995	89	2003	2007+
1994	86	1999	2002
1993	95	2005	2013
1992	89	1997	2000
1991	91	1999	2003

'i'

RMB 555 Old Moorooduc Road, Tuerong Vic 3933. Tel: (03) 5974 4400. Fax: (03) 5974 1155.
Website: www.dromanaestate.com.au Email: info@dromanaestate.com.au
Regions: **Alpine Valleys, Mornington Peninsula** Winemaker: **Rollo Crittenden** Viticulturist: **Rollo Crittenden**
Chief Executive: **Richard Green**

Made by Dromana Estate, this range of Italian varieties is among the best and most convincing collections of its kind. Like all Australian efforts with these varieties, the concept is still very much a 'work in progress', but as a group the wines reliably display genuinely varietal flavours and textures. The range was initially developed through the inspirational work and endeavour of Garry Crittenden.

ARNEIS

King Valley,		2004	87	2006	2009
Mornington Peninsula	$20–$29	2003	90	2003	2004
Current vintage: 2004	**87**	2002	77	2002	2003

Dusty aromas of pears and dried herbs precede a forward, round and juicy palate whose tangy pear/apple flavours finish dusty and savoury with a lingering core of fruit.

2001	89	2003	2006
2000	89	2001	2002+
1999	86	2000	2001

BARBERA

Alpine Valleys	$20–$29	2002	80	2004	2007
Current vintage: 2002	**80**	2001	89	2003	2006

Cooked, meaty and varnishy, revealing under-and over-ripe sweet and moderately intense flavours of black and red berries with greenish, herbaceous undertones. Medium in weight, its spicy palate lacks length and structure, finishing with a varnishy and tomatoey aspect.

2000	89	2001	2002+
1999	86	2000	2001
1998	84	2000	2003
1997	89	2002	2005
1996	89	1998	2001+
1995	90	2000	2003

DOLCETTO RATING 5

Alpine Valleys $12–$19
Current vintage: 2002 87

A minty, spicy dolcetto with a musky aroma of red cherries, rhubarb and red earth over nuances of mint and eucalypt. Medium in weight, it's a fine and elegant early-drinker, with pleasing fruitiness framed by dusty tannins. Finishes clean and savoury.

Year	Score	From	To
2002	87	2003	2004
2001	77	2001	2002
2000	88	2002	2005
1999	83	2001	2004
1998	87	2000	2003
1997	82	1998	1999
1996	87	1998	2001

NEBBIOLO RATING 4

Alpine Valleys $20–$29
Current vintage: 2000 88

Wild and spicy suggestions of rose petals, cooked meats and raisins precede a long, firm and savoury palate of weight structure and integrity. While its earthy and currant fruit is a little faded and dull, its meaty and leathery development and firm astringency offer some genuine varietal quality.

Year	Score	From	To
2000	88	2005	2008
1999	89	2007	2011
1998	93	2003	2006+
1997	91	2002	2005+
1996	88	2004	2008
1995	89	2002	2007
1994	87	2002	2006
1993	83	1998	2001

SANGIOVESE RATING 4

Alpine Valleys $20–$29
Current vintage: 2003 87

Dusty, spicy aromas of slightly candied cherries and plums overlie a meaty, earthy funkiness and undertones of menthol. Medium in weight, it's smooth and elegant, delivering searingly intense flavours of red cherries and plums with a tomatoey aspect. Framed by drying, fine tannins, it finishes with suggestions of overcooked fruit and some meaty, greenish edges.

Year	Score	From	To
2003	87	2004	2005+
2002	84	2004	2007
2001	90	2003	2006
2000	89	2001	2002
1999	94	2004	2007
1998	93	2000	2003+
1997	89	1999	2002
1996	90	2001	2004

Irvine Wines

Roeslers Road, Eden Valley SA 5235. Tel: (08) 8564 1046. Fax: (08) 8546 1314.
Website www.irvinewines.com.au Email: merlotbiz@irvinewines.com.au

Region: **Eden Valley** Winemaker: **James Irvine** Viticulturist: **James Irvine** Chief Executive: **Marjorie Irvine**

James Irvine has achieved an international reputation for his robust and extensively oak-matured Grand Merlot. Made in a traditional Australian fashion, it has made a habit of collecting major international awards. He has recently introduced The Baroness, a merlot-based wine whose first two releases have also contained cabernet sauvignon and cabernet franc. Making the matter slightly confusing, these wines are also multi-vintage blends encompassing a range between 1998 and 2001. Regrettably, a series of unfortunate incidents will delay the release of the next Grand Merlot.

GRAND MERLOT RATING 4

Eden Valley $50–$99
Current vintage: 2002 87

A smooth and carefully handled merlot whose slightly jammy expression of blackcurrant, dark plum and mulberry flavour can't quite conceal an underlying thread of herbaceousness. There's a meaty and vegetal aspect about its violet-like perfume, while its plump and succulent palate of vibrant fruit and restrained cedar/chocolate oak finishes with a disappointing note of capsicum and green bean.

Year	Score	From	To
2002	87	2007	2010+
1999	90	2007	2011
1998	91	2003	2006+
1997	87	2005	2009
1996	89	2004	2008
1995	92	2003	2007
1994	95	2006	2014
1993	95	2005	2013
1992	89	2000	2004
1991	94	1999	2003
1990	93	2002	2010

Jacob's Creek

Barossa Valley Way, Rowland Flat SA 5352. Tel: (08) 8521 3111. Fax: (08) 8521 3100.
Website www.jacobscreek.com.au
Region: **Southern Australia** Winemakers: **Philip Laffer, Bernard Hickin, Susan Mickan**
Viticulturist: **Joy Dick** Chief Executive: **Laurent Lacassgne**

With its complex and almost convoluted extension into Reserve and Limited Edition wines, which have since
been replaced by a diversity of individual vineyard and branded ultra-premium (of considerable class, I might
add), Jacob's Creek is no longer the little modest Australian brand of yesteryear. It now contains the Steingarten
Riesling (deservedly now a '1' rating wine), the excellent Johann Shiraz Cabernet and the occasionally brilliant
individual vineyard Centenary Hill Shiraz from the Barossa. Mind you, the basic Shiraz Cabernet '04 is just terrific.

CENTENARY HILL SHIRAZ RATING 3

Barossa Valley $50–$99
Current vintage: 1999   95

A sumptuous, concentrated and slightly jammy
shiraz in typical velvet-smooth 1999 style. Its sweet
and perfumed fragrance of blackberries, dark plums
and cedar/vanilla oak reveals musky, spicy undertones of cloves and cinnamon. Smooth and
unctuous, its luscious expression of jammy and
slightly juicy and meaty shiraz is ably supported
by a restrained but structured measure of pliant
tannins. Finely honed and balanced, it is beginning
to show the rewards of bottle-age.

2002	97	2022	2032
1999	95	2011	2019
1998	88	2006	2010
1997	90	2009	2017
1996	94	2008	2016
1995	94	2003	2007
1994	96	2006	2014+

CHARDONNAY

Southern Australia $5–$11
Current vintage: 2005   86

Vibrant, juicy and slightly candied aromas of peach,
grapefruit and lemon sherbet precede a vibrant,
tangy palate with a soft, clean and chalky finish
of refreshing acidity. Simple, confectionary and
clean.

2005	86	2005	2006+
2004	89	2005	2006+
2003	86	2004	2005
2002	82	2002	2003
2001	82	2001	2002

JOHANN SHIRAZ CABERNET (formerly Limited Release) RATING 2

Southern Australia $50–$99
Current vintage: 2001   95

Massively concentrated, this sumptuous and
deeply layered wine is profoundly but elegantly
crafted. Its minty aromas of blackberries, raspberries,
cassis, dark chocolate and vanilla are backed by
peppery notes of cloves and cinnamon. Lavishly
coated with firm but pliant tannins, its long and
seamless palate reveals layers of deep, dark
flavours of plums, berries, mint and menthol before
a lingering spicy finish.

2001	95	2013	2021+
2000	93	2012	2020
1999	96	2011	2019+
1998	96	2010	2018
1997	86	1999	2002
1996	94	2008	2016
1994	88	1999	2002

MERLOT RATING 5

Southern Australia $5–$11
Current vintage: 2004   87

A genuinely varietal merlot with a spicy perfume
of vibrant dark plums, cherries and currants over
earthy undertones of riverland fruit. Its smooth,
measured and even palate delivers a lively
expression of earthy and rather minty flavour before
a firm and savoury finish.

2004	87	2005	2006+
2003	88	2005	2008
2002	81	2003	2004
2001	82	2002	2003+

REEVES POINT CHARDONNAY
(formerly Limited Release)

Padthaway $20–$29
Current vintage: 2004 94

A vibrant and tightly focused chardonnay of elegance and complexity. Zesty, floral aromas of grapefruit, melon and lime juice are backed by very restrained and dusty vanilla oak. Long and silky, its generously fruited palate seamlessly integrates with fresh oak and crisp acids, with a persistent core of intense flavour. Excellent balance and potential.

2004	94	2009	2012
2003	94	2005	2008+
2002	86	2004	2007
2001	90	2003	2006+
2000	88	2002	2005
1999	82	2000	2001
1998	86	1999	2000
1996	88	1997	1998

RESERVE CABERNET SAUVIGNON

RATING **5**

Southern Australia $12–$19
Current vintage: 2002 84

Greenish aromas of snow peas, blackberries, mulberries and plums overlie nuances of chocolate and vanilla oak, with a whiff of silage. Forward and green-edged, it delivers some lively cassis/plum fruit but is both raw-edged and sappy, lacking smoothness and tightness. Its tannins are slightly metallic.

2002	84	2004	2007
2001	86	2003	2006
2000	89	2005	2008
1999	87	2001	2004+
1998	87	2000	2003

RESERVE CHARDONNAY

RATING **5**

Southern Australia $12–$19
Current vintage: 2003 88

Spotlessly clean, finely crafted, refreshing and flavoursome, but just a tad sterile. Juicy aromas of melon and lemon rind are backed by light vanilla oak, before a moderately full, round and generous palate of juicy fruit backed by nuances of tobacco. Soft and creamy, with refreshing acids.

2003	88	2005	2008
2002	90	2004	2007
2001	88	2003	2006
2000	87	2002	2005
1999	88	2001	2004

RESERVE RIESLING

RATING **3**

Southern Australia $12–$19
Current vintage: 2004 93

An intense, musky perfume of vibrant lime juice and lemon rind, with faint undertones of kerosene and spice. Exceptionally long and austere, it reveals a palate of searing intensity, bursting with citrus flavour and supported by chalky, baby powder-like phenolics. Tightly sculpted with racy acids, it's youthful and finely balanced, likely to cellar well.

2004	93	2009	2012+
2003	93	2008	2011+
2002	92	2007	2010
2001	88	2003	2006

RESERVE SHIRAZ

RATING **4**

Southern Australia $12–$19
Current vintage: 2003 90

Sumptuously ripened, dark and tarry, this smooth and richly fruited shiraz reflects the warmth of its vintage without being overcooked. Its vibrant and lightly smoky aromas of raspberries, cherries, plums and fresh mocha/vanilla oak reveal slightly confectionary undertones of raisins and currants. Firm and powerfully flavoured, its thick treacle-like palate of juicy fruit finishes with length and balance.

2003	90	2008	2011+
2002	93	2007	2010+
2001	89	2006	2009
2000	87	2002	2005+
1999	89	2001	2004+
1998	87	2000	2003

A B C D E F G H I J K L M N O P Q R S T U V W X Y Z

RIESLING

Southern Australia $5–$11
Current vintage: 2005 88

This fragrant and estery riesling has a candied, spicy and floral perfume of lime juice and lemon rind. Round and generous, with a finely textured, chalky undercarriage, its juicy, tangy and slightly confectionary palate of lime-like flavour finishes with length and refreshing acids.

2005	88	2007	2010+
2004	89	2005	2006+
2003	89	2005	2008+
2002	86	2003	2004+
2001	89	2003	2006
2000	88	2005	2008
1999	89	2001	2004
1998	86	1999	2000
1997	88	1999	2002
1996	89	2001	2004

SHIRAZ CABERNET

RATING 5

Southern Australia $5–$11
Current vintage: 2004 90

A profound, almost powerful expression of this benchmark Australian red wine whose deeply fruited and spicy aromas of plums and cassis precede a vibrant and sumptuous palate of surprising depth and intensity. Retaining its typical elegance, its lingering core of small berry and cherry fruit flavours is handsomely partnered by sweet oak influences and fine, firm tannin. It's fuller and more assertive than its predecessors.

2004	90	2009	2012+
2003	87	2008	2011
2002	90	2010	2014
2001	87	2006	2009
2000	86	2002	2005+
1999	90	2007	2011+
1998	89	2003	2007+
1997	82	1999	2002
1996	85	1998	2001+

ST HUGO CABERNET SAUVIGNON

RATING 3

Coonawarra $30–$49
Current vintage: 2002 88

An honest, uncomplicated and firmish young cabernet with an earthy, spearmint-like bouquet of dark plums and sweet berries backed by dark chocolate/cedary oak and herbal nuances. Robust and quite concentrated, its minty palate of dark berries, plums and assertive sweet oak is firmly gripped by tight-knit tannins, but finishes with lingering green edges.

2002	88	2010	2014
2001	93	2009	2013+
2000	87	2005	2008
1999	90	2007	2011
1998	95	2010	2018
1997	89	2005	2009
1996	93	2008	2016
1994	95	2006	2014+
1993	91	2001	2005
1992	88	1997	2000
1991	95	2003	2011+
1990	94	2002	2010
1989	94	1997	2001
1988	91	1996	2000
1987	89	1995	1999
1986	90	1994	1998
1985	92	1990	1993

STEINGARTEN RIESLING

RATING 1

Eden Valley $20–$29
Current vintage: 2003 98

What a follow-on from the superlative 2002 vintage! Its penetrative, floral and smoky aromas of pure lime, lemon and apple overlie a slightly funky and minerally background of chalky, earthy complexity. Fine, taut and shapely, its wonderfully open expression of pristine riesling flavours are tightly punctuated by sherbet-like acids and underpinned by fine, chalky phenolics. Superbly long and structured, it's an essay in balance and concentration. World class.

2003	98	2015	2023+
2002	97	2014	2022
2001	96	2009	2013+
2000	95	2008	2012+
1999	94	2007	2011
1998	95	2010	2018
1997	95	2005	2009
1996	96	2008	2016
1995	91	2000	2003
1994	96	1999	2002+
1992	93	2004	2012
1991	96	2003	2011
1990	95	1998	2002+
1989	88	1991	1994
1988	90	1993	1996
1987	90	1999	2004
1979	94	1987	1991+

Jamiesons Run

Riddoch Highway, Coonawarra SA 5263. Tel: (08) 8736 3380. Fax: (08) 8736 3071.
Website www.jamiesonsrun.com.au Email: cellardoor@jamiesonsrun.com.au

Regions: **Coonawarra, Limestone Coast** Winemaker: **Andrew Hales** Viticulturist: **Brendan Provis**
Chief Executive: **Jamie Odell**

Jamiesons Run began as a single red blend of Coonawarra shiraz, cabernet and merlot, evolved into a range
of similarly labelled wines (as product managers are wont to do), went upmarket with a plethora of fancy
labels, and is now being adjusted into its latest premium incarnation of 'Country Label' wines. It wouldn't be
difficult to be confused by all this, but like everyone else, I will wait and see. I think there's a lesson beneath
all of this, that says that mistakes tend to last longer than product managers in big companies ...

CHARDONNAY

RATING **5**

Limestone Coast	$12–$19
Current vintage: 2005	**81**

Simple, peachy, greenish, lightly tropical and
estery aromas with a background of light vanilla
and buttery oak precede a juicy, forward palate
of peachy, citrus flavours that finishes short and
skinny, with herbaceous undertones.

2005	81	2005	2006
2004	85	2004	2005+
2003	89	2003	2004+
2002	89	2003	2004
2001	87	2002	2003

MERLOT

RATING **5**

Coonawarra	$12–$19
Current vintage: 2003	**89**

Spicy, slightly gamey and confection-like aromas
of dark cherries, plums and creamy
vanilla/chocolate oak precede a smooth and deeply
flavoured palate. Round and generous, its ripe
cherry/plum fruit intermeshes neatly with
assertive oak and a firm structure of pliant
tannins. Competent, even and measured, but
perhaps lacking a little vivaciousness.

2003	89	2005	2008
2002	86	2004	2007
2001	88	2003	2006
2000	77	2001	2002
1999	82	2001	2004
1998	88	2000	2003

RESERVE COONAWARRA CABERNET BLEND

RATING **4**

Coonawarra	$30–$49
Current vintage: 2001	**95**

Deeply perfumed with violets, cassis, sweet
plums and mulberries, with attractively integrated cedar/vanilla oak and a pronounced suggestion of peppermint. Its smooth, plush palate
sumptuously marries deeply flavoured small
berry fruits with harmoniously integrated oak.
Pleasingly long and complete, with just the
merest hint of salty/stressed 2001 characters.

2001	95	2009	2013
2000	89	2005	2008
1999	88	2004	2007
1998	93	2006	2010+
1996	84	1998	2001
1995	82	1997	2000

Jansz

1216B Pipers Brook Road, Pipers Brook Tas 7254. Tel: (03) 6382 7066. Fax: (03) 6382 7088.
Website: www.jansztas.com Email: info@jansztas.com
Region: **Pipers River** Winemaker: **Natalie Fryar** Viticulturist: **Robin Nettelbeck**
Chief Executive: **Robert Hill Smith**

Owned by S. Smith & Son of Yalumba fame, Jansz is a cutting-edge Australian sparkling label able to source exceptional cool-climate fruit from northern Tasmania. With its new interactive wine visitor centre in Pipers Brook and a developing track record of fine, tightly sculpted and beautifully presented sparkling wines, Jansz is going to take some beating. However, I must admit to a trace of disappointment that the Late Disgorged effort from 1997 has developed just too much tropical and herbaceous influence to live up to the expectations developed by the outstanding 'standard' wine from the same vintage.

VINTAGE CUVÉE (formerly Brut Cuvée) — RATING 3

Northern Tasmania	$30–$49
Current vintage: 2001	**86**

A meaty and rather evolved sparkling wine whose slightly flat, dull and herbaceous aromas of tropical fruits, dried flowers, mealy suggestions and oatmeal reveal some aldehydic undertones. Initially forward and juicy, it becomes rather hollow by mid palate and finishes with greenish and metallic edges, lacking its customary length and freshness.

2001	86	2006	2009
2000	91	2005	2008
1999	93	2007	2011+
1997	95	2005	2009+
1996	89	2001	2004+
1995	87	2000	2003
1994	95	2002	2006
1993	86	1998	2001
1992	94	1997	2000+
1991	89	1996	1999+
1990	95	1998	2002

LATE DISGORGED CUVÉE — RATING 4

Northern Tasmania	$30–$49
Current vintage: 1997	**90**

Fragrant and tropical, with faintly angular and estery aromas of pineapple, citrus fruits and creamy leesy undertones, it's long, fine and savoury. There's a hint of sweetness about its creamy and slightly herbaceous palate of citrusy fruit and bakery yeast, while it finishes with some greenish edges. Given its age and treatment, it's very much driven by primary fruit.

1997	90	2005	2009
1996	87	2001	2004
1995	90	2003	2007
1992	95	2000	2004

Jasper Hill

Drummonds Lane, Heathcote Vic 3523. Tel: (03) 5433 2528. Fax: (03) 5433 3143.
Website: www.jasperhill.com
Region: **Heathcote** Winemaker: **Ron Laughton** Viticulturist: **Ron Laughton** Chief Executive: **Ron Laughton**

Jasper Hill is a dryland vineyard, so several recent seasons — which have witnessed the death of many large trees on the property — have naturally been more difficult from the perspective of making balanced and brightly-fruited wine. It's something of a concern that even the 2004 reds, made in a significantly cooler season than several of its recent predecessors, lack brightness and intensity of fruit. I sincerely hope that Jasper Hill is able to recover its former health. Like many dryland vineyards, it needs healthy rain, and plenty of it.

EMILY'S PADDOCK SHIRAZ CABERNET FRANC — RATING 3

Heathcote	$50–$99
Current vintage: 2004	**90**

This wine needs loads of time for its reserved expression of spicy, currant-like flavours of cranberries, blackberries and cassis to emerge. Profoundly smoky and chocolate-like, its aromas are initially oak-dominated, but then reveal pleasing floral and spicy influences. Framed by very firm, drying and astringent tannins, its impressively structured palate slowly unfolds the sweetness to match its dehydrated currant-like notes.

2004	90	2012	2016
2003	90	2011	2015+
2002	88	2010	2014
2001	95	2013	2021+
2000	93	2008	2012+
1999	86	2004	2007
1998	90	2006	2010+
1997	94	2009	2017
1996	89	2000	2008
1995	87	2000	2003
1994	88	2002	2006
1993	93	2001	2005+
1992	87	2012	2022
1991	96	2003	2011
1990	94	2002	2010

GEORGIA'S PADDOCK NEBBIOLO

RATING **3**

Heathcote	$50–$99
Current vintage: 2004	94

Firm, drying and very complex, this meaty young nebbiolo should open up delightfully over the next few years. Its wild and briary aromas of meaty, herbal and raspberry-like fruit precede a powerfully constructed palate. Its very spicy and slightly spirity expression of plum and berry flavours is framed by tight, bony tannins, finishing long and savoury.

2004	94	2009	2012+
2003	91	2008	2011+
2002	83	2010	2014
2001	92	2006	2009+
2000	92	2005	2008+

GEORGIA'S PADDOCK RIESLING

RATING **4**

Heathcote	$20–$29
Current vintage: 2005	93

Fine and elegant, this chalky young riesling has a lightly floral perfume of lemon rind, lime juice and green apples. Its juicy and deliciously vibrant palate of fresh citrus and apple flavour is tightly sculpted around crunchy acids and bath powder-like phenolics, finishing with effortless length and persistence.

2005	93	2010	2013+
2004	89	2006	2009+
2003	90	2008	2011+
2002	90	2007	2010+
2001	87	2006	2009+
2000	91	2005	2008
1998	90	2003	2006
1997	93	2005	2009
1996	87	1998	2001

GEORGIA'S PADDOCK SHIRAZ

RATING **3**

Heathcote	$50–$99
Current vintage: 2004	89

A firm, powerful and linear shiraz whose somewhat varnishy aromas of raspberries, red cherries, dark plums and cedar/vanilla oak are backed by slightly meaty and funky kirsch-like suggestions of spirity fruit with spicy, floral undertones. Framed by firm, fine-grained and powdery tannins, it's a strong, rather cooked and meaty shiraz that delivers some lively fruit sweetness, but also reveals some stressed and dried out influences.

2004	89	2009	2012+
2003	95	2015	2023
2002	90	2014	2022
2001	95	2009	2013+
2000	90	2008	2012+
1999	87	2004	2007
1998	88	2006	2010+
1997	93	2009	2017
1996	94	2008	2016
1995	96	2007	2015
1994	95	2002	2006+
1993	96	2005	2013
1992	95	2004	2012
1991	89	1999	2003
1990	94	2002	2010

Jim Barry

Craigs Hill Road (off Main North Road), Clare SA 5453. Tel: (08) 8842 2261. Fax: (08) 8842 3752.
Email: jbwines@jimbarry.com
Region: **Clare Valley** Winemaker: **Mark Barry** Viticulturist: **Peter Barry** Chief Executive: **Peter Barry**

Jim Barry is a well-established and traditional maker of Clare Valley reds, although it has recently developed a vineyard on the former Penola cricket ground in the southern sector of Coonawarra. Its stable includes the redoubtable The Armagh Shiraz, long considered to be one of the genuine rivals to Penfolds Grange. Recent vintages have seen it take a turn towards more concentrated and alcoholic styles, of which the 2002 is a classic and high-quality example. Its premier rieslings are bottled under 'The Florita' label.

THE ARMAGH SHIRAZ

RATING **2**

Clare Valley	$50–$99
Current vintage: 2002	95

Impressively concentrated and powerfully structured, this is a warm, spirity and not insignificantly dehydrated expression of modern, oaky shiraz with some alcoholic hotness and sweetness. It achieves its high rating because it's genuinely balanced and not too overcooked. It offers astonishing depth of dark, spicy cherry, plum and cassis-like fruit, highlighted by exotically musky undertones of pepper, cloves and cinnamon. It's deep and heady, tarry and chocolate-like, and its undertones of raisins and currants are overshadowed by an impressive core of dark, minty and vibrant ripe fruit. Finishes long and firm, with suggestions of mint, menthol and dried herbs.

2002	95	2014	2022
2001	89	2009	2013
2000	91	2005	2008+
1999	95	2011	2019
1998	92	2006	2010
1997	95	2005	2009+
1996	93	2004	2008
1995	95	2003	2007+
1994	93	2006	2014
1993	88	1998	2001+
1992	94	2004	2012
1991	93	2003	2011
1990	95	2010	2020
1989	94	2009	2019
1988	93	2000	2005
1987	93	2007	2017

THE LODGE HILL SHIRAZ

RATING 4

Clare Valley $12–$19
Current vintage: 2004   87

Supple, smooth and early-drinking, this fruity, spicy and short-term shiraz has a lightly herbal, violet-like and minty aroma of cranberries, red plums and redcurrants. Framed by a fine and approachable cut of tannin, its vibrant and juicy palate of black and red berries, plums and restrained cedar/vanilla oak is backed by nuances of white pepper.

2004	89	2006	2009
2003	89	2005	2008+
2002	90	2004	2007+
2001	92	2006	2009+

THE McRAE WOOD SHIRAZ

RATING 5

Clare Valley $30–$49
Current vintage: 2003   86

Oaky and drying out, this fast-maturing shiraz provides a big, smoky, mocha-like mouthful of meaty, currant-like fruit with a treacle-like aspect in place of fruit sweetness. Cooked and stressed, it shows how tough a vintage 2003 was for the Clare Valley.

2003	86	2005	2008
2002	88	2007	2010+
2001	82	2003	2006+
2000	87	2002	2005+
1999	88	2004	2007
1998	89	2003	2006
1997	84	2002	2005
1996	93	2004	2008
1995	91	2000	2003
1994	94	2002	2006
1993	87	1995	1998
1992	93	2000	2004+

WATERVALE RIESLING

RATING 4

Clare Valley $12–$19
Current vintage: 2005   91

Spicy floral and slightly candied, its lemony aromas and tangy, juicy palate of lime/apple flavour culminate in a clean, crunchy finish of refreshing acids. It's long, fresh and tightly focused, with pleasing shape and generosity.

2005	91	2010	2013
2004	91	2009	2012+
2003	89	2005	2008
2002	94	2007	2010+
2001	92	2009	2013
2000	89	2005	2008
1999	95	2004	2007
1998	93	2003	2006+
1997	93	2005	2009
1996	89	2004	2008
1995	91	2003	2007+
1994	88	1999	2002
1993	91	2001	2005

Katnook Estate

Riddoch Highway, Coonawarra SA 5263. Tel: (08) 8737 2394. Fax: (08) 8737 2397.
Website: www.katnookestate.com.au   Email: katnook@wingara.com.au
Region: **Coonawarra** Winemakers: **Wayne Stehbens, Tony Milanowski** Viticulturist: **Chris Brodie**
Chief Executive: **David Yunghanns**

While Katnook Estate has access to some Coonawarra vineyards of genuine maturity, most of its fruit is now sourced from comparatively recent plantings from different sites to those whose fruit helped create its reputation. Its wines continue to be made with high levels of skill and care by Wayne Stehbens, and the company takes great trouble to ensure that the fruit used for its premier wines is of the highest possible standard. It is still a struggle for modern Katnook wine to match the standard of the vintages that made it famous.

CABERNET SAUVIGNON

RATING 3

Coonawarra $30–$49
Current vintage: 2003   90

A finely constructed and elegant Coonawarra cabernet whose vibrant aromas of blackberries, mulberries and cedar reveal nuances of dried herbs and capsicum, with earthy and slightly muddy undertones. Medium to full in weight, it's fine and restrained, with a moderate length of vibrant cassis, mulberry, dark plum and cherry flavours framed by slightly green-edged and metallic tannins. Very well made, but lacking genuine fruit intensity and density.

2003	90	2011	2015
2002	86	2007	2010+
2001	92	2009	2013+
2000	86	2002	2005
1999	95	2007	2011
1998	95	2010	2018
1997	95	2009	2017
1996	95	2008	2016
1995	88	2000	2003
1994	94	2002	2006
1993	94	2005	2013
1992	87	2004	2012
1991	94	2003	2011
1990	92	2002	2010

CHARDONNAY

RATING 4

Coonawarra	$30–$49
Current vintage: 2003	**90**

A finely structured and assembled chardonnay with a toasty, buttery aroma of melon, quince and cumquat-like fruit backed by vanilla oak. Smooth and even, its palate marries a lingering core of stonefruit flavour with assertive, but well-balanced and polished oak. It finishes with just a hint of metallic acidity.

2003	90	2005	2008+
2002	92	2004	2007+
2001	88	2003	2006+
2000	86	2002	2005
1999	87	2001	2004
1998	90	2000	2003
1997	89	1999	2002
1996	93	2001	2004
1995	94	2000	2003
1994	94	1999	2002
1993	94	1998	2001

CHARDONNAY BRUT

RATING 5

Coonawarra	$20–$29
Current vintage: 2004	**86**

Lightly toasty, buttery and peachy aromas reveal creamy undertones of melon and lemon. Its toasty, rather broad and awkward palate of rich nectarine and tropical fruit flavours lacks genuine tightness and freshness.

2004	86	2006	2009
2002	87	2004	2007
2001	85	2003	2006
1996	93	2001	2004
1995	90	2000	2003
1994	82	1996	1999
1993	90	1995	1998
1990	94	1995	1998

MERLOT

RATING 5

Coonawarra	$30–$49
Current vintage: 2004	**86**

Evolving quite quickly, with slightly meaty, leathery aromas of stewed plums, cherries and blackberries backed by sweet oak and herbal undertones. Its forward, currant and raisin-like expression of fruit tends to lack sweetness. Given stuffing though mocha and chocolate oak, its dries out towards the finish, lacking much brightness. Tiring.

2004	86	2006	2009
2002	88	2007	2010
2001	82	2003	2006
2000	87	2002	2005
1999	82	2001	2004
1998	96	2006	2010+
1997	93	2002	2005+
1996	94	2004	2008
1995	87	1997	2000
1994	94	1999	2002
1993	94	1998	2001
1992	93	1997	2000

ODYSSEY

RATING 3

Coonawarra	$50–$99
Current vintage: 2001	**91**

A well-structured, complex and savoury cabernet of full to medium weight. Its slightly sweaty, gamey bouquet of lively plum and blackcurrant fruit, cedar/vanilla/chocolate oak and meaty, dried herbal undertones has a jammy aspect. Initially vibrant and juicy, its dark-fruited palate is firm and oaky, becoming more savoury and cedary towards its long and firm finish. A complex wine, with balanced and slightly reductive influences. Should develop well.

2001	91	2009	2013
2000	87	2008	2012
1999	95	2011	2019
1998	90	2006	2010
1997	90	2005	2009+
1996	97	2008	2016+
1994	95	2006	2014
1992	94	2004	2012
1991	96	2003	2011+

PRODIGY SHIRAZ

RATING 4

Coonawarra	$50–$99
Current vintage: 2002	**92**

Juicy, ripe and oaky, this assertive, peppery and intensely flavoured shiraz presents deep, smooth and vibrant varietal flavours in a slightly old-fashioned and jammy style. Smoky, vanilla and chocolate-like oak and pristine cassis, currant, dark plum and violet-like fruit culminate in a slightly salty and savoury finish of minerally complexity. Already quite leathery, it is very expressive but lacks genuine sophistication.

2002	92	2010	2014
2001	89	2006	2009
2000	88	2002	2005+
1999	89	2004	2007
1998	97	2006	2010
1997	91	2005	2009

RIESLING

Coonawarra	$12–$19
Current vintage: 2005	**88**

A lean, taut, high-acid expression of young riesling with a floral perfume of lime juice and lemon rind. It's clean and refreshing, penetrative and citrusy, with a tangy, lemony finish and a lightly chalky texture.

2005	88	2010	2013
2004	86	2006	2009
2003	89	2005	2008+
2002	90	2004	2007+
2001	87	2003	2006+
2000	89	2005	2008
1999	82	2001	2004
1998	91	2003	2006+
1997	86	1999	2002
1996	87	2001	2004
1995	82	2000	2003

SAUVIGNON BLANC

Coonawarra	$20–$29
Current vintage: 2005	**86**

A rather tight and focused sauvignon blanc whose lightly grassy and passionfruit-like aromas and modest expression of herbal gooseberry and lemony flavour just lacks genuine punch, fruit and brightness.

2005	86	2005	2006
2004	90	2005	2006
2003	90	2004	2005+
2002	90	2003	2004
2001	88	2001	2002
2000	82	2001	2002
1999	82	1999	2000
1998	88	1998	1999

SHIRAZ

Coonawarra	$20–$29
Current vintage: 2003	**88**

A smooth, soft, oaky and early-drinking shiraz whose minty aromas of spicy plums, leather and menthol-like undertones precede a supple, fine-grained palate. Its restrained flavours of small black and red berries, plums and cedar/vanilla/chocolate oak leave a lingering brightness and charm. Finishes with a hint of greenish flavour and extract.

2003	88	2005	2008+
2002	87	2004	2007+
2001	89	2003	2006+
2000	88	2002	2005+
1999	88	2001	2004+
1998	86	2006	2010

Killerby

Caves Road, Willyabrup WA 6285. Tel: 1-800 655 722. Fax: 1-800 679 578.
Website: www.killerby.com.au Email: grapevine@killerby.com.au
Regions: **Geographe, Margaret River** Winemaker: **Simon Keall** Viticulturist: **Michael Brocksopp**
Chief Executive: **Ben Killerby**

Killerby is an ambitious small winery whose recent red releases have been impaired by over-ripe and cooked fruit influences, and whose white wines have lacked their customary tightness and finesse. It's a business that could go places, but it will need to keep a stricter eye on its offerings to the market if it's to do so.

CABERNET SAUVIGNON

Geographe	$20–$29
Current vintage: 2003	**80**

Meaty, rather varnishy aromas of prune and currant-like fruit are backed by meaty, mocha-like oak. While moderately rich, the palate lacks focus and brightness, delivering earthy, leathery and chocolate-like flavours framed by firm, gritty tannins.

2003	80	2005	2008+
2002	89	2007	2010
2001	89	2009	2013
2000	93	2008	2012+
1999	87	2004	2007
1998	86	2003	2006+
1997	86	2002	2005
1996	83	2004	2008
1995	87	2003	2007
1994	82	1999	2002
1993	93	2005	2013
1992	94	2000	2004
1991	87	2003	2011

CHARDONNAY

Geographe, Margaret River $20–$29
Current vintage: 2003   87

Rather cooked and buttery, this peachy, citrusy chardonnay is pungent, broad and generous, delivering rich, spicy stonefruit flavours backed by nuances of wheatmeal and resiny oak. It's juicy and slightly oily, but finishes savoury with soft acids. Could perhaps have used some better oak.

RATING 4

2003	87	2005	2008
2002	92	2007	2010
2001	89	2003	2006
2000	92	2005	2008
1999	80	2000	2000
1998	86	2000	2003+
1997	84	1999	2002
1996	93	2001	2004
1995	93	2000	2003

SAUVIGNON BLANC

Geographe, Margaret River $20–$29
Current vintage: 2005   83

Simple, herbal and slightly confectionary, with lightly grassy lemon sherbet-like aromas and a forward, rather thinly fruited palate of under-ripe fruit.

RATING 4

2005	83	2005	2006+
2004	88	2005	2006+
2003	92	2004	2005+
2002	93	2004	2007
2001	88	2003	2006

SEMILLON

Geographe, Margaret River $20–$29
Current vintage: 2004   90

Complex, almost pungent aromas of green melon, honeysuckle and dried flowers overlie creamy, pastry-like leesy nuances, with a touch of funkiness. Its long, supple palate of delicate and charming melon-like fruit and refreshing lemony acidity is tightly knit with dusty vanilla oak, finishing smooth and savoury.

RATING 4

2004	90	2006	2009+
2003	90	2005	2008+
2002	91	2004	2007+
2001	90	2003	2006
1999	93	2004	2007
1998	84	2000	2003
1997	90	2002	2005
1996	93	2001	2004
1995	94	2000	2003
1994	91	2002	2006
1993	90	1998	2001
1992	91	1997	2000
1991	91	1999	2003
1990	87	1995	1998

SHIRAZ

Geographe, Margaret River $20–$29
Current vintage: 2003   91

A sumptuous but neatly balanced combination of meaty shiraz fruit and chocolate-like, almost gamey oak. With a sweet oaky fragrance of small black and red berries, spices and vanilla oak plus a juicy ripe and slightly tarry palate of deep plum currant-like flavour, it's smoothly framed by velvet tannins.

RATING 4

2003	91	2011	2015
2001	89	2009	2013
2000	89	2005	2008+
1999	95	2007	2011
1998	93	2006	2010
1997	86	2002	2005
1996	89	2001	2004
1995	94	2003	2007
1994	94	2002	2006
1993	89	2001	2005
1992	82	1997	2000
1991	94	1999	2003
1989	89	1997	2001

Knappstein

2 Pioneer Avenue, Clare SA 5453. Tel: (08) 8842 2600. Fax: (08) 8842 3831.
Website: www.knappsteinwines.com.au Email: knappsteinwines@knappstein.com.au
Region: **Clare Valley** Winemaker: **Paul T. Smith** Viticulturist: **Kate Strachan** Chief Executive: **Peter Cowan**

The redevelopment of Knappstein continues apace, driven by the appearance of the new Single Vineyard category, which to date includes two excellent vintages of Ackland, or Single Vineyard Riesling. I have tasted the Single Vineyard Cabernet Sauvignon 2003 on two occasions, and while it has failed to impress, the 2002 wine is very good. The issue now facing Knappstein is maintaining the quality of the rest of its range.

CABERNET MERLOT

Clare Valley $20–$29
Current vintage: 2004 86

Slightly cooked and clunky, with minty, floral and menthol-like aromas of apparently stressed and somewhat meaty currant, prune, cassis, and blackberry-like fruit over sweet vanilla oak. Medium to full in weight, its rather dehydrated fruit is supported by a firm spine of drying, powdery tannins. Honest and early-drinking, but lacking charm and tightness.

2004	86	2006	2009
2003	86	2008	2011
2002	88	2004	2007+
2001	86	2003	2006+
2000	82	2002	2005
1999	88	2004	2007
1998	90	2003	2006
1997	89	2002	2005
1996	91	2001	2004
1995	89	2000	2003
1994	89	2002	2006
1993	87	1998	2001
1992	88	1997	2000
1991	91	1999	2003
1990	90	1992	1995

SINGLE VINEYARD CABERNET SAUVIGNON
(formerly Enterprise)

RATING

Clare Valley $50–$99
Current vintage: 2003 89

A firm and typically long-term Clare Valley red based around sumptuously ripe cabernet, excellent oak and firm, drying tannins. There's a minty, meaty and musky aspect to its menthol-like aromas of cassis, prunes and plums, which are ably supported by sweet cedar/vanilla oak. Deeply fruited, its slightly confectionary palate of jammy raspberries, blackcurrants and red plums is tightly woven around newish oak and a powdery spine of drying tannin. It finishes savoury, with nutty, dusty undertones.

2003	89	2011	2015+
2002	93	2014	2022
2000	86	2002	2005+
1999	89	2004	2007+
1998	95	2010	2018+
1997	93	2005	2009+
1996	95	2008	2016+
1995	90	2003	2007+
1994	89	2006	2014

ENTERPRISE SHIRAZ

RATING

Clare Valley $50–$99
Current vintage: 2000 88

Meaty, concentrated shiraz whose minty, menthol-like expression of pruney, plummy and currant-like fruit is reliant for sweetness and depth on its rather assertive chocolate/mocha oak. It's rich, soft and generous, fine for early drinking, but lacks the length, freshness and structure for longer cellaring.

2000	88	2005	2008
1999	95	2007	2011+
1998	91	2003	2006+
1997	94	2005	2009+
1996	95	2004	2008+
1995	93	2003	2007
1994	95	2006	2014

HAND PICKED RIESLING

RATING 2

Clare Valley $12–$19
Current vintage: 2005   **88**

A savoury and quite heavily worked riesling with delicate, floral and lime juice aromas backed by stony, earthy and slightly reductive nuances of wet slate and talcum powder. It's generously flavoured, with a succulent and chewy palate of apple, pear and lime flavours that becomes fractionally coarse and viscous towards its slightly hot and cooked finish. Lacks its usual freshness.

2005	88	2007	2010
2004	91	2009	2012
2003	94	2008	2011
2002	93	2007	2010+
2001	94	2009	2013+
2000	95	2008	2012
1999	93	2004	2007
1998	95	2006	2010
1997	94	2005	2009
1996	93	2004	2008+
1995	90	2003	2007
1994	94	2006	2014
1993	95	2001	2005
1992	91	1997	2000
1991	90	1996	1999

SHIRAZ

RATING 4

Clare Valley $20–$29
Current vintage: 2003   **85**

Meaty, rather cooked aromas of dark plums, cherries, blackberries and cedar/chocolate oak are lifted by floral undertones. Deep, rich and smoky, its charry, meaty palate is round and very ripe, generous and chunky. A crowd-pleasing style, but finishes too aggressive and drying for its weight of fruit.

2003	85	2008	2011
2002	90	2007	2010+
2001	89	2006	2009+
2000	86	2002	2005
1999	90	2004	2007
1998	92	2003	2006+
1997	88	2002	2005
1996	83	1998	2001

Kooyong

110 Hunts Road, Tuerong Vic 3933. Tel: (03) 5989 7355. Fax: (03) 5989 7677.
Website: www.kooyong.com Email: wines@kooyong.com
Region: **Mornington Peninsula** Winemaker: **Sandro Mosele** Viticulturist: **Sandro Mosele**
Chief Executive: **Giorgio Gjergja**
Kooyong is a significant maker of complex, savoury Chardonnay and brightly lit and perfumed Pinot Noir. Quite surprisingly for such a young operation, it has already evolved an upper tier of labels that feature specific matches of several of the vineyard blocks on the Kooyong site with these two varieties. The best of these, particularly the Chardonnays, are outstanding. Kooyong also releases a very respectable earlier-drinking duo of Massale Pinot Noir and Clonale Chardonnay.

CHARDONNAY

RATING 3

Mornington Peninsula $30–$49
Current vintage: 2004   **93**

Particularly Francophilic, this very floral, mealy and citrusy chardonnay is a finely crafted wine already showing plenty of secondary flavour development. Its aromatic perfume of peach, quince and grilled nuts reveals herbal undertones and deeply scented vanilla oak. Round, smooth and creamy, its generous palate of peach and melon flavour culminates in a tightly focused finish with lingering mineral and butterscotch undertones.

2004	93	2006	2009
2003	93	2005	2008+
2001	95	2006	2009
2000	94	2002	2005+
1999	92	2001	2004

PINOT NOIR

RATING 3

Mornington Peninsula $30–$49
Current vintage: 2004   **94**

An elegant, deeply flavoured and finely crafted pinot whose vibrant perfume of rose petals, cherries and slightly candied red berries reveal pungent, reductive charcuterie-like undertones. Fine and supple, smooth and polished, its restrained but juicy flavours of small red cherries and berries are tightly wound around a fine-grained structure of powdery tannins. Likely to develop richness and weight with time in the bottle.

2004	94	2009	2012+
2003	93	2008	2011
2001	95	2006	2009+
2000	90	2005	2008
1999	92	2001	2004+

Labyrinth

PO Box 7372, Shepparton Vic 3622 (postal only). Tel: (03) 5831 2793. Fax: (03) 5831 2982.
Website: www.labyrinthwine.com Email: ajhill@labyrinthwine.com

Region: **Yarra Valley** Winemaker: **Ariki Hill** Chief Executive: **Ariki Hill**

Operated by American winemaker Ricki Hill, Labyrinth is a small but international pinot noir brand that produces another wine from the Bien Nacido vineyard in California's Santa Maria Valley. The Yarra Valley sites comprise the coolish Viggers Vineyard and the higher elevated but warmer Valley Farm Vineyard. In each of the three vintages bottled to date, I believe that the Viggers site has ripened its fruit more evenly and successfully.

VIGGERS VINEYARD PINOT NOIR

RATING 4

Yarra Valley	$30–$49	2004	93	2009	2012
Current vintage: 2004	93	2003	88	2008	2011
		2002	91	2005	2008+

Supple, fine and delicate, this tightly focused pinot is simply waiting to flower. Its delicate perfume of raspberries, cherries and restrained cedar/vanilla oak suggests a dustiness, while its sweet, round and seamless palate of juicy red cherry and raspberry fruit finishes with nuances of spice and cedar. Moderately firm, with velvet-like tannins, it should acquire more depth and richness.

Lake's Folly

Broke Road, Pokolbin NSW 2320. Tel: (02) 4998 7507. Fax: (02) 4998 7322.
Website: www.lakesfolly.com.au Email: wine@lakesfolly.com.au

Region: **Lower Hunter Valley** Winemaker: **Rodney Kempe** Viticulturist: **Jason Locke** Chief Executive: **Peter Fogarty**

Lake's Folly is a small and iconic Hunter winery and vineyard whose followers are doubtless rejoicing in the remarkable consistency and quality being achieved by the team headed by Rodney Kempe. Its silky, fine and superbly balanced Chardonnay is among the finest now made in Australia, while the Cabernets blend sensitively marries an unusual set of varieties by Hunter standards with the region's inherent elegance and ability to encourage complexity with time in the bottle.

LAKE'S FOLLY (Cabernet blend)

RATING 2

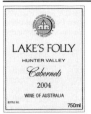

Lower Hunter Valley	$50–$99	2004	92	2006	2024
Current vintage: 2004	92	2003	93	2011	2015
		2002	95	2014	2022
		2001	96	2013	2021+
		2000	96	2012	2020+
		1999	93	2011	2019
		1998	95	2010	2018
		1997	89	2005	2009+
		1996	82	2001	2004
		1995	88	2003	2007
		1994	95	2002	2006+
		1993	94	2001	2005
		1992	87	1997	2000
		1991	90	2003	2011
		1990	87	1998	2002+
		1989	92	2001	2009

A supple, elegant cabernet blend whose floral perfume of violets, cassis and small red berries overlies fine-grained cedar/vanilla oak, plus suggestions of spice and sage. Long, fine and silky, its precise and pristine expression of small red berries, cherries and plums is tightly knit with clean, restrained oak and framed by fine but slightly raw-edged tannins that should settle with time.

CHARDONNAY

RATING 2

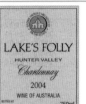

Lower Hunter Valley	$30–$49	2004	96	2012	2016
Current vintage: 2004	96	2003	96	2008	2011+
		2002	95	2007	2010+
		2001	96	2009	2013
		2000	95	2005	2008
		1999	89	2001	2004
		1998	94	2003	2006+
		1997	89	1999	2002
		1996	95	2001	2004+
		1995	89	2000	2003
		1994	90	1999	2002
		1993	89	1998	2001+
		1992	92	2000	2004

A smooth, stylish and spotlessly clean chardonnay right on the style of the new Lake's Folly. Its delicate fragrance of peach, honeydew melon and lightly buttery oak has a distinctive floral aspect, while its seamlessly integrated palate marries a lightly tobaccoey expression of pristine fruit with creamy oak and lightly mineral acids. It's tightly focused, exceptionally long and well defined.

Langmeil

Corner Langmeil & Para Roads, Tanunda SA 5352. Tel: (08) 8563 2595. Fax: (08) 8563 3622.
Website: www.langmeilwinery.com.au Email: info@langmeilwinery.com.au

Region: **Barossa Valley** Winemaker: **Paul Lindner** Viticulturist: **Carl Lindner** Chief Executive: **Chris Bitter**

As expected, Langmeil has begun to release some very good red wine from the 2004 vintage, and has done itself proud with a firm and briary Freedom Shiraz from 2003 that has managed to avoid much of the cooked and dehydrated character so evident in many Barossa shirazes of this vintage. Put that down to the quality of the ancient vineyard as well as its management regime. Langmeil continues to impress.

THE BLACKSMITH CABERNET SAUVIGNON

RATING **5**

Barossa Valley $20–$29
Current vintage: 2004 90

Charming, supple but deeply flavoured, this elegant and sweet-fruited shiraz has a lifted perfume of violets, dark plums, blackberries and cedar/vanilla oak, with a herbal undercurrent of rosemary and sage. It's silky-smooth palate reveals suggestions of mulberries and cassis beneath its vibrant berry/plum fruit, while a fine-grained spine of drying tannin provides tightly integrated support.

2004	90	2012	2016+
2003	87	2008	2011
2002	87	2004	2007
2001	86	2003	2006+
2000	88	2005	2008
1999	91	2007	2011+
1998	90	2006	2010

THE FIFTH WAVE GRENACHE

RATING **4**

Barossa Valley $20–$29
Current vintage: 2003 90

A fine effort from this hot vintage, with spicy, earthy and leathery aromas of dark plums, blueberries, cinnamon cake and dark chocolate. It's fractionally cooked and stewy, but offers a richly flavoured and slightly meaty palate of medium to full weight whose plum and blueberry flavours have a currant-like aspect. Framed by firm, drying and bony tannins, it's long and savoury.

2003	90	2005	2008+
2001	90	2006	2009
1999	91	2004	2007

THE FREEDOM SHIRAZ

RATING **3**

Barossa Valley $50–$99
Current vintage: 2003 94

Very wild, briary and spicy, with confiture-like aromas of blackberries, plums and redcurrants and perfumed, floral notes revealing faint suggestions of tar and treacle, pepper and cloves. Stained with vibrant and deeply concentrated flavours of blackberries, cassis and plums, the palate moves towards a fine and savoury finish whose lingering fruit sweetness is backed by nuances of dark olives and bitumen. Framed by firm, bony tannins, it's slightly spirity but an excellent result from a very hot vintage.

2003	94	2015	2023
2002	93	2010	2014+
2001	91	2006	2009+
2000	91	2005	2008+
1999	96	2011	2019
1998	93	2006	2010+
1997	90	2002	2005+

THREE GARDENS (Shiraz Grenache Mourvèdre)

RATING **4**

Barossa Valley $20–$29
Current vintage: 2004 89

An honest, modern and early-drinking expression of the southern Rhône blend with a jammy, floral and confection-like aroma of raspberries, cherries, plums and gentle spices. Juicy-smooth and spicy, it's powered by its grenache component, but backed by some meaty mourvèdre strength at the back of the palate. It finishes with a lingering core of dark fruit and a spicy, licorice-like flavour.

2004	89	2006	2009
2003	89	2005	2008
2002	90	2004	2007
2001	91	2006	2009
2000	90	2005	2008

VALLEY FLOOR SHIRAZ

RATING 5

Barossa Valley $20–$29
Current vintage: 2004 90

Juicy, slightly jammy aromas of dark plums, berries and cherries are backed by sweet vanilla and cedar/chocolate oak plus undertones of cloves and cinnamon. Long, smooth and polished, its deep expression of pristine, confiture-like flavour finishes long and bright, with lingering blueberry-like undertones. It's framed by fine, smooth tannins that provide genuine structure.

2004	90	2009	2012
2003	86	2005	2008
2002	88	2004	2007
2001	89	2003	2006+
2000	88	2002	2005
1999	93	2011	2019
1998	89	2003	2006+

Leasingham

7 Dominic Street, Clare SA 5453. Tel: (08) 8842 2555. Fax: (08) 8842 3293.
Website: www.leasingham-wines.com.au Email: cellardoor@leasingham-wines.com.au
Region: **Clare Valley** Winemakers: **Kerri Thompson, Simon Cole, Simon Osicka, Stephen Hall**
Viticulturist: **Marcus Woods** Chief Executive: **David Woods**

Part of The Hardy Wine Company, Leasingham is a major Clare Valley producer with long traditions of fine riesling and shiraz, plus its popular Bin 56 Cabernet Malbec blend. While the Classic Clare Riesling is a state-of-the-art wine, the Shiraz and Cabernet Sauvignon in this range are looking rather old-fashioned and oaky. The Bastion wines continue to offer excellent value for money.

BASTION SHIRAZ CABERNET

RATING 5

Clare Valley $12–$19
Current vintage: 2003 88

A grippy, focused and brightly flavoured red blend with a pungent, spicy and slightly meaty aroma of dark plums and blackberries, cloves and cinnamon, mint and menthol. Backed by creamy and cedary oak, its elegant but moderately firm palate of bright cassis, chocolate, blackberry and plum flavour is framed by powdery tannins. Wonderful value for money.

2003	88	2005	2008+
2002	88	2007	2010
2001	86	2002	2003
2000	87	2005	2008

BIN 7 RIESLING

RATING 3

Clare Valley $12–$19
Current vintage: 2005 94

Brittle and tightly focused, this finely crafted young riesling has a floral perfume of fresh lime and lemon rind, with delicate undertones of minerals and rose petals. Its long, mineral palate of lemon sherbet and lime juice overlies a tight, bath powdery texture before a lingering, dry and tightly integrated schisty finish.

2005	94	2010	2013+
2004	89	2009	2012
2003	95	2008	2011
2002	88	2004	2007
2001	91	2003	2006
2000	94	2008	2012
1999	89	2004	2007
1998	92	2006	2010
1997	85	2002	2005
1996	90	2001	2004+

BIN 56 CABERNET MALBEC

RATING 4

Clare Valley $20–$29
Current vintage: 2002 91

Rustic, briary and earthy aromas of dark berries, plums and cedar/chocolate oak reveal lightly floral undertones of dried herbs, mint and menthol. Smooth, elegant and creamy, the palate marries vibrant black and red fruits with earthy, herbal malbec influences and fine-grained tannins. It's full to medium in weight, with a lingering core of fruit and a herbal, rosemary-like finish.

2002	91	2010	2014+
2001	87	2006	2009+
2000	84	2002	2005
1999	90	2004	2007+
1998	92	2006	2010
1997	86	2002	2005+
1996	90	2004	2008
1995	96	2000	2003
1994	90	1999	2002
1993	89	2001	2005
1992	93	2000	2004
1991	90	1999	2003+
1990	90	1998	2002
1989	86	1994	1997

BIN 61 SHIRAZ

RATING 4

Clare Valley $20–$29
Current vintage: 2004 **91**

A polished, smooth and supple marriage of musky, lightly minty, dark-fruited shiraz with assertive, lightly toasty dark chocolate, cedar and vanilla oak influences and velvet-fine tannin. Floral and spicy, scented with pristine aromas of cassis, dark plums and blackberries, it's long and savoury, with a slightly raisined and currant-like aspect.

2004	91	2012	2016
2003	89	2008	2011+
2002	83	2007	2010
2001	90	2006	2009
2000	88	2005	2008
1999	93	2004	2007+
1998	94	2003	2006+
1997	91	2005	2009
1996	90	2001	2004
1995	93	2003	2007
1994	93	1999	2002
1993	89	2001	2005
1992	87	1997	2000

CLASSIC CLARE CABERNET SAUVIGNON

RATING 4

Clare Valley $30–$49
Current vintage: 2003 **89**

An old-fashioned, dark, ripe and brooding cabernet whose slightly meaty aromas of cassis, dark plums and violets overlie fresh cedar/vanilla oak. Very closed, its deep-fisted core of black and red berry fruits and dark chocolate/cedar oak is framed by firm, powdery tannins. It finishes long and persistent, with lingering meaty and jammy fruit.

2003	89	2015	2023
2002	83	2004	2007+
2001	89	2009	2013
1999	94	2011	2019
1998	92	2006	2010+
1997	86	2002	2005
1996	91	2004	2008
1995	87	2000	2003
1994	91	2002	2006
1993	93	2001	2005

CLASSIC CLARE RIESLING

RATING 2

Clare Valley $20–$29
Current vintage: 2005 **95**

A long, restrained and finely honed riesling of delicacy, poise and finesse. Its complex perfume of fresh flowers, apple, lime and minerals precedes a taut, powdery and fine-grained palate with exceptional length of pristine, almost juicy fruit. Punctuated by fresh, vibrant acids and finishing with austerity and tautness, it is simply waiting to explode with fruit and flavour.

2005	95	2013	2017+
2002	96	2010	2014+
2000	93	2008	2012
1998	88	2000	2003
1996	93	2004	2008
1995	94	2003	2007
1994	95	2002	2006+

CLASSIC CLARE SHIRAZ

RATING 3

Clare Valley $30–$49
Current vintage: 2002 **93**

This big, oaky shiraz is bursting with intense cassis, raspberry flavours and deeply scented with exotic spices. There are some earthy, meaty and slightly reductive notes beneath its voluminous fragrance, while the palate reveals a similar aspect that might also be linked to some unusually assertive oak. That aside, the wine is sumptuous and smooth, with a profoundly juicy presence of dark, peppery fruit framed by a fine-grained but almost creamy extract.

2002	93	2010	2014+
2001	91	2006	2009+
1999	90	2004	2007
1998	95	2006	2010+
1997	93	2005	2009
1996	95	2001	2004+
1995	92	2003	2007
1994	95	2006	2014
1993	94	2001	2005
1992	88	1997	2000
1991	94	2003	2011

CLASSIC CLARE SPARKLING SHIRAZ

RATING 3

Clare Valley $30–$49
Current vintage: 1996 **92**

Elegant, fine and tightly integrated, this very polished, smooth and creamy sparking shiraz marries intense, vibrant and youthful fruit qualities with delightful cigarboxy bottle-aged complexity. Slightly herbal and meaty, its gamey aromas of cassis, dark plums, cherries and chocolates precedes a long and silky palate whose vibrant fruit is underpinned by leathery development and herbal undertones.

1996	92	2004	2008
1995	93	2007	2015
1994	95	2006	2012+
1992	93	2000	2004+
1991	88	1999	2003

Leconfield

Riddoch Highway, Coonawarra SA 5263. Tel: (08) 8737 2326. Fax: (08) 8737 2285.
Website: www.leconfieldwines.com Email: coonawarra@leconfieldwines.com
Regions: **Coonawarra, McLaren Vale** Winemaker: **Paul Gordon** Viticulturist: **Bendt Rasmussen**
Chief Executive: **Richard Hamilton**

2004 is the vintage that followers of Leconfield have been waiting for. Its Cabernet Sauvignon, the vineyard's best since 1982, is a tightly focused and finely crafted wine based on a thoroughly ripe core of vibrant cabernet flavour. One now hopes that this standard can be maintained, since the vines occupy some of the best land in the region. While I also really enjoy the very spicy and savoury Shiraz from 2004, it makes little sense to me why this wine was sourced from McLaren Vale and not Coonawarra. It seems folly to attempt to deregionalise the Leconfield name, which I believe should be associated with its own vineyard and region.

CABERNET SAUVIGNON
RATING **5**

Coonawarra	$30–$49
Current vintage: 2004	**93**

A significant improvement for this label. A floral perfume of cassis, raspberries and violets overlies cedar, dark chocolate and vanilla oak influences. Long, fine and tightly focused, its brightly lit palate of cassis and dark plums, fine-grained oak and powdery tannin offer depth and elegance, finishing with varietal undertones of dried herbs.

2004	93	2012	2016+
2003	82	2008	2011
2002	83	2007	2010
2001	91	2009	2013+
2000	84	2002	2005
1999	84	2001	2004+
1998	83	2003	2006
1997	86	2009	2011
1996	87	2001	2004
1995	82	2000	2003
1994	89	1999	2002

CHARDONNAY
RATING **5**

Coonawarra	$20–$29
Current vintage: 2003	**82**

Light buttery, tropical aromas of melon and banana are juicy and confected, while the palate is lean, relatively simple and green-edged.

2003	82	2003	2004
2002	88	2003	2004+
2000	86	2002	2005
1999	84	2000	2001
1998	90	2000	2003

MERLOT
RATING **5**

Coonawarra	$30–$49
Current vintage: 2004	**90**

Charming, elegant and varietal, this vibrant young merlot has a violet-like fragrance of dark cherries and cedar/mocha oak over restrained nuances of undergrowth. Supported by fine and tight-knit tannin, it's long and supple, delivering a lingering core of intense fruit.

2004	90	2009	2012+
2003	89	2008	2011+
2002	81	2004	2007
2001	87	2006	2009
2000	88	2002	2005
1998	90	2003	2006
1997	92	2005	2009
1996	95	2004	2008

OLD VINES RIESLING
RATING **4**

Coonawarra	$20–$29
Current vintage: 2005	**87**

Clean and refreshing, but rather confectionary and estery, this lively young riesling has a spicy, floral perfume and a moderate length of citrusy fruit that finishes with lemon rind-like acids.

2005	87	2007	2010
2004	88	2006	2009
2003	90	2008	2011
2002	93	2004	2007+
2001	88	2003	2006
1999	77	2000	2001
1998	89	2003	2006+
1997	90	2002	2005
1996	87	2001	2004
1995	91	2000	2003

SHIRAZ

RATING **5**

McLaren Vale (formerly Coonawarra) $20–$29
Current vintage: 2004 92

Spicy, slightly meaty aromas of dark plums, blackberries and leather overlie nuances of dark pepper, cloves and cinnamon. Smooth and sumptuous, its sour-edged expression of dark plums and berries, cedar/vanilla oak and firm but silky tannin shows pleasing integration and harmony. It finishes long, spicy and savoury, with a lingering core of jujube-like fruit and hints of mineral.

2004	92	2012	2016+
2003	89	2008	2011+
2002	83	2003	2006
2001	82	2003	2006
2000	87	2002	2005
1999	81	2001	2004
1998	85	2003	2006
1997	92	2002	2005
1996	92	1998	2001
1995	93	2003	2007
1994	92	1999	2002
1993	93	2001	2005
1992	93	1997	2000
1990	95	1998	2002

Leeuwin Estate

Stevens Road, Witchcliffe WA 6285. Tel: (08) 9759 0000. Fax: (08) 9750 0001.
Website: www.leeuwinestate.com.au Email: info@leeuwinestate.com.au
Region: **Margaret River** Winemakers: **Paul Atwood, Damien North** Viticulturist: **David Winstanley**
Chief Executive: **Tricia Horgan**

Leeuwin Estate is a long-established elite maker of Margaret River wine that is best known for its iconic Art Series Chardonnay. This is an exemplary wine that, almost regardless of vintage, has performed at very high levels on each and every vintage since its first in 1980. The 2003 release marries the best qualities of the two excellent prior vintages of 2001 and 2002. The slightly under-rated Sauvignon Blanc is the pick of the wines released to date from 2005.

ART SERIES CABERNET SAUVIGNON

RATING **5**

Margaret River $30–$49
Current vintage: 2001 87

A rustic and meaty cabernet whose sweet red berry and plum-like fruit overlies wild, farmyard and reductive influences suggestive of horse hide. Smooth and elegant, its slightly green-edged expression of black and red berries and plums is framed by firmish but sappy tannins, and supported by creamy oak. It finishes with lingering fruit, but also with notes of menthol and licorice.

2001	87	2009	2013+
2000	85	2005	2008+
1999	87	2004	2007+
1998	89	2006	2010+
1997	82	2005	2009
1996	83	2001	2004
1995	80	2003	2007
1994	89	2006	2014
1993	88	2001	2005
1992	95	2000	2004
1991	95	2003	2011+
1990	95	2002	2010
1989	95	2001	2009
1988	86	2000	2008
1987	87	1999	2004

ART SERIES CHARDONNAY

RATING **1**

Margaret River $50–$99
Current vintage: 2003 97

A classic Leeuwin Estate Chardonnay whose perfectly focused citrus, stonefruit and tropical fruit qualities are interwoven with tightly knit oak and crystalline acidity. There's a suggestion of lemon tart, cloves, vanilla and mineral beneath its penetrative aromas of grapefruit, peach and lemon butter. Exceptionally long and pronounced, its taut and persistent palate knits pristine layers of pineapple, banana, lemon and grapefruit with the purest, brightest acidity. Exemplary.

2003	97	2011	2015+
2002	97	2010	2014+
2001	96	2009	2013+
2000	95	2008	2012
1999	95	2007	2011
1998	95	2006	2010
1997	97	2005	2009
1996	95	2004	2008
1995	97	2003	2007
1994	94	2002	2006
1993	93	1998	2001
1992	93	1997	2000
1991	93	1999	2003
1990	95	2002	2010
1989	94	1997	2001
1988	93	1996	2000
1987	97	1999	2007
1986	97	1998	2006
1985	94	1993	1997+
1984	91	1992	1996+
1983	95	1995	2003
1982	95	1990	1994+

ART SERIES RIESLING

RATING 5

| Margaret River | $20–$29 |
| Current vintage: 2005 | 88 |

Zesty, floral aromas of lemon rind and lime juice reveal a slight confectionary aspect, while its fresh, if marginally sweet palate of intense and tangy lemon/lime fruit overlies pleasingly chalky/bath powdery notes.

2005	88	2007	2010+
2004	89	2006	2009+
2003	89	2008	2011
2002	88	2004	2007+
2001	89	2006	2009
2000	87	2002	2005
1999	87	2001	2004
1998	83	1999	2000
1997	87	2002	2005
1996	90	2001	2004
1995	89	2000	2003
1994	87	1999	2002

ART SERIES SAUVIGNON BLANC

RATING 4

| Margaret River | $20–$29 |
| Current vintage: 2005 | 92 |

Fragrant, lightly grassy and talcum powder-like aromas of ripe gooseberries, passionfruit reveal undertones of nettles and minerals. Juicy, round and generous, it's also long and elegant, finishing with a savoury, briney quality and minerality. Pleasingly taut, deep and shapely.

2005	92	2006	2007
2004	86	2005	2006
2003	88	2004	2005
2002	91	2003	2004
2001	93	2002	2003+
2000	87	2001	2002
1999	91	2000	2001+
1998	93	1999	2000
1997	94	1999	2002
1996	95	1998	2001
1995	94	1997	2000

ART SERIES SHIRAZ

RATING 4

| Margaret River | $30–$49 |
| Current vintage: 2003 | 87 |

Slightly confectionary aromas of small red berries, cherries and plums are backed by assertive vanilla oak and herbal, earthy undertones. Medium to full in weight, it's smooth and sappy, with intense berry flavours becoming more herbal towards the slightly spirity finish.

2003	87	2008	2011
2002	91	2007	2010+
2001	90	2006	2009
2000	83	2002	2005
1999	90	2007	2011

PRELUDE CHARDONNAY

RATING 5

| Margaret River | $20–$29 |
| Current vintage: 2004 | 87 |

Delicate floral aromas of wheatmeal, sweet vanilla and buttery oak and undertones of grilled nuts precede a smooth, elegant and juicy palate of moderate depth and intensity. Its restrained peachy and lightly herbal fruit and creamy oak culminate in a slightly thin and spirity finish.

2004	87	2006	2009
2003	89	2005	2008
2002	87	2004	2007
2001	93	2003	2006+
2000	90	2002	2005
1999	90	2001	2004+
1998	92	2000	2003+
1997	87	1999	2002
1996	82	1997	1998
1994	92	1999	2002
1993	93	1998	2001
1992	89	1997	2000

SIBLINGS SAUVIGNON BLANC SEMILLON

RATING 4

| Margaret River | $12–$19 |
| Current vintage: 2005 | 88 |

Dusty, herbal and asparagus-like scents of lychee and honeydew melon reveal smoky chevre-like undertones, while its juicy, vibrant palate of fresh melon and gooseberry flavour finishes clean and fractionally sweet. Moderately long, juicy and a trifle sappy, it's forward and lively, with a finish of slightly metallic acids.

2005	88	2005	2006
2004	92	2004	2005+
2003	88	2003	2004+
2002	92	2002	2003+
2001	89	2001	2002

Lenton Brae

Caves Road, Willyabrup Valley, Margaret River WA 6295. Tel: (08) 9755 6255. Fax: (08) 9755 6268.
Website: www.lentonbrae.com Email: info@lentonbrae.com
Region: **Margaret River** Winemaker: **Edward Tomlinson** Viticulturist: **Mark Groat**
Chief Executive: **Jeanette Tomlinson**

Lenton Brae is a small family-owned operation that has proven capable of making outstanding wine from the typical Margaret River mix of varieties. Its wines are rarely poor, but typically just fall short of true excellence. The current-release Cabernet Merlot is a delightfully vibrant, finely crafted and easy-drinking wine that certainly reflects its regional origins.

CABERNET MERLOT

RATING 5

Margaret River	$20–$29
Current vintage: 2004	**90**

Delicate floral aromas of light berry fruits and cedary oak precede an enticingly bright and sweet-fruited palate whose dark plum, cassis and cherry flavours are backed by a fine-grained structure of drying tannin. Delightful elegance, roundness and generosity.

2004	90	2009	2012
2003	88	2005	2008
2002	87	2004	2007
2001	87	2003	2006
2000	90	2002	2005+
1999	89	2004	2007
1998	87	2000	2003
1997	82	1998	1999
1996	87	2001	2004
1995	89	2000	2003
1993	82	1995	1998

CABERNET SAUVIGNON

RATING 5

Margaret River	$30–$49
Current vintage: 2001	**87**

While it's a little greenish around the edges, this is a fine and elegant cabernet whose restrained expression of cassis and dark plums is lifted by a perfume of violets and sweet vanilla oak. There's an underlying regional earthiness, plus rather a leafy aspect to the nose and palate.

2001	87	2006	2009+
2000	89	2008	2012
1999	94	2007	2011+
1998	88	2006	2010
1997	87	2002	2005
1996	95	2004	2008+
1995	93	2003	2007
1994	92	2006	2014

CHARDONNAY

RATING 4

Margaret River	$20–$29
Current vintage: 2004	**88**

A toasty young chardonnay with a smooth, creamy and attractive palate of buttery, figgy and grapefruit flavours. It is somewhat overawed by a powerful malolactic presence of butterscotch and bacony aromas, and rather overblown toffee-like characters on the palate, before finishing slightly metallic.

2004	88	2006	2009
2003	92	2005	2008+
2002	88	2004	2007+
2001	94	2003	2006+
2000	91	2002	2005+
1999	93	2001	2004+
1998	92	2000	2003
1997	89	1999	2002+
1996	89	2001	2004

SEMILLON SAUVIGNON BLANC

RATING 5

Margaret River	$20–$29
Current vintage: 2005	**86**

A lightly grassy and passionfruit-like fragrance of gooseberry, melon and delicate tropical under-tones precedes a palate that begins with juicy, generous flavours, but which then becomes leaner and rather dilute towards the finish. There are some powdery, mineral undertones, but the wine needs more intensity and brightness.

2005	86	2006	2009
2004	89	2005	2006
2003	89	2004	2005+
2002	90	2003	2004+
2001	90	2001	2002+
2000	91	2001	2002
1999	89	1999	2000
1998	86	2000	2003
1997	88	1999	2002
1996	93	2001	2004

Leo Buring

Tanunda Road, Nuriootpa SA 5355. Tel: (08) 8568 9389. Fax: (08) 8562 1669.
Website: www.leoburing.com.au

Regions: **Eden Valley, Clare Valley** Winemaker: **Matthew Pick** Viticulturist: **Greg Pearce**
Chief Executive: **Jamie Odell**

Leo Buring is a benchmark riesling brand noted for the excellence and longevity of its wines from the Eden and Clare valleys of South Australia. Recent years have seen Eden Valley take centre stage, since it is the source of a more regular release of top-level Leonay wine. The brand's owners, Foster's, have augmented its range in 2005 with a musky and very shapely Mount Barker Riesling (94, drink 2013–2017), plus a very floral and Germanic Tamar Valley Riesling (90, drink 2007–2010+). All Buring rieslings are excellent value for money.

CLARE VALLEY RIESLING
RATING 3

Clare Valley $12–$19
Current vintage: 2005 **91**

An open, generous and very regional Clare Valley riesling with an opulent aroma of lime, lemon and floral aromatics and an assertively rich, flavoursome palate underpinned by fine but firmish phenolics. Excellent length and intensity.

2005	91	2013	2017
2004	94	2009	2012+
2003	94	2011	2015+
2002	93	2010	2014
2000	87	2005	2008
1999	93	2007	2011
1998	89	2000	2003
1997	91	2005	2009
1996	91	2004	2008
1995	86	2000	2003
1994	93	2002	2006
1993	94	2001	2005

LEONAY EDEN VALLEY RIESLING
RATING 1

Eden Valley $30–$49
Current vintage: 2005 **95**

A big, stylish riesling with some weight and punch. Its perfumed, minerally fragrance of heady lemon blossom and floral aromas precedes a long, brightly flavoured and austere palate supported by fine-grained and chalky phenolics. There's wonderful depth, tightness and an accent of citrusy flavour plus plenty of underlying slate-like texture and shape. A little less alcohol, and the score would be even higher.

2005	95	2017	2025
2004	96	2012	2016+
2003	97	2015	2023
1999	95	2007	2011+
1998	92	2006	2010
1997	93	2005	2009
1995	96	2003	2007
1994	96	2006	2014+
1993	93	2001	2005
1991	96	2003	2011
1990	94	2002	2010
1984	93	1996	2004+

LEONAY WATERVALE RIESLING
RATING 2

Clare Valley $30–$49
Current vintage: 2002 **95**

A stylish, assertive and focused riesling with substance and longevity. Its rose garden perfume of apple, guava, baby powder and wet slate precedes a fine and powdery palate whose concentration and fruit is tightly harnessed by appropriately bracing acidity. Wonderful lenth and balance, especially for a dry riesling of 13% alcohol.

2002	95	2010	2014+
1994	92	2002	2006
1992	94	2000	2004
1991	95	2003	2011
1990	93	1998	2002
1988	93	1996	2000
1981	80	1989	1993
1980	87	1988	1992
1973	94	1981	1985
1972	96	1992	1997

Lillydale Estate

Lot 10 Davross Court, Seville Vic 3139. Tel: (03) 5964 2016. Fax: (03) 5964 3009.
Website: www.mcwilliams.com.au Email: liloffice@mcwilliams.com.au

Region: **Yarra Valley** Winemakers: **Max McWilliam, Jim Brayne** Viticulturist: **Alex Van Driel**
Chief Executive: **George Wahby**

One of the larger operations in the Yarra Valley, Lillydale is owned by the McWilliam family. While its wines are typically elegant, flavoursome and ready to drink at or shortly after release, it would be interesting to see what this highly capable wine producer could achieve if it decided to take the brand up-market. Yet again, the spicy, floral and racy Gewürztraminer is my pick of the current releases.

CHARDONNAY

RATING **5**

Yarra Valley	$12–$19	2004	88	2006	2009
Current vintage: 2004	**88**	2003	87	2004	2005+

While this young chardonnay presently reveals some slightly raw oak and underlying greenish and metallic notes, it should flesh out and develop neatly. It offers some punchy, peachy and tropical fruit with bubblegum and vanilla oak undertones, and there is a slightly disappointing finish of light fruit and green cashews. Give it a little time.

2004	88	2006	2009
2003	87	2004	2005+
2002	89	2004	2007
2001	84	2002	2003+
2000	87	2002	2005
1999	87	2001	2004
1998	88	1999	2000
1997	90	1999	2002
1996	87	1998	2001
1995	86	1997	2000
1994	82	1996	1999

GEWÜRZTRAMINER

RATING **4**

Yarra Valley $12–$19
Current vintage: 2005 **93**

A delightful traminer that presents deliciously spicy and intensely aromatic varietal qualities without the excessive fatness or oiliness usually found in wines of such intensity. A musky, floral perfume of lychees and rose oil precedes a juicy, bright and crunchy palate whose pristine fruit is tightly bound by crackly acids. Excellent shape and future.

2005	93	2010	2013
2004	82	2004	2005
2003	90	2005	2008+
2002	83	2002	2003
2000	92	2002	2005
1998	89	2000	2003
1996	90	2001	2004
1995	94	2000	2003
1993	85	1995	1996

PINOT NOIR

RATING **5**

Yarra Valley $20–$29
Current vintage: 2005 **89**

A pretty, spotlessly clean young pinot whose minty aromas of spicy red cherries, raspberries and restrained vanilla/bubblegum oak reveal faint undertones of eucalypt. Supple and sappy, its vibrant and juicy palate of fresh cherry/raspberry fruit overlies a restrained spine of genuine structure and tightly knit cedary oak.

2005	89	2007	2010
2004	86	2006	2009
2003	87	2008	2011
2002	89	2004	2007
2001	86	2003	2006
2000	83	2002	2005
1999	89	2001	2004
1998	85	1999	2000
1997	89	1999	2002
1996	90	1998	2001
1995	87	1997	2000
1994	88	1996	1999

Lindemans

Karadoc Winery, Edey Road, Karadoc via Red Cliffs Vic 3496. Tel: (03) 5051 3285. Fax: (03) 5051 3390.
Website: www.lindemans.com.au

Regions: **Coonawarra, Padthaway, South Australia, Victoria** Winemaker: **Wayne Falkenberg**
Viticulturist: **Marcus Everett** Chief Executive: **Jamie Odell**

It seems the fate of Lindemans Coonawarra is forever to be a brand in limbo. A previous ownership and management slashed its price and its profile in the mid 1990s after which, thanks in large measure to its extraordinary 1998 vintage, it managed to recover its profile in full. It has since been affected by a combination of poor vintages and another change in ownership and appears to have fallen through some corporate cracks. The vineyards are as good as ever, and hopefully the seasons of 2004 and 2005 will ultimately see a return to past glory.

BIN 65 CHARDONNAY

Southern Australia $5–$11
Current vintage: 2005 80

Lightly toasty aromas of melon, fig, vanilla and slightly acrid oak influences precede rather a hot, broad and juicy palate whose honeyed expression of peach/apricot fruit finishes with a toasty sweetness. A little too flat and stale.

2005	80	2005	2006
2004	83	2004	2005
2003	83	2003	2004+
2002	86	2002	2003
2001	81	2001	2002

LIMESTONE RIDGE SHIRAZ CAB. SAUVIGNON   RATING

Coonawarra $50–$99
Current vintage: 2001 93

Spicy, slightly meaty and leathery, this brightly flavoured and dark-fruited shiraz reveals a hint of herbaceousness. Closed and brooding, its violet-like perfume of cassis, dark plums and mulberries reveals smoky undertones of cedar/mocha oak and capsicum. Its deep, dark flavours of plums, cassis and mulberries knit tightly with pencil shavings-like cedar/chocolate oak, before a persistent savoury finish of lingering mineral and meaty qualities.

2001	93	2013	2021
2000	86	2005	2008
1999	95	2011	2011+
1998	96	2006	2010+
1997	90	2005	2009+
1996	94	2004	2008+
1994	95	2014	2024
1993	91	2001	2005
1992	88	1997	2000
1991	94	2003	2011
1990	88	1995	1998

PYRUS   RATING 3

Coonawarra $50–$99
Current vintage: 2000 90

Fine-grained, tight and supple cabernet blend with a herbal note beneath its aromas of slightly stewed plums, small berries and sweet vanilla oak. Forward and lively, its palate of attractive red cherry, cassis and plum flavours and dusty cedar/vanilla oak presents both length and elegance.

2000	90	2005	2008
1999	93	2007	2011+
1998	95	2006	2010+
1997	89	2002	2005+
1996	89	2004	2008
1995	88	2000	2003+
1994	90	2002	2006+
1993	89	1998	2001
1992	88	1997	2000

ST GEORGE CABERNET SAUVIGNON   RATING

Coonawarra $50–$99
Current vintage: 2001 88

Showing signs of over-ripeness, this slightly dis-jointed cabernet of medium to full weight and firmish tannin lacks sufficient fruit intensity to last its customary distance. Its plummy aromas reveal leathery development, while the cassis, plum and mulberry fruits present on the palate are forward and beginning to dry out. Fine-grained cedar/chocolate oak does lend sweetness and mouthfeel.

2001	88	2006	2009
2000	88	2005	2008
1999	94	2007	2019
1998	95	2010	2018
1997	90	2002	2005+
1996	94	2008	2016
1995	94	2003	2007+
1994	94	2006	2014
1993	87	1998	2001
1992	89	2000	2004
1991	95	2003	2011
1990	92	2002	2010
1989	87	1994	1997
1988	93	1993	1996
1987	82	1989	1992
1986	94	1998	2006

Madew

Lake George via Collector NSW 2581. Tel: (02) 4848 0165. Fax: (02) 4848 0164.
Website: www.madewwines.com.au Email: cellardoor@madewwines.com.au

Region: **Canberra** Winemaker: **David Madew** Chief Executive: **David Madew**

Madew is forging a fine reputation for its very European-styled rieslings, most of which ably carry some residual sweetness as part of their style. This edition sees the introduction of perhaps Australia's finest slightly sweet and Germanic riesling, the aptly-named 'Belle'. Madew is also doing very well with its perfumed and gentle Pinot Gris.

BELLE LATE PICKED RIESLING

RATING **3**

Canberra $30–$49
Current vintage: 2006 **94**

A delightfully racy, juicy and crisp young riesling of halbtrocken-like 'off-dry'-ness whose vibrant and slightly sweet expression of stonefruit, lime juice, pear and apple flavours finishes with crunchy acidity. It's floral and perfumed, long and smooth, with delightful palate weight and texture supported by a fine, chalky spine of powdery phenolics.

2006	94	2008	2011+
2004	95	2006	2009
2003	91	2008	2011
2002	95	2007	2010

RIESLING

RATING **4**

Canberra $20–$29
Current vintage: 2005 **90**

Pungent, youthful and estery floral aromas of apple and pear precede a juicy and fleshy palate bursting with vibrant flavour. Its intense core of apple, pear and lemon zest culminates in a marginally sweet and refreshing finish of slightly mineral acids. Excellent shape and balance. Quite Alsatian.

2005	90	2010	2013
2003	88	2005	2008
2002	94	2010	2014
2001	86	2002	2003
2000	90	2002	2005

Maglieri

Sturt Highway, Nuriootpa SA 5355. Tel: (08) 8383 2211. Fax: (08) 8383 0735.
Website: www.fosters.com.au

Region: **McLaren Vale** Winemaker: **Alex Mackenzie** Viticulturist: **Chris Dundon** Chief Executive: **Jamie Odell**

After what will hopefully not prove to be a false start with some very promising wines from red Italian varieties, Maglieri has released a firm and meaty Cabernet Sauvignon plus a deeply fruited Shiraz from 2004. Its future, in the exceptionally large and diverse Foster's wine portfolio, perhaps remains uncertain. When bought by Mildara Blass, Maglieri was one of the hottest wine brands in McLaren Vale.

CABERNET SAUVIGNON

RATING **5**

McLaren Vale $12–$19
Current vintage: 2004 **81**

A firm and grippy red whose slightly cooked, meaty aromas of plums and currants overlie cedary, chocolate oak. Simple, forward and raisined, its rather dehydrated and stressed palate tends to lack fruit sweetness, revealing a hollowness and some raw edges.

2004	81	2006	2009
2003	88	2005	2008+
2002	88	2004	2007+
2001	81	2003	2006
2000	82	2002	2005
1999	83	2001	2004
1997	90	2002	2005
1995	91	2003	2007

SHIRAZ

RATING **5**

McLaren Vale $12–$19
Current vintage: 2004 **89**

Ripe aromas of blackberries, redcurrants, dark plums and toasty vanilla oak overlie nuances of raisins, clove and nutmeg, with a suggestion of dark olives and licorice. Moderately long and gritty of extract, it's still rather closed with a slightly salty, mineral finish. Given time, its somewhat overcooked and spirity expression of dark fruits and firm tannins should flesh out.

2004	89	2009	2012+
2003	90	2008	2011
2002	77	2003	2004
2001	88	2003	2006
2000	82	2002	2005
1999	83	2001	2004
1998	87	2000	2003
1997	90	2002	2005
1996	89	2004	2008
1995	91	2003	2007

Main Ridge Estate

80 William Road, Red Hill Vic 3937. Tel: (03) 5989 2686. Fax: (03) 5931 0000.
Website: www.mre.com.au Email: mrestate@mre.com.au
Region: **Mornington Peninsula** Winemaker: **Nat White** Viticulturist: **Nat White**
Chief Executives: **Rosalie & Nat White**

Main Ridge Estate was one of the first vineyards on Victoria's much-hyped Mornington Peninsula, but through thick and thin, this tiny estate has justified all the accolades it has collected. Its 2004 vintage is a step up even from its exceptional 2003 and expectations for 2005 are high. Main Ridge is a tiny producer whose handcrafted wines reflect decades of care, learning and nurturing by Nat and Rosalie White and their family.

CHARDONNAY

RATING 3

Mornington Peninsula $30–$49
Current vintage: 2004 94

A fine, elegant and deeply flavoured chardonnay whose pristine, spotless perfume of citrus/melon fruit and lightly dusty vanilla oak reveals a hint of spice and a funky whiff of leesy undertone. Richly fruited but extremely stylish, its vibrant core of melon, cumquat and tangerine is supported by perfectly integrated oak, butterscotch and nuances of clove. Long and savoury, with a lingering fruit presence framed by refreshing acids, it should develop very well.

2004	94	2009	2012+
2003	93	2008	2011
2002	86	2004	2007
2001	89	2003	2006+
2000	93	2005	2008
1999	93	2004	2007
1998	95	2006	2010
1997	88	1999	2002+
1996	88	1998	2001
1995	82	1997	2000
1994	94	1999	2002
1993	89	1998	2001

HALF ACRE PINOT NOIR

RATING 2

Mornington Peninsula $50–$99
Current vintage: 2004 97

The finest pinot noir yet made at Main Ridge Estate has a heady floral perfume of musky rose petals, red and black cherries, cloves and cinnamon, with a background of dusty new cedar/vanilla oak. Alluringly and profoundly flavoured, its pristine expression of dark cherries, plums and berries is delivered by a palate already round and luscious in its texture, but which is likely acquire more depth and richness over the next three years. Cloaked by firm, powdery tannins, it balances its assertiveness and intensity with an aspect of elegance and refinement.

2004	97	2009	2012+
2003	96	2008	2011+
2002	90	2004	2007+
2001	95	2006	2009+
2000	95	2008	2012
1999	94	2007	2011
1998	93	2003	2006
1997	95	2002	2005+
1996	87	2001	2004
1995	88	1997	2000
1994	93	2002	2006
1993	90	2001	2005

THE ACRE PINOT NOIR

RATING 3

Mornington Peninsula $30–$49
Current vintage: 2004 91

A supple and deeply flavoured pinot of medium weight, whose spicy perfume of maraschino cherries, raspberry confection and cedar/vanilla oak is enticingly floral and aromatic. Fine, smooth and supple, its silky palate of vibrant red cherry/berry flavours is framed by tightly knit tannins that provide genuine backbone and support. It should build in the bottle over the next two years.

2004	91	2006	2009+
2003	93	2005	2008+
2002	87	2004	2007
2001	93	2003	2006

Majella

Lynn Road, Coonawarra SA 5263. Tel: (08) 8736 3055. Fax: (08) 8736 3057.
Website: www.majellawines.com.au Email: prof@majellawines.com.au

Region: **Coonawarra** Winemaker: **Bruce Gregory** Viticulturist: **Anthony Lynn** Chief Executive: **Brian Lynn**

Majella is an expanding family owned and operated wine business in the heart of Coonawarra. It's a red specialist, with significant holdings of mature red vineyards, although it still releases a Riesling. It has recently released a very affordable blend of cabernet sauvignon and shiraz labelled 'The Musician'. By and large, the principal Majella wines are today significantly more elegant and less concentrated than those of the late 1990s.

CABERNET SAUVIGNON

RATING **3**

Coonawarra	$20–$29
Current vintage: 2004	**93**

Delicate violet-like aromas of ripe blackberries, plums and cedary oak precede a long, fine and elegant palate. Its intense and expressive blackberry and dark plum flavours are tightly knit with sweet cedar/vanilla oak and framed by fine and firmish tannins. It finishes with an attractive dustiness and lingering nuances of dark fruit and dried herbs.

2004	93	2012	2016+
2003	86	2005	2008
2002	88	2010	2014
2001	95	2009	2013+
2000	93	2005	2008
1999	90	2004	2007
1998	95	2006	2010+
1997	93	2005	2009
1996	93	2001	2004
1995	86	1997	2000
1994	82	1996	1999

SHIRAZ

RATING **3**

Coonawarra	$30–$49
Current vintage: 2004	**90**

A very elegant, measured and restrained Majella red whose violet-like fragrances of cassis, blueberries and dark plums are backed by white pepper and spice, fragrant vanilla oak and complex meaty undertones. Supple and restrained, its gentle palate of vibrant dark berry flavours and measured oak finishes with just a hint of herbal complexity.

2004	90	2012	2016
2003	92	2008	2011+
2002	87	2004	2007
2001	95	2009	2013
2000	89	2005	2008
1999	90	2004	2007
1998	95	2003	2006+
1997	94	2002	2005+
1996	94	2001	2004
1995	87	1997	2000
1994	93	2002	2006
1993	86	1995	1998
1992	84	1994	1997
1991	86	1993	1996

THE MALLEEA

RATING **4**

Coonawarra	$50–$99
Current vintage: 2003	**89**

A smooth and elegant Coonawarra red whose spicy aromas of blackberries, dark cherries and plums reveal minty, herbal undertones and smoky and slightly gluey new oak influences. There's a minty, herbal aspect to its smooth and intense palate of dark berries and plums that becomes more herbal, salty and metallic towards the finish. A little varnishy and green-edged, just lacking conviction.

2003	89	2011	2015
2002	90	2010	2012
2001	91	2009	2013+
2000	87	2005	2008
1999	92	2004	2007
1998	95	2006	2010+
1997	92	2002	2005+
1996	94	2001	2004

Margan

1238 Milbrodale Road, Ceres Hill, Broke NSW 2330. Tel: (02) 6579 1317. Fax: (02) 6579 1267.
Website: www.margan.com.au Email: di@margan.com.au

Region: **Lower Hunter Valley** Winemaker: **Andrew Margan** Viticulturist: **Andrew Margan**
Chief Executive: **Andrew Margan**

Margan is a family-owned wine business in the Hunter Valley. Its wines are made by Andrew Margan to be enjoyed without a period of cellaring, although every now and again the season dictates that wines like the firm and astringent Shiraz and Cabernet Sauvignon from 2003 should be kept before drinking. Margan wines are typically bright, fresh, neatly balanced and bottled with refreshing acidity.

BOTRYTIS SEMILLON

RATING 4

Lower Hunter Valley $12–$19 (375 ml)
Current vintage: 2005　　　　　　　**91**

Quite a charmer, this fragrant and harmonious young dessert wine has a floral and slightly honeyed perfume of grapefruit, melon and citrus aromas with undertones of butter and traminer-like muskiness. Long and fine, it's intensely flavoured but remains clean and refreshing. Its moderate sweetness is ably balanced by clean and refreshing acids, and the wine never becomes cloying.

2005	91	2006	2007
2004	90	2005	2006+
2003	93	2005	2008
2002	89	2004	2007
2001	86	2003	2006+

CABERNET SAUVIGNON

RATING 5

Lower Hunter Valley　　　　**$20–$29**
Current vintage: 2003　　　　　　　**90**

A brightly and generously flavoured cabernet whose juicy aromas of cassis, plums and dark olives overlie cedary oak plus nuances of dried herbs and mint. Full to medium in weight, it's long and vibrant, with pleasing fruit richness, a slightly mineral edge and an assertive but integrated chassis of drying, powdery tannins.

2003	90	2008	2011+
2002	87	2004	2007+
2001	87	2003	2006
2000	90	2005	2008
1999	87	2001	2004+
1997	84	2002	2005

CHARDONNAY

RATING 5

Lower Hunter Valley　　　　**$12–$19**
Current vintage: 2005　　　　　　　**88**

A charming, early-drinking chardonnay whose fresh peachy, citrusy fruit reveals light tropical undertones. Matched to sweet, buttery cashew/vanilla oak, its long, smooth palate of stonefruit flavours finishes with refreshing acidity. Attractive elegance and brightness.

2005	88	2006	2007
2004	86	2005	2006
2003	88	2004	2005+
2002	86	2003	2004+
2001	82	2002	2003+
2000	86	2001	2002
1998	91	1999	2000

SEMILLON

RATING 5

Lower Hunter Valley　　　　**$12–$19**
Current vintage: 2005　　　　　　　**88**

Delicate, dusty aromas of melon, lemon rind and pawpaw precede a juicy, slightly candied and generously flavoured palate whose tangy, vibrant and lightly tropical fruit is wound up by a lively cut of citrusy acid.

2005	88	2007	2010
2004	88	2005	2006
2003	90	2008	2011+
2002	90	2004	2007
2001	85	2001	2002+
2000	89	2002	2005
1998	87	2003	2006

SHIRAZ

RATING 4

Lower Hunter Valley　　　　**$20–$29**
Current vintage: 2004　　　　　　　**89**

An attractive and moderately rich Hunter shiraz with a spicy and slightly meaty fragrance of dark plums, cherries and cassis supported by cedar/chocolate oak. Framed by firmish, powdery and pliant tannins, its brightly lit palate of dark berry/plum flavour finishes with a lingering sour-edged aspect.

2004	89	2009	2012
2003	90	2008	2011
2002	90	2004	2007
2001	89	2003	2006
2000	92	2005	2008+
1999	90	2004	2007
1998	85	2000	2003
1997	89	2002	2005

McAlister Vineyards

RMB 6810 Golden Beach Road, Longford South-East Gippsland Vic 3851. Tel: (03) 5149 7229.
Fax: (03) 5149 7229

Region: **Gippsland** Winemaker: **Peter Edwards** Viticulturist: **Peter Edwards** Chief Executive: **Peter Edwards**

The McAlister is a single-vineyard blend of red Bordeaux varieties that typically exhibits vibrant, complex flavours delivered in a refined and elegant package. The 2001 is a classic example, now looking very much like a fine wine from the Margaux district. The dramatic climatic variations of recent vintages have certainly made it challenging for Peter Edwards to maintain the style he is seeking.

THE McALISTER

RATING

Gippsland	$50–$99
Current vintage: 2003	88

A complex, smoky and autumnal cabernet blend whose leathery bouquet of dark cherries, plums and blackberries reveals meaty, cedary and herbal undertones. Quite evolved, it's smooth and supple, medium to full in weight, with dark, earthy flavours and herbal, leathery undertones framed by firmish but slightly sappy tannins.

2003	88	2008	2011+
2002	87	2007	2010+
2001	94	2009	2013
2000	91	2005	2008
1999	87	2004	2007
1998	85	2003	2006+
1997	87	2005	2009
1996	84	1998	2001
1995	87	2000	2003
1994	95	2002	2006
1993	90	1998	2001
1992	93	2000	2004
1991	93	1999	2003
1990	94	2002	2010
1989	87	1997	2001
1988	93	2000	2005
1987	92	1999	2004
1986	90	1994	1998

McWilliam's

Doug McWilliam Road, Yenda NSW 2681. Tel: (02) 6968 1001. Fax: (02) 6968 1312.
Website: www.mcwilliams.com.au Email: mcwines@mcwilliams.com.au

Regions: **Various SA, WA & NSW** Winemakers: **Jim Brayne, Russell Cody** Viticulturists: **Terry McLeary, Jeoff McCorkelle** Chief Executive: **George Wahby**

Most of the wines in this McWilliam's regional range offer terrific but inexpensive drinking. The company's current highlights include a rather closed and long-living 1877 flagship blend of cabernet sauvignon and shiraz, a taut and limey 2005 Clare Valley Riesling and yet another exceptional vintage of its consistently high-performing dessert style, the Riverina Botrytis Semillon.

1877 CABERNET SAUVIGNON SHIRAZ

RATING

Coonawarra, Hilltops	$50–$99
Current vintage: 2002	93

Dusty, leafy aromas of mulberries, cassis and plums are backed by handsome, assertive mocha and cedar/vanilla oak plus lightly minty, menthol-like herbal undertones and suggestions of smoked meats. Long, firm and powerfully structured, it slowly unveils vibrant flavours of small dark berries and plums framed by fine, bony tannin and backed by impressive oak. It needs time.

2002	93	2014	2022
2001	93	2009	2013
2000	87	2005	2008
1999	87	2004	2007
1998	95	2006	2010+

CLARE VALLEY RIESLING

RATING

Clare Valley	$12–$19
Current vintage: 2005	92

A very stylish, taut and limey riesling whose punchy floral perfume of citrus, musk and mineral precedes a long and pristine palate with a slightly chalky undercarriage. Its tangy fruit and rose oil undertones culminate in a clean, refreshing and sculpted finish with a lingering core of intense fruit.

2005	92	2010	2013+
2004	91	2009	2012+
2003	82	2004	2005+
2002	87	2004	2007+
2001	90	2006	2009+

EDEN VALLEY RIESLING

RATING 5

Eden Valley	$12–$19	2005	82	2007	2010
Current vintage: 2005	**82**	2004	89	2006	2009+
		2003	91	2008	2011+

Rather awkward and disjointed, with slightly spirity aromas of lime juice and lemon zest. Its palate appears grippy and phenolic despite some residual sweetness. There's some attractive fruit and racy acidity, but it's hard to find pleasure from this wine which appears to be hard, hot and skinsy.

2002	86	2004	2007
2001	89	2006	2009
1996	89	2001	2004

MARGARET RIVER SEMILLON SAUVIGNON BLANC

RATING 5

Margaret River	$12–$19	2004	84	2006	2009
Current vintage: 2004	**84**	2003	89	2004	2005
		2002	88	2003	2004
		2001	86	2002	2003

Rather green-edged, raw and sweaty, with asparagus-like aromas of shaded green melon and gooseberry fruit matched by toasty vanilla oak. Quite generous and juicy, finishing with clean acids, its palate is also excessively herbaceous and rather let down by simple toasty vanilla oak influences.

RIVERINA BOTRYTIS SEMILLON

RATING 2

Riverina	$20–$29 (375 ml)	2004	95	2009	2012
Current vintage: 2004	**95**	2003	90	2005	2008
		2001	95	2003	2006

A classically elegant, stylish and shapely dessert wine whose restrained melon, lime and grapefruit flavours are augmented by delightfully complex pastry-like, nutty, beeswaxy and honeyed complexity. It's fragrant and floral, with tightly interwoven oak-derived creamy vanilla properties. Fine and elegant, it finishes clean and savoury, with refreshing acids. Very sophisticated and clearly influenced by Sauternes.

2000	94	2005	2008
1999	96	2004	2007
1998	95	2003	2006
1997	92	2002	2005
1996	88	1998	2001

Meadowbank

699 Richmond Road, Cambridge Tas 7170. Tel: (03) 6248 4484. Fax: (03) 6248 4485.
Website: www.meadowbankwines.com.au Email: bookings@meadowbankwines.com.au

Region: **Derwent Valley** Winemaker: **Andrew Hood** Viticulturist: **Adrian Hallam** Chief Executive: **Gerald Ellis**

2005 was always tipped to be a fine vintage in Tasmania, and has helped Meadowbank to produce its best wines for several years. Its collection of white wines includes a tangy and briney Sauvignon Blanc, a floral and chalky Riesling, plus a delightful unwooded Chardonnay. Its other highlight is a very pretty and perfumed Henry James Pinot Noir.

CHARDONNAY

Derwent Valley	$20–$29	2005	90	2006	2007+
Current vintage: 2005	**90**	2004	84	2005	2006
		2003	86	2004	2005

A very good unwooded chardonnay whose aromas of peach, melon, pineapple, passionfruit and guava precede a creamy and vibrant palate of genuine length and freshness. Punctuated by refreshingly soft and tingly acids, it's very clean and persistent.

2002	77	2002	2003
2001	88	2002	2003
1999	87	2001	2004
1998	86	2000	2003
1997	82	1998	1999
1995	87	1997	2000
1994	88	1999	2002
1993	90	1998	2001

GRACE ELIZABETH CHARDONNAY

RATING 5

Derwent Valley $30–$49
Current vintage: 2005 89

A restrained, smooth, lightly oaked and silky chardonnay whose delicate, dusty aromas of citrusy fruit, green olives and vanilla oak precede a long and almost slippery palate brightly flavoured with peachy, tropical fruit. It finishes savoury and nutty, with lingering fruit and clean acids.

2005	89	2007	2010
2004	81	2005	2006+
2003	87	2005	2008
2002	89	2004	2007
2000	87	2002	2005
1998	82	2000	2003
1997	83	1998	1999
1995	95	2003	2007

HENRY JAMES PINOT NOIR

RATING 5

Derwent Valley $30–$49
Current vintage: 2005 91

A pretty, fine-grained and sappy pinot that is likely to build in weight and intensity with time in the bottle. Its floral fragrance of red cherries, raspberries and sweet oak has a confiture-like aspect, with underlying nuances of cinnamon, butter and cloves. Framed by very fine tannins, its silky palate of medium depth is charmingly lit with flavours of red cherries and blackberries, finishing with suggestions of dried herbs and mint.

2005	91	2007	2010+
2003	77	2004	2005+
2001	88	2003	2006
2000	91	2002	2005
1999	89	2001	2004+
1998	82	2000	2003+
1997	84	1999	2002

mesh

Tel: (08) 8561 3200. Fax: (08) 8561 3465
Website: www.meshwine.com Email: marketing@meshwine.com

Region: **Eden Valley** Winemakers: **Jeff Grosset, Robert Hill Smith** Viticulturists: **Jeff Grosset, Robert Hill Smith**
Chief Executives: **Jeff Grosset, Robert Hill Smith**

mesh is the joint venture between an unlikely couple of riesling devotees in Jeff Grosset and Robert Hill Smith. The fruit is equally divided between the two parties but then, after vintage; the finished components are compared to define the final blend. mesh is heady and perfumed, remarkably floral and citrusy, with the classic lime juice qualities and chalky tightness expected of Eden Valley riesling.

RIESLING

RATING 2

Eden Valley $30–$49
Current vintage: 2005 97

An incredible riesling in the classically stylish and powdery Eden Valley style, with a purity of accent and simply exceptional delivery. There's something of the wild, mineral and exotic about its heady perfume of floral, citrus and stonefruit aromas. Long, tight and tangy, its clear lime juice palate builds towards a crescendo of flavour prior to a taut and mineral finish of wonderful length. Grand Cru stuff.

2005	97	2017	2025+
2004	95	2009	2012
2003	95	2011	2015
2002	97	2014	2022+

Metala

Nuriootpa Road, Angaston SA 5353. Tel: (08) 8564 3355. Fax: (08) 8564 2209.
Website: www.fosters.com.au

Region: **Langhorne Creek** Winemaker: **Nigel Dolan** Viticulturists: **Tom & Guy Adams** Chief Executive: **Jamie Odell**

Metala is an historic Australian brand made by Nigel Dolan and sourced from a very old vineyard in Langhorne Creek. In better vintages its oldest vines contribute to the Black Label Shiraz, which shows the effects of extreme heat in the 2001 release. The rather charming 'standard' white label blend of shiraz with cabernet sauvignon from 2004 is typically supple, minty and packed with intense berry flavour.

BLACK LABEL SHIRAZ

RATING 3

Langhorne Creek		$30–$49
Current vintage: 2001		88

Firm, grippy and flavoursome, this early-drinking shiraz dries out a shade at the back of the palate. Its slightly cooked aromas of cherries, raspberries and sweet vanilla/coconut American oak reveal violet-like and meaty undertones, while its fullish and forward palate lacks its customary length and brightness. Its rather stewed expression of dark berry fruit is backed by sweet oak and suggestions of mint and eucalypt.

2001	88	2006	2009
2000	94	2008	2012
1998	90	2003	2006
1996	95	2004	2008
1995	90	2003	2007
1994	95	2002	2006

SHIRAZ CABERNET

RATING 4

Langhorne Creek		$12–$19
Current vintage: 2004		90

Elegant and supple, with a spicy and minty fragrance of cassis, redcurrants, slightly stewed plums and vanilla oak over nuances of cloves, cinnamon and violets. Vibrant flavours of cassis, raspberries, redcurrants and plums knit tightly with cedary oak and fine tannins, culminating in a long, firm finish. Charmingly balanced.

2004	90	2012	2016
2002	82	2004	2007
2001	89	2006	2009
2000	90	2005	2008
1999	86	2001	2004
1998	93	2006	2010
1997	89	2002	2005
1996	91	2001	2004
1995	90	2000	2003
1994	91	2002	2006
1993	92	2001	2005
1992	91	2000	2004
1991	87	1999	2003
1988	80	1993	1996

Mildara Coonawarra

Riddoch Highway, Coonawarra SA 5263. Tel: (08) 8736 3380. Fax: (08) 8736 3307.
Website: www.fosters.com.au

Region: **Coonawarra** Winemaker: **Andrew Hales** Viticulturist: **Brendan Provis** Chief Executive: **Jamie Odell**

Those who persevered with Mildara's white label Coonawarra reds are now collecting their reward. Not only is the enduring Cabernet Sauvignon label in the form of its life with a succulent and minty 2004 release, but it has been augmented by three very worthy wines from the 2003 vintage, being a smooth and charming Cabernet Merlot (92, drink 2008–2011+), a savoury and peppery Shiraz (90, drink 2008–2011+) and deeply flavoured, silky and spotless Cabernet Shiraz (94, drink 2015–2023).

CABERNET SAUVIGNON

RATING 3

Coonawarra		$20–$29
Current vintage: 2004		94

Very stylish and contemporary, this first-rate young cabernet has a piercingly intense and violet-like aroma of cassis-like fruit backed by cedar/dark chocolate oak and minty undertones. Long, supple and velvet-smooth, its firm and fine-grained palate is deeply stained by flavours of dark berries and plums, with dusty suggestions of herbs and mint, tightly knit with bony tannins. Excellent structure, focus and balance.

2004	94	2016	2024
2003	92	2011	2015+
2002	92	2010	2014
2000	87	2005	2008
1999	88	2004	2007+
1998	93	2006	2010+
1997	83	1999	2002
1996	88	2004	2008
1995	87	2000	2003
1994	93	2002	2006
1993	95	2001	2005
1992	94	2000	2004
1991	90	1996	1999
1990	94	1995	1998
1989	87	1994	1997

Mitchell

Hughes Park Road, Sevenhill via Clare SA 5453. Tel: (08) 8843 4258. Fax: (08) 8843 4340.
Website: www.mitchellwines.com.au Email: amitchell@mitchellwines.com

Region: **Clare Valley** Winemaker: **Simon Pringle** Viticulturist: **Leon Schramm**
Chief Executives: **Andrew Mitchell & Jane Mitchell**

A small producer of compelling Clare Valley wines, Mitchell is one of the leading makers of the region's white speciality, riesling. The 2005 release has a powdery texture and sculpted tightness akin to the Eden Valley's finest, and should cellar superbly. Mitchell recently introduced a portion of tight and fine-grained sangiovese (as well as mourvèdre) into its popular grenache blend. The second release of the McNicol Shiraz should find a welcome home on restaurant lists.

GSM GRENACHE SANGIOVESE MOURVÈDRE   RATING 5
(formerly The Growers Grenache)

	Clare Valley	$20–$29
	Current vintage: 2002	90

Spicy, meaty and herbal, its fragrance of sour cherry liqueur, blueberries and dark plums reveals undertones of dark chocolate. Its fine-grained and elegant palate offers a juicy but measured expression of intense raspberry, cherry and plum-like fruit tightly knit by slightly drying and fine-grained tannins. A carefully constructed and harmonious blend that carries its alcoholic strength remarkably well, finishing long and savoury with lingering notes of aniseed and dried herbs.

2002	90	2007	2010
2001	86	2003	2009
2000	87	2002	2005
1999	86	2001	2004
1998	88	2000	2003
1997	90	1999	2002
1996	86	1998	2001

McNICOL SHIRAZ   RATING 3

	Clare Valley	$50–$99
	Current vintage: 1998	93

A classic old-style Australian shiraz with a restrained, complex and minty perfume of smoky fruit and spices, and earthy, meaty undertones of polished old furniture. Backed by cedar/vanilla oak, it's smooth, soft and generous, deeply flavoured with spicy plums, berries and dark chocolates. Framed by firm, pliant tannins, it finishes with a lingering core of fruit and leathery undertones.

2002	94	2014	2022+
1999	91	2007	2011+
1998	93	2010	2018+
1997	90	2005	2009+

PEPPERTREE VINEYARD SHIRAZ   RATING 4

	Clare Valley	$20–$29
	Current vintage: 2004	93

A very well handled wine that opens slowly to reveal brightness and length. Its meaty, spicy aromas of red berries and plums are backed by peppery undertones of cinnamon and nutmeg, with charcuterie-like notes. Long and vibrant, its deeply ripened palate of black and red berry flavours and minty, menthol-like regional qualities is wound around a firmish but fine-grained and powdery spine of pliant tannin. Just marginally too cooked and stressed for a higher rating.

2004	93	2012	2016+
2003	90	2011	2015
2002	87	2007	2010+
2001	85	2003	2006
2000	81	2005	2008
1999	90	2007	2011
1998	92	2010	2018
1997	82	2002	2005
1996	93	2001	2004
1995	82	2000	2003
1994	90	1999	2003
1993	93	2001	2005
1992	92	2000	2004
1991	91	1996	1999

SEMILLON   RATING 5

	Clare Valley	$12–$19
	Current vintage: 2004	88

An unusually heady, wild and tropical bouquet clearly reminiscent of Belgian beer, with suggestions of fresh flowers and dried herbs. Its tangy palate of juicy and highly accentuated tropical fruit is long, clean and racy, finishing with an impression of sweetness and herbal undertones.

2004	88	2006	2009
2002	90	2004	2007+
2001	89	2003	2006
2000	88	2002	2005
1999	89	2001	2004+
1998	88	2000	2003
1997	89	2002	2005
1996	90	2001	2004
1995	88	2000	2003
1994	93	2002	2006
1993	95	2001	2005

SEVENHILL VINEYARD CABERNET SAUVIGNON

RATING 3

Clare Valley $20–$29
Current vintage: 2001   93

A fine-grained and stylish cabernet of focus, depth and structure. Its intense aromas of violets, cassis and plums are backed by sweet cedar/vanilla oak and undertones of mint and menthol. Long and finely balanced, the vibrant fruit is tightly framed by slightly drying and bony tannins. Pleasing elegance, focus and longevity.

2001	93	2013	2021+
2000	87	2008	2012
1999	94	2011	2019
1998	94	2010	2018+
1997	87	2005	2009
1996	92	2008	2016
1995	82	2000	2003
1994	91	2002	2006
1992	91	2004	2012
1991	93	2003	2011
1990	94	2002	2010
1988	88	1996	2000

WATERVALE RIESLING

RATING 2

Clare Valley $12–$19
Current vintage: 2005   95

A very classy young riesling whose bony, stony fragrance of rose petals, lime juice and lemon have a slightly confectionary and musky aspect. Long, fine and tightly sculpted, its chalky palate has a bony presence pierced by pristine citrus and apple-like flavours, culminating in an austere and lingering finish. In its youth it looks more like an Eden Valley riesling than one from Watervale (Clare Valley), although it should flesh out beautifully with time in the bottle.

2005	95	2013	2017+
2004	95	2012	2016+
2003	92	2011	2015
2002	86	2004	2007+
2001	94	2009	2013+
2000	91	2005	2008+
1999	80	2001	2004
1998	94	2006	2010+
1997	92	2005	2009
1996	87	2001	2004
1995	94	2003	2007
1994	88	1999	2003
1993	93	2001	2005
1992	91	1997	2000

Mitchelton

Mitcheltonstown Road, Nagambie Vic 3608. Tel: (03) 5736 2222. Fax: (03) 5736 2266.
Website: www.mitchelton.com.au Email: mitchelton@mitchelton.com.au

Region: **Nagambie Lakes** Winemaker: **Toby Barlow** Viticulturist: **John Beresford** Chief Executive: **Neville Rowe**

A monumental Victorian winery that has struggled to cement a place in the hearts of Australian wine drinkers, Mitchelton is moving towards a Rhône Valley set of varieties and blends with some success. While it needs to release the white Airstrip blend at a significantly younger age than it is presently doing, the Shiraz, Crescent and Parish reds deserve to do well. Unsurprisingly, the Print Shiraz struggled in the hot 2003 season.

AIRSTRIP (Marsanne Viognier Roussanne blend)

RATING 3

Nagambie Lakes $20–$29
Current vintage: 2003   89

Already rather developed and ready to drink, with honeysuckle-like aromas of lime marmalade, with toasty and spicy undertones of sweet corn, wheatmeal and butter. Showing plenty of toasty bottle-age, it's juicy, round and generous, with a candied expression of fruit culminating in a fresh, tangy and lemony finish. A good wine that should have been released earlier.

2003	89	2005	2008
2002	93	2004	2007
2001	93	2003	2006
2000	89	2002	2005+
1999	90	2001	2005+
1998	85	2000	2003
1994	92	1999	2002+

BLACKWOOD PARK RIESLING

RATING 4

Nagambie Lakes $12–$19
Current vintage: 2005   89

A pretty, clean and shapely riesling with a fresh, penetrative and floral perfume of lime juice and lemon rind. Fresh and juicy, with a slightly confectionary aspect, its tangy, citrusy palate delivers a pleasing length of lingering limey fruit backed by chalky, powdery undertones. Finishes crisp and refreshing.

2005	89	2010	2013+
2004	93	2009	2012+
2003	90	2008	2011
2002	90	2007	2010+
2001	88	2003	2006+
2000	93	2008	2012
1999	87	2001	2004
1998	93	2006	2010
1997	90	2002	2005+
1996	93	2004	2008
1995	93	2000	2003
1994	93	1999	2002
1993	91	1998	2001

SHIRAZ

Heathcote $20–29
Current vintage: 2004   **84**

A simple, meaty and early-drinking shiraz that appears to have been made from over-cropped and over-ripened fruit. Its cooked, porty aromas of currants, raisins and blackberries overlie sweet suggestions of slightly gluey cedar/vanilla oak with undertones of mint and menthol. Rather dried-out, thin and lacking fruit ripeness, its palate is dominated by raw-edged tannins.

2004	84	2006	2009
2003	92	2005	2008+
2002	93	2007	2010+
2001	90	2006	2009+
2000	92	2005	2008
1999	89	2004	2007
1997	85	1999	2002
1996	83	1998	2001
1995	87	2000	2003
1994	85	1996	2001

VIOGNIER

RATING **5**

Nagambie Lakes $20–$29
Current vintage: 2005   **83**

Candied aromas of nectarines, apricots and tropical fruits with undertones of cloves and cinnamon precede a forward, juicy and rather broad palate that delivers sumptuous fruit but lacks brightness and penetration of flavour. Honeyed, buttery and toasty, it needs a more convincing presence of bright, varietal fruit and finishes a little hard-edged. Caricature-like.

2005	83	2005	2006+
2003	90	2004	2005+
2002	89	2003	2004+
2001	88	2002	2003+
2000	79	2000	2001
1998	84	1999	2000

CLASSIC RELEASE MARSANNE

RATING **5**

Nagambie Lakes $20–$29
Current vintage: 1998   **89**

A mature dry white for drinking now with a developed, toasty and buttery bouquet whose sweet vanilla oak slightly dominates its waxy, nutty and spicy fruit qualities. Round and generous, its lightly sappy and oily palate of butter, toast and grilled nut flavours finishes a little sweet and alcoholic, with clean soft acids. Not hugely varietal.

1998	89	2003	2006
1997	89	1999	2002+
1996	90	2000	2003
1995	88	1997	2000+
1994	82	1995	1998
1993	95	1998	2001
1992	94	2000	2004

CRESCENT (Shiraz Mourvèdre Grenache blend)

RATING **4**

Nagambie Lakes $20–$29
Current vintage: 2001   **91**

A sweet, slightly confected and spicy perfume of plums, blueberries, raspberries and cassis is scented with white pepper, cinnamon and cloves over dusty vanilla oak. A moderately firm chassis of grippy tannins finishes long and minty. Earthy, savoury undertones frame its smooth and generous palate of lively berry and currant flavours with pleasing depth and integration.

2001	91	2006	2009
2000	93	2005	2008
1999	89	2004	2007+
1998	89	2003	2006+
1997	84	1999	2002

PRINT SHIRAZ

RATING **3**

Nagambie Lakes $50–$99
Current vintage: 2003   **89**

Dark, brooding aromas of plums and black berries, cedar/vanilla oak and spices reveal some varnishy and meaty aspects suggestive of shrivelled fruit. Firm and powdery, it's long and tightly astringent, delivering a rich, minty expression of currants, raisins, blackberries and plums framed by chalky tannins. A little varnishy, it lacks the fruit brightness for a higher rating.

2003	89	2011	2015
2002	95	2010	2014+
2001	93	2009	2013+
2000	90	2005	2008+
1999	92	2007	2011
1998	93	2010	2018
1997	91	2005	2009
1996	89	2001	2004
1995	92	2003	2007
1994	88	2002	2006
1993	94	2005	2013
1992	88	2000	2004+
1991	94	2003	2011
1990	90	1998	2002

Mitolo

34 Barossa Valley Way, Tanunda SA 5352. Tel: (08) 8292 9012. Fax: (08) 8282 9062.
Website: www.mitolowines.com.au Email: enquiries@mitolowines.com.au
Regions: **Barossa Valley, McLaren Vale** Winemaker: **Ben Glaetzer** Chief Executive: **Frank Mitolo**

While its premier Savitar Shiraz from McLaren Vale produced a fine, if alcoholic red wine in 2004, I can't help thinking that Mitolo let this vintage short of its high expectations. The G.A.M. is tarry and dehydrated, while the Reiver appears rather disjointed and raw. The Serpico Cabernet Sauvignon from McLaren Vale — not an area noted for the variety — is a very soupy, vegetal wine that falls well short of the region's best examples from this unusually favourable vintage.

G.A.M. SHIRAZ

RATING **5**

McLaren Vale	$50–$99
Current vintage: 2004	**89**

Slightly cooked, meaty and evolved, with a spicy, leathery and floral bouquet of cassis, plums and redcurrants backed by sweet, lightly gluey and mocha-like American oak. Full to medium in weight, it's savoury and quite tarry, with a confectionary and partially dehydrated expression of cassis and plums backed by sweet dark chocolate/vanilla oak and supported by slightly gritty tannin. Quite well mannered, but with some dead fruit qualities.

2004	89	2009	2012+
2003	87	2005	2008
2002	89	2004	2007+
2001	88	2006	2009+

REIVER SHIRAZ

RATING **3**

Barossa Valley	$50–$99
Current vintage: 2004	**89**

Gluey, slightly raw and cedary oak detracts marginally from the sweet aromas of cassis, dark plums and dark chocolate oak. Initially succulent and juicy, the palate delivers a spirity expression of jujube-like red berry, redcurrant, cassis and plum flavours, with distinct mint and menthol influences. There's some overt over-ripeness seen in the currant-like finish. It has all the components, but they might have been put together a little more carefully.

2004	89	2009	2012
2003	92	2008	2011+
2002	92	2007	2010
2001	90	2006	2009

SAVITAR SHIRAZ

RATING **3**

McLaren Vale	$50–$99
Current vintage: 2004	**93**

A very good wine in the modern alcoholic style that would have been better still with about a percent less alcohol to enable its fruit to express itself more clearly and intensely. Its heady perfume of cassis, dark plums and dark olives overlies fine-grained, roast walnut-like oak. Massively concentrated, its smooth and luscious palate is deeply stained with sour-edged flavours of plums, cassis, dark olives and blackberries, and backed by nuances of mint and menthol. It finishes tarry and smoky, with slightly overt raw, spirity influences and lingering suggestions of salt and mineral.

2004	93	2009	2012+
2003	94	2008	2011+
2002	91	2004	2007+
2001	89	2006	2009

Montalto

33 Shoreham Road, Red Hill South Vic 3937. Tel: (03) 5989 8412. Fax: (03) 5989 8417.
Website: www.montalto.com.au Email: info@montalto.com.au
Region: **Mornington Peninsula** Winemaker: **Robin Brockett** Viticulturist: **Geoff Clarke**
Chief Executive: **John Mitchell**

After a very bright start with its first four vintages, Montalto has slipped back into the pack. Montalto is a very diverse business, with a high-level restaurant, an olive grove and wetland development, but the flame that saw the making of some tightly focused wine of comparable stature to its other endeavours appears to be dwindling. The actual wine processing takes place at Scotchman's Hill on the Bellarine Peninsula.

CHARDONNAY   RATING 3

Mornington Peninsula	$30–$49
Current vintage: 2005	89

An honest and uncomplicated chardonnay whose fresh aromas of peaches, pineapple, cashew and vanilla oak herald a smooth and creamy palate whose vibrant, juicy stonefruit flavours are backed by nuances of citrus, melon and grilled nuts. Wrapped in clean but soft acids, it's likely to become quite rich and generous.

2005	89	2007	2010
2004	89	2006	2009
2003	94	2008	2011
2001	93	2003	2006+
2000	92	2002	2005
1999	91	2001	2004

PINOT NOIR   RATING 4

Mornington Peninsula	$30–$49
Current vintage: 2005	87

Floral, spicy and rather stewed aromas of plums, currants and raspberries precede a moderately rich, smooth and generous palate whose slightly cooked red berry and currant-like fruit flavours finish a little short, with minty/menthol undertones. Just lacks a little fruit brightness and expression, finesse and polish.

2005	87	2007	2010+
2004	86	2005	2006+
2003	93	2005	2008+
2001	93	2003	2006+
2000	90	2002	2005
1999	80	2001	2004

Montrose

Poet's Corner Wines, Craigmoor Road, Mudgee NSW 2850. Tel: (02) 6372 2208. Fax: (02) 6372 4464.
Website: www.poetscorner.com.au Email: info@poetscornerwines.com
Region: **Mudgee** Winemakers: **Trent Nankivell, Ben Bryant** Viticulturist: **Kirily Rimmer**
Chief Executive: **Laurent Lacassgne**

Montrose is a long-established brand that has been part of the Orlando-Wyndham group for a considerable time. It offers two tiers of wines: some from traditional French varieties and others such as Barbera and Sangiovese from Italy. Unless seasons dictate otherwise, as they have indeed done for several recent Mudgee vintages, each of the wines is reliably well made, flavoursome, true to type and offers great value for money.

BARBERA   RATING 4

Mudgee	$20–$29
Current vintage: 2002	92

Vibrant, elegant and varietally correct barbera, with some regional notes of eucalypt and mint. Sweet and spicy, its briary aromas of tomato bush, small red berries, nicotine and diesel oil are backed by sweet, sumptuous and pristine, it offers a long and lingering palate of piercing small red berries, plums and cherries, evenly matched to restrained vanilla oak and framed by powder-fine tannins.

2002	92	2004	2007+
2000	83	2002	2005
1999	91	2001	2004+
1997	92	2002	2005+
1996	89	2001	2004+

BLACK SHIRAZ

RATING **5**

Mudgee	**$20–$29**	2002	90	2010	2014

Mudgee	$20–$29
Current vintage: 2002	**90**

Cooked, porty and spirity aromas of dark plums, berries and lightly smoky vanilla oak precede a fullish palate whose meaty, dehydrated expression of stressed fruit lacks genuine fruit sweetness, for which some assertive oak influence fails to compensate.

2002	90	2010	2014
2001	81	2002	2003
1999	90	2004	2007+
1998	84	2000	2003
1997	89	2005	2009
1996	89	1998	2001
1995	88	1997	2000
1994	87	1996	1999

SANGIOVESE

RATING **5**

Mudgee	$20–$29
Current vintage: 2004	**89**

A stylish and shapely sangiovese that needs to age a little to enable its fruit to emerge. Its dusty, spicy aromas of sweet raspberries, cherries, white pepper and cloves precede a supple and juicy palate framed by appropriately tight and fine-grained tannins. Quite long and savoury, with a slightly sour-edged note to its cherry/plum fruit, it just lacks a little cut and definition.

2004	89	2009	2012
2002	90	2003	2004+
1998	89	2000	2003+
1997	90	1999	2002
1996	89	2001	2004

STONY CREEK CHARDONNAY

RATING **4**

Mudgee	$12–$19
Current vintage: 2004	**89**

Juicy aromas of ripe melon and lemon zest reveal a toasty, buttery background of sweet vanilla and biscuit-like oak. Its vibrant, tangy palate of melon, grapefruit and white peach finishes with limey acids and a mineral, sherbet and bath powder-like aspect.

2004	89	2006	2009
2002	90	2007	2010
2001	88	2003	2006
1999	90	2001	2004+
1997	91	2002	2005
1996	90	1998	2001+
1994	90	1999	2002

Moondah Brook

Dale Road, Middle Swan WA 6056. Tel: (08) 9274 9547. Fax: (08) 9274 8949.
Website: www.moondahbrook.com.au

Region: **Western Australia** Winemaker: **Ross Pamment** Viticulturist: **Diane Stewart**
Chief Executive: **David Woods**

Moondah Brook has been slowly downgraded to a generic Western Australian brand of cheap, cheerful and well-made wines of lively varietal flavours and short-term appeal. With a shade of residual sweetness, its ripe, tropical and peachy 2005 Verdelho is clearly its best current release.

CABERNET SAUVIGNON

RATING **5**

Western Australia	$12–$19
Current vintage: 2002	**83**

Quite firm and chalky, this lightly herbal and stewy cabernet lacks the depth of ripe fruit to handle its extract. There's a light presence of berry and dark plum flavour, but the fruit is essentially nondescript, finishing greenish and metallic.

2002	83	2007	2010
2001	77	2003	2006
2000	86	2002	2005+
1999	88	2004	2007
1998	88	2003	2006+
1997	82	1999	2002
1996	90	2004	2008
1995	87	2000	2003
1993	84	1995	1998

SHIRAZ

Western Australia $12–$19
Current vintage: 2004   87

A flavoursome, slightly jammy and herbal shiraz with a violet-like perfume. Lightly toasty mocha/chocolate oak backs its perfume of violets and cassis, plums and blackberries, while its palate is almost confectionary, with sweet berry-like fruit and cedar/mocha oak framed by somewhat sappy, but pliant tannins. It finishes with pleasing length and a light herbal sappiness.

2004	87	2006	2009+
2002	81	2004	2007
2001	83	2003	2006
2000	86	2002	2005+
1999	88	2004	2007
1998	87	2003	2006
1997	86	1999	2002
1996	88	2001	2004

VERDELHO

RATING 5

Western Australia $12–$19
Current vintage: 2005   88

Generous and varietal, this lightly sweet verdelho delivers vibrant flavours of mango-like tropical fruits, peach and apricot. Its intense, round and fleshy mouthfeel precedes a long, clean and lingering finish.

2005	88	2005	2006+
2004	77	2004	2005+
2003	87	2004	2005+
2002	88	2003	2004
2001	89	2002	2006
2000	89	2002	2005
1999	87	2001	2004+
1998	89	2000	2003+
1997	83	1999	2002

Moondarra

Browns Road, Moondarra via Erica Vic 3825. Tel: (03) 9598 3049. Fax: (03) 9598 0766.
Region: **Gippsland** Winemakers: **Sandro Mosele, Neil Prentice** Viticulturist: **Neil Prentice**
Chief Executive: **Neil Prentice**

Moondarra is a tiny Gippsland vineyard whose wines are among the many others made at Kooyong on the Mornington Peninsula. Its premier wines, the complex, long-living and profoundly structured Conception and Samba Side pinot noirs, have quickly acquired cult status. Neil Prentice decided not to release any wine from the pitifully small 2002 vintage.

CONCEPTION PINOT NOIR

RATING 4

Gippsland $50–$99
Current vintage: 2003   93

A pretty, supple and willowy pinot whose tightly focused and musky perfume of sweet red cherries and berries reveals meaty, earthy undertones of hazelnuts and flowers. Smooth and silky, it presents a slightly fatty palate of penetrative cherry/berry flavour over a fine-grained chassis of powdery tannin. It finishes with just a hint of meaty and leathery complexity, plus a herbal hint of tomato stalk.

2003	93	2008	2011+
2001	90	2006	2009
2000	90	2005	2008
1999	88	2004	2007

A B C D E F G H I J K L M N O P Q R S T U V W X Y Z

Moorilla Estate

655 Main Road, Berriedale Tas 7011. Tel: (03) 6277 9900. Fax: (03) 6249 4093.
Website: www.moorilla.com.au Email: wine@moorilla.com.au
Region: **Southern Tasmania** Winemaker: **Alan Ferry** Viticulturist: **Alan Ferry**
Chief Executive: **Tim Goddard**

Based at Berriedale, close to central Hobart, Moorilla Estate is a serious maker of cool-climate table wines. It regularly achieves success with pinot noir and chardonnay, also with often very perfumed and musky expressions of riesling and gewürztraminer. Its Pinot Noir can also be surprisingly long-living. The Claudio's Reserve Pinot Noir 2005 was tasted just after bottling and has every chance of developing beyond my initial expectations.

CABERNET SAUVIGNON

RATING 4

Southern Tasmania	**$20–$29**		
Current vintage: 2003	**90**		

A cedary, fine-grained and tightly knit cabernet whose sweet, slightly varnishy aromas of small berries and cedary oak gradually opens to reveal bright-ness and freshness. Moderately rich and firm, its intensely juicy palate of red berries, blackberries, plums and cedary oak has a drying spine of fine tannins, finishing with dusty, herbal undertones beneath its vibrant fruit.

2003	90	2011	2015
2002	77	2004	2007+
2001	86	2003	2006
2000	91	2008	2012
1999	88	2004	2007
1998	88	2003	2006
1997	86	2002	2005+
1995	81	2000	2003
1994	93	2002	2006
1993	82	2001	2005

CHARDONNAY

Southern Tasmania	**$20–$29**		
Current vintage: 2003	**87**		

Nutty aromas of tropical and melon-like fruit are backed by creamy, buttery oak with undertones of green cashew. Smooth and juicy, its generous palate of white peach, apple, pear and lime flavours reveals buttery nuances of vanilla oak and a slightly green-edged and metallic cut of acidity.

2003	87	2005	2008
2002	84	2004	2007
2001	85	2003	2006
2000	87	2002	2005
1999	83	2001	2004
1998	81	2000	2003+
1996	83	1998	2001
1995	94	2003	2007

CLAUDIO'S RESERVE PINOT NOIR

RATING 4

Southern Tasmania	**$30–$49**		
Current vintage: 2005	**91**		

A very minty and powerfully fruited young pinot that needs time to settle in the bottle and for its aromas and flavours to build further. Its briary, con-centrated aromas of sweet raspberries, cherries and plums overlies nuances of cedar/vanilla oak. Silky-fine and sumptuous, its minty, brambly and intensely fruited palate is backed by a slightly raw extract of cedary oak, but should smooth out and become more luxuriant as it ages.

2005	91	2013	2017
2002	90	2004	2007+
2001	93	2006	2009
2000	91	2002	2005+
1999	91	2004	2007
1998	83	2000	2003
1997	88	2002	2005
1996	87	1998	2001

GEWÜRZTRAMINER

RATING 5

Southern Tasmania	**$20–$29**		
Current vintage: 2005	**83**		

While this delicately perfumed, spicy and floral young gewürztraminer has an appealing scent of rosewater and lychees, its palate begins sweet and confectionary, before drying out towards a powdery finish that appears stripped of fruit. While not appearing to want a bet each way, I'd like to see this again in a year.

2005	83	2007	2010
2003	86	2004	2005+
2001	83	2002	2003
2000	94	2005	2008
1999	90	2004	2007
1998	89	2003	2006
1997	90	2002	2005
1996	82	1997	1998

PINOT NOIR

Southern Tasmania	$20–$29
Current vintage: 2004	86

Backed by musky nuances of dried herbs, this firm and rather polished pinot has a delicate, floral and cedary perfume of menthol-like red cherries and berries. Its structured, meaty palate of red plums and berries is supported by cedar/vanilla oak, with undertones of dried herbs. It's a fraction green, and lacks genuine varietal impact.

2004	86	2006	2009+
2003	81	2004	2005+
2002	86	2004	2007
2001	89	2003	2006+
2000	90	2005	2008
1999	87	2001	2004
1998	87	2000	2003
1997	92	2002	2005
1996	90	2001	2004
1995	88	2000	2003
1994	91	1999	2002

RIESLING

RATING 5

Southern Tasmania	$20–$29
Current vintage: 2005	92

Penetrative musky aromas of lemon blossom, citrus juices and fresh lime zest reveal mineral and steely undertones. Long, lean and refreshing, the restrained and slightly smoky palate of citrus and apple flavour overlies some tight, chalky texture, finishing with plenty of focus, minerality and tightness.

2005	92	2010	2013+
2004	88	2006	2009
2003	84	2005	2008+
2002	80	2003	2004+
2001	93	2006	2009+
2000	87	2008	2012
1999	87	2004	2007
1998	90	2003	2006
1997	87	1999	2002
1996	91	2001	2004
1995	88	1997	2000
1994	95	2006	2014

Moorooduc Estate

501 Derril Road, Moorooduc Vic 3933. Tel: (03) 5971 8506. Fax: (03) 5971 8550.
Website: www.moorooduc-estate.com.au Email: us@moorooduc-estate.com.au

Region: **Mornington Peninsula** Winemaker: **Richard McIntyre** Chief Executive: **Richard McIntyre**

Moorooduc Estate was one of the first makers from the Mornington Peninsula to fashion table wines of genuine class. After some years of struggling to regain its early form, it is edging its way back with some very flavoursome and adventurous wines. 2004 has seen the making of two significantly better reserve level 'The Moorooduc' wines, although the 'standard' labels are both lacking the intensity expected from a season of that quality.

CHARDONNAY

Mornington Peninsula	$30–$49
Current vintage: 2004	84

Slightly stale, buttery and confectionary aromas of peach and mango are backed by nuances of cashew and herbal, tropical undertones. Juicy, generous and forward, the palate of tropical and melon-like fruit is sweet and chewy but slightly hollow in the middle, with a greenish, sappy and toffee-like finish lacking freshness and bite.

2004	84	2006	2009
2003	89	2005	2008
2002	83	2003	2004
2001	77	2002	2003
2000	77	2002	2005
1999	87	2001	2004
1998	92	2000	2003
1997	88	2002	2005
1996	93	2001	2004
1995	93	2000	2003
1994	95	1999	2002

PINOT NOIR

RATING 4

Mornington Peninsula	$30–$49
Current vintage: 2004	89

Spicy, floral and herbal aromas of raspberry and red cherry confection are backed by nuances of cloves and cinnamon, while the palate presents a joyfully bright core of intense small berry and cherry flavours backed by fine, powdery tannin. It finishes with pleasing intensity, and a hint of currant.

2004	89	2006	2009+
2003	91	2005	2008+
2002	91	2004	2007+
2001	84	2003	2006
2000	84	2002	2005
1998	88	2003	2006
1997	93	2002	2005
1996	87	2001	2004
1995	93	2000	2003
1994	92	1999	2002
1993	93	1998	2001
1992	95	2000	2004
1991	84	1996	1999

THE MOOROODUC CHARDONNAY

Mornington Peninsula $50–$99
Current vintage: 2004   92

Smooth, supple and creamy, this restrained and elegant wine reveals a typically wild, meaty and slightly reductive aspect. Its perfume of dried flowers, peaches, quince and melon is subtly backed by spicy, fine-grained oak with dusty, earthy undertones. Its soft and savoury palate marries peachy fruit with newish oak and slightly funky complexity, finishing with concentration and a trace of bitterness.

2004	92	2006	2009+
2002	84	2004	2007+
2001	86	2003	2006
2000	76	2002	2005
1999	84	2001	2004
1998	91	2003	2006

THE MOOROODUC PINOT NOIR

RATING **5**

Mornington Peninsula $50–$99
Current vintage: 2004   90

Distinctly varietal but a little edgy all the same, this smooth and richly textured pinot carries a significant load of funky complexity. There's a meaty, charcuterie aspect beneath its spicy, assertively floral and slightly candied aromas of raspberries, red cherries, plums, cinnamon and cloves. Long and even, it presents tightly focused but ripe fruit over white pepper-like influences, dusty fine tannins and restrained oak.

2004	90	2009	2012
2003	87	2005	2008
2001	87	2003	2006
2000	81	2002	2005
1998	77	2000	2003
1997	94	2005	2009

Morris

Mia Mia Road, Rutherglen Vic 3685. Tel: (02) 6026 7303. Fax: (02) 6026 7445.
Website: www.morriswines.com.au Email: morriswines@orlando-wyndham.com
Region: **Rutherglen** Winemakers: **David Morris, Mick Morris** Chief Executive: **Laurent Lacassgne**
Morris is one of the traditional makers of red wines in Victoria's warm-to-hot and northeasterly Rutherglen region. Despite the fact that it is owned by one of the world's largest beverage companies in Pernod-Ricard, Morris makes its reds quite autonomously. The results are everything you'd hope for — traditionally crafted 'country' wines of integrity, character and authenticity. The 2002 reds are typically generous, exceptionally ripe and meaty, and honestly and simply balanced with firm tannins and restrained oak. Morris is also one of the elite makers of Rutherglen's unique tokay and muscat.

BLUE IMPERIAL

RATING **5**

Rutherglen $20–$29
Current vintage: 2002   88

An honest, but lighter wine whose meaty, spicy aromas of plums and blueberries, prunes and currants have sweet vanilla oak and floral undertones. Ripe and forward, then slightly hollow, its sweet, rather cooked and meaty prune/currant fruit qualities overlie nuances of blueberries and blackberries, before finishing soft and smooth.

2002	88	2010	2014+
2001	89	2006	2009
1999	88	2007	2011
1998	86	2003	2006

CABERNET SAUVIGNON

RATING **5**

Rutherglen $12–$19
Current vintage: 2002   89

A rustic, old-fashioned and largely over-ripe cabernet that has the depth and structure to last for some time. Its meaty, earthy and gamey aromas of plums, prunes and currants suggests plenty of time hanging to develop sugar sweetness, while its chewy and astringent palate offers sufficient vibrant plum and berry flavour to complement its firm extract.

2002	89	2010	2014+
2001	89	2009	2013
2000	86	2008	2012
1999	89	2007	2011+
1998	89	2006	2010
1997	82	1999	2002+
1996	88	2004	2008+
1995	87	2003	2007
1994	89	2006	2014
1993	87	2005	2013
1992	88	2000	2004
1990	91	2002	2010
1989	91	2001	2009
1988	91	2000	2005
1987	88	1995	1999

Rutherglen $12–$19
Current vintage: 2005   89

A big, generous and juicy chardonnay whose uncompromisingly ripe flavour of juicy, peachy fruit is handsomely backed by creamy vanilla oak before a lingering and tangy finish of lively acids and a hint of minerality. Clean and refreshing despite its ripeness, this is a very fine effort from this warmer region.

2005	89	2007	2010+
2003	88	2005	2008
2002	89	2004	2007
2001	87	2003	2006
2000	88	2002	2005
1999	87	2000	2001
1998	86	2000	2003
1997	83	1999	2002

DURIF   RATING 4

Rutherglen $20–$29
Current vintage: 2002   90

Long, firm and gamey, this typically meaty, briary and sumptuously flavoured durif has a heady bouquet of deep, spicy berry and plum aromas backed by restrained nuances of older oak. Lacking the weight and occasional heaviness of wines from warmer years, it still presents a raisined, currant-like expression of fruit over more vibrant dark plum and berry flavours. Framed by chalky tannins, it finishes long and savoury.

2002	90	2014	2022
2001	90	2013	2021
2000	90	2012	2020
1999	87	2007	2011
1998	85	2010	2018+
1997	91	2009	2017
1996	88	2004	2008+
1995	93	2007	2015
1994	93	2002	2006
1993	87	2001	2005
1992	90	2004	2012
1991	93	2003	2011
1990	93	2002	2010
1989	88	2001	2009

SHIRAZ   RATING 4

Rutherglen $12–$19
Current vintage: 2002   90

An honest, old-fashioned Rutherglen shiraz that combines typically spicy and leathery regional qualities with the elegance of a cooler vintage. Its meaty, chocolatey aromas of deep plummy and dark berry fruit reveal undertones of licorice and treacle, while its velvet-smooth, gamey and deeply ripened palate of plums and berries, prunes and currants is very true to type.

2002	90	2014	2022
2001	90	2009	2013
2000	85	2005	2008
1999	88	2004	2007+
1998	89	2003	2006+
1997	85	2005	2009
1996	89	2004	2008+
1995	87	2000	2003
1994	87	2002	2006
1993	82	1998	2001
1992	91	2004	2012
1991	90	2003	2011

Moss Wood

Metricup Road, Willyabrup WA 6280. Tel: (08) 9755 6266. Fax: (08) 9755 6303.
Website: www.mosswood.com.au Email: mosswood@mosswood.com.au
Regions: **Margaret River, Pemberton** Winemakers: **Keith Mugford, Ian Bell** Viticulturist: **Josh Bahen**
Chief Executives: **Keith & Clare Mugford**

Moss Wood has produced another superb Cabernet Sauvignon of its own style in 2003. It's a spectacular wine for its sheer opulence and seamlessness, but would rate even higher were it not for a slight confiture-like aspect and a fraction too much alcohol. That's how close Moss Wood is getting to perfection. The same can't be said for two very ordinary chardonnays from 2005 that are simply right out of style and off the pace. I can only assume that a serious technical difficulty was encountered in their making. Of some concern is the repeated failure of the Ribbon Vale Vineyard Merlot to meet expectations.

AMY'S CABERNET SAUVIGNON   RATING 5
(formerly Glenmore Vineyard)

Margaret River $30–$49
Current vintage: 2004   89

Jammy, rather confectionary and herbal aromas of raspberries and plums are pierced by a spirity note of alcohol and backed by sweet cedar/vanilla oak. Spotlessly clean, plush and smooth, its juicy palate of relatively simple, boiled lolly-like cassis and dark cherry fruit and smooth oak are framed by soft, pliant and firmish tannins.

2004	89	2006	2009+
2003	89	2008	2011
2002	86	2004	2007+
2001	89	2003	2006+
2000	93	2008	2012
1999	93	2004	2007+

CABERNET SAUVIGNON

RATING 2

Margaret River $50–$99
Current vintage: 2003   96

Luxuriantly smooth, this deeply fragrant, firmly structured, plush and seamless wine marries deep, ripe fruit with superb oak and tannin. Its heady bouquet of cassis, dark plums, blueberries and plain chocolate overlies assertive cedar/vanilla oak, with nuances of forest floor. Steeped in sumptuous cassis and dark cherry-like flavour, the palate has a plumpness and richness of fruit tightly interwoven with cedar/dark chocolate oak and a powdery spine of drying tannin. There's a hint of confiture about the fruit, while it finishes very slightly spirity, with lingering nuances of dark olives.

2003	96	2015	2023+
2002	95	2014	2022
2001	97	2013	2021+
2000	93	2008	2012+
1999	93	2011	2021
1998	90	2006	2010+
1997	89	2005	2009
1996	96	2008	2016
1995	96	2015	2025
1994	95	2014	2024
1993	87	2001	2005
1992	89	2000	2004
1991	96	2003	2011+
1990	95	2002	2010+
1989	91	2001	2009
1988	89	2000	2008
1987	89	1999	2007
1986	95	2006	2016
1985	97	2005	2015

CHARDONNAY

RATING 2

Margaret River $50–$99
Current vintage: 2005   87

Rather flat, dull and oxidative, with buttery aromas of peach, grapefruit and lemon backed by nuances of nougat, sweet vanilla oak and wet hessian. It's initially forward and citrusy, but becomes leaner and thinner down the palate, finishing with quite assertive oak influences and tight, lemony and mineral acids. Lacks length and depth of fruit.

2005	87	2007	2010
2004	96	2009	2012
2003	95	2008	2011
2002	95	2007	2010+
2001	95	2006	2009
2000	91	2005	2008
1999	96	2007	2011
1998	90	2003	2006+
1997	95	2002	2005
1996	93	1998	2001
1995	93	2003	2007
1994	95	2002	2006
1993	92	1998	2001
1992	94	2000	2004
1991	91	2003	2011
1990	94	2002	2010

LEFROY BROOK VINEYARD CHARDONNAY

RATING 4

Pemberton $30–$49
Current vintage: 2005   81

A very herbaceous chardonnay whose restrained aromas of dried flowers, chardonnay and melon are overshadowed by assertively herbal, sweaty and silage-like nuances, with creamy, butterscotch undertones. Vegetal and forward, it lacks length and mid-palate brightness and freshness.

2005	81	2006	2007
2004	89	2006	2009
2003	93	2005	2008+
2002	89	2004	2007+
2001	91	2003	2006
1997	92	1999	2002

PINOT NOIR

RATING 5

Margaret River $30–$49
Current vintage: 2003   88

Slightly minty, earthy and floral aromas of red cherries and plums are backed by funky, spicy leesy undertones. Smooth and elegant, it's fine and supple, delivering a soft-centred palate of sweet raspberry, red cherry and currant-like fruit over a silky-fine spine of dusty tannin. An east-drinking soft dry red with some pinot character.

2003	88	2008	2011
2002	89	2004	2007+
2001	87	2006	2009
2000	81	2002	2005
1999	81	2004	2007
1998	88	2003	2006
1997	86	2002	2005
1996	89	2001	2004
1995	93	2003	2007
1994	87	1999	2002
1993	83	1998	2001

RIBBON VALE VINEYARD CABERNET BLEND RATING 3

Margaret River $30–$49
Current vintage: 2004 90

A stylish, modern cabernet blend with pleasing elegance, depth and brightness of fruit. Its oaky, menthol-like aromas of mulberries, dark cherries, plums and cranberries reveal smoky, meaty and herbal undertones. Smooth and silky, its faintly sour-edged expression of cassis, cherries and blue-berries is framed by slightly sappy tannins and backed by lightly smoky cedar/vanilla oak.

2004	90	2012	2016
2003	93	2011	2015+
2002	91	2010	2014+
2001	92	2009	2013
2000	93	2008	2012
1999	90	2011	2019
1998	77	2000	2003
1997	93	2005	2009
1996	90	2004	2008+
1995	87	2003	2007+
1994	87	2002	2006
1993	84	1995	1998

RIBBON VALE VINEYARD MERLOT RATING 5

Margaret River $30–$49
Current vintage: 2004 87

Rustic, reductive and meaty aromas of stewed plums and cherries reveal earthy and leathery under-tones. Handsomely coated with sweet cedar/vanilla oak but otherwise simple and jammy, the palate frames a moderately juicy and rustic expression of plum and cherry fruit with smooth, firmish but slightly sappy and metallic tannins.

2004	87	2006	2009+
2003	88	2008	2011
2002	88	2007	2010+
2001	90	2006	2009+
2000	91	2005	2008
1999	92	2007	2011
1998	77	2000	2003
1997	91	2002	2005
1996	90	2004	2008
1995	90	2000	2003
1994	80	1999	2002
1993	89	2001	2005
1992	92	2000	2004
1991	93	1999	2003

SEMILLON RATING 3

Margaret River $30–$49
Current vintage: 2005 86

Rather overcooked, warm and spirity, lacking its typical brightness and length. Dullish apple-like aromas precede a palate whose initially vibrant melon and citrus flavour finishes a little short, raw and oaky.

2005	86	2007	2010
2004	89	2006	2009
2003	93	2005	2008+
2001	95	2006	2009
2000	92	2002	2005+
1999	91	2001	2004
1998	87	2000	2003
1997	84	1998	1999
1994	86	1996	1999
1993	87	1998	2001
1992	90	2000	2004

Mount Horrocks

The Old Railway, Station Curling Street, Auburn SA 5451. Tel: (08) 8849 2202. Fax: (08) 8849 2265.
Website: www.mounthorrocks.com Email: sales@mounthorrocks.com

Region: **Clare Valley** Winemaker: **Stephanie Toole** Chief Executive: **Stephanie Toole**

Mount Horrocks is an energetic Clare Valley wine producer whose proprietor and maker, Stephanie Toole, is relentlessly working to refine her wines towards classic status. Looking at my ratings, it's impossible for me not to conclude that the vineyards are better suited to white varieties than reds, although the reds still meet a high standard. As ever, I have a very large soft spot for the Semillon, which in 2005 was as good as ever.

CABERNET MERLOT RATING 4

Clare Valley $30–$49
Current vintage: 2002 90

A fine, elegant, tightly balanced and stable wine with pleasing fruit depth and structure. Its vibrant, floral and faintly herbal aromas of black and red berries are tightly knit with cedary suggestions of spicy vanilla oak. Its supple, smooth palate of vibrant berry/plum flavour, cedary oak and herbal undertones finishes long and persistent, with under-tones of dried herbs.

2002	90	2010	2014+
2001	90	2009	2013
2000	89	2005	2008
1999	91	2007	2011
1998	90	2003	2006+
1996	94	2004	2008+
1995	90	2000	2003
1994	91	1999	2002
1993	87	1998	2001
1992	89	1997	2000

CHARDONNAY

RATING 4

Clare Valley $20–$29
Current vintage: 2004   89

Floral and lightly spicy, with a peachy fragrance of orange blossom and creamy, nutty undertones. Smooth and elegant, it's an early-drinking wine with pristine stonefruit flavours wrapped in citrusy acids, with a lingering note of reductive complexity.

2004	89	2005	2006+
2003	85	2003	2004+
2002	90	2004	2007
2000	90	2002	2005+
1999	90	2001	2004
1998	80	1999	2000

CORDON CUT

RATING 2

Clare Valley $20–$29 (375 ml)
Current vintage: 2005   95

Intensely flavoured, smooth and luscious, this very stylish and youthful dessert wine finishes with freshness and brightness. Its limey aromas of white peaches, apricots and minerals have a lifted floral quality, while its unctuous tropical and citrusy palate is backed by a dusty, chalky undercarriage and wrapped up by a clean and balanced acidity.

2005	95	2010	2013
2004	93	2006	2009
2003	90	2004	2005+
2002	96	2002	2007
2001	94	2003	2006
2000	95	2002	2005
1999	91	2001	2004
1998	90	1999	2000
1997	87	1999	2002
1996	93	2001	2004

RIESLING

RATING 2

Clare Valley $20–$29
Current vintage: 2005   93

This tightly focused and bone-dry riesling offers a heady aroma of lime, lemon and floral perfume. Slightly confectionary, its long and finely sculpted palate of juicy citrus fruit is tightly focused and balanced by refreshing acids. Should develop beautifully.

2005	93	2013	2017
2004	96	2012	2016+
2003	95	2011	2015
2002	95	2010	2014+
2001	92	2006	2009+
2000	87	2002	2005
1999	93	2004	2007
1998	93	2003	2006
1997	90	2002	2005
1996	90	1998	2001
1995	90	1997	2000
1994	93	1999	2002
1993	94	2001	2005
1992	91	2000	2004

SEMILLON (formerly blended with Sauvignon Blanc)

RATING 2

Clare Valley $20–$29
Current vintage: 2005   95

A fabulously fresh and pristine young semillon whose fragrant, lightly toasty and almost perfumed scents of melon, white peach and citrus fruit reveal a light grassiness. Explosively flavoured, its long, smooth and silky palate of pristine melon and citrusy fruit is neatly tied up with a tangy finish of refreshing acidity. It retains a lingering core of vibrant flavour.

2005	95	2010	2013+
2004	94	2006	2009+
2003	94	2005	2008+
2002	91	2004	2007
2001	95	2006	2009
2000	90	2002	2005
1999	92	2004	2007+
1998	90	2000	2003

SHIRAZ

RATING 4

Clare Valley $30–$49
Current vintage: 2003   83

A dusty aroma of dried herbs and musky spices underpins a briary expression of cassis, raspberries and plums with undertones of cedar and capsicum. Initially forward, round and fleshy, the palate then becomes greenish, thin and sappy, lacking genuine length. Some well-handled oak doesn't quite conceal its stressed and green-edged nature.

2003	83	2005	2008
2002	87	2004	2007
2001	88	2006	2009
2000	92	2005	2008+
1999	91	2004	2007
1998	93	2003	2006+
1997	82	1999	2002
1996	86	1998	2001

Mount Ida

Northern Highway, Heathcote Vic 3523. Tel: (03) 9730 1022.
Website: www.fosters.com.au

Region: **Victoria** Winemaker: **Mark Robertson** Viticulturist: **George Taylor** Chief Executive: **Jamie Odell**

Mount Ida is a tiny Heathcote vineyard that, through a series of historical accidents, has ended up in the hands of Beringer Blass, one of the world's largest wine producers. It was planted in 1975 by Melbourne artist Len French, the designer of the National Gallery of Victoria's remarkable (and recently cleaned) ceiling. Its wines are typically better balanced, more fruit-driven and elegant than the modern dry port for which Heathcote is sadly becoming known in these allegedly enlightened days. They're great value and they live well.

SHIRAZ

RATING **3**

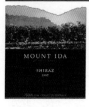

Heathcote	$20–$29				
Current vintage: 2003	**93**	2003	93	2015	2023
		2002	93	2010	2014+
Slightly meaty but certainly not overcooked; this		2001	84	2003	2006
is a tightly balanced Heathcote shiraz of moderate		1999	92	2004	2007
firmness and weight. Its spicy perfume of violets,		1998	96	2003	2006+
blackberries, plums and cassis overlies dark		1997	91	2002	2005
chocolate/vanilla oak and a whiff of menthol/mint.		1996	93	2001	2004
Long, firm and pliant, it's deeply flavoured, pen-		1995	96	2003	2007
etrative and spicy, with a lingering peppery		1994	94	1999	2002
finish.		1992	95	1997	2000
		1991	94	1999	2003
		1990	93	1995	1998

Mount Langi Ghiran

80 Vine Road, Bayindeen Vic 3375. Tel: (03) 5354 3207. Fax: (03) 5354 3277.
Website: www.langi.com.au Email: sales@langi.com.au

Region: **Grampians** Winemakers: **Trevor Mast, Dan Buckle** Viticulturist: **Damien Sheehan**
Chief Executive: **Gordon Gebbie**

Mount Langi Ghiran is best known for its modern, stylish and peppery expression of western Victorian shiraz, and was right there when the American market discovered top-notch Australian wine. It is now in the hands of the Rathbone family, owners of Yering Station and, more recently, Parker Coonawarra and Xanadu. Sadly, the much-awaited 2003 vintage of Langi Shiraz is not up to anticipated standard, instead reflecting the high levels of stress experienced across many southern Australian vineyards in that exceptionally hot vintage.

BILLI BILLI (Shiraz & Grenache)

Victoria	$12–$19				
Current vintage: 2003	**87**	2003	87	2005	2008
		2002	82	2004	2007
A charmingly spicy and early-drinking shiraz		2001	83	2003	2006+
with generosity, softness and structure. Its meaty		2000	92	2005	2008
and slightly peppery scents of dark cherries and		1999	86	2001	2004
cassis reveal musky undertones of cloves and		1998	82	2000	2003
cinnamon, dark chocolate and cedar/vanilla oak.					
There's also a suggestion of earth and leather.					
Smooth and peppery, with pleasingly persistent					
fruit supported by sweet oak and fine tannins, it					
finishes soft and savoury.					

CLIFF EDGE SHIRAZ

RATING **5**

Grampians	$20–$29				
Current vintage: 2002	**87**	2002	87	2004	2007+
		2001	88	2003	2006
A pleasingly soft, spicy and early-drinking shiraz		2000	92	2002	2005
whose attractive jujube-like fruit reveals spicy, licorice-		1999	86	2001	2004
like qualities. Fresh aromas of raspberries, cassis					
and mulberries are backed by sweet vanilla and					
coconut oak, with dusty, herbaceous under-					
tones. Uncomplicated, soft and pliant its spicy, lightly					
herbal palate finishes with slightly varnishy acids.					

LANGI CABERNET SAUVIGNON MERLOT

Grampians $30–$49
Current vintage: 2000   81

Evolved, meaty and herbal, this rather hollow and smoky cabernet blend has a lightly floral and forest floor-like bouquet of dried herbs, small berries and cedary oak. While its tannins are quite firm, they're also hard, sappy and green-edged, supporting a tiring expression of herbaceous berry flavours.

2000	81	2005	2008
1999	93	2007	2011+
1998	88	2006	2010
1997	91	2005	2009+
1996	90	2004	2008+
1994	95	2006	2014
1993	94	2001	2005
1992	95	2000	2004
1991	93	1999	2003
1990	92	1995	1998
1989	91	1997	2001
1988	90	1993	1996

LANGI SHIRAZ

Grampians $50–$99
Current vintage: 2003   87

A powerful, assertive and juicy shiraz with both under-and over-ripe influences. Its spicy, peppery aromas of cassis, dark plums and chocolate/mocha/vanilla oak are lifted by a violet-like perfume and spicy, leathery undertones. There's also a hint of spirit. Meaty, ripe and juicy, its forward and slightly confectionary palate does reveal some stressed, greenish and raw aspects which some sweet mocha/chocolate oak attempts to shield. Firm and astringent, its finish is flat and spirity, lacking freshness and vitality.

2003	87	2008	2011
2000	94	2008	2020
1999	88	2001	2004+
1998	90	2003	2006
1997	86	2002	2005
1996	94	2004	2008
1995	94	2003	2007
1994	97	2006	2014
1993	93	2001	2005
1992	93	2004	2012
1991	90	1999	2003
1990	93	2002	2010
1989	95	2001	2009
1988	91	1996	2000

PINOT GRIS

Grampians $20–$29
Current vintage: 2005   90

Very delicate, lightly spicy and citrusy aromas precede a long, savoury, dusty and nutty palate of pleasing length and balance. It's a very attractive food style, with lingering citrusy flavours and refreshing acids.

2005	90	2006	2007
2004	90	2005	2006+
2003	90	2004	2005+
2002	86	2003	2004+
2001	89	2001	2002+

RIESLING

Grampians $20–$29
Current vintage: 2005   93

Open and generous, this rather modern and distinctly Germanic riesling has a floral, honeysuckle-like fragrance whose delicate perfume of citrus and pear precede a smooth, generous and supple palate that culminates in a clean, refreshing halbtrocken-like finish. It ends with lingering fresh flavours of apple and pear backed by a slightly oxidative complexity.

2005	93	2010	2013+
2004	90	2009	2012
2003	93	2008	2011
2002	93	2007	2010
2000	92	2005	2008
1999	80	2000	2001
1998	83	2000	2003
1997	82	1999	2002
1996	94	2004	2008
1995	94	2003	2007

Mount Mary

Coldstream West Road, Lilydale Vic 3140. Tel: (03) 9739 1761. Fax: (03) 9739 0137.
Region: **Yarra Valley** Winemakers: **John Middleton, Rob Hall**
Viticulturists: **John Middleton, Jamie McGlade** Chief Executive: **David Middleton**

John Middleton, doctor, winemaker, intellectual, champion of bombast, scientist and scientific eccentric, friend and antagonist par excellence died just over a week prior to my writing these words. To suggest that he will be sorely missed by Australian wine — including the many who couldn't stomach him — is an understatement of massive proportions. John Middleton was a visionary and a purist who adhered doggedly to his particular set of ideas. While some would say he succeeded despite them, he leaves behind a legacy of great work and achievement in Australian wine. Furthermore, he leaves Mount Mary exactly as he wanted to — at the very top of its form, and in the hands of his family and a new generation of talented young employees.

CABERNET 'QUINTET'   RATING 1

Yarra Valley $100–$199
Current vintage: 2004   97

A top-drawer Mount Mary red that would appear to contain significantly more merlot than its mere eleven percent. Its deep, dark and briary aromas of violets, cassis, blackberries, dark plums and plain chocolate reveal undertones of dried herbs and bramble. Beautifully controlled and contained, its silky and elegant palate conceals its ample power and strength beneath an exterior of spotlessly fresh, pure blackcurrant and dark cherry fruit, camera-shy oak and tannin so delicate and fine that its genuine impact could easily be ignored. Evenly ripened, it also reveals classic nuances of dried herbs.

2004	97	2016	2024+
2003	96	2015	2023
2002	94	2014	2022
2001	97	2013	2021
2000	97	2012	2020+
1999	97	2011	2019
1998	97	2010	2018
1997	91	2002	2005+
1996	95	2004	2008+
1995	91	2007	2015
1994	96	2006	2014
1993	90	2001	2005
1992	95	2000	2004
1991	95	2009	2003
1990	97	2002	2010
1989	85	1994	1997
1988	97	2000	2008
1987	90	1995	1999
1986	95	1998	2006

CHARDONNAY   RATING 2

Yarra Valley $50–$99
Current vintage: 2005   95

A beautifully composed, complete and finely crafted chardonnay that simply needs time to flesh out and deliver on its considerable early promise. A floral, nutty perfume of peach, melon, grapefruit and guava reveals undertones of wheatmeal, vanilla, cloves and cinnamon. Silky, long and supple, its tightly crafted marriage of lingering stonefruit, grapefruit and melon-like flavour and restrained oak culminates in a taut and persistent finish of refreshing acidity.

2005	95	2010	2013+
2004	97	2009	2012
2003	96	2008	2011+
2002	95	2007	2010+
2001	96	2006	2009+
2000	95	2008	2012
1999	94	2004	2007
1998	92	2003	2006+
1997	90	2002	2005
1996	93	2004	2008
1995	92	2003	2007
1994	90	1997	2002
1993	90	1998	2001

PINOT NOIR   RATING 2

Yarra Valley $50–$99
Current vintage: 2004   96

An exemplary Mount Mary pinot and a classic example of this variety. Slightly stewed, floral and briary aromas of quince, cherries and raspberries are lifted by scents of rose petals, five spice and nutmeg. Silky, smooth and seamless, its unctuous, sappy palate of juicy sweet cherries and plums is tightly wrapped in the finest of tannins, finishing with savoury spices. Its balance, intensity and texture are simply delightful, and will only develop with time in the bottle.

2004	96	2012	2016
2003	95	2008	2011+
2002	92	2004	2007+
2001	93	2006	2009
2000	97	2008	2012
1999	95	2007	2011
1998	89	2003	2006
1997	89	2002	2005+
1996	89	1998	2001
1995	88	2000	2003
1994	94	2002	2006
1993	88	1998	2001
1992	94	2000	2004
1991	93	1999	2003
1990	92	1995	1998

RATING 2

Yarra Valley $50–$99
Current vintage: 2005 96

A piercing fragrance of citrus and gooseberry-like fruit, dried flowers and dusty herbal and mineral undertones precedes a long, taut, trim and chalky palate of exemplary shape, brightness and freshness. Mineral, dusty and chalky qualities underpin its lingering flavours of tangy lemon and melon, before a steely, briney finish of refreshing citrusy acids.

2005	96	2010	2013+
2004	96	2009	2012
2003	95	2005	2008+
2002	95	2007	2010
2001	95	2006	2009
2000	95	2005	2008
1999	94	2004	2007
1998	95	2003	2006+
1997	92	2002	2005
1996	95	2001	2004
1995	95	2000	2003
1994	93	1999	2002
1993	95	1995	1998
1992	95	1997	2000+
1991	94	1996	1999
1990	94	1998	2002

Mount Pleasant

Marrowbone Road, Pokolbin NSW 2321. Tel: (02) 4998 7505. Fax: (02) 4998 7761.
Website: www.mcwilliams.com.au Email: mcwines@mcwilliams.com.au
Region: **Lower Hunter Valley** Winemaker: **Phillip Ryan** Viticulturist: **Peter Rohr**
Chief Executive: **George Wahby**

Mount Pleasant is the McWilliams family's beachhead in the Hunter Valley, and home to classic, traditional wines made from ancient and historic vineyards. Its efforts with semillon under the Elizabeth and Lovedale labels are the stuff of legend, while the rustic, earthy and typically regional reds from the OP & OH and Rosehill Vineyards can be spectacular. While the Lovedale Semillon effortlessly cruised through the 2002 season, delivering another charming and silky-smooth wine (for slightly shorter term cellaring than usual), it was the OP & OH Shiraz that really performed during the hot 2003 red vintage.

CLASSIC CHARDONNAY
(formerly Hunter Valley Chardonnay)

RATING 5

Lower Hunter Valley $12–$19
Current vintage: 2005 87

Juicy, exuberant and overtly oaky, this flavoursome and refreshing young chardonnay matches its ripe, vibrant flavours of peach, nectarine, quince and grapefruit with toasty vanilla oak. Wrapped in clean and refreshing acids, it's overt, showy and right in your face, but makes delightful, if uncomplicated drinking.

2005	87	2006	2007
2004	90	2005	2006+
2003	88	2005	2008
2002	87	2002	2003
2001	89	2003	2006
2000	87	2002	2005
1999	89	2001	2004
1997	88	1999	2002
1996	90	2001	2004
1995	87	2000	2003
1994	85	1996	1999

ELIZABETH (Semillon)

RATING 4

Lower Hunter Valley $12–$19
Current vintage: 2003 89

A toasty, smoky and forward Elizabeth from a hot vintage. Its evolving melon and citrusy aromas are backed by rather a funky, meaty and reductive quality, while its unusually robust palate has more texture and ripeness than usual. There's a rich core of sumptuous fruit, plenty of developed complexity and a persistent and tangy finish.

2003	89	2008	2011+
2002	95	2010	2014+
2001	89	2006	2009
2000	90	2005	2008+
1999	89	2001	2004+
1998	90	2003	2006+
1997	93	2005	2009
1996	95	2008	2016
1995	93	2003	2007+
1994	95	2006	2014
1993	93	2001	2005
1992	87	2000	2004
1991	88	1993	1996
1990	87	1995	1998
1989	93	2001	2009
1988	88	1990	1993
1987	91	1995	1999+
1986	95	1998	2006+

THE AUSTRALIAN WINE ANNUAL
www.jeremyoliver.com.au **2007**

RATING **2**

	Lower Hunter Valley	$50–$99
	Current vintage: 2002	**94**

A classically smooth and silky Lovedale semillon with some toasty development. Its delicate floral and wheatmeal aromas of lemon rind and melon precede a long, almost fluffy palate whose vibrant but restrained honeydew melon flavours are neatly bound by lemony acids. Very good indeed, but not for the super-long term.

2003	95	2015	2023
2002	94	2010	2014
2001	91	2009	2013
2000	93	2008	2012
1998	95	2010	2018
1997	91	2005	2009+
1996	96	2008	2016
1995	90	2007	2015
1986	95	1998	2006+
1984	96	1996	2004
1979	94	1991	1999+

MAURICE O'SHEA SHIRAZ

RATING **3**

	Lower Hunter Valley	$30–$49
	Current vintage: 2003	**88**

Deep aromas of blackberries, dark plums and plain chocolate are backed by very smoky, ashtray and Kahlua-like aromas of either unusually distinctive oak or the bushfire taint not uncommon in Lower Hunter wines of this vintage. A firm, rod-like spine of drying tannin coats its powerfully structured and richly fruited palate, which reveals faint undertones of lanolin and herbal qualities.

2003	88	2011	2015
2000	94	2012	2020
1999	92	2007	2011
1998	93	2006	2010+
1997	91	2005	2009
1996	88	2001	2004+
1994	88	2002	2006
1993	91	1998	2001

OLD PADDOCK & OLD HILL SHIRAZ

RATING **4**

	Lower Hunter Valley	$30–$49
	Current vintage: 2003	**94**

Charmingly old-fashioned and balanced, this is powerfully ripened, slightly meaty Hunter shiraz of unusual concentration and richness. Its smoky, leathery and rustic bouquet of blackberries, plums and red berries precedes a sumptuous and sweet-fruited palate whose deliciously rich fruit is unobtrusively supported by oak and framed by firm but velvet-smooth tannins.

2003	94	2015	2023
2002	90	2010	2014
2001	89	2009	2013+
1999	89	2004	2007
1998	94	2006	2010+
1997	88	2002	2005
1996	92	2004	2008+
1995	90	2003	2007

PHILIP (Shiraz)

RATING **5**

	Lower Hunter Valley	$12–$19
	Current vintage: 2003	**89**

A considerably richer and more profoundly structured Philip than most of its predecessors, with an earthy, leathery bouquet whose delicate aromas of spicy cherries and plums overlie violet-like nuances. Full to medium in weight, it's smooth and elegant, with undertones of mint and menthol beneath its juicy fruit and smooth tannins. It finishes pleasingly long and savoury.

2003	89	2008	2012
2002	88	2007	2010+
2000	85	2005	2008
1999	88	2004	2007
1998	83	2003	2006
1997	82	1999	2002
1996	84	1998	2001
1995	88	2000	2003
1994	83	1999	2002
1993	77	1995	1998

ROSEHILL SHIRAZ

RATING **4**

	Lower Hunter Valley	$20–$29
	Current vintage: 2003	**90**

Spicy, rather spirity aromas of fresh sweet berries, plums, menthol and mint overlie mocha-like nuances of prunes and currants. Firm and meaty, its sumptuous and treacle-like palate of fresh plum and rather more dehydrated prune and currant-like characters is framed by firm and slightly blocky tannin. Clearly reflective of a hot vintage, it's very awkward right now, but should settle down and age well over the medium term.

2003	90	2011	2015+
2001	85	2006	2009
2000	84	2005	2008
1999	91	2004	2007+
1998	93	2006	2010+
1997	93	2002	2005
1996	93	2004	2008
1995	84	1997	2000
1991	91	1996	1999
1990	80	1992	1995

A B C D E F G H I J K L **M** N O P Q R S T U V W X Y Z

Mountadam

High Eden Road, Eden Valley SA 5235. Tel: (08) 8564 1900. Fax: (08) 8564 1999.
Website: www.mountadam.com Email: office@mountadam.com.au

Region: **Eden Valley** Winemaker: **Con Moshos** Viticulturist: **Con Moshos** Chief Executive: **David Brown**

After a few years in which it struggled under the ownership of Veuve Clicquot (part of the French LVMH giant), Mountadam was sold to David Brown, for a fraction of the outrageous amount LVMH paid. Today, with a new team headed by unheralded but experienced Petaluma winemaker Con Moshos, Mountadam is set, ready and raring to go. It still has all the tools that matter — an excellent vineyard of mature vines, a fine winemaking facility and the resources to push through changes and developments. Watch this space, closely.

CHARDONNAY
RATING 5

Eden Valley	$30–$49
Current vintage: 2004	**89**

Brassy, toasty aromas of peachy, citrusy fruit are backed by a complex array of wheatmeal, buttery and reductive leesy undertones. Long, smooth and creamy, it delivers a slightly oily expression of citrus and melon flavour with tightly knit suggestions of wheatmeal and butter. Just lacks the definition and focus of fruit for a higher score.

2004	89	2006	2009+
2002	89	2004	2007+
2001	77	2002	2003
2000	86	2002	2005
1999	87	2001	2004
1998	87	2000	2003+
1997	80	1999	2002
1996	86	1998	2001
1995	87	1997	2000
1994	94	1999	2002
1993	88	1998	2001

PINOT NOIR
RATING 5

Eden Valley	$30–$49
Current vintage: 2002	**89**

Meaty, youthful pinot with a spicy, rose petal perfume of maraschino cherries and red plums before a soft, stalky palate of medium weight and some grip. Likely to build in the bottle, acquiring a good depth of varietal flavour.

2002	89	2004	2007+
2001	86	2006	2009
1999	89	2004	2007
1998	92	2003	2006
1997	87	2002	2005
1996	87	2004	2008
1995	87	2000	2003
1994	89	1999	2002
1993	90	2001	2005
1992	89	1997	2000
1991	93	1999	2002

SHIRAZ (formerly Patriarch)
RATING 4

Eden Valley	$30–$49
Current vintage: 2002	**87**

Spicy, herbal aromas of mulberries, raspberries, red plums and rather toasty vanilla oak overlie briary, forest floor-like nuances and a meaty, leathery aspect. Firm, oaky and rather herbal, its relatively simple palate of mulberry, cassis and plum-like flavour just lacks genuine brightness and depth of fruit, finishing with greenish edges.

2002	87	2007	2010
2001	91	2009	2013+
1999	85	2001	2004
1998	92	2006	2010
1997	88	2002	2005
1996	88	2004	2008
1995	94	2003	2007
1994	92	1999	2002
1993	92	2001	2005
1992	91	2002	2004
1991	94	1999	2003
1990	92	1998	2002

THE RED (Cabernet Sauvignon & Merlot)
RATING 5

Eden Valley	$30–$49
Current vintage: 2002	**83**

Vegetal, herbaceous and shaded fruit aromas of mulberries, cassis and capsicum soup are backed by minty undertones. Medium to full in weight, its herbal, jammy expression of forward berry fruit and sweet, creamy vanilla oak is framed by a firmish cut of sappy tannin that lacks structure and emphasis.

2002	83	2007	2010
2001	89	2009	2013
1999	83	2004	2007
1998	87	2003	2006
1997	82	1999	2002+
1996	86	2001	2004
1995	90	2000	2003
1994	94	2006	2014
1992	89	2000	2004
1990	93	1995	1998
1989	87	1994	1997
1988	90	1996	2000

Mr Riggs

McLaren Vale SA 5171. Tel: (08) 8556 4460. Fax: (08) 8556 4462.
Website: www.mrriggs.com.au Email: mrriggs@pennyshill.com.au

Region: **McLaren Vale** Winemaker: **Ben Riggs** Viticulturist: **Toby Bekkers** Chief Executive: **Ben Riggs**

Former Wirra Wirra winemaker-turned-consultant Ben Riggs now has his own brand, making a delightfully Germanic and slightly sweet Riesling, a spicy and fragrant Shiraz Viognier, a very rustic Tempranillo, a juicy Viognier and a voluptuous and fine-grained Shiraz that is steadily growing in stature. The 2004 Shiraz just about encapsulates the Mr Riggs approach to red wine: ripe, rich and silky-smooth.

SHIRAZ

RATING **3**

McLaren Vale	$30–$49
Current vintage: 2004	93

A meaty, chocolate-like fragrance of cranberries, blueberries and cassis overlies nuances of violets and currants, sweet vanilla/mocha oak and spicy influences of cloves and cinnamon. A sumptuous, smooth and vibrant palate of juicy cassis, mulberry, raspberries, plums and dark cherries has a confiture-like sweetness and a slightly cooked, currant-like aspect. Supported by tight-knit oak and framed by fine, pliant tannins, it's a fine, modern, generous and earlier-maturing style.

2004	93	2009	2012
2003	94	2011	2015+
2002	92	2007	2010+
2001	92	2006	2009+

Nepenthe

Jones Road, Balhannah SA 5242. Tel: (08) 8388 4439. Fax: (08) 8398 0488.
Website: www.nepenthe.com.au Email: cellardoor@nepenthe.com.au

Region: **Adelaide Hills** Winemakers: **Peter Leske, Michael Paxton** Viticulturist: **Murray Leake**
Chief Executive: **James Tweddell**

Nepenthe's diverse and imaginative range of wines, which include two separate zinfandels and a tempranillo from the Adelaide Hills, reflects a creative and original approach to winemaking, not to mention a fair measure of eccentricity. Winemaker Peter Leske appears to have a deft touch with the white varieties of sauvignon blanc and chardonnay, not to mention a flair for his small-run Tempranillo. There's a refreshing element within Nepenthe of 'anything goes', which stands it apart from so many Australian wine companies whose ranges are limited to classic French varieties.

ITHACA CHARDONNAY

RATING **5**

Adelaide Hills	$20–$29
Current vintage: 2003	91

A fine, supple and elegant chardonnay whose dusty, lightly herbal aromas of honeydew melon and tropical fruits reveal nuances of matchstick and vanilla oak. There's a babyfat-like juiciness about the palate, but it retains plenty of tightness and integration with spicy oak and refreshing acids. It finishes long and smooth, with lingering fruit sweetness.

2003	91	2008	2011
2002	87	2003	2004
2000	86	2002	2005
1999	88	2001	2004+
1998	90	2000	2003
1997	87	1998	1999

LENSWOOD ZINFANDEL

RATING **5**

Adelaide Hills	$30–$49
Current vintage: 2003	87

A surprisingly restrained zinfandel that has little in common with the American model of the variety. Its spicy, meaty perfume of red cherries and apricot precedes a dusty, slightly hollow and powdery palate backed by cedary oak and framed by fine and powdery tannins.

2003	87	2008	2011
2001	89	2003	2006+
2000	76	2002	2005
1999	91	2004	2007
1998	81	2000	2003
1997	87	1999	2002+

PINOT GRIS

	Adelaide Hills	$20–$29
	Current vintage: 2005	**86**

Buttery aromas of citrus fruits, apple and pear with a lightly creamy, leesy background precede a juicy, forward palate whose nutty fruit thins out towards a slightly metallic and green-edged finish. There's some pleasing tightness and austerity, but the wine lacks sufficient brightness, finishing salty and herbal.

2005	86	2005	2006+
2004	89	2005	2006
2003	88	2004	2005+
2002	92	2003	2004+
2001	77	2001	2002
2000	82	2000	2001

SAUVIGNON BLANC

RATING 4

	Adelaide Hills	$20–$29
	Current vintage: 2005	**88**

A vibrant, chewy and slightly phenolic sauvignon blanc whose lightly cooked aromas of juicy, rather sweaty and herbaceous fruit precede a generous and forward palate that thins out a little towards a greenish finish. Lively and clean, it just lacks a pure core of flavour.

2005	88	2005	2006+
2004	91	2004	2005+
2003	91	2004	2005
2002	91	2002	2003+
2001	91	2002	2003
2000	87	2001	2002
1999	94	2000	2001
1998	92	1999	2000+
1997	92	1997	1998

CHARLESTON PINOT NOIR

RATING 5

	Adelaide Hills	$20–$29
	Current vintage: 2004	**88**

A rather herbal, evolved, meaty and leathery pinot whose slightly stewed and stemmy aromas of dark plums and cherries precede a juicy but firmish palate of medium weight. Framed by slightly hard, kernel-like tannins, it's honest and flavoursome, but lacks genuine charm, complexity and silkiness.

2004	88	2006	2009
2003	85	2004	2005+
2002	89	2004	2007
2001	86	2003	2006
2000	86	2002	2005
1999	87	2001	2004+
1998	88	2000	2003+
1997	81	1998	1999

THE FUGUE (Cabernet Sauvignon Merlot Cabernet Franc)

RATING 4

	Adelaide Hills	$20–$29
	Current vintage: 2002	**90**

A polished, balanced and elegant red whose minty aromas of cassis, mulberries and cedar/vanilla oak reveal lightly herbal undertones. Its bright, forward expression of cassis, mulberries and plums is supported by a dusty, powdery suggestion of vanilla oak underpinned by firmish tannins. Pleasingly long, with brightness and ripeness, it shows some herbal edges without appearing greenish.

2002	90	2010	2014
2000	85	2005	2008
1999	90	2007	2011
1998	89	2003	2006
1997	93	2005	2009

THE ROGUE (Cabernet Sauvignon Merlot Shiraz)

RATING 5

	Adelaide Hills	$20–$29
	Current vintage: 2003	**88**

Supple, restrained and willowy, this lightly herbal and floral wine has a minty and cedary bouquet of small red and black berries. Its smooth, juicy palate of intense blackcurrant, dark plum and mulberry fruit is partnered by creamy, cedary oak and backed by earthy nuances of forest floor. It finishes with slightly herbal undertones.

2003	88	2008	2011
2002	82	2004	2007
2001	90	2006	2009+
2000	88	2002	2005+

192 — **THE AUSTRALIAN WINE ANNUAL**
www.jeremyoliver.com.au **2007**

Ninth Island

1216 Pipers Brook Road, Pipers Brook Tas 7252. Tel: (03) 6382 7527. Fax: (03) 6382 7226.
Website: www.pipersbrook.com Email: enquiries@pipersbrook.com

Region: **Tasmania** Winemaker: **Rene Bezemer** Viticulturist: **Bruce McCormack** Managing Director: **Paul de Moor**

Sourced from several Tasmanian regions, Ninth Island is Pipers Brook's second label. It usually offers a range of fresh and flavoursome early-drinking table wines of brightness and vitality, but aside from the Pinot Noir, the current releases fall well short of this mark.

PINOT NOIR

RATING **5**

Tasmania		$20–$29
Current vintage: 2005		87

A pretty, vibrant and slightly confectionary pinot whose floral aromas of raspberries and cherries reveal lightly herbal and minty undertones. Forward and fruity, with some genuine underlying structure, it does dry out a little towards the finish, becoming a tad herbal, green-edged and metallic. It might yet, however, flesh out further in the bottle.

2005	87	2007	2010
2004	87	2005	2006+
2003	87	2004	2005+
2001	89	2002	2003
2000	87	2001	2002
1999	87	2000	2001+
1998	88	2000	2003

Oakridge

864 Maroondah Highway, Coldstream Vic 3770. Tel: (03) 9739 1920. Fax: (03) 9739 1923.
Website: www.oakridgeestate.com.au Email: info@oakridgeestate.com.au

Region: **Yarra Valley** Winemaker: **David Bicknell** Viticulturist: **Daniel Dujic** Chief Executive: **Martin Johnson**

One of the tragedies behind a corporate catastrophe such as its parent Evans & Tate is experiencing is that the innocent get caught up in the net. Oakridge has operated independently under the winemaking guidance of the very talented Dave Bicknell, and its wines have performed way over expectation given the likely pressure on budgets. Atop the excellent collection of releases covered in this edition sits the first-rate 864 collection, of which the Chardonnay and Riesling are exemplary. At time of writing, Oakridge is for sale.

CABERNET MERLOT

RATING **5**

Yarra Valley		$20–$29
Current vintage: 2004		89

A pretty, fruit-driven wine with some sappy and unfinished aspects. Its slightly minty, floral aromas of violets, cranberries, cassis, cherries and mulberries reveal oaky undertones of cedar and vanilla. Medium to full in weight, it's fine and supple palate of slightly confection-like red berries, cherries and blackberries overlies a firmish, fine-grained backbone.

2004	89	2009	2012
2003	88	2008	2011
2001	86	2003	2006
2000	89	2005	2008
1999	87	2001	2004
1998	87	2000	2003
1997	84	2002	2005
1995	87	1997	2000
1994	82	1996	1999
1993	87	1998	2001
1992	93	2000	2004

CABERNET SAUVIGNON (formerly Reserve)

RATING **3**

Yarra Valley		$30–$49
Current vintage: 2004		92

A pristine, dusty and savoury cabernet whose heady, violet-like perfume of blackcurrant, mulberries, dark cherries and plums is backed by slightly gamey and cedary oak. Framed by firm and fine-grained tannins, its measured and elegant palate of vibrant fruit and cedary oak finishes with length and depth.

2004	92	2012	2016
2003	93	2015	2023
2001	86	2003	2006
2000	90	2008	2012+
1999	93	2007	2011+
1997	88	2005	2009+
1995	89	2000	2003+
1994	93	2002	2006
1991	96	2003	2011
1990	94	2002	2010
1987	82	1992	1995
1986	94	1994	1998

CHARDONNAY

RATING 5

Yarra Valley $20–$29
Current vintage: 2005 89

Imbued with less winemaker-derived complexity than previous vintages, this restrained and elegant chardonnay has an oaky, but subdued bouquet of pristine grapefruit and melon aromas backed by dusty vanilla oak. Austere and citrusy, its pleasingly tight and refreshing palate finishes with crisp acidity.

2005	89	2007	2010
2004	86	2006	2009+
2003	93	2005	2008+
2002	92	2007	2010
1999	82	2001	2004
1998	89	2003	2006
1997	93	2002	2005
1996	94	2001	2004
1995	85	1997	2000

PINOT NOIR

RATING 5

Yarra Valley $20–$29
Current vintage: 2005 91

A supple, smooth and juicy pinot that should flesh out with more fruit richness, colour and structure. Its fresh, floral perfume of raspberries, cherries and restrained vanilla oak precedes a vibrant, supple and soft palate of pleasing length, balance and underlying structure.

2005	91	2010	2013
2004	81	2005	2006
2003	89	2005	2008
2002	80	2004	2007
2000	87	2002	2005
1999	81	2000	2001
1998	82	1999	2000
1997	89	1999	2002+

SHIRAZ

RATING 5

Yarra Valley $20–$29
Current vintage: 2004 92

A modern, elegant and tightly integrated savoury, spicy and peppery shiraz whose lively aromas of small black and red berries, anise and licorice, cinnamon and cloves are assertively backed by smoky vanilla oak. Long and supple, its stylish palate of juicy small berry fruit is packed with pepper and spice and framed by fine, silky tannins. Attractively balanced and harmonious.

2004	92	2006	2009+
2003	90	2008	2011
2002	86	2004	2007
2000	81	2002	2005
1999	83	2001	2004
1998	89	2003	2006

Omrah

Albany Highway, Mount Barker WA 6324. Tel: (08) 9851 2150. Fax: (08) 9851 1839.
Website: www.plantagenetwines.com Email: sales@plantagenetwines.com
Region: **Great Southern** Winemaker: **Richard Robson** Viticulturist: **Jaysen Gladish** Chairman: **Tony Smith**
Omrah is the highly rated second label of Plantagenet, one of the Great Southern's leading wineries. As the current releases illustrate, its rather tomatoey Shiraz offers plenty of peppery, spicy dark fruit and richness, while its Sauvignon Blanc is vibrant, tight, herby and tropical.

SAUVIGNON BLANC

RATING 5

Western Australia $12–$19
Current vintage: 2005 90

Lightly herbal aromas of accentuated gooseberry, melon and tropical fruits with lightly sweaty undertones precede a generous, round and juicy palate whose tangy fruits and refreshing acids overlie a fine chalkiness. Attractively varietal and slightly herbaceous.

2005	90	2005	2006+
2004	87	2005	2006+
2003	91	2003	2004+
2002	88	2003	2004
2000	86	2001	2002
1999	77	1999	2000

SHIRAZ

RATING 5

Western Australia $12–$19
Current vintage: 2004 86

A medium-weight and rather tomatoey Western Australian shiraz with a floral and slightly confectionary aroma of red berries, sweet vanilla oak, pepper and spice. Fine, silky tannins frame its briary and powdery palate of blackberry, blueberry and cranberry flavour. Everything in the right place except for a tomatoey taste on the palate.

2004	86	2006	2009
2003	86	2004	2005
2002	89	2004	2007+
2001	87	2003	2006
2000	89	2001	2002+
1999	90	2001	2004
1998	82	2000	2003

UNOAKED CHARDONNAY

Western Australia	$12–$19
Current vintage: 2005	**83**

Relatively clean and refreshing, with lightly candied and herbal aromas of tropical fruit, peaches and cashew before a sweet, forward and juicy palate whose retrained expression of lemon and peachy flavours finishes slightly herbal and spirity.

2005	83	2005	2006
2004	86	2005	2006
2003	88	2004	2005
2002	88	2003	2004
2001	84	2001	2002
2000	87	2001	2002

Orlando

Barossa Valley Way, Rowland Flat SA 5352. Tel: (08) 8521 3111. Fax: (08) 8521 3100.
Website: www.pernod-ricard-pacific.com Email: contact_us@orlando-wyndham.com
Region: **South Australia** Winemakers: **Don Young, Hylton McLean, Nick Bruer** Viticulturist: **Joy Dick**
Chief Executive: **Laurent Lacassgne**

With several wines transferred to its stablemate Jacob's Creek brand, the Orlando collection is diminished in diversity and cohesion, perhaps, but certainly not quality. The wines represented here include one of Coonawarra's finest cabernets, Padthaway's best (minty) red, an exceptional and very affordable Riesling and a smooth, measured Chardonnay. Quite what will happen to the names of St Hilary and St Helga now that St Hugo has 'defected' to Jacob's Creek, only time will tell.

JACARANDA RIDGE CABERNET SAUVIGNON

Coonawarra	$50–$99
Current vintage: 1999	**94**

A firm, deeply fruited and astringent cabernet whose dusty and lightly herbal and briary aromas of blackberries, cassis, dark plums and cedar/vanilla oak reveal meaty and autumnal undertones. Its long and tightly structured palate of deep plum and berry fruits, cedary oak and drying astringency reveals some herbal notes that are progressively becoming more cigarboxy. A fine marriage of strength, structure and dark varietal fruit.

1999	94	2011	2019+
1998	97	2010	2018+
1997	92	2009	2017
1996	97	2008	2016
1994	95	2006	2014
1992	89	2000	2004
1991	94	2003	2011
1990	94	2002	2010
1989	93	1997	2001
1988	91	1993	1996
1987	91	1995	1999

LAWSON'S SHIRAZ

Padthaway	$50–$99
Current vintage: 2000	**89**

A minty Padthaway shiraz, with a healthy dose of menthol and eucalypt beneath its dark berry and maraschino cherry flavours. There's a whiff of black pepper, violets and cassis beneath its oaky aromas, while the palate is fine-grained, polished and silky. Creamy oak adds roundness and generosity, while there's a faint impression of saltiness about the finish.

2000	89	2008	2012
1999	93	2007	2011+
1998	94	2010	2018
1997	93	2005	2009+
1996	95	2004	2008+
1995	90	2003	2007
1994	96	2006	2014+
1993	90	2001	2005
1992	86	2004	2012
1991	95	2003	2011
1990	93	2002	2010

ST HELGA RIESLING

Eden Valley	$12–$19
Current vintage: 2005	**95**

Long, tight and finely balanced, this intensely flavoured riesling reveals a floral perfume of rose petals, lime juice and hints of baby powder, backed by faint mineral undertones. Juicy, long and intense, with a slightly candied aspect, its explosively flavoured palate of pristine and tangy citrus fruit overlies a fine, chalky backbone, before culminating in a lingering and tightly sculpted finish.

2005	95	2013	2017
2004	95	2012	2016
2003	90	2011	2015
2002	95	2010	2014+
2001	94	2006	2009+
2000	88	2002	2005+
1999	95	2007	2011
1998	94	2006	2010
1997	89	2002	2005
1996	95	2004	2010
1995	89	2003	2007
1994	95	2002	2006+
1993	87	1995	1998
1992	95	2000	2004+

ST HILARY CHARDONNAY

RATING **5**

Padthaway	$12–$19		
Current vintage: 2003	**88**		

Pleasing, if rather oaky chardonnay with a lemon bathpowder fragrance suggestive of grapefruit, melon and creamy vanilla oak. Smooth, restrained and even, there is a herbal note beneath its lively peach, apple and grapefruit and melon flavours. Finishes quite tightly, with refreshing lemony acids.

2003	88	2005	2008
2002	89	2004	2007
2001	86	2002	2003+
2000	90	2002	2005+
1999	88	2001	2004
1998	90	2003	2006
1997	90	1999	2002
1996	90	2001	2004
1995	85	1996	1997

Oxford Landing

PMB 31 Waikerie SA 5330. Tel: (08) 8561 3200. Fax: (08) 8561 3393.
Website: www.oxfordlanding.com Email: info@oxfordlanding.com
Region: **Riverlands** Winemaker: **Teresa Heuzenroeder** Viticulturist: **Bill Wilksch** Chief Executive: **Robert Hill Smith**
Not unexpectedly, the 2003 reds display some of the cooked and meaty characters typical of this exceptionally hot Riverland vintage, but the 2005 Chardonnay is right on song for its tightness, generosity and approachability. I rate Oxford Landing highly among the more competitively priced Australian brands.

CABERNET SAUVIGNON SHIRAZ

South Australia	$12–$19		
Current vintage: 2003	**85**		

A pliant and slightly candied warm-year wine that is beginning to dry out. Its floral aromas of raspberries, cherries, plums and blackberries are backed by restrained cedar/vanilla oak. Juicy and forward, its palate offers a pleasing weight of berry/plum flavour and earthy undertones, framed by firmish tannins.

2003	85	2005	2008
2002	89	2004	2007
2001	86	2003	2006
2000	84	2002	2005
1999	84	2000	2001
1998	81	1999	2000
1997	89	1998	1999
1996	87	1998	2001
1995	80	1996	1997

CHARDONNAY

RATING **5**

Riverlands	$12–$19		
Current vintage: 2005	**88**		

Sweet peachy, tropical and melon-like aromas backed by vanilla oak precede a surprisingly fine, elegant and tightly focused palate. Its bright, lively fruit flavours and restrained creamy vanilla oak deliver a long, persistent palate punctuated by clean and refreshing acids. Great value.

2005	88	2006	2007
2004	88	2005	2006
2003	80	2003	2004
2002	81	2002	2003
2001	80	2001	2002
2000	88	2001	2002
1999	86	2000	2001
1998	87	1999	2000+
1997	87	1998	1999

Panorama

1848 Cygnet Coast Road, Cradoc Tas 7109. Tel: (03) 6266 3409. Fax: (03) 6266 3482.
Website: www.panoramavineyard.com.au Email: panoramavineyard@bigpond.com
Region: **Huon Valley** Winemaker: **Michael Vishacki** Viticulturist: **Michael Vishacki**
Chief Executives: **Michael & Sharon Vishacki**
Panorama has emerged as one of the most sought-after makers of Tasmanian pinot noir. The richly flavoured, soundly structured and meaty 2001 Reserve Pinot Noir has won a number of accolades, while I found more brightness and less herbal influence in the very worthy 'standard' release of that year. There's no doubt in my mind that this vineyard is worth keeping an eye out for.

PINOT NOIR

RATING **4**

Huon Valley	$50–$99		
Current vintage: 2004	**89**		

This meaty and vegetal pinot has a musky, floral and confectionary perfume of red cherries, raspberries and redcurrants with undertones of cloves and cinnamon. Moderately long, smooth and elegant, it's framed by firmish, powdery tannins, offering a pleasing length of intense cherry/berry fruit before a lingering savoury and tightly structured finish.

2004	89	2006	2009+
2003	92	2008	2011+
2001	90	2006	2009
2000	88	2002	2005+

Paringa Estate

44 Paringa Road, Red Hill South Vic 3937. Tel: (03) 5989 2669. Fax: (03) 5931 0135.
Website: www.paringaestate.com.au Email: paringa@cdi.com.au
Region: **Mornington Peninsula** Winemaker: **Lindsay McCall** Viticulturists: **Lindsay McCall, Nick Power**
Chief Executives: **Lindsay & Margaret McCall**

Paringa Estate has made a name for its deeply ripened, coloured, dark-fruited and spicy Pinot Noir, and its fragrant and peppery Shiraz, both of which are typically given generous treatment in new oak, qualities that are regularly appreciated on the Australian wine show circuit. Simply because it's such a high-profile maker and because the introduction of its Reserve Pinot Noir and Shiraz wines was so recent (from the 2003 vintage) I feel I must comment on how the new wines have affected the overall performance of the vineyard. I honestly believe that Paringa would be making better pinot and shiraz if it was only making one of each.

CHARDONNAY
RATING 5

Mornington Peninsula	$30–$49
Current vintage: 2005	**88**

Juicy aromas of lemon rind, pineapple and grapefruit with slightly herbal undertones precede a smooth, elegant palate whose tropical and citrusy fruit finishes just a little sweet and cloying.

2005	88	2007	2010+
2003	86	2004	2005+
2002	85	2004	2007
2001	90	2003	2006
2000	89	2002	2005
1999	89	2001	2004
1998	91	2000	2003
1997	93	2002	2005
1996	84	1997	1998
1995	92	2000	2003
1994	93	1996	1999
1993	92	1998	2001
1992	89	1997	2000

PINOT NOIR
RATING 5

Mornington Peninsula	$50–$99
Current vintage: 2004	**89**

A sweet fragrance of red berries, cherries with floral, spicy and slightly varnishy undertones precedes a smooth and sappy palate framed by firmish, fine and powdery tannins. There's weight and structure aplenty, with lively flavours of red berries, cherries and plums finishing long and savoury. A little more fruit intensity would see a higher score.

2004	89	2006	2009+
2003	83	2005	2008
2002	88	2004	2007
2001	89	2003	2006
2000	93	2002	2005+
1999	89	2004	2007
1998	95	2003	2006+
1997	95	2002	2005
1996	87	1998	2001
1995	93	2000	2003
1994	87	1996	1999

SHIRAZ
RATING 4

Mornington Peninsula	$50–$99
Current vintage: 2004	**91**

Scented with violets, white pepper and spices, this firmish and oaky shiraz has a bouquet of ripe red and black berries and dark chocolate. Fine, smooth and elegant, its moderately rich expression of plum and berry flavour is quite restrained and meaty, but should flesh out with time. Framed by fine-grained tannins, it finishes long and savoury.

2004	91	2009	2012+
2003	87	2005	2008+
2001	88	2003	2006+
2000	90	2005	2008
1999	88	2001	2004+
1998	88	2003	2006
1997	95	2005	2009
1996	88	2001	2004
1995	88	2000	2003
1994	94	1999	2002
1993	93	2001	2005
1992	86	2000	2004
1991	91	1999	2003

Parker Coonawarra Estate

Riddoch Highway, Coonawarra SA 5263. Tel: (08) 8737 3525. Fax: (08) 8737 3527.
Website: www.parkercoonawarraestate.com.au Email: cellardoor@parkercoonawarraestate.com.au
Region: **Coonawarra** Winemaker: **Peter Bissell** Viticulturist: **Doug Balnaves** Chief Executive: **Gordon Gebbie**

Parker Coonawarra Estate is the brainchild of the late John Parker. It was Parker's aim to create a definitive marque of Coonawarra red wines, offering the depth of fruit and longevity for which the region is famous. The business was then acquired by the Rathbone family, owners of Yering Station and Mount Langi Ghiran. It's encouraging to see such good 2004 reds under this brand, which suggest a full resurgence is imminent.

TERRA ROSSA CABERNET SAUVIGNON   RATING 5

Coonawarra $20–$29
Current vintage: 2004   90

Minty and floral, its fragrance of cassis, violets, dark chocolate and cedar/vanilla oak precedes a fine, elegant and slightly one-dimensional palate. Framed by firmish but pliant tannins, its intense blackberry, plum and cassis-like fruit is handsomely backed by fine-grained oak, finishing with tightness and focus.

2004	90	2012	2016
2003	86	2005	2008
2002	83	2004	2007+
2001	89	2006	2009
1999	90	2001	2004+
1998	87	2003	2006
1997	86	1999	2002+
1996	84	1998	2001
1995	87	2000	2003
1994	84	1999	2002
1992	82	1997	2000
1991	88	1999	2003
1989	87	1991	1994

TERRA ROSSA FIRST GROWTH   RATING 2

Coonawarra $50–$99
Current vintage: 2001   93

A firm, long-living and complete cabernet. Its dark, deep and concentrated leathery aroma of meaty merlot and plummy/cassis fruit opens into a powerful, plush palate of length, concentration and firmness. Deep, dark berry fruits are tightly knit with new oak and fine, astringent tannins.

2001	93	2013	2021
2000	95	2008	2012+
1999	88	2004	2007
1998	95	2018	2028
1996	97	2008	2016+
1994	84	1999	2002
1993	90	2001	2005
1991	95	2003	2011+
1990	97	2002	2010
1989	92	1997	1991
1988	95	2000	2008

TERRA ROSSA MERLOT   RATING 4

Coonawarra $30–$49
Current vintage: 2004   92

Firm and concentrated, but rather brooding all the same, this handsomely structured merlot has a brightly lit perfume of dark cherries and plums dusted with hints of tobacco and backed by sweet newish vanilla/mocha oak. Its lingering core of intense fruit is supported by dark chocolate/mocha oak, framed by a firm and fine-grained astringency. It finishes long and savoury.

2004	92	2012	2016
2001	83	2006	2009
2000	91	2002	2005+
1999	89	2004	2007
1998	93	2006	2010

Passing Clouds

Kurting Road, Kingower Vic 3517. Tel: (03) 5438 8257. Fax: (03) 5438 8246.

Region: **Bendigo** Winemaker: **Graeme Leith** Viticulturist: **Graeme Leith**
Chief Executives: **Graeme Leith, Sue Mackinnon**

Passing Clouds has long been an important and consistent maker of central Victorian red wines of immense depth and longevity. There's barely a concession to modernity, as the style has hardly altered since I was first attracted by them more than two decades ago. The exceptional quality of the palate-staining 2004 Reserve Shiraz comes as no surprise, although in all honesty it will be another two decades before this delicious little monster is seen at its best.

ANGEL BLEND (Cabernet Sauvignon Merlot) RATING 4

Bendigo $30–$49
Current vintage: 2003 90

A dusty floral perfume of raspberries, cassis, sweet cedar/vanilla oak and dried herbs overlies nuances of menthol and tea leaves. Full in weight, its slightly jammy flavours of blackcurrant, red cherries, plums and blackberries deliver a lingering fruit sweetness. Framed by supple tannins and backed by restrained oak, it finishes firm and dusty. Balanced and stable, but could have used some better oak.

2003	90	2015	2023
2002	89	2010	2014+
2001	86	2006	2009+
2000	87	2005	2008
1999	91	2007	2011
1998	90	2010	2018
1997	93	2005	2009+
1996	90	2008	2016
1995	94	2007	2015
1994	91	2006	2014
1992	93	2000	2004
1991	90	1999	2003
1990	89	2002	2010
1987	87	1995	1999
1985	93	1993	1997
1984	87	1989	1992

GRAEME'S BLEND (Shiraz Cabernet Sauvignon) RATING 4

Bendigo $20–$29
Current vintage: 2003 88

An honest, smooth and approachable red blend with a rustic, menthol-like bouquet of sweet plums, red berries and hints of cassis backed by slightly meaty, leathery undertones, cedar/vanilla oak and undertones of forest floor. Its moderately long and slightly minty palate of cranberries, blackberries and plums is supported by restrained older oak influences and supported by supple tannins.

2003	88	2008	2011
2002	92	2014	2022
2001	87	2006	2009
2000	83	2002	2005+
1999	89	2011	2019
1998	91	2006	2010+
1997	90	2005	2009
1996	89	2004	2008+
1995	94	2003	2007
1994	88	2006	2014
1992	94	2004	2012
1991	91	1996	1999
1990	88	2002	2010
1989	85	1994	1997

RESERVE SHIRAZ RATING 3

Bendigo $50–$99
Current vintage: 2004 96

A superb, oaky and minty shiraz of first-rate balance and focus. Its heady perfume of cassis, dark plums, blackberries and violets has a rather polished oaky underswell of dark chocolate and vanilla, with spicy nuances of cloves and cinnamon. Its sumptuous and palate-staining expression of dark, minty fruit is tightly knit with fine-grained oak and framed by firm but velvet-smooth tannins.

2004	96	2016	2024+
2003	93	2011	2015+
2002	93	2014	2022
2001	91	2013	2021

SHIRAZ

RATING 4

Bendigo	$30–$49
Current vintage: 2004	**90**

Richly flavoured, balanced and likely to build in the bottle, this honest and minty shiraz has a slightly herbal and meaty bouquet of dark plums and cherries backed by older cedary oak. Firm, long and astringent, its drying, chalky palate of bright minty small berry/plum fruit has a lingering finish with menthol-like undertones. Give it time.

2004	90	2012	2016+
2002	90	2010	2014+
2001	93	2009	2013+
1998	87	2010	2018
1997	87	2005	2009
1996	89	2004	2008
1994	93	2002	2006+

Pauletts

Polish Hill Road, Polish Hill River SA 5453. Tel: (08) 8843 4328. Fax: (08) 8843 4202.
Website: www.paulettwines.com.au Email: info@paulettwines.com.au
Region: **Clare Valley** Winemaker: **Neil Paulett** Viticulturist: **Matthew Paulett** Chief Executive: **Neil Paulett**

Pauletts is a small maker of a typically regional selection of Clare Valley wines. It's little surprise to those of us who follow the seasons that the 2005 Riesling is a delightful expression of taut and tangy varietal flavour, while the reds from the significantly hotter and more challenging 2003 season are rather less memorable. Such are the vicissitudes of small vineyard wine production.

CABERNET MERLOT

RATING 5

Clare Valley	$20–$29
Current vintage: 2003	**80**

A rather soupy red blend whose dull, meaty and oaky aromas of plum-like fruit and cooked palate of sugar-ripe but flavour-deficient fruit lack intensity and brightness. It finishes sappy, thin and herbal.

2003	80	2005	2008
2002	90	2010	2014
2001	88	2006	2009+
2000	89	2008	2012
1999	88	2004	2007
1998	81	2000	2003
1997	88	2002	2005
1996	93	2004	2008
1995	89	2000	2003
1994	90	1996	1999
1993	84	1995	1998
1992	93	2000	2004
1991	93	1999	2003

RIESLING

RATING 5

Clare Valley	$12–$19
Current vintage: 2005	**93**

A brightly flavoured, taut and elegant Clare riesling whose flowery scents of lemon and lime precede a supple and tightly focused palate of length and restraint. Its lingering core of tangy citrus flavour builds steadily on the palate before a refreshing finish of clean and lightly mineral acids.

2005	93	2013	2017
2004	87	2009	2012
2003	88	2008	2011+
2001	85	2003	2006
2000	87	2005	2008
1999	89	2004	2007
1998	89	2000	2003+
1997	82	2002	2005
1996	88	2001	2004
1995	93	2003	2007
1994	93	2002	2006
1993	90	1995	1998

SHIRAZ

RATING 5

Clare Valley	$20–$29
Current vintage: 2003	**83**

Meaty, menthol-like aromas of dark plums, raisins and currants are slightly cooked and porty, while its forward and spicy palate lacks length and intensity. Finishing rather flat and dull, it reflects another very hot season.

2003	83	2005	2008+
2002	86	2007	2010
2001	89	2009	2013+
2000	90	2005	2008
1999	90	2004	2007
1998	86	2000	2003+
1997	86	2002	2005
1996	88	2001	2004
1995	89	2000	2003
1994	91	1999	2002
1993	94	2001	2005
1992	91	2000	2004
1991	91	1996	1999

Paxton

Sand Road, McLaren Vale SA 5171. Tel: (08) 8323 8645. Fax: (08) 8323 8903.
Website: www.paxtonvineyards.com Email: paxton@paxtonvineyards.com
Region: **McLaren Vale** Winemaker: **Michael Paxton** Viticulturist: **Toby Bekkers** Chief Executive: **David Paxton**

Paxton is a McLaren Vale label developed by one of Australia's leading viticulturists. Its 2004 Shiraz is right on the company's chosen style button of rich, chocolatey and pruney fruit, made into a sumptuous and voluptuous style for short to medium-term cellaring.

JONES BLOCK SHIRAZ

RATING **4**

McLaren Vale	$30–$49
Current vintage: 2004	**90**

A very ripe and meaty shiraz whose sumptuous expression of plummy, raisin, prune and currant-like fruit retains just enough bright cassis and raspberry-like flavour. Backed by smoky, mocha and smoked oyster-like new oak, it's velvet-smooth and very approachable, with nuances of dark chocolate, licorice, tar and treacle before its lingering, slightly salty and mineral finish. A little ultra-ripe for long-term cellaring.

2004	90	2009	2012
2003	90	2011	2015
2002	92	2010	2014
2001	86	2003	2006
2000	87	2002	2005+
1999	88	2001	2004+
1998	90	2000	2003+

Penfolds

Magill Estate Winery, 78 Penfold Road, Magill SA 5072. Tel: (08) 8301 5569. Fax: (08) 8364 3961.
Website: www.penfolds.com.au Email: penfolds.bv@cellar-door.com.au
Region: **South Australia** Winemaker: **Peter Gago** Viticulturist: **Tim Brooks** Chief Executive: **Jamie Odell**

Penfolds is Australia's most significant maker of red wine, and is a lynchpin brand within the expanded Foster's Wine Estates empire. Today it is recognised around the world for its famous hierarchy of red wines that begins with the budget Rawson's Retreat label and extends all the way upwards to the country's most feted wine, Grange. The 2001 Grange, without being a great example of the wine, restores a measure of credibility to the brand after what I believe was an ill-advised decision to release the 2000 vintage. Other signs for Penfolds are good, however, with steadily improving wines under the near-icon labels of Yattarna and St Henri.

BIN 04A CHARDONNAY

RATING **3**

Adelaide Hills	$50–$99
Current vintage: 2004	**93**

A shapely, smoky and rather funky chardonnay whose floral aromas of peach, grapefruit and cumquat are backed by sweet vanilla oak and leesy, bacony undertones. Its long and powdery palate reveals a tangy core of juicy peach, grapefruit and lemon zest, culminating in a lingering mineral and fractionally spirity finish of lime juice and baby powder.

2004 04A	93	2006	2009+
2003 03A	92	2005	2008+
2000 00A	94	2005	2008
1998 98A	92	2003	2006
1995 95A	93	2000	2003
1994 94A	93	1999	2002

BIN 128 COONAWARRA SHIRAZ

RATING **4**

Coonawarra	$20–$29
Current vintage: 2003	**89**

A very well handled wine whose firm structure and depth of fruit just lack the sweetness, charm and length to really impress. Its spicy fragrance of restrained red and black berries and violets is backed by cedary nuances of vanilla oak, with light undertones of menthol. There's also a note of leather than remains throughout the handsomely oaked and firmly constructed palate.

2003	89	2015	2023
2002	88	2007	2010
2001	93	2009	2013+
2000	83	2002	2005
1999	90	2004	2007
1998	93	2010	2018
1997	87	2002	2005
1996	94	2008	2016
1995	86	2000	2003
1994	93	2002	2006
1993	88	2001	2005
1992	93	2000	2004
1991	89	1999	2003
1990	92	1998	2002
1989	86	1994	1997
1988	90	2000	2005
1987	82	1992	1995
1986	93	1994	1998

BIN 138 OLD VINE RHÔNE BLEND

Barossa Valley $20–$29
Current vintage: 2004 90

A spicy, polished and deeply flavoured red blend whose juicy suggestions of blackberries, blueberries and red plums reveal a slightly confectionary and jujube aspect. The nose is slightly cooked, but reveals pleasing meaty and earthy undertones. Smooth and velvet-like, the palate is similarly meaty, with jammy fruit backed by rustic influences. It finishes rather chunky, with licorice-like spices. It should settle down with time, becoming one of the better wines under this label.

2004	90	2009	2012
2003	87	2005	2008
2002	91	2004	2007+
2001	88	2003	2006+
1999	89	2004	2007
1998	92	2006	2010
1997	90	2005	2009
1996	92	2004	2008
1995	86	1997	2000
1994	92	2002	2006
1993	89	2001	2005

BIN 389 CABERNET SHIRAZ

South Australia $30–$49
Current vintage: 2003 94

An evolution in 389's style, this artfully structured red blend has moved away from the overtly charming mocha/chocolate oak of the 1990s towards a finer and more perfumed oak extract, as well as revealing some herbal, bay leaf aromas largely unfamiliar to the label. Its rich, dark and meaty aromas of dark plums, cassis and cedar/vanilla oak reveal delightfully assertive and complex suggestions of dark chocolate, spice, game and leather. Smooth and polished, its palate backs its ripe, clean expression of cassis/blackberry fruit, with a drying and rather chalky backbone of firm tannin, finishing with warm, lingering nuances of polished oak and minerals. It's very good, but below gold medal standard.

2003	94	2015	2023+
2002	93	2014	2022
2001	91	2009	2013
2000	89	2005	2008+
1999	92	2007	2011
1998	96	2010	2018+
1997	93	2005	2009+
1996	97	2008	2016
1995	92	2004	2008
1994	95	2006	2014+
1993	93	2005	2013
1992	92	2004	2012
1991	94	2003	2011
1990	95	2002	2010
1989	87	1994	1997
1988	93	1996	2000
1987	91	1995	1999
1986	95	1998	2006

BIN 407 CABERNET SAUVIGNON

South Australia $30–$49
Current vintage: 2003 93

A very un-Penfolds-like cabernet of elegance and style. Its uncharacteristic greenish aspect comes across as a dried herb aroma and a hint of capsicum on the palate. Its dusty and perfumed aromas of sweet red and black berries, dark cherries, cedar and cigarboxy oak reveal delicate suggestions of violets and cassis. Supple and smooth, it presents a cool climate-like array of intense jujube-like cabernet flavour combined with smart, newish and lightly toasted cedar/vanilla oak and supported by a tight, firm and powdery extract. Good depth and structure.

2003	93	2011	2015+
2002	89	2010	2014
2001	87	2006	2009
2000	87	2005	2008
1999	90	2004	2007+
1998	91	2006	2010
1997	89	2005	2009
1996	95	2004	2008
1995	90	2003	2007+
1994	94	2002	2006
1993	93	2001	2005
1992	88	1997	2000
1991	94	2003	2011
1990	93	2002	2010

BIN 707 CABERNET SAUVIGNON

South Australia $50–$99
Current vintage: 2002 96

A welcome return to form for this important wine. It slowly unfolds a very closed and deeply layered bouquet of intense small black and red berries, plums and slightly meaty, deep mocha/dark chocolate and cedary oak. Its deeply ripened and sumptuously concentrated palate of dark plums and berries, chocolates and cassis is firmly structured around a supremely fine-grained cut of bony, kernelly tannins. Finer and more elegant than either 1996 or 1998 vintages, without a hint of over-ripeness, it's deep and brooding, with an exceptional cellaring potential.

2002	96	2022	2032
2001	93	2013	2021+
1999	95	2007	2011+
1998	97	2010	2018+
1997	93	2005	2009+
1996	96	2008	2016+
1994	94	2006	2014
1993	95	2005	2013
1992	94	2004	2012
1991	97	2003	2011+
1990	95	2010	2018
1989	91	1997	2001
1988	95	2000	2008
1987	93	1999	2007
1986	95	2006	2016
1985	91	1997	2005
1984	93	1996	2004

GRANGE

RATING 1

Barossa Valley (predominantly) $200+
Current vintage: 2001   95

A very fragrant, richly structured and flavoursome Grange whose deep, heady and smoky aromas of blackberry confiture, dark chocolate, violets and treacle reveal faint undertones of bitumen. Richly ripened and sumptuous, it gradually reveals its layers of deep, dark plums, cranberries and blackberries, steadily building in structure and intensity down the palate. Supported by drying, powdery tannins and first-rate oak, it's a surprisingly good wine from a tough vintage, with just a hint of stewed fruit, and finishing with a lingering core of licorice-like flavour.

2001	95	2021	2031
2000	87	2008	2012
1999	96	2019	2029+
1998	97	2018	2028+
1997	95	2017	2027+
1996	98	2026	2036+
1995	95	2025	2035+
1994	95	2014	2024+
1993	89	2005	2013
1992	94	2012	2022
1991	97	2021	2031
1990	97	2020	2030
1989	95	2001	2009+
1988	91	2000	2008+
1987	91	1999	2007
1986	95	2016	2026
1985	92	2005	2015
1984	90	2004	2014
1983	96	2023	2033
1982	93	2002	2012
1981	88	2001	2011
1980	90	2000	2010
1979	87	1991	1999
1978	94	1998	2008+
1977	92	1997	2007
1976	94	1986	1996+
1975	89	1987	1995
1974	89	1986	1994+
1973	83	1981	1985
1972	90	1984	1992
1971	97	2001	2011
1970	93	1980	1990
1969	91	1989	1994
1968	94	1988	1998
1967	92	1987	1997
1966	97	1996	2006
1965	95	1995	2005+
1964	96	1984	1994+
1963	95	1983	1993+
1962	97	1992	2002+
1961	95	1991	2001

KALIMNA BIN 28 SHIRAZ

RATING 5

South Australia $20–$29
Current vintage: 2003   93

Rich, meaty and deeply scented, this is a powerful, smooth and balanced shiraz of sweetness and charm. There's a brooding aspect to its spicy aromas of red plums and berries, cedar/vanilla oak, shoe leather and meaty shiraz undertones. A sumptuous palate of slightly sour-edged fruit and mouth-coating tannin packs plenty of flavour, before a lingering savoury and slightly salty/mineral finish. Give it some time.

2003	93	2011	2015+
2002	88	2010	2014
2001	87	2006	2009
2000	88	2005	2008
1999	86	2004	2007+
1998	95	2010	2018+
1997	91	2005	2009
1996	94	2008	2016
1995	90	2003	2007
1994	92	2002	2006
1993	84	1998	2001
1992	92	2000	2004
1991	93	1999	2003
1990	93	1998	2002
1989	87	1994	1997
1988	89	1996	2000
1987	88	1995	1999
1986	93	1998	2003
1985	87	1993	1997
1984	85	1989	1992
1983	82	1995	2000
1982	88	1990	1994

KOONUNGA HILL SHIRAZ CABERNET SAUVIGNON

South-Eastern Australia $12–$19
Current vintage: 2003   **87**

More of a forward, juicy Rosemount-like red style, with a sweet, floral perfume of mulberries, plums and blackberries, backed by lightly smoky vanilla oak and earthy, peppery undertones. Its soft, smooth and vibrant palate of jammy, jujube-like fruit and sweet oak are backed by a gentle undercurrent of fine tannins.

2003	87	2005	2008
2002	82	2004	2007
2001	81	2003	2006
2000	86	2002	2005+
1999	87	2004	2007
1998	87	2003	2006+
1997	86	2002	2005
1996	90	2004	2008
1995	87	2000	2003
1994	87	1999	2002
1993	88	2001	2005
1992	88	2000	2004
1991	92	1999	2003
1990	90	1998	2002
1989	88	1997	2001
1988	90	1996	2000
1987	82	1995	1999
1986	93	1998	2006
1985	84	1993	1997
1984	90	1996	2004
1983	89	1995	2003
1982	90	1994	2002
1981	88	1993	2001
1980	89	1992	2000+
1979	87	1987	1991
1978	93	1990	1998
1977	91	1989	1997
1976	88	1988	1996

MAGILL ESTATE SHIRAZ   RATING **3**

Adelaide Metropolitan $50–$99
Current vintage: 2003   **89**

Slightly lacking in genuine length and ripeness, this cultivated but somewhat cooked shiraz reveals richly concentrated aromas of blueberries, cassis and dark plums backed by suggestions of pepper and cloves. Meaty and juicy, it's smooth and cultivated, delivering a slightly salty expression of deep, dark and slightly sour-edged plums and cranberries breaking up just fractionally at the smoky, mineral finish.

2003	89	2011	2015
2002	88	2007	2010
2001	93	2013	2021
2000	90	2005	2008+
1999	95	2011	2019
1998	93	2010	2018
1997	92	2005	2009+
1996	95	2008	2016
1995	93	2003	2007
1994	91	2002	2012
1993	93	2005	2013
1992	90	2000	2004
1991	95	2011	2021
1990	94	2002	2010
1989	93	1997	2001
1988	91	2000	2005
1987	93	1995	1999
1986	94	1998	2003
1985	93	1993	1997
1984	90	1989	1992

RAWSON'S RETREAT CABERNET SAUVIGNON

South Australia $12–$19
Current vintage: 2004   **86**

A very good quaffing red with some elegance and smoothness. Its relatively simple earthy aromas of slightly confectionary blackberries, raspberries and plums reveal minty and menthol-like undertones while its long and silky palate of earthy riverland fruit delivers plenty of fruit sweetness and balance.

2004	86	2005	2006+
2002	83	2003	2004
2001	86	2002	2003+
2000	86	2002	2005
1999	85	2001	2004
1998	86	2000	2003
1997	82	1998	1999
1996	85	1998	2001

RESERVE BIN EDEN VALLEY RIESLING

RATING 3

Eden Valley			$20–$29	2005	91	2010 2013+
Current vintage: 2005			**91**	2004	93	2009 2012+

Intense, penetrative lime juice and lemon rind aromas with a floral, mineral and bath powder-like background precede a long, tangy and tightly focused palate punctuated by refreshing acidity. There's a slightly candied and over-ripe aspect about the fruit, but it's still a delightful wine that finishes long, lean and stylishly taut.

Year	Rating	Year	Drink
2005	91	2010	2013+
2004	93	2009	2012+
2003	93	2008	2011
2002	92	2007	2010
2001	92	2003	2006+
2000	93	2002	2005+
1999	94	2004	2007+

RWT SHIRAZ

RATING 3

Barossa Valley $100–$199
Current vintage: 2003 **90**

A perfumed, floral and slightly meaty shiraz whose cedary fragrance of dark plums, blueberries, blackcurrant, vanilla and chocolate precede a long, tightly knit and focused shiraz that just lacks the brightness and vitality of the best years. It offers deep, dark berry flavours, which, despite a balanced spine of fine-grained tannin, just breaks up a fraction at the finish, leaving a slightly rubbery and reductive aftertaste.

Year	Rating	Year	Drink
2003	90	2011	2015
2002	93	2010	2014+
2001	88	2009	2013+
2000	91	2005	2008+
1999	96	2011	2019
1998	97	2010	2018+
1997	95	2005	2009

ST HENRI SHIRAZ

RATING 2

South Australia $50–$99
Current vintage: 2002 **97**

One of the finest releases ever of this benchmark shiraz, with an alluring and slightly meaty fragrance of dark plums, blackberries, dark chocolate, backed by spicy and smoky undertones. Made in the traditional velvet-smooth Australian 'burgundy' style, it's soft and juicy, with a deeply flavoured and layered palate whose deep, dark core of vibrant dark fruit flavours is tightly wrapped in fine, approachable tannins. Marvellously long, it finishes with freshness and acidity, revealing underlying hints of mineral.

Year	Rating	Year	Drink
2002	97	2022	2032+
2001	90	2009	2013
2000	89	2008	2012
1999	95	2011	2019
1998	94	2018	2028
1997	93	2005	2009
1996	95	2008	2016
1995	91	2003	2007+
1994	94	2006	2014
1993	92	2003	2007
1992	90	2000	2004
1991	94	2003	2011
1990	96	2002	2010
1989	94	2001	2009
1988	93	2000	2005
1987	93	1999	2004
1986	96	1998	2008+
1985	91	1997	2002
1984	80	1992	1996
1983	90	1995	2003
1982	90	1990	1994
1981	82	1993	1998
1980	90	1992	1997
1979	77	1987	1991
1978	80	1990	1995
1977	82	1989	1994
1976	93	1996	2006+

YATTARNA CHARDONNAY

RATING 2

Adelaide Hills $100–$199
Current vintage: 2003 **95**

Fine and elegant, this supple and sappy chardonnay is all about delicacy, balance and suppleness. Its floral fragrance of restrained melon and citrus fruit reveals mealy, almost cheesy undertones, with undertones of smoky, minerally lees-derived complexity. Smooth and savoury, it's long and fine-grained, with an intense sweet spot of lime, lemon and cumquat flavour right in the middle of its lingering palate.

Year	Rating	Year	Drink
2003	95	2008	2011
2002	90	2007	2010
2001	96	2006	2009+
2000	95	2005	2008
1999	95	2004	2007+
1998	97	2006	2010
1997	95	2002	2005+
1996	95	2001	2004+
1995	94	2000	2003

Penley Estate

McLeans Road, Coonawarra SA 5263. Tel: (08) 8736 3211. Fax: (08) 8736 3124.
Website: www.penley.com.au Email: penley@penley.com.au
Region: **Coonawarra** Winemaker: **Kym Tolley** Viticulturist: **Michael Wetherall** Chief Executive: **Kym Tolley**
Penley Estate is a small and serious maker of Coonawarra wines, principally rich and briary reds from cabernet sauvignon, merlot and shiraz. The 2004 vintage reds released to date present lively, bright and pristine varietal flavours and luxuriantly smooth textures, with just a hint of the meatiness and richness for which Penley is well known.

CHARDONNAY

RATING 5

Coonawarra $20–$29
Current vintage: 2004 **88**

Moderately intense, fresh and varietal, this very competent chardonnay has a fresh, zesty aroma of estery tropical fruit, peaches and cashews backed by a whiff of lemon detergent and vanilla oak. Its sweet and slightly spirity palate presents fresh flavours of grapefruit, lemon and peach wrapped up in clean acidity.

2004	88	2006	2009
2003	86	2004	2005
2002	88	2004	2007
2001	90	2003	2006
2000	81	2001	2002
1999	82	2001	2004

HYLAND SHIRAZ

RATING 4

Coonawarra $20–$29
Current vintage: 2004 **90**

Firm and fine-grained, this flavoursome and tightly structured shiraz has a spicy fragrance of violets, dark chocolate, blackberries and dark plums backed by nuances of cloves and cinnamon. Smooth and supple despite its moderately astringent spine of fine-grained tannin, it's packed with flavours of blackberries, dark plums, redcurrants and sweet chocolate/vanilla oak.

2004	90	2009	2012
2003	86	2005	2008
2002	87	2004	2007
2001	91	2006	2009
2000	88	2002	2005+
1999	91	2004	2007
1998	87	2003	2006
1997	89	1999	2002+
1996	89	2001	2004
1994	82	1996	1999

MERLOT

RATING 5

Coonawarra $20–$29
Current vintage: 2004 **89**

Earthy, slightly meaty aromas of dark plums, cherries and lightly toasty cedar/vanilla oak precede a fine, smooth and elegant palate framed by moderately firm and pliant tannins. It's meaty and savoury, with a lingering core of sour-edged dark plum and cherry flavour. The oak is certainly assertive, but reasonably integrated and balanced.

2004	89	2006	2009+
2002	87	2004	2007+
1999	87	2001	2004
1998	83	2000	2003
1997	86	1999	2002
1996	80	1997	1998

PHOENIX CABERNET SAUVIGNON

RATING 5

Coonawarra $20–$29
Current vintage: 2004 **90**

A delicious cabernet whose vibrant aromas of cassis, dark plums and violets are supported by chocolate and cedary oak with undertones of dried herbs. Round and sumptuous, it's a ripe and generous wine whose deep, dark favours of berries and plums are tightly knit with cedar/vanilla oak and mineral undertones. Framed by supple, dusty tannins, it's genuinely varietal and focused, even if, at 14.5% alcohol, it's a fraction warm and spirity.

2004	90	2012	2016
2003	87	2005	2008+
2002	89	2007	2010
2001	93	2006	2009+
2000	82	2002	2005
1999	82	2001	2004
1998	89	2003	2006
1997	89	1999	2002+
1996	90	1998	2001+

RESERVE CABERNET SAUVIGNON

RATING 4

Coonawarra	$50–$99
Current vintage: 2002	89

A well-handled but slightly herbaceous cabernet whose dusty, leafy aromas of cassis and dark plums overlie nuances of menthol, green beans and camphor. Sumptuous and fleshy, the palate is long, silky-smooth and creamy, delivering vibrant small berry fruit flavours tightly knit with vanilla and cedar/chocolate oak. Its finish is lightly green-edged.

2002	89	2007	2010
2000	88	2005	2008
1999	93	2007	2011
1998	91	2006	2010
1997	90	2002	2005+
1996	91	2004	2008
1995	87	2000	2003
1994	90	1998	2002
1993	93	2005	2013
1992	93	2000	2004
1991	95	2003	2011
1990	94	1998	2002

SHIRAZ CABERNET

RATING 5

Coonawarra	$30–$49
Current vintage: 2002	87

Intense aromas of blackberries and currants are backed by an unusually minty expression of menthol and chocolate. Long and smooth, its distinctive and well-handled palate is saturated with searingly intense cassis, blackberry and currant-like flavours before culminating in a clean and minty finish.

2002	87	2007	2010
2001	87	2003	2006+
2000	88	2005	2008
1999	88	2001	2004+
1998	88	2003	2006
1997	82	1999	2002
1996	87	1998	2001
1995	89	1997	2000
1994	92	2002	2006
1993	89	1995	1998
1992	90	1997	2000
1991	93	1999	2003
1990	91	1995	1998

Penny's Hill

Ingleburne, Main Road, McLaren Vale SA 5171. Tel: (08) 8556 4460. Fax: (08) 8556 4462.
Website: www.pennyshill.com.au Email: info@pennyshill.com.au

Region: **McLaren Vale** Winemaker: **Ben Riggs** Viticulturists: **Toby Bekkers, David Paxton**
Chief Executive: **Tony Parkinson**

Penny's Hill is a newcomer to McLaren Vale that has deployed the experienced duo of David Paxton and Ben Riggs to create its wine. All the fruit used for its wines is estate-grown, and the range includes a typical McLaren Vale mix of shiraz, grenache, semillon plus a 'Specialized' release of shiraz, cabernet and merlot.

SHIRAZ

RATING 4

McLaren Vale	$30–$49
Current vintage: 2004	90

2004	90	2009	2012
2003	90	2008	2011
2002	90	2007	2010
2000	81	2002	2005

Deeply ripened and flavoured, this full-bodied, savoury and carefully constructed McLaren Vale shiraz just borders on meaty, currant-like over-ripeness. Its earthy, violet-like fragance of blueberries, dark plums and creamy, cedary oak precedes a sumptuous but silky-fine palate. Its deep core of juicy and slightly sour-edged shiraz fruit, cinnamon-like spiciness and classy oak reveal a slightly dehydrated aspect that detracts marginally from its length and finish.

A B C D E F G H I J K L M N O P Q R S T U V W X Y Z

Pepper Tree

Halls Road, Pokolbin NSW 2320. Tel: (02) 4998 7539. Fax: (02) 4998 7746.
Website: www.peppertreewines.com.au Email: ptwinery@peppertreewines.com.au

Regions: **Lower Hunter Valley, Coonawarra, Various** Winemakers: **Chris Cameron, Janelle Zerk**
Viticulturist: **Derek Smith** Chief Executive: **John Martini**

With a winery based in downtown Hunter Valley, Pepper Tree produces wine from local fruit as well as a significant number of labels from South Australia's southeast. It releases wines under a range of assumptive and confusing levels such as 'Reserve', 'Reserve Classics' and 'Limited Release'. As the vegetal 'Reserve Classics' red Bordeaux blend from Coonawarra might suggest, the same amount of creativity also needs to be applied in the vineyard.

RESERVE CLASSICS
(formerly Grand Reserve Cabernet Sauvignon)

RATING 5

Coonawarra		**$50–$99**	2002	80	2004	2007
Current vintage: 2002		**80**	2001	87	2006	2009

Coonawarra $50–$99
Current vintage: 2002 — 80

Greenish, capsicum and geranium-like aromas are backed by some nuances of under-ripe berries and plums, plus a cedary whiff of oak. Sappy and vegetal, the palate suggests heavily shaded and under-ripe grapes that leave a hard, green-edged finish.

2002	80	2004	2007
2001	87	2006	2009
2000	92	2008	2012
1999	84	2001	2004
1998	87	2006	2010+
1996	83	2001	2004

GRAND RESERVE MERLOT

RATING 3

Coonawarra $50–$99
Current vintage: 2000 — 89

An early-maturing merlot whose slightly closed bouquet of sweet red and black cherries, dark plums and new cedar/vanilla oak reveals hints of undergrowth. Rich and generous, it's forward and oaky, with some reserved but sweet and slightly candied raspberry, cherry and plum flavours. While there's a reasonable length of fruit and some very assertive oak, the palate is showing signs of drying out.

2000	89	2005	2008
1998	95	2006	2010
1996	92	2001	2004
1995	88	1997	2000

Pepperjack

Saltram Estates, Nuriootpa-Angaston Road, Angaston SA 5353. Tel: (08) 8564 3355. Fax: (08) 8564 2209.

Region: **Barossa** Winemaker: **Nigel Dolan** Chief Executive: **Jamie Odell**

Pepperjack is a Beringer Blass-owned brand spawned out of the Saltram business. While its very approachable, soft and flavoursome Barossa Valley reds are richly flavoured, generously oaked and usually ready to drink by release, there's also an opportunity with the 2004 Shiraz to enjoy the benefits of cellaring.

CABERNET SAUVIGNON

RATING 5

Barossa Valley $20–$29
Current vintage: 2004 — 87

Floral aromas of violets and jammy red and black berry fruits are backed by herbal nuances and cedary oak. Full to medium in weight, it's smooth and supple, with some richness and presence of uncomplicated fruit, with a firmish spine of powdery tannins.

2004	87	2006	2009+
2003	87	2005	2008
2000	81	2001	2002
1999	87	2001	2004+
1998	81	2000	2003

SHIRAZ

RATING 5

Barossa Valley $12–$19
Current vintage: 2004 — 89

A typically honest, generous and slightly jammy Barossa shiraz with a minty, menthol-like fragrance of sweet red berries, plums and cedar/vanilla oak. Its bright, vibrant palate of sweet red and black berry confiture and sweet oak is framed by firmish, fine tannins, finishing long and persistent.

2004	89	2009	2012+
2002	88	2005	2008
2001	86	2003	2006
2000	86	2002	2005
1999	86	2001	2004
1998	89	2003	2006
1997	82	1999	2002
1996	89	2001	2004+

Pertaringa

Corner Hunt & Rifle Range roads, McLaren Vale SA 5171. Tel: (08) 8323 8125. Fax: (08) 8323 7766.
Website: www.pertaringa.com.au Email: wine@pertaringa.com.au

Region: **McLaren Vale** Winemakers: **Geoff Hardy, Ben Riggs** Viticulturist: **Ian Leask**
Chief Executives: **Ian Leask & Geoff Hardy**

Geoff Hardy and Ian Leask are major grape growers whose fruit is largely used for the Pertaringa and K1 wine brands. Their Pertaringa label comprises a range of typically ripe, meaty and generous McLaren Vale wines. The 2004 releases are typically sumptuous and raisined, smooth and handsomely oaked.

OVER THE TOP SHIRAZ
RATING **5**

McLaren Vale	$30–$49
Current vintage: 2004	**90**

Slightly overcooked, this sumptuous and porty shiraz does retain sufficient fruit brightness and sweetness. Its smoky, charcuterie-like aromas of small black berries, cassis and dark plums overlie toasty, dark chocolate oak and an exotic spiciness. Smooth and velvet-like, its palate of plums, blackberries, raisins and currants is handsomely supported by newish mocha oak and coated by firm, drying tannins. It finishes long and gamey, with lingering notes of licorice and prune.

2004	90	2012	2016
2002	87	2007	2010+
2001	89	2006	2009
2000	83	2002	2005
1999	90	2004	2007
1998	88	2003	2006+

RIFLE AND HUNT CABERNET SAUVIGNON
RATING **5**

Adelaide	$30–$49
Current vintage: 2004	**89**

Sweet, briary aromas of blackberries, plums, cassis and raisins, with minty, herbal undertones, precede a juicy, ripe and forward palate of plummy, currant-like fruit. Velvet smooth, it's sumptuously ripened, a fraction cooked, with rich plum and blackberry fruit dressed in dusty, vanilla oak and framed by fine, powdery tannins. It's persistent, slightly dusty and herbal, with meaty undertones.

2004	89	2012	2016
2002	87	2007	2010
2001	88	2003	2006
2000	82	2002	2005
1999	87	2001	2004

Petaluma

Spring Gully Road, Piccadilly SA 5151. Tel: (08) 8339 4122. Fax: (08) 8339 5253.
Website: www.petaluma.com.au Email: petaluma@petaluma.com.au

Regions: **Adelaide Hills, Clare Valley, Coonawarra** Winemaker: **Andrew Hardy** Viticulturist: **Mike Harms**
Chief Executive: **Peter Cowan**

Perhaps it's because so few of its wines conform to widely held expectations of Australian styles that Petaluma's profile is significantly lower than it merits. But by any measure, Petaluma is an outstanding wine company, and one that until recently operated under the very personal control of Brian Croser. With Croser's departure, and with the more recent loss of winemaker Con Moshos to Mountadam, Andrew Hardy has some big boots to fill. That said, I have every confidence that he has what it takes to continue to develop Petaluma's ever-increasing range of wines. The unctuous 2004 Chardonnay is the pick of the current releases.

CHARDONNAY
RATING **2**

Adelaide Hills	$30–$49
Current vintage: 2004	**95**

Seamless, smooth and generous, this complex and savoury chardonnay has a lightly soapy fragrance of peach, melon and grapefruit supported by sweet nutty, buttery and spicy undertones of lemon, vanilla, dried flowers, cloves and nutmeg. Richly fruited, its unctuous and surprisingly powerful palate of lingering stonefruit, citrus and mealy flavours culminates in a lingering savoury and nutty finish. Very restrained and complex.

2004	95	2009	2012+
2003	95	2008	2011+
2002	93	2007	2010
2001	94	2006	2009
2000	92	2005	2008
1999	95	2004	2007
1998	94	2006	2010
1997	95	2005	2009
1996	95	2004	2008
1995	95	2003	2007
1994	94	2002	2006
1993	93	1995	1998
1992	95	2000	2004
1991	91	1996	1999
1990	93	1998	2002
1989	90	1991	1994

COONAWARRA (Cabernet Sauvignon & Merlot)

RATING 2

Coonawarra $50–$99
Current vintage: 2002 91

Sweet aromas of cassis, dark cherries and mulberries are backed by cedar/vanilla oak with nuances of game meats and dried herbs. There's a hint of currant-like over-ripeness. Smooth and succulent, the palate has a plump, juicy expression of blackberry, mulberry and cherry-like fruit supported by sweet oak that becomes rather more cedary and drying towards the finish. Lacking the length of genuinely vibrant fruit for a higher score, it should settle down into a pleasingly elegant style.

2002	91	2010	2014+
2001	95	2013	2021
2000	94	2008	2012
1999	91	2007	2011
1998	98	2018	2028
1997	97	2009	2017+
1996	95	2016	2026
1995	93	2007	2015
1994	95	2006	2014+
1993	92	2005	2013
1992	95	2012	2022
1991	95	2003	2011+
1990	95	2002	2010
1988	92	2000	2008+
1987	87	1995	1999
1986	91	1998	2006
1985	82	1990	1993
1984	81	1986	1989
1982	87	1987	1990

CROSER (Sparkling wine)

RATING 4

Adelaide Hills $30–$49
Current vintage: 2003 91

Rather a modern Californian style of sparkling wine whose generous, fruit-driven qualities are backed by restrained yeast-derived influences and finished with a smooth, soft acidity. Its delicate aromas of lemon, apple and pear reveal mildly creamy undertones, while its intensely flavoured but silky palate of white peach, pear and lemon delivers a lingering soft creaminess. It finishes with pleasing freshness and brightness.

2003	91	2005	2008
2002	89	2004	2007+
2001	93	2003	2006+
2000	89	2005	2008
1999	93	2001	2004+
1998	91	2000	2003+

HANLIN HILL RIESLING

RATING 2

Clare Valley $20–$29
Current vintage: 2005 93

Very floral and perfumed, this generously flavoured and structured riesling has an open, heady aroma of lime juice and rose petals, apples and pears. Its quite broad and almost oily palate presents a pleasing length of concentrated, slightly spicy and confectionary citrus flavours before an austere and dry finish.

2005	93	2013	2017
2004	95	2012	2016
2003	93	2008	2011+
2002	96	2010	2014
2001	95	2009	2013
2000	91	2005	2008
1999	95	2011	2019
1998	91	2006	2010
1997	94	2009	2017
1996	95	2008	2016
1995	96	2007	2015
1994	94	2006	2014
1993	87	2001	2005
1992	90	2000	2004
1991	93	2003	2011
1990	95	2002	2010+
1989	90	1997	2001+
1988	92	2000	2008

MERLOT

RATING 2

Coonawarra $50–$99
Current vintage: 2003 87

A firm and slightly over-made merlot that lacks its customary intensity and brightness. Its meaty, earthy aromas of cherries, plums and cedar/vanilla oak have a herbal, minty aspect, while its creamy palate becomes rather sappy and hollow towards the choc-mint-like finish of red cherries and firmish, drying and tight-knit tannins.

2003	87	2008	2011
2001	96	2009	2013+
2000	93	2008	2012+
1999	94	2007	2011+
1998	93	2006	2010
1997	96	2009	2017
1996	94	2004	2008
1995	90	2003	2007
1994	93	2006	2014+
1993	89	2001	2005+
1992	95	2004	2012+
1991	90	2003	2011
1990	92	2002	2010

SHIRAZ

RATING 4

	Adelaide Hills	$30–$49
	Current vintage: 2003	87

Unusually fat and chunky, this meaty, almost soupy shiraz has a cooked bouquet of dried plums, prunes and currants. Lacking much fruit brightness, its leathery palate presents a dehydrated and jammy expression of stewed fruit, before finishing with sweet vanilla oak and without much length of fruit.

2003	87	2005	2008+
2002	93	2010	2014
2001	95	2009	2013
2000	91	2005	2008
1999	89	2004	2007
1998	91	2003	2006

SUMMERTOWN CHARDONNAY

RATING 2

	Piccadilly Valley	$50–$99
	Current vintage: 2002	94

A juicy, oily chardonnay whose fragrance of nectarine and pineapple reveals sweet nutty oak and green cashew aromas. Up-front and sumptuous, with undertones of cashews and green olives, it delivers in length and generosity what it might lack in elegance, culminating in a marzipan-like finish of minerality.

2003	96	2008	2011
2002	94	2007	2010
2001	94	2003	2006+

TIERS CHARDONNAY

RATING 1

	Piccadilly Valley	$100–$199
	Current vintage: 2002	93

Lacking the length, ripeness and structure usually associated with this vineyard, this cool-year wine has a tropical fragrance of pineapple and grapefruit over herbal nuances and sweet oak. Very forward and juicy, its generous and fleshy palate of peaches and tropical fruits, green olives and cashews is rather viscous and cloying.

2002	93	2004	2007+
2001	96	2009	2013
2000	96	2005	2008+
1999	93	2004	2007
1998	97	2005	2008
1997	97	2002	2005+
1996	96	2004	2008

VIOGNIER

RATING 4

	Adelaide Hills	$30–$49
	Current vintage: 2005	83

Simple, estery aromas of pineapples, lemon detergent and sherbet-like confection are backed by floral and spicy nuances. Juicy, sweet and tropical, its rather candied fruit lacks length and intensity, finishing simple and sweet. Possibly a stuck ferment?

2005	83	2006	2007
2003	89	2005	2008
2002	91	2004	2007
2001	89	2003	2006
2000	90	2001	2002+
1999	90	2001	2004
1998	90	2000	2003+

Peter Lehmann

Off Para Road, Tanunda SA 5352. Tel: (08) 8563 2100. Fax: (08) 8563 3402.
Website: www.peterlehmannwines.com.au Email: plw@lehmannwines.com.au

Region: **Barossa Valley** Winemakers: **Andrew Wigan, Leonie Lange & Ian Hongell**
Viticulturist: **Peter Nash** Chief Executive: **Douglas Lehmann**

Peter Lehmann has a hard-earned reputation for the quality and consistency of its Barossa-based table wines. While its red wines have performed well, if not spectacularly in the cooler seasons of 2002 and 2004 (from which I have tasted a few but not all wines), its performance in the hotter seasons of 2000, 2001 and 2003 does leave much to be desired. Most of the company's fruit is bought from a very loyal assembly of growers, many of whom, it would appear, might need to revisit their strategies.

BAROSSA CABERNET SAUVIGNON   RATING **5**

Barossa Valley $12–$19
Current vintage: 2003   84

Rather hollow, forward and early-maturing, this uncomplicated Barossa cabernet has a violet-like fragrance of raspberries and cassis backed by sweet vanilla and cedary oak. Its initially vibrant and generous palate of juicy berry and plum-like flavour thins out, finishing rather short and incomplete. It does offer varietal qualities and some fruit sweetness, but will dry out fairly quickly.

2003	84	2005	2008
2002	91	2007	2010
2001	83	2003	2006
2000	88	2002	2005+
1999	87	2001	2004+
1998	93	2006	2010
1997	93	2002	2005+
1996	90	2001	2004
1995	88	2000	2003
1994	93	1999	2002
1993	93	2001	2005
1992	94	2000	2004
1991	89	1999	2003
1990	93	2002	2010
1989	91	1997	2001
1988	93	2000	2008

BAROSSA CHARDONNAY   RATING **5**

Barossa Valley $12–$19
Current vintage: 2005   87

Creamy, peachy aromas of nectarine, cashew and sweet vanilla oak precede a juicy and vibrant palate whose smooth expression of stonefruit flavours is deftly balanced with restrained and lightly toasty vanilla oak. It finishes long and fresh.

2005	87	2006	2007+
2004	89	2006	2009
2002	87	2004	2007
2001	84	2002	2003
2000	81	2001	2002

BAROSSA RIESLING (formerly Eden Valley Riesling)   RATING **4**

Barossa Valley $12–$19
Current vintage: 2005   89

Refreshingly tight and chalky, this juicy, tangy and pristine young riesling has a floral aroma of lime juice and powdery undertones. Fine and elegant, its lively palate of lime juice and lemon rind is long and elegant, finishing with refreshingly tight and citrusy acids.

2005	89	2007	2010+
2004	92	2009	2012
2003	90	2005	2008+
2002	90	2004	2007+
2001	88	2003	2006
2000	86	2001	2005
1999	85	2000	2001
1998	90	2003	2006
1997	87	1999	2002
1996	90	2001	2004
1995	82	1997	2000
1994	88	1999	2002
1993	93	1998	2001
1992	92	1997	2000

BAROSSA SEMILLON

Barossa Valley $5–$11
Current vintage: 2005   88

A vibrant and varietal semillon whose fresh aromas of green melon and lemon juice precede a refreshing and lively palate whose bright, tangy fruit finishes with clean and zesty acidity.

2005	88	2007	2010
2004	89	2006	2009+
2003	92	2008	2011
2002	91	2004	2007+
2001	89	2001	2002+
2000	92	2002	2005
1999	89	2001	2004
1998	89	2000	2003
1997	90	1999	2002
1996	89	1998	2001

BAROSSA SHIRAZ

Barossa Valley $12–$19
Current vintage: 2004   90

Vibrant aromas of fresh blackberries, redcurrant, cassis and raspberries overlie fresh coconut/vanilla oak and undertones of violets and white pepper. Medium to full in weight, it's smooth but firmish, with pleasingly long and juicy flavours of spicy small berry and redcurrant fruit backed by cedar/vanilla oak and framed by fine, powdery tannins.

2004	90	2009	2012
2002	90	2007	2010
2001	90	2003	2006
2000	89	2002	2005+
1999	88	2001	2004+
1998	92	2003	2006
1997	93	2002	2005+
1996	91	1998	2001
1995	87	1997	2000
1994	91	1999	2002
1993	90	2001	2005
1992	93	2000	2004
1991	91	1996	1999

BOTRYTIS SEMILLON (formerly Noble Semillon)

Barossa Valley $12–$19 (375 ml)
Current vintage: 2005   86

A moderately luscious, confectionary and rather delicate dessert wine whose floral aromas of apricot, lemon rind and lime marmalade reveal light undertones of minerality. Lightly chalky, its sweet but restrained palate is long and tangy, with a lemony finish of clean acids.

2005	86	2007	2010
2002	91	2004	2007+
2001	87	2003	2006+
2000	90	2002	2005+
1999	82	2001	2004
1998	84	2003	2006
1997	86	1999	2002
1996	81	1997	1998
1995	87	2000	2003
1994	91	1999	2002
1992	84	1997	2000

CLANCY'S (Shiraz Cabernet Sauvignon Merlot)

Barossa Valley $12–$19
Current vintage: 2004   86

Rather simple, earthy and slightly thin, with lightly spicy and peppery aromas of fresh small black and red berries and violets over restrained cedar/vanilla oak. Smooth and supple, with an initially vibrant expression of blueberries and dark plums, it thins out towards a dusty, chalky finish with earthy undertones.

2004	86	2006	2009
2003	87	2005	2008
2002	89	2004	2007
2000	80	2002	2005
1999	81	2000	2001
1998	85	2000	2003
1997	92	2002	2005
1996	89	1998	2001
1995	89	1997	2000
1994	90	1996	1999

EDEN VALLEY RIESLING (formerly Blue Eden Riesling)

Eden Valley $12–$19
Current vintage: 2005   93

A well-defined, chalky and complex young Eden Valley riesling whose slightly confectionary expression of lime juice, lemon and honeysuckle-like flavours overlie appealingly schisty and mineral influences. It's very floral and pleasingly complex, with classical varietal and regional flavours and textures.

2005	93	2013	2017+
2004	90	2006	2009+
2003	95	2008	2011+
2002	95	2007	2010
2001	95	2009	2013
2000	89	2005	2008

EIGHT SONGS SHIRAZ

RATING 4

Barossa Valley	$30–$49
Current vintage: 2002	90

A substantial, ripe and meaty medium to long-term Barossa shiraz. Its deep, gamey aromas of blackberries and plums are handsomely backed by sweet, smoky oak and black pepper, with nuances of cinnamon and cloves. Deeply spiced, its sumptuous, smooth and slightly overcooked palate of earthy shiraz fruit is thickly coated with firm, grippy tannin before finishing long, persistent and savoury.

2002	90	2010	2014
2001	88	2006	2009
2000	89	2005	2008
1999	92	2004	2007+
1998	94	2006	2010+
1997	88	2002	2005+
1996	96	2004	2008+

MENTOR

RATING 3

Barossa Valley	$30–$49
Current vintage: 2002	93

An elegant, smooth and silky cabernet blend whose dusty, floral perfume of violets, cassis, cedar and vanilla oak reveals undertones of dried herbs, mint and menthol. Full to medium weight, it's long and vibrant, with intense flavours of mulberries, plums and blackberries backed by creamy oak and framed by powdery, bony tannins. It finishes with lingering minty dark fruits and nuances of menthol.

2002	93	2014	2022
2001	88	2009	2013
2000	88	2005	2008+
1999	91	2004	2007
1998	93	2010	2018
1997	91	2005	2009
1996	95	2008	2016
1995	87	2007	2015
1994	93	2006	2014
1993	87	2001	2005+
1992	93	2000	2004+
1991	93	1999	2003
1990	94	2002	2010
1989	94	2001	2006
1986	95	1998	2003

RESERVE RIESLING

RATING 3

Eden Valley	$20–$29
Current vintage: 2001	92

A delightful if earlier-maturing example of this wine, whose fragrant toasty, buttery aromas of lemon and lime juice reveal subtle and developing nuances of kerosene. Generous and slightly candied, this rather old-fashioned riesling has a luscious and mouthfilling palate whose toasty, buttery flavours reveal beeswax-like undertones over a slightly chalky backbone. It finishes with fresh, vibrant acids.

2001	92	2009	2013+
2000	90	2005	2008+
1998	95	2006	2010+
1997	90	2005	2009
1996	90	2001	2004
1995	92	2000	2003
1994	93	2002	2006
1993	96	2005	2013
1992	93	2000	2004
1991	93	1996	1999

STONEWELL (Shiraz)

RATING 3

Barossa Valley	$50–$99
Current vintage: 2001	85

A dehydrated and porty shiraz whose cooked, treacle-like aromas of raisins, prunes and plums overlie smoky nuances of dark chocolate and mocha oak, plus spicy, marzipan-like influences. Its sumptuous, jammy and fruitcake-like palate is chewy, rich and ultra-ripe, finishing meaty and savoury.

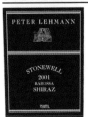

2001	85	2006	2009
2000	89	2008	2012
1999	95	2007	2011+
1998	89	2006	2010
1997	93	2005	2008+
1996	96	2008	2016+
1995	91	2003	2007+
1994	96	2002	2006+
1993	95	2005	2013
1992	93	2000	2004
1991	95	2011	2021
1990	89	1998	2002+
1989	95	2001	2006+
1988	95	2000	2008
1987	94	1999	2004

Pewsey Vale

Browns Road, Pewsey Vale SA 5235. Tel: (08) 8561 3200. Fax: (08) 8561 3393.
Website: www.pewseyvale.com Email: info@pewseyvale.com

Region: **Eden Valley** Winemaker: **Louisa Rose** Viticulturist: **Robin Nettelbeck** Chief Executive: **Robert Hill Smith**

Pewsey Vale is a riesling vineyard in the Eden Valley whose consistently reliable wines are made by the very talented Louisa Rose into perfumed, delicate expressions of the dry Australian style. While the 2005 Riesling is typically fine and chalky, the very generous 2000 The Contours needs more time to reveal what it's all about.

RIESLING

RATING 4

Eden Valley	$12–$19
Current vintage: 2005	**93**

A fine, smooth and fluffy riesling whose delicate floral perfume of lemon rind and fresh tropical undertones precedes a moderately full palate of fineness and generosity. There's a juicy aspect to its lime juice and lemon rind flavours, which is underpinned by a typical Eden Valley tightness and chalkiness. Beautifully open, lively and stylish.

2005	93	2013	2017
2004	87	2006	2009
2003	93	2008	2011+
2002	91	2007	2010+
2001	90	2006	2009
2000	91	2005	2008+
1999	95	2007	2011+
1998	88	2003	2006
1997	94	2005	2009
1996	94	2008	2016
1995	92	2003	2007
1994	93	2006	2014
1993	94	1998	2001
1992	93	1997	2000
1991	93	1999	2003
1990	94	1998	2002
1989	89	1997	2001
1988	90	1993	1996

THE CONTOURS RIESLING

RATING 2

Eden Valley	$20–$29
Current vintage: 2000	**91**

Perhaps tasted in its adolescence, this maturing riesling is clearly finely crafted and tightly focused, but is presently a little simple and candied, lacking in great complexity. Toasty, keroseney aromas of lime marmalade and honey precede a generous, ripe and fruity palate whose powdery chassis contributes to its long and assertive presence in the mouth. It just needs another couple of years.

2000	91	2008	2012
1999	94	2007	2011+
1998	95	2006	2010+
1997	89	2002	2005
1996	95	2008	2016
1995	92	2003	2007+

Pierro

Caves Road, Willyabrup via Cowaramup WA 6284. Tel: (08) 9755 6220. Fax: (08) 9755 6308.
Website: www.pierro.com.au Email: pierro@iinet.net.au

Region: **Margaret River** Winemaker: **Mike Peterkin** Viticulturist: **Mike Peterkin** Chief Executive: **Mike Peterkin**

Mike Peterkin is a leader among Australian makers of chardonnay. Pierro's has traditionally been one of the country's more opulent and powerful chardonnays, but since 2002 it has acquired additional dimensions of tightness and silkiness. Peterkin recently introduced another red to the Pierro stable, the LTC Cabernet Merlot (which also includes Cabernet Franc). The first release was from 2003 (88, drink 2008–2011+), and is a supple, fine-grained and moderately firm wine with a meaty, currant-like aspect to its berry and plum flavours.

CABERNET SAUVIGNON MERLOT

RATING 3

Margaret River	$50–$99
Current vintage: 2001	**92**

Sumptuous, modern and well-ripened cabernet blend with some slightly reductive and meaty complexity. Its delicate perfume of small red berries and sweet vanilla/cedar oak precedes a plush, very smooth and rounded palate whose intense small berry flavours are married to an assertive combination of oak and firm, fine tannins. Some ultra-ripe currant-like nuances lead me to question its ultimate longevity.

2001	92	2009	2013+
2000	87	2002	2005+
1999	93	2007	2011+
1998	90	2006	2010+
1997	86	2002	2005
1996	93	2004	2008+
1995	87	2000	2003

RATING 1

Margaret River $50–$99
Current vintage: 2004 90

A well-handled wine that is not quite up to its usual exemplary standard. Its smoky fragrance of grapefruit, lime juice and clove-like oak reveals just a hint of spice and spikiness. Smooth and juicy, its tightly focused palate of citrus, tropical fruit and melon-like flavours are backed by undertones of minerals, butterscotch and meaty smallgoods-like influences. It finishes slightly sweet with a hint of sourness, suggesting a similar issue to that possibly stuck ferment found in the Cullen Chardonnay of 2003 and several other Margaret River chardonnays from 2004.

2004	90	2006	2009
2003	97	2008	2011+
2002	96	2005	2008
2001	89	2003	2006
2000	95	2005	2008+
1999	96	2007	2011
1998	93	2000	2003+
1997	95	2002	2005+
1996	97	2001	2004
1995	93	2000	2003
1994	95	2002	2006
1993	95	2001	2005
1992	96	2000	2004
1991	94	1996	1999
1990	94	1998	2002

PINOT NOIR

RATING 5

Margaret River $30–$49
Current vintage: 2003 84

Meaty, smoky and herbaceous, this rather funky, complex and oily pinot noir presents a sappy, green-edged expression of candied, plummy fruit before a finish of capsicum and asparagus.

2003	84	2008	2011
2002	87	2004	2007
2001	86	2003	2006
2000	81	2002	2005+
1999	90	2004	2007
1998	87	2000	2003+
1997	89	2002	2005
1996	88	2001	2004
1995	84	2000	2003
1994	87	1999	2002
1993	90	2001	2005
1992	90	2000	2004
1990	94	1995	1998

SEMILLON SAUVIGNON BLANC (LTC)

RATING 3

Margaret River $20–$29
Current vintage: 2005 91

Vibrantly fruited and spotlessly clean, this elegant Margaret River blend has plenty of flavour and a genuine backbone of powdery extract. There's a hint of herbaceousness and dustiness beneath its lifted aromas of passionfruit and mango, with a subtle background of vanilla oak. Finely crafted, it's long and powdery, with nutty, citrusy fruit culminating in a lightly mineral finish with a suggestion of sweetness.

2005	91	2007	2010+
2004	94	2006	2009+
2003	91	2005	2008+
2002	91	2004	2007
2001	92	2003	2006+
2000	94	2002	2005
1999	89	2001	2004
1998	91	2000	2003
1997	93	2002	2005
1996	94	2001	2004
1995	93	1997	2000
1994	93	1999	2002
1993	93	1998	2001

Pike & Joyce

Polish Hill River Road, Sevenhill via Clare SA 5453. Tel: (08) 8843 4370. Fax: (08) 8843 4353.
Website: www.pikeswines.com.au/pikeandjoyce Email: pikeandjoyce@pikeswines.com.au

Region: **Lenswood** Winemakers: **Neil Pike, John Trotter** Viticulturists: **Andrew Pike, Sam Luke, Mark Joyce**
Chief Executives: **Neil Pike, Andrew Pike & Mark Joyce**

This joint venture between Pikes Wines (Clare Valley) and Joyson Orchards (Lenswood) produced a deliciously wild, savoury and funky Chardonnay in 2004 and a refreshingly tangy Sauvignon Blanc in 2005. Its Pinot Noir is steadily gaining some respectability, while its 2005 Pinot Gris is a crisp, mineral and supple wine with lingering crystal-clear pear/apple flavours.

CHARDONNAY

RATING **4**

Lenswood	$20–$29	2004	93	2006	2009+
Current vintage: 2004	**93**	2003	92	2005	2008
		2002	82	2003	2004+
		2001	87	2003	2006

A complex, funky and enjoyable chardonnay with a pleasing core of melon, grapefruit and quince-like fruit. Its rustic, rather wild and heavily worked bouquet reveals meaty undertones of hessian and vanilla oak, while its juicy and quite viscous palate still finishes with clean acidity and a lingering mineral note. Oak is abundant, but carefully deployed, and the wine delivers plenty of chewy, savoury and complex chardonnay charm.

SAUVIGNON BLANC

RATING **4**

Lenswood	$20–$29	2005	90	2006	2007
Current vintage: 2005	**90**	2004	83	2004	2005+
		2003	89	2003	2004+
		2002	93	2003	2004

A juicy, fresh and intensely flavoured sauvignon blanc whose lively aromas of gooseberry, passionfruit and asparagus-like undertones of capsicum have a slightly candied aspect. Its pleasing length of pristine, lightly grassy fruit culminates in a tangy finish of bright acidity.

Pikes

Polish Hill River Road, Sevenhill SA 5453. Tel: (08) 8843 4370. Fax: (08) 8843 4353.
Website: www.pikeswines.com.au Email: info@pikeswines.com.au

Region: **Clare Valley** Winemakers: **Neil Pike, John Trotter** Viticulturist: **Andrew Pike**
Chief Executives: **Neil Pike & Andrew Pike**

Pikes is an energetic family-owned and operated winery in Clare. Its 2004 Luccio red blend of sangiovese, merlot and cabernet sauvignon is smooth and juicy, with a deliciously dusty, fine-grained and earthy finish. The Eastside Shiraz has also delivered in 2004, creating a pliant and smooth wine of deep spicy flavour. 2005 produced yet another stellar and steely expression of The Merle Riesling. This wine is fast achieving top status for its precise balance, exemplary tightness and minerality, and its amazing varietal purity.

EASTSIDE SHIRAZ

RATING **5**

Clare Valley	$20–$29	2004	94	2012	2016+
Current vintage: 2004	**94**	2003	89	2008	2011
		2002	86	2007	2010
		2001	89	2006	2009
		2000	87	2005	2008
		1999	89	2004	2007
		1998	88	2006	2010+
		1997	90	2005	2009
		1996	87	2001	2004
		1995	93	2000	2003
		1994	91	1999	2002
		1993	90	2001	2005
		1992	94	2000	2004
		1991	94	2003	2011
		1990	94	2002	2010

A smooth, soft and supple shiraz likely to reveal more mint and menthol character as it ages. Its heady fragrance of violets, cassis, raspberries and redcurrants has a spicy, peppery aspect of cloves and cinnamon. Backed by slightly toasty cedar/vanilla oak, it's a full to medium weight Australian burgundy style whose spicy ripe black and red berry flavours, pepper and spice overlie a powdery chassis of pliant tannins. It finishes long and savoury, with a lingering core of fruit.

RIESLING

Clare Valley	$12–$19		
Current vintage: 2005	**92**		

A measured, stylish and restrained riesling whose floral, limey aromas of lemon juice and bath powder are fresh and penetrative. Long, chalky and austere, its tightly focused, clean and refreshing palate of vibrant lemon/lime fruit and crisp acidity finishes with excellent length and dryness.

2005	92	2010	2013+
2004	92	2009	2012
2003	94	2008	2011+
2002	94	2007	2010
2001	92	2006	2009
2000	94	2008	2012
1999	95	2007	2011
1998	93	2003	2006+
1997	89	2002	2005
1996	90	2001	2004
1995	81	1997	2000
1992	87	1997	2000
1990	93	1998	2002
1988	93	1993	1996

THE HILL BLOCK CABERNET

Clare Valley	$20–$29		
Current vintage: 2004	**87**		

Moderately rich and round, this approachable but lightly herbal and leafy cabernet has a delicate and dusty fragrance of small black and red berries backed by lightly cedary vanilla oak. Generously flavoured, its smooth palate presents cranberry and blackberry fruit with undertones of menthol, cedar and vanilla. Elegant and quite long, it finishes with greenish edges.

2004	87	2009	2012
2002	86	2007	2010
2001	87	2006	2009
2000	86	2002	2005+
1999	89	2004	2007
1998	91	2006	2010+
1997	89	2005	2009
1996	91	2004	2008+
1995	87	1997	2000
1994	94	2002	2006
1993	93	1998	2001
1992	94	2000	2004
1991	93	1999	2003
1990	93	1998	2002

THE MERLE RESERVE RIESLING

Clare Valley	$20–$29		
Current vintage: 2005	**95**		

A very classy and long-term riesling whose musky, floral perfume of rose petal and lime aromas reveals undertones of minerals. Fine, long and chalky, the palate is deliciously concentrated and presents an open, almost juicy expression of pristine, essential varietal flavour before an austere but refreshing finish.

2005	95	2017	2025
2004	96	2016	2024
2002	96	2010	2014+
2001	94	2009	2013+
1997	95	2005	2009

Pipers Brook

1216 Pipers Brook Road, Pipers Brook Tas 7254. Tel: (03) 6382 7527. Fax: (03) 6382 7226.
Website: www.pipersbrook.com Email: enquiries@pipersbrook.com

Region: **Pipers River** Winemaker: **Rene Bezemer** Viticulturist: **Bruce McCormack** Chief Executive: **Paul de Moor**

2005 looks like a signature year for one of the best-known Tasmanian wineries. Its 'Alsatian' collection of Riesling, Gewürztraminer and Pinot Gris each delivered exceptional wines. The Pinot Gris is one of the freshest, most vibrant and tightly focused yet made in Australia. The 2004 vintage also saw a brilliant Reserve Pinot Noir whose opulence and seamless quality has changed the way I view Pipers Brook reds. The 2002 The Summit is typically wild and woolly, but does have the concentration to get away with it.

CUVÉE CLARK RIESLING (Late Harvest)

Pipers River	$30–$49 (375 ml)		
Current vintage: 2003	**93**		

Nutty, pastry-like scents of fresh flowers, melon and mango, pear and apple, backed by confection-like baby powder undertones. Pure, bright and lively, it offers a sweet and luscious palate whose concentrated flavours of apricots, lime and pear finish savoury and clean, with racy and refreshing acidity.

2003	93	2005	2008+
2001	95	2006	2009+
2000	96	2005	2008+

ESTATE CHARDONNAY

PIPERS BROOK VINEYARD
2000 CHARDONNAY
TASMANIA

ESTATE

Pipers River $30–$49
Current vintage: 2003 88

Lacking great density and length of fruit, this slightly sweaty, coolish chardonnay has a delicate bouquet of apple and peach, clove and vanilla oak over spicy nuances of marzipan, dried flowers and honeysuckle. Its initially intense flavours of quince, melon and apple thin out towards a slightly herbal, spirity and metallic finish, backed by assertive vanilla oak.

Year	Score		
2003	88	2005	2008
2002	86	2004	2007
2001	94	2006	2009
2000	93	2005	2008
1999	88	2001	2004
1998	90	2003	2006
1997	92	1999	2002
1996	86	1998	2001
1995	94	2003	2007
1994	82	1996	1999
1993	93	1998	2001
1992	93	1997	2000

ESTATE GEWÜRZTRAMINER

ESTATE

PIPERS BROOK VINEYARD
2001 GEWÜRZTRAMINER
TASMANIA

Pipers River $20–$29
Current vintage: 2005 95

A classic traminer, whose delicate, highly floral scents of rose oil and lychees precede a smooth, juicy and sumptuous palate of essence-like flavour that never loses its restraint and tight focus. An exemplary wine that finishes long, clean and savoury, with genuine dryness. It should develop superbly without becoming coarse or excessively oily.

Year	Score		
2005	95	2010	2013+
2004	95	2006	2009+
2003	93	2008	2011+
2001	93	2006	2009
2000	94	2005	2008
1999	89	2004	2007
1998	94	2003	2006+
1997	90	1999	2002
1996	94	2001	2004
1995	94	2000	2003
1993	90	1995	1998
1992	93	2000	2004

ESTATE PINOT GRIS

ESTATE

PIPERS BROOK VINEYARD
2001 PINOT GRIS
TASMANIA

Pipers River $20–$29
Current vintage: 2005 95

A brilliant pinot gris, in both its sheer class and the lustre of its fruit. Its dusty fragrance of pear and lemon oil reveals spicy, nutty undertones, while its palate is long, bright and crunchy. Deliciously accentuated varietal fruit overlies a fine chalkiness, delivering plenty of length and a refreshingly chalky and savoury finish of lemony acids. It raises the bar for this variety.

Year	Score		
2005	95	2007	2010+
2004	84	2005	2006
2003	82	2003	2004
2001	77	2002	2003
2000	90	2002	2005
1999	94	2001	2004
1998	87	1999	2000

ESTATE PINOT NOIR (formerly Pellion)

PIPERS BROOK VINEYARD
2000 PINOT NOIR
TASMANIA

ESTATE

Pipers River $30–$49
Current vintage: 2004 88

A herbal and tight-grained pinot whose slightly dull aromas of red cherries, flowers and cedary oak reveal minty undertones. Assertively backed by firmish and bony tannins, it lacks great fleshiness and sappiness, with a brooding core of cherry-like fruit presently finishing slightly greenish and metallic. Should evolve quickly.

Year	Score		
2004	88	2006	2009
2003	90	2008	2011
2002	87	2004	2007
2001	81	2002	2003
2000	90	2002	2005
1999	90	2004	2007
1998	86	2000	2003+
1997	89	2002	2005
1996	82	2001	2004
1995	89	1997	2000
1994	90	1999	2002
1993	89	1995	1998
1992	91	1997	2000

A B C D E F G H I J K L M N O P Q R S T U V W X Y Z

ESTATE RIESLING

RATING 3

PIPERS BROOK VINEYARD
2001 RIESLING
TASMANIA

Tasmania $20–$29
Current vintage: 2005 95

A superb, round and generous riesling whose musky, floral perfume of pear, apple and white peach reveals rose oil-like nuances. Exceptionally intense and brightly flavoured, its juicy, long and bone-dry palate of apple/pear fruit has an Alsace-like sumptuousness, finishing with great length and a terrific balance with lemony acids.

2005	95	2013	2017
2004	93	2009	2012
2003	89	2005	2008
2002	90	2004	2007
2001	93	2003	2006+
2000	95	2012	2020
1999	93	2007	2011
1998	95	2006	2010
1997	90	2002	2005
1996	93	2004	2008
1995	93	2003	2007
1994	91	2002	2006

RESERVE PINOT NOIR

RATING 3

PIPERS BROOK VINEYARD
1998 PINOT NOIR RESERVE
Tasmania

Pipers River $50–$99
Current vintage: 2003 96

A superb pinot driven by the sheer power of its opulent fruit but still managing to exude finesse and balance. Its pristine aromas of cherries and raspberries are lifted by a heady rose garden perfume and undertones of caramel, butter and delicate spices. Deeply and richly flavoured, it's smooth and seamless, with a sumptuous core of vibrant fruit integrated with tight-grained oak and fine, silky tannins. It finishes long and savoury, with lingering meaty and nutty influences.

2003	96	2008	2011
2002	93	2007	2010+
1998	79	2000	2003

THE SUMMIT CHARDONNAY

RATING 4

PIPERS BROOK VINEYARD
1998 SUMMIT CHARDONNAY
Tasmania

Pipers River $50–$99
Current vintage: 2002 93

Very evolved, savoury, meaty and intellectual, this highly concentrated and complex chardonnay has received plenty of winemaking attention, but lacks the great length of fruit and the precise ripeness to carry it off perfectly. A honeyed and slightly varnishy bouquet of butterscotch, smoky vanilla oak and mealy undertones dominates its apple and melon fruit, while there are greenish and metallic edges around its syrupy, rather cloying and unctuous palate. Far from flawless and very hard to score, it could be sensational in the right environment.

2002	93	2007	2010
2000	89	2002	2005
1999	88	2001	2004
1998	91	2000	2003
1997	82	1999	2002

Pizzini

175 King Valley Road, Whitfield Vic 3678. Tel: (03) 5729 8278. Fax: (03) 5279 8495.
Website: www.pizzini.com.au Email: pizzini@bigpond.com
Region: **King Valley** Winemakers: **Joel & Alfred Pizzini** Chief Executives: **Alfred & Katrina Pizzini**
Pizzini is just the sort of winery Australia needs more of. It's working hard to develop authentic expressions of Italian varieties in Australia, sells what it makes at a very fair price, and is prepared to cellar its reds until they're ready for sale. With wines like the 1998 Nebbiolo and deliciously sour-edged and savoury 2004 Sangiovese, its early steps are very positive ones indeed.

NEBBIOLO

RATING 4

pizzini
Nebbiolo
2000
KING VALLEY

King Valley $30–$49
Current vintage: 2000 91

Rich, rustic and savoury, this firm and astringent red marries lightly herbal, meaty and leathery complexity with a deep core of slightly jammy plum and cherry flavour. There's some smokiness about the palate, plus a hint of camphor and mature cheddar cheese. It's long and drying, with some herbal undertones, but it's ready to enjoy with an appropriately flavoursome and rustic dish.

2000	91	2005	2008+
1999	90	2007	2011+
1998	92	2010	2018

RIESLING

King Valley	$12–$19
Current vintage: 2005	**84**

A flavoursome young riesling that lacks great focus and definition. Its floral, estery perfume of lime, lemon and mineral undertones is somewhat spicy, while its juicy palate finishes rather awkward and spicy, without much cut and shape.

2005	84	2007	2010
2004	90	2009	2012
2003	90	2008	2011
2002	87	2007	2010+

SANGIOVESE

RATING 5

King Valley	$20–$29
Current vintage: 2004	**93**

A bony, savoury and varietally correct sangiovese whose deep, chocolatey aroma of dark plums and cherries overlies suggestions of spice and sweet vanilla oak. It's sumptuous and meaty, delivering a long and astringent palate of dark, sour-edged plums and cherries backed by spicy nuances of cloves and cinnamon. Great shape and structure.

2004	93	2009	2012+
2003	82	2005	2008
2002	89	2004	2007+

SHIRAZ

King Valley	$20–$29
Current vintage: 2001	**86**

Slightly sappy and herbal, this developing shiraz has a lightly meaty bouquet of plums and berries backed by sweet vanilla oak and undertones of spice. There's more life and vitality on the palate, although the flavours of red plums, raspberries and redcurrants finish a little flat, with green-edged tannins. Lacks genuine ripeness.

2001	86	2003	2006
2000	80	2002	2005
1999	89	2007	2011

Plantagenet

Albany Highway, Mount Barker WA 6324. Tel: (08) 9851 3111. Fax: (08) 9851 1839.
Website: www.plantagenetwines.com Email: sales@plantagenetwines.com

Region: **Mount Barker** Winemaker: **Richard Robson** Viticulturist: **Jaysen Gladish** Chairman: **Tony Smith**

Plantagenet is a well-established small winery with good access to mature vineyards. Over the years it has proven capable of exceptional Riesling, Shiraz and Cabernet Sauvignon. The fine and savoury 2002 Shiraz was an extremely impressive inclusion in several major tastings of Australian shiraz I helped to stage in Japan in 2006, and demonstrated the wide range of shirazes presently being made in this country. Recent Plantagenet Rieslings have been perfumed, musky, tight and exemplary.

CABERNET SAUVIGNON

RATING 5

Mount Barker	$30–$49
Current vintage: 2003	**87**

A cooler year cabernet whose slightly leafy and cedary aromas of red and black berries overlie meaty nuances of blue cheese and leather. Its moderate length of plum and berry flavour is supported by quite a firm grip of slightly sappy tannin and sweet underlying oak. Finishing with a hint of capsicum, but not too green.

2003	87	2008	2011+
2002	90	2007	2010+
2001	89	2009	2013
1999	89	2004	2007+
1998	88	2003	2006+
1997	88	2005	2009
1996	87	2001	2004
1995	88	2003	2007
1994	95	2006	2014
1993	93	2005	2013+
1992	94	2000	2004+
1991	91	1999	2003+
1990	89	1998	2002
1989	95	2001	2009+

CHARDONNAY

RATING 3

Mount Barker	$20–$29
Current vintage: 2005	**93**

A finely weighted, balanced and tightly integrated chardonnay that marries its fresh citrusy and tropical fruit with restrained creamy, leesy complexity, dusty vanilla oak and refreshing acidity. It opens with a fresh and lightly toasty nose of quince, cumquat, grapefruit and pineapple, while its palate is long, supple and elegant, delivering juicy, slightly meaty and creamy fruit plus matchstick-like oak before a warm, savoury and wheatmeal-like finish.

2005	93	2010	2013
2004	86	2006	2009
2003	94	2008	2011
2001	85	2003	2006
2000	93	2005	2008
1999	94	2004	2007+
1998	89	2003	2006
1997	91	2002	2005
1996	87	2001	2004
1995	93	2000	2003

RIESLING

RATING 2

Great Southern	$12–$19
Current vintage: 2005	**95**

Intense and musky, with a delightfully floral perfume of lime juice, lemon rind, apple and pear backed by spicy bath powder-like influences. Taut and trim, its long, tight and sculpted palate reveals layers of finely honed mineral and citrus flavours, culminating in a bony, dry and schisty finish.

2005	95	2013	2017
2004	95	2009	2013+
2003	92	2011	2015
2002	90	2007	2010
2001	94	2009	2013
2000	95	2005	2008
1999	94	2007	2011
1998	95	2006	2010
1997	93	2005	2009
1996	95	2004	2008
1995	94	2003	2007
1994	94	2006	2014
1993	94	1998	2001

SHIRAZ

RATING 3

Great Southern	$30–$49
Current vintage: 2003	**89**

A floral, spicy shiraz from a milder season whose lightly minty aromas of small black and red berries are assertively backed by mocha and dark chocolate oak influences with a suggestion of fennel. Brooding, meaty and slightly overcooked, it retains undertones of vibrant berry fruits beneath its raisin and currant-like flavours. The palate is slightly overawed by overt oak.

2003	89	2008	2011+
2002	93	2014	2022
2001	93	2000	2013+
2000	90	2005	2008
1999	91	2007	2011
1998	90	2006	2010+
1997	86	1999	2002
1996	87	2002	2008
1995	90	2003	2007+
1994	96	2002	2006
1993	93	2005	2013
1991	89	1996	1999+
1990	92	2002	2010
1989	90	2001	2009
1988	90	2000	2008
1987	90	1999	2007
1986	88	1994	1998+

Poet's Corner

Craigmoor Road, Mudgee NSW 2850. Tel: (02) 6372 2208. Fax: (02) 6372 4464.
Website: www.poetscornerwines.com Email: info@poetscornerwines.com.au
Region: **Mudgee** Winemakers: **Trent Nankivell, Ben Bryant** Viticulturist: **Kirily Rimmer**
Chief Executive: **Laurent Lacassgne**

Poet's Corner is an Orlando Wyndham-owned Mudgee brand that has evolved out of a pair of very good and affordable red and white table wines. It has recently gone upmarket with some reasonably good 'Henry Lawson' wines, of which the Chardonnay has been quite classy and the reds rather old-fashioned and rustic.

HENRY LAWSON SHIRAZ

RATING **5**

Mudgee	$20–$29
Current vintage: 2002	**89**

A rustic, spicy medium-term red with an earthy honesty. Its restrained bouquet of redcurrants, briary cassis, plums and blackberries reveals undertones of nutty, cedary/vanilla oak with hints of game meat. Slightly cooked, with confectionary red berry fruit, it's smooth and generous, with up-front earthy, spicy fruit and sweet cedary oak framed by soft tannins.

2002	89	2007	2010+
2001	88	2006	2009
1998	89	2006	2010+
1997	83	2002	2005

SEMILLON SAUVIGNON BLANC

RATING **5**

Mudgee	$5–$11
Current vintage: 2005	**87**

Lightly toasty, fragrant aromas of gooseberry, melon and grassy undertones precede a smooth, forward and juicy palate whose creamy texture and lingering fruit sweetness are finished by clean, tangy and refreshing acids. Uncomplicated, clean and lively.

2005	87	2006	2007
2004	81	2005	2006
2003	87	2004	2005
2002	88	2003	2004+
2000	87	2001	2002
1999	82	2001	2004
1998	82	1999	2000
1997	87	1998	1999
1996	87	1997	1998

SHIRAZ CABERNET BLEND

Various	$5–$11
Current vintage: 2004	**86**

An honest wine whose vibrant, floral and earthy aromas of raspberries and plums are backed by lightly charry cedar/vanilla oak, with undertones of cloves, nutmeg and white pepper. Fine, supple and elegant, it's pleasingly long, juicy and slightly jammy, with a restrained background of cedar/vanilla oak and a firmish grip.

2004	86	2006	2009+
2003	86	2005	2008
2002	87	2004	2007+
2001	85	2002	2003
1999	82	2000	2001
1998	83	2000	2003
1997	86	1999	2002
1996	88	2001	2004
1995	87	1997	2000

UNWOODED CHARDONNAY

Various	$12–$19
Current vintage: 2005	**85**

Slightly under-ripe but clean and refreshing, with a dusty, cashew-like aroma of peach, nectarine, butter and quince. Fruity and forward, it's creamy, round and generous, lacking great length, before finishing with soft acids and citrusy, melon-like flavours.

2005	85	2006	2007
2004	86	2005	2006
2003	86	2004	2005
2001	83	2002	2003
2000	80	2000	2001
1999	87	2000	2001
1998	88	1999	2000

Poole's Rock

DeBeyers Road, Pokolbin NSW 2320. Tel: (02) 4998 7389. Fax: (02) 4998 7682.
Website: www.poolesrock.com.au Email: info@poolesrock.com.au
Region: **Lower Hunter Valley** Winemaker: **Patrick Auld** Viticulturist: **Evan Powell** Chief Executive: **Peter Russell**
With the purchase of the Tulloch winery from Southcorp in 2002, Poole's Rock acquired a base in the heart of the Hunter Valley. Then, with the appointment of former Tulloch winemaker Patrick Auld, it bought itself an inestimable resource of Hunter Valley experience and talent. Poole's Rock is owned by investment banker David Clarke.

CHARDONNAY
RATING 5

Lower Hunter Valley	$20–$29
Current vintage: 2003	**72**

Clearly affected by a serious case of bushfire taint, this potentially ripe, flavoursome chardonnay does reveal a depth of melon and fig-like flavour, but is totally dominated by its ashtray-like smokiness. It's far from the only 2003 Hunter wine to exhibit this problem.

2003	72	2004	2005
2002	86	2004	2007
2001	89	2003	2006
1999	89	2001	2004
1998	90	2003	2006
1997	90	2002	2005
1996	92	1998	2001
1995	87	1997	2000

Port Phillip Estate

261 Red Hill Road, Red Hill South Vic 3937. Tel: (03) 5989 2708. Fax: (03) 5989 3017.
Website: www.portphillip.net Email: sales@portphillip.net
Region: **Mornington Peninsula** Winemaker: **Sandro Mosele** Viticulturist: **Doug Wood**
Chief Executive: **Giorgio Gjergja**
Port Phillip Estate is a tiny Mornington Peninsula producer now part of the same stable as the Kooyong winery. The only real glitch among its 2004 offerings is a very green and skinny Chardonnay, while the Pinot Noir is far and away the best wine yet from this now-mature estate. The 2005 Sauvignon Blanc has cut and flavour.

PINOT NOIR
RATING 5

Mornington Peninsula	$30–$49
Current vintage: 2004	**95**

Powerfully constructed, with brooding layers of dark, spicy fruit and a drying astringency, this bruising young pinot will emerge as a wine of considerable class. Its floral, spicy and confiture-like aromas of redcurrants, raspberries and strawberries are handsomely backed by cedary oak. Chewy, almost sinewy, its robust palate will flesh out, giving full rein to its presently closed expression of dark plum and blackberry fruit.

2004	95	2009	2012+
2003	89	2005	2008
2002	87	2003	2004+
2001	89	2003	2006
2000	82	2002	2005
1999	91	2001	2004+
1998	88	1999	2000

SAUVIGNON BLANC
RATING 4

Mornington Peninsula	$20–$29
Current vintage: 2005	**93**

Tightly structured over a powdery spine of mineral texture, this generously flavoured young sauvignon blanc has freshness and flavour aplenty. Scented with passionfruit and gooseberries, it presents a lingering core of pristine flavour before finishing with genuine cut and definition.

2005	93	2006	2007+
2004	92	2005	2006
2003	81	2003	2003

SHIRAZ
RATING 5

Mornington Peninsula	$30–$49
Current vintage: 2004	**88**

Delicate meaty, spicy and herbal aromas and briary dark berries and plums are lifted by tight-grained oak aromatics, but leave an impression of under- and over-ripened fruit. Fractionally porty, with a slightly hollow palate of dark fruit and sweet chocolate oak, it's backed by a rather green-edged and metallic spine of firm tannins. Well handled, but a little disjointed.

2004	88	2006	2009+
2003	90	2005	2008+
2001	79	2003	2006
2000	89	2002	2005+
1999	86	2000	2003
1998	89	2002	2005+

Preece

Mitchelton, Nagambie Vic 3608. Tel: (03) 5736 2222. Fax: (03) 5736 2266.
Website: www.mitchelton.com.au Email: mitchelton@mitchelton.com.au
Region: **Goulburn Valley** Winemaker: **Toby Barlow** Viticulturist: **John Beresford**
Chief Executive: **Peter Cowan**

Preece is a Mitchelton brand comprising a number of varietal table wines grown in the Nagambie Lakes region.
Several of the current releases, the Merlot especially, offer great value at their modest price-points.

CABERNET SAUVIGNON

RATING **5**

Nagambie Lakes		**$12–$19**	2005	81	2007	2010
Current vintage: 2005		**81**	2003	80	2005	2008

2005	81	2007	2010
2003	80	2005	2008
2002	90	2007	2010
2001	88	2006	2009
2000	89	2005	2008
1999	89	2001	2004+
1998	87	2000	2003+
1997	83	2002	2005

Drying and dehydrated, this is a hard, sinewy red with spearmint-like aromas of mulberries and cassis, plums and cranberries with meaty, menthol-like undertones. Its cooked, minty palate of currants and prunes culminates in a flat, stale finish.

MERLOT

RATING **5**

Nagambie Lakes **$12–$19**
Current vintage: 2005 **87**

2005	87	2007	2010+
2003	88	2005	2008+
2002	90	2004	2007+
2000	88	2002	2005+
1999	89	2001	2004+
1998	87	2003	2006
1997	89	2002	2005
1996	83	1998	2001

Dark, minty and faintly eucalypt-like aromas of plums, cherries and blackberries, with spicy undertones of cloves and cinnamon precede a moderately intense and oaky palate, whose sweet, ripe and minty fruit is underpinned by a dusty spine of firmish tannins. It's a pleasing varietal that would have been marked higher if not for some rather card-boardy oak.

SAUVIGNON BLANC

RATING **5**

Nagambie Lakes **$12–$19**
Current vintage: 2005 **88**

2005	88	2005	2006+
2004	87	2004	2005+
2003	90	2003	2004+
2002	86	2002	2003
2001	87	2002	2003
2000	87	2001	2002
1999	89	2000	2001

A dry, shapely and slightly briny sauvignon blanc with a zesty, lightly herbal and grassy aroma of lychees and gooseberries plus a long, lean and pleasingly tight palate whose juicy, spicy passionfruit-like flavours are finished by appropriately powdery acids.

SHIRAZ

RATING **5**

Nagambie Lakes **$12–$19**
Current vintage: 2004 **86**

2004	86	2006	2009
2003	87	2005	2008
2002	89	2004	2007
2001	81	2003	2006
2000	87	2002	2005
1999	87	2001	2004
1998	86	2000	2003

A sweaty, meaty and animal-like shiraz whose restrained expression of black and red berries and plums reveals nuances of suede and farmyard. Moderately firm and savoury, its rustic complexity overshadows some rather attractive and spicy fruit.

Primo Estate

Old Port Wakefield Road, Virginia SA 5120. Tel: (08) 8380 9442. Fax: (08) 8380 9696.
Website: www.primoestate.com.au Email: info@primoestate.com.au
Region: **Adelaide** Winemakers: **Joe Grilli, David Tait** Chief Executive: **Joe Grilli**

Never content to rest on his laurels, Joe Grilli is developing new and innovative wines for his Joseph collection. This edition welcomes the Angel Gully Shiraz, a wine sourced from a company-owned site near Clarendon in McLaren Vale, which happens to feature a lonely gum tree that looks almost identical to that on the Primo Estate label. The site also grows outstanding shiraz. Primo Estate continues to thrive at the cutting edge of Australian wine.

IL BRICCONE SHIRAZ SANGIOVESE

RATING **5**

Various, South Australia	$12–$19
Current vintage: 2004	88

Spicy, earthy and lightly meaty aromas of stewed red cherries, plums and floral undertones are backed by nuances of dried herbs. Supple, smooth and fine-grained, the palate makes up for what it might lack in length and complexity with delightful flavours of sour cherries, plums and raspberries. Framed by firm, fine tannins, it finishes savoury, with a light meatiness.

2004	88	2006	2009
2003	91	2005	2008
2002	86	2004	2007
2001	92	2003	2006+
2000	89	2002	2005
1999	89	2001	2004
1998	82	1999	2000

JOSEPH ANGEL GULLY SHIRAZ

RATING **3**

McLaren Vale	$50–$99
Current vintage: 2003	90

A very slightly cooked, meaty but smooth, supple and deeply flavoured shiraz whose deep, leathery aromas of cassis, plums and dark chocolate are backed by nuances of cloves, cinnamon and vanilla. Its long, elegant and savoury palate of small berries, plums and currants finishes with lingering earthy and charcuterie-like undertones.

2003	90	2008	2011
2002	95	2010	2014+
2001	93	2009	2013

JOSEPH LA MAGIA RIESLING GEWÜRZTRAMINER

RATING **2**

Eden Valley, Clare Valley,	
Coonawarra	$20–$29 (375 ml)
Current vintage: 2005	93

A smooth, silky dessert wine whose musky floral perfume of rose petals, pear and citrus is backed by minerally wet slate undertones. Long, tangy and concentrated, its vibrant palate of lime juice, lemon rind and apple-like flavour culminates in a refreshingly clean and persistent finish of balanced sweetness. Its 15% traminer content contributes suggestions of musk and spice, without making the palate excessively oily.

2005	93	2007	2010
2003	89	2005	2006+
2002	95	2004	2007+
2001	94	2003	2006+
1998	86	2000	2003+
1996	90	2001	2004
1995	95	2000	2003
1994	94	1999	2002
1993	95	2001	2005
1991	94	1999	2003
1989	88	1994	1998

JOSEPH MODA CABERNET SAUVIGNON MERLOT

RATING **3**

McLaren Vale	$50–$99
Current vintage: 2002	90

Likely to fill out and develop pleasing complexity, this concentrated and slightly drying cabernet blend is presently a little spirity and lacking in great length. There are meaty, earthy undertones beneath its slightly confectionary aromas of red berries and cedar/vanilla oak, while a firm spine of tannins lurks beneath its smooth, fleshy and expressive palate of dark plums, dark berries and forest floor influences. There's some licorice-like complexity but also some greenish, sappy edges to the finish. Keep it.

2002	90	2010	2014
2001	93	2009	2013+
2000	92	2008	2012
1999	95	2011	2019
1998	89	2003	2006
1997	88	2002	2005
1996	93	2008	2016
1995	94	2007	2015
1994	97	2006	2014
1993	95	2005	2013
1992	92	2004	2012
1991	97	2003	2011
1990	94	2002	2010
1989	94	2001	2009

LA BIONDINA COLOMBARD (with Sauv. Blanc in 2006) RATING 5

South Australia	$12–$19				
Current vintage: 2006	**87**				

A faintly salty and mineral wine whose fresh, slightly confectionary aromas of passionfruit and pineapple reveal nuances of herbs and lemon. Juicy and mouthfilling, its tangy but rather syrupy palate finishes long and clean, despite a trace of residual sugar.

2006	87	2006	2007
2005	88	2005	2006
2004	83	2004	2005+
2003	89	2004	2005
2002	87	2002	2003
2001	88	2002	2003
1999	83	2000	2001
1997	86	1997	1997

Prince Albert

100 Lemins Road, Waurn Ponds Vic 3216. Tel: (03) 5241 8091. Fax: (03) 5241 8091.

Region: **Geelong** Winemaker: **Bruce Hyett** Viticulturist: **Bruce Hyett** Chief Executive: **Bruce Hyett**

Prince Albert was the first Victorian vineyard to be entirely devoted to pinot noir. It has produced some excellent wines, but remains particularly vulnerable to seasonal fluctuation. Clearly, the vineyard experienced significant stress before the 2005 harvest. At the time of writing, there is a question mark over the future of this vineyard. One hopes it will be able to continue.

PINOT NOIR RATING 4

PRINCE ALBERT
GEELONG

PINOT NOIR
2001

PRODUCE OF AUSTRALIA

Geelong	$30–$49		
Current vintage: 2005	**82**		

Lifted by some floral undertones and backed by cedar/vanilla oak, its pruney, currant-like and plummy aromas are rather stressed and candied. Cooked and raisined, its smooth and developing palate is framed by slightly gritty fine tannins and beginning to dry out.

2005	82	2007	2010
2004	90	2009	2012
2003	87	2005	2008
2002	84	2004	2007
2001	92	2006	2009
2000	95	2005	2008
1999	89	2007	2011
1998	91	2003	2006
1997	93	2002	2005
1996	82	1998	2001
1995	93	2000	2003
1994	90	1999	2002
1993	86	1995	1998
1992	94	1997	2000

Radenti

Freycinet, 15919 Tasman Highway, Bicheno Tas 7215. Tel: (03) 6257 8574. Fax: (03) 6257 8454.
Website: www.freycinetvineyard.com.au

Region: **East Coast Tasmania** Winemakers: **Claudio Radenti & Lindy Bull** Viticulturist: **Claudio Radenti** Chief Executive: **Geoff Bull**

The sparkling wine from the highly rated Freycinet vineyard, Radenti is usually made in rather a wild, earthy and complex style with ultra-long maturation on lees. This was certainly the case with the very rich and chewy 1999 edition.

CHARDONNAY PINOT NOIR RATING 3

East Coast Tasmania	$30–$49		
Current vintage: 1999	**88**		

A complex, nutty and mineral fragrance of lime, grapefruit and apple reveals developing nuances of wheatmeal, toast, honey and butter. Slightly sweet and awkward to finish, it's chewy, rich and creamy, with a generous complement of depth and character, but would have been better if left a little drier.

1999	88	2004	2007
1998	93	2003	2006+
1997	92	2002	2005+
1996	89	2001	2004
1995	93	2000	2003
1994	95	1999	2002
1993	88	1998	2001

Redbank Winery

1 Sally's Lane, Redbank Vic 3478. Tel: (03) 5467 7255. Fax: (03) 5467 7248.
Website: www.sallyspaddock.com.au Email: info@sallyspaddock.com.au
Region: **Pyrenees** Winemaker: **Neill Robb** Viticulturist: **Scott Hutton** Chief Executive: **Neill Robb**

Redbank is a maker of several small production, small individual vineyard wines from the Pyrenees region in central Victoria. Most famous is Sally's Paddock, an acclaimed blend of cabernet sauvignon, shiraz, cabernet franc and merlot from a dryland vineyard at the front of the Redbank property. Now with significant vineage, this wine is really coming into its own with a series of first-rate vintages in 1998, 2000, 2002 and 2004. Better order your 2006 now?

SALLY'S PADDOCK

RATING 2

Pyrenees	$50–$99
Current vintage: 2004	**96**

A beautifully crafted and balanced red of inert strength that slowly unfolds layers of penetrative flavour. Its heady bouquet of brambly blackcurrant and redcurrant aromas, violets and sweet, cedar/gamey oak overlie slightly wild and meaty nuances. Long, sumptuous and fine-grained, its brightly lit palate of pristine berry, cherry and plumlike fruit knits tightly with smooth oak and a mouthcoating presence of fine, firm tannins. Effortlessly natural, with lingering juicy and meaty qualities.

2004	96	2016	2024+
2003	89	2011	2015
2002	93	2014	2022+
2001	88	2009	2013+
2000	93	2012	2020+
1999	88	2007	2011+
1998	96	2010	2018+
1997	88	2005	2009
1996	90	2004	2008+
1995	95	2007	2015
1994	94	2006	2014
1993	94	2005	2013
1992	92	2000	2004
1991	91	2003	2011
1990	93	2020	2030
1989	87	2001	2009
1988	95	2000	2008
1987	82	1999	2004
1986	93	2006	2016
1985	88	1997	2005
1984	85	1989	1992
1983	87	2003	2013
1982	93	2002	2012
1981	94	2001	2011

Redgate

Boodjidup Road, Margaret River WA 6285. Tel: (08) 9757 6488. Fax: (08) 9757 6308.
Website: www.redgatewines.com.au Email: info@redgatewines.com.au
Region: **Margaret River** Winemaker: **Simon Keall** Viticulturist: **Paul McGrath** Chief Executive: **Paul Ullinger**

While Redgate's herbaceous and occasionally sweaty white wines are offering more intensity and brightness, its reds still tend towards excessive greenish, leaner styles. The Reserve Sauvignon Blanc from 2005 is a very good and rare example of how oak can gently contribute to the texture and richness of this variety. Redgate's citrusy 2005 Chardonnay is another very good effort, and a considerable improvement.

CHARDONNAY

RATING 5

Margaret River	$30–$49
Current vintage: 2005	**91**

Vibrant floral and mineral aromas of fresh citrus and melon fruit overlie restrained nuances of fresh vanilla oak. Smooth and polished, its sumptuous but elegant palate of peach, grapefruit and melon flavours reveals dusty undertones of vanilla and cashew-like oak. It finishes with refreshing and lively acids, and a lingering core of tangy, lemony fruit.

2005	91	2007	2010+
2004	82	2005	2006+
2003	87	2005	2008
2002	89	2004	2007
2001	87	2003	2006
1999	82	1999	2000

RESERVE SAUVIGNON BLANC

RATING 5

Margaret River	$12–$19
Current vintage: 2005	91

A lifted and herbal bouquet of gooseberries, passionfruit and grassy undertones is carefully knit with lightly smoky vanilla oak. Supple and juicy, its long and elegant palate of vibrant, tangy fruit and neatly balanced toasty oak culminates in a racy finish of bright, refreshing acids. Manages to retain plenty of fruit freshness in an oaked style.

2005	91	2007	2010
2004	89	2005	2006+
2003	89	2004	2005
2002	86	2002	2003
2001	86	2002	2003+
2000	87	2002	2005
1999	82	1999	2000
1998	90	1999	2000
1997	87	1998	1999

SAUVIGNON BLANC SEMILLON

RATING 5

Margaret River	$12–$19
Current vintage: 2005	86

Dusty, herbal and grassy aromas of gooseberries, melon and white cheese mould precede a long and vibrant palate whose tangy expression of citrus/melon fruit has a peppery quality and a hint of sweetness at the finish.

2005	86	2006	2007
2004	88	2005	2006
2003	88	2004	2005+
2002	88	2004	2007
2001	83	2002	2003
2000	87	2002	2005
1999	88	1999	2000

Redman

Riddoch Highway, Coonawarra SA 5263. Tel: (08) 8736 3331. Fax: (08) 8736 3013. Website: www.redman.com.au

Region: **Coonawarra** Winemakers: **Bruce & Malcolm Redman** Viticulturists: **Bruce & Malcolm Redman**
Chief Executives: **Bruce & Malcolm Redman**

Unlike most Coonawarra producers, which enjoyed a season out of the box in 2004, Redman's wines reveal distinctive unevenness of ripening, causing herbal characters in the Shiraz and a meaty, currant-like aspect in the Cabernet Sauvignon. It will be interesting to see, in the course of the year, how the red blend dealt with this. Redman's vineyards are among the oldest and best in Coonawarra, and on occasion produce this exceptional intensity and length of flavour.

CABERNET SAUVIGNON

RATING 5

Coonawarra	$20–$29
Current vintage: 2004	88

Framed by fine, firm and bony tannins and backed by rather restrained and cedary oak, this is a typically smooth and supple Coonawarra cabernet of medium to full weight. Its dusty, spicy and herbal aromas of violets, dark plums, blackcurrants, red berries and dark chocolate reveal a slight meatiness, while its palate is finely balanced but reveals a somewhat cooked aspect.

2004	88	2012	2016
2003	93	2015	2023
2002	88	2014	2022
2001	89	2006	2009
2000	88	2008	2012
1999	90	2007	2011
1998	89	2006	2010
1997	88	2002	2005
1996	89	2004	2008
1994	93	2002	2006
1993	93	2001	2005
1992	92	2004	2012
1991	84	2003	2011
1990	93	2002	2010
1989	82	1997	2001
1988	88	2000	2008
1987	88	1999	2004

CABERNET SAUVIGNON MERLOT

RATING 4

Coonawarra	$20–$29
Current vintage: 2003	87

Ripe aromas of dark berries, plums and restrained cedary and lightly smoky oak precede a smooth and slightly herbal palate whose pleasing depth of fruit and balanced oak are framed by rather green-edged tannins and flavours.

2003	87	2008	2011
2001	95	2013	2021+
2000	89	2008	2012
1999	86	2004	2007+
1998	94	2010	2018
1997	83	1999	2002
1996	90	2004	2008+
1995	86	2000	2003
1994	93	2006	2014
1993	93	2001	2005
1992	94	2000	2004
1991	91	1999	2003

SHIRAZ

RATING **5**

Coonawarra $12–$19
Current vintage: 2004   88

There's a slightly herbal thread beneath this savoury, spicy and fine-grained shiraz. Its sweet red cherry, raspberry and currant-like perfume overlies lightly smoky vanilla oak. Medium in weight, its smooth palate of lively red berry flavours and sweet oak is framed by gentle tannins.

2004	88	2009	2012
2003	81	2005	2008
2002	89	2010	2014
2001	89	2003	2006+
2000	89	2003	2006+
1999	82	2001	2004
1998	86	2003	2006
1997	81	1998	1999
1996	84	1998	2004+
1995	86	1997	2000
1994	84	1996	1999
1993	90	2001	2005
1992	91	2000	2004
1991	88	1993	1996
1990	91	1995	1998

Reilly's

Corner Burra & Hill streets, Mintaro SA 5415. Tel: (08) 8843 9013. Fax: (08) 8843 9013.
Website: www.reillyswines.com   Email: pip@reillyswines.com
Region: **Clare Valley** Winemaker: **Justin Ardill** Viticulturist: **Robert Smyth** Chief Executive: **Justin Ardill**

Based at Mintaro, in the Clare Valley, Reilly's is a small maker of traditional regional table wines led by its firm, minty and assertively oaked 'Dry Land' Shiraz and Cabernet Sauvignon varietals. The 2003 Shiraz is ultra-ripe but certainly not overcooked, and dealt very well with the season, while the 2005 Riesling is a fine and tightly sculpted expression of the variety.

DRY LAND CABERNET SAUVIGNON

RATING **5**

Clare Valley $30–$49
Current vintage: 2003   88

Assertive, concentrated, slightly unpolished and sinewy, this rich, meaty cabernet has a dark, choc-mint-like bouquet of cooked, plums, currants, menthol and eucalypt. Its ultra-ripe palate is thick and powerful, if lacking in brightness and sweetness. Very firm, its rough edges should soften with time.

2003	88	2011	2015
2002	88	2010	2014+
2001	86	2006	2009+
2000	89	2005	2008
1999	82	2001	2004
1998	88	2003	2006+

DRY LAND SHIRAZ

RATING **5**

Clare Valley $20–$29
Current vintage: 2003   91

Impressively concentrated and oaky, this powerful shiraz fits into the ultra-ripe spectrum of flavour without showing overcooked characters. Its meaty, tarry aromas of currants, plums and violets reveal earthy undertones and spicy, fine-grained nuances of sweet vanilla/coconut oak. Its sumptuous palate of vibrant small berry and plum-like fruit is framed by fine, firm and tightly knit tannins, finishing with a vibrant length of minty fruit backed by exotic spices.

2003	91	2015	2023
2002	85	2004	2007
2001	89	2009	2013
2000	88	2005	2008
1999	92	2004	2007
1998	89	2003	2006+

WATERVALE RIESLING

RATING **5**

Clare Valley $12–$19
Current vintage: 2005   93

A pretty, tightly sculpted, long and dry riesling with a delicate floral and citrusy perfume and a long, smooth and supple palate. Its bright, fresh and juicy expression of lime and lemon fruit and under-lying musky influences finishes crisp and long.

2005	93	2010	2013+
2004	88	2006	2009+
2003	89	2008	2011
2002	88	2004	2007+
2001	83	2002	2003

Reynell

Reynell Road, Reynella SA 5161. Tel: (08) 8392 2222. Fax: (08) 8392 2202.
Region: **McLaren Vale** Winemakers: **Paul Lapsley, Robert Mann** Viticulturist: **Brenton Baker**
Chief Executive: **David Woods**

The Reynell label is now home to the Basket Pressed series of traditional McLaren Vale red varieties. Recent vintages of these wines have evidently been made from extremely ripe and dehydrated fruit, and the 2004 Cabernet Sauvignon is no exception. I'm not sure its makers made the most of this very good vintage for McLaren Vale cabernet, but they certainly did with the stellar and delightfully old-fashioned Shiraz.

BASKET PRESSED CABERNET SAUVIGNON   RATING 4

McLaren Vale	$30–$49
Current vintage: 2004	**88**

Framed by very firm and powdery tannin, this cooked and meaty cabernet lacks brightness and sweetness of fruit and charm. Its heady aromas of confiture-like blackberries, dark plums, black-currants and older vanilla/cedar oak are backed by earthy, leathery and meaty undertones. Forward and very ripe, its substantial palate of raisined, currant-like fruit tastes riper and more alcoholic than the 13.5% declared on the label. Probably made from stressed fruit.

2004	88	2009	2012
2002	88	2010	2014
1998	95	2010	2018+
1997	89	2005	2009+
1996	92	2008	2016
1995	91	2007	2015

BASKET PRESSED SHIRAZ   RATING 2

McLaren Vale	$50–$99
Current vintage: 2004	**95**

Slightly jammy and old-fashioned, with heady, ripe and briary aromas of dark plums, red and black berries backed by chocolate/vanilla oak and musky nuances of cinnamon and cloves. Coated by firm and tightly knit tannins, its palate-staining, sour-edged expression of dark berries and plums reveal a tangy and faintly mineral saltiness. Very full and rich, but also balanced and harmonious.

2004	95	2016	2024
2003	88	2008	2011
2000	90	2002	2005
1998	94	2018	2028
1997	93	2009	2017
1996	95	2008	2016
1995	94	2007	2015

Richard Hamilton

Corner Main and Johnston roads, McLaren Vale SA 5171. Tel: (08) 8323 8830. Fax: (08) 8323 8881.
Website: www.leconfieldwines.com Email: info@leconfieldwines.com
Region: **McLaren Vale** Winemaker: **Paul Gordon** Viticulturist: **Lee Harding**
Chief Executive: **Richard Hamilton**

Just as he is now doing with the Leconfield reds, Paul Gordon is beginning to imbue the Richard Hamilton wines with the fruit intensity and sweetness (not to be confused with sugar sweetness) that they have traditionally lacked. The results are there to be seen in the 2004 reds, which are also bottled with more flair and polish. Finally, I believe, the Richard Hamilton wine company is settling into an easily understood range of very enjoyable wines. Even the Slate Quarry Riesling 2005 is well above expectations for this variety from McLaren Vale.

BURTON'S VINEYARD (Grenache Shiraz Blend)   RATING 5

McLaren Vale	$20–$29
Current vintage: 2002	**88**

A meaty, treacle-like blend of shiraz and grenache whose spicy and rather old-fashioned aromas of dark plums, blackberries and briar are backed by nuances of minerals and cedar. Initially plump and fruitcake-like, its spicy, chocolatey palate is firm and earthy, with currant and prune-like fruit given sweetness by assertive chocolate/vanilla oak. A good wine, perhaps lacking genuine length, but packed with meaty flavour.

2002	88	2007	2010
2001	86	2006	2009
1999	88	2004	2007
1998	93	2003	2006+
1997	86	2005	2008
1996	89	2001	2004
1995	93	2003	2007
1994	88	1999	2002
1992	86	1998	2001

CENTURION SHIRAZ

RATING 3

McLaren Vale $30–$49
Current vintage: 2002 93

Minty, meaty and spicy, its deep aromas of dark, plummy and blackberry-like shiraz are backed by chocolate/vanilla oak and suggestions of iodide and menthol. Long and firm, its briary, spicy palate is saturated by dark berry and plum flavours framed by a fine-grained and well-balanced extract, finishing earthy and savoury. Its oak is especially well handled and integrated.

2002	93	2010	2014+
2001	91	2009	2013
2000	87	2002	2005+
1999	93	2007	2011+
1998	93	2006	2010+
1996	88	2001	2004+
1995	94	2003	2007
1994	91	2002	2006
1992	87	2000	2004

GUMPRS' SHIRAZ

RATING 4

McLaren Vale $20–$29
Current vintage: 2004 92

A polished, harmonious and typically regional shiraz whose sweet, heady and confiture-like aromas of blackberries, cassis and dark plums overlie sweet cedar and vanilla oak. Full to medium in weight, its slightly sour-edged palate of dark plums and berries is framed by smooth, fine-grained tannins and backed by chocolate-like oak.

2004	92	2009	2012+
2003	90	2008	2011+
2002	89	2007	2010
2001	89	2006	2009
2000	90	2008	2012
1999	89	2001	2004+
1998	91	2006	2010
1997	89	1999	2002
1996	83	1998	2001+

HUT BLOCK CABERNET SAUVIGNON

RATING 4

McLaren Vale $20–$29
Current vintage: 2004 91

A deliciously juicy but elegant wine of tightness and brightness. Its intense floral aromas of cassis, dark plums and lightly smoky, walnut-like oak reveal layers of depth and perfume. Pristine flavours of blackberries, dark plums, mulberries and black-currant are backed by tight-knit cedar/vanilla oak and framed by a lightly sappy extract of fine tannins.

2004	91	2012	2016
2003	91	2011	2015
2002	81	2007	2010
2001	93	2009	2013+
2000	90	2005	2008+
1999	91	2004	2007+
1998	94	2006	2010
1997	88	2002	2005
1996	84	2004	2008
1995	91	2003	2007
1994	89	1999	2002
1993	87	1998	2001
1992	90	2000	2004
1991	94	1999	2003

LOT 148 MERLOT

RATING 4

McLaren Vale $12–$19
Current vintage: 2004 90

A floral and fragrant merlot whose earthy, leathery and violet-like aromas reveal an underlying core of dark cherries, plums and cedar/vanilla oak. Smooth and elegant, its long and fine-grained palate marries sour-edged cherry/plum fruit with restrained oak and a spine of fine and bony tannins. Bound by refreshing acids, it has weight, balance and a pleasing medium-term future.

2004	90	2009	2012+
2002	86	2004	2007+
2001	89	2006	2009
2000	90	2005	2008+
1999	90	2001	2004+
1998	87	2003	2006
1997	89	2002	2005

SIGNATURE CHARDONNAY

RATING 5

McLaren Vale $12–$19
Current vintage: 2003 87

Restrained, lightly oaked aromas of melon and lemon rind, peach and banana precede a soft and surprisingly elegant palate. There's plenty of texture, but refreshingly crisp acids neatly punctuate the wine's generous and vibrant peach/apple flavours.

2003	87	2004	2005
2002	89	2004	2007
2000	89	2001	2002
1999	84	2001	2004
1998	87	2000	2003
1997	87	1999	2000

SLATE QUARRY RIESLING

RATING 5

McLaren Vale	$12–$19	2005	89	2007	2010+
Current vintage: 2005	**89**	2003	89	2005	2008
		2002	87	2004	2007

A powdery and sculpted riesling whose pristine floral aromas of lime juice, lemon rind and wet slate precede a generously ripened and juicy palate of elegance and tightness. Remarkably trim and focused for this region, it's long and shapely, punctuated by a clean and refreshing acidity.

2001	80	2002	2003
2000	89	2002	2005
1999	87	2001	2004
1998	86	2000	2003

Richmond Grove

Para Road, Tanunda SA 5352. Tel: (08) 8563 7300. Fax: (08) 8563 7330.
Website: www.richmondgrovewines.com Email: info@richmondgrove.com.au

Region: **Various** Winemakers: **John Vickery, Steve Clarkson, Steve Meyer** Viticulturist: **Joy Dick**
Chief Executive: **Laurent Lacassgne**

Richmond Grove is a popular Orlando Wyndham brand that comprises honest, well-made wines blended and sourced from a number of prominent Australian regions. By some distance, its finest and most consistent wine is its tangy, citrusy and perfumed Watervale Riesling, from South Australia's Clare Valley. The 2001 release of the Barossa Shiraz is rich, meaty and well made. It has certainly appreciated another year in the bottle.

FRENCH CASK CHARDONNAY

RATING 5

Various	$12–$19	2005	82	2006	2007
Current vintage: 2005	**82**	2003	84	2004	2005+
		2002	87	2003	2004+

A fine, elegant and lightly oaked inland chardonnay whose delicate, lightly smoky and nutty fragrance of tropical, peachy fruit and tangy, citrusy palate finishes clean and lean.

2001	87	2002	2003
2000	87	2002	2005
1997	80	1998	1999

LIMITED RELEASE BAROSSA SHIRAZ

RATING 5

Barossa Valley	$12–$19	2001	90	2009	2013
Current vintage: 2001	**90**	2000	81	2002	2005
		1999	88	2001	2004+

A rich, rather brassy shiraz in a slightly meaty style. Its sweet, spicy aromas of black and red berries, plums and currants overlie smoky suggestions of toasty mocha oak. Sumptuous and creamy, its spicy, slightly jammy and raisin-like palate is backed by balanced, but assertive oak and framed by smooth, firmish tannins. Very ripe, bordering on cooked, but with plenty of fruit sweetness.

1998	88	2000	2003+
1997	87	1999	2002
1996	90	2001	2004
1995	87	1997	2000
1994	91	1999	2002

LIMITED RELEASE CABERNET SAUVIGNON

RATING 5

Coonawarra	$12–$19	2001	88	2006	2009
Current vintage: 2001	**88**	2000	83	2002	2005
		1999	88	2004	2007

Restrained, lightly floral cassis, mulberry and violet-like aromas, with light cedar/vanilla oak over tobaccoey hints of greenish fruit. Full to medium weight, with good length and slightly gritty firmness, it reveals some attractive primary fruit and oak over an underlying greenish thread.

1998	86	2003	2006
1997	82	1999	2002
1996	88	1998	2001
1995	87	2000	2003
1994	94	2002	2006
1993	88	1998	2001
1992	89	1997	2000

PADTHAWAY CHARDONNAY

RATING 5

Padthaway	$12–$19
Current vintage: 2004	**88**

A fresh, brightly lit and citrusy chardonnay whose lifted aromas of pineapple, grapefruit and sweet, spicy vanilla oak precede a measured, clean and tangy palate of appealing length and crispness. Great value.

2004	88	2006	2009
2003	89	2005	2008
2002	86	2004	2007
2001	88	2003	2006

WATERVALE RIESLING

RATING 3

Clare Valley	$12–$19
Current vintage: 2004	**90**

A floral perfume of lime juice, baby powder and lemon rind precedes a round, fleshy and generous, if slightly candied palate that just lacks genuine length. Lively and forward, its flavours of orange peel, lemon rind and apple finish with gentle acids.

2004	90	2006	2009
2003	93	2008	2011
2002	95	2010	2014
2001	93	2006	2009
2000	93	2008	2012
1999	94	2004	2007+
1998	93	2006	2010
1997	89	2006	2010
1996	92	2001	2004
1995	94	2003	2007
1994	91	1999	2002

Riddoch

Riddoch Highway, Coonawarra SA 5263. Tel: (08) 8737 2394. Fax: (08) 8737 2397.
Website: www.riddoch.com.au Email: riddoch@wingara.com.au

Region: **Coonawarra** Winemakers: **Wayne Stehbens, Tony Milanowski** Viticulturist: **Chris Brodie**
Chief Executive: **David Yunghanns**

Riddoch is the second label for Coonawarra high-flier Katnook Estate. Its best wines are its reds, typically sound wines that offer moderate weight, with pleasing fruit and oak qualities. The 2002 red releases are lighter and faster to mature than usual, while there is more weight and richness about the 2004 Shiraz. The 2004 Chardonnay is well worth looking at, and might well surprise in masked tastings.

CABERNET SHIRAZ

Coonawarra	$12–$19
Current vintage: 2002	**82**

Dusty herbal and white pepper-like aromas of light berry/plum fruit with cedar/vanilla oak precede a forward, but dilute palate lacking fruit and richness, finishing slightly thin with sappy, metallic tannins.

2002	82	2004	2007
2001	87	2003	2006+
2000	81	2002	2005
1999	79	2000	2001
1998	88	2000	2003+
1997	81	1998	1999
1996	88	1998	2001
1995	84	1997	2000
1994	90	1996	1999

CHARDONNAY

RATING 5

Coonawarra	$12–$19
Current vintage: 2004	**89**

An elegant, restrained and surprisingly sophisticated young chardonnay. Its floral aromas of peach, quince and pineapple reveal undertones of grilled nuts and wheatmeal, while its tightly knit, long and savoury palate is backed by creamy, nutty complexity.

2004	89	2006	2009
2003	86	2004	2005+
2002	87	2003	2004+
2001	87	2002	2003+
1999	87	2000	2001
1998	82	1999	2000

Robertson's Well

Riddoch Highway, Coonawarra SA 5263. Tel: (08) 8736 3380. Fax: (08) 8736 3071. Website: www.fosters.com.au

Region: **Coonawarra** Winemaker: **Andrew Hales** Viticulturist: **Stuart McNab** Chief Executive: **Jamie Odell**

Robertson's Well is one of a large number of Foster's Wine Group brands based in the south-eastern corner of South Australia. The 2004 Cabernet Sauvignon is disappointing, while the Shiraz delivers more brightness and character. Otherwise, they are both fairly honest and represent reasonable value for money.

CABERNET SAUVIGNON

RATING 5

Coonawarra	$20–$29
Current vintage: 2004	86

Jammy and lightly herbal, this leathery and evolving young wine has a modest depth of dark berry, currant, blackberry and plum-like fruit backed by cedary oak. It's just a fraction cooked and sweaty, lacking some brightness, and finishes a little blocky and hard-edged.

2004	86	2009	2012
2003	89	2008	2011+
2000	86	2002	2005+
1999	89	2004	2007+
1998	91	2006	2010
1996	87	2001	2004
1995	88	2000	2003
1994	94	2002	2006
1993	91	2001	2005
1992	92	2000	2004

SHIRAZ

RATING 5

Coonawarra	$20–$29
Current vintage: 2004	88

Polished, smooth and evenly ripened, this fragrant young shiraz presents a fruit-driven aroma of blueberries, blackberries and dark plums backed by gamey, cedary oak and lightly herbaceous undertones. Supple and forward, medium to full in weight, its smooth and approachable palate of jujube-like black and red berry flavours reveals plenty of sweet, newish oak. Framed by fine, pliant tannins, it's drinking now.

2004	88	2006	2009+
2003	91	2005	2008+
2000	81	2002	2005
1999	81	2001	2004
1998	91	2003	2006
1997	87	1999	2002
1996	89	1998	2001

Rochford

Corner Maroondah Highway & Hill Road, Coldstream Vic 3770. Tel: (03) 5962 2119. Fax: (03) 5962 5319. Website: www.rochfordwines.com Email: info@rochfordwines.com

Regions: **Macedon Ranges, Yarra Valley** Winemaker: **David Creed** Chief Executive: **Helmut Konecsny**

Rochford is an energetic small wine business that acquired Eyton On Yarra in 2001 to complement its existing vineyards in the cool Macedon Ranges region. At this stage I am more impressed with its white wines, of which the most consistent is the Pinot Gris from Macedon. The company has big ambitions for its pinot noirs from both regions, but needs to work the vineyards better in order to minimise their levels of herbaceous influence.

MACEDON RANGES CHARDONNAY

RATING 5

Macedon Ranges	$20–$29
Current vintage: 2004	91

A fine, elegant chardonnay likely to flesh out well. Its delicate aromas of melon and tangy citrus fruit reveal nutty oak and spicy undertones of cloves and cinnamon, while its juicy, creamy expression of peach/nectarine fruit is long and harmonious, freshly punctuated by citrusy acids.

2004	91	2006	2009
2002	83	2003	2004+
2000	87	2002	2005
1999	82	2001	2004

MACEDON RANGES PINOT GRIS

RATING 5

Macedon Ranges	$20–$29
Current vintage: 2005	91

Dusty, crisp and generous, this is a zesty young wine with some Alsatian characteristics. Its nutty fragrance of pear, apple and dried flowers precedes a juicy, concentrated and almost crunchy rose oil-like palate whose lychee, pear and apple flavours finish clean and tangy. It reveals excellent shape and depth of varietal fruit.

2005	91	2006	2007+
2004	84	2004	2005
2003	90	2004	2005
2001	88	2002	2003

MACEDON RANGES PINOT NOIR

RATING 4

Macedon Ranges $30–$49
Current vintage: 2003 88

An early-drinking, slightly under-and over-ripened pinot whose confection-like expression of red cherry and berry flavour is backed by herbaceous and herbal undertones as well as meaty, somewhat medicinal influences. Silky-smooth, it reveals a pleasingly expressive palate of red berries and plums backed by some stalk-derived aspects and framed by firmish, but fine-grained tannins.

2003	88	2005	2008+
2002	78	2003	2004
2001	90	2006	2009
2000	90	2005	2008
1999	83	2001	2004
1996	86	1998	2001
1995	91	2000	2003
1994	87	2002	2006
1993	94	2001	2005
1992	94	2000	2004
1991	92	1999	2003

YARRA VALLEY SAUVIGNON BLANC

RATING 5

Yarra Valley $20–$29
Current vintage: 2005 87

Vibrant, spicy and slightly spiky, its estery, tropical and passionfruit-like aromas reveal lightly grassy undertones. Driven by intense juicy fruit, it's mouthfilling and generously flavoured and while it finishes with some tightness, it lacks a little shape and finesse.

2005	87	2005	2006
2004	90	2005	2006
2003	84	2003	2004
2002	90	2003	2004+

Rockford

Krondorf Road, Tanunda SA 5352. Tel: (08) 8563 2720. Fax: (08) 8563 3787. Email: info@rockfordwines.com.au
Region: **Barossa Valley** Winemakers: **Robert O'Callaghan, Chris Ringland** Chief Executive: **David Kalleske**

Rockford is a dedicated small Barossa maker and a committed supporter of the region's small vineyards and their owners. Its wines are made with a refreshing disregard for trends and fashion and are bottled without artefact or manipulation. That is not to suggest that they are made and assembled without great care, experience and dedication, but these are essentially 'natural' wines that faithfully reflect their sites and seasons. Given the extreme heat encountered in 2003, Rockford's reds show the benefits of having mature vineyards and considerable experience in the region.

BASKET PRESS SHIRAZ

RATING 2

Barossa Valley $50–$99
Current vintage: 2003 93

A finely crafted, very meaty and leathery wine from a challenging vintage. Its pungent, meaty and slightly cooked, currant-like aromas reveal reductive, earthy undertones, restrained cedar/vanilla oak and nuances of dried herbs, mint and menthol. Its sumptuous, long and richly flavoured palate of cassis, plums and faintly dehydrated suggestions of currant and raisins is tightly supported by oak and pliant tannins. Has enough fruit to age well, and should become very meaty and leathery.

2003	93	2011	2015
2002	96	2014	2022
2001	89	2009	2013
2000	93	2005	2008+
1999	96	2007	2011+
1998	96	2008	2018
1997	93	2005	2009
1996	96	2016	2026
1995	90	2003	2007
1994	93	2002	2006+
1993	88	2005	2013
1992	89	2000	2004
1991	96	2011	2021
1990	91	1998	2002+
1989	87	1997	2001
1988	93	2000	2004+

BLACK SHIRAZ

RATING 2

Barossa Valley $100–$199
Current disgorging: 2005 93

Silky-smooth, this fine, supple and piercingly intense sparkling shiraz has a spicy, leathery perfume of small dark berries, cherries and plums over meaty, leathery nuances. Its deep flavours of berries, cherries and plums reveal undertones of currants and raisins, roast meats and dried herbs, with a background of forest floor-like complexity.

2005 dis	93	2007	2010+
2004 dis	95	2005	2009
2003 dis	90	2005	2008
2002 dis	96	2006	2010
2001 dis	95	2004	2008
2000 dis	97	2006	2010
1998 dis	91	1999	2003

HAND PICKED RIESLING

Eden Valley	$12–$19
Current vintage: 2003	**86**

A fragrant, confectionary and rather citrusy riesling whose minerally aromas of lime and lemon precede a soft, juicy and forward palate that finishes with soft acids, but slightly thin and dilute.

RATING 3

2003	86	2005	2008
2002	93	2007	2010+
2001	93	2009	2013
2000	95	2005	2008+
1999	93	2004	2007
1998	94	2003	2006+
1997	88	1999	2002
1996	92	2004	2008
1995	93	2000	2003+

LOCAL GROWERS SEMILLON

Barossa Valley	$20–$29
Current vintage: 2003	**89**

Juicy, slightly candied aromas of melon, lemon and honeysuckle overlie dusty nuances of vanilla oak, with creamy and leesy undertones. Smooth and supple, its buttery palate of restrained, tobaccoey melon-like fruit and vanilla oak finishes soft and easy.

RATING 3

2003	89	2005	2008+
2002	92	2007	2010
2001	87	2003	2006
2000	92	2002	2005+
1999	92	2004	2007
1998	93	2003	2006+
1997	91	2005	2009
1996	90	2001	2004
1995	94	2000	2003+
1994	92	1999	2002

MOPPA SPRINGS (Grenache Shiraz Mataro)

Barossa Valley	$20–$29
Current vintage: 2002	**89**

Soft and spirity, this slightly porty, tarry and old-fashioned red has already developed earthy and leathery complexity. Its slightly meaty, prune-like aromas of plums, raisins and cinnamon/clove spices precede a smooth and gentle palate whose spicy and slightly herbal flavours of dark plums and red berries are framed by slightly green-edged and metallic tannins.

RATING 5

2002	89	2007	2010
2001	89	2003	2006+
2000	88	2002	2005
1999	90	2004	2007
1998	89	2003	2006+

RIFLE RANGE CABERNET SAUVIGNON

Barossa Valley	$30–$49
Current vintage: 2003	**92**

A surprisingly rich and concentrated cabernet from a very difficult season for this variety. Its lightly herbal, violet-like aromas of small black and red berries are backed by restrained vanilla/cedary oak with reductive, meaty undertones. Smooth and juicy, framed by velvet tannins, its lively expression of vibrant blackberries, dark plums and sweet cedary oak finishes long and persistent, without a sign of over-ripeness or stress.

RATING 3

2003	92	2011	2015
2002	91	2010	2014
2001	90	2009	2013+
2000	89	2005	2008
1999	94	2007	2011+
1998	94	2010	2018
1997	89	2005	2009
1996	94	2004	2008+
1995	91	2000	2003+
1994	89	1999	2002

ROD & SPUR (Shiraz Cabernet Sauvignon)

Barossa Valley	$30–$49
Current vintage: 2003	**88**

Dusty, herbal aromas of violets, blackcurrants, raspberries, plums and sweet vanilla oak are backed by slightly cooked undertones of currants and tea leaves. Revealing both under-and over-ripe influences, the palate is moderately rich and long, with herbal, dusty and currant-like characters framed by pliant but slightly sappy tannins and backed by secondary oak. The fruit is beginning to show signs of breaking up.

RATING 5

2003	88	2005	2008+
2002	89	2004	2007+
2001	87	2003	2006
2000	91	2005	2008
1999	87	2004	2007

Rosemount Estate

Rosemount Road, Denman NSW 2328. Tel: (02) 6549 6400. Fax: (02) 6549 6499.
Website: www.rosemountestate.com.au Email: rosemountestates.hv@cellardoor.com.au
Regions: **Various** Winemakers: **Charles Whish, Matthew Johnson**
Viticulturists: **Sam Hayne, Nigel Everingham** Chief Executive: **Jamie Odell**

At the time of writing, Foster's was shortly to relaunch the Rosemount brand. Peter Taylor has been actively involved in reshaping the wines in a bid to recapture its excitement and relevance. The overall collection is a mixed bag, with a number of high-profile brands such as Balmoral and Roxburgh not really doing enough in recent years to justify their elevated status. Not that it affects the wines in any way, but the Rosemount winery at Denman, in the Upper Hunter Valley, has been put on the market by Foster's.

BALMORAL SYRAH

RATING **4**

McLaren Vale			$50–$99
Current vintage: 2002			**87**

A very oaky and unsophisticated wine of short-term charm and appeal made from unevenly ripened fruit. Its deep, briary and confiture-like aromas of blackberries, plums and cassis are backed by smoky dark chocolate/vanilla oak with lightly herbal tones. Full to medium in weight, it's jammy and forward, reliant on sweet oak and alcohol for palate intensity. It is underpinned by a greenish thread and lacks genuine definition.

2002	87	2007	2010
2001	91	2009	2013
2000	89	2005	2008
1999	90	2004	2007
1998	97	2010	2018
1997	90	2002	2005
1996	94	2004	2008
1995	97	2007	2015
1994	95	2002	2006+
1993	88	1998	2001
1992	96	2000	2004+
1991	95	2003	2011
1990	94	2002	2010
1989	94	1997	2003+

CABERNET SAUVIGNON

RATING **5**

Various			$5–$11
Current vintage: 2003			**89**

A lively and flavoursome cabernet with fruit and structure. Its sweet, lightly jammy aromas of cassis and plums reveal earthy undertones of mint and violets, with a background of creamy vanilla oak. Smooth and elegant, its vibrant palate of minty, jujube-like blackberry fruit and vanilla/chocolate oak is supported by a firm undercarriage of assertive, bony tannins.

2003	89	2005	2008+
2001	80	2002	2003
2000	81	2002	2005
1999	87	2000	2001
1998	87	2000	2003
1996	84	1998	2001

CHARDONNAY

Various			$5–$11
Current vintage: 2005			**86**

Sweet peachy, creamy and buttery aromas of juicy chardonnay fruit and vanilla oak precede a flavoursome, round and generous mouthful of fruit. Soft and smooth, it's spotlessly clean and vibrant, finishing with lingering flavour.

2005	86	2006	2007
2004	86	2004	2005+
2003	82	2004	2005+
2002	87	2003	2004+
2001	83	2002	2003
2000	87	2001	2002
1999	87	2000	2001
1998	90	2000	2003

GIANTS CREEK CHARDONNAY

RATING **4**

Upper Hunter Valley			$30–$49
Current vintage: 2004			**87**

Its wild, slightly meaty, oxidative and floral aromas reveal a pungent, leesy and funky charcuterie-like element with an underlying depth of citrus, melon and tobaccoey fruit and restrained vanilla oak. Initially round and juicy, its ripe, forward expression of cumquat, peach and nectarine fruit becomes more savoury and meaty down the palate, finishing with soft acids and suggestions of green melons. Slightly lacking in length and acidity, and possibly with some stuck ferment influences.

2004	87	2006	2009
2002	93	2007	2010
2001	90	2003	2006+
1999	93	2004	2007
1998	90	2003	2006
1997	87	2002	2005
1996	90	2001	2004
1995	89	1997	2000
1994	90	1999	2002
1993	94	1998	2001
1992	84	1994	1997

GSM

McLaren Vale	$20–$29
Current vintage: 2002	90

A more savoury and very spicy expression of this Southern Rhône blend whose meaty, leathery aromas of dark plums, prunes and blackberries are backed by undertones of dark chocolate and treacle. Round and juicy, its firm and sumptuous palate bursts with vibrant but slightly shrivelled plum and blueberry fruits, finishing with soft tannins and lingering suggestions of currants and treacle.

2002	90	2007	2010
2001	91	2006	2009
1999	93	2007	2011
1998	90	2003	2006
1997	88	1999	2002+
1996	90	2001	2004
1995	86	2003	2007
1994	88	1999	2002

MOUNTAIN BLUE

Mudgee	$30–$49
Current vintage: 2001	95

A welcome return to form for this important Mudgee label, delivering a firm, complete and savoury palate of depth and structure. Its spicy white pepper fragrance of blackberries and violets is backed by sweet gamey chocolate/vanilla oak and a meaty, slightly reductive and smoky suggestion of animal hide. Full to medium in weight, it's smooth and polished, delivering a plump, juicy expression of dark plums and berries framed by a drying extract and finishing with lingering meaty and sour-edged fruit qualities.

2001	95	2013	2021
2000	87	2005	2008+
1999	82	2001	2004+
1998	96	2010	2018
1997	95	2005	2009
1996	95	2008	2016
1995	95	2007	2015
1994	93	2006	2014

ORANGE VINEYARD CABERNET SAUVIGNON

Orange	$20–$29
Current vintage: 2002	84

Thin, green and sappy, with a closed, herbal aroma of plums, cedar/vanilla oak and vegetal undertones. Meaty and herbaceous, its slightly soupy palate begins with some sweet, forward red and black berry flavours but thins out towards a greenish finish of metallic tannins.

2002	84	2004	2007+
2000	90	2008	2012+
1999	86	2001	2004+
1998	87	2003	2006
1997	87	2002	2005
1996	91	2004	2008
1995	87	2003	2007

ORANGE VINEYARD CHARDONNAY

Orange	$20–$29
Current vintage: 2003	93

Quite a punchy but shapely and elegant chardonnay with a deep, vibrant core of peach and citrusy flavours that culminate in a lingering savoury and wheatmeal-like finish. There's a hint of dried flowers and a smoky meatiness beneath its cumquat and stonefruit aromas, while its soft and supple palate presents finely integrated fruit and butterscotch-like malolactic qualities.

2003	93	2005	2008+
2002	89	2004	2007+
2001	95	2006	2009
2000	94	2002	2005+
1999	95	2004	2007
1998	93	2003	2006
1997	94	2005	2009
1996	93	2001	2004
1995	93	2003	2007
1994	94	1999	2002

ORANGE VINEYARD MERLOT

Orange	$20–$29
Current vintage: 2001	89

Savoury, but herbal merlot with a meaty, earthy bouquet of plums and tobacco underpinned by fine-grained cedary oak. Elegant, supple and tightly knit, its gentle palate delivers plum and dark cherry flavours and undergrowth-like complexity over sappy, tobaccoey influences.

2001	89	2006	2009+
2000	89	2005	2008
1999	83	2001	2004
1998	93	2003	2006+

ROXBURGH CHARDONNAY

Upper Hunter Valley	$50–$99
Current vintage: 2003	90

Backed by slightly edgy and splintery oak, intense aromas of grapefruit and mango show some toasty development. Slightly oily, its long, creamy palate has a nougat-like quality, delivering concentrated and generous flavours of ripe juicy fruit. It finishes slightly sweet, with some raw-edged oak, but should settle down with time.

2003	90	2008	2011
2002	94	2004	2007
2001	91	2003	2006+
1999	91	2004	2007
1998	95	2003	2006+
1997	91	2002	2005
1996	94	2002	2006
1995	94	2000	2003
1994	91	1999	2001
1993	88	1998	2001
1992	88	1997	2000
1991	94	2003	2011

SHIRAZ

Various	$5–$11
Current vintage: 2004	87

An honest, spicy and slightly confectionary shiraz whose aromas of cassis, raspberries and plums are backed by sweet vanilla and cedary oak plus a whiff of white pepper. Smooth and supple, its vibrant, jammy palate of intense plum and small black and red berry flavours has a pliant spine of fine tannin and lingering earthy undertones.

2004	87	2006	2009
2003	88	2005	2008
2002	86	2003	2004+
2001	86	2002	2003+
2000	86	2001	2002
1999	87	2000	2001
1998	89	2000	2003+
1997	87	1999	2002

SHOW RESERVE CABERNET SAUVIGNON

Coonawarra	$20–$29
Current vintage: 2003	83

Simple, lightly dusty and herbal aromas of cassis, mulberries and cedar/vanilla oak reveal undertones of capsicum. Medium to full in weight, its green-edged palate begins with some light and attractive forward fruit quality, but becomes quite hollow and dilute, lacking richness and depth. Framed by drying, powdery tannins, it finishes with dusty, tobaccoey nuances.

2003	83	2005	2008+
2002	88	2007	2010
2001	87	2006	2009
2000	93	2008	2012
1999	91	2007	2011+
1998	94	2010	2018
1997	90	2002	2005+
1996	95	2004	2008+
1995	88	2000	2003
1994	95	2006	2014
1993	93	2001	2005
1992	94	2004	2012
1991	87	2003	2011

SHOW RESERVE CHARDONNAY

Upper Hunter Valley	$20–$29
Current vintage: 2004	89

Pungent aromas of honeydew melon are backed by nuances of marmalade and undertones of sweet vanilla and lightly charry oak. Smooth and creamy, it's round and soft, with a delicate expression of melon, peach and nectarine that lacks great length and becomes a little eggy. Oak is restrained, while the wine is underpinned by fine-grained phenolics.

2004	89	2006	2009
2002	91	2004	2007
2001	87	2002	2003
2000	95	2005	2008+
1999	94	2004	2007
1998	93	2006	2010
1997	93	2002	2005+
1996	95	2004	2008+
1995	93	2003	2007
1994	90	2002	2006
1993	91	1998	2001

SHOW RESERVE SEMILLON

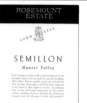

Hunter Valley	$20–$29
Current vintage: 2003	90

This oak-matured semillon will appreciate a little more time in the bottle. Its melon and lemon juice-like aromas have a sweet and lightly toasty butter/vanilla oak background, with complex meaty undertones of creamy, leesy influences. Richly textured and slightly oily, it's round and generous, presenting a seamless length of juicy green melon fruit and sweet, buttery vanilla oak.

2003	90	2008	2011
2002	90	2007	2010
2000	92	2005	2008
1998	92	2006	2010
1997	91	2005	2009
1996	93	2004	2008
1995	93	2003	2007
1991	89	1996	1999
1990	93	1998	2002
1989	94	1997	2001+

SHOW RESERVE SHIRAZ

RATING **5**

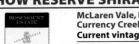

McLaren Vale, Langhorne Creek, Currency Creek $20–$29
Current vintage: 2001 90

Rather meaty, cooked and stewy aromas of mocha, chocolate, prunes and currants are backed by nuances of white pepper, cloves and cinnamon, with leathery, animal hide-like undertones. Its palate is rich and chunky, delivering a powerful, show-stopping expression of super-ripe meaty and leathery shiraz lifted by sweet oak. A very impressive example of its type, but hasn't the depth of fruit to cellar.

2001	90	2006	2009
2000	87	2002	2005+
1999	86	2004	2007
1998	88	2003	2006
1997	88	2002	2005
1996	95	2004	2008
1995	91	2003	2007

TRADITIONAL (Cabernet blend)

RATING **5**

McLaren Vale, Langhorne Creek $20–$29
Current vintage: 2002 88

Minty, vegetal and meaty aromas of stewed and under-ripe berry/plum fruit with greenish undertones precede an assertive but slightly herbaceous palate given richness and flavour, thanks to its meaty component of petit verdot. While it offers a good depth of minty, plummy and blackberry-like fruit, it is somewhat stressed and lacking in brightness.

2002	88	2007	2010
2001	89	2003	2006+
2000	87	2002	2005+
1999	88	2001	2004
1998	93	2006	2010
1997	90	2002	2005
1996	91	2004	2008

Rosily Vineyard

RSM 488 Yelverton Road, Busselton WA 6280. Tel: (08) 9755 6336. Fax: (08) 9755 6336.
Website: www.rosily.com.au Email: info@rosily.com.au
Region: **Margaret River** Winemaker: **Mike Lemmes** Chief Executives: **Mike Scott & Ken Allan**

Rosily is an emergent Margaret River vineyard whose Cabernet Sauvignon turned over a positive leaf in 2004, producing a deeply flavoured wine framed by smooth tannin, thanks to a favourable vintage and increasing vine age. The whites continue to impress, especially the tightly focused and lightly mineral Chardonnay 2005.

CABERNET SAUVIGNON

RATING **5**

Margaret River $20–$29
Current vintage: 2004 90

Intense, confiture-like aromas of blackberries, raspberries and cassis are backed by sweet chocolate/vanilla oak, with attractive undertones of violets. Smooth and creamy, and supported by a fine spine of pliant tannins, it delivers deep flavours of mulberries, blackberries and cassis tightly knit with creamy mocha/vanilla oak. Likely to develop more complexity with time.

2004	90	2009	2012
2003	87	2005	2008+
2002	88	2010	2014
2001	87	2003	2006
2000	81	2002	2005

CHARDONNAY

RATING **4**

Margaret River $20–$29
Current vintage: 2005 91

Finely crafted, complex and likely to build nicely in the bottle, this savoury and tightly focused young chardonnay has an assertive aroma of grapefruit, peach and tropical fruits plus toasty vanilla oak with undertones of wheatmeal. Smooth and restrained, its generous weight of fruit overlies slightly meaty and mineral complexity, with buttery vanilla oak in support.

2005	91	2007	2010+
2004	88	2006	2009
2001	93	2003	2006+
2000	92	2002	2005+

A
B
C
D
E
F
G
H
I
J
K
L
M
N
O
P
Q
R
S
T
U
V
W
X
Y
Z

SAUVIGNON BLANC

Margaret River $20–$29
Current vintage: 2005 87

Sound, honest and flavoursome, with a lightly grassy aroma of melon-like fruit and a moderately long, fresh and juicy palate. Lively passionfruit and green melon flavours are generous enough without being especially complex.

2005	87	2005	2006+
2004	82	2004	2005
2003	91	2003	2004+
2002	88	2002	2003
2001	82	2001	2002

Ross Estate

Barossa Valley Highway, Lyndoch SA 5351. Tel: (08) 8524 4033. Fax: (08) 8524 4533.
Website: www.rossestate.com.au Email: rossestate@rossestate.com.au
Region: **Barossa Valley** Winemaker: **Rod Chapman** Chief Executive: **Darius Ross**

In 1993 the Ross family bought a 110 hectare vineyard near Lyndoch in the Barossa Valley. It hasn't taken long for their reds to evolve into a house style I greatly admire, especially since it's the opposite of what too many Barossa vignerons are doing today. These wines are focused on ripe but not overcooked fruit, are tightly integrated with oak and tannins, and deliver a long, seamless palate of vibrant flavour. They cellar well without being heavy or extracted. The 2004 Shiraz is very ripe, but retains plenty of brightness.

CABERNET SAUVIGNON

Barossa Valley $20–$29
Current vintage: 2003 82

Richly flavoured, firm and relatively fast-maturing, this is a slightly cooked and currant-like cabernet. Its bouquet is raisined and meaty, while the palate offers a rather hollow and raw-edged expression of plum, currant and blackberry-like fruit.

2003	82	2008	2011
2002	90	2007	2010+
2001	88	2006	2009
2000	89	2005	2008
1999	83	2001	2004+

OLD VINE GRENACHE

Barossa Valley $20–$29
Current vintage: 2004 82

Confiture-like aromas of sweet raspberries, blackberries and spice precede a simple, juicy and uninspiring palate that falls away towards a thin, sweet and confectionary finish.

2004	82	2006	2009
2003	92	2005	2008+
2002	83	2004	2007
2001	89	2003	2006+
2000	88	2002	2005
1999	81	2001	2004

SHIRAZ

Barossa Valley $20–$29
Current vintage: 2004 90

An elegant, deeply flavoured and finely structured Barossa shiraz that would have been even better with some finer cooperage. Its lightly floral, spicy fragrance of blackberries, blackcurrants, dark plums overlies nuances of dried herbs. Long and savoury, its slightly meaty aspect of currants, prunes and treacle reflects considerable ripeness, but there is a powerful presence of vibrant dark berry and plum flavours. It finishes with underlying herbal notes and a salty hint of mineral.

2004	90	2009	2012+
2002	93	2007	2010+
2001	90	2006	2009+
2000	88	2005	2008
1999	86	2001	2004+

Rothbury Estate, The

Broke Road, Pokolbin NSW 2320. Tel: (02) 4998 7555. Fax: (02) 4998 7553.
Website: www.fosters.com.au

Region: **Lower Hunter Valley** Winemaker: **Mike DeGaris** Chief Executive: **Jamie Odell**

Some honest, if unspectacular, releases under the Neil McGuigan label have been overshadowed by some fine and very regional Brokenback wines — especially the Semillon and Chardonnay, of which the 2002 editions are a big step forward. Just prior to printing this edition, Rothbury's physical presence, but not the wine brand, was sold to Hope Estate. Its owner, Michael Hope, intends to return the facility to its former glory as a home of wine education and festivities.

BROKENBACK CHARDONNAY
RATING 5

Lower Hunter Valley	$20–$29	2002	92	2004	2007
Current vintage: 2002	**92**	2001	86	2002	2003
		2000	87	2002	2005
		1996	88	1998	2001

A smooth, charmingly elegant and flavoursome young chardonnay with a floral and lightly nutty aroma of peachy fruit and restrained vanilla oak, backed by creamy suggestions of extended lees contact. A gentle, supple and fluffy palate of stone-fruits and creamy oak finishes with soft acidity.

BROKENBACK SEMILLON
RATING 4

Lower Hunter Valley	$20–$29	2002	90	2007	2010+
Current vintage: 2002	**90**	2001	82	2003	2006
		2000	91	2008	2012
		1998	92	2003	2006
		1997	94	2005	2009

Likely to evolve into a richer style, its floral aromas of lemon, apple and melon are well ripened, without a hint of grassiness. Initially round and juicy, it becomes tighter and more restrained down the palate, finishing chalky, with lemony acids. Tight and focused.

Rufus Stone

Tyrrell's, Broke Road, Pokolbin NSW 2320. Tel: (02) 4993 7000. Fax: (02) 4998 7723.
Website: www.tyrrells.com.au Email: tyrrells@tyrrells.com.au

Regions: **Heathcote, McLaren Vale** Winemakers: **Andrew Spinaze, Mark Richardson** Chief Executive: **Bruce Tyrrell**

A brand owned by Tyrrell's that features red wines sourced from outside the company's native Hunter Valley, Rufus Stone is a well-priced source of medium to full-bodied reds usually made without excessive ripeness or extract, although the 2004 Heathcote Shiraz does stray into over-ripeness. When an ampellographer recently discovered that its McLaren Vale plantings of 'merlot' were actually malbec, the Merlot was discontinued in favour of a Cabernet Sauvignon Malbec, whose 2004 vintage is easily the pick of the current releases.

HEATHCOTE SHIRAZ
RATING 5

Heathcote	$20–$29	2004	86	2006	2009
Current vintage: 2004	**86**	2003	88	2008	2011
		2002	88	2004	2007
		2001	87	2003	2006
		2000	92	2005	2008+
		1999	91	2004	2007
		1998	88	2006	2010
		1997	92	2002	2005+

Rather a contrived shiraz with meaty, Bovril-like aromas of red and black berries and smoky oak plus a spicy, assertive and dehydrated palate whose currant-like fruit lacks richness and presence in mid palate. Framed by firmish tannins with metallic edges and revealing a faintly salty aspect, it does deliver some ripe fruit but remains meaty and hollow.

McLAREN VALE CABERNET SAUVIGNON MALBEC
RATING 5

McLaren Vale	$20–$29	2004	91	2012	2016+
Current vintage: 2004	**91**	2003	83	2005	2008
		2002	89	2007	2010+

Vibrant aromas of black and red berries are backed by dark chocolate, cedar and vanilla oak, with earthy undertones of mocha and dark olives. It's smooth, measured and deeply flavoured, bursting with intense forest berry flavours with meaty undertones offset by a mineral saltiness. Bound by fine-grained and powdery tannins, it's harmoniously structured, with length and balance, finishing dry and savoury.

McLAREN VALE SHIRAZ

RATING 4

McLaren Vale	$20–$29
Current vintage: 2004	88

Spicy and slightly jammy, this fruit-driven McLaren Vale shiraz has a fresh aroma of small dark berries and plums backed by cedar/mocha/vanilla oak and nutmeg/clove-like spices. Full to medium weight, its briary and spicy palate of small fruit flavours and cedar/vanilla oak is framed by fine, supple tannins.

2004	88	2006	2009+
2003	90	2008	2011
2002	91	2010	2014+
2000	87	2002	2005+
1999	90	2004	2007
1998	93	2003	2006+
1997	93	2002	2005
1996	84	2001	2004

Russet Ridge

Corner Caves Road & Riddoch Highway, Naracoorte SA 5271. Tel: (08) 8762 0114. Fax: (08) 8762 0341
Website: www.russetridge.com.au Email: contact_us@orlando.com
Region: **Limestone Coast** Winemakers: **Don Young, Hylton McLean, Nick Bruer** Viticulturist: **Martin Wirper**
Chief Executive: **Laurent Lacassgne**

Russet Ridge is a Limestone Coast-sourced brand of Orlando Wyndham red wine. The tightly focused 2002 vintage represents a strong return to its mid-1990s form.

CABERNET SHIRAZ MERLOT

RATING 5

Coonawarra	$12–$19
Current vintage: 2002	92

A fine, elegant, flavoursome and smoothly structured wine whose lively berry/plum fruits are cleverly integrated into a modestly generous and harmonious palate of freshness and focus. Its sweet oak and fine tannins appropriately offset its vibrant fruit.

2002	92	2007	2010+
1999	82	2001	2004+
1998	88	2003	2006
1997	86	2002	2005
1996	92	2001	2004+
1995	85	2000	2003
1994	92	1999	2002
1993	90	2001	2005
1992	89	2000	2004

Rymill

Riddoch Highway, Coonawarra SA 5263. Tel: (08) 8736 5001. Fax: (08) 8736 5040.
Website: www.rymill.com.au Email: winery@rymill.com.au
Region: **Coonawarra** Winemakers: **John Innes, Sandrine Gimon** Viticulturist: **Grant Oschar**
Chief Executive: **John Innes**

Rymill is a small to medium-sized Coonawarra operation with some significant vine plantings within the region's newly-designated boundaries but well outside its traditionally tighter-focused bounds around the Hundreds of Comaum and Penola. Perhaps the introduction of young vine material from these new vineyards is the cause of the very herbaceous nature of its current release reds. If not, the management of the older Rymill vineyards clearly need a rethink.

CABERNET SAUVIGNON

RATING 5

Coonawarra	$20–$29
Current vintage: 2002	81

Leafy, capsicum-like aromas of shaded fruit precede a green and sappy palate whose modest fruit sweetness is entirely overshadowed by its under-ripe influences.

2002	81	2007	2010
2001	88	2009	2013
2000	84	2005	2008
1999	86	2004	2007
1998	91	2006	2010
1997	86	2002	2005
1996	90	2004	2008
1995	88	2000	2003+
1994	89	2002	2006+
1993	83	1995	1998
1992	88	2000	2004+

MC² MERLOT CABERNETS

RATING 5

Coonawarra	$12–$19
Current vintage: 2003	81

An ethereal and herbaceous red whose meaty, vegetal and brackish aromas of ageing plum-like fruit and cedary oak precede a sappy and lightly fruited palate of medium weight, framed by green-edged tannins.

2003	81	2005	2008
2001	89	2006	2009+
2000	89	2005	2008
1999	88	2001	2004
1998	81	2000	2003
1997	91	1999	2002
1996	89	1998	2001
1995	88	1997	2000

SHIRAZ

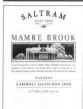

Coonawarra	$20–$29	2002	84	2004	2007+
Current vintage: 2002	**84**	2001	87	2006	2009

Spicy, herbal and leathery aromas of dark berries and plums overlie earthy nuances of undergrowth and capsicum. Smooth and gentle, its palate begins with a lively expression of blackberry and plum flavours, but finishes slightly short, with herbal undertones and lingering cedar/vanilla oak influences. Lacks length of fruit and genuine ripeness.

2000	77
1999	92
1998	91
1997	91
1996	89
1995	88
1994	82

2002	2005
2004	2007+
2003	2006
2002	2006+
2004	2005
2000	2003
1999	2002+

Saltram

Nuriootpa-Angaston Road, Angaston SA 5353. Tel: (08) 8564 3355. Fax: (08) 8564 2209.
Website: www.saltramwines.com.au Email: cellardoor@saltramestate.com.au

Region: **Barossa** Winemaker: **Nigel Dolan** Viticulturist: **Murray Heidenreich** Chief Executive: **Jamie Odell**

Saltram's premier wines from the 2004 vintage showcase the best that its Mamre Brook label can deliver. This was one of those perfect cabernet vintages in the Barossa, and the Mamre Brook Cabernet Sauvignon is not only a classic expression of Barossa cabernet, but perhaps the best-value red in Australia today. The Shiraz, while not having quite the same cut and polish, is excellent. Tracking back to 2002, the No. 1 Shiraz is almost predictably finely balanced, smooth and concentrated.

MAMRE BROOK CABERNET SAUVIGNON

RATING **4**

Barossa Valley	$20–$29
Current vintage: 2004	**95**

A stunningly varietal cabernet whose highly aromatic perfume of cassis, violets and restrained cedar/vanilla oak is underpinned by minty nuances of crushed leaves. Full to medium in weight, its fine and pristine palate of crystalline cassis/plum flavours is tightly knit with sweet, creamy vanilla oak and supported by a chalky spine of powdery tannins. There's a suppleness and softness about this stylish and exceptionally varietal wine, with a lingering finish of star anise.

2004	95	2024	2034
2003	90	2011	2015
2002	95	2014	2022
2001	88	2006	2009
2000	88	2005	2008
1999	90	2004	2007
1998	95	2010	2018
1997	93	2005	2009
1996	93	2008	2016
1995	88	1997	2000
1994	90	2002	2006
1993	91	1998	2001
1988	85	1993	1998
1986	93	2006	2016

MAMRE BROOK CHARDONNAY

RATING **5**

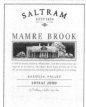

South Australia	$20–$29
Current vintage: 2004	**88**

A pleasingly succulent, round shorter-term wine of freshness and depth. Its slightly brassy, peachy and creamy aromas reveal some buttery, honeyed development over nuances of wheatmeal. Its generous palate of juicy ripe fruit and toasty vanilla oak finishes with attractive length and soft acids.

2004	88	2006	2009
2003	87	2005	2008
2002	90	2004	2007
2001	89	2003	2006
2000	90	2002	2005+
1999	87	2000	2001
1998	87	2000	2003
1997	83	1998	1999
1996	89	1998	2001

MAMRE BROOK SHIRAZ

RATING **4**

Barossa Valley	$20–$29
Current vintage: 2004	**93**

A supple, deeply flavoured and crowd-pleasing shiraz of the early-drinking Barossa style. Its heady, floral and slightly minty aromas of wild blueberries, raspberry confection and pristine blackcurrant fruit overlie nuances of plums and sweet vanilla oak. Silky-smooth and luscious, its juicy expression of blackberries, raspberries and creamy vanilla oak is supported by fine tannins and finished with bright, refreshing acids. It leaves a spicy fennellike aftertaste.

2004	93	2009	2012+
2003	89	2008	2011
2002	93	2010	2014
2001	88	2003	2006+
2000	89	2005	2008
1999	93	2007	2011+
1998	95	2006	2010
1997	95	2005	2009+
1996	90	2001	2004

NO. 1 SHIRAZ

RATING **2**

Barossa Valley $50–$99
Current vintage: 2002   95

Heady, briary aromas of crushed violets, cassis, raspberries and redcurrants overlie suggestions of blood plums, lightly smoky vanilla oak, plus a whiff of tar and treacle. Smooth and silky, it's a supremely focused, sumptuous and seamless Barossa shiraz whose slightly spicy and sour-edged deep fruit flavours are matched by restrained oak and framed by velvet-like tannins. It's finely balanced and very expressive, but might reveal more than a faint touch of rustic meatiness in years to come.

2002	95	2014	2022
2001	94	2009	2013
2000	90	2005	2008+
1999	94	2007	2011+
1998	96	2010	2018
1997	88	2005	2009
1996	94	2008	2016
1995	93	2003	2007+
1994	93	2002	2006

Sandalford

3210 West Swan Road, Caversham WA 6055. Tel: (08) 9374 9374. Fax: (08) 9274 2154.
Website: www.sandalford.com   Email: sandalford@sandalford.com

Region: **Margaret River** Winemaker: **Paul Boulden** Viticulturist: **Peter Traeger** Chief Executive: **Grant Brinklow**

Sandalford is a moderately large Margaret River-based producer whose wines have traditionally been very affordably priced. The pick of its current releases is the tightly crafted 2004 Cabernet Sauvignon. Somehow I get the feeling that for Sandalford to become a really solid business, it will have to take its wines either upward and more pricey and profitable, or make them cheaper and more competitive against the larger makers. I hope it selects the former.

CABERNET SAUVIGNON

RATING **4**

Margaret River $30–$49
Current vintage: 2004   90

A lively young cabernet whose attractive dark plum, cherry and berry flavours are backed by cedary oak and a firmish spine of powdery but pliant tannins. The nose is lifted by floral suggestions of violets, redcurrants and raspberries, while the palate is finely honed, balanced and supple.

2004	90	2012	2026
2003	90	2008	2011
2002	90	2007	2010+
2001	90	2009	2013
2000	88	2005	2008
1999	87	2004	2007
1998	84	2000	2003
1997	84	1999	2002+
1996	81	1998	2001
1995	92	2000	2003
1994	92	2002	2006
1993	81	1998	2001
1992	87	1994	1997
1991	87	1999	2003
1990	90	2002	2010
1989	85	2001	2009

CHARDONNAY

RATING **5**

Margaret River $30–$49
Current vintage: 2004   85

An honest, if rather cloying and confectionary chardonnay whose buttery, grapefruit and pineapple-like aromas precede a forward, flavoursome and rather coarse palate that finishes rather deficient in genuine freshness.

2004	85	2005	2006+
2003	89	2005	2008
2002	90	2004	2007
2001	87	2003	2006
1999	94	2004	2007
1998	84	2000	2003
1997	84	1998	1999
1996	89	1998	2001
1994	90	1999	2002

RIESLING

RATING **5**

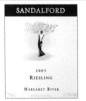

Margaret River $20–$29
Current vintage: 2005   88

A generous and crisply defined riesling with fresh, floral aromas of apple, pear and lemon zest and a juicy, almost crunchy palate of vibrant, tangy fruit. Its pleasing length of citrusy fruit culminates in a lingering and refreshing finish with lingering nuances of lime marmalade.

2005	88	2007	2010+
2004	89	2006	2009+
2003	89	2005	2008
2002	90	2007	2010
2001	83	2002	2003
2000	93	2005	2008+
1998	90	2006	2010

SHIRAZ

Margaret River $30–$49
Current vintage: 2003 88

A very woody shiraz whose old-fashioned and leathery bouquet of jammy blackberries, plums and cassis is backed by minty undertones and toasty vanilla/hocolate oak. Very ripe, juicy and oaky, without any real regional distinction, it's forward and meaty, with a moderately long expression of blackberry and plum fruit that finishes with a firm grip of drying tannin and plenty of sweet oak.

2003	88	2005	2008+
2002	84	2003	2004+
2001	89	2006	2009
1999	81	2001	2004
1998	83	2000	2003
1997	82	1999	2002+
1996	87	2001	2004
1995	89	2003	2007
1994	90	2002	2006
1993	89	1998	2001

VERDELHO

RATING 4

Margaret River $20–$29
Current vintage: 2005 86

Rather a coarse and broad verdelho with herbal, cashew-like aromas of dusty tropical fruit. Rather simple, its oily, somewhat flabby palate lacks cut and definition, but the wine is clean and approachable.

2005	86	2006	2007
2004	90	2006	2009
2003	90	2005	2008
2002	90	2004	2007
2001	84	2006	2009
2000	77	2001	2002
1999	89	2001	2004
1998	88	2003	2006
1997	83	1998	1999

Sandstone

PO Box 346, Cowaramup WA 6284. Tel: (08) 9755 6271. Fax: (08) 9755 6292. Email: info@sandstonewines.com.au

Region: **Margaret River** Winemaker: **Jan McIntosh** Chief Executive: **Jan McIntosh**

Jan McIntosh is an immensely talented winemaker whose two Margaret River wines are varietal expressions of Semillon and Cabernet Sauvignon. Typically, these are generously flavoured, smooth and seamlessly oaked and integrated. Both these wines have established long track records in the cellar.

CABERNET SAUVIGNON

RATING 4

Margaret River $30–$49
Current vintage: 2003 87

An unusual cabernet that marries youthful, ageing and herbaceous aspects of the variety. Its minty, herbal, floral and menthol-like aromas of sweet berries and plums are backed by flat, cedary oak. Its juicy palate of cassis, cranberry and plum-like fruit is framed by sappy tannins and finished with slightly green-edged acids. It shows some leathery development.

2003	87	2008	2011
2002	87	2007	2010+
2000	86	2002	2005+
1999	95	2011	2019
1998	92	2006	2010
1996	89	2004	2008
1995	87	2003	2007
1993	88	2001	2005
1992	92	2004	2012
1991	90	2003	2011
1990	89	1998	2002
1989	91	1997	2001

SEMILLON

RATING 4

Margaret River $20–$29
Current vintage: 2004 93

A luscious, smooth and carefully honed oak-fermented semillon whose dusty, lightly herbal and grassy aromas of melon and gooseberry are tightly knit with smoky vanilla oak. Its long, creamy palate of sumptuous melon and honeysuckle-like fruit and beautifully crafted, lightly charry oak extends towards a clean, soft and persistent silky finish.

2004	93	2009	2012
2003	95	2008	2011
2002	87	2007	2010
2001	91	2006	2009
2000	84	2002	2005+
1999	90	2004	2007
1998	94	2003	2006
1997	94	2002	2005
1995	94	2003	2007
1994	93	1999	2002
1993	93	2001	2005

Scotchmans Hill

190 Scotchmans Road, Drysdale Vic 3222. Tel: (03) 5251 3176. Fax: (03) 5253 1743.
Website: www.scotchmanshill.com.au Email: info@scotchmans.com.au

Region: **Geelong** Winemaker: **Robin Brockett** Viticulturist: **Robin Brockett**
Chief Executives: **David & Vivienne Browne**

Scotchmans Hill is a successful small winery business located near Geelong, on Melbourne's Port Phillip Bay. The drought hasn't made viticulture easy for the last few years yet its wines are typically very true to variety, honest and generous. The best are the firm and slightly herbal Pinot Noir and the luscious and grassy Sauvignon Blanc.

CHARDONNAY

Geelong	$20–$29
Current vintage: 2004	**87**

A creamy, peachy and citrusy chardonnay with assertive caramel and butterscotch-like malolactic influences that perhaps detract from its freshness and brightness. Heavily worked, with creamy, leesy undertones, it's smooth and generous, with slightly candied melon, peach and sweet vanilla oak flavours, but finishes slightly flat, with soft acids.

2004	87	2005	2006+
2003	81	2004	2005
2002	86	2004	2007
2001	83	2002	2003
2000	86	2002	2005
1999	82	2000	2001
1998	87	1999	2000
1997	91	1998	2002

PINOT NOIR

RATING **5**

Geelong	$20–$29
Current vintage: 2004	**88**

Flavoursome, honest and varietal, this firm and slightly gritty young pinot just lacks cut and polish. Its sweet floral aromas of rose petals, spicy cherries, cinnamon and restrained oak precede a moderately rich palate whose vibrant cherry, raspberry and plum-like fruit reveals some herbal undertones. The tannins are just a little disjointed and unresolved for its weight of fruit.

2004	88	2006	2009
2003	88	2005	2008
2002	88	2004	2007
2001	89	2002	2006
2000	84	2001	2002
1999	87	2000	2001+
1998	86	1999	2000
1997	93	2002	2005

SAUVIGNON BLANC

RATING **5**

Geelong	$12–$19
Current vintage: 2005	**89**

A lively, well made and refreshing sauvignon blanc whose herbaceous aromas of gooseberries, passionfruit and cut grass precede a juicy, forward and vibrant palate. Lacking great length, its lychee and passionfruit flavours thin out a little towards the finish, but remain clean and refreshing.

2005	89	2006	2007
2004	85	2005	2006
2003	89	2003	2004+
2002	89	2003	2004
2001	90	2002	2003+
2000	88	2001	2002

SHIRAZ

RATING **4**

Geelong	$20–$29
Current vintage: 2004	**81**

Autumnal and slightly meaty aromas of decaying leaves, blackberries, plums and currants with spicy and herbal undertones. Lacking mid-palate stuffing, its under-and over-ripe expression of currant, prunes, raisins and plums is bound by a metallic cut of green-edged tannin.

2004	81	2006	2009
2003	90	2005	2008+
2000	91	2002	2005+
1999	89	2001	2004+

Seppelt

Moyston Road, Great Western Vic 3377. Tel: (03) 5361 2222. Fax: (03) 5361 2200.
Website: www.seppelt.com.au Email: gwcd@cellar-door.com.au
Seppeltsfield Road, Seppeltsfield via Nuriootpa SA 5355. Tel: (08) 8568 6200. Fax: (08) 8562 8333.
Website: www.seppelt.com.au Email: seppelt.bv@cellar-door.com.au
Regions: **Great Western, Drumborg, Barooga, Barossa**
Winemakers: **Arthur O'Connor, James Godfrey** Viticulturist: **Paul Dakis** Chief Executive: **Jamie Odell**

While it is with plenty of regret that Foster's recently announced its imminent sale of the Seppeltsfield fortified wines and the unique Seppeltsfield facility in the Barossa, the underlying sense behind the move is obvious. Fortunately it has no such plans to divest itself of the Great Western arm of the brand, which, under Arthur O'Connor, is going from strength to strength. Recently in Melbourne, bottles of Chalambar Shiraz 2004 were advertised for less than $20 a bottle by one of Australia's larger retailers. This makes no sense, for the wine would still be a perfect bargain at twice that price. It's one thing for Seppelt to deliberately over-achieve to re-establish its market presence, but another thing entirely to allow people to steal some of the crown jewels of modern Victorian wine.

BELLFIELD MARSANNE ROUSSANNE   RATING 4

Pyrenees	$20–$29
Current vintage: 2005	**90**

Lightly candied aromas of honeysuckle, cinnamon and dusty oak reveal nutty and herbal undertones. Long and elegant, the palate is supple, honeyed, nutty and savoury, pleasingly rich, quite viscous and soft before a tangy finish of citrusy acids. Given some very restrained oak treatment, it's tightly focused, with a lingering hint of mineral.

2005	90	2007	2010+
2004	93	2009	2012+
2003	93	2005	2008+

CHALAMBAR SHIRAZ   RATING 2

Great Western, Bendigo	$20–$29
Current vintage: 2004	**96**

A powerful, deeply fruited shiraz of weight, density, length and structure. Its deeply aromatic and peppery scents of black fruits, violets, dried herbs, dark chocolate, cedar/vanilla oak, musk and mint precede a substantial palate of poise and restrained power. There's massive depth of fruit sweetness, a deep core of dark, spicy flavour and a long, fine-grained and savoury finish. Framed by silky-fine but astringent and drying tannins, it exudes strength and style.

2004	96	2016	2024+
2003	95	2015	2023
2002	96	2014	2022
2001	93	2009	2013+
2000	93	2008	2012+
1999	86	2001	2004+
1998	93	2006	2010+
1997	89	2002	2005+
1996	83	1998	2001
1995	91	2003	2007
1994	88	1999	2002
1993	84	1995	1998

DRUMBORG RIESLING   RATING 2

Drumborg	$20–$29
Current vintage: 2005	**97**

A very taut, fine and minerally riesling with a deep citrusy perfume and a powerfully concentrated palate. Scented with green apples, lime and minerals, its remarkably long and vibrant palate marries pristine, crystalline fruit with chalky phenolics and steely, schisty acids. Needing time to show its best, it's like a tightly coiled spring, waiting to explode.

2005	97	2017	2025
2004	96	2016	2024
2003	95	2011	2015+
2000	94	2008	2012
1999	94	2011	2019
1998	89	2003	2006+
1997	87	2002	2005
1996	90	2001	2004
1993	94	2001	2005
1991	89	1999	2003
1988	88	1996	2000

JALUKA CHARDONNAY   RATING 4

Drumborg	$20–$29
Current vintage: 2005	**94**

A major step forward for this label, and one of the tightest and most refreshing Australian chardonnays on the market. Its floral, lemony, limey and mineral aromas reveal hints of matchstick oak with lightly funky leesy undertones. Taut and focused, its long and lean palate of intense lemon and grapefruit flavour reveals wheatmeal undertones and delivers some babyfat-like richness in the middle before a sculpted and almost austere finish of limey acids.

2005	94	2007	2010+
2004	93	2006	2009+
2003	90	2005	2008+
2002	88	2003	2004+

ORIGINAL SPARKLING SHIRAZ

RATING **3**

Victoria $12–$19
Current vintage: 2002 89

Lacking the customary lees-derived maturity of many Seppelt sparkling reds, this is more like a carbonated shiraz, albeit a flavoursome and elegant one. Its lightly earthy, spicy aromas of white pepper and cloves, dark red and black berries, cassis and plums reveal light cedary oak, undergrowth and violet-like fragrances. There's plenty of generous primary fruit on the palate, which remains long and fine before a lingering savoury finish.

2002	89	2004	2007+
1998	90	2006	2010
1996	93	2004	2008
1995	94	2003	2007
1994	93	2002	2006+
1993	92	2001	2005
1992	87	1997	2000
1991	93	2003	2011
1990	91	1998	2002
1989	85	1997	2001
1988	88	1996	2000

SALINGER

RATING **4**

Victoria, Southern Australia $30–$49
Current vintage: 2002 88

A green-edged cool-season wine whose rather floral and herbal aromas of tropical fruit, quince and sweet corn reveal creamy, yeasty undertones. Smooth, fine and silky, with a terrifically tight and creamy bead, it's pleasingly toasty and honeyed. Supple and restrained, it finishes with a very apparent herbaceousness.

2002	88	2007	2010
2001	90	2006	2009
2000	91	2005	2008
1999	94	2004	2007
1998	94	2003	2006
1997	93	2002	2005+
1996	91	2001	2004
1995	91	2003	2007
1994	92	1999	2002+

SHOW SPARKLING SHIRAZ

RATING **2**

Great Western $50–$99
Current vintage: 1994 92

Earthy, rather rustic sparkling shiraz with attractive fruit sweetness, undergrowth-like complexity and firmness, but a suggestion of under-ripened fruit. There's a greenish, sweet corn-like note beneath its peppery, spicy perfume of earthy cassis, plums and cigarboxy influences. Smooth and elegant, its sweet, chewy palate reveals meaty, forest floor and savoury complexity beneath its lingering jujube-like expression of black and red berries.

1994	92	2006	2014
1993	93	2005	2013
1990	95	2002	2010+
1987	90	1995	1999+
1986	95	1998	2006
1985	91	1993	1997
1984	94	1999	2001

ST PETERS SHIRAZ (formerly Great Western Shiraz)

RATING **1**

Great Western $50–$99
Current vintage: 2004 97

A brilliant combination of pristine, dark-fruited and deeply spiced shiraz with firm, fine-grained tannin that will live long into the future. Heavily scented with black pepper and spice, its dense, still rather closed bouquet of deep, dark berry aromas reveals assertive meaty, charcuterie-like complexity. Silky-smooth, its supremely elegant palate of sour-edged blackberry, mulberry and dark plum flavours and subdued and tightly knit oak builds towards a long, licorice-like finish.

2004	97	2024	2034
2003	96	2015	2023
2002	98	2014	2022+
2001	96	2013	2021+
2000	95	2012	2020+
1999	90	2004	2007+
1998	95	2010	2018+
1997	92	2009	2017
1996	95	2008	2016
1995	95	2007	2015
1993	95	2005	2013
1992	90	2000	2004
1991	96	2003	2011+
1988	88	1996	2000

VICTORIAN CABERNET SAUVIGNON MERLOT
(formerly Harpers Range)

RATING **4**

Victoria $12–$19
Current vintage: 2003 87

A minty Victorian cabernet blend whose attractive aromas of mulberries, cassis and dark plums are backed by sweet cedar/chocolate oak and dusty, herbal undertones of eucalypt and forest floor. Moderately long, it's vibrant, ripe and smooth, showing good palate sweetness and balance, finishing with a hint of menthol.

2003	87	2005	2008+
2000	91	2008	2012
1998	90	2006	2010
1997	91	2002	2005+
1996	87	2001	2004
1995	89	2003	2007
1994	88	1999	2002
1993	82	1995	1998
1992	90	1997	2000

VICTORIA SHIRAZ

Victoria	$12–$19
Current vintage: 2004	**90**

2004	90	2009	2012
2003	90	2008	2011
2002	92	2010	2014
2001	87	2003	2006+

More exceptional value from this over-achieving label. Its dark, spicy perfume of dark cherries, plums and blackberries is backed by appealingly peppery suggestions of musk and spice, with undertones of cedar/vanilla oak. Medium to full in weight, it's smooth and supple, with a lively palate of fresh plum, cassis and redcurrant flavour revealing just a hint of raisins and creamy chocolate/vanilla cooperage. Framed by firm, fine tannins, it has plenty of potential to develop further.

Sevenhill

College Road, Sevenhill via Clare SA 5453. Tel: (08) 8843 4222. Fax: (08) 8843 4382.
Website: www.sevenhillcellars.com.au Email: sales@sevenhillcellars.com.au
Region: **Clare Valley** Winemakers: **Lis Heidenreich & Brother John May** Viticulturist: **Craig Richards**
Chief Executive: **Paul McClure**

Clare's oldest winery, Sevenhill, is still operated by the same order of Jesuit priests who bought the land it occupies in 1851. Recent years have seen the emergence of more cut and polish about its wines, which today, more than ever, provide a lively and vibrant reflection of their vineyards and seasons. The pick of its current releases is the slatey and flavoursome 2005 St Aloysius Riesling.

CABERNET SAUVIGNON

Clare Valley	$20–$29
Current vintage: 2003	**86**

2003	86	2008	2011
2002	87	2007	2010+
2001	87	2006	2009
2000	83	2002	2005
1999	88	2007	2011
1998	86	2003	2006
1997	86	2002	2005+
1996	88	2004	2008
1995	84	1997	2000
1994	90	2006	2014
1993	90	2005	2013
1992	90	2000	2004
1991	87	1999	2003

A rustic mouthful of ripe cabernet, with a jammy and lightly minty aroma of blackberries, raspberries, plums and sweet vanilla oak. Moderately rich and juicy, with some smooth, creamy oak, it's vibrant and forward before a slightly cooked and greenish finish of under-and over-ripened influences.

ST ALOYSIUS RIESLING

Clare Valley	$12–$19
Current vintage: 2005	**92**

2005	92	2013	2017+
2004	91	2009	2012+
2003	89	2008	2011
2002	87	2004	2007
2001	90	2006	2009
2000	91	2005	2008+
1999	88	2004	2007
1998	91	2003	2006
1997	93	2002	2005
1996	93	2004	2008
1995	94	2000	2003
1994	93	2002	2006

Slightly confectionary, with a fresh, floral perfume of lemon rind and wet slate. Long and tightly focused, it's particularly taut, austere and steely, with lingering lime and lemon flavours persisting through a finish of abrupt acidity. A genuinely long-term wine with a surprising depth of fruit.

SEMILLON

Clare Valley	$12–$19
Current vintage: 2005	**87**

2005	87	2007	2010+
2004	89	2006	2009
2003	87	2005	2008
1999	90	2005	2007+
1998	89	2003	2006
1996	87	1998	2001
1995	82	1997	2000
1994	87	1999	2002

Rather spirity and alcoholic, this clean and mineral semillon does, however, reveal a lifted, floral and apple-like aroma with undertones of lemon detergent and wet slate. Round and generous, its rich, melon-like palate is flavoursome and varietal, finishing with powdery mineral nuances.

SHIRAZ

RATING **5**

Clare Valley	$20–$29	2003	86	2008	2011
Current vintage: 2003	86	2002	89	2010	2014

2003	86	2008	2011
2002	89	2010	2014
2001	89	2009	2013
1999	87	2004	2007
1998	90	2003	2006
1997	89	2002	2005+
1996	91	2001	2004
1995	91	2003	2007
1994	91	2002	2006
1993	93	2005	2013
1992	90	2000	2004

Clare Valley $20–$29
Current vintage: 2003 86

Pruney, treacle-like and jammy, this faster-maturing shiraz has a briary, prune and currant-like bouquet plus a moderately firm and chewy palate whose rich but rather dehydrated fruit does lack a little freshness and brightness.

Seville Estate

Linwood Road, Seville Vic 3139. Tel: 1300 880 561. Fax: (03) 5964 2633.
Website: www.sevilleestate.com.au Email: wine@sevilleestate.com.au

Region: **Yarra Valley** Winemaker: **Dylan McMahon** Viticulturist: **Margaret van der Muelen**
Chief Executives: **Graham & Margaret van der Muelen**

Seville Estate is a mature vineyard with one of the cooler sites in the Yarra Valley. Its original plantings of nearly 30-year-old vines provide a rare and valuable resource. Having said that, with the exception of the mealy and savoury 2004 Chardonnay, the present releases are nowhere near the quality of even two years ago. The 2004 Shiraz is sub-par and should never have been released. Hard-won reputations can diminish in the blink of an eye. I sincerely hope that normal levels of transmission resume at Seville Estate, and quickly.

CHARDONNAY

RATING **5**

Yarra Valley $20–$29
Current vintage: 2004 91

A smooth, creamy chardonnay whose heavily worked aromas of dried flowers, smoked meats and nutty, mealy nuances precede a generous, nutty and savoury palate. Quite complex and evolved, with more of an emphasis on complexity and development than primary fruit, it finishes clean and refreshing. Pleasing texture and balance.

2004	91	2009	2012
2003	90	2005	2008
2002	87	2004	2007
2001	88	2003	2006
2000	87	2002	2005
1999	89	2001	2004
1998	89	2003	2006
1997	94	2002	2005+
1996	91	2001	2004
1995	92	2000	2003

PINOT NOIR

RATING **5**

Yarra Valley $20–$29
Current vintage: 2003 88

Honest and flavoursome if rather simple pinot whose aroma of raspberries, cherries and red plums reveals sweet vanilla/cedary oak and nuances of dried herbs. Smooth and pretty, its supple and juicy palate delivers a vibrant mouthful of tangy, candied cherry and plum flavours backed by smoky vanilla oak, finishing with soft tannins and fresh acids.

2003	88	2005	2008
2002	86	2004	2007
2001	88	2003	2006+
2000	89	2002	2005
1999	87	2001	2004
1998	87	2000	2003+
1995	87	2000	2003
1993	93	1998	2001
1992	88	2000	2004

RESERVE CABERNET SAUVIGNON

RATING **3**

Yarra Valley $30–$49
Current vintage: 2003 86

Meaty, greenish and rather flat, lacking genuine brightness of fruit, with minty, earthy aromas supported by assertive chocolate/mocha oak. Framed by firm, but sappy tannins, its meaty expression of rather simple and confection-like red and black berries and mocha/vanilla oak is rather overwhelmed by its extract and greenness.

2003	86	2008	2011
2001	92	2009	2013+
2000	93	2012	2020
1999	90	2001	2004
1998	84	2000	2003+
1997	89	2005	2009
1995	86	2002	2006
1994	89	2002	2006
1992	94	2004	2012

RESERVE SHIRAZ

Yarra Valley	$50–$99
Current vintage: 2004	88

A supple, smoky and relatively simple shiraz whose sweet flavours of black and red berries and cherries are lifted by assertive oak influences. Its spicy, caramel-like and vanilla aromas of raspberries, cranberries and cherries precedes a round and juicy palate of medium to full weight. Backed by meaty and reductive undertones, with hints of tomato stalk, it finishes with lingering fruit and spices.

2004	88	2009	2012
2003	87	2005	2008+
2001	95	2013	2021
2000	95	2008	2012+

SHIRAZ

Yarra Valley	$20–$29
Current vintage: 2004	77

Flat, oxidised and aldehydic, with dull, meaty aromas of stewed plums and cranberries. Its simple, thin palate of cooked cherries and cranberries finishes short and dilute, with undertones of dried herbs.

2004	77	2006	2009
2003	89	2008	2011
2002	93	2010	2014+
2001	93	2006	2009
2000	86	2002	2005
1999	92	2004	2007
1997	93	2005	2009
1996	93	2004	2008
1995	93	2003	2007
1994	90	2002	2006
1993	95	2001	2005
1992	94	2004	2012+

Shadowfax

K Road, Werribee Vic 3030. Tel: (03) 9731 4420. Fax: (03) 9731 4421.
Website: www.shadowfax.com.au Email: cellardoor@shadowfax.com.au
Regions: **Various** Winemaker: **Matt Harrop** Viticulturist: **Andrew Tedder**

Located on the grounds of Werribee Park, Shadowfax is steadily acquiring vineyard sites and long-term relationships with growers all over Australia to provide its diverse range of regional specialty wines. They're all very competently made by Matt Harrop; typically spotlessly clean and very true to variety and region. Of most interest to me are the two Heathcote shirazes, especially the refined, elegant, silky and deeply flavoured Pink Cliffs from 2002. The second wine, the curiously named One Eye, is a little more assertive and rustic.

CHARDONNAY

Various, Victoria	$20–$29
Current vintage: 2005	87

Buttery, toasty and lightly varnishy aromas of assertive oak and citrus, melon and banana-like fruit precede a round, generous and juicy palate whose slightly candied melon-like fruit reflects some under-and over-ripe influences. Finished by clean acids, it lacks genuine brightness and focus.

2005	87	2006	2007+
2004	93	2006	200?+
2003	89	2005	2008
2002	90	2004	2007
2001	87	2003	2006
2000	89	2002	2005
1999	93	2001	2004

ONE EYE SHIRAZ

Heathcote	$50–$99
Current vintage: 2003	87

Charry, oaky aromas of cloves and cinnamon underpin a rather cooked and meaty bouquet of plums, prunes and blackberry confiture. Round and generous, its rich, meaty and somewhat porty palate of dark plums, cassis and blackberries is firmly coated by fine, loose-knit tannin and relies a little on oak for its sweetness. It finishes long and minty, with lingering hints of menthol and mocha-like oak.

2003	87	2005	2008+
2002	92	2010	2014
2001	91	2009	2013

PINK CLIFFS SHIRAZ

Heathcote	$50–$99
Current vintage: 2003	80

Minty, meaty aromas of cooked plums, licorice and menthol overlie varnishy suggestions of pencil-shavings oak. Over-ripe, cooked and leathery, its hard-edged palate of dehydrated fruit lacks brightness and length.

2003	80	2005	2008
2002	95	2010	2014+
2001	95	2009	2013

PINOT GRIS

Adelaide Hills	$20–$29
Current vintage: 2005	86

Estery, nutty and spicy aromas of apple, lemon and pear precede a rather dull and spiky palate whose slightly cooked and cloying fruit lacks genuine freshness, finishing herbal and cashew-like.

2005	86	2006	2007
2004	88	2005	2006
2003	91	2003	2004+
2002	83	2003	2004
2001	84	2002	2003
2000	91	2002	2005

PINOT NOIR

Geelong, Gippsland, Yarra Valley	$30–$49
Current vintage: 2004	87

A firm, minty and rather candied pinot whose menthol-like aromas of sweet red cherries, rasp-berries and plums are backed by a lightly herbal, undergrowth-like complexity and sweet vanilla oak. Moderately rich and ripe, with rather stewed and forward fruit framed by slightly sappy and metallic tannins, it's firm and drying, lacking real brightness and silkiness.

2004	87	2006	2009+
2003	90	2005	2008
2002	86	2004	2007
2001	89	2003	2006
2000	93	2002	2005

SAUVIGNON BLANC

Adelaide Hills	$12–$19
Current vintage: 2005	88

Slightly sweaty and herbaceous, this moder-ately elegant and juicy sauvignon blanc reveals some reductive rubbery influences beneath its marginally cooked expression of gooseberry and honeydew melon flavours. It's long and grassy, with a lingering finish of lemon-like acidity and a chalky texture, but lacks the brightness and freshness for a higher rating.

2005	88	2006	2007
2004	92	2005	2006
2003	92	2003	2004+
2002	84	2003	2004
2001	90	2002	2003+

SHIRAZ

Various	$20–$29
Current vintage: 2003	87

Rather cooked, meaty and slightly porty aromas of currants, raisins, treacle and bitumen are backed by nuances of dried herbs and dark olives. Full to medium in weight and framed by smooth tannins, its surprisingly restrained and elegant palate of blackberries, currants and prune/plum-like fruit dries out a little towards the rather green-edged, salty and spicy finish. Simple and early-maturing.

2003	87	2005	2008
2002	90	2007	2010+
2000	84	2002	2002+
1999	91	2004	2007

Shaw and Smith

Lot 4 Jones Road, Balhannah SA 5242. Tel: (08) 8398 0500. Fax: (08) 8398 0600.
Website: www.shawandsmith.com Email: info@shawandsmith.com
Region: **Adelaide Hills** Winemaker: **Martin Shaw** Viticulturist: **Wayne Pittaway**
Chief Executives: **Martin Shaw, Michael Hill Smith**

Shaw and Smith recently announced a major change in direction. It intends to focus on just three wines —
its Sauvignon Blanc, Shiraz and M3 Vineyard Chardonnay. I'm sorry to hear this, because I had formed the view
that this was one of the few Australian wineries likely to make a genuine success of Merlot, as my marks below
might confirm. That said, it's high time most Australian producers started thinking seriously about which wines
they should and should not make, doing something about the unnecessary fruit salad of grapes making wine
that doesn't sell and contributing to the country's oversupply.

M3 VINEYARD CHARDONNAY RATING 2

Adelaide Hills $30–$49
Current vintage: 2005 93

An unctuous, stylish and very showy young
chardonnay whose sweet, oaky aromas of peach,
nectarine and citrusy fruit reveal undertones of
vanilla, cloves, and cinnamon. Long and smooth,
its seamless palate of melon, grapefruit, lemon
and apple flavour is tightly knit with assertive
butter/vanilla oak, finishing long and creamy, with
smooth, soft acids. Very focused and tightly integrated, but at this stage lacks wow factor.

2005	93	2010	2013
2004	95	2009	2012
2003	94	2008	2011
2002	95	2007	2010
2001	93	2003	2006+
2000	94	2002	2005+

MERLOT RATING 3

Adelaide Hills $20–$29
Current vintage: 2003 93

A full-flavoured, stylish and well-balanced merlot
whose fragrant perfume of dark cherries, plums
and blackberries reveals undertones of cedary, dusty
and vanilla-like new oak qualities. Medium to full
in weight, it presents length and intensity, with an
undercarriage of smooth, silky and fine-grained
tannins that allows its fruit to build in the mouth.

2003	93	2008	2011+
2002	94	2010	2014
2001	93	2006	2009
2000	90	2002	2005
1999	87	2004	2007

SAUVIGNON BLANC RATING 4

Adelaide Hills $20–$29
Current vintage: 2006 90

A juicy, smooth and generous sauvignon blanc
whose heady aromas of fresh gooseberries, passionfruit and lychees reveal just a hint of grassiness. Very ripe, round and mouthfilling, its essence-
like palate of intense, pure fruit finishes with lingering
soft acids. Just lacks the shape and bite for a higher
score.

2006	90	2006	2007+
2005	93	2006	2007
2004	91	2004	2005
2003	88	2003	2004
2002	95	2003	2004+
2001	91	2002	2003+
2000	87	2000	2001
1999	88	2000	2001
1998	91	1998	1999

SHIRAZ RATING 4

Adelaide Hills $30–$49
Current vintage: 2004 91

A meaty and fractionally jammy shiraz whose heady,
musky perfume is laden with cassis, redcurrant
and dark plum aromas over spicy undertones of
pepper with cedar, vanilla and dark chocolate oak.
Full to medium weight, it's smooth and sumptuous,
delivering a slightly cooked, meaty and savoury
palate whose dark flavours of plums and berries
are backed by assertive new oak and framed by
firmish tannins.

2004	91	2009	2012+
2003	91	2005	2008+
2002	95	2007	2010+

Shottesbrooke

Bagshaws Road, McLaren Flat SA 5171. Tel: (08) 8383 0002. Fax: (08) 8383 0222.
Website: www.shottesbrooke.com.au Email: admin@shottesbrooke.com.au

Region: **McLaren Vale** Winemaker: **Nick Holmes** Viticulturist: **Hamish Maguire** Chief Executive: **Nick Holmes**

Shottesbrooke is a well-established winery whose smoothly structured reds have traditionally been finer and more elegant than most in McLaren Vale. Its Sauvignon Blanc is usually pungent and arrestingly varietal.

CABERNET SAUVIGNON (or blend)

RATING 5

McLaren Vale	**$20–$29**	2004	82	2006	2009+
Current vintage: 2004	**82**	2002	86	2007	2010
		2001	88	2009	2013
Jammy aromas of briary cassis, blackberries and		1999	83	2001	2004+
plums reveal herbal undertones. Rather cooked		1998	94	2006	2010
and forward, its early impression of fruit becomes		1997	89	2005	2009
leaner, while the finish is quite skinny and metallic.		1996	86	2001	2004
Reflects both over-and under-ripe fruit charac-		1995	84	2000	2003
ters.		1994	92	2002	2006
		1993	87	1998	2001
		1992	93	2000	2004

MERLOT

RATING 5

McLaren Vale	**$20–$29**	2004	88	2009	2012
Current vintage: 2004	**88**	2003	82	2005	2008
		2002	83	2004	2007+
A moderately rich and flavoursome, but not		2001	86	2006	2009
entirely convincing merlot whose slightly stewed		2000	89	2008	2012
aromas of plums, red and black cherries reveal		1999	89	2004	2007
smoky, charcuterie-like undertones. Framed by		1998	90	2003	2006
firmish and faintly sappy and metallic tannins, its		1997	92	2002	2005
honest, smoky expression of cherry/plum fruit is		1996	90	2001	2004
underpinned by oak sweetness, but lacks genuine		1995	90	2000	2003
varietal definition.					

SAUVIGNON BLANC

 RATING 5

Fleurieu, Adelaide Hills	**$12–$19**	2005	84	2006	2007
Current vintage: 2005	**84**	2004	77	2004	2004
		2003	87	2004	2005
Lightly herbaceous, sweaty aromas of gooseberries		2002	89	2003	2004
and estery tropical fruits precede a simple,		2001	91	2002	2003+
forward and candied palate whose tangy flavours		2000	88	2002	2005
of citrus, melon and gooseberries finish rather		1999	86	2000	2001
cloying, lacking freshness and shape.					

Skillogalee

Trevarrick Road, Sevenhill via Clare SA 5453. Tel: (08) 8843 4311. Fax: (08) 8843 4343.
Email: skilly@chariot.net.au Website: www.skillogalee.com

Region: **Clare Valley** Winemaker: **Dan Palmer** Viticulturist: **Craig McLean** Chief Executive: **Dave Palmer**

Skillogalee is one of the Clare Valley's small family-run vineyards. Its rustic, earthy reds are typically less ripe and assertive than others of the region, but became rather overcooked during the hot 2003 season. Pick of the releases are the tighly focused 2005 Riesling and the very spicy, savoury and slightly meaty 2005 Gewürztraminer, which will become wilder and more adventurous the longer you leave it.

GEWÜRZTRAMINER

 RATING 5

Clare Valley	**$12–$19**	2005	90	2007	2010
Current vintage: 2005	**90**	2004	86	2005	2006+
		2003	84	2004	2005
A generous, clean and savoury wine whose slowly		2002	93	2004	2007
evolving but rather pungent and bath powdery		1999	87	2004	2007
aromas of musky, spicy and floral traminer char-					
acters of lychees and rose oil reveal faint hints of					
toastiness. Rather round, broad and generous, with					
a hint of meatiness, its juicy palate of pronounced					
varietal fruit culminates in a fractionally sweet but					
clean and savoury finish of some length.					

RIESLING

RATING **5**

Clare Valley	$12–$19				
Current vintage: 2005	**90**				

Well made, very clean and honest, this floral, dry and juicy young riesling has a very open and musky perfume of dried flowers, spices and lime juice. Smooth and evenly flavoured, its vibrant palate of tangy lemon and lime flavour finishes with length and persistence.

Year	Score		
2005	90	2010	2013+
2004	88	2006	2009+
2003	87	2005	2008
2002	89	2007	2010
2001	93	2006	2008+
2000	89	2002	2005+
1999	90	2004	2007
1998	90	2003	2006
1997	92	2005	2009
1996	91	2001	2004
1995	93	2003	2007
1994	94	2006	2014
1993	90	2001	2005
1992	93	1997	2000

SHIRAZ

RATING **5**

Clare Valley	$20–$29
Current vintage: 2003	**88**

Slightly pruney and currant-like, lacking genuine tightness and focus, this still makes rather a good fist of a hot year. Its rather cooked and stewed fruit and raspberry aromas are backed by mint and menthol, with undertones of violets, iodide and herbaceous influences. Full to medium in weight, its sumptuous and generously flavoured minty palate of dark fruit and cedar/vanilla oak dries out a little towards the finish.

Year	Score		
2003	88	2005	2008
2002	87	2007	2010
2001	87	2003	2006+
2000	81	2002	2005+
1999	85	2007	2011
1998	84	2000	2003+
1997	92	2002	2005+
1996	88	1998	2001
1995	90	2000	2003
1994	91	1999	2002
1993	91	2001	2005
1992	91	2000	2004

THE CABERNETS

Clare Valley	$20–$29
Current vintage: 2003	**83**

Rather a cooked and meaty red from a very hot vintage. Its briary, earthy and raisined aromas of blackberries, mocha and chocolate are backed by earthy, minty and menthol-like undertones. Its forward, but hollow and dehydrated palate of raisins, cassis and plums finishes without much focus or freshness.

Year	Score		
2003	83	2005	2008
2001	85	2006	2009
2000	86	2005	2008
1999	85	2007	2011
1998	88	2003	2006
1997	91	2002	2005+
1996	92	2004	2008
1995	87	2000	2003
1994	91	2002	2006
1993	88	2001	2005
1992	89	2000	2004
1991	90	1996	1999

Smithbrook

Smithbrook Road, Pemberton WA 6260. Tel: (08) 9772 3557. Fax: (08) 9772 3579.
Website: www.smithbrook.com.au Email: smithbrk@karriweb.com.au

Region: **Pemberton** Winemakers: **Mike Symons, Jonathan Farrington** Viticulturists: **Mike Symons, Jonathan Farrington** Chief Executive: **Peter Cowan**

Lion Nathan's Western Australian outpost is a large vineyard in Pemberton that delivers one of Australia's finest Sauvignon Blancs, as well as an earthy, leathery Merlot of some charm. This issue sees the debut of its reserve red, the merlot-based The Yilgarn. There is also a slightly oaky but very smooth and creamy The Yilgarn Sauvignon Blanc from 2004 (90, drink 2006–2009).

MERLOT

RATING **5**

Pemberton	$20–$29
Current vintage: 2003	**87**

A polished, well-made wine that, despite some stewy and under-ripe influences, presents pleasing merlot fruit harnessed with cedar/vanilla/chocolate oak and chalky tannins. It offers a slightly cooked expression of meaty dark plum, cherry and cranberry flavour.

Year	Score		
2003	87	2008	2011
2002	88	2007	2010
2001	87	2003	2006+
2000	89	2005	2008
1999	89	2001	2004

SAUVIGNON BLANC

RATING 4

Pemberton	$12–$19
Current vintage: 2005	**86**

A chalky, phenolic sauvignon blanc whose juicy, candied aromas of citrus and lightly grassy undertones have a floral, riesling-like quality. Forward and simple, it lacks its customary intensity and length, but finishes with a touch of austerity.

2005	86	2005	2006
2004	93	2004	2005+
2003	93	2004	2005+
2002	90	2003	2004
2001	87	2002	2003
2000	91	2000	2001

THE YILGARN (Merlot Blend)

RATING 5

Pemberton	$20–$29
Current vintage: 2004	**90**

A minty, rather firm and traditional red wine whose earthy and lightly herbal aromas of dark plums, cherries and sweet cedar/vanilla oak are backed by suggestions of menthol. Its juicy, dark-fruited palate of dark plum and cherry flavours is framed by drying tannins, finishing minty and savoury, with genuine length of flavour and attractive spiciness. Should age well.

2004	90	2012	2016
2001	93	2006	2009+
2000	87	2005	2008

Sorrenberg

Alma Road, Beechworth Vic 3747. Tel: (03) 5728 2278. Fax: (03) 5728 2278. Website: www.sorrenberg.com

Region: **Beechworth** Winemaker: **Barry Morey** Viticulturist: **Barry Morey** Chief Executive: **Barry Morey**

Sorrenberg is a small and highly rated maker of distinctive and complex wines in the Beechworth hills of north-east Victoria. Its finest wine is its savoury, mineral Sauvignon Blanc Semillon blend, which in certain years is uncannily Bordeaux-like. Sorrenberg can also make astoundingly sophisticated Chardonnay and wild, briary Gamay. Several of its wines were not released from the bushfire-affected 2003 vintage.

CABERNET BLEND

RATING 5

Beechworth	$20–$29
Current vintage: 2004	**89**

Fine, elegant and dusty, this slightly herbal and minty red has a restrained aroma of cassis, dark plums and redcurrants backed by cedar/vanilla oak and forest floor undertones. Supple, fine and willowy, its measured and silky palate of brightly lit plum and small berry flavours is framed by fine, smooth tannins, finishing with balance, stability and fresh acidity.

2004	89	2009	2012+
2002	93	2014	2022
2001	87	2006	2009
2000	90	2005	2008+
1999	88	2004	2007
1998	87	2003	2006
1997	83	1999	2002
1994	88	1998	2003

CHARDONNAY

RATING 4

Beechworth	$30–$49
Current vintage: 2004	**89**

A developing young chardonnay whose toasty citrus and melon qualities are enhanced by nutty and creamy complexit and buttery and toasty oak. Its floral bouquet reveals faint nuances of sweet corn, while its smooth and silky palate delivers a mouthfilling expression of juicy fruit before finishing long and savoury, with light mineral notes.

2004	89	2006	2009
2003	84	2005	2008
2002	90	2004	2007
2001	95	2003	2006+
2000	94	2005	2008
1999	90	2004	2007
1998	86	2000	2003
1997	93	2002	2005

GAMAY

RATING 5

Beechworth	$20–$29
Current vintage: 2004	**91**

Wild and briary, with depth and brightness of fruit, plus genuine structure. Its spicy floral perfume of stewed redcurrants, red cherries and raspberry confiture reveals rose petal-like undertones. Smooth and silky, its supple expression of juicy fresh cherries and spicy red berries is underpinned by fine-grained tannins, finishing meaty and savoury.

2004	91	2005	2006+
2002	87	2004	2007
2001	88	2003	2006
2000	91	2002	2005
1999	84	2000	2001
1998	87	1999	2000

SAUVIGNON BLANC SEMILLON

RATING **3**

Beechworth	$20–$29	2005	86	2006	2007
Current vintage: 2005	**86**	2004	95	2006	2009+

Vibrant, spicy and mineral aromas of citrus, gooseberries and lime juice precede a juicy, slightly candied, simple and cloying palate that finishes with lemony acids.

2003	91	2005	2008
2002	95	2007	2010
2001	93	2006	2009
2000	90	2002	2005
1999	87	2001	2004
1998	88	2000	2003

St Hallett

St Hallett's Road, Hallet Valley, Tanunda SA 5352. Tel: (08) 8563 7000. Fax: (08) 8563 7001.
Website: www.sthallett.com.au Email: sthallett@sthallett.com.au

Region: **Barossa Valley** Winemakers: **Stuart Blackwell, Matt Gant** Viticulturist: **Chris Rogers**

Two of the best value shirazes around are the Faith and Blackwell Shirazes from St Hallett. The Blackwell 2004 is yet another vibrant, smooth and seamless wine, qualities that were once readily apparent in its more expensive stablemate, the Old Block Shiraz. Barossa semillon is never an easy sell, so if you're wondering what it's all about, invest in a bottle of the rather drinkable 2003 edition from St Hallett.

BLACKWELL SHIRAZ

RATING **3**

Barossa Valley	$20–$29	2004	94	2012	2016+
Current vintage: 2004	**94**	2003	93	2008	2011

A delightful Barossa shiraz whose deep, dark and spicy aromas of plums, blackberries and redcurrants are backed by nuances of white pepper, spice and a meaty shade of fine-grained oak. Velvet smooth, luscious and seamless, it's long, gamey and dark-fruited, saturated with pristine but meaty flavours of cassis and dark plums handsomely supported by chocolate/vanilla oak and framed by a firm, cut of silky tannins.

2002	93	2007	2010+
2001	92	2006	2009+
1999	92	2004	2007+
1998	95	2006	2010+
1997	88	2002	2005
1996	91	2004	2008
1995	87	2000	2003
1994	92	1999	2002+

EDEN VALLEY RIESLING

RATING **4**

Eden Valley	$12–$19	2005	89	2010	2013
Current vintage: 2005	**89**	2004	87	2006	2009

A rather reductive perfume cleans up to reveal fragrant, if rather confectionary notes of lime, lemon and minerals, with nettle-like undertones. Long, fine and steely, its concentrated and shapely palate of tangy citrus, pear and apple flavours culminates in an austere but slightly sweet and phenolic finish punctuated by lime juice-like acidity.

2003	92	2008	2011+
2002	93	2007	2010
2001	89	2006	2009
2000	90	2005	2008
1999	90	2004	2007
1998	90	2003	2006+
1997	93	2002	2005+
1996	88	2001	2004

FAITH SHIRAZ

RATING **5**

Barossa Valley	$12–$19	2004	87	2006	2009
Current vintage: 2004	**87**	2003	90	2005	2008

A pleasing, early-drinking soft and juicy red that appears to have been boosted by an assertive blueberry-like grenache component. Its slightly earthy, muddy and meaty aromas of spicy and stewy dark plums, cassis, raspberries and blueberries precede a forward and juicy palate of moderate length. Framed by fine, smooth tannins, it's brightly flavoured and persistent.

2002	89	2004	2007
2001	86	2003	2006
2000	82	2002	2005
1999	92	2004	2009
1998	90	2003	2006
1997	88	1998	1999
1996	86	1998	2001
1995	88	2000	2003
1994	89	1996	1999+

OLD BLOCK SHIRAZ

Barossa Valley $50–$99
Current vintage: 2002   89

Smooth and elegant, but lacking its customary length and richness, this fine-grained and supple shiraz has a perfume of sweet violets and mulberries backed by slightly charry nuances of tight-grained oak and suggestions of capsicum, dried herbs and licorice. Toasty chocolate/vanilla oak backs its silky but slightly sappy palate of cassis, blackberry and plum-like fruit, before a lightly green-edged finish.

2002	89	2007	2010
2001	89	2009	2013
2000	84	2002	2005+
1999	94	2007	2011
1998	95	2010	2018
1997	82	1999	2002
1996	89	2001	2004
1995	89	2000	2003+
1994	94	2002	2006
1993	91	1998	2001
1992	92	1997	2000
1991	95	2003	2011
1990	95	2002	2010
1989	91	1997	2001
1988	95	2000	2008

SEMILLON (formerly Semillon Select and Blackwell Semillon)

RATING 5

Barossa Valley $12–$19
Current vintage: 2003   92

Tight, racy and refreshing, this tangy and vibrant Barossa semillon reveals a sweet, smoky bouquet whose juicy melon and lemony fruit overlies vanilla and bubblegum-like barrel ferment influences and nuances of lemon detergent. Long and smooth, its mouthfilling melon/citrus flavours knit tightly with toasty vanilla oak, finishing with clean and zesty acids.

2003	92	2008	2011+
2002	86	2004	2007+
2001	87	2003	2006
1999	84	2001	2004
1998	88	2000	2003
1997	90	1999	2002
1996	88	1998	2001
1995	83	1996	1997

St Huberts

St Huberts Road, Coldstream Vic 3770. Tel: (03) 9739 1118. Fax: (03) 9739 1096.
Website: www.fosters.com.au

Region: **Yarra Valley** Winemaker: **Shavaughn Wells** Viticulturist: **Damien de Castella**
Chief Executive: **Jamie Odell**

St Huberts is a Yarra Valley brand that was redeveloped in the late 1970s by the Cester family. It shares its name and much of its identification with one of the three grand properties that dominated Yarra viticulture in the 1800s, even though its vineyards are planted next to, and not on the original St Huberts site. Today the brand is one of several owned by the Foster's Wine Group in the region, along with Yarra Ridge and Coldstream Hills. St Huberts wines are generally very reliable, classically elegant and excellent value, especially the under-rated Cabernet Sauvignon.

CABERNET SAUVIGNON

RATING 3

Yarra Valley $20–$29
Current vintage: 2003   93

A stylish wine of genuine presence and potential. Its dusty, cedary aromas of violets, cassis, dark plums and plain chocolate precede a polished, silky palate whose piercing mulberry and cassis-like expression of classic cool-climate fruit is framed by fine, but firmish tannins. Exceptional value, it's long and balanced, with a structure and depth of fruit worth ageing.

2003	93	2011	2015
2001	90	2009	2013+
2000	90	2008	2012+
1999	90	2004	2007
1998	93	2006	2010
1997	92	2005	2009+
1996	87	1998	2001
1995	92	2000	2003
1994	94	2002	2006
1993	90	1998	2003
1992	93	2000	2004

CHARDONNAY

RATING 4

Yarra Valley $20–$29
Current vintage: 2005   89

A fresh, balanced and stylish chardonnay likely to build depth and richness in the bottle for a short while. Its delicate aromas of lime, grapefruit, apple and melon reveal suggestions of mineral and vanilla oak. Its pristine, silky palate of peach flavour, butterscotch and sweet oak has a delightful fluffy quality, before finishing smooth and creamy with soft acids.

2005	89	2007	2010+
2004	91	2006	2009+
2003	91	2005	2008+
2002	86	2003	2004
2001	87	2002	2003
2000	90	2002	2005+
1999	92	2004	2007
1998	87	2000	2003
1997	84	1999	2002
1996	87	1998	2001

260
THE AUSTRALIAN WINE ANNUAL
www.jeremyoliver.com.au
2007

PINOT NOIR

RATING 5

		Yarra Valley	$20–$29

Current vintage: 2004 — **89**

An honest, flavoursome pinot with richness, firmness and weight. Its rather oaky, bubblegum-like bouquet of dark rose petals, cherries and raspberries precedes a round, smooth and generous palate framed by firm, bony tannins. Slightly stewed flavours of plums and cherries finish long and savoury.

2004	89	2006	2009
2003	89	2005	2008
2002	90	2007	2010
2001	89	2003	2006
2000	86	2002	2005
1999	89	2001	2004
1998	87	2000	2003
1997	87	2002	2005
1996	87	1998	2001

ROUSSANNE

RATING 4

Yarra Valley — $20–$29
Current vintage: 2004 — **91**

Long, chalky and savoury, this delicate and minerally roussanne has a floral and nutty aroma of perfumed fruit backed by cinnamon, clove and nutmeg. Its taut and refreshing palate of lingering citrus, wheatmeal and nutty flavours finishes with persistence and austerity. Good shape and definition.

2004	91	2006	2009+
2003	90	2005	2008+
2002	90	2003	2004+
2000	86	2002	2005
1999	89	2001	2004
1998	87	1999	2000+

Stanton & Killeen

Murray Valley Highway, Rutherglen Vic 3685. Tel: (02) 6032 9457. Fax: (02) 6032 8018.
Website: www.stantonandkilleenwines.com.au Email: sk_wines@netc.net.au

Region: **Rutherglen** Winemaker: **Chris Killeen** Viticulturist: **Paul Geddes** Chief Executive: **Chris Killeen**

Stanton & Killeen is a long-established maker of the traditionally rich and smooth Rutherglen dry reds and luscious fortified wines. Some of the currently available reds are significantly more rustic and meaty than is typical for this maker, while the benchmark Vintage Port didn't fare quite as well in the heat of 2001 as it has done in recent years.

CABERNET BLEND

Rutherglen — $20–$29
Current vintage: 2003 — **87**

Smooth, earthy Rutherglen red with a spicy, floral aroma of blackcurrants, redcurrants and plums, with undertones of cherries and restrained cedar/vanilla oak. Its vibrant, juicy palate of cherry/plum flavours is slightly stewy, but offers pleasing softness and sweetness, framed by smooth tannins.

2003	87	2005	2008+
2002	80	2004	2007
2001	83	2003	2006
2000	82	2002	2005
1999	86	2004	2007
1998	86	2006	2010+
1996	87	2000	2003
1995	88	2000	2003
1992	92	2004	2012
1991	91	1999	2003
1990	88	2002	2010

CABERNET SHIRAZ

RATING 5

Rutherglen — $20–$29
Current vintage: 2004 — **90**

A richly flavoured but finely balanced Rutherglen red whose deeply spiced and alluring aromas of blackberries, dark plums, chocolate, cedar and vanilla are backed by peppery nuances of cloves and cinnamon. Fully but not over-ripened, its sumptuous and well-integrated palate of intense black and red berries, cedar/vanilla oak and firm but pliant tannin finishes long, spicy and slightly meaty.

2004	90	2012	2016+
2003	89	2008	2011
2001	88	2006	2009+
1998	88	2006	2010
1997	90	2005	2009+
1996	90	2004	2008+
1995	88	2007	2015
1994	88	2006	2014
1992	91	2004	2012

DURIF

RATING 4

Rutherglen $20–$29
Current vintage: 2003   82

A tiring red now beginning to dry out, with rustic, meaty and leathery aromas of berries and plums and horsehair undertones. Medium to full in weight, it's forward and spicy, with berry and plum-like fruit becoming more spicy and meaty down the palate. Barnyard-like characters dominate the finish.

2003	82	2005	2008
2002	92	2014	2022
2000	92	2008	2012+
1999	90	2007	2011
1998	87	2010	2018
1997	89	2009	2017
1996	90	2008	2016
1995	90	2007	2015
1994	88	2006	2014
1992	92	2004	2012
1991	86	1999	2003
1990	93	2002	2010
1988	93	2000	2008

JACK'S BLOCK SHIRAZ

RATING 3

Rutherglen $30–$49
Current vintage: 2004   87

Deep, spicy, earthy and leathery aromas of slightly cooked and juicy small berries reveal musky undertones of clove s and cinnamon, with underlying cedar/vanilla oak and meaty, rather horsy and herbal undertones. Framed by firm, fine tannins, its rich, meaty palate of dark plums, cherries and licorice is supported by fine oak but finishes raw and bitter, with a metallic hardness and Bandaid-like notes.

2004	87	2009	2012
2000	93	2012	2020
1998	94	2006	2010+
1997	93	2009	2017
1993	88	2001	2005+

MOODEMERE SHIRAZ

RATING 5

Rutherglen $20–$29
Current vintage: 2004   89

A typically rich and earthy Rutherglen shiraz whose spicy, meaty aromas of dark plums, redcurrants and lightly smoky oak precede a bright, smooth and silky palate of medium to full weight. Supported by restrained oak, its jujube-like flavours of blackberries and raspberries finish with fresh acids and lingering nuances of licorice and bitumen.

2004	89	2009	2012+
2003	88	2008	2011
2002	87	2004	2007+
2001	82	2003	2006+
2000	86	2005	2008
1999	87	2004	2007
1996	90	2004	2008
1995	89	2007	2015
1993	91	2005	2013
1992	94	2004	2012
1991	88	1999	2003
1990	92	2002	2010
1988	85	1996	2000

VINTAGE PORT

RATING 2

Rutherglen $20–$29
Current vintage: 2001   92

A rich, smooth and soft vintage port whose floral and earthy aromas of dark plums, treacle and bitumen are lifted by spicy fresh spirit and reveal underlying meaty, gamey undertones. Its succulent, but fine and elegant palate delivers meaty, currant and raisin-like fruit with plenty of meaty and leathery complexity. It finishes quite savoury, with moderate length and balanced sweetness. Rather more Australian in style than the Portuguese-inspired releases of recent years.

2001	92	2009	2013+
2000	95	2008	2012+
1999	93	2007	2011+
1998	96	2010	2018+
1997	95	2009	2017
1996	95	2008	2016+
1995	95	2015	2025
1994	93	2006	2014
1993	94	2005	2013
1992	95	2004	2012
1991	94	2003	2011
1990	93	1998	2002
1989	90	1997	2001
1988	94	2000	2005

Starvedog Lane

Ravenswood Lane, Hahndorf SA 5245. Tel: (08) 8388 1250. Fax: (08) 8388 7233.
Website: www.thelane.com.au Email: john@thelane.com.au

Region: **Adelaide Hills** Winemaker: **Genevieve Stols** Viticulturist: **Alex Sas** Chief Executive: **David Woods**

Aside from the observation that there is too much viognier influence in the Shiraz Viognier blend, Starvedog Lane delivers a thoroughly contemporary collection of cooler climate wines. The tight, citrusy and often quite mineral Chardonnay, which often punches well above its weight (especially in terms of price) consistently rates well in my tastings and is also something of a darling of the wine show circuit. The briny Sauvignon Blanc is one of this country's finest.

CABERNET MERLOT (formerly Cabernet Sauvignon) RATING 5

| Adelaide Hills | $20–$29 |
| Current vintage: 2004 | 91 |

Supple, long and stylish, this fine and lightly chalky cabernet blend elegantly marries full flavour ripeness with sweet chocolate and cedary oak and a pliant spine of loose-knit tannin. There's an earthy and slightly meaty note beneath its perfume of blackberries, dark plums and violets, while its moderately full palate of pristine dark cherries, plums and blackberries neatly marries the qualities of both varieties.

2004	91	2012	2016
2003	83	2005	2008
2001	93	2009	2013+
2000	89	2008	2012
1999	87	2004	2007
1998	89	2010	2018

CHARDONNAY RATING 3

| Adelaide Hills | $20–$29 |
| Current vintage: 2004 | 92 |

A fine and polished chardonnay with appealing reductive and toasty complexity beneath its juicy presence of citrus, melon and apple-like flavour. Floral, nutty, matchstick and wheatmeal-like influences underpin its citrusy bouquet. Its smooth, silky and creamy palate of melon, peach and apple reveals some buttery malolactic influences before finishing with tangy, citrusy acids and lingering sweet toasty oak.

2004	92	2006	2009+
2003	93	2005	2008+
2002	95	2004	2007+
2001	90	2003	2006+
2000	91	2002	2005+
1999	93	2001	2004+
1998	87	2000	2003

SAUVIGNON BLANC RATING 3

| Adelaide Hills | $12–$19 |
| Current vintage: 2005 | 94 |

A juicy, intensely flavoured sauvignon blanc with cut and shape. Its penetrative fragrance of gooseberries, passionfruit and cut grass reveals mineral, baby powder-like undertones. Long and tangy, its taut and tightly sculpted palate presents clear, vibrant fruit before a persistent and slightly briny finish of refreshing acidity.

2005	94	2006	2007+
2004	93	2005	2006+
2003	93	2003	2004+
2002	95	2003	2004+
2001	91	2002	2003
1999	90	2000	2001
1998	90	2000	2003

SHIRAZ VIOGNIER (formerly Shiraz) RATING 5

| Adelaide Hills | $20–$29 |
| Current vintage: 2004 | 88 |

Spicy, floral and perfumed, its sweet and slightly jammy aromas of red cherries, berries and dark plums reveal undertones of apricot-like viognier. Smooth and creamy, its elegant and polished palate of pristine blackberry, raspberry and cranberry flavour is framed by silky tannins, finishing with length and brightness, but perhaps a shade too much viognier influence.

2004	88	2006	2009+
2003	84	2005	2008
2002	88	2007	2010
2001	87	2006	2009
2000	80	2002	2005
1999	82	2001	2004+
1998	84	2003	2006
1997	87	2002	2005

Stefano Lubiana

60 Rowbottoms Road, Granton Tas 7030. Tel: (03) 6263 7457. Fax: (03) 6263 7430.
Website: www.slw.com.au Email: wine@slw.com.au

Region: **Southern Tasmania** Winemaker: **Steve Lubiana** Chief Executive: **Steve Lubiana**

Two stunning wines, the 2004 Pinot Noir and 2005 Riesling, are the current highlights from Stefano Lubiana, a small and highly committed maker of cool-climate Tasmanian wine. The Pinot Noir is very sophisticated, revealing several layers of flavour and texture, while the Riesling is tightly sculpted and refreshing, with a lingering minerality. The Primavera continues its very impressive recent form, while the Pinot Gris is just marginally hot and oily. Lubiana's current non-vintage sparkling wine is wonderfully rich, chewy and toasty.

CHARDONNAY

RATING **3**

Southern Tasmania	$30–$49	2003	92	2005	2008
Current vintage: 2003	**92**	2002	85	2004	2007
		2001	94	2006	2009
		2000	93	2005	2008
		1999	91	2004	2007
		1998	91	2000	2003

Heavily worked and early-maturing, its brassy, toffee-like bouquet of sweet melon, peach and citrus aromas is backed by hints of honeysuckle and funky, creamy and leesy undertones. Round and juicy, its soft and generous core of nectarine, citrus and peach-like fruit and undertones of butterscotch, grilled nuts and vanilla oak are neatly tied together by tangy lime-juice acids.

PINOT GRIGIO

RATING **5**

Tasmania	$20–$29	2004	89	2006	2007
Current vintage: 2005	**89**	2003	90	2005	2008
		2002	83	2002	2003+
		2001	87	2002	2003+

An oily, unctuous grigio style whose slightly herbaceous and cashew-like aromas of citrus and melon precede a tangy palate of slightly confectionary flavour and lemony acidity. It finishes dusty and dry, with a hint of spirity warmth.

PINOT NOIR

RATING **4**

Southern Tasmania	$30–$49	2004	95	2009	2012+
Current vintage: 2004	**95**	2003	88	2005	2008
		2002	87	2004	2007+
		2001	92	2003	2006+
		2000	87	2002	2005
		1999	86	2001	2004
		1998	88	2000	2003

Sophisticated and deeply layered, its delicate, rustic perfume of red cherries, rose petal and plums reveals meaty, musky undertones. Supple and silky, its focused palate of sweet cherry, plum and berry fruit knits tightly with savoury oak and a fine-grained underswell of firm tannins.

PRIMAVERA PINOT NOIR

RATING **3**

Southern Tasmania	$20–$29	2005	92	2007	2010+
Current vintage: 2005	**92**	2004	89	2005	2006+
		2003	94	2005	2008+
		2002	93	2007	2010
		2001	89	2003	2006+

A spicy, floral and confiture-like aroma of red and black cherries, redcurrants, plums and blackberries overlies dusty cedar/vanilla oak and spicy nuances of cinnamon and cloves. Long and vibrant, its generous and juicy palate has a pleasing sappiness and elegance, but also a powdery undercarriage of bony tannins.

RIESLING

RATING **4**

Tasmania	$20–$29	2005	94	2010	2013+
Current vintage: 2005	**94**	2003	90	2008	2011
		2002	77	2002	2003+
		2001	93	2006	2009+

A lightly musky and spicy perfume of lime juice and lemon precedes a pristine palate whose round and juicy expression of vibrant limey flavour is tightly bound by a sculpted and refreshing lemon-like acidity. Very long and persistent, with an appealing minerality at the finish, it presents traminer-like aspects of muskiness and oiliness.

Stonehaven

Riddoch Highway, Padthaway SA 5271. Tel: (08) 8765 6140. Fax: (08) 8765 6137.
Website: www.stonehavenvineyards.com.au Email: info@stonehavenvineyards.com.au

Region: **Padthaway** Winemakers: **Susanne Bell, Paul Kernich, Garth Cliff**
Viticulturists: **Kerry DeGaris, Graham Kay, Peter Bird, Shane Mills** Chief Executive: **David Woods**

Stonehaven has replaced its Limestone Coast label with one called Hidden Sea. What that is supposed to mean is anyone's guess, but it brings back a 25-year-old memory of when I worked at Padthaway, for Lindemans. Standing atop a hill I could see a huge body of water, where none had been indicated on the map I had studied. 'It's Lake Padthaway,' I was told, which confused me further. My consternation doubled a day later, when I saw that 'Lake Padthaway' had disappeared entirely. Some locals used to flood-irrigate the place. Crazy.

HIDDEN SEA CHARDONNAY (formerly Limestone Coast)   RATING 5

Limestone Coast	$12–$19		
Current vintage: 2005	**85**		

2005	85	2007	2010
2004	88	2002	2005
2003	81	2005	2008
2001	91	2003	2006
2000	90	2002	2005
1999	89	2001	2004
1998	87	2000	2003

Closed and reductive, with smoky aromas of peach and melon fruit backed by wheatmeal-like complexity and lightly toasty vanilla oak. Elegant, moderately long and restrained, its peachy, lemon and tropical flavours however lack definition. It finishes a little too soft and lacking in tightness.

HIDDEN SEA SHIRAZ (formerly Limestone Coast)   RATING 5

Limestone Coast	$12–$19		
Current vintage: 2002	**84**		

2002	84	2007	2010
2001	89	2006	2009+
2000	90	2008	2012
1999	87	2004	2007
1998	89	2003	2006+
1997	88	2002	2005
1996	91	2004	2008

Juicy, soft and generous, this old-fashioned, ripe and jammy shiraz lacks real complexity and charm. Its spicy aromas of blackberries and plums are assertively backed by chocolate, vanilla and coconut-like oak, with undertones of tar and treacle. It's smooth and fruity, with plenty of smoky vanilla oak, but finishes with an excessive saltiness.

LIMITED VINEYARD RELEASE CABERNET SAUVIGNON   RATING 5

Padthaway	$20–$29		
Current vintage: 2002	**89**		

2002	89	2007	2010
1999	89	2004	2007+
1998	90	2006	2010

A typically firm, polished and minty Padthaway cabernet whose menthol-like aromas of blackberries, dark plums and sweet cedar/vanilla oak reveal undertones of dried herbs. Full to medium in weight, its dark-fruited palate is framed by measured but drying tannin and finishes with a lingering smoky and minty impression of sweet red berry fruit.

LIMITED VINEYARD RELEASE CHARDONNAY   RATING 4

Padthaway	$20–$29		
Current vintage: 2002	**85**		

2002	85	2004	2007
2001	91	2006	2009
2000	92	2005	2008
1999	82	2001	2004

An ageing and evolved chardonnay whose slightly brassy and oxidative aromas of citrus, honeysuckle, dried flowers are backed by dusty vanilla oak. Sweet and honeyed, the palate is nearing the end of its drinking life, with very developed, confectionary and sugary characters that lack fruit intensity, definition and freshness.

LIMITED VINEYARD RELEASE SHIRAZ   RATING 5

Padthaway	$20–$29		
Current vintage: 2002	**90**		

2002	90	2010	2014
2001	87	2006	2009
2000	87	2002	2005+
1999	92	2007	2011
1998	89	2003	2006+
1997	89	2009	2017
1996	89	2008	2016

A spicy, floral and peppery bouquet of raspberries, red cherries, plum and fine-grained cedar/vanilla oak is backed by faint minty and menthol-like undertones. Smooth and polished, its elegant expression of small black and red berries, tight-knit cedary oak, leather and spices overlies earthy, meaty complexity. A charmingly soft and old-fashioned red, it should age well.

Stoney Vineyard

105 Tea Tree Road, Campania Tas 7026. Tel: (03) 6260 4174. Fax: (03) 6260 4390.
Website: www.domaine-a.com.au Email: althaus@domaine-a.com.au
Region: **Coal River Valley** Winemaker: **Peter Althaus** Viticulturist: **Peter Althaus** Chief Executive: **Peter Althaus**
Stoney Vineyard is the recently expanded Coal River Valley vineyard whose best fruit is carefully meted into
the Domaine A label, with the Stoney Vineyard name used as a pretty solid and interesting second brand.
The Sauvignon Blanc can be racy and vivacious, the Cabernet Sauvignon elegant and structured, and the Pinot
Noir complex and textured. Like other Tasmanian vineyards, it tends to produce its best wine in warmer seasons.

PINOT NOIR

RATING **4**

| Coal River Valley | $20–$29 |
| Current vintage: 2004 | 89 |

Likely to become quite meaty and savoury with
age, this fragrant and fine-grained pinot has a charmingly smooth palate supported by fine-grained,
bony tannins. Scented with kernel-like aromas of
red cherries, dark plums and marzipan over
spicy nuances of cinnamon, it steadily builds on
the palate, finishing long and dusty and leaving
a lingering core of vibrant fruit.

2004	89	2006	2009+
2003	90	2005	2008
2001	90	2006	2009
1996	90	1998	2001+

SAUVIGNON BLANC

RATING **5**

| Coal River Valley | $12–$19 |
| Current vintage: 2005 | 89 |

A very herbaceous sauvignon blanc whose
lightly sweaty aromas of gooseberries, melon reveal
chalky undertones. Round and generous, with a
tangy, slippery and full-flavoured palate of gooseberry and passionfruit flavour, it finishes very dry
and mineral, with clean acids.

2005	89	2006	2007+
2003	90	2004	2005+
2002	89	2003	2004+
2001	87	2002	2003+
2000	87	2002	2005+
1999	86	1998	1999+
1998	93	1999	2000+

Stonier

2 Thompsons Lane, Merricks Vic 3916. Tel: (03) 5989 8300. Fax: (03) 5989 8709.
Website: www.stoniers.com.au Email: stoniers@stoniers.com.au
Region: **Mornington Peninsula** Winemaker: **Geraldine McFaul** Viticulturist: **Stuart Marshall**
Chief Executive: **Peter Cowan**
Owned by Lion Nathan, Stonier has augmented its premier Reserve label and its 'standard' brand with the
introduction of individual vineyard wines under the KBS and Windmill labels. The 2004 KBS Chardonnay (96,
drink 2006–2009+) is a stunning, sumptuous and concentrated wine of great tightness, while the 2004 KBS
Pinot Noir (95, drink 2009–2012) is substantial, gamey and very savoury, with a backbone of silky tannins. The
2004 Windmill Pinot Noir (96, drink 2009–2012) is very smooth, lightly stalky and deeply fruited.

CHARDONNAY

RATING **5**

| Mornington Peninsula | $20–$29 |
| Current vintage: 2004 | 90 |

A sophisticated, smooth and finely crafted young
chardonnay whose vibrant tropical aromas of
mango and pineapple are backed by suggestions
of honey, butterscotch, creamy and nutty lees-
derived influences and dried flowers. It's fluffy and
creamy, and while its tropical and melon-like fruit
is presently slightly overshadowed by bacon/but-
terscotch malolactic influences, there's sufficient
length of fruit and balance with soft acidity to
suggest its fruit will build in the bottle.

2004	90	2006	2009
2003	87	2003	2004
2002	82	2003	2004
2001	87	2003	2006
2000	89	2002	2005
1999	89	2001	2004
1998	88	1999	2000
1997	88	1998	2001

PINOT NOIR

RATING 4

Mornington Peninsula	**$30–$49**	2004	87	2006	2009
Current vintage: 2004	**87**	2003	90	2004	2005+

An honest early-drinking pinot whose slightly cooked and tomato-like expression of fruit and metallic edges detract from some otherwise pleasing pinot characters of rose petals, red cherries and dark plums. There's some meatiness and cinnamon/clove-like spice beneath the bouquet, while the palate offers good length and a fine structure of tight tannins. This wine could flesh out and refocus over the next year, so the score might well be a little hard. Right now, it's frankly hard to tell.

2002	88	2003	2004+
2001	88	2002	2003+
2000	91	2002	2005
1999	89	2001	2004
1998	88	1999	2000
1997	88	1999	2002
1996	91	2001	2004
1995	87	1997	2000

RESERVE CHARDONNAY

RATING 2

Mornington Peninsula	$30–$49	2004	93	2009	2012
Current vintage: 2004	**93**	2003	93	2005	2008+

A smooth, supple and seamless chardonnay with a slightly candied expression of buttery, melon and citrusy fruit. Its nutty and lightly toasty bouquet is laced with cloves and cinnamon, with a background of smoky vanilla oak and lemon sherbet. Finishing with a hint of tinned pineapple and taut minerality, it's long, elegant and slightly spirity.

2002	93	2007	2010
2001	95	2006	2009
2000	95	2005	2008
1999	92	2001	2004
1998	95	2003	2006
1997	95	2002	2005
1996	92	1998	2001
1995	92	2003	2007
1994	93	1996	1999

RESERVE PINOT NOIR

RATING 3

Mornington Peninsula	**$30–$49**	2004	93	2009	2012
Current vintage: 2004	**93**	2003	94	2008	2011+

Likely to develop well, this very floral and perfumed young pinot is scented with red and black cherries, rose petals and restrained cedar/vanilla oak with complex undertones of forest floor, cloves and cinnamon. Supple and silky, it's piercingly intense, delivering pristine varietal fruit backed by a fine undercarriage of dusty tannin. It finishes long and savoury, with lingering hints of herbs and meatiness.

2001	84	2003	2006
2000	91	2002	2005
1999	93	2004	2007
1998	94	2003	2006
1997	95	2002	2005
1995	77	1997	2000
1994	93	1996	1999
1993	95	1998	2001
1992	93	1997	2000
1991	88	1993	1996

Stringy Brae

Sawmill Road, Sevenhill SA 5453. Tel: (08) 8843 4313. Fax: (08) 8843 4319.
Website: www.stringybrae.com.au Email: sales@stringybrae.com.au

Region: **Clare Valley** Winemaker: **Contract** Viticulturist: **Hannah Rantanen** Chief Executive: **Donald Willson**

Stringy Brae is a small Clare Valley maker whose Rieslings are slightly broader, more candied and fractionally sweeter than those typical of the region, while its Shiraz is usually minty, robust and briary.

RIESLING

RATING 4

Clare Valley	$20–$29	2005	91	2010	2013+
Current vintage: 2005	**91**	2004	90	2009	2012+

Restrained and waiting to emerge, this long, dry and seamless riesling has a slightly reductive and candied bouquet that soon clears away, leaving a lime juice and lemon detergent fragrance. Vibrant and juicy, its crunchy apple-like palate has a smoothness and richness, but finishes with a lingering, clean and citrusy finish.

2003	89	2008	2011
2002	91	2007	2010+
2001	90	2009	2013
2000	87	2002	2005+

A B C D E F G H I J K L M N O P Q R S T U V W X Y Z

SHIRAZ

RATING **5**

		Clare Valley	$20–$29
		Current vintage: 2002	89

Assertive aromas of briary cassis, dark plums and blackberries penetrate a liniment-like background of menthol, mint and sweet cedar/vanilla oak. Soft and juicy, its smooth and measured palate is deeply flavoured, generous and supple. It's a question of how much you enjoy its deeply accentuated and medicinal regional cut of mint and menthol.

2002	89	2007	2010+
2001	88	2003	2006+
2000	87	2002	2005+
1999	86	2001	2004+

Suckfizzle

Lot 4 Gnaraway Road, Margaret River WA 6290. Tel: (08) 9757 6377. Fax: (08) 9757 6022.
Website: www.stellabella.com.au Email: wines@stellabella.com.au
Region: **Margaret River** Winemaker: **Janice McDonald** Viticulturist: **Shelly Brennan** Chief Executive: **John Britton**
Suckfizzle is a brand associated with a significant planting near Augusta, in the cooler, southerly reaches of the Margaret River region. Its white blend of Bordeaux varieties counters its significant oak-derived creaminess with wonderful length and racy austerity, while its Cabernet Sauvignon is rather herbaceous.

SAUVIGNON BLANC SEMILLON

RATING **3**

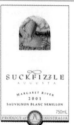

	Margaret River	$30–$49
	Current vintage: 2004	93

A charming New World white blend that flaunts its smoky vanilla oak influences. Its lifted, floral and dusty aromas of passionfruit, gooseberries, grapefruit and lemon are backed with nettle-like herbal undertones, and oak. Round and smooth, with a sumptuous viscosity, its handsomely oaked palate of intense, juicy and herbal fruit finishes long and clean, with supple acids.

2004	93	2006	2009
2003	94	2005	2008
2002	91	2004	2007
2001	89	2002	2003+
1998	93	2000	2003
1997	95	1999	2002

Summerfield

5967 Stawell-Avoca Road, Moonambel Vic 3478. Tel: (03) 5467 2264. Fax: (03) 5467 2380.
Website: www.summerfieldwines.com Email: info@summerfieldwines.com
Region: **Pyrenees** Winemakers: **Ian & Mark Summerfield** Viticulturist: **Ian Summerfield**
Chief Executive: **Ian Summerfield**
Summerfield is a small, mature and family-owned vineyard in the Pyrenees area whose super-ripe Reserve Cabernet Shiraz and Reserve Shiraz have not been able to avoid some of the stress associated with the region's severe recent vintages. The 2004 Tradition (90, drink 2016–2024), a cabernet-based red blend, is significantly more vibrant and better-structured than the more expensive 2003 Reserve reds.

RESERVE CABERNET SHIRAZ (formerly Reserve Cabernet)

RATING **5**

	Pyrenees	$50–$99
	Current vintage: 2003	87

Sumptuous and robust, this lusciously proportioned and lavishly oaked wine just lacks the charm and brightness to rate more highly and drink more easily. Its spirity aromas of raisins, currants, prunes and licorice overlie suggestions of treacle and mocha/dark chocolate-like oak. Exaggerated and powerful, the palate is reliant on its new oak for sweetness, as its flavours of prunes and cooked plums finish tarry and toffee-like.

2003	87	2008	2011+
2002	86	2007	2010
2001	86	2003	2006
2000	89	2005	2008+
1999	86	2004	2007

RESERVE SHIRAZ

RATING **5**

Pyrenees	$50–$99
Current vintage: 2003	**89**

A smooth and juicy shiraz of the ultra-ripe style with just enough fruit sweetness and freshness to counter its sweet and spicy vanilla oak. Its meaty fragrance of cassis, blackberries and plums reveals cooked currant and prune-like aspects, while its sumptuous palate of ripe and jammy fruit finishes with a note of licorice and treacle. Framed by fine and silky tannins, it lacks the presence of genuinely ripe (ie not over-ripe) fruit for a higher rating

2003	89	2008	2011
2002	87	2004	2007+
2001	88	2003	2006
2000	88	2002	2005
1999	89	2004	2007

Summit Estate

291 Granite Belt Drive, Thulimbah Qld 4377. Tel: (07) 4683 2011. Fax: (07) 4683 2600.
Website: www.summitestate.com.au Email: stanwine@halenet.com.au
Region: **Granite Belt** Winemaker: **Paola Cabezas Rhymer** Viticulturist: **William Higgins**
Chief Executive: **William Ryan**
Summit Estate is an emergent winery that has made a couple of ripe, oaky and assertive Reserve Shirazes, a rather funky 2004 Verdelho and a delightfully restrained and fluffy 2004 Chardonnay. Its Shiraz is typically smooth, ripe and slightly meaty.

SHIRAZ

Granite Belt	$20–$29
Current vintage: 2003	**88**

A vibrant and generously flavoured shiraz of charm and balance. Its sweet, spicy aromas of raspberries, cassis and chocolate/vanilla oak reveal spicy undertones of cloves and white pepper. Smooth and silky, its spicy berry/plum fruit overlies slightly cooked and meaty influences, finishing with charm and balance.

2003	88	2005	2008
2002	83	2004	2007
2001	82	2003	2006

Tahbilk

Off Goulburn Valley Highway, Tahbilk Vic 3608. Tel: (03) 5794 2555. Fax: (03) 5794 2360.
Website: www.tahbilk.com.au Email: admin@tahbilk.com.au
Region: **Nagambie Lakes** Winemakers: **Alister Purbrick, Neil Larson, Alan George** Viticulturist: **Ian Hendy**
Chief Executive: **Alister Purbrick**
Tahbilk is an historic vineyard and winery on the banks of the Goulburn River in central Victoria, which is operated by Alister Purbrick, the third generation member of this family to do so. The winery is blessed with large old cellars replete with very large old cooperage, which Purbrick feels is essential to the make-up and identity of Tahbilk red wine. Because of this, Tahbilk's reds hark back to a bygone era whose wines are less vibrant and juicy than most modern red wines, and rely on their typically firm tannins for their structure and longevity.

1860 VINES SHIRAZ (formerly Claret)

RATING **4**

Nagambie Lakes	$100–$199
Current vintage: 2001	**90**

Richly fruited by Tahbilk standards, this remains an old-fashioned, firm and sinewy shiraz that demands cellaring. Backed by a delicate floral perfume, it reveals a bouquet of cherries and red plums, coach leather and dusty, cedary oak. Backed by bony tannins, there's a good length of fruit sweetness before a rather drying, firm and savoury finish.

2001	90	2013	2021+
2000	86	2008	2012+
1999	91	2011	2019
1998	95	2010	2018+
1997	90	2009	2017+
1996	93	2008	2016+
1995	91	2007	2015
1994	90	2002	2006
1992	93	2012	2022
1991	90	2011	2021
1990	90	2010	2020
1989	82	2001	2011
1988	88	2000	2010
1987	92	2007	2017

CABERNET SAUVIGNON

Nagambie Lakes $12–$19
Current vintage: 2003   89

A very old-fashioned red that needs a very long time. Its minty, eucalypt-like aromas of blackberry jam, dark plums and menthol precede a firm, heavy and powerfully astringent palate whose jammy fruit is coated by hard, sinewy tannins. It should, however, repay those with the cellaring conditions and the patience.

2003	89	2015	2023
2002	91	2014	2022
2001	83	2003	2006+
2000	90	2008	2012+
1999	88	2007	2011
1998	86	2006	2010
1997	86	2005	2009
1996	83	2001	2004
1995	92	2015	2025
1994	90	2006	2014
1993	91	2005	2013
1992	93	2004	2012
1991	93	2011	2021
1990	93	2010	2020

CHARDONNAY

Nagambie Lakes $12–$19
Current vintage: 2004   77

Lacklustre nutty, peachy aromas are backed by rather clunky cardboard-like oak that dulls its freshness. It's forward and simple but dries out towards a flat finish of papery oak influence.

2004	77	2005	2006
2002	89	2004	2007
2001	89	2003	2006+
2000	83	2003	2005
1999	81	2001	2004
1998	83	2000	2003
1997	85	1999	2002

MARSANNE

Nagambie Lakes $12–19
Current vintage: 2005   89

Spicy aromas of honeysuckle and lemon sherbet precede a generous and juicy palate whose mouthfilling flavours of lemon rind and honeydew melon are backed by nuances of minerals and tangerine. It finishes long and clean, with a bright, vibrant and citrusy acidity.

2005	89	2010	2013
2004	92	2012	2016
2003	92	2011	2015
2002	91	2007	2010+
2001	87	2006	2009
2000	88	2005	2008
1999	90	2004	2007
1998	87	2003	2006+
1997	90	2005	2009
1996	93	2004	2008
1995	90	2007	2015
1994	92	2006	2014

RESERVE CABERNET SAUVIGNON

Nagambie Lakes $50–$99
Current vintage: 2001   89

Ripe and meaty, this substantial but slightly overcooked cabernet backs its baked and currant-like fruit with an astringent backbone of firm tannins. There is a varnishy aspect to the nose, while the raisined palate reveals undertones of plums and red berries, with lingering fruit sweetness. It might lack consistency of ripeness, but could cellar well and slowly into an interesting wine of idiosyncratic Tahbilk style.

2001	89	2013	2021
2000	93	2012	2020+
1998	93	2010	2018+
1997	93	2009	2017+
1996	90	2008	2016+
1994	89	2014	2024
1993	88	2005	2013
1992	91	2012	2022

RESERVE SHIRAZ

Nagambie Lakes $50–$99
Current vintage: 2001   91

Robust and meaty, earthy and extracted, with a leathery bouquet of dark chocolate, dried herbs, cedar and vanilla tending to lack primary fruit. Its rustic palate does reveal some deep, dark plum-like fruit beneath its cask and bottle-aged development. Drinking considerably older than its age, but with the depth of flavour and structure of cherry kernel-like tannin to go considerably further.

2001	91	2013	2021+
2000	89	2012	2020
1999	92	2011	2019+
1998	95	2018	2028
1997	92	2009	2017
1996	90	2004	2008+
1994	90	2002	2006+

RIESLING

RATING **5**

Nagambie Lakes	$12–$19
Current vintage: 2005	**87**

A generous, early-drinking riesling whose flesh aromas of lemon sherbet, baby powder and lime juice overlie nuances of lemon rind and minerals. Juicy, fresh and slightly candied, it's forward and relatively simple, but clean and refreshing.

2005	87	2007	2010
2004	92	2009	2012+
2003	88	2005	2008
2001	83	2003	2006
2000	90	2005	2008
1999	87	2001	2004
1998	82	2003	2006+
1997	93	2005	2009
1996	92	2004	2008
1995	90	2003	2007
1994	91	2002	2006

SHIRAZ

RATING **5**

Nagambie Lakes	$12–$19
Current vintage: 2003	**91**

A very ripe, sumptuous and powerfully constructed shiraz suited to long-term cellaring. Its porty aromas of cooked plums and blackberries reveal underlying nuances of cassis and sweet red berries, plus hints of sage and cloves, tar and treacle. Unusually concentrated for a Tahbilk red, its thick, firm and astringent palate of meaty blackberry and plum flavours has a slightly stewy but not overcooked aspect. Framed by somewhat gritty tannins, it finishes long, drying and savoury.

2003	91	2015	2023+
2002	88	2014	2022
2001	88	2009	2013
2000	89	2008	2012+
1999	87	2004	2007
1998	87	2006	2010+
1997	87	2005	2009
1996	82	2001	2004
1995	89	2007	2015
1994	90	2014	2024
1993	86	1998	2001
1992	93	2004	2012
1991	92	2011	2021
1990	89	2002	2010

Tallarook

2 Delaney's Road, Warranwood Vic 3134. Tel: (03) 9876 7022. Fax: (03) 9876 7044.
Website: www.tallarook.com Email: info@tallarook.com

Region: **Upper Goulburn** Winemaker: **Trina Smith** Viticulturist: **Daniel Ebert** General Manager: **Anthony Woollams**
Tallarook makes interesting and complex Chardonnay and Marsanne, each of which is given full Burgundian treatment in the cellar. The best releases are those with the depth of fruit to handle the significant level of artefact they acquire along the way. The reds I have tasted are greenish, minty and medicinal.

CHARDONNAY

RATING **5**

Upper Goulburn	$20–$29
Current vintage: 2004	**84**

A rich, juicy and heavily worked chardonnay that lacks the intensity and length of fruit to handle the amount of winemaker-derived complexity it has acquired. Very oaky and slightly varnishy, its buttery and toffee-like aromas of quince, cumquat, peaches and varnishy vanilla oak are backed by meaty, leesy undertones. Forward and unctuous, its fruit struggles for attention throughout its cloying and caramel-like palate.

2004	84	2006	2009
2002	88	2004	2007
2001	87	2003	2006
2000	93	2002	2005+
1999	87	2001	2004
1998	89	2000	2003

MARSANNE

RATING **5**

Upper Goulburn	$20–$29
Current vintage: 2004	**87**

A powerfully winemaker-influenced wine whose interesting complexity somewhat overshadows its varietal identity. Meaty, mineral and lanolin-like aromas of lime juice, musky spices and matchstick/vanilla oak precede a richly textured and reductive palate. Long and smooth, it dries out a little quickly, and was perhaps bottled with too high a level of reduction for a screwcap seal.

2004	87	2006	2009
2003	88	2005	2008
2002	88	2004	2007
2001	91	2003	2006+
2000	82	2002	2005

Taltarni

Taltarni Road, Moonambel Vic 3478. Tel: (03) 5459 7900. Fax: (03) 5467 2306.
Website: www.taltarni.com.au Email: enquiries@taltarni.com.au
Region: **Pyrenees** Winemakers: **Leigh Clarnette, Loic le Calvez, Louella McPhan**
Viticulturist: **Kym Ludvigsen** Chief Executive: **Adam Torpy**

Taltarni is gradually re-emerging as a maker of a rounder, and more forward expression of red wine than the very firm and astringent long-term wines of yesteryear. A fine example of this is the peppery and ethereal 2002 Shiraz, whose palate reveals plenty of brightness and intensity. Sparkling wine production has long been a part of Taltarni's business, and the rich, creamy and slightly meaty 2003 Brut is a delicious reminder of how proficient it has become.

BRUT

RATING **5**

Victoria, Tasmania	$20–$29
Current vintage: 2004	**90**

A very fine, elegant and stylish sparkling wine of restraint and freshness, whose delicate, lightly herbal aromas of peach and citrus fruits reveal pleasingly creamy undertones. It's long, creamy and slightly chalky, delivering vibrant peach, melon and citrusy fruit all the way to its refreshing, quite dry and tangy finish. Generous and restrained, its bead is pleasingly fine and crackly.

2004	90	2006	2009
2003	92	2005	2008
2002	88	2004	2007
2001	87	2003	2006
2000	88	2003	2006
1999	89	2001	2004+

CABERNET SAUVIGNON

RATING **5**

Pyrenees	$30–$49
Current vintage: 2002	**88**

Slightly herbal, but fine and grainy, this moderately full-bodied cabernet marries delicate black and red berry flavours with cedary oak and meaty, autumnal undertones. Its dusty aromas and supple, almost sappy palate show some finesse and elegance but the wine is a little too herbaceous for a higher rating.

2002	88	2010	2014
2001	93	2013	2021
2000	84	2008	2012
1998	94	2006	2010+
1997	86	2002	2005+
1996	88	2004	2008
1995	89	2003	2007
1994	93	2006	2014+
1993	91	2005	2013
1992	93	2004	2012+
1991	91	2011	2021
1990	93	2002	2010+
1989	87	1997	2001
1988	94	2000	2008
1987	89	1999	2007
1986	89	1998	2006

SAUVIGNON BLANC

RATING **4**

Pyrenees	$12–$19
Current vintage: 2005	**87**

An attempt at a more reductive, mineral and savoury Old World style whose slightly dull, flat and confectionary aromas of citrus and gooseberry fruit reveal floral and cheesy undertones. Long, chalky and austere, the palate is more convincing, with genuine flintiness and cut.

2005	87	2005	2006
2004	90	2005	2006+
2003	87	2004	2005
2002	91	2003	2004
2001	90	2001	2002
2000	90	2001	2002
1999	93	2000	2001+
1998	87	1999	2000
1997	86	1997	1998
1996	88	1998	2001

SHIRAZ (formerly French Syrah)

RATING 3

Pyrenees	$30–$49
Current vintage: 2002	91

Taltarni has taken advantage of the cooler Victorian 2002 season to fashion a deeply flavoured but shapely shiraz of medium to full weight, but genuine cellaring potential. It's a stylish and harmonious wine that marries the pepper, spice and intense dark plum and berry qualities of shiraz with restrained but lightly smoky oak and the minty/menthol undertones typical of the Pyrenees region. There's an ethereal quality about its peppery and deeply fruited fragrance, while the palate reveals genuine refinement and elegance, as its vibrant depth of red and black berry fruit is enhanced by fresh acids and supported by fine, grainy tannins. Keep it for at least five years.

2002	91	2010	2014+
2001	90	2009	2013
2000	93	2008	2012+
1999	93	2007	2011
1998	95	2006	2010
1997	95	2005	2009+
1996	95	2004	2008
1995	87	2000	2003
1994	92	1999	2002
1993	94	2001	2005
1992	94	2004	2012
1991	93	2003	2011
1990	89	1998	2002+

THREE MONKS CABERNET MERLOT

RATING 5

Victoria	$12–$19
Current vintage: 2004	90

A stylish and elegant young wine should develop with charm. Its fresh, minty fragrance of black berries, plums, dark cherries and cedar/vanilla oak overlies a hint of meatiness. Tightly supported by firmish, chalky tannins, the palate is fine and drying, with a pleasing length of cassis/plum fruit and a lingering and slightly salty/mineral finish.

2004	90	2012	2016
2003	90	2011	2015
2002	88	2007	2010+
2001	89	2006	2009
2000	91	2005	2008
1999	82	2001	2004
1998	84	2000	2003
1997	82	2002	2005

TarraWarra Estate

Healesville Road, Yarra Glen Vic 3775. Tel: (03) 5962 3311. Fax: (03) 5962 3887.
Website: www.tarrawarra.com.au Email: enq@tarrawarra.com.au

Region: **Yarra Valley** Winemaker: **Clare Halloran** Viticulturist: **Stuart Sissins** General Manager: **Simon Napthine**

This dedicated and ambitious small winery operation in the Yarra Valley is owned by the Besen family, who set it up in the early 1980s with the help of David Wollan, today one of the world's foremost wine technologists. The richness, complexity and elegance of the 2004 Chardonnay is totally faithful to Wollan's original ambitions for the style. The 2004 Pinot Noir wasn't made from fruit with the same intensity and ripeness.

CHARDONNAY

RATING 2

Yarra Valley	$30–$49
Current vintage: 2004	96

A sumptuous, spotless and smoky chardonnay whose slightly funky bouquet of creamy grapefruit, melon and mineral aromas overlies nuances of butterscotch. Richly flavoured, meaty and chewy, this is a full orchestra chardonnay based on a powerful expression of ripe, juicy fruit tightly interwoven with savoury oak and lemony acids. It finishes with exceptional length and balance.

2004	96	2012	2016
2003	94	2008	2011
2002	94	2007	2010
2001	92	2005	2008
2000	90	2002	2005
1999	90	2004	2007
1998	94	2006	2010
1997	95	2005	2009
1996	91	2001	2004
1995	91	2000	2003+

PINOT NOIR

RATING 5

Yarra Valley	$50–$99
Current vintage: 2004	89

A pretty, sappy and autumnal pinot whose leafy aromas of red cherries, raspberries, plums and forest floor reveal gamey undertones. Medium to full in weight, it's forward and juicy, with a good length of vibrant fruit framed by greenish tannins. Already showing some development, and likely to age quickly.

2004	89	2006	2009
2003	93	2008	2011
2002	89	2004	2007
2001	89	2003	2006+
2000	83	2002	2005
1999	88	2001	2004
1998	95	2006	2010
1997	90	2002	2005
1996	95	2001	2004+
1995	93	2000	2003
1994	93	1999	2002
1993	89	1998	2001
1992	95	2000	2004

Tatachilla

151 Main Road, McLaren Vale SA 5171. Tel: (08) 8323 8656. Fax: (08) 8323 9096.
Website: www.tatachillawines.com.au   Email: enquiries@tatachillawines.com.au

Region: **McLaren Vale**   Winemaker: **Fanchon Ferrandi**   Chief Executive: **Peter Cowan**

Tatachilla has been a successful Lion Nathan brand, but there are some indications that it is experiencing difficulty selling its wine. As my scores might suggest, there's not a huge and obvious quality difference between its more expensive wines and those considerably cheaper. Making the comparison even more difficult is that while the older vintages of expensive labels hanging around are now showing signs of tiredness, the more youthful cheaper labels, like the 2004 McLaren Vale Shiraz, are simply bursting with fruit and vitality.

1901 CABERNET SAUVIGNON

RATING **4**

South Australia	$30–$49		
Current vintage: 2002	92		

Firm, structured and deeply flavoured, this lightly herbal and minty cabernet has a fragrance of dark plums, blackcurrants, vanilla and dark chocolate, with lightly vegetal and capsicum-like undertones. Long and smooth, its pristine expression of black-berries, cassis and plums is framed by drying tannins. Likely to become more elegant and complex.

2002	92	2010	2014+
2000	82	2002	2005+
1999	89	2004	2007+
1998	91	2006	2010+

CLARENDON VINEYARD MERLOT

RATING **4**

McLaren Vale	$30–$49		
Current vintage: 2001	87		

A rather blocky and forward merlot whose sweet, jammy aromas of red berries and plums reveal a cedar/vanilla oak background with suggestions of mint and menthol. A firm spine of hard-edged tannins underpins its sweet, but slightly short expression of berry/plum flavours. Should soften quickly.

2001	87	2006	2009
2000	90	2002	2005+
1999	87	2001	2004
1998	90	2003	2006
1997	87	2002	2005
1996	92	2001	2004+

FOUNDATION SHIRAZ

RATING **5**

McLaren Vale	$30–$49		
Current vintage: 2001	89		

A more restrained expression of this wine despite presenting a slightly cooked aspect. Its gamey, rather baked and porty aromas of plums and red-currants, cloves and nutmeg are supported by sweet cedar/vanilla oak. Smooth and leathery, its palate of red plums, currants and dark olives lacks great length, but finishes with powdery tannins, some greenish edges and a lingering note of chocolate.

2001	89	2006	2009+
2000	88	2002	2005+
1999	88	2001	2004+
1998	91	2006	2010
1997	89	1999	2002+
1996	89	1998	2001
1995	90	1997	2000

KEYSTONE GRENACHE SHIRAZ

RATING **5**

McLaren Vale	$12–$19		
Current vintage: 2002	85		

Honest, flavoursome and uncomplicated, with a sweet, slightly cooked and jammy aroma of plums and raspberries with spicy undertones. Its forward, licorice-like expression of plum, raspberry and blueberry flavours is wrapped in soft tannins but loses freshness and brightness towards the finish.

2002	85	2003	2004+
2001	87	2003	2006
2000	87	2001	2002+
1999	82	2000	2001
1998	86	2000	2003
1997	86	1999	2002+
1996	87	2001	2004

McLAREN VALE CABERNET SAUVIGNON

RATING **5**

McLaren Vale	$20–$29		
Current vintage: 2003	87		

A modest, uncomplicated cabernet whose lightly herbal aromas of berries and plums are backed by restrained cedar/vanilla oak. It's moderately intense, juicy and long, with dark berry/plum fruit and sweet vanilla oak framed by simple tannins. Acceptable, flawless but straightforward.

2003	87	2005	2008+
2002	90	2007	2010
2001	87	2003	2006
2000	89	2002	2005+
1999	82	2001	2004
1998	91	2003	2006+
1997	89	1999	2002
1996	87	2001	2004
1995	87	2000	2003
1994	82	1996	1999

McLAREN VALE SHIRAZ

RATING **5**

McLaren Vale	$20–$29
Current vintage: 2004	**90**

A delicious young shiraz whose spicy, peppery fragrance of blackberries, cassis and dark plums overlies sweet coconut ice-like oak and scents of violets. Sumptuous, smooth and silky, its long and lively palate is packed with juicy berry and plum flavours. Framed by smooth, creamy tannin and backed by rather smart and lightly smoky oak, it finishes with length and brightness of fruit, and a refreshing acidity. Terrific value.

2004	90	2006	2009+
2002	89	2007	2010+
2001	88	2003	2006
2000	81	2002	2005
1999	82	2001	2004
1998	90	2006	2010
1997	89	2002	2005
1996	90	2004	2008

PADTHAWAY CABERNET SAUVIGNON

RATING **5**

Padthaway	$20–$29
Current vintage: 2001	**80**

Skinny, stewy and herbal red with a minty, eucalypt aroma of cassis, raspberries and light vanilla oak, plus a simple, cooked palate whose cassis/plum flavours thin out towards a green, dilute finish.

2001	80	2003	2006
2000	87	2002	2005
1999	84	2001	2004
1998	90	2003	2006

Taylors

Taylors Road, Auburn SA 5451. Tel: (08) 8849 1100. Fax: (08) 8849 1199.
Website: www.taylorswines.com.au Email: cdoor@taylorswines.com.au
Region: **Clare Valley** Winemakers: **Adam Eggins, Helen McCarthy** Viticulturists: **Ken Noack, Colin Hinze**
Chief Executive: **Mitchell Taylor**

Taylors is a comparatively large Clare Valley maker that has lifted the standard of its popular range of varietal table wines. By and large it has succeeded in this, but by comparison, its premier St Andrews reds now look rather over-ripe, clunky and over-priced. Where Taylors really delivers is in its cheaper range of young, fresh varietal wines (except the 2004 Merlot) and with the deliciously racy 2004 Jaraman Riesling.

CABERNET SAUVIGNON

RATING **5**

Clare Valley	$12–$19
Current vintage: 2004	**89**

Not hugely complex but built to last, this firm but pliant young cabernet is based on a ripe, juicy and minty expression of intense blackcurrant, dark plum and blackberry flavour backed by sweet cedar/vanilla oak. Tightly integrated and finely structured, it reveals an attractive violet-like perfume and a long, smooth and deeply flavoured, drying palate.

2004	89	2009	2012+
2003	88	2008	2011+
2002	88	2007	2010
2001	90	2009	2013
2000	88	2008	2012
1999	93	2004	2007+
1998	90	2003	2006
1997	81	1999	2002
1996	82	1998	2001
1995	86	1997	2000
1994	87	1999	2002
1993	81	2001	2005
1992	83	2000	2004

JARAMAN RIESLING

RATING **5**

Clare Valley, Eden Valley	$12–$19
Current vintage: 2005	**94**

Supple, smooth and silky, this powdery and elegant riesling has a fresh perfume of lime, lemon juice and musky rose petal. Its long and vibrant palate reveals a pleasingly juicy core of flavour, finishing with clean, refreshing acidity.

2005	94	2013	2017
2004	88	2006	2009
2992	82	2004	2007

MERLOT

Clare Valley	$12–$19
Current vintage: 2004	80

A raisined and pruney merlot clearly made from stressed or over-ripened grapes. Its minty, menthol-like aromas rely on creamy vanilla oak for sweetness, while the thick, moderately tannic and dehydrated palate lacks brightness and elegance. No amount of sweet oak could revive these dead grapes.

2004	80	2005	2006
2003	87	2005	2008
2002	89	2004	2007
2001	81	2002	2003+

RIESLING

Clare Valley	$12–$19
Current vintage: 2005	88

An honest, richly flavoured and varietal riesling whose rather candied fragrance of lemon meringue and lime juice is backed by musky, spicy nuances. Round and juicy, it's smooth and generous, with slightly confection-like fruit over a chalky backbone that culminates in a clean, but fractionally sweet finish.

2005	88	2005	2013
2004	89	2006	2009
2003	88	2005	2008
2002	83	2003	2004
2001	93	2006	2009
2000	92	2005	2008
1999	86	2001	2004
1998	85	2000	2003
1997	85	1999	2002
1996	92	2004	2008
1994	93	2002	2006
1993	89	1995	1998

SHIRAZ

Clare Valley	$12–$19
Current vintage: 2004	88

Honest, ripe and flavoursome, this oaky and spicy shiraz has a smoky aroma of cassis, plums and prunes over peppery spices and smoky mocha/coconut ice oak. Long and juicy, its vibrant palate of spicy blackberries, plums and redcurrants fits well with its generous measure of sweet oak. It's framed by moderately firm tannins and finishes with some tight and refreshing acidity.

2004	88	2006	2009+
2003	88	2005	2008
2002	89	2004	2007
2001	91	2003	2006+
2000	89	2002	2005+
1999	88	2001	2004
1998	90	2003	2006
1997	88	2002	2005
1996	87	2001	2004
1995	88	2000	2003
1994	87	1996	1999
1993	87	1998	2001

ST ANDREWS CABERNET SAUVIGNON

Clare Valley	$50–$99
Current vintage: 2000	91

A firm, savoury cabernet of strength and depth. Its earthy, dusty and cedary aromas of violets, blackberries, mint and dark chocolate/cedar/vanilla oak precede a ripe, well-proportioned but not over-cooked palate framed by fine-grained and powdery tannins. There's just a hint of currant beneath its dark plum and berry flavours, while sweet oak plays second fiddle.

2000	91	2012	2020
1999	90	2007	2011
1998	87	2003	2006
1997	84	2002	2005

ST ANDREWS RIESLING

Clare Valley	$30–$49
Current vintage: 2001	90

Toasty, honeyed aromas of floral, citrusy fruit backed by buttery, keroseney and lightly smoky, beeswax-like nuances introduce a flavoursome, sumptuous riesling developing reasonably quickly. Round and creamy, its long and generous palate finishes long and citrusy.

2001	90	2009	2013
2000	92	2008	2012
1998	91	2003	2006
1996	92	2004	2008

ST ANDREWS SHIRAZ

RATING **5**

Clare Valley	**$50–$99**		
Current vintage: 2001	**88**		

Meaty and robust, this sumptuously ripened shiraz presents a spicy, clove and cinnamon-like bouquet of red and black berries backed by sweet vanilla oak. On the tarry, currant-like side of ripeness, it offers profound fruit depth and astringency, but lacks genuinely vibrant fruit sweetness.

2001	88	2009	2013
2000	87	2005	2008+
1999	93	2007	2011
1998	90	2003	2006+
1997	89	2002	2005

The Lane Vineyard

Ravenswood Lane, Hahndorf SA 5245. Tel: (08) 8388 1250. Fax: (08) 8388 7233.
Website: www.thelane.com.au Email: cellar@thelane.com.au

Region: **Adelaide Hills** Winemaker: **Robert Mann** Viticulturist: **John Edwards** Chief Executive: **John Edwards**

This brand has changed its name from Ravenswood Lane to The Lane. It should perhaps be given more credit than it receives for its consistently classy and racy Sauvignon Blanc, of which the 2005 vintage is typically tight and mineral. The 2004 Chardonnay is under-fruited, while the 2003 Reunion Shiraz is overworked and overcooked. The company releases some very herbal and dark-fruited 19th Meeting Cabernet Sauvignon.

BEGINNING CHARDONNAY

RATING **5**

Adelaide Hills	**$30–$49**		
Current vintage: 2004	**87**		

A supple and citrusy chardonnay with a delicate lemony, grapefruit-like aroma of tropical fruit and nutty/vanilla oak and a smooth, restrained palate that just lacks genuine length and intensity. It's soft and creamy, with stonefruit and citrus flavours before a savoury finish.

2004	87	2006	2009+
2002	84	2004	2007
2001	90	2006	2009
2000	93	2002	2005
1999	88	2000	2001
1998	82	1999	2000

GATHERING SAUVIGNON SEMILLON

RATING **3**

Adelaide Hills	**$30–$49**		
Current vintage: 2005	**93**		

A complex, flavoursome and tightly crafted but oak-enhanced blend of some class. Its pungent aromas of gooseberries, passionfruit and cassis overlie floral, mineral and lightly herbal complexity, with restrained undertones of vanilla oak. There's also a hint of oak beneath its soft and generously flavoured palate, whose vibrant fruit and mineral, baby powder-like complexity finishes with excellent length and refreshing acidity.

2005	93	2007	2010+
2002	93	2003	2004+
2001	94	2003	2006
2000	75	2000	2001

REUNION SHIRAZ

RATING **5**

Adelaide Hills	**$30–$49**		
Current vintage: 2003	**86**		

Tightly crafted but cooked and meaty, this smooth and fine-grained shiraz just lacks the fruit brightness and intensity to counter its oak and extract. Pungent mocha and dark chocolate-like aromas of blackberries, currants, plums and raisins with undertones of pepper and musk precede a moderately rich palate whose currant and raisin-like fruit are framed by fine-grained but drying tannins.

2003	86	2008	2011
2001	90	2006	2009+
2000	80	2002	2005
1999	87	2007	2011
1998	86	2000	2003+
1997	84	1999	2002
1996	88	1998	2001

Thompson Estate

Lot 10 Harmans Road South, Willyabrup WA 6280. Tel: (08) 9755 6406. Fax: (08) 9386 1708.
Website: www.thompsonestate.com.au Email: peterlthompson@bigpond.com

Region: **Margaret River** Winemakers: **Michael Peterkin, Mark Messenger, Mark Lane & Harold Osborne**
Viticulturist: **Ian Bell** Chief Executive: **Peter Thompson**

Thompson Estate is a very different wine business whose owner, Peter Thompson, has been able to persuade some of the best winemakers around to assist with the making of their own speciality varieties. The Chardonnay, which easily earns its place here, is made by Pierro's Michael Peterkin. The 2004 release is beautifully crafted, finely balanced, generous and mineral.

CHARDONNAY

RATING 3

Margaret River	$20–$29	2004	94	2006	2009+
Current vintage: 2004	**94**	2003	89	2005	2008
		2002	87	2004	2007
		2001	93	2003	2006

Fine, elegant and beautifully integrated chardonnay, whose delicate creamy aromas of grapefruit, peach and suggestions of tropical fruit are accompanied by fresh creamy oak and undertones of grilled nuts. Its juicy, elegant palate delivers a delightfully fluffy expression of fresh tropical and citrusy fruit shaped by clean and refreshing acids, finishing with nuances of minerals and a persistent and finely integrated core of fruit and oak.

Tim Adams

Warenda Road, Clare SA 5453. Tel: (08) 8842 2429. Fax: (08) 8842 3550.
Website: www.timadamswines.com.au Email: sales@timadamswines.com.au

Region: **Clare Valley** Winemaker: **Tim Adams** Viticulturist: **Mick Plumridge**
Chief Executives: **Tim Adams, Pam Goldsack**

2004 looks to be a ripe and generous year for Tim Adams' red wines. The Aberfeldy is a substantially riper and significantly more opulent and luscious expression of this wine. While it's a delicious shiraz that will develop very well, it perhaps lacks the finely honed tightness and focus of the very best vintages. This edition welcomes the lively and varietally correct Pinot Gris, and basically offers the same message as virtually every edition of this book: that the wines from Tim Adams are among the best and most affordable of their kind.

CABERNET

RATING 3

Clare Valley	$20–$29	2003	89	2008	2011+
Current vintage: 2003	**89**	2002	94	2010	2014+
		2001	93	2013	2021
		2000	88	2005	2008
		1999	87	2004	2007+
		1998	90	2010	2018
		1997	89	2002	2005
		1996	89	2004	2008
		1995	89	2003	2007
		1994	88	2002	2006
		1993	90	2001	2005
		1992	92	2000	2004
		1991	90	2003	2011

Fresh, lightly herbal and violet-like aromas of blackcurrant and cedar/vanilla oak are lightly dusted with nuances of dried herbs and mint. Smooth and supple, its fresh palate of cassis, blackberry and plum-like fruit is coated with fine, powdery tannins. It offers length of fruit and brightness, elegance and tightness.

PINOT GRIS

RATING 5

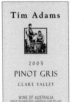

Clare Valley	$20–$29	2006	91	2007	2008+
Current vintage: 2006	**91**	2005	89	2006	2007+
		2004	89	2004	2005+

A pinot gris full of varietal expression and freshness, whose tangy perfume of lemon rind, cloves and cinnamon reveals lightly chalky nuances of pear and apple. It's long and concentrated, with rather an unctuous and fleshy mid-palate of pear, apple and citrus flavours finishing briney and spicy, with length of fruit, lemony acids and hints of dried herbs.

RIESLING

Clare Valley $20–$29
Current vintage: 2005   **95**

An intense, focused and tightly sculpted wine with a fragrant perfume and a racy, chalky palate that finishes long, dry and minerally. Its slatey aromas of lime and lemon juice have an almost exaggerated floral aspect, while the palate presents a lingering core of citrus and apple flavour.

2005	95	2013	2017
2004	92	2009	2012
2003	95	2011	2015
2002	96	2010	2014+
2001	90	2006	2009
2000	93	2008	2012
1999	93	2007	2011
1998	92	2006	2010
1997	93	2005	2009
1996	91	2004	2008
1995	84	1997	2000
1994	93	2002	2006

SEMILLON

Clare Valley $20–$29
Current vintage: 2005   **93**

Enticingly and brightly flavoured, carefully oaked and tightly integrated, this is a tangy and finely crafted semillon whose lightly grassy expression of melon and lemon flavour reveals smoky, herbal undertones against a background of lightly toasty vanilla oak. It's lightly floral and mineral, long and refreshing, with fresh leesy complexity and a racy acid finish.

2005	93	2010	2013
2004	92	2009	2012
2003	93	2005	2008
2002	94	2007	2010
2001	86	2003	2006
2000	88	2002	2005
1999	90	2004	2007
1998	88	2003	2006
1997	94	2002	2005+
1996	92	2004	2008
1995	84	1997	2000
1994	94	2006	2014

SHIRAZ

Clare Valley $20–$29
Current vintage: 2004   **91**

A fine, balanced and elegant regional shiraz of delightful freshness and intensity. Its cracked pepper fragrance of raspberries, cassis, blackberries and plums knits tightly with cedar/vanilla oak and nuances of cloves and cinnamon, mint and menthol. Long and smooth, its brightly lit palate of black and red berries is framed by fine, silky tannins.

2004	91	2012	2016
2003	90	2008	2011
2002	94	2010	2014+
2001	94	2009	2013
2000	91	2002	2005+
1999	91	2007	2011
1998	93	2003	2006+
1997	92	2002	2005
1996	86	2001	2004
1995	91	2003	2007
1994	92	1999	2002
1993	90	1995	1998
1992	92	2000	2004

THE ABERFELDY

Clare Valley $50–$99
Current vintage: 2004   **95**

Deeply ripened and luscious, this spicy and powerfully concentrated shiraz reveals a heady perfume of jujube-like blackberries, dark plums and cassis backed by clove, cinnamon, white pepper and assertive dark chocolate/vanilla oak. Its luscious palate of searingly intense dark berry fruit and polished, creamy vanilla oak is framed by firm but smooth tannins, finishing long and briary, with suggestions of mint and mineral.

2004	95	2016	2024
2003	95	2015	2023+
2002	97	2014	2022
2001	95	2013	2021
2000	92	2008	2012+
1999	95	2007	2011+
1998	97	2010	2018+
1997	91	2005	2009+
1996	94	2008	2016
1995	90	2007	2015
1994	95	2006	2014+
1993	87	1998	2001+
1992	90	2004	2012
1991	94	2003	2011+
1990	91	2002	2010
1988	90	2000	2008

THE FERGUS GRENACHE

RATING **3**

| Clare Valley | $20–$29 |
| Current vintage: 2004 | 91 |

A restrained expression of grenache that holds its more overt and confectionary varietal instincts in check. Its vibrant, floral and spicy perfume of raspberries, cherries and blueberries has a lightly minty background, while its smooth, supple, long and silky palate is tightly framed by dusty, powdery tannins. It finishes fresh and lively, with lingering cherry and blueberry flavours.

2004	91	2009	2012
2003	92	2008	2011
2002	93	2004	2007+
2001	85	2003	2006
2000	87	2002	2005+
1999	90	2004	2007
1998	93	2003	2006+
1997	92	2002	2005
1996	91	2001	2004
1995	93	2000	2003
1994	92	2002	2006
1993	93	1998	2001

Tin Cows

Healesville Road, Yarra Glen Vic 3775. Tel: (03) 5962 3311. Fax: (03) 5962 3887.
Website: www.tincows.com.au Email: enq@tincows.com.au

Region: **Yarra Valley** Winemaker: **Clare Halloran** Viticulturist: **Stuart Sissins** General Manager: **Simon Napthine**

Tim Cows is TarraWarra's second label, which once was known rather ingloriously as Tunnel Hill. Its juicy and early-drinking Chardonnay remains its best wine, while its Pinot Noir made a significant improvement in 2005.

CHARDONNAY

RATING **5**

| Yarra Valley | $12–$19 |
| Current vintage: 2005 | 87 |

A tangy, citrusy young chardonnay for the shorter term. Its vibrant, spicy aromas of pineapple, grapefruit and melon overlie creamy, nutty nuances, with suggestions of butter and vanilla. Ripe and juicy, its spicy and slightly herbal expression of peach, melon and grapefruit flavour is backed by assertive and slightly varnishy oak. It should flesh out.

2005	87	2006	2007+
2003	88	2004	2005+
2002	86	2004	2007
2001	87	2003	2006
2000	83	2001	2002

TK Wines (formerly Lenswood Vineyards)

Croft Road, Lenswood SA 5240. Tel: (08) 8843 4377. Fax: (08) 8843 4246.
Website: www.tkwines.com.au Email: admin@tkwines.com.au

Region: **Adelaide Hills** Winemaker: **Tim Knappstein** Viticulturist: **Paul Smith** Chief Executive: **Nathan Waks**

TK is an Adelaide Hills-based producer with a track record across a number of varieties. The present offerings have clearly been affected by the very cool 2002 and the extremely hot 2003 vintages. Quite why the 2005 Sauvignon Blanc is so far beneath normal standards escapes me, especially since this is a first-rate vintage for Adelaide Hills sauvignon blanc.

CHARDONNAY

RATING **3**

| Adelaide Hills | $20–$29 |
| Current vintage: 2003 | 92 |

Complex, smoky aromas of citrus, melon and pineapple, with meaty and cream undertones of spicy vanilla oak and a hint of mineral. Smooth and silky, it's long and seamless, delivering a restrained and creamy, lightly smoky palate of citrus and melon flavour. While it might lack the concentration of the best vintages, it's a very stylish effort.

2003	92	2005	2008+
2001	87	2002	2003+
2000	94	2005	2008
1999	93	2001	2004+
1998	93	2003	2006
1997	90	1999	2002
1996	92	2001	2004
1995	95	2000	2003+
1994	91	1999	2002

GEWÜRZTRAMINER

RATING **3**

| Adelaide Hills | $20–$29 |
| Current vintage: 2004 | 92 |

Rather a subdued but medium-term traminer with a hint of sweetness. Its delicate spicy perfume of rose petals and lychees precedes a smooth and slightly oily palate of length and restraint. Vibrant rose water and lychee flavours are framed by lively, refreshing acids.

2004	92	2006	2009
2003	93	2005	2008+
2001	91	2003	2006
1999	86	2001	2004+

PINOT NOIR

RATING 3

Adelaide Hills	$30–$49
Current vintage: 2003	**88**

Slightly stewed, meaty aromas of plums and cherries with spicy and lightly stalky herbal undertones. Medium to full in body, it's smooth, soft and elegant, with a green-edged expression of red cherries, raspberries and forest floor-like complexity. It's a little advanced, and finishes with sappy and herbal edges.

2003	88	2005	2008
2002	91	2007	2010+
2000	95	2005	2008+
1999	93	2007	2011
1998	95	2003	2006+
1997	87	2002	2005
1996	92	2004	2008
1995	87	1997	2000
1994	91	1999	2002+
1993	90	1998	2001+

SAUVIGNON BLANC

RATING 3

Adelaide Hills	$20–$29
Current vintage: 2005	**87**

An honest, slightly sweaty and refreshing sauvignon blanc whose very herbaceous aromas of gooseberries, passionfruit lack great fruit intensity. Forward, fruity and then slightly dilute, its moderately long palate of herbaceous gooseberry fruit culminates in a clean, refreshing and lemony finish. Lacks impact and cut.

2005	87	2006	2007
2004	89	2005	2006
2003	93	2003	2004+
2002	95	2003	2004+
2001	93	2001	2002+
2000	89	2000	2001
1999	94	2001	2004
1998	94	1999	2000
1997	91	1998	1999

THE PALATINE (Merlot Malbec Cabernet Sauvignon)

RATING 3

Adelaide Hills	$30–$49
Current vintage: 2002	**86**

Floral, minty and herbaceous aromas of cassis, plums and violets overlie cedary/vanilla undertones. Fine and elegant, its juicy flavours of cassis, plums and mulberries thin out before a moderately firm grip of drying tannin. Too green and cool, lacking conviction and length of truly ripe fruit.

2002	86	2010	2014
2001	90	2009	2013+
1999	95	2007	2011+
1998	94	2006	2010
1997	89	2005	2009

Torbreck

Roennfeldt Road, Marananga SA 5356. Tel: (08) 8562 4155. Fax: (08) 8562 4195.
Website: www.torbreck.com Email: dave@torbreck.com

Region: **Barossa Valley** Winemakers: **David Powell, Dan Standish** Viticulturist: **Michael Wilson**
Chief Executive: **David Powell**

Few wineries have done more than this Barossa-based producer to inspire its neighbours to create deeply fruited, spicy and savoury red wines with genuine regional character. Since its first vintage in 1996, Torbreck has encouraged many others down the path of Rhône-like complexity and character. As one might expect, the early releases suggest a stellar 2004.

CUVÉE JUVENILES

RATING 5

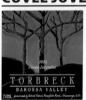

Barossa Valley	$20–$29
Current vintage: 2005	**87**

Just a fraction sweet for a higher rating, this vibrant, soft and lusciously flavoured young red Rhône blend has an enticingly spicy and floral aroma of raspberries and blackberries. Framed by silky fine tannins, its jujube-like palate of juicy black and red berries has plenty of depth and brightness.

2005	87	2006	2007
2004	89	2005	2006+
2003	89	2004	2005+
2002	90	2003	2004
2001	89	2001	2002
2000	90	2001	2002
1999	90	2001	2004+

A B C D E F G H I J K L M N O P Q R S T U V W X Y Z

DESCENDANT SHIRAZ VIOGNIER

RATING **2**

Barossa Valley	$100–$199
Current vintage: 2004	95

Complex, brooding and meaty, and lifted by heady, fragrant and spicy viognier, this is a first-class wine whose sumptuous fruit, high-quality oak and firm, powdery tannins are finely balanced and tightly integrated. Its deep and youthful perfume of berry and plum-like fruit reveals reductive, charcuterie-like undertones and apricot-like suggestions of viognier. Long, alluring and silky, with glimmers of mint and menthol beneath its vibrant, juicy fruit.

2004	95	2012	2016+
2003	93	2011	2015
2002	96	2010	2014+
2001	94	2006	2009
2000	91	2002	2005
1999	95	2004	2007+
1998	92	2003	2006+

RUNRIG SHIRAZ VIOGNIER

RATING **2**

Barossa Valley	$200+
Current vintage: 2003	93

Concentrated and powerfully structured, with musky, smoky aromas of deeply spiced, heady and floral notes of dark cherries, plums and blackberries laced with earthy and mineral undertones and backed by chocolate and vanilla oak. Smooth and elegant, this sumptuous and liqueur-like expression of luscious and slightly over-ripe fruit is lavishly coated with dark, smoky new oak, finishing with nuances of menthol, game meats and mocha.

2003	93	2008	2011+
2002	92	2007	2010
2001	94	2009	2013
1999	96	2007	2011
1998	97	2010	2018+
1997	93	2005	2009+
1996	95	2008	2016+

THE FACTOR

RATING **2**

Barossa Valley	$100–$199
Current vintage: 2003	90

Finely crafted from rather overcooked fruit, with meaty, exotically spiced and briary aromas of dark pepper, prunes and currants over a treacle-like presence of Kahlua, cinnamon and musk. There's an underlying smokiness and a suggestion of dried herbs. Ultra-ripe and concentrated, the palate is profoundly thick and juicy, delivering a dark, briary spectrum of ripe and rather dehydrated fruit flavours supported by sweet chocolatey oak and firm, pliant tannins.

2003	90	2008	2011+
2002	96	2010	2014+
2001	91	2003	2006
2000	95	2005	2008+
1999	97	2007	2011+
1998	93	2006	2010+

THE STEADING

RATING **3**

Barossa Valley	$30–$49
Current vintage: 2003	93

Heady and perfumed, its licorice-like aromas of blueberries, cranberries and raspberries overlie spicy notes of cloves, cinnamon and nutmeg and restrained cedary oak. It's wild and brambly, with a juicy palate deeply stained with flavours of red and black fruits, plus a powerful blueberry grenache influence. Framed by fine and pliant tannins, it's an artfully composed and controlled riper style, culminating in a lingering savoury finish of sour cherries and star anise.

2003	93	2008	2011+
2002	95	2007	2010+
2001	90	2003	2006
2000	93	2005	2008
1999	95	2004	2007+
1998	87	2003	2006
1997	94	2002	2005+

THE STRUIE (Shiraz)

RATING **3**

Barossa Valley, Eden Valley	$50–$99
Current vintage: 2004	93

Deeply flavoured and silky, with gamey, reductive and charcuterie-like flavours of cassis, blackberries and dark plums backed by herbal suggestions of slightly greenish fruit plus some somewhat overcooked and meaty nuances. Its floral perfume of peppercorns, dark fruits and musky spices has an ethereal Rhône-like quality. Its sumptuous core of fruit, molasses and crème caramel-like oak finishes long and savoury with velvet tannins.

2004	93	2009	2012+
2003	90	2008	2011+
2002	95	2004	2007+
2001	93	2003	2006+

Tower Estate

Corner Halls and Broke Road, Pokolbin NSW 2320. Tel: (02) 4998 7989. Fax: (02) 4998 7919.
Website: www.towerestate.com Email: sales@towerestate.com
Regions: **Various** Winemaker: **Scott Stephens** Chief Executive: **Len Evans**

While its cabernet sauvignons from Coonawarra and Margaret River and its pinot noirs from Tasmania and the Yarra Valley have left much to be desired, Tower Estate does create a wide spread of diverse marriages of major varieties with their signature Australian regions. Its shirazes from the Barossa and Hunter Valley are both very faithful to their regional origins, while the Hunter Valley whites, Semillon especially, are very sound.

ADELAIDE HILLS SAUVIGNON BLANC   RATING 5

Adelaide Hills $20–$29
Current vintage: 2005   **83**

Slightly sweet and awkward, with an herba-ceous, lightly sweaty and nettle-like aroma of pas-sionfruit and gooseberries followed by a juicy, tropical and grassy palate that finishes finishes with a tin-like acidity.

2005	83	2006	2007
2004	94	2005	2006+
2003	87	2003	2004+
2002	89	2002	2003
2001	81	2002	2003
2000	88	2000	2001
1999	94	2000	2001+

BAROSSA SHIRAZ   RATING 3

Barossa Valley $30–$49
Current vintage: 2004   **93**

An artfully balanced shiraz laced with mint, cloves and white pepper. Its violet-like fragrance of rasp-berries, cassis and plums is supported by restrained and sweet cedar/vanilla oak. Silky-fine, its smooth and moderately full palate of concentrated sour-edged small berry fruit is smartly wrapped in mocha oak and framed by thick, soft tannins.

2003	93	2011	2015+
2002	94	2010	2014+
2001	92	2006	2009+
2000	93	2005	2008+
1999	94	2007	2011

CLARE VALLEY RIESLING   RATING 4

Clare Valley $20–$29
Current vintage: 2005   **91**

A fine, elegant and well-made Clare Valley riesling whose delicate floral and crystalline perfume of lime and lemon precedes a long, fine and supple palate. Its citrusy fruit builds towards a clean, crunchy and crackly finish of refreshing lemon sherbet-like acids.

2005	91	2010	2013+
2004	89	2009	2012
2003	90	2005	2008+
2002	90	2007	2010
2001	89	2003	2006
2000	77	2001	2002
1999	91	2004	2007+

HUNTER VALLEY CHARDONNAY   RATING 4

Lower Hunter Valley $20–$29
Current vintage: 2004   **89**

A heavily worked, funky, complex and early-drinking chardonnay whose peach and cumquat aromas overlie sweet buttery and vanilla oak plus sug-gestions of honey, wheatmeal and grilled nuts. Smooth, elegant and savoury, its leesy, meaty palate offers a rich mouthful of quince, cumquat, peach and melon-like flavour backed by plenty of winemaking artefact and faint undertones of wet wool.

2004	89	2006	2009
2003	87	2005	2008+
2002	93	2004	2007
2001	91	2006	2009
2000	91	2002	2005+
1999	90	2001	2004+

HUNTER VALLEY SEMILLON   RATING 3

Lower Hunter Valley $20–$29
Current vintage: 2006   **93**

A delicate, fresh and dusty fragrance of lemon sherbet and honeydew melon precedes a long, tangy and vibrant palate whose slightly broad and oily expression of fresh varietal semillon finishes with refreshing acidity. A classical low-alcohol- style, it should age finely and gracefully.

2006	93	2014	2018
2005	87	2010	2013+
2004	94	2012	2016
2003	91	2005	2008
2002	92	2004	2007+
2001	91	2003	2006+
2000	90	2005	2008
1999	93	2007	2011

HUNTER VALLEY SHIRAZ

RATING 4

Lower Hunter Valley	$30–$49
Current vintage: 2004	88

2004	88	2009	2012
2003	81	2005	2008
2002	87	2004	2007
2001	93	2009	2013+
2000	95	2008	2012
1999	93	2007	2011

Meaty, spicy nuances of cloves and cinnamon underpin sweet, leathery aromas of red plums, cherries and cedar/vanilla oak. Initially bright and intensely focused, the palate falls away fractionally towards a tart, very savoury and slightly metallic finish. It reveals chocolate-like and faintly cardboardy undertones, and remains just a little sappy and greenish for a higher score.

CABERNET SAUVIGNON

RATING 5

Margaret River or Coonawarra	$30–$49
Current vintage: 2003	86

2003	86	2004	2007+
2001	87	2006	2009
2000	85	2002	2005
1999	94	2007	2011+

Pungent and meaty, with animal and iodide-like aromas plus herbaceous undertones. Weedy, greenish and thin, framed by edgy tannins.

Tuck's Ridge

37 Shoreham Road, Red Hill South Vic 3937. Tel: (03) 5989 8660. Fax: (03) 5989 8579.
Website: www.tucksridge.com.au Email: cellardoor@tucksridge.com.au
Region: **Mornington Peninsula** Winemaker: **Michael Kyberd** Viticulturist: **Tyson Lewis**
Chief Executive: **Peter Hollick**

Tuck's Ridge is one of the larger makers on the Mornington Peninsula, where its best wines are typically made from the Burgundian varieties. While its 'standard' wines are typically round, juicy and suited to early enjoyment, the company is steadily releasing more wines with single vineyard designations. The smooth and silky 2004 Buckle Vineyard Chardonnay (90, drink 2006–2009) and the citrusy and mineral 2005 Turramurra Vineyard Chardonnay (90, drink 2007–2010) are two delightful examples.

CHARDONNAY

RATING 5

Mornington Peninsula	$20–$29
Current vintage: 2004	89

2004	89	2006	2009
2003	89	2005	2008
2002	92	2004	2007
2001	92	2003	2006
2000	89	2002	2005
1999	85	2000	2001
1998	86	2000	2003
1997	90	1999	2002

A charming early-drinking chardonnay whose lightly herbaceous and sweaty aromas of peach, melon and dusty vanilla oak reveal undertones of cloves and cinnamon. Smooth and soft, its gentle palate is deeply flavoured with peach and nectarine-like fruit and creamy oak, finishing with soft, clean acids. Lively and very approachable.

PINOT NOIR

RATING 5

Mornington Peninsula	$20–$29
Current vintage: 2004	86

2004	86	2005	2006
2003	88	2005	2008
2002	89	2004	2007
2001	90	2003	2006+
2000	90	2002	2005
1999	88	2001	2004
1998	87	2000	2003
1997	91	1999	2002
1996	87	1998	2001

An honest, early-maturing pinot whose sweet floral fragrance of raspberries and cherries reveals herbal undertones of tomato stalk and lightly creamy vanilla oak. Slightly sappy and herbaceous, its juicy mid palate of tangy red cherry and berry flavours finishes with an angular, green-edged grip of tannin.

Turkey Flat

Bethany Road, Tanunda SA 5352. Tel: (08) 8563 2851. Fax: (08) 8563 3610.
Website: www.turkeyflat.com.au Email: turkeyflat@bigpond.com

Region: **Barossa Valley** Winemaker: **Peter Schulz** Viticulturist: **Peter Schulz** Chief Executive: **Christie Schulz**

Turkey Flat boasts some of the oldest vineyards still in commercial production in Australia, which means about as old as any still being used for serious wine anywhere in the world. By contrast, its winery is the oenological equivalent of a new Maserati. As a group, the 2004 reds are slightly overcooked and raisined. The pick is the Shiraz, a very modern wine whose fruit was assertively and unashamedly ultra-ripe.

BUTCHERS BLOCK

RATING **5**

Barossa Valley $30–$49
Current vintage: 2004   87

Wild, meaty and rather stewy, this moderately rich Barossa blend of Rhône varieties has a grenache-driven aroma of blueberries, plums and mulberries with spice undertones of cloves and cinnamon. Sweet, juicy and very forward, its concentrated and rustic expression of intense, jammy flavour is framed by drying, slightly gritty tannins.

2004	87	2006	2009
2003	88	2005	2008
2002	90	2004	2007
2001	89	2003	2006
2000	89	2002	2005+
1999	90	2001	2004+
1998	88	2000	2003
1997	85	1998	1999

CABERNET SAUVIGNON

RATING **4**

Barossa Valley $30–$49
Current vintage: 2004   89

Meaty, firm and briary, this complex wine should become even more wild and intriguing. While it's a little cooked for a higher score, it's still worthy of attention. Meaty aromas of currants, cassis, plums and prunes are backed by sweet, ethereal oak, with nuances of rosemary and violets. Firm and drying, it's cedary, tightly focused and should develop further.

2004	89	2012	2016+
2003	83	2005	2008
2002	91	2010	2014+
2001	85	2003	2006+
2000	89	2008	2012
1999	92	2004	2007
1998	90	2003	2006
1997	91	2002	2005
1996	88	2001	2004+

GRENACHE

RATING **5**

Barossa Valley $20–$29
Current vintage: 2004   85

Slightly overcooked, currant-like and lacking a genuine core of ripe, vibrant fruit. Its spicy, meaty aromas of raisins, blueberries and plum jam have a light floral lift, while its firmish, initially forward and penetrative palate becomes rather hollow and loses brightness towards the finish.

2004	85	2006	2009
2003	87	2005	2008
2002	89	2007	2010+
2001	88	2003	2006
2000	81	2002	2005
1999	90	2001	2004+
1998	87	2000	2003
1997	84	1998	1999
1996	89	2001	2004
1994	89	2002	2006

SEMILLON MARSANNE BLEND

RATING **5**

Barossa Valley $20–$29
Current vintage: 2003   84

A complex, savoury, honeyed and nutty wine whose delicate floral and wheatmeal complexity and generous, round palate of creamy citrus and melon fruit reveal pungent reductive influences that in all likelihood have been exacerbated by the screwcap used to seal this wine.

2003	84	2004	2005+
2002	89	2003	2004+
2001	87	2002	2003
2000	90	2002	2005
1999	87	2001	2004
1998	82	1999	2000
1997	89	1999	2002+

SHIRAZ

RATING **3**

Barossa Valley $30–$49
Current vintage: 2004   90

A typical modern ultra-ripe wine whose heady, wild and briary aromas of deep dark berry and plum-like fruit are backed by meaty, very spicy and treacle-like undertones of raisins, prunes and currants. It's a little sweet and spirity, packed with luscious, slightly shrivelled but not overcooked flavours, with undertones of bitumen and a pleasingly firm grip.

2004	90	2012	2016
2003	91	2008	2011
2002	94	2010	2014
2001	90	2006	2009
2000	90	2005	2008
1999	93	2007	2011
1998	95	2006	2010
1997	89	2002	2005
1996	94	2004	2008+
1993	89	2001	2005

Tyrrell's

Broke Road, Pokolbin NSW 2320. Tel: (02) 4993 7000. Fax: (02) 4998 7723.
Website: www.tyrrells.com.au Email: info@tyrrells.com.au

Region: **Lower Hunter Valley** Winemakers: **Andrew Spinaze, Mark Richardson**
Viticulturists: **Cliff Currie, Rob Donoghue** Chief Executive: **Bruce Tyrrell**

Tyrrell's is a custodian of the traditional Hunter Valley wine styles of early-harvested, unwooded semillon and meaty, leathery shiraz of medium to full weight. In this it succeeds admirably, with a stable full of semillons, each with different terroirs and stories to tell. Resuming normal transmission in 2004, the Vat 47 Chardonnay is an idiosyncratic wine of immense quality and rare longevity. Tyrrell's also releases some unusual wines (in addition to the mysterious Vat 6 Pinot Noir), such as the DB24 Shiraz, a sumptuous and juicy McLaren Vale offering from 2003 that has received two separate 12-month maturations in small new oak.

BROKENBACK SHIRAZ

RATING 5

Lower Hunter Valley $20–$29
Current vintage: 2004 87

A sweet leathery fragrance of red plums, cherries, berries and spices with floral undertones precedes a supple and elegant palate of modest weight and structure. Framed by rather fragile, fine tannins, it's pretty but ethereal. While it should flesh out a little, it lacks real depth on the palate.

2004	87	2009	2012
2003	89	2008	2011+
2002	89	2007	2010+
2001	87	2003	2006
2000	86	2002	2005
1999	89	2004	2007
1998	90	2006	2010
1997	85	1999	2002
1996	83	1998	2001
1995	89	2000	2003
1994	90	2002	2006

LOST BLOCK SEMILLON

RATING 5

Lower Hunter Valley $12–$19
Current vintage: 2005 88

A lively and vibrant young semillon whose dusty, powdery and lightly herbal aromas of melon and lemon reveal a hint of tobacco. Its tangy and lightly tropical palate delivers plenty of juicy flavour with almost a hint of effervescence. It finishes long and clean, with lingering citrus flavours.

2005	88	2006	2007
2004	87	2006	2009+
2003	88	2005	2008+
2002	92	2007	2010+
2001	90	2003	2006
1999	89	2001	2004
1998	94	2003	2006+
1997	90	2002	2005+
1996	92	2004	2008
1995	89	2000	2003+

'QUINTUS' MOON MOUNTAIN CHARDONNAY

RATING 4

Lower Hunter Valley $20–$29
Current vintage: 2004 90

A very good chardonnay whose pleasing peachy, citrus, green olive and cashew flavours are backed by restrained vanilla oak and suggestions of lime marmalade. Vibrant, spicy and brightly lit, its creamy melon and citrus-like palate has a babyfat quality in mid palate, before finishing clean and refreshing with slightly mineral acids.

2004	90	2005	2006+
2003	75	2003	2004
2002	90	2004	2007
2000	90	2002	2005
1998	85	1999	2000
1997	82	1998	1999
1996	90	1998	2001

RESERVE STEVENS SEMILLON

RATING 3

Lower Hunter Valley $20–$29
Current vintage: 2001 87

Very round and generous despite a mere 10% alcohol by volume, this juicy and buttery wine is just a little cooked and flat. It offers a fragrance of lemon, lime, rosemary and honeydew melon fruit developing toasty, buttery marmalade-like influences. Its creamy palate is rather unusual, and it looks to be developing quite quickly.

2001	87	2006	2009
2000	95	2012	2020
1999	93	2007	2011+
1998	94	2006	2010+
1997	94	2005	2009
1996	86	2001	2004
1995	90	2003	2007+

RESERVE STEVENS SHIRAZ

Lower Hunter Valley $20–$29
Current vintage: 2002   92

Silky and smooth, this typical old-fashioned Australian 'burgundy' style has an earthy, floral and meaty fragrance of lightly herbal sweet red berries and cassis. Framed by velvet-like tannins, it's ethereal and almost fragile, only medium to full in body. Finishing long and savoury, its sweet and earthy expression of berries, plums and chocolates is delightfully vibrant and offset by chocolate/cedary oak.

2002	92	2007	2010+
2000	89	2005	2008+
1999	87	2001	2004+
1998	92	2006	2010+
1997	88	2002	2005
1996	84	1998	2001
1995	87	2000	2003

VAT 1 SEMILLON

Lower Hunter Valley $30–$49
Current vintage: 1999   97

Long and seamless, this slowly maturing Hunter semillon has a faintly buttery and toasty bouquet of melon and citrus, backed by delicate floral aromas. Its smooth and savoury palate reveals a deep core of fruit with tobacco-like and chalky undertones. Exceptionally tight and focused, it finishes with refreshingly tangy acidity.

1999	97	2007	2011+
1998	95	2010	2018
1997	96	2009	2017
1996	95	2004	2008
1995	95	2007	2015
1994	96	2002	2006+
1993	95	2001	2005+
1992	95	2004	2012
1991	92	1999	2003
1990	88	1998	2002
1989	86	1991	1994
1988	88	1993	1996
1987	93	1995	1999
1986	95	1998	2008
1985	88	1993	1997
1984	93	1996	2004

VAT 6 PINOT NOIR

Lower Hunter Valley $30–$49
Current vintage: 2002   82

An ageing, tiring pinot whose earthy, floral and simple herbal aromas of plums and raspberries are backed by nuances of mint and menthol. Underpinned by sweet cedar/vanilla oak, its simple and forward palate of cherry-like fruit dries out towards a thin, lean finish.

2002	82	2004	2007
2001	81	2003	2006+
2000	82	2002	2005
1999	88	2001	2004
1998	87	2003	2006
1997	92	2002	2005
1996	84	2001	2004
1994	90	1999	2002

VAT 8 SHIRAZ CABERNET

**Lower Hunter Valley,
Mudgee** $30–$49
Current vintage: 2003   90

Leathery and old-fashioned, this richly fruited and earthy red has a subtle, rather gamey fragrance of dark plums and black berries backed by hints of raisin and iodide. Deeply stained by flavours of dark berries and plums, backed by cedary oak, its minty and tightly composed, rather closed and chewy palate finishes with lingering spicy and slightly meaty, currant-like nuances.

2003	90	2011	2015
2002	87	2007	2010
2000	87	2005	2008
1999	89	2004	2007+
1998	95	2006	2010
1997	92	2005	2009+
1996	91	2001	2004
1995	93	2003	2007
1994	92	2002	2006

VAT 9 SHIRAZ

Lower Hunter Valley $30–$49
Current vintage: 2002   88

Sweet cedar/vanilla oak lifts a typically regional and earthy bouquet of red plums, dark cherries, violets, dried herbs and polished leather. Medium to full in weight, it's smooth, silky and vibrant, delivering a slightly old-fashioned expression of tarry blackberry and rhubarb-like flavour backed by sweet oak and framed by smooth tannins. Lacks its usual length and texture, and reveals some prune/currant notes.

2002	88	2007	2010+
2001	87	2006	2009
1999	88	2007	2011+
1998	94	2010	2018
1997	89	2002	2005+
1996	88	2004	2008
1995	80	1997	2000
1994	91	2002	2006+
1993	87	1998	2001
1992	93	1997	2000
1991	95	2003	2011

VAT 47 CHARDONNAY

Lower Hunter Valley $30–$49
Current vintage: 2004 96

A finely tuned, classic Vat 47 whose dusty, nutty aromas of melon, quince and cumquat reveal a hint of tangerine, lightly creamy leesy undertones and a delicate whiff of vanilla oak. Long, smooth and comparatively juicy for this wine, its chalky expression of melon and citrus fruit is tightly focused with lime juice acids and a powdery, mineral influence. Exceptionally well balanced and stylish.

2004	96	2012	2016
2003	88	2005	2008+
2002	96	2010	2014
2001	95	2009	2013
2000	96	2008	2012
1999	94	2001	2004+
1998	95	2006	2010+
1997	90	1999	2002+
1996	94	2001	2004+
1995	93	2003	2007+
1994	94	2002	2006+
1993	94	2001	2005

Vasse Felix

Corner Caves Road, and Harmans Road, South Cowaramup WA 6284. Tel: (08) 9756 5000.
Fax: (08) 9755 5425. Website: www.vassefelix.com.au Email: info@vassefelix.com.au
Region: **Margaret River** Winemakers: **David Dowden, Travis Clydesdale** Viticulturist: **Bruce Pearce**
Chief Executive: **Bob Baker**

Vasse Felix is one of the Margaret River region's leading wineries whose recent performance suggests it will finally cement a place among the elite. The 2004 wines are very solid indeed, especially the first-class Shiraz and Heytesbury Chardonnay. Vasse Felix produced the best ever Heytesbury cabernet blend in 2003, a powerful and slightly angular young wine that should develop exceptionally well over a long time.

CABERNET MERLOT

Margaret River $20–$29
Current vintage: 2004 88

Delicate floral and cedary aromas of black plums, cherries and mocha oak reveal capsicum-like herbal undertones. Full to medium weight, it's long, smooth and supple, with black berries, plums and cherry fruit firmly framed by pliant tannins. Elegant and harmonious, with a lingering core of flavour that almost conceals its thread of greenness.

2004	88	2009	2012
2003	88	2005	2008+
2002	80	2004	2007
2001	89	2003	2006
2000	88	2002	2005+
1999	82	2001	2004
1998	83	2000	2003
1997	88	2002	2005
1996	88	2001	2004
1995	87	2000	2003
1994	88	1996	1999

CABERNET SAUVIGNON

Margaret River $20–$29
Current vintage: 2004 93

A very good, elegant and fully ripened cabernet whose lively aromas of small black and red berries, red plums and dark cherries are backed by dusty notes of chocolates and dried herbs. Supple, fine and stylish, it's quite full in weight, deeply flavoured with a lingering core of blackberry and mulberry flavour and framed by firm, assertive tannins. Fine balance and potential.

2004	93	2016	2024
2003	89	2008	2011+
2002	83	2004	2007
2001	90	2006	2009
2000	93	2008	2012
1999	93	2007	2011+
1998	96	2010	2018
1997	89	2002	2005+
1996	86	2001	2004+
1995	87	2003	2007
1994	93	2006	2014
1993	88	1995	1998
1991	93	2003	2011

CHARDONNAY

Margaret River $20–$29
Current vintage: 2005 87

Complex and heavily worked aromas of grapefruit, melon and green cashew reveal suggestions of wheatmeal and matchstick, with some spicy, almost spiky nuances. Presently forward and slightly cloying, its ripe, juicy palate of peach, melon and tropical fruit is handsomely backed by spicy vanilla oak, finishing with tangy citrus flavours. Likely to flesh out further.

2005	87	2007	2010
2004	89	2006	2009
2003	89	2005	2008
2002	87	2004	2007
2001	92	2006	2009
2000	90	2002	2005+
1999	89	2001	2004
1998	80	1999	2000
1997	87	1999	2002
1996	88	1998	2001
1995	91	2000	2003

HEYTESBURY (Cabernet blend)

RATING 4

	Margaret River	$50–$99
	Current vintage: 2003	95

A deep, powerful, rather closed and brooding wine whose layers of flavour and texture should come together in time. Assertive dark chocolate and vanilla oak slightly overshadows its restrained aromas of blackberry, dark plum and dark cherry fruit, while nuances of rosemary and violets slowly emerge. Sumptuous, dark-fruited and intensely flavoured, it's still coming to grips with its powerful oak and very firm and slightly awkward malbec-driven extract.

2003	95	2015	2023
2002	87	2004	2007+
2001	91	2006	2009+
2000	90	2005	2008
1999	91	2004	2007
1998	89	2003	2006
1997	93	2005	2009
1996	89	2002	2008
1995	94	2003	2007+

HEYTESBURY CHARDONNAY

RATING 2

	Margaret River	$30–$49
	Current vintage: 2004	94

A modern and stylish chardonnay whose complex, spicy aromas of melon and grapefruit are backed by smoky vanilla oak, hints of lime and creamy, leesy undertones. Long and sumptuous, its smooth, creamy palate of grapefruit, melon and peach is underpinned by a chalky minerality and punctuated by a tangy, citrusy finish. Very complex and stylish.

2004	94	2009	2012
2003	95	2008	2011
2002	89	2004	2007
2001	95	2006	2009
2000	90	2002	2005
1999	90	2001	2004
1998	88	2000	2003+
1996	86	1997	1998

SEMILLON

RATING 4

	Margaret River	$20–$29
	Current vintage: 2005	81

Estery, spicy and varnishy, with herbal, melon-like aromas and a slightly sweet, oily and forward palate that lacks depth, balance and freshness. Possibly the result of a stuck ferment.

2005	81	2005	2005
2004	86	2005	2006
2002	93	2004	2007
2001	89	2003	2006+
2000	90	2005	2008
1999	91	2004	2007
1998	86	2000	2003

SHIRAZ

RATING 3

	Margaret River	$20–$29
	Current vintage: 2004	92

A modern, intensely varietal, almost exaggerated shiraz with a vibrant, peppery and slightly tomatoey aromas of spicy red berries and plums backed by lightly toasty mocha/vanilla oak. Elegant and tightly structured, its pristine and spicy palate of opulent small berry, plum and cassis flavour has a wild, almost feral aspect. Neatly bound about a fine spine of pliant tannins, it finishes with a salty, mineral note.

2004	92	2012	2016
2003	88	2008	2011
2002	93	2010	2014+
2001	93	2006	2009
2000	93	2008	2012
1999	93	2004	2007+
1998	82	2000	2003
1997	93	2005	2009
1996	90	2001	2004
1995	94	2000	2003
1994	93	2002	2006

Voyager Estate

Stevens Road, Margaret River WA 6285. Tel: (08) 9757 6354. Fax: (08) 9757 6494.
Website: www.voyagerestate.com.au Email: wine@voyagerestate.com.au
Region: **Margaret River** Winemaker: **Cliff Royle** Viticulturist: **Steve James** Chief Executive: **Michael Wright**

A spectacular Margaret River winery development, Voyager Estate has become one of the region's leading makers. Its current releases are uniformly strong, especially the 2004 Chardonnay, its best and most sophisticated white wine yet made. The supple and silky 2002 Cabernet Sauvignon Merlot provides a finer and more elegant follow-on from the excellent 2001 wine, while the 2004 Shiraz shows class and polish.

CABERNET SAUVIGNON MERLOT   RATING 2

Margaret River $30–$49
Current vintage: 2002   **95**

Very stylish, measured and elegant, this supple and long-term cabernet blend has a fragrant perfume of redcurrants, violets, mulberries over cedary, chocolate and vanilla-like oak and musky nuances of dried herbs. Smooth and silky, its tightly focused and evenly balanced palate of pristine cassis, red berry and dark chocolate is neatly enmeshed with fine-grained oak and an under-current of fine tannin.

2002	95	2014	2022
2001	97	2013	2021
2000	91	2008	2012
1999	92	2011	2019
1998	96	2010	2018
1997	91	2005	2009
1996	95	2004	2008+
1995	95	2003	2007+
1994	94	2006	2014

CHARDONNAY   RATING 2

Margaret River $30–$49
Current vintage: 2004   **96**

A poised, stylish and tightly focused chardonnay whose delicate, nutty aromas of honeydew melon, vanilla oak and butterscotch overlie nuances of bacon and hessian. Silky-smooth, its succulent and mouthfilling palate of apple, pear, lime juice and creamy peach-like fruit is supported by tight-knit vanilla oak and undertones of cinnamon and clove. It finishes, long, savoury and very refreshing.

2004	96	2009	2012
2003	93	2005	2008+
2002	95	2007	2010
2001	93	2006	2009
2000	93	2005	2008
1999	94	2001	2004
1998	88	2000	2003
1997	90	1999	2002
1996	91	1998	2001

SAUVIGNON BLANC SEMILLON   RATING 3

Margaret River $12–$19
Current vintage: 2005   **91**

A fine and restrained blend whose pristine expression of lightly herbal and tropical flavours is supported by a fine underlying chalkiness. Lightly dusty, with herbaceous undertones of green beans and nettles, its melon and tropical fruit aromas precede a smooth and fruit-driven palate framed by crisp, tangy acids. Long, fine and pleasingly intense, it finishes with an appealing austerity.

2005	91	2007	2010+
2004	92	2004	2005+
2003	93	2004	2005+
2002	90	2004	2007
2001	87	2002	2003
2000	94	2005	2008
1999	95	2001	2004+
1996	95	2001	2004

SEMILLON   RATING 4

Margaret River $20–$29
Current vintage: 2002   **94**

A very graceful, fine and silky semillon whose delicate herbal and lightly citrusy aromas precede a smooth and creamy palate. Backed by slightly charry oak, its pristine melon and lightly herbal/green pea fruit is tautly bound by crisp and refreshing acid.

2002	94	2004	2007+
2001	88	2003	2006
2000	91	2002	2005+
1999	90	2001	2004
1998	88	2000	2003
1997	92	2002	2005

SHIRAZ

RATING 3

Margaret River	$20–$29
Current vintage: 2004	90

A balanced and well made shiraz whose deeply spiced, peppery fragrance of sweet red and black berries, cassis, plums and sweet vanilla/cedar oak reveals musky undertones of animal hide and a tomatoey aspect. Its long and firmish palate delivers tightly focused but slightly sharp-edged, tomatoey and herbal fruit and smart new oak framed by fine tannins.

2004	90	2009	2012
2003	94	2008	2011+
2002	82	2007	2010
2001	94	2006	2009
2000	88	2005	2008
1999	92	2004	2007

TOM PRICE CABERNET SAUVIGNON

RATING 5

Margaret River	$50–$99
Current vintage: 1995	87

Leafy, capsicum and pea-like aromas with undertones of dusty, cedary and minty small red berries and menthol. Its assertive, but under-ripe tannins shroud its herbal fruit qualities and tight-knit cedar/vanilla oak, culminating in a grippy, but sappy finish.

1995	87	2003	2007
1994	89	2002	2006+
1992	89	1997	2000

TOM PRICE WHITE BLEND

RATING 4

Margaret River	$30–$49
Current vintage: 2000	90

Cut grass Margaret River semillon and lively, nutty vanilla oak aromas precede a juicy and lightly toasty palate of shape and elegance. Very herbal and supported by sweet vanilla oak, it's long and tangy, culminating in a lemony finish of mineral acids.

2000	90	2002	2005+
1997	89	1999	2002
1996	93	2001	2004

Wandin Valley Estate

Wilderness Road, Lovedale, NSW 2320. Tel: (02) 4930 7317. Fax: (02) 4930 7814.
Website: www.wandinvalley.com.au Email: sales@wandinvalley.com.au
Region: **Lower Hunter Valley** Winemaker: **Matthew Burton** Viticulturist: **Scott Ling**
Chief Executives: **James & Philippa Davern**

A small Hunter vineyard and winery, Wandin Valley Estate's leading two wines are its regional specials of Bridie's Shiraz and Reserve Semillon. These wines are typically true to the Hunter traditions of leathery and elegant shirazes and long-living, taut and refreshing but low-alcohol semillons. Wandin Valley Estate also boasts a very attractive private cricket ground that is available for social fixtures.

BRIDIE'S RESERVE SHIRAZ

RATING 4

Lower Hunter Valley	$20–$29
Current vintage: 2004	92

A typical older-style Hunter shiraz whose meaty, leathery and earthy expression of dark berry and plum-like shiraz is tightly crafted into a fine, supple and silky wine with very restrained vanilla oak and a delightful lingering sour edge to the fruit. It's very perfumed and spicy, long and supple, with plenty of rustic character.

2004	92	2012	2016
2003	90	2008	2011+
2001	83	2003	2006
2000	90	2008	2012
1998	93	2006	2010+

RESERVE SEMILLON

RATING 4

Lower Hunter Valley	$20–$29	2006	90	2011	2014+
Current vintage: 2006	90	2005	91	2010	2013+
		2002	91	2010	2014

Fresh, slightly estery and spicy aromas of honeydew melon and lemon precede a juicy, tangy and lemony palate whose pleasing length of fruit overlies baby powder-like chalkiness. Its lingering melon/lemon fruit extends down the palate before a tight and refreshing finish. Likely to develop into a slightly fuller expression of traditional Hunter semillon.

Wantirna Estate

10 Bushy Park Lane, Wantirna South Vic 3152. Tel: (03) 9801 2367. Fax: (03) 9887 0225.
Website: www.wantirnaestate.com.au Email: wantirnaestate@bigpond.com.au
Region: **Yarra Valley** Winemakers: **Maryann Egan, Reg Egan** Viticulturist: **Reg Egan** Chief Executive: **Reg Egan**

Wantirna Estate's spotlessly crafted, elegant and fine-grained table wines typically reveal deeply scented perfumes of pristine fruit and fine-grained oak, before poised, supple and seamless palates of intensity and integration. The latest releases comprise the vineyard's finest collection yet. They are seamless, spotless, profoundly fruited and superbly crafted. My only concern is that because they are so immediately drinkable, little will live to see their full maturity and potential.

AMELIA CABERNET SAUVIGNON MERLOT

RATING 2

Yarra Valley	$50–$99	2004	97	2016	2024
Current vintage: 2004	97	2003	91	2008	2011+
		2002	93	2010	2014+
		2001	95	2009	2013
		2000	95	2008	2012+
		1999	94	2007	2011+
		1998	90	2006	2010
		1997	96	2009	2017
		1996	92	2004	2008
		1995	94	2003	2007+

Deeply and alluringly charming; a wine that will only become more seductive. Its fragrant perfume of violets, cassis, mulberries, blackberries and cedar/vanilla oak reveals nuances of dark chocolates and forest floor. Silky, fine and exceptionally elegant, it is a remarkable fusion of pristine and beautifully ripened flavours of dark cherries, berries and plums with powder-fine tannins, presented with poise and sensitivity. Long and seamless, it's likely to build in the bottle before settling down in the future.

HANNAH CABERNET FRANC MERLOT

RATING 2

Yarra Valley	$100–$199	2004	96	2012	2016+
Current vintage: 2004	96	2003	91	2008	2011
		2002	93	2007	2010+
		2001	95	2009	2013+
		2000	95	2008	2012+
		1999	95	2007	2011

A willowy and beautifully presented wine whose heady fragrance of red cherries, dark plums and cedar/vanilla oak reveals undertones of cloves and cinnamon, plus a background of meaty and forest floor-like complexity. Framed by firm, drying and fine tannins, it is full to medium in weight. Long, tight and supple, its vibrant, juicy berry/cherry fruit is backed by spicy, cedary oak over nuances of briar and undergrowth.

ISABELLA CHARDONNAY

RATING 2

Yarra Valley	$30–$49	2005	97	2010	2013
Current vintage: 2005	97	2004	95	2009	2012+
		2003	95	2008	2011
		2002	96	2007	2010
		2000	93	2005	2008
		1999	90	2001	2004+
		1998	95	2003	2006+
		1997	93	2002	2005+
		1996	96	2004	2008
		1994	94	2002	2006

An exceptionally generous and complete chardonnay of elegance and complexity. Its creamy fragrance of grapefruit, melon, lemon sherbet and vanilla/matchstick oak reveals spicy undertones of cloves and grilled nuts. Its sumptuous, soft and juicy palate of brightly lit citrus and melon fruit is neatly tied by refreshing and natural acids, finishing long, tight and savoury with a lingering core of fruit and butter.

LILY PINOT NOIR

RATING 2

Yarra Valley $50–$99
Current vintage: 2005 96

Scented with rose petals, red and black cherries, spicy cedar/vanilla oak laced with nuances of cloves and nutmeg, this fine and silky pinot reveals undertones of forest floor and an appealing meatiness. Highlighted by a burst of pristine blackcurrant-like fruit and framed by a genuinely tight-knit but surprisingly firm and assertive structure, its succulent palate of juicy cherry/berry flavour is likely to build considerably with time in the bottle. It finishes with excellent length and persistence, plus a hint of spirity warmth.

2005	96	2010	2013+
2004	94	2009	2012+
2003	94	2008	2011
2002	95	2007	2010
2001	94	2006	2009
2000	95	2005	2008
1999	97	2004	2007+
1998	94	2003	2006
1997	95	2002	2005
1996	92	2001	2004+
1995	92	2000	2003

Warrenmang

Mountain Creek Road, Moonambel Vic 3478. Tel: (03) 5467 2233. Fax: (03) 5467 2309.
Website: www.bazzani.com.au/warrenmang Email: mail@pyreneeswines.com.au

Region: **Pyrenees** Winemaker: **Brett Duffin** Viticulturist: **Luigi Bazzani** Chief Executive: **Luigi Bazzani**

Perhaps the largest and most pleasant surprise I experienced in the research of this guide was my tasting of the two Warrenmang shirazes from 2004. These are naturally robust wines of remarkable, searing fruit intensity. The Black Puma is simply opulent and alluring, while the 'standard' Shiraz carries less weight but delivers deliciously wild, briary and peppery shiraz character. It is marvellous to see this mature vineyard live up to its potential.

BLACK PUMA SHIRAZ

RATING 4

Pyrenees $30–$49
Current vintage: 2004 95

A sumptuous, exceptionally concentrated and harmoniously constructed shiraz of remarkable depth and longevity. Wild, ripe and briary, its dense and alluringly complex aromas of violets, dark berries and plums are supported by cedar/vanilla oak. Black and brooding, its rich palate is lavishly coated with firm, powerful tannins. While its oak is perhaps a little basic, this wine will develop very well thanks to the sheer brightness, intensity and penetration of its fruit.

2004	95	2016	2024+
2001	87	2006	2009
1998	90	2006	2010+

ESTATE SHIRAZ

RATING 4

Pyrenees $30–$49
Current vintage: 2004 93

A firm, long-term and rustic shiraz likely to develop gamey complexity. Finely crafted, its intense perfume of sweet dark berries, plums and violets reveals meaty, spicy and sage-like undertones, plus a whiff of black pepper. Its searingly intense and vibrant fruit and polished cedary oak influences overlie a firm, drying backbone of powdery tannin.

2004	93	2016	2024
2002	81	2007	2010+
2001	89	2006	2009
2000	93	2012	2020
1999	92	2004	2007+
1998	81	2003	2006
1997	90	2002	2005+
1996	89	2004	2008
1995	80	2000	2003
1994	88	1999	2002
1993	90	2001	2005
1992	93	2004	2012

GRAND PYRENEES

RATING 5

Pyrenees $30–$49
Current vintage: 2002 87

Rustic, meaty and earthy, this robust, drying and slightly unpolished red blend needs time for its palate-staining array of minty dark berry and plum flavours to integrate with its firm rod of kernel-like tannins. There's a hint of menthol and iodide beneath its concentrated and meaty flavours, while the finish reveals a note of onion skin.

2001	89	2009	2013
2000	84	2005	2008+
1999	88	2007	2011+
1998	89	2006	2012
1997	86	2005	2009
1996	87	2004	2008
1995	87	2003	2007
1993	89	2001	2005
1992	88	2000	2004

Water Wheel

Raywood Road, Bridgewater-on-Loddon Vic 3516. Tel: (03) 5437 3060. Fax: (03) 5437 3082.
Website: www.waterwheelwine.com Email: info@waterwheelwine.com

Region: **Bendigo** Winemakers: **Peter Cumming, Bill Trevaskis** Viticulturist: **Peter Cumming**
Chief Executive: **Peter Cumming**

Water Wheel is an operation of surprising scale given its relatively modest winemaking facility. Its typically ripe and forward varietal table wines are usually well-made, fresh and fruity, with a generous length of palate flavour. Its 2004 reds are typically richly fruited, smooth and finely crafted, each able to cellar well into the future. It's easy to see why Water Wheel is a benchmark for quality and value for so many people.

CABERNET SAUVIGNON

RATING **5**

Bendigo $12–$19
Current vintage: 2004 90

A very elegant, smooth and polished cabernet whose deep, dark aromas of berries, plums and black olives are backed by fresh cedar/chocolate and vanilla oak. Long and sumptuous, its palate unfolds layers of juicy blackberry, cassis and dark plum flavour backed by nuances of mint, eucalypt and cedar/vanilla oak. Framed by smooth, loose-knit tannins, it's fresh, finely balanced and persistent.

2004	90	2012	2016
2003	89	2013	2017
2002	87	2007	2010
2001	88	2009	2013
2000	89	2008	2012
1999	87	2004	2007+
1998	91	2006	2010
1997	92	2002	2005+
1996	91	2001	2004
1995	90	2000	2003

SHIRAZ

RATING **4**

Bendigo $12–$19
Current vintage: 2004 90

Deeply and evenly ripened, this fresh and deeply flavoured shiraz clearly reflects its variety and region. Its aromas of raspberries, blackberries and dark plums are backed by sweet vanilla/chocolate oak, with undertones of mint and menthol. Richly flavoured but smooth and round, its sweet suggestions of blackberries, plums and raspberries are tightly knit with sweet oak and firmish but pliant tannins.

2004	90	2009	2012+
2003	90	2008	2011+
2002	92	2007	2010
2001	87	2006	2009
2000	89	2005	2008+
1999	88	2004	2007
1998	94	2007	2010
1997	90	2005	2009+
1996	93	2004	2008
1995	89	2003	2007
1994	93	1999	2002+

Wedgetail

40 Hildebrand Road, Cottles Bridge Vic 3099. Tel: (03) 9714 8661. Fax: (03) 9714 8676.
Website: www.wedgetailestate.com.au Email: info@wedgetailestate.com.au

Region: **Yarra Valley** Winemaker: **Guy Lamothe** Viticulturist: **Guy Lamothe**
Chief Executives: **Dena Ashbolt & Guy Lamothe**

Guy Lamothe, who previously worked in wineries in France and on the Mornington Peninsula, produces small volumes of handcrafted wine at Cottles Bridge, just 40 kilometres north-east of Melbourne. His best wine is his Pinot Noir, whose easterly aspect enables it to capture the early morning sunshine.

PINOT NOIR

RATING **5**

Yarra Valley $30–$49
Current vintage: 2003 92

Charmingly evolved and rustic, this is an early-drinking pinot of genuine character and depth. Its slightly stewy and gamey aromas of sweet red plums, raspberries and cherries reveal an undercurrent of earthy, leathery and undergrowth-like complexity. Rich and smooth, it presents a fine, supple and slightly sappy palate whose generous, meaty fruit is framed by fine tannins.

2003	92	2005	2008
2002	88	2007	2010
2001	86	2003	2006

Wellington

Corner Richmond & Denholms roads, Cambridge Tas 7170. Tel: (03) 6248 5844. Fax: (03) 6248 5855.
Email: wellington@hoodwines.com

Region: **Southern Tasmania** Winemaker: **Andrew Hood** Chief Executive: **Graeme Allen**

Made by one of Tasmania's finest winemakers in Andrew Hood, Wellington's wines are long and intensely flavoured, but fine and restrained. The whites are pleasingly crisp and acidic, exemplified by the slightly sweet but mineral 2004 Riesling and the refreshing 2003 Chardonnay. The Iced Riesling, which is concentrated in the winery, produced a deliciously flavoursome and essence-like wine in 2004.

CHARDONNAY

RATING 4

Southern Tasmania	$20–$29
Current vintage: 2003	**90**

Clean and tangy, this shapely, lean and austere cool-climate chardonnay presents a fresh aroma of melon and citrus fruit backed by nuances of flowers, wheatmeal and vanilla oak, with minerally undertones. Taut and trim, its crisp palate of citrus and mineral influences is punctuated by clean and refreshing acids, without any evident presence of malolactic influences.

2003	90	2005	2008+
2002	88	2004	2007
2001	87	2003	2006
2000	91	2005	2008
1999	90	2004	2007
1998	90	2003	2006+
1997	87	2002	2005
1996	86	1998	2001
1995	89	2000	2003
1994	87	1996	1999

ICED RIESLING

RATING 4

Southern Tasmania $20–$29 (375 ml)	
Current vintage: 2005	**93**

Estery, honeyed aromas of pear, apple and lime juice precede a luscious, sweet and very smooth palate that finishes long, clean and finely balanced. Its lingering, vibrant and essence-like expression of pear and citrus flavours are wrapped in refreshing and lively acids. It's not excessively sweet, and it's easy to enjoy.

2005	93	2007	2010
2004	82	2006	2009
2003	83	2004	2005+
2000	93	2005	2008
1999	92	2004	2007
1998	83	1999	2000
1997	89	1999	2002

PINOT NOIR

RATING 5

Southern Tasmania	$20–$29
Current vintage: 2004	**88**

A pretty, varietal pinot whose dark cherry-like fruit is backed by restrained cedar/vanilla oak and meaty, funky undertones. Its floral, rose petal perfume overlies earthy suggestions, spicy nuances of cinnamon and capsicum-like herbaceous notes. Complex and elegant, with a pleasing presence and weight of fruit backed by some genuine fine-grained structure, it's just a fraction too herbaceous for a higher rating.

2004	88	2009	2012
2003	80	2005	2008
2002	90	2004	2007
2001	88	2003	2006
2000	89	2002	2005
1999	89	2001	2004
1998	92	2000	2003
1997	89	2002	2005
1994	90	1999	2002

RIESLING

RATING 3

Southern Tasmania	$20–$29
Current vintage: 2004	**92**

Rather a stylish expression of a modern German trocken style, framed by minerality and scented with rose petals, lime juice, white peaches and apricots. Fractionally sweet for an Australian palate but brightly flavoured and refreshingly finished with clean, citrusy acids, it's a charming wine of moderate length and intensity.

2004	92	2006	2009
2003	92	2008	2011
2000	91	2005	2008
1999	95	2007	2011
1998	89	2000	2003+
1997	89	2002	2005

Wendouree

Wendouree Road, Clare SA 5453. Tel: (08) 8842 2896.

Region: **Clare Valley** Winemakers: **Tony & Lita Brady** Viticulturist: **I Cerchi** Chief Executive: **Tony Brady**

Wendouree is an iconic maker of small volumes of deeply flavoured, firmly structured and finely crafted red wine from its historic dryland Clare Valley vineyard. As the 2004 vintage again illustrates, it is no longer the case that you need to wait forever to appreciate these wines, although if I could, I most certainly would.

SHIRAZ

RATING **1**

Clare Valley	$100–$199
Current vintage: 2004	**97**

Heady floral notes and suggestions of clove and cinnamon-like spices overlie a brooding bouquet whose aromas of blackberries, blueberries, cassis and dark plums are tightly knit with fine-grained oak. Framed by firm, powdery tannin, it unfolds layers of searingly intense and slightly sour-edged, juicy plum and berry fruit backed by spicy, minty nuances and restrained oak. Very firm and astringent, it is already very approachable, entirely natural and finely balanced.

2004	97	2024	2023+
2003	95	2015	2023
2002	97	2022	2032
2001	89	2009	2013+
2000	88	2008	2012
1999	96	2019	2029
1998	97	2018	2028+
1997	89	2009	2017+
1996	95	2008	2016+
1995	94	2015	2025
1994	91	2006	2014+
1993	86	2001	2005+
1992	91	2012	2022
1991	96	2021	2031
1990	90	2010	2020+
1989	93	2009	2019
1988	93	2008	2018
1987	88	1999	2007
1985	95	2005	2015
1983	89	2003	2013+

SHIRAZ MATARO

RATING **3**

Clare Valley	$50–$99
Current vintage: 2003	**92**

Dusty and slightly meaty, its fragrance of spicy redcurrants, plums and blackberries, with restrained cedar/vanilla undertones has a perfumed, floral quality. Full-bodied, firm and linear, its chewy palate of meaty, dark-fruited and earthy influences overlies a powerful, rod-like and mouth-coating spine of bony tannin. It finishes long and savoury, with lightly herbal undertones.

2003	92	2011	2015+
2002	95	2014	2022+
2001	90	2021	2031
2000	87	2008	2012+
1999	95	2019	2029
1998	96	2018	2028+
1997	88	2009	2017
1996	94	2016	2026
1995	94	2005	2015+
1994	87	2004	2014
1991	95	2011	2021
1988	93	2000	2008+
1987	89	1999	2007

Westend

1283 Brayne Road, Griffith NSW 2680. Tel: (02) 6969 0800. Fax: (02) 6962 1673.
Website: www.westendestate.com.au Email: westend@webfront.net.au

Region: **Riverina** Winemakers: **William Calabria, Bryan Currie** Viticulturist: **Anthony Trimboli**
Chief Executive: **William Calabria**

Bill Calabria's family business continues to make Griffith's finest range of wine. The 3 Bridges range reflects his desire to put Riverina wines on the same stage as the finest from the more fashionable regions. The current releases include his best-ever Chardonnay, a wine whose richness and finesse could easily eclipse many significantly dearer wines. Similarly, the Reserve Shiraz 2003 is typically sumptuous, deeply flavoured and assertive, a wine of which many other makers would rightly be proud.

3 BRIDGES CABERNET SAUVIGNON

RATING **4**

Riverina	$20–$29
Current vintage: 2002	**88**

Sweet violet and cassis aromas with mocha/cedary oak and minty undertones of eucalypt and dried herbs precede an oaky, forward and earthy palate of up-front jammy fruit. It's plummy, minty and vibrant, with a slightly hollow centre, and lacks the depth and structure for longer cellaring.

2002	88	2004	2007+
2001	91	2006	2009+
2000	87	2002	2005+
1999	89	2004	2007
1998	90	2003	2006+
1997	90	1999	2002+

3 BRIDGES CHARDONNAY

Riverina $12–$19
Current vintage: 2004 90

Big, broad but balanced, this smooth and harmonious chardonnay reveals a delicate perfume of peach and melon over nutty, dusty and lightly toasty nuances of vanilla oak. Smooth and buttery, its generous, juicy expression of peaches, cream and grapefruit-like flavour, sweet vanilla oak and buttery malolactic undertones finishes with a soft but tightly knit acidity.

2004	90	2006	2009
2003	87	2004	2005+
2002	87	2003	2004
2001	84	2002	2002
2000	88	2001	2002+
1999	87	2000	2001
1998	87	1999	2000

3 BRIDGES DURIF

RATING 5

Riverina $20–$29
Current vintage: 2004 88

Briary, meaty aromas of blackberries, blueberries, dark plums and treacle overlie nuances of bitumen, currants and raisins. Rich and forward, its modest richness of slightly cooked durif flavour thins out towards the finish, leaving the wine a little too reliant on assertive oak and firmish tannins for length down the palate.

2004	88	2006	2009
2003	89	2005	2008
2002	93	2007	2010
2001	87	2003	2006+
2000	91	2005	2008+

3 BRIDGES GOLDEN MIST BOTRYTIS SEMILLON

RATING 5

Riverina $20–$29 (375 ml)
Current vintage: 2003 87

Rather varnishy and developed, with toasty, honeyed aromas of marmalade and cumquat before an almost cloying, luscious and sugar-coated palate. Quite thick and citrusy, but beginning to lose some freshness.

2003	87	2005	2008
2002	89	2003	2004+
2001	88	2002	2003
1999	91	2001	2004+
1998	87	1999	2000
1997	94	1999	2002+
1996	90	1998	2001
1995	84	1996	1997

3 BRIDGES RESERVE SHIRAZ

RATING 4

Riverina $20–$29
Current vintage: 2003 90

A plush, smooth and oaky modern wine with the depth of vibrant, juicy fruit to carry it with ease. Its spicy fragrance of white pepper, sweet red and black berries and chocolate/vanilla oak precedes a plush and deeply flavoured palate. Framed by pliant, firm tannins, its carefully integrated and lingering palate evenly marries intense fruit and oak, finishing with nuances of licorice and blackberry.

2003	90	2005	2008+
2002	91	2007	2010+
2001	90	2006	2009
2000	91	2005	2008+
1999	86	2001	2004

A B C D E F G H I J K L M N O P Q R S T U V **W** X Y Z

2007 **THE AUSTRALIAN WINE ANNUAL**
www.jeremyoliver.com.au 297

Willow Creek

RMB 6535, 166 Balnarring Road, Merricks North Vic 3926. Tel: (03) 5989 7448. Fax: (03) 5989 7584.
Website: www.willow-creek.com.au Email: admin@willow-creek.com.au

Region: **Mornington Peninsula** Winemaker: **Phil Kerney** Viticulturist: **Robert O'Leary** Chief Executive: **Phil Kerney**

Willow Creek has been part of the Mornington Peninsula scene for some time. It is making sound, well-structured and handsomely crafted wines that reflect some fine work in the cellar. These relatively faultless wines could improve in the vineyard, for all they are lacking is top-class density of fruit and depth of flavour. I remain entirely mystified why a specialist pinot noir maker would introduce a top-tier wine (in this case the 2004 Benedictus, 87, drink 2006–2009+) without a single reference to its main identity (Willow Creek) on its label or bottle.

TULUM CHARDONNAY

RATING 5

Mornington Peninsula	$30–$49
Current vintage: 2005	90

Stylish and concentrated, with a fruit-driven aroma of pineapple, peach and nectarine backed by sweet vanilla oak. Round, generous and juicy, its smooth and fluffy palate of bright stonefruit, citrus and melon flavours reveals a background of vanila oak, but not a lot of winemaking artefact. It finishes long and clean, with refreshing acids.

2005	90	2007	2010+
2004	90	2006	2009
2003	87	2005	2008
2002	89	2004	2007

TULUM PINOT NOIR

RATING 5

Mornington Peninsula	$30–$49
Current vintage: 2004	88

Fine-grained, supple and smooth; a genuinely varietal pinot with a fresh, floral perfume of sweet, confiture-like red cherries and plums lifted by a spicy background of cloves, cinnamon and vanilla oak. Medium in weight, its juicy, sappy expression of berry/cherry flavour overlies a pliant spine of fine-grained tannin.

2004	88	2006	2009+
2003	88	2005	2008
2002	88	2004	2007

WCV PINOT NOIR

RATING 5

Mornington Peninsula	$20–$29
Current vintage: 2005	90

A plush, smooth and oaky modern wine with the depth of vibrant, juicy fruit to carry it with ease. Its spicy fragrance of white pepper, sweet red and black berries and chocolate/vanilla oak precedes a plush and deeply flavoured palate. Framed by pliant, firm tannins, its carefully integrated and lingering palate evenly marries intense fruit and oak, finishing with nuances of licorice and blackberry.

2004	90	2006	2009
2003	87	2005	2008
2002	88	2004	2007

Wilson Vineyard, The

Polish Hill Road, Sevenhill via Clare SA 5453. Tel: (08) 8843 4310. Website: www.wilsonvineyard.com.au

Region: **Clare Valley** Winemakers: **Daniel Wilson, John Wilson** Viticulturist: **John Wilson** Chief Executive: **John Wilson**

While the Wilson Vineyard is one of the Clare Valley's long-established producers of classic Australian riesling, I was surprised to see the extent of broadness and thickness in the proprietory Riesling. The DJW Riesling is made by the second generation of winemaking Wilsons, Daniel, who appears to have a flair for a more adventurous and evolved style.

DJW RIESLING

RATING 5

Clare Valley	$12–$19
Current vintage: 2005	89

Rather toasty, developed and buttery, with varietal aromas of lime juice and lemon rind. Broad, juicy and generous, with a pleasing length of zesty apple, lime and lemon-like fruit, it settles into a long, smooth and dry finish.

2005	89	2010	2013
2004	88	2006	2009+
2003	93	2011	2015
2002	82	2004	2007
2001	89	2005	2008

RIESLING (formerly Gallery Series)

Clare Valley	**$12–$19**	2005	83	2007	2010+
Current vintage: 2005	**83**	2004	90	2009	2012+
		2003	91	2011	2015+

A powerful, broad-shouldered riesling that is developing rather quickly. Its floral and tea tin-like aromas of slightly cooked and spicy fruit precede a broad, juicy palate supported by some rather raw and assertive phenolic extract. A little too thick, and lacking in brightness and freshness.

2002	89	2007	2010
2001	88	2006	2009
2000	91	2005	2008+
1999	94	2007	2011+
1998	95	2006	2010+
1997	87	2002	2005
1996	93	2004	2008
1995	94	2003	2007

Wirra Wirra

McMurtrie Road, McLaren Vale SA 5171. Tel: (08) 8323 8414. Fax: (08) 8323 8596.
Website: www.wirra.com.au Email: info@wirra.com.au
Regions: **McLaren Vale, Various SA** Winemaker: **Samantha Connew** Viticulturist: **Tony Hoare**
Chief Executive: **Tim James**

The immediate story for Wirra Wirra today is the excellent return to red wine form in 2004. This has resulted in excellent wines under the RSW Shiraz and The Angelus Cabernet Sauvignon labels and a soft, meaty and briary Woodhenge Shiraz. The Chardonnay and the Riesling are appreciating the relocation of its source to the Adelaide Hills, while the Church Block and Scrubby Rise labels are offering great value.

CHARDONNAY

RATING 5

Adelaide Hills	**$20–$29**	2005	91	2007	2010+
Current vintage: 2005	**91**	2004	91	2006	2009
		2002	86	2004	2007

An elegant and finely crafted chardonnay with a fresh, nutty bouquet of honeydew melon, peach and citrus aromas supported by lightly toasty vanilla oak. Its refreshing palate of lemon sherbet, apple, pear and peach-like flavour is backed by assertive but well integrated smoky oak and finished with brisk acidity.

2000	81	2001	2002
1999	87	2001	2004
1998	88	2000	2003
1997	89	1999	2002

CHURCH BLOCK

RATING 5

McLaren Vale	**$20–$29**	2004	89	2009	2012+
Current vintage: 2004	**89**	2003	81	2005	2008
		2002	86	2003	2004+

Deep, dark-fruited and earthy aromas with undertones of dark chocolate and polished leather precede a smooth and savoury palate of full to medium weight. There's attractive rustic, meaty and spicy complexity beneath its plum and dark berry-like flavours, with a drying and tannic finish of mineral-like nuances. Good weight and structure.

2001	81	2002	2003+
2000	83	2002	2005
1999	92	2004	2007
1998	93	2003	2006+
1997	93	2002	2005+
1996	87	1998	2001
1995	88	2000	2003

HAND PICKED RIESLING

RATING 5

Adelaide Hills	**$12–$19**	2005	90	2010	2013
Current vintage: 2005	**90**	2004	88	2006	2009
		2003	86	2004	2005

Flavoursome, juicy and elegant, this polished expression of Adelaide Hills riesling has a musky perfume of pear and lime before a slightly oily, viscous palate whose vibrant pear, apple, lemon and lime flavours culminate in a tangy finish of crystalline acidity.

2002	82	2003	2004+
2001	87	2003	2006+
2000	82	2002	2005
1999	88	2001	2004+
1998	85	2003	2006
1997	86	1999	2002

RSW SHIRAZ

RATING 3

McLaren Vale $50–$99
Current vintage: 2004 94

A very stylish, finely honed modern shiraz whose assertive and deeply flavoured fruit is handsomely oaked and framed by firm, fine-grained tannins. Perfumed and floral, with intense small, dark berries and forthright cedary oak backed by spicy, dusty nuances of cloves and cinnamon, it's also meaty, very slightly varnishy and scented with white pepper. Full in body, silky of texture, sumptuous of weight, it's a luxuriant drop whose intense small berry and currant-like fruit is backed by assertive but measured chocolatey, gamey new oak and framed by firm, fine-grained tannins. There's a salty, mineral tang at the finish, and a lingering sour-edged note to the fruit.

2004	94	2012	2016+
2003	93	2011	2015+
2002	94	2010	2014+
2001	91	2006	2009
2000	87	2002	2005+
1999	87	2004	2007
1998	94	2003	2006+
1997	90	2002	2005
1996	96	2004	2008
1995	92	2000	2003
1994	94	1999	2002
1993	91	1998	2001
1992	93	2000	2004

SCRUBBY RISE (Sauvignon Blanc Semillon Viognier)

Various SA $12–$19
Current vintage: 2005 87

Fresh pineapple and passionfruit flavours reveal a lightly grassy and herbal thread. Clean and tangy, it's juicy, generously flavoured, slightly phenolic and fruit-driven, offering length and richness.

2005	87	2005	2006
2004	86	2004	2005
2003	86	2004	2005
2002	87	2003	2004
2001	86	2001	2002
2000	80	2000	2001
1999	80	1999	2000
1998	87	2000	2003

THE ANGELUS CABERNET SAUVIGNON

RATING 3

McLaren Vale $50–$99
Current vintage: 2004 94

Tightly astringent, long and harmonious, this firm but supple McLaren Vale cabernet has a floral perfume of violets, cassis, sweet dark plums and fine-grained cedar/vanilla oak. Supple, tightly integrated and dusty, its pristine palate of fresh blackberries, dark plums and cassis is backed by dark chocolate, cedar and vanilla oak influences and bound by firm but finely grained tannins. It's a deep, long-term wine of power, style and harmony.

2004	94	2016	2024
2003	90	2011	2015
2002	93	2014	2022
2001	87	2006	2009
2000	90	2005	2008
1999	88	2004	2007
1998	95	2006	2010+
1997	86	2002	2005
1996	95	2004	2008+
1995	91	2003	2007
1994	88	1999	2002
1993	93	2001	2005
1992	93	2000	2004

WOODHENGE SHIRAZ

RATING 5

McLaren Vale $20–$29
Current vintage: 2004 91

Briary aromas of blackberries, raspberries, plums and cranberries with sweet undertones of vanilla and dark chocolate oak precede a spicy, fullish and velvet-like palate. Framed by soft, pliant tannin, its sumptuous palate of juicy dark fruit has a slightly jammy and meaty edge, finishing smooth and savoury with lingering nuances of licorice. Nicely oaked and balanced.

2004	91	2009	2012
2003	88	2008	2011+
2002	88	2007	2010
2001	87	2003	2006
2000	82	2002	2005
1999	85	2001	2004+

Wolf Blass

Sturt Highway, Nuriootpa SA 5355. Tel: (08) 8568 7303. Fax: (08) 8568 7380.
Website: www.wolfblass.com.au Email: cellardoor@wolfblass.com.au

Regions: **Langhorne Creek, Barossa Valley, Various SA** Winemakers: **Caroline Dunn, Chris Hatcher, Kirsten Glaetzer, Wendy Stuckey** Viticulturist: **Stuart McNab** Chief Executive: **Jamie Odell**

Wolf Blass is a steadily resurgent wine range that presently offers excellence throughout its tiered hierarchy, with only a few exceptions: the wines I have tasted from the Yellow Label range. A significant recent vertical tasting of all Black Label wines conveyed a number of messages, including how well grown and constructed were vintages like 1973, 1975, 1976 and 1977, and that it is only recently that the wine has again achieved such consistency and quality. These days, though, its Langhorne Creek component has reduced significantly and shiraz has replaced cabernet as the wine's principal variety.

BLACK LABEL   RATING 3

| Various, SA | | $100–$199 |
| Current vintage: 2002 | | 97 |

A modern classic. Its opulent, heady perfume of wild, briary dark berries, plums and redcurrants reveals layers of deeply scented oak, pepper and spice. Smooth and luscious, its silky-fine palate is steeped in pure, joyous dark fruit, handsomely partnered by creamy and slightly caramelised cedar/vanilla oak. It's effortless and refined, beautifully balanced with firm, fine tannins, finishing with length and persistence.

2002	97	2022	2032+
2001	92	2009	2013
2000	88	2005	2008+
1999	89	2007	2011
1998	94	2010	2018+
1997	86	2002	2005
1996	92	2008	20016
1995	93	2007	2015+
1994	89	2000	2003
1993	81	1998	2001
1992	90	2000	2004+
1991	93	2003	2011+
1990	93	2002	2010+
1989	88	1997	2001+
1988	90	1993	1996+
1987	87	1995	1999+
1986	93	1999	2006+

GOLD LABEL CHARDONNAY   RATING 3

| Adelaide Hills | | $20–$29 |
| Current vintage: 2005 | | 91 |

Slightly funky, meaty and floral, scented with white peaches and melon backed by sweet vanilla oak, this complex young chardonnay has a long, mineral and savoury palate. Its brightly lit and juicy flavours of tangerine, melon and mango finish with nutty undertones and soft, refreshing acids. Should develop well.

2005	91	2007	2010
2004	94	2006	2009
2003	93	2005	2008
2002	94	2004	2007+

GOLD LABEL RIESLING   RATING 3

| Clare Valley, Eden Valley | | $12–$19 |
| Current vintage: 2005 | | 87 |

Spicy and slightly confectionary, its citrusy perfume reveals nuances of talcum powder and bath salts. Juicy and forward, it's smooth and brightly flavoured but finishes a little sweet and cloying, flat and metallic, with a phenolic chalkiness and mineral undertones.

2005	87	2007	2010
2004	93	2006	2009
2003	92	2005	2006
2002	94	2007	2010
2001	95	2006	2009+
2000	90	2002	2005
1999	90	2001	2004
1998	94	2003	2006
1997	91	2002	2005
1996	94	2004	2008

GOLD LABEL SHIRAZ VIOGNIER   RATING 4

| Adelaide Hills | | $20–$29 |
| Current vintage: 2004 | | 93 |

Viognier plays a subdued role in this deeply flavoured, spicy and savoury red, whose complex and smoky perfume of blackberries, dark plums and cherries is carefully matched with cedar/vanilla oak. Its sumptuous, palate-staining expression of spicy black fruits and dark chocolate oak is remarkably smooth and silky, finishing with a persistent core of peppery and slightly meaty flavour.

2004	93	2009	2012+
2003	88	2005	2008+
2002	90	2004	2007

GREY LABEL CABERNET SAUVIGNON

RATING **4**

Langhorne Creek $30–$49
Current vintage: 2004 93

Firmly structured, deeply ripened and intensely flavoured, this slightly old-fashioned red should age well. Its musky, floral perfume of confiture-like cassis and dark plums, mint, cloves and menthol overlies toasty aromas of sweet vanilla oak. Its penetrative, pristine and jujube-like fruit and toasty oak are framed by firm, chalky tannins, finishing long and strong.

2004	93	2016	2024+
2003	93	2011	2015+
2002	88	2010	2014
2001	90	2006	2009
1999	87	2004	2007
1997	84	1999	2002
1996	90	2001	2004+
1995	93	2002	2007
1994	94	2002	2006
1993	89	2001	2005
1992	93	2000	2004
1991	94	1999	2003
1990	91	1995	1998

GREY LABEL SHIRAZ (formerly Brown Label)

RATING **3**

McLaren Vale $30–$49
Current vintage: 2004 93

A finely crafted and elegant modern shiraz whose spicy, peppery and slightly jammy fragrance of cassis, raspberries and sweet red plums is backed by oaky suggestions of vanilla, coconut ice, dark chocolate and cedar. Its long and stylish palate of cassis, dark plums and blackberries is tightly knit with firm, drying and bony tannins. There's a hint of saltiness, with a background of cinnamon and nutmeg.

2004	93	2016	2024
2003	92	2008	2011+
2002	94	2010	2014+
2001	88	2003	2006
2000	86	2002	2005
1999	88	2001	2004
1998	89	2006	2010
1997	88	2002	2005
1996	91	2004	2008
1995	87	2000	2003
1994	92	2002	2006
1993	89	1998	2001
1992	90	2000	2004
1990	92	1998	2002

PLATINUM LABEL SHIRAZ

RATING **1**

Various, SA $100–$199
Current vintage: 2003 95

Heady, meaty and peppery aromas of blackber-ries, raspberries, cassis and mulberries are lifted by lightly smoky/cedary oak, black pepper and spicy nuances of clove and nutmeg. Velvet smooth and quite restrained despite its 15.5% alcohol, it reveals a meaty, raisined and leathery aspect and a spirity warmth. Handsomely oaked and framed by fine, mouth-coating tannin, it's strong and powerful, finishing with a lingering core of vibrant berry/plum fruit.

2003	95	2015	2023
2002	96	2009	2013+
2001	97	2013	2021+
2000	95	2008	2012
1999	95	2011	2019+
1998	96	2010	2018+

RED LABEL SHIRAZ CABERNET SAUVIGNON

Various $5–$11
Current vintage: 2004 86

Juicy aromas of blackberries, plums and smoky, cedar/vanilla/chocolate oak reveal spicy and earthy undertones. Medium to full in weight, its slightly sweet, jujube-like flavours of dark berries and plums reveal a hint of currants and raisins, assertively backed by very toasty mocha/chocolate oak. Backed by soft, approachable tannins, it has genuine texture and length.

2004	86	2006	2009
2003	80	2004	2005+
2002	89	2004	2007
2001	86	2003	2006
1999	82	2000	2001
1998	81	2002	2003
1997	87	1999	2002
1996	82	1997	1998

YELLOW LABEL CABERNET SAUVIGNON

RATING **5**

South Australia $12–$19
Current vintage: 2004 82

A rather thin, simple and under-ripened wine whose dusty, herbal aromas of small berries, plums and cedar/vanilla oak precede a straightforward palate whose light berry fruit thins out towards a herbal finish. Lacks weight and conviction.

2004	82	2006	2009
2003	88	2005	2008
2002	88	2005	2008+
2001	87	2003	2006
2000	88	2002	2005+
1998	89	2003	2006
1997	81	1999	2002
1996	88	1998	2001
1995	87	2000	2003

YELLOW LABEL RIESLING

Various, SA	$5–$11
Current vintage: 2005	**82**

Slightly cooked, candied aromas of lime, lemon and tea leaves lack much freshness and lift. Sweet and confectionary, it lacks its usual tightness and varietal qualities. Very simple and disappointing.

2005	82	2006	2007+
2004	87	2004	2005
2003	82	2003	2004
2002	83	2003	2004
2001	92	2005	2008
2000	87	2001	2002
1999	86	2000	2001
1998	92	2000	2003
1997	87	1999	2002

Woodlands

Lot 1 Caves Road, Willyabrup WA 6280. Tel: (08) 9755 6226. Fax: (08) 9755 6236.
Website: www.woodlandswines.com Email: mail@woodlandswines.com

Region: **Margaret River** Winemaker: **Stuart Watson** Viticulturist: **Nick Clark** Chief Executive: **David Watson**

Established in 1973, Woodlands might not be terribly well known, but it was among the first wave of plantings in Margaret River. Developed by David and Heather Watson, it is undergoing a renaissance in the hands of their son Stuart, whose first vintage at the winery was 2002. To put it mildly, the Woodlands reds from 2004 are brilliant. If you take your Australian wine seriously, you need to try them.

BARREL RESERVE CABERNET FRANC

RATING **3**

Margaret River	$50–$99
Current vintage: 2005	**95**

A finely crafted and supple cabernet franc with a distinctively floral perfume of rose petals, raspberries, redcurrants and plums backed by restrained cedary oak and nuances of cinnamon. Long and savoury, its penetrative flavours of blackberries, small red berries and cranberries are framed by fine, dusty tannins. Likely to become quite spicy and meaty with age.

2005	95	2013	2017
2004	90	2009	2012
2003	93	2011	2015+
2002	87	2007	2010+

BARREL RESERVE MALBEC

RATING **3**

Margaret River	$50–$99
Current vintage: 2005	**95**

Quite a mind-blowing wine for an Australian malbec; hardly a category populated by superstars. A spicy fragrance of fruit salad, guava, dark plums and cherries reveals undertones of sweet cedar/chocolate oak and a whiff of banana. Its sumptuous, brooding dark plum and berry flavours are sure to evolve significantly from this, a very youthful state, but it should retain its lingering core of brightness and varietal integrity. Terrific length, richness and structure of bony, firm tannin.

2005	95	2017	2025
2004	95	2016	2024
2003	91	2008	2011+
2002	90	2007	2010+

CABERNET MERLOT

RATING **3**

Margaret River	$12–$19
Current vintage: 2005	**91**

A brambly fragrance of sweet blackberries and plums reveals slightly gamey undertones of ripe cherry-like merlot and cedary oak. Full to medium in weight, it's supple and silky, with a deeply flavoured palate of juicy, briary berry and plum flavours backed by cedar/vanilla oak and framed by smooth and dusty tannins.

2005	91	2010	2013
2004	93	2009	2012+
2003	92	2011	2015+
2002	82	2007	2010+

CABERNET SAUVIGNON

| Margaret River | $50–$99 | 2004 | 97 | 2016 | 2024+ |
| Current vintage: 2004 | 97 | 2003 | 96 | 2015 | 2023 |

| | 2002 | 95 | 2014 | 2022 |
| | 2001 | 87 | 2006 | 2009 |

A beautifully elegant and structured cabernet of considerable class. Its floral perfume of sweet small black and red berries, fresh cedar/vanilla oak and undertones of dried herbs precedes a tightly focused palate of exceptional length and restrained power. Beneath its pristine expression of berry fruits and cedary oak lie nuances of dried herbs and forest floor, while its fine, superbly integrated tannins have a measured, polished quality.

MARGARET RESERVE CABERNET MERLOT

| Margaret River | $30–$49 | 2004 | 97 | 2016 | 2024 |
| Current vintage: 2004 | 97 | 2003 | 90 | 2011 | 2015 |

| | 2002 | 87 | 2007 | 2010+ |
| | 2001 | 88 | 2009 | 2012 |

Sweet aromas of violets, blackberries, redcurrants and dark cherries are handsomely backed by cedar/vanilla oak, with delicate underlying nuances of tobacco, damp forest floor and dark chocolates. Supple, fine and willowy, the palate presents a succulent, generous expression of sweet blackcurrant, dark plum and blackberry fruit tightly knit with new vanilla/cedar oak and dusty tannins. Beautifully integrated, and finishing with a lingering note of mineral.

Woodstock

Douglas Gully Road, McLaren Flat SA 5171. Tel: (08) 8383 0156. Fax: (08) 8383 0437.
Website: www.woodstockwine.com.au Email: woodstock@woodstockwine.com.au
Regions: **McLaren Vale, Limestone Coast, Langhorne Creek** Winemaker: **Ben Glaetzer**
Viticulturist: **Scott Collett** Chief Executive: **Scott Collett**

If Scott Collett was happy last year, the standard of Woodstock's 2004 wines should put him over the moon. It's clearly a signature vintage for the region, and Ben Glaetzer has made the most of it. Slightly riper than it traditionally used to be, The Stocks Shiraz is a first-rate modern wine, with all the spicy, oaky and fruit-powered bells and whistles. The imaginatively labelled Botrytis Sweet White could comprise chenin blanc, riesling and semillon on any given year. The 2004 edition is a delicious straight Semillon, and is clean, vibrant and fresh enough for more than just a single glass.

BOTRYTIS SWEET WHITE

| Various | $20–$29 (375 ml) | 2004 | 94 | 2006 | 2009+ |
| Current vintage: 2004 | 94 | 2003 | 94 | 2005 | 2008+ |

	1999	87	2001	2004
	97/98	81	2000	2003
	1996	92	2001	2004
	1995	93	2000	2003
	1994	91	2002	2006
	1993	90	1995	1998

A lightly spicy fragrance of white peach, apricot, custard crème and citrus reveals nuances of marzipan and brulée. Luscious, sweet and very intense, its pristine and vibrant palate reveals undertones of lemon tart and marmalade. It has good but not great length, and finishes with lingering flavours of citrus, melon and stonefruit neatly wrapped by a clean and refreshing acidity.

CABERNET SAUVIGNON

| McLaren Vale | $20–$29 | 2004 | 90 | 2009 | 2012+ |
| Current vintage: 2004 | 90 | 2002 | 91 | 2010 | 2014+ |

	2001	86	2006	2009
	2000	81	2002	2005
	1999	84	2001	2004+
	1998	86	2003	2006
	1997	89	2005	2009
	1996	87	2001	2004
	1995	87	2000	2003
	1994	93	2002	2006
	1993	91	2001	2005
	1992	93	2004	2012
	1991	95	2003	2011

A supple, pliant and approachable cabernet whose minty, briary fragrance of cassis, plums and blackberries overlies cedary oak, cloves and dried herbs. Its long, dusty palate delivers vibrant, confiture-like dark berry fruit neatly meshed with cedar/vanilla oak and framed by fine tannins, finishing with undertones of dried herbs and peppermint.

SHIRAZ

RATING 4

Limestone Coast, Langhorne Creek, McLaren Vale $20–$29
Current vintage: 2004 91

Charmingly smooth and silky, this vibrant, spicy and intensely fruity young shiraz has a deep aroma of dark berries and plums backed by mocha and dark chocolate-like oak, with undertones of spearmint. It's supple, approachable and tightly focused, with a deliciously vibrant palate of small berries, tight oak and fine tannins, finishing with lingering nuances of cinnamon, clove and licorice.

2004	91	2012	2016
2002	91	2007	2010+
2001	86	2003	2006+
2000	90	2005	2008
1999	83	2001	2004
1998	92	2006	2010
1997	90	2002	2005+
1996	92	2004	2008
1995	86	2000	2003
1994	88	1999	2002
1993	93	2001	2005

THE STOCKS

RATING 3

McLaren Vale $30–$49
Current vintage: 2004 96

A superb modern shiraz that marries explosively flavoured and sour-edged fruit with smoky, mocha-like oak and velvet tannin. It's heady and ethereal, with a spicy, peppery fragrant of blackberries, blueberries and cassis backed by meaty, gamey, leathery and chocolate-like undertones. Easily soaking up its showy and charry new oak and a lavish array of spices, it's opulent expression of perfectly ripened berry flavours finish long and smooth, with just a faint hint of currant. Give it time.

2004	96	2016	2024
2002	93	2010	2014
2001	90	2003	2006+
2000	89	2002	2005+
1999	89	2001	2004+
1998	96	2010	2018
1997	87	1999	2002
1996	95	2004	2008
1995	92	2003	2007
1994	95	2002	2006
1993	93	2001	2005
1991	89	1999	2003

Wyndham Estate

Dalwood Road, Dalwood NSW 2335. Tel: (02) 4938 3444. Fax: (02) 4938 3555.
Website: www.wyndhamestate.com.au

Regions: **Various, Lower Hunter Valley** Winemakers: **Sam Kurtz, Tony Hooper, Andrew Miller**
Viticulturist: **Stephen Guilbaud-Oulton** Chief Executive: **Laurent Lacassgne**

While Wyndham Estate continues to release impressively flavoursome and polished wines under its Bin labels, the real quality story here lies in the Show Reserve wines, of which the Shiraz is usually considerably more polished and better presented than the rather clunky and overcooked 2003 edition. On the other hand the Show Reserve Semillon is a fine expression of this idiosyncratic regional style.

BIN 222 CHARDONNAY

RATING 5

Various $12–$19
Current vintage: 2005 87

A clean, crisp and shapely chardonnay whose peachy, lightly tropical and buttery fruit and fresh cashew/vanilla oak combine in a juicy and moderately intense palate that finishes refreshingly long and creamy.

2005	87	2005	2006+
2004	88	2005	2006
2003	88	2004	2005+
2002	89	2003	2004+
2001	88	2003	2006
2000	79	2001	2002

BIN 555 SHIRAZ

Various $12–$19
Current vintage: 2003 87

A balanced and vibrant young shiraz whose spicy, peppery fragrance of red berries, plums, cassis, cloves and cinnamon overlies smoky nuances of vanilla oak. It's fresh and lively, fine and supple, with a pleasing length of juicy berry fruit and well-handled oak.

2003	87	2005	2008+
2002	86	2004	2007
2001	87	2003	2006
2000	82	2001	2002
1999	86	2001	2004+
1998	82	2000	2003
1997	88	1999	2002
1996	86	1998	2001
1995	86	2000	2003

SHOW RESERVE CABERNET MERLOT

RATING **4**

Lower Hunter Valley	$20–$29
Current vintage: 2001	86

Rather straightforward, minty and slightly cooked, with menthol-like aromas of sweet, jammy red-currants, plums and blackberries over cedar/vanilla oak. Full to medium in weight, it reveals a moderately long, juicy and minty expression of jammy red berry, cassis and plum-like fruit framed by chalky tannins.

2001	86	2009	2013
1998	90	2006	2010+
1997	90	2002	2005
1996	86	1998	2001

SHOW RESERVE SEMILLON

RATING **4**

Lower Hunter Valley	$20–$29
Current vintage: 1999	92

Another fine wine in this series, whose toasty aromas of melon and pastry are backed by a pleasing fragrance of honeysuckle and roasted nuts. Generous, round and juicy, it's long, dry and savoury, delivering a slightly honeyed expression of melon, brioche and nutty flavours. Still has a way to travel.

1999	92	2007	2011
1997	88	2005	2009
1996	90	2004	2009
1995	90	2003	2007+
1994	87	1999	2002

SHOW RESERVE SHIRAZ

RATING **3**

Lower Hunter Valley	$20–$29
Current vintage: 2003	87

A raisined, tarry, very oaky and alcoholic shiraz whose juicy aromas of blackberries, plums and blueberries are assertively backed by chocolate/mocha oak and reveal reductive, charcuterie-like undertones. Smooth and creamy, its voluptuous palate of concentrated dark berries, chocolate and cedar/cigarboxy oak is framed by firm, drying tannins and finishes warm and spirity with smoky oak influences.

2003	87	2005	2008+
1999	94	2007	2011+
1998	95	2010	2018+
1997	88	2002	2005+
1996	87	2001	2004+
1995	87	2000	2003
1993	95	2001	2005+

Wynns Coonawarra Estate

Memorial Drive, Coonawarra SA 5263. Tel: (08) 8736 3266. Fax: (08) 8736 3202.
Website: www.wynns.com.au
Region: **Coonawarra** Winemaker: **Sue Hodder** Viticulturist: **Suzanne McLoughlin** Chief Executive: **Jamie Odell**

The return to the marketplace of the John Riddoch Cabernet Sauvignon and the Michael Shiraz with two top-drawer wines from 2003 is the first really positive indication to the wine public that the massive reworking of the Wynns Coonawarra Estate vineyards is having a major effect. These are complex, stylish and deeply flavoured and perfumed wines of some class. The recent appearance of the 2004 Cabernet Sauvignon, a marked improvement over the very acceptable 2003 vintage, leads one to suggest that the process is ongoing.

CABERNET SAUVIGNON

RATING **3**

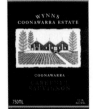

Coonawarra	$20–$29
Current vintage: 2004	93

An elegant and lightly herbal cool-year Coonawarra cabernet whose slightly leafy expression of small black and red berries, mulberries and plums knits effortlessly with fine-grained and loose-knit tannin and smooth, creamy oak. It opens slowly to reveal a violet-like perfume, while its smooth, restrained and supple palate of vibrant fruit overlies a wonderfully tight spine and pleasing cedary undertones.

2004	93	2016	2024
2003	92	2015	2023
2002	93	2014	2022+
2001	90	2013	2021
2000	87	2008	2012
1999	94	2011	2019+
1998	91	2010	2018+
1997	90	2005	2009+
1996	96	2016	2026+
1995	91	2007	2015
1994	95	2014	2024+
1993	87	2001	2005
1992	82	2000	2004
1991	96	2011	2021
1990	94	2010	2020
1989	87	1994	1997
1988	88	1996	2000
1987	86	1996	1999+
1986	90	1998	2006

CABERNET SHIRAZ MERLOT

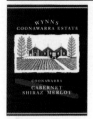

Coonawarra $12–$19
Current vintage: 2003 86

A moderately firm red that just lacks richness and depth of fruit. Its rather herbal, lightly minty aromas of cranberry jam, dark plums and cedary oak overlie herbal, meaty and greenish elements. Medium in weight, with a chalky undercarriage, its initially confection-like expression of dark plum and cassis-like fruit becomes meaty and savoury as it dries out towards the finish.

2003	86	2008	2011
2002	87	2004	2007
2000	82	2002	2005
1999	82	2001	2004
1998	85	2000	2003
1997	83	1999	2002
1996	88	2004	2010
1995	90	2000	2003
1994	89	1999	2002

CHARDONNAY
RATING 5

Coonawarra $12–$19
Current vintage: 2005 90

Well made, elegant and refreshing, this is a fine contemporary Australian chardonnay whose lightly herbal aromas of white peach, grapefruit and nectarine overlie cashew and vanilla oak influences. Long, fine and savoury, its vibrant and spotlessly clean palate of melon and stonefruit flavour has a delightfully fluffy texture and finishes with balance and brightness.

2005	90	2007	2010
2004	88	2005	2006+
2003	88	2005	2008
2002	84	2002	2004+
2001	88	2003	2006
2000	82	2001	2002
1999	87	2001	2004
1998	89	2000	2003
1997	88	1999	2002

JOHN RIDDOCH CABERNET SAUVIGNON
RATING 2

Coonawarra $50–$99
Current vintage: 2003 94

A very elegant, tightly structured and refined John Riddoch that, from a stylistic perspective, is the closest release to the inaugural 1982 vintage of the wine. Its cedary aromas of cassis, plums and dark chocolate are backed by hints of dark olives and a capsicum-like herbaceousness. The firm, dusty palate reveals pristine berry and plum-like fruit tightly knit with very fine and stylish tannins and dark chocolate oak. It's long, firm and tight, but also reveals leafy and herbal undertones that are just a little too evident at the finish for a higher rating. Terrific winemaking from an improving vineyard resource.

2003	94	2015	2023+
1999	95	2019	2029
1998	95	2010	2018+
1997	89	2005	2009
1996	95	2016	2026
1994	95	2006	2014
1993	94	2001	2005
1992	93	2004	2012
1991	94	2003	2011
1990	96	2010	2020
1988	91	2000	2005
1987	93	1999	2004
1986	94	1998	2006
1985	90	1993	1997
1984	89	1992	1996
1982	96	1994	2002+

MICHAEL SHIRAZ
RATING 2

Coonawarra $50–$99
Current vintage: 2003 95

A very good and stylish shiraz of full to medium weight that gradually opens to reveal a very musky perfume of cassis, dark plums and raspberries, backed by white pepper, cloves, cinnamon and sweet chocolate/vanilla oak. Very smooth, supple and elegant for a Michael, its succulent and charmingly pristine and spicy shiraz flavour is supported by an artfully crafted spine of firm but loose-knit tannins. Very elegant and sophisticated; likely to cellar exceptionally well.

2003	95	2015	2023
1999	89	2007	2011
1998	95	2010	2018
1997	87	2002	2005
1996	94	2008	2016
1994	96	2006	2014
1993	95	2005	2013
1991	95	2003	2011
1990	94	2002	2010
1955	97	1975	1985

RIESLING

RATING 4

	Coonawarra	$12–$19
	Current vintage: 2005	**87**

Smoky and slightly candied, this ripe and vibrant riesling has a floral, rose petal perfume of apple, pear and lemon sherbet. Rather round and forward, it's soft and juicy, with a fine powdery underswell of phenolic influence beneath its lively and slightly confectionary fruit.

2005	87	2010	2013+
2004	90	2006	2009+
2002	90	2007	2010
2001	90	2006	2009
2000	90	2005	2008
1999	86	2001	2004
1998	90	2003	2006
1997	86	2002	2005
1996	90	2001	2004
1995	85	1997	2000
1994	91	1999	2002

SHIRAZ

RATING 5

	Coonawarra	$12–$19
	Current vintage: 2004	**89**

A spicy fragrance of sweet red berries, cassis and fresh cedary oak precedes a smooth, supple and sweet-fruited palate framed by fine, silky tannins. Long and elegant, its vibrant redcurrant and raspberry flavours are backed by fine-grained cedar/vanilla and finish with lingering fruit sweetness and delicate nuances of dried herbs.

2004	89	2009	2012
2003	88	2008	2011
2002	91	2004	2007+
2001	86	2003	2006
2000	87	2002	2005
1999	89	2004	2007
1998	89	2003	2006
1997	88	2002	2005
1996	84	1998	2001
1995	89	2000	2003
1994	87	1996	1999
1993	88	1998	2001
1992	91	2000	2004
1991	89	1996	1999

Xanadu

Boodjidup Road, Margaret River WA 6285. Tel: (08) 9757 2581. Fax: (08) 9757 3389.
Website: www.xanadunormans.com.au Email: info@xanadunormans.com.au

Region: **Margaret River** Winemaker: **Jurg Muggli** Viticulturist: **Peter Gherardi** Chief Executive: **Sam Atkins**

While Xanadu remains a publicly listed company, its brand and assets have been bought by Doug Rathbone, with the intention of folding them into the marketing operations of his wine business, which already includes Yering Station, Mount Langi Ghiran and Parker Coonawarra.

CHARDONNAY

RATING 4

	Margaret River	$20–$29
	Current vintage: 2004	**87**

A complex, heavily worked and very ripe chardonnay likely to mature quite quickly. Its slightly candied aromas of grapefruit, nectarines, peaches and melon are backed by creamy barrel-ferment influences and slightly meaty suggestions of wild yeast. Smooth and creamy, its slightly thick and textured palate of juicy grapefruit, lime and tropical flavours is a little clunky and cloying. Just needs more cut and polish.

2004	87	2006	2009
2003	88	2005	2008
2002	90	2004	2007
2001	88	2003	2006+
2000	93	2005	2008
1999	87	2001	2004
1998	92	2003	2006
1997	90	2002	2005
1996	94	2004	2008
1995	91	1997	2000
1994	94	2002	2006

SEMILLON

RATING 3

	Margaret River	$20–$29
	Current vintage: 2003	**87**

Heavily oaked, toasty and slightly brassy semillon whose herby, melon-like fruit is slightly subdued by creamy, toasty barrel-ferment influences. Broad and charry, its generous, oaky palate of oily green melon flavours has roundness and texture, before a long, but charry finish.

2003	87	2005	2008
2002	94	2004	2007+
2001	92	2003	2006+
2000	89	2002	2005
1999	82	2001	2004
1998	93	2003	2006
1997	93	2002	2005
1996	94	2001	2004
1995	87	1996	1997

Yabby Lake

112 Tuerong Road, Tuerong Vic 3933. Tel: (03) 9251 5375. Fax: (03) 9639 1540.
Website: www.yabbylake.com Email: info@yabbylake.com

Region: **Mornington Peninsula** Winemakers: **Tod Dexter, Larry McKenna**
Viticulturist: **Keith Harris** Chief Executives: **Robert & Mem Kirby**

Yabby Lake is a new and highly feted entrant to the Mornington Peninsula's crowded wine industry. The early wines were made by Larry McKenna, while Tod Dexter recently joined the business (which also cooperates closely with Heathcote Estate) as Group Winemaker. To date the Pinot Noirs have shown promise, but tend to be heavily worked and blocky, lacking tightness and finesse. The complex and meaty 2004 Chardonnay is clearly its best wine to date, avoiding some of the overblown, cloying and flabby characters of previous releases.

CHARDONNAY

RATING 5

Mornington Peninsula	$30–$49
Current vintage: 2004	**93**

2004	93	2006	2009
2003	89	2005	2008
2002	82	2003	2004+

Assertive, ripe and generous, this full-blown chardonnay is destined for a relatively short, but happy existence. There's a pungent meaty, nutty and charmingly reductive background beneath its funky aromas of peach, nectarine, wheatmeal and bacon, while its rich, viscous and seamless palate marries ripe stonefruit and pineapple fruit with the full gamut of winemaking artefact. Sweet but slightly blocky oak with nutty, creamy lees-derived qualities contributes plenty of texture and complexity.

PINOT NOIR

RATING 5

Mornington Peninsula	$30–$49
Current vintage: 2004	**87**

2004	87	2006	2009
2003	90	2005	2008+
2002	89	2004	2007

Rather varnishy aromas of ripe red cherries, rose petals and plums overlie sweet cedary oak and nuances of cloves and cinnamon. Very intense and spicy, its luscious and richly fruited palate of red cherry and plum-like flavour is backed by a firm and powdery cut of slightly overworked tannin plus some blocky oak. Too overblown, extracted and volatile for a higher score.

Yalumba

Eden Valley Road, Angaston SA 5353. Tel: (08) 8561 3200. Fax: (08) 8561 3393.
Website: www.yalumba.com Email: info@yalumba.com

Regions: **Barossa, Coonawarra, Eden Valley** Winemakers: **Alan Hoey, Kevin Glastonbury, Louisa Rose, Natalie Fryar, Peter Gambetta** Viticulturist: **Robin Nettelbeck** Chief Executive: **Robert Hill Smith**

This large, historic and family-owned winery has made itself the home of Australian viognier, with a terrific series of wines made by Louisa Rose. Astride them sits The Virgilius, an impressively concentrated and perfumed wine whose very musky and sumptuous 2004 and 2005 releases are two of the leading viogniers yet made in Australia. The spectacular return to form in 2002 of The Octavius is another 'best yet' for Yalumba's team, while the ultra-consistent The Signature blend of Cabernet Sauvignon and Shiraz lived up to expectations.

BAROSSA CABERNET SAUVIGNON SHIRAZ

RATING 5

Barossa Valley	$12–$19
Current vintage: 2002	**89**

2002	89	2007	2010+
2001	85	2003	2006
2000	87	2002	2005+
1999	82	2001	2004
1998	85	2000	2003

A typically elegant Yalumba red wine whose fragrant aromas of violets, cassis, raspberries and blood plums overlie sweet chocolate/cedar/vanilla oak and undertones of earthiness and spice. Ripe and juicy, the palate delivers slightly sour-edged berry and plum-like fruit framed by firmish powdery tannins and smoothed over by well-managed oak. Full to medium in weight, finishing with lingering suggestions of mint and dried herbs.

BAROSSA SHIRAZ

RATING 5

Barossa Valley $12–$19
Current vintage: 2002 88

Meaty and reductive, with dark aromas of plums, berries chocolate/vanilla oak and charcuterie-like undertones. Earthy, quite full and spicy, its pleasingly long palate of lively cassis, plum and blackberry flavours is neatly wrapped in sweet oak and fine-grained but moderately firm tannins. Good balance and elegance, but with attractive regional qualities.

2002	88	2004	2007+
2001	87	2003	2006
2000	87	2002	2005
1999	87	2001	2004+
1998	87	2000	2003
1997	90	2002	2005
1996	86	1998	2001
1995	89	1997	2000

BAROSSA SHIRAZ VIOGNIER

RATING 4

Barossa Valley, Eden Valley $30–$49
Current vintage: 2004 89

Rich, luscious and finely integrated, brightly flavoured and aromatic, presenting a flavoursome if confectionary marriage of floral, spicy and well-ripened fruit with carefully managed cedar/vanilla oak. Backed by firmish but smooth tannins, its juicy flavours of dark plums and black and red berries have a sour-edged finish.

2004	89	2009	2012
2003	93	2008	2011
2002	91	2007	2010
2000	88	2002	2005
1999	88	2004	2007
1998	87	2000	2003+

BUSH VINE GRENACHE

RATING 5

Barossa Valley $12–$19
Current vintage: 2005 90

Smooth, spicy and rather polished, this brambly expression of redcurrant, blueberry and plum-like fruit is neither too jammy nor confectionary. Floral and spicy, it's backed by restrained oak and a fine, silky undercarriage of gentle, pliant tannin, finishing long, dusty and savoury.

2005	90	2007	2010+
2002	89	2004	2007+
2001	89	2003	2006+
2000	88	2002	2005
1999	86	2001	2004+
1998	89	2003	2006
1997	90	2002	2005
1996	87	1998	2001

'D' CUVÉE

RATING 4

Tasmania, Victoria,
South Australia $30–$49
Current vintage: 2002 91

Attractive and refreshing, with a creamy fragrance of citrus fruit, dried flowers and lemon sherbet over nutty and bakery-like undertones. Long and tangy, it's fine and elegant, with a clean, creamy and citrusy palate finishing with bread-like nuances and a hint of greenish and tropical fruit.

2002	91	2004	2007+
2001	90	2003	2006+
1999	95	2004	2007
1998	89	2003	2006
1997	90	1999	2002
1996	93	2001	2004
1995	90	2000	2003
1994	94	1999	2002

EDEN VALLEY VIOGNIER

RATING 4

Eden Valley $20–$29
Current vintage: 2005 88

A flavoursome, savoury and meaty viognier whose pungent, floral bouquet of apricots, honeysuckle, cloves and cinnamon overlie creamy, leesy nuances. Rather complex, wild and woolly, its chewy palate begins with lively forward fruit but becomes quite smoky and charcuterie-like.

2005	88	2006	2007
2004	90	2005	2006
2003	90	2004	2005+
2002	89	2003	2004+
2001	88	2003	2006
2000	88	2001	2002
1999	86	2000	2001
1998	90	1999	2000

HAND PICKED EDEN VALLEY RIESLING

RATING 2

Eden Valley $20–$29
Current vintage: 2004 95

A supple, fine and beautifully presented young riesling scented with a delicate, lightly toasty and honeyed perfume of dried flowers, blossom, rosewater, honeysuckle and lime juice. Pristine, smooth and supple, its long and effortless palate is utterly charming, with ripe, restrained and juicy fruit wrapped in clean, bright acids and finishing with seamless length.

2004	95	2009	2012+
2003	83	2005	2006+
2002	94	2007	2010
2001	95	2009	2013+
2000	94	2008	2012

THE MENZIES CABERNET SAUVIGNON

RATING 5

Coonawarra $20–$29
Current vintage: 2002 87

A polished and elegant wine that has received some first-rate oak treatment, but which remains underpinned by a thread of green fruit. Its delicate perfume of raspberries, cassis, plums and sweetly scented vanilla/dark chocolate oak reveals dusty, leafy undertones of dried herbs. Its supple palate of juicy fruit has richness and weight, but its astringency has a metallic edge.

2002	87	2010	2014
2001	87	2009	2013
2000	86	2005	2008
1999	89	2004	2007+
1998	88	2003	2006
1997	87	2002	2005
1996	94	2004	2008+
1995	89	2000	2003
1994	87	2006	2014
1993	89	2001	2005
1992	93	2002	2004

THE OCTAVIUS SHIRAZ

RATING 3

Barossa Valley $50–$99
Current vintage: 2002 96

Marvellously tight, restrained, elegant and finely crafted for such an overt and showy shiraz. Its meaty, black pepper-like aromas of blackberries, redcurrants, dark plums and cinnamon/clove spices are backed by assertive, toasty but tightly integrated influences of cedar and vanilla. Long, firm and concentrated, its sumptuous and multi-layered palate of brooding dark fruit easily carries its showy new oak, framed by tight, powdery and mouth-coating tannins. It finishes savoury, with lingering musky spices.

2002	96	2014	2022
2001	92	2009	2013+
2000	89	2008	2012
1999	93	2011	2019
1998	95	2006	2010
1997	87	2002	2005
1996	89	2004	2008
1995	93	2003	2007
1994	95	2002	2006+
1993	91	1998	2001
1992	95	2000	2004
1990	95	2002	2010

THE RESERVE (Cabernet Sauvignon & Shiraz)

RATING 5

Barossa Valley $50–$99
Current vintage: 1998 86

Varnishy aromas of meaty, pruney and currant-like fruit with crushed bull ant-like undertones. Suggestive of substantial hang-time, its strongly raisined fruit lacks vitality and freshness. Offering richness and generosity, it's framed by firm and drying tannins.

1998	86	2003	2006+
1996	87	2001	2004+
1992	87	2000	2004
1990	94	2002	2010+

THE SIGNATURE (Cabernet Sauvignon & Shiraz)

RATING 2

Barossa Valley $30–$49
Current vintage: 2002 95

A finely crafted and balanced red blend likely to cellar very well indeed. Its violet-like perfume of blackberries, plums and aromatic vanilla and cedary oak overlie nuances of spice, game and mocha. Firm and fine-grained, its pleasingly long palate of vibrant, briary and sour-edged plum and juicy black and red berries reveals nuances of cloves, dried herbs and a deep underswell of cedar/vanilla and dark chocolate oak.

2002	95	2014	2022
2001	86	2006	2009
2000	89	2008	2012
1999	94	2011	2019
1998	95	2010	2018+
1997	89	2005	2009
1996	95	2008	2016
1995	90	2003	2007
1994	94	2006	2014
1993	93	2001	2005
1992	95	2004	2012
1991	94	2003	2011
1990	94	2002	2010
1989	93	1994	1997

THE VIRGILIUS VIOGNIER

RATING 3

Eden Valley $30–$49
Current vintage: 2005 93

Pungent, wild, very reductive and rubbery aromas blow away to reveal spicy, honeysuckle-like scents of apricot-like fruit with undertones of wheatmeal. It's long, smooth and unctuous, delivering a seamless and almost silky expression of juicy flavour that culminates in a savoury, smoky finish. Likely to flesh out nicely.

2005	93	2007	2010+
2004	95	2006	2009+
2003	93	2005	2008
2002	90	2003	2004+
2001	91	2003	2006+
2000	87	2002	2005

TRICENTENARY VINES GRENACHE

Barossa Valley $30–$49
Current vintage: 2003 92

Firm and savoury, with pleasingly deep red fruit flavours, this spicy, perfumed and floral grenache avoids the exaggerated varietal characters of so many from this region. Scented with flowers, cloves and cinnamon, red plums and cherries, it's fresh and juicy, with a generous but medium-bodied palate of vibrant spicy fruit framed by firmish tannins.

2003	92	2008	2011
2002	88	2004	2007
2001	87	2003	2006+
2000	89	2005	2008
1999	86	2001	2004

Yarra Burn

60 Settlement Road, Yarra Junction Vic 3797. Tel: (03) 5967 1428. Fax: (03) 5967 1146.
Website: www.yarraburn.com.au Email: cellardoor@yarraburn.com.au
Region: **Yarra Valley** Winemakers: **Mark O'Callaghan, Ed Carr (sparkling)** Viticulturist: **Ray Guerin**
Chief Executive: **David Woods**

Yarra Burn is The Hardy Wine Company's Yarra Valley brand, and it has access to some of the region's largest vineyards. Why, then, it needs to incorporate fruit from Heathcote and the Pyrenees in its Shiraz is totally beyond me. Furthermore, Hardy's has launched a mid-priced multi-regional brand under the Yarra Burn name called Third Light, whose wines will be sourced from the Heathcote and the Pyrenees. And the Yarra Valley as well. I remain convinced that if a wine brand includes a region's name, it should come exclusively from that region.

BASTARD HILL CHARDONNAY

RATING 2

Yarra Valley $30–$49
Current vintage: 2004 95

An intense, smooth and mineral chardonnay of considerable class. Bright aromas of melon and grapefruit are backed by smoky, toasty undertones of grilled nuts plus creamy leesy nuances. Its long, vibrant palate bursts with juicy, crystalline melon and citrus flavour over a wet slate-like texture and reductive complexity. It's clean, crisp, delightfully balanced and precisely honed.

2004	95	2009	2012+
2000	93	2005	2008+
1999	95	2004	2007
1998	96	2003	2006
1997	90	2002	2004
1996	87	1997	1998
1994	91	1996	1999

CABERNET SAUVIGNON

RATING 3

Yarra Valley $20–$29
Current vintage: 2003 87

Both meaty and herbal, this plummy and cedary cabernet has an earthy, leathery bouquet of small dark berries with greenish undertones. Simple, forward and sappy to finish, it's an honest but uncomplicated wine whose plum and blackberry fruit reveal under-and over-ripe characters.

2003	87	2008	2011
2002	89	2007	2010+
2001	92	2009	2013+
2000	90	2008	2012
1999	95	2011	2019
1998	93	2006	2010
1997	89	2002	2005
1995	94	2003	2007
1994	89	1999	2002
1993	89	1998	2001
1992	94	2000	2004

CHARDONNAY

RATING 4

Yarra Valley $20–$29
Current vintage: 2005 88

A pretty, restrained and harmonious young wine whose delicate aromas of peach, grapefruit, melon and tropical fruits overlie lightly spicy and vanilla oak-derived characters. It's a little closed and tight, with pretty, delicate citrusy and nutty flavours backed by vanilla and oak beginning to flesh out, but finishing dusty and savoury.

2005	88	2007	2010
2003	92	2005	2008+
2002	87	2003	2004+
2001	90	2003	2006+
2000	91	2005	2008
1999	91	2001	2004
1998	87	1999	2000
1997	93	2002	2005
1996	90	2001	2004

PINOT NOIR

RATING **5**

Yarra Valley	$20–$29
Current vintage: 2005	**86**

Floral and slightly confectionary aromas of raspberries and cherries are backed by lightly toasty cedar/vanilla oak with meaty, musky, animal-like undertones. Simple and smooth, soft and forward, it's a little hollow and dilute, revealing the outlines, but not the stuffing of a real pinot.

2005	86	2006	2007+
2004	86	2006	2009
2002	82	2004	2007
2001	89	2003	2006
2000	87	2002	2005
1999	82	2001	2004
1998	87	2003	2006
1997	92	2002	2005
1994	75	1999	2002

SHIRAZ

RATING **5**

Heathcote, Pyrenees, Yarra Valley	$20–$29
Current vintage: 2002	**89**

Honest, rustic shiraz with some Rhôney pretensions. Its meaty, spicy and musky aroma of animal hide reveals lightly greenish berry/plum fruit and cedar/vanilla oak. Slightly raw and green-edged, its earthy palate of meaty blackberry and plum flavour is rather reserved, but finishes with some hard edges.

2002	89	2007	2010
2001	86	2003	2006+
2000	87	2003	2005+
1999	87	2001	2004+
1998	89	2003	2006+

SPARKLING PINOT NOIR CHARDONNAY

RATING **4**

Yarra Valley	$20–$29
Current vintage: 2002	**85**

A relatively simple and herbaceous sparking wine that lacks length and freshness. Very floral and tropical, its grassy aromas of under-ripe fruit precede a palate that offers some buttery creaminess and lively fruit, but finishes with slightly raw and herbal edges.

2002	85	2004	2007
2001	92	2006	2009
2000	88	2002	2005
1999	88	2001	2004
1998	93	2000	2003
1997	95	1999	2002+
1996	85	1998	2001
1993	87	1995	2000

Yarra Ridge

Racecourse Vineyard, Yarra Glen Vic 3775. Tel: 1800 186 456. Website: www.yarraridge.com.au

Region: **Yarra Valley** Winemaker: **Shavaughn Wells** Viticulturist: **Damien de Castella**
Chief Executive: **Jamie Odell**

Unlike its St Huberts brand, whose wines will repay cellaring, Beringer Blass produces early-drinking, flavoursome and up-front wines of pleasing varietal characters under its Yarra Ridge label. I am greatly interested in watching how Foster's Wine Estates deals with its trio of Yarra labels, which now includes Yarra Ridge, St Huberts and Coldstream Hills, each of which is producing varietal Yarra wines at similar price-points.

CHARDONNAY

RATING **5**

Yarra Valley	$12–$19
Current vintage: 2004	**89**

Fresh aromas of peaches and grilled nuts, with a background of wheatmeal, precede a soft, elegant and restrained palate whose generous stonefruit and melon flavours finish with some assertive vanilla oak. Should flesh out over the short term.

2004	89	2005	2006+
2003	87	2004	2005+
2001	90	2002	2003+
2000	87	2001	2002
1999	86	1999	2000
1998	87	1999	2000
1997	89	1998	1999

PINOT NOIR

RATING **5**

Yarra Valley	$12–$19
Current vintage: 2004	**89**

A fresh, floral and spicy young pinot whose slightly confectionary expression of cherries, raspberries and caramel delivers a perfumed fragrance backed by sweet vanilla oak and a juicy, fleshy palate framed by pliant tannins. It's uncomplicated but generous, packed with lively flavour and finished by soft but refreshing acidity.

2004	89	2006	2009
2003	87	2005	2008
2002	88	2004	2007
2001	82	2003	2006
2000	89	2002	2005
1999	85	2000	2001
1998	84	2000	2003
1997	87	1999	2002
1996	90	1998	2003

Yarra Yarra

239 Hunts Lane, Steels Creek Vic 3775. Tel: (03) 5965 2380. Fax: (03) 5965 2086.
Email: wine@yarrayarravineyard.com.au

Region: **Yarra Valley** Winemaker: **Ian Maclean** Viticulturist: **Ian Maclean** Chief Executives: **Ian & Anne Maclean**

Yarra Yarra is a small and dedicated maker of finely crafted Yarra Valley table wines from the Bordeaux varieties. The reserve level Yarra Yarra cabernet blend is a spectacular wine, the best yet from this winery and a red that shows that Australian vineyards can indeed marry the key attributes of cabernet sauvignon: depth of perfume and flavour, with strength and inherent structure. Ian Maclean suggested I rerate the 2003 Syrah Viognier, which I have happily done. Its overt greenness has subsided considerably, and the wine is today showing a much better balance.

CABERNETS   RATING **3**

Yarra Valley	**$50–$99**		
Current vintage: 2003	**93**		

A fine-grained and very elegant cabernet that should build handsomely in the bottle. Dusty, floral and aromatic, its concentrated perfume of small berries and plums overlies herbal nuances and tight-grained cedar/vanilla oak. Smooth and stylish, its firm and lingering palate delivers an intense core of pristine dark fruit backed by cedar/tobaccoey oak.

2003	93	2011	2015
2002	88	2007	2010
2000	93	2012	2020
1999	93	2007	2011
1998	90	2003	2006
1997	91	2005	2009+
1996	87	1998	2001+
1995	92	2003	2007+
1994	93	2002	2006+
1993	90	2003	2007
1992	91	2003	2007
1991	95	1999	2003+
1990	95	2002	2010+

SAUVIGNON BLANC SEMILLON   RATING **4**

Yarra Valley	**$30–$49**		
Current vintage: 2003	**88**		

Pungent, lightly grassy, creamy and toffee-like aromas of slightly candied melon and gooseberry fruit are backed by toasty, slightly varnishy and bubblegum-like oak. Smooth, gentle and oaky, its slightly cloying and buttery palate of herbal passionfruit and melon flavours is already showing some development. Complex and full of character, but ageing, very oaky and lacking a little freshness.

2003	88	2005	2008
2002	94	2004	2007
2001	88	2003	2006
2000	83	2002	2005
1999	95	2004	2007+
1998	88	2003	2006
1997	94	2002	2005
1996	92	2001	2004
1995	95	2003	2007
1994	87	1999	2002
1993	86	1995	1998

SYRAH VIOGNIER (with Viognier since 2003)   RATING **5**

Yarra Valley	**$50–$99**		
Current vintage: 2004	**88**		

Very herbaceous and rather funky for its vibrant but modest impression of fruit. Its spicy, floral perfume is quite viognier-driven at this time, with pronounced aromas of honeysuckle, sweet red berries, dark plums and cherries over restrained cedary oak. Framed by firm, grippy tannins, its smooth and savoury palate of lively dark berry/plum fruit overlies meaty, dusty and herbal nuances, finishing with a slightly sappy and metallic aspect.

2004	88	2009	2012+
2003	90	2008	2011+
2002	87	2007	2010
2001	92	2009	2013

THE YARRA YARRA (formerly Reserve Cabernet Sauvignon)   RATING **2**

Yarra Valley	**$50–$99**		
Current vintage: 2003	**97**		

An aristocratic cabernet of depth, power, balance and longevity. Its deep, brooding and very primary aromas of alluringly fragrant and briary dark berries, violets and cedar/vanilla oak precede a classically long, firm palate. Layers of dark and red berry flavour knit seamlessly with excellent new oak and assertive, powdery tannins, delivering exceptional length and depth of flavour and structure.

2003	97	2015	2023+
2002	93	2014	2022
2001	88	2013	2021
2000	96	2012	2020
1999	95	2007	2011+
1998	90	2003	2006
1997	89	2002	2005+
1995	95	2007	2015
1994	89	2002	2006+
1993	89	1998	2001

Yarrabank

38 Melba Highway, Yering Vic 3775. Tel: (03) 9730 1107. Fax: (03) 9739 0135. Website: www.yering.com
Regions: **Various, Victoria** Winemakers: **Michael Parisot, Tom Carson** Viticulturist: **John Evans**
Chief Executives: **Doug Rathbone, Laurent Gillet**
From the small house of Devaux, Champagne winemaker Claude Thibaut collaborates with Tom Carson of
Yering Station in the making of this blend from different Victorian cool-climate regions. The exceptional 1999
vintage is a very classy, elegant and minerally wine, while the 2000 is earlier-maturing and rounder.

YARRABANK CUVÉE   RATING **3**

Various, Victoria		$30–$49				
Current vintage: 2000		**91**				

2000	91	2005	2008
1999	95	2004	2007
1998	89	2000	2003+
1997	88	2002	2005
1996	89	2001	2004
1995	96	2003	2007
1994	89	1996	1999+
1993	94	1998	2001+

Opulent and powerful, it delivers in punchiness and character what it might lack in elegance and finesse. Its fragrant aromas of honeysuckle and creamy, buttery undertones of complex spices precede a long, rich and juicy palate with a lingering chewy and crackly texture.

Yarra Yering

Briarty Road, Gruyere via Coldstream, Vic 3770. Tel: (03) 5964 9267. Fax: (03) 5964 9239.
Website: www.yarrayering.com Email: info@yarrayering.com
Region: **Yarra Valley** Winemaker: **Bailey Carrodus** Chief Executive: **Bailey Carrodus**
Yarra Yering is one of the wineries that began the rebirth of the Yarra Valley as a wine region in the early 1970s.
It is owned and operated by the redoutable Dr Bailey Carrodus, who has done very well in recent years to
introduce a younger team to assist with the vineyard and winery operations. The modern Yarra Yering wines
are considerably more polished and technically reliable than they were a decade ago, and there's every indication
that with future redevelopment in the vineyard, that the trend might continue. The two shiraz-based reds
are comfortably the vineyard's best and most consistent, but all its reds are capable of excellence.

DRY RED NO. 1 (Cabernet Blend)   RATING **4**

Yarra Valley		$50–$99
Current vintage: 2004		**91**

2004	91	2012	2016
2003	89	2008	2011+
2002	86	2004	2007
2001	96	2013	2021
1998	91	2006	2010
1997	92	2009	2017
1996	87	2001	2004
1995	80	2000	2003
1994	93	2006	2014
1993	94	2001	2005
1992	91	2000	2004
1991	95	1999	2003
1990	97	2010	2020+

Dusty, lightly herbal aromas of small black and red berries, crushed violets and cedar/vanilla oak reveal hints of vegetal undertones. Long, smooth and complete, its fine, powdery palate delivers a fresh expression of forest berry flavour, backed by cedar/vanilla oak and framed by dusty tannins. There's an undercurrent of dried herbs and forest floor-like complexity. Very stylish, but too herbal for a higher score.

DRY RED NO. 2 (Shiraz Viognier blend)   RATING **2**

Yarra Valley		$50–$99
Current vintage: 2004		**97**

2004	97	2016	2024
2003	96	2011	2015+
2001	96	2009	2013+

A classic wine of silkiness, perfume and elegance. Its heady, floral bouquet of vibrant black and red berries, dark chocolate, cedar and vanilla oak, musky spices and meaty undertones precedes a smooth, delightfully fine-grained and surprisingly sumptuous palate. Its intense, spicy dark fruits extend well down towards the lingering, savoury finish, while the viognier smoothes over the fine and slightly powdery tannins with ease. Very balanced and complete.

MERLOT

RATING 4

Yarra Valley $100–$199
Current vintage: 2004   93

Finely honed, supple and willowy merlot with a floral perfume of black cherries, cassis and mulberries, backed by cedar/vanilla oak and herbal and tobaccoey undertones. Long and smooth, its vibrant cherry/plum/cassis fruit and restrained oak reveal some faint dusty, leafy undertones. It's tightly integrated and brightly flavoured but lacks the length for a higher rating.

2004	93	2009	2012
2003	89	2005	2008+
2001	94	2009	2013
1994	95	2002	2006
1993	94	1998	2001
1992	91	1997	2000
1990	90	1996	1998

PINOT NOIR

RATING 3

Yarra Valley $50–$99
Current vintage: 2004   95

A classic Yarra pinot with a silky, supple texture supported by fine, dusty tannins. Its floral, rose petal perfume of sweet red cherries, cedar/vanilla oak and exotic spices precedes a fleshy but fragile and fine-grained palate. Its vibrant fruit extends long, smooth and silky, with underlying nuances of dried herbs. Very stylish and understated, but likely to build more richness in the bottle.

2004	95	2009	2012
2003	93	2008	2011+
2001	95	2006	2009
1996	86	2001	2004
1995	87	2000	2003
1994	90	1999	2002
1993	82	1998	2001
1992	95	2000	2004
1991	95	1999	2004

UNDERHILL SHIRAZ

RATING 2

Yarra Valley $50–$99
Current vintage: 2004   90

Intense aromas of blackberries, sweet mulberries and cranberries are backed by undertones of minerals, cedar/vanilla oak and light herbal nuances. Long, smooth and creamy, its vibrant, almost jujube-like red and black berry fruit overlies a supple chassis of somewhat sappy, fine tannins. It's very pretty, a little leafy and very elegant.

2004	90	2009	2012
2003	96	2011	2015
2001	97	2013	2021
1999	96	2007	2011
1997	94	2005	2009+
1996	87	2001	2004
1995	90	2000	2003+
1994	89	1999	2002
1993	89	1998	2001
1992	96	1997	2000

Yering Station

38 Melba Highway, Yering Vic 3775. Tel: (03) 9730 0100. Fax: (03) 9739 0135.
Website: www.yering.com Email: info@yering.com
Region: **Yarra Valley** Winemaker: **Tom Carson** Viticulturist: **John Evans** Chief Executive: **Gordon Gebbie**
Yering Station is one of the most impressive new facilities in the Yarra Valley and it has set its sights unquestionably high. The Reserve Chardonnay and Reserve Shiraz Viognier have quickly evolved into classic styles, while the 'standard' wines are finding more consistency and character. The 2005 Chardonnay and 2004 Shiraz Viognier are quite delicious. Yering Station offers one of the finest visitor experiences in Australian wine.

CABERNET SAUVIGNON

RATING 5

Yarra Valley $20–$29
Current vintage: 2003   86

A jammy fragrance of mulberries, blackcurrants, plums and vanilla oak reveals herbaceous undertones, while the palate of sweet berry fruit is similarly sappy and green-edged. It's helped along by some sweet oak, but is framed by thin tannins and finished with greenish acids. Drink soon.

2003	86	2005	2008
2001	87	2003	2006+
2000	83	2002	2005
1999	89	2004	2007
1998	82	2000	2003

CHARDONNAY

Yarra Valley $20–$29
Current vintage: 2005 90

A measured, restrained and delightfully flavoured young chardonnay whose lightly floral aromas of fresh peach, melon and grapefruit are backed by hints of spices and dusty, nutty and vanilla oak. Long, smooth and even, the palate is gently oaked and bursts with spicy and pristine fruit. It has a charmingly fluffy texture and finishes with soft, refreshing acids.

2005	90	2007	2010
2004	89	2006	2009
2002	87	2003	2004
2001	87	2003	2006
2000	84	2001	2002
1999	87	2000	2001
1998	93	2000	2003+
1997	90	1999	2002
1996	80	1997	1998

PINOT NOIR

Yarra Valley $20–$29
Current vintage: 2004 88

Smooth, simple and approachable, this lively young pinot marries vibrant raspberry, cherry and plum-like fruit with restrained cedar/vanilla oak and silky, sappy tannin. There's a hint of stewed fruit, but plenty of confectionary brightness and a structured, savoury finish.

2004	88	2006	2009
2003	86	2004	2005
2002	86	2004	2007
2001	80	2002	2003
2000	88	2002	2005
1999	83	2000	2001
1998	89	2000	2003
1997	87	1998	1999

RESERVE CHARDONNAY

Yarra Valley $50–$99
Current vintage: 2002 95

Very delicate, perfumed, almost fragile chardonnay whose aromas of melon, grapefruit and grainy oak are presently rather closed and floral. Its long, creamy palate of stonefruit and citrus, apple and pear culminates in soft acids and lingering suggestions of quince and cumquat. Its flavours are bright and clear, while its slightly babyfat-like texture finishes with tightness and elegance.

2002	95	2007	2010+
2001	95	2006	2009
1999	95	2004	2007+
1997	95	2002	2005

RESERVE PINOT NOIR

Yarra Valley $50–$99
Current vintage: 2003 89

A flavoursome and complex pinot perfumed with sweet oak and spicy, slightly confectionary red cherries and plums, with gamey undertones of undergrowth and sage. Sappy and juicy, it's smooth, silky and refined, delivering a willowy palate whose sweet cherry/plum fruit and smoky cedary oak reveals just a hint of under/over-ripe influences.

2003	89	2005	2008+
2002	88	2004	2007+
2000	90	2002	2005+
1998	87	2000	2003+
1997	93	2002	2005

RESERVE SHIRAZ VIOGNIER

Yarra Valley $50–$99
Current vintage: 2003 93

Its ethereal musky fragrance of vibrant small red and black berries, cloves and cinnamon reveals nuances of white pepper, dark cherries and marzipan. Firmish, silky and refined, with a sweet apricot viognier influence matched with raspberry and blackcurrant flavours. It's slightly confectionary, and backed by herbal undertones.

2003	93	2008	2011
2002	96	2014	2022
2001	93	2006	2009+
1998	90	2003	2006+
1997	95	2005	2009

SHIRAZ VIOGNIER

Yarra Valley $20–$29
Current vintage: 2004   91

Deeply aromatic and flavoured, this silky-fine, smooth and stylish red tightly marries the best of both varieties with some pleasing reductive complexity. Its meaty, charcuterie-like aromas of blackberries, dark plums, plain chocolate and cinnamon/clove spices are lifted by fresh, blueberry-like nuances. Medium to full in weight, with piercing cherry, plum and berry flavours backed by restrained cedar/chocolate/vanilla oak, it's framed by smooth but firm tannins.

2004	91	2009	2012
2003	92	2005	2008+
2002	94	2007	2010
2001	92	2003	2006+
2000	86	2002	2005
1999	81	2000	2001

Yeringberg

Maroondah Highway, Yeringberg, Coldstream Vic 3770. Tel: (03) 9739 1453. Fax: (03) 9739 0048.

Region: **Yarra Valley** Winemakers: **Guill & Sandra De Pury** Viticulturist: **David De Pury** Chief Executive: **Guill De Pury**

Yeringberg makes small volumes of fastidiously grown and produced wine in the cellars beneath its historic 19th century winery. The 2005 whites and 2004 reds perhaps comprise the finest and most consistent release yet for Yeringberg. The 2005 Chardonnay is a supremely restrained wine that opens layer after layer of fruit and complexity. The other real highlight is the intensely perfumed and ethereal but sappy and fragile 2004 Pinot Noir.

CHARDONNAY

Yarra Valley $30–$49
Current vintage: 2005   96

Very classy indeed, this smooth and seamless chardonnay has a delicate fragrance of peach, melon and tightly knit vanilla oak with undertones of spice and wheatmeal. Long and creamy, it's an essay in elegance and restraint, unfolding layers of grapefruit, melon and peachy flavours that mesh neatly with a measured oak background and zesty acids. Terrific focus and shape, and excellent potential.

2005	96	2010	2013+
2004	94	2009	2012
2003	93	2008	2011
2002	94	2007	2010
2001	93	2006	2009+
2000	95	2005	2008+
1999	89	2004	2007
1998	95	2003	2006
1997	94	2005	2009
1996	94	2004	2008
1995	92	2003	2007

MARSANNE ROUSSANNE

Yarra Valley $30–$49
Current vintage: 2005   94

Tighter and leaner than most of its predecessors, this finely focused, delicate and pristine young wine has raciness and structure. Its nutty aromas of tangerine and honeysuckle reveal mineral undertones, while its finely honed palate neatly wraps its grapefruit-like flavours in nervy acidity. Likely to evolve with appealing complexity.

2005	94	2010	2013+
2004	94	2009	2012
2003	94	2008	2011+
2002	90	2007	2010+
2001	93	2009	2013
2000	93	2008	2012
1999	93	2007	2011
1998	93	2003	2006
1997	94	2005	2009
1996	91	2004	2008
1995	88	2003	2007
1994	94	2002	2006

PINOT NOIR

Yarra Valley $50–$99
Current vintage: 2004   95

A finely crafted, supple and brightly flavoured young pinot whose floral, rose petal-like perfume of red cherries, plums and berries reveals spicy undertones of forest floor backed by caramel-like vanilla oak. Supported by almost a fragile spine of smooth tannin, its vibrant palate of sweet cherry and berry flavour has a charmingly sappy, silky quality, finishing with intense and lingering fruit, plus nuances of cloves and star anise.

2004	95	2009	2012+
2003	92	2008	2011
2002	94	2007	2010+
2001	90	2003	2006
2000	92	2005	2008
1999	89	2004	2007
1998	82	2000	2003
1997	96	2005	2009
1996	94	2004	2008
1995	90	2000	2003
1994	92	2002	2006
1993	91	1995	1998

YERINGBERG CABERNET BLEND

RATING **2**

Yarra Valley $50–$99
Current vintage: 2004 93

A violet-like perfume of fresh blackberries, raspberries and sweet cedar/vanilla oak reveals a slightly meaty complexity. Smooth, supple and vibrant, its elegant but quite succulent and juicy palate of plums and dark cherries, mulberries and cassis is framed by supple and powdery tannins. There's just a hint of under-and over-ripeness, with herbal undertones and some suggestions of jamminess, but this finely crafted wine has plenty to offer.

2004	93	2012	2016
2003	90	2011	2015
2002	89	2010	2014
2001	96	2013	2021
2000	94	2012	2020+
1999	92	2007	2011
1998	95	2010	2018
1997	95	2005	2009+
1996	93	2004	2008
1995	88	2003	2007
1994	94	2006	2014
1993	91	2001	2005
1992	95	2012	2022
1991	93	2003	2011
1990	95	2002	2010+
1989	86	1994	1997
1988	95	2000	2008+

Zema Estate

Riddoch Highway, Coonawarra SA 5263. Tel: (08) 8736 3219. Fax: (08) 8736 3280.
Website: www.zema.com.au Email: zemaestate@zema.com.au
Region: **Coonawarra** Winemaker: **Greg Clayfield** Viticulturist: **Nick Zema** Chief Executive: **Demetrio Zema**

Zema Estate is a small, family-owned winery whose growth in size and stature has been measured and even, despite a slight and hopefully temporary drop in the quality of its 'standard' reds thanks to some challenging vintages. Zema recently appointed well-known Coonawarra winemaker Greg Clayfield to look after production, and have also opened a dramatic extension of their winery complex. The Zema story is one of hard work and deserved success by an unassuming family.

CABERNET SAUVIGNON

RATING **5**

Coonawarra $20–$29
Current vintage: 2004 93

A delightfully intense, elegant and tightly focused cabernet whose floral perfume of cassis, plums and small red berries overlies fresh cedar/vanilla oak. Smooth, supple and silky, its long, pristine palate of intense dark, briary berry fruits knits tightly with powder-fine tannins, finishing with a sour-edged definition of flavour. It's long, persistent and finely crafted, reflecting truly even fruit ripeness.

2004	93	2016	2024
2003	89	2011	2015+
2002	84	2010	2014
2001	86	2009	2013
2000	87	2008	2012
1999	87	2007	2011
1998	89	2006	2010+
1997	84	2005	2009
1996	80	2001	2004
1995	81	2000	2003
1994	84	2002	2006+
1993	83	2001	2005
1992	87	2004	2012+
1991	89	2003	2011
1990	86	1995	1998

CLUNY (blend of red Bordeaux varieties)

RATING **5**

Coonawarra $20–$29
Current vintage: 2004 94

A supple, finely balanced and elegant blend whose violet-like fragrance of fresh black and red berries and restrained cedar/vanilla oak are lifted by a light mintiness. Smooth and fine-grained, its surprisingly plush palate of pristine fresh berries, cherries and dark plums knits tightly with fine oak. It finishes long and smooth, with a lingering reminder of its fine texture and structure.

2004	94	2016	2024
2003	89	2011	2015
2002	82	2004	2007+
2001	82	2003	2006+
2000	87	2005	2008
1999	89	2007	2011+
1998	93	2010	2018
1997	80	1999	2002
1996	89	2004	2008+
1995	83	2000	2003+
1994	90	2002	2006+

FAMILY SELECTION CABERNET SAUVIGNON

Coonawarra	$30–$49
Current vintage: 2002	**87**

An honest wine, but one made from unevenly ripened fruit. Its sweet, simple and jammy fruits are backed by assertively toasty cedar, chocolate and vanilla oak, with herbal undertones. Initially powerful, rich and flavoursome, the palate moves towards a sappy and metallic finish, with slightly cooked and green-edged fruit.

2002	87	2010	2014
2001	93	2013	2021+
2000	88	2005	2008+
1999	91	2011	2019
1998	93	2010	2018
1996	90	2006	2016
1994	86	1999	2002
1993	81	1998	2001
1992	82	2000	2004
1991	92	2003	2011+
1988	88	2000	2008

FAMILY SELECTION SHIRAZ

Coonawarra	$30–$49
Current vintage: 2002	**89**

A bright, lively and spicy bouquet of small berry and plum-like fruit and restrained oak reveals meaty and herbal undertones. It's long and restrained, with a pleasing core of concentrated spicy and peppery berry flavour backed by slightly varnishy oak and framed by fine, powdery tannins. It finishes savoury, with a hint of meatiness and a lingering undercurrent of lightly herbal influences.

2002	89	2010	2014
2001	87	2009	2013
2000	88	2008	2012+

MERLOT

Coonawarra	$20–$29
Current vintage: 2004	**91**

An elegant and fine-grained merlot with richness and plumpness of sweet berry, cherry and plum-like fruit. Its fresh, floral aromas of dark cherries, mulberries and cassis overlie restrained and lightly toasty cedar/vanilla oak. Medium to full in weight, it's supple and juicy, with a lingering chocolatey finish. It should develop well.

2004	91	2009	2012+
2001	87	2009	2013
2000	88	2005	2008+

SHIRAZ

Coonawarra	$20–$29
Current vintage: 2004	**95**

Exemplary, elegant, deeply flavoured and finely balanced Coonawarra shiraz whose fresh spicy, peppery and violet-like aromas of cassis, cherries and violets overlie restrained nuances of cedar/vanilla oak. Its long, smooth and juicy palate of essence-like shiraz fruit is neatly supported by a fine-grained spine of tightly interwoven tannin, delivering a lingering core of flavour before a meaty, savoury finish.

2004	95	2016	2024
2003	86	2005	2008+
2002	88	2007	2010
2001	91	2013	2021
2000	87	2005	2008
1999	90	2011	2019
1998	96	2010	2018+
1997	86	2002	2005
1996	90	2008	2016
1995	80	1997	2000+
1994	88	2002	2006+
1993	90	2005	2013
1992	89	2004	2012
1991	87	1999	2003+
1990	89	2002	2010
1989	81	1994	1997
1988	88	1996	2000+
1987	94	1992	1997+
1986	90	1998	2006